BUSINESS AND GOVERNMENT IN AMERICA SINCE 1870

*A Twelve-Volume Anthology
of Scholarly Articles*

Series Editor

ROBERT F. HIMMELBERG

Fordham University

A GARLAND SERIES

SERIES CONTENTS

VOLUME

5

BUSINESS-GOVERNMENT COOPERATION 1917–1932

THE RISE OF CORPORATIST POLICIES

Edited with introductions by

ROBERT F. HIMMELBERG

GARLAND PUBLISHING, INC.
New York & London
1994

Library of Congress Cataloging-in-Publication Data

Business-government cooperation, 1917–1932 : the rise of corporatist policies / edited with introductions by Robert F. Himmelberg.
    p.   cm. — (Business and government in America since 1870 ; v. 5)
    Articles previously published 1973–1989.
    ISBN 0-8153-1407-8 (alk. paper)
    1. Industry and state—United States—History—20th century.
2. Corporate state—United States—History—20th century.
3. United States—Politics and government—1901–1953.
4. United States—Economic policy—To 1933.   I. Himmelberg, Robert F.   II. Series.
HD3616. U46B858   1994
338.973'009'041—dc20   93–47242
                                           CIP

Printed on acid-free, 250-year-life paper
Manufactured in the United States of America

Contents

SERIES INTRODUCTION

This compilation of articles provides a very broad and representative selection of the scholarly literature found in learned journals on the subject of government-business relations in the age of industry, the period since 1870. The scope of this collection is wide, covering all the arenas of business-government interaction. Sectorially, the focus is on manufacturing and transportation, upon whose rapid expansion after the Civil War the modern industrial economy was founded.

For the volumes covering the years from 1870 to 1965 (Volumes I through IX) it has been possible, while exercising selectivity, to include a very high proportion of everything published within the past thirty years. This literature is found largely in historical journals. More selectivity had to be employed for Volumes X through XII, which cover the period since 1965. Historians have not yet trodden much on the ground of the very recent past but social scientists and legal scholars have offered abundant materials, so abundant as to require a relatively severe selectivity. By choosing articles that appear to have a long-term analytical value and by excluding those too narrow in scope, too preoccupied with methodological questions or otherwise unsuitable for a non-specialized audience, an extensive and accessible body of writing has, however, been assembled for the post-1965 period, mainly from economics and legal periodicals.

The volumes are designed to contain articles relating to a particular period and to one or more topics within a period. The literature of business-government relations has four logically distinct major topics: antitrust, regulation, promotion, and cooperation. These topics define distinctive aspects of the relationship. Yet, the distinctions sometimes in practice blur, the ostensible, publicly proclaimed purposes of policy sometimes differing from the actually intended purposes or the actual outcomes.

Antitrust policy emerges in Volume I, which covers the era 1870–1900 when big business appeared, and figures prominently throughout the series. Several volumes are devoted entirely to it. Uniquely American, at least until relatively recently, antitrust policy has a complex history and much of what scholars have discovered about its origin and evolution is recorded only in the articles gathered in this collection. The literature reproduced here makes clear that the intent and impact of antitrust policy has varied enormously during its one-hundred-year history, which dates from the Sherman Act of 1890. Tension between competing objectives has existed from the outset. Should the "trusts" be broken up on the grounds that super-corporations inevitably conflict with democratic government and entrepreneurial opportunity? Or should only "bad trusts", those guilty of crushing competitors through unfair methods, suffer dissolution? Is cartelistic behavior always an illegal restraint of trade, or should it sometimes be tolerated if it helps small business to survive? Put most broadly, should the aim of antitrust policy be simply promoting competition, or should other conflicting social and economic values be recognized?

Business regulation also arose during the early stages of industrialization, appearing at the federal level with the enactment of the Interstate Commerce Act in 1887. The term "regulation" is used here to denote government policies intended, not to promote or restore competition, but to require specific behavior from business. The classic justification for regulation was the argument that in some situations the public interest could be served only through governmental prescription, that in some instances a remedy simply could not be obtained through the workings of the marketplace. Theoretically there are two such instances. The first occurs in the case of "natural monopoly," market situations in which competition would be wasteful and competing firms do not and should not exist. Railroads and public utilities were early identified as industries of this sort and were the first targets of government regulation. Would-be regulators early discovered a second justification for applying the regulatory approach, the situation in which competition fails to provide rival firms with incentives to avoid methods that may injure public health or well being. The argument found early expression in regulation of the meat-packing industry and has over the course of the twentieth century created a remarkable body of federal regulatory practices. The history of regulation, however, has not unfolded, any more than the history of antitrust, according to the logic of theory. It has been determined by the interplay between many factors, including the ideas of reformers, the complaints of those who have felt injured, policy rivalries among businessmen themselves, and the capacity or incapacity of government to execute planned reform. A major focus of recent literature on regulation, and to an extent on antitrust also, is the thesis of capture, the notion that regulatory efforts have often fallen captive to the interests they were intended to oppose.

The third theme of relations between government and business, promotion and encouragement, also emerged during the initial stages of the industrial era. Railroad subsidies abounded during the age of building the transcontinentals, of course, and protective tariffs were almost as old as the Republic itself. In the early twentieth century government support of trade expansion abroad enlarged and gradually became a major thread of government policy. Resembling promotion but logically distinct in many respects is the fourth category of business-government interaction, the area of cooperative relationships. Few scholars, even those who believe ongoing conflict has chiefly characterized business-government relations, would deny that cooperation has occurred at certain points, as during American participation in the major wars of the twentieth century. But in recent years many writers who conceive of business-government relations as taking place within a "corporatist" framework have perceived the scope and continuity of cooperative tendencies as very broad.

These four categories describe the subjects or topics around which scholarly investigation of business-government relations has revolved. There is, however, another approach to analyzing the literature of this relationship, one in which we ask about a writer's interpretive perspective, the conceptualizations the writer brings to the subject. All historians and social scientists, including those who created the literature collected here, adopt an interpretive standpoint from which to view society and its workings. An interpretive standpoint is a way of understanding the structure of society and the way those structural elements relate and interact; in other words, it is a "model" of society. Several rival models have competed for acceptance among scholars in recent times. Readers will be better equipped for informed reading of the literature assembled in these volumes if they are knowledgeable about these interpretive standpoints and the aim here therefore is to define the most important of these and give them appropriate labels.

Until the 1950s the prevailing interpretation of business-government relations—indeed, of American history generally—was the progressive viewpoint. The term progressive refers in the first place to the reform ideology and activity of the early twentieth century, the period before World War I. The perspective of the progressive generation continued for many years to dominate historical writing, not only on the period itself but on the whole of American history. According to the progressive perspective, the rise of big business during the late nineteenth and early twentieth centuries created a radical shift in the balance of economic and political power in America in favor of concentrated wealth. The rise of the "trusts", the powerful firms that came to predominate in many industries in the years after 1880, and the creation of cartels and other arrangements for suppressing competition, threatened independent capitalists and consumers with raw economic exploitation. This concentration of economic power threatened to utterly suborn representative political institutions as well and reduce American democracy to a plutocracy. In the progressive view the predominating tone of business-government relations was therefore necessarily antagonistic and conflictual.

The progressive paradigm became deeply embedded in the American consciousness. Reformist politicians have often reverted to it in shaping their ideological and rhetorical appeals. Franklin D. Roosevelt's attack in the campaign of 1936 upon "economic royalists" and John Kennedy's denunciation in 1962 of Big Steel during the controversy over price guidelines as "utterly contemptuous of the public interest" are vivid examples. The progressive outlook is evidently a persistent element in the popular historical consciousness. The power of the progressive conception of American history is in fact readily confirmed by reference to the way twentieth-century history is periodized, in textbooks and popular histories, into epochs of reform (the Progressive, New Deal, Fair Deal and Great Society periods) and of reaction (the Twenties, the Eisenhower and Reagan eras).

But if the progressive interpretation of business government relations retains some force among some historians and in the consciousness of liberal opinion makers and the public, its hold on much of the academic mind has long since weakened. A reaction among historians and other academics against the progressive paradigm emerged soon after the end of the Second World War and gathered force during the 1950s. The reaction was especially sharp among historians writing business history. Writing at a time when a reinvigorated American economy appeared to have overcome the doldrums of the 1930s and to be demonstrating the superiority of capitalism over other systems, energetic business and economic historians completely revised the progressive interpretation of the founders of American big business. The revisionists interpreted the founders not as greedy robber barons but as heroes of the entrepreneurial spirit, the spirit of enterprise and productivity. This revisionist interpretation proved too one-dimensional and celebratory to be maintained without modification. Revisionism, however, did succeed in thoroughly discrediting the progressive point of view. This circumstance, together with the impact of interpretive concepts emanating from post-war social science, moved historians to replace the progressive paradigm with a new and more sophisticated framework for understanding American political economy, the pluralist framework.

Pluralism as the dominant interpretive mode replaced progressivism in the 1950s and 60s. Speaking broadly, the pluralist model understands public policy as the result of struggle between economic and social groups. A major by-product of industrialization is the sharpening of differences between groups playing distinctive economic roles and a heightened articulation of self-interested goals and purposes on the part of such groups. Thus, government-business relations, that is, the shape of government policies towards business, are the result of rivalries among the major interest groups, business, labor, consumers, and so on. But the nature of the struggle is complex because the major groups are themselves divided into more or less rivalrous sub-groups. Business itself is divided; both intra- and inter-industry rivalries exist, sometimes in acute forms. Government policy is not merely the result of nonbusiness groups seeking to shape that policy but also of some business interests seeking to impose their own wishes on others.

During the 1960s pluralist interpretation became more complex. One important source of this heightened complexity was what some commentators have called the "organizational" outlook. Again influenced by currents in American social science, this time sociology, practitioners employing the organizational perspective are struck by the ever-increasing importance of large bureaucratic organizations in American life since the onset of industrialization. Business has continuously evolved in terms of an ever larger role for the large corporation, but other spheres, including government and the professions, also are organized in terms of large hierarchical bureaucracies. Borrowing from Weberian sociological traditions, writers impressed by the organizational perspective have explored the thesis that large bureaucracies wherever situated have similar requirements and tend to develop in those who manage them similar values and expectations. Thus, this brand of pluralism stresses the extent to which group leaders, including the managers and technicians who run the large corporations, developed accommodative as well as merely self-seeking motives. Business leaders, many of them at least, came to share certain values, such as respect for stability in the overall economy, which leads them to seek harmonious and cooperative relationships between interest groups and between them and the government. Government is assigned the role, in this construct, of facilitating and stimulating cooperative modes of behavior and umpiring conflicts. In the literature on business and government, figures who have advocated this kind of polity are often dubbed "corporatists" or "corporate liberals." Broadly defined, corporatism is the practice of cooperation between government and the corporate world to resolve economic issues. The existence and the importance of corporatist relationships has been one of the major emphases of recent scholarship but there is much disagreement as to the intentions of its practitioners and its impact. Some scholars have interpreted corporatism in a more or less positive light, as an ideology and a practice entailing cooperation rather than conflict between government and business, as an alternative to an adversarial relationship, a way of obtaining desirable economic performance from business without resorting to governmental coercion.

But others, especially but not only those writing in the vein of the "New Left", have argued that members of the corporate elite have frequently pursued their own narrow interests under the cover of ostensibly cooperative endeavors. The New Leftists emerged in the 1960s, expounding a more radical criticism of business than the progressive-liberal historians had advanced. The New Leftists doubted or denied outright that the American system was pluralist at all in any meaningful sense. Control of public policy might appear as a contest between social groups, but in fact one group, or rather class, those who controlled big business, enjoyed such lopsided power that the contest was apparently not real. Behind the facade of political infighting over government policy toward business, the masters of the corporate world quietly steered events toward outcomes which cemented in place control of the economy by monopoly capital.

These four conceptualizations, the progressive, the pluralist, the corporatist, and the New Leftist, are essentially theories of the structure and process of American political economy. However, rarely are researchers slavishly devoted to a theoretical perspective. Thus, those who see, in the progressive vein, an ongoing conflictual relationship between the people and business sometimes argue against the reformers and in favor of the businessmen. Even more significant and widespread is the conclusion of many writers using the pluralist or corporatist modes of interpretation, that regulation has not fostered equity and economic progress but rather has hardened the economy's vital arteries. Pluralists initially assumed that policies arising from a political arena to which all organized interests have access will inevitably achieve benign results, that the policy outputs will construct a system of "countervailing power" among organized interest groups. The assumption of acceptable outcomes is still prevalent, but a skeptical version of the results of interest group rivalries became manifest in the late

1960s, holding that both in origin and ongoing impact, business regulation was too often subject to "capture." In this view, regulatory measures and agencies and other policies seeking to guide business behavior toward balanced and generally acceptable outcomes readily fall under the control of the very interests they were intended to regulate.

There has emerged in recent years still another approach to the origin and process of social-economic policy that has been applied to the business-government connection. In this interpretation of the connection, a few examples of which will be found in articles collected here, emphasis is placed on the relative autonomy of government administrators and regulators. Seen by the pluralists as merely the creatures of the organizational struggles that result in public policies, in this new view regulators are seen as possessing substantial room for independent action. Thus the state is not merely to be seen as a passive receptor and executor of outcomes that social forces determine but as having a partially autonomous role which the officers of the state presumably will use to extend their own interests rather than the interests articulated by social groups.

These categories, progressivism, pluralism, corporatism, Leftism and the "autonomous officialdom" viewpoint, represent the major schools of thought and interpretation that readers will discover in the literature reproduced in these volumes. Writers investigating specific historical incidents, trends or problems have, in most cases, written through the framework provided by one or another of these interpretive models. As an alert reader will discover, most writers do have certain assumptions about the structure and dynamics of social relationships, and these assumptions stem from one of the models that have been described.

Interpretation of the relationship between business and government in the age of industry has given rise to a literature that is large and complex. It presents a stimulating intellectual challenge and is certainly relevant for anyone seeking understanding of contemporary business-government relations and endeavoring to predict, or to shape, their future course.

INTRODUCTION

Modern research on this era of war, boom and bust has discovered that the reality of business-state relations did not match the portrayal provided by liberal historiography. Pictured by progressive historians as the reign of a business-dominated Republicanism that sought the restoration of laissez-faire, the era's meaning has undergone profound revision. According to this new portrayal, the most important development in business-government relations was the growing acceptance, by business and government elites alike, of an ideology calling upon the two groups to cooperate in order to achieve social-economic stability and progress. In the government the central figure is Herbert Hoover, wartime head of the Food Administration, Secretary of Commerce under Presidents Harding and Coolidge and, finally, president during the Great Depression. In business there is no one central figure. During World War I, Bernard Baruch, the Wall-Street financier who served as Chairman of the War Industries Board, was especially prominent, while during the 1920s and 30s corporate leaders such as Gerard Swope and Owen Young, both of General Electric, trade association executives such as George Sloan of the Cotton Textile Institute, and representatives of major business organizations such as the Chamber of Commerce of the United States, played key roles.

The ideology they sought to purvey was an American version of corporatism, a social philosophy prominent everywhere in the Western world during the postwar epoch. In America the corporatist outlook envisioned a society organized according to its functional parts, business, labor, agricultural, and so on. For business this would mean organization by industry through trade associations that could formulate plans for achieving the industry's stability and progress. Through cooperation among these units, a cooperation coordinated and facilitated by government, the entire society could effectively pursue these goals. For success such a system depended, of course, upon high-minded leadership from elites accustomed to the methods of science, technology and management.

The discovery of the broad extent to which this corporatist philosophy found expression, both in word and deed, is the major contribution recent scholarship has made to the reinterpretation of business-government interactions during the period between the onset of the war and the arrival of the New Deal in 1933. These expressions in fact now appear to form a basic theme of the period, giving it a previously unrecognized unity. The most influential writer elaborating this theme has been Ellis Hawley, several of whose articles are included in this section. Hawley's work has revealed the remarkable scope of Hoover's efforts during the 1920s. Through the Department of Commerce, and his role as an influential advisor to Harding and Coolidge in other spheres, Hoover sought to stimulate the formation and the activities of trade associations and other types of functionally organized cooperative units. Cooperation among competitors to improve economic information, the efficiency of production and distribution, and the acceptance of the goal of stabilization over rugged individualism could, according to Hoover, raise living standards and avoid periodic depressions. At the heart of Hoover's corporatism was the goal of solving social and economic problems through the methods of voluntarism and cooperationism. If this method worked, social conflict would be minimized and a directing role for the state could be avoided. Thus, the creativity and capacity for innovation Hoover thought characteristic of American life would be preserved and the class conflict and stifling bureaucratic controls, which in Hoover's view were the cause of Europe's postwar travail, could be indefinitely avoided. In the materials reproduced in this section, Hawley clarifies the remarkably broad scope of Hoover's activities during the 1920s and, in "Herbert Hoover and American Corporatism, 1929-1933," demonstrates how central to Hoover's Depression presidency was his commitment to solving economic ills through government coordination of voluntary cooperative efforts by businessmen.

Many other writers represented in this collection have explored these themes. Kim McQuaid's work illuminates the role of major business figures who enthusiastically supported welfare capitalist programs and economy-wide stabilization plans. Many writers have centered their work on trade associations and their governmental patrons, and their mutual endeavors to solve productivity and stabilization problems, or to establish the basis for sustained growth.

Not all commentators, however, have fully accepted the positive assessment of the corporatist developments of the 1920s that Hawley's interpretive stance implies. Two issues especially have troubled some researchers. Even if sincerity and conviction is taken for granted on Hoover's part, and on the part of many of the major business figures who followed his ideological and programmatic lead, the question nevertheless arises whether the cooperative ideal may have functioned as much to mask ulterior motives as to promote altruistic harmony. Secondly, there is the issue of effectiveness. What results did the method of business-government cooperation secure?

In numerous articles Robert Cuff has probed the function and meaning of the associational or corporatistic ideology emphasized by government war mobilizers during World War I. His findings indicate that key figures such as Bernard Baruch preferred voluntarist-corporatist methods because they wanted to shield business from the growth of state bureaucracy. Moreover, the methods were not really as successful as Baruch and others claimed in persuading businessmen to subordinate their own welfare to the common interests of the nation. On the question of effectiveness, William Robbins in his study of the lumber trade associations underscores how incapable the voluntary programs Hoover and industry leaders urged upon the lumbermen were of solving the trade's overproduction and price instability problems.

However one judges its merits, the building of an associative state was hindered not only by the difficulties obviously inherent in persuading conflicting interests to cooperate but also by well-established and contradictory national policies, notably antitrust, which continued to function as a restraint on cooperation. This problem is the subject of the preceding volume of this series. Unity escaped government policy in other words, as Hoover's vision of a new order had to compete with the traditional policies based on the conviction that government-business relations in some ways were inescapably adversarial.

Government-business relations during this period from war to Depression emerges then in quite a new light in recent scholarship. Important leaders from both sectors sought to reorder the relationship and make it explicitly cooperative. Though flawed in some respects, this effort established precedents that deeply and permanently influenced the course of government-business interaction.

HARRY GARFIELD, THE FUEL ADMINISTRATION, AND THE SEARCH FOR A COOPERATIVE ORDER DURING WORLD WAR I

ROBERT CUFF

Johns Hopkins University

HARRY AUGUSTUS GARFIELD, CHAIRMAN OF THE FUEL ADMINISTRATION during World War I, is one of the least known of the major Wilsonian war administrators. This is not surprising. Garfield's jurisdiction as Fuel Administrator was comparatively limited; he could not intervene in the broad range of economic and foreign policy issues open to contemporaries such as Newton D. Baker, Secretary of War, or Josephus Daniels, Secretary of the Navy, or William Gibbs McAdoo, Secretary of the Treasury. Nor did Garfield even seek the kind of status as theoretician of industrial mobilization that his wartime colleague Bernard Baruch achieved in the postwar years. He did not take the same care to shape public attitudes toward his wartime administration. Compared with the War Industries Board chairman, indeed, or with Food Administrator Herbert Hoover, Garfield showed remarkably little appetite for power or capacity for self-promotion — a tribute, perhaps, to character, but a barrier, apparently, to recognition.[1]

Such historical oversight, if understandable, is unfortunate. Garfield's Fuel Administration supervised a crucial segment of the industrial economy. Its policies dramatically affected the government's stabilization policies; its

[1] There is no scholarly biography of Harry Garfield, nor did he leave any published memoirs. *Harry Garfield's First Forty Years: Man of Action in a Troubled World* (New York: Vantage Press, 1965) by Lucretia G. Comer, Garfield's daughter, is a useful introduction, however. It elaborates upon the author's earlier, slimmer volume, *Strands From The Weaving* (New York: Vantage Press, 1959).

evolution exemplifies characteristic patterns of administrative growth and personnel recruitment in emergency government; its interaction with labor and management in the coal fields illuminates a variety of general themes in business–government relations during the war.[2]

Garfield's own story, moreover, is intrinsically instructive. Born in 1863, Garfield was the son of assassinated Republican president James A. Garfield, and a shocked witness to the fatal shooting of 1881. Garfield spent the rest of his life coming to terms with the personal and political implications of this tragic heritage. An anxious concern with personal meaning pervaded all his public activities, from the false start in private school teaching, through an absorbing business career and law practice in Cleveland, to a dramatic decision at middle age to accept Woodrow Wilson's call to a Princeton professorship, and to assume next the presidency of Williams College, a post he held from 1908 until 1934.

Garfield campaigned actively for McKinley in 1896 and attended Republican presidential conventions thereafter. But he never committed himself to national party politics like his brother James Rudolph, who became Civil Service Commissioner and Commissioner of Corporations under Roosevelt, and Secretary of the Interior under Taft. More significantly, Garfield left the Republican party altogether after falling under Wilson's spell at Princeton. By 1916, Garfield, like so many progressives of his generation, had followed his fellow college president into the Democratic camp. By 1917 he had become Wilson's Fuel Administrator.

What ideas and values did Garfield urge on Wilson after 1916? How can we characterize the symbolic meanings he later attached to his activities as Fuel Administrator? What did Wilson, the war, and the Fuel Administration mean for Garfield? These are important questions, for if Garfield's biography is idiosyncratic, his ideology is symptomatic. It is symptomatic of the view that Wilsonian war managers constructed and shared in the daily rounds of their disparate, frequently contradictory, administrative tasks. More specifically, it is symptomatic of the search for community which lay at the heart of the Wilsonian vision.

My central argument is that from 1916 forward Garfield searched for a new cooperative order both inside and outside the United States. This argument situates Garfield in the context of recent historical interest in corporate modes of American social thought. Jean B. Quandt and R. Jackson Wilson have explored this impulse among progressive intellectuals, for

---

[2] The Fuel Administration still awaits historical description and analysis. The generalizations in this paragraph are based upon a reading of relevant primary sources, particularly issues of *The Coal Trade Journal*, an industry trade paper. I have also benefited from reading an unpublished manuscript by James P. Johnson, "Rationalization Under the Fuel Administration, 1917-1918."

example; James Weinstein and William Appleman Williams, among others, have explored the forms it took among business ideologues; and Robert Wiebe, in his influential book, *The Search for Order*, has described its intellectual consequences for burgeoning professional groups. But nowhere else within recent scholarship have the effects of this growing appreciation been so dramatically felt as in the reinterpretation of Herbert Hoover's career currently underway. If once regarded as a rigid spokesman for an outmoded model of laissez faire, Hoover, after scrutiny by Ellis Hawley and Barry Karl and others, has now emerged as an intellectual innovator and apostle of a corporate vision.[3]

But to situate Garfield's war experience in the context of recent scholarship on neglected strands of corporate thinking is to say both too much and too little. It says far too much if it presumes a common definition and interpretation of the implications of corporate thought among its analysts. Jean Quandt's progressives are far more suspicious of bureaucracy than are Robert Wiebe's, for example; William Appleman Williams' Hoover is far more sensitive to capitalist imperatives than is Ellis Hawley's. Such a claim says too little, on the other hand, if it fails to specify the particular experiences out of which Garfield shaped his personal variations on the theme, or if it fails to specify the kinds of administrative forms in which Garfield sought to embody his particular view.

Garfield shared a number of parallel experiences with wartime colleagues who drifted into the Wilsonian war organization — a fling at the politics of municipal reform like Newton D. Baker and George Creel, head of the Committee on Public Information; a professional training and cosmopolitan background like Herbert Hoover — but he probably shared most of all with Wilson. There is the personal connection at Princeton and the common problems of academic administrators at private Eastern colleges. But more importantly, Garfield and Wilson also shared a common commitment to

[3] Jean B. Quandt, *From the Small Town to the Great Community: The Social Thought of Progressive Intellectuals* (New Brunswick: Rutgers Univ. Press, 1970); R. Jackson Wilson, *In Quest of Community: Social Philosophy in the United States, 1860-1920* (New York: Wiley, 1968); James Weinstein, *The Corporate Ideal in The Liberal State, 1900-1918* (Boston: Beacon Press, 1968); William Appleman Williams, *The Contours of American History* (Chicago: Quadrangle, 1966), 425 ff; Robert Wiebe, *The Search For Order 1877-1920* (New York: Hill and Wang, 1967), chs. 5 and 6; Ellis Hawley, "Herbert Hoover, the Commerce Secretariat, and the Vision of an 'Associative State,' 1921-1928," *Journal of American History*, 61 (June 1974), 116-40; Barry D. Karl, "Presidential Planning and Social Science Research. Mr. Hoover's Experts," *Perspectives in American History*, 3 (1969), 347-409. For an introduction to the corporate perspective in recent American history, see Ellis Hawley, "Techno-Corporatist Formulas in the Liberal State, 1920-1960: A Neglected Aspect of America's Search For a New Order," unpublished manuscript.

liberal academic culture, an elitist view of education, and, most significant of all, an evolutionary organic view of social change.[4]

From the rather belated start of his academic career, Garfield held that the University stood ideally as a "body of cultivated men, earnest & seeking by all ways to advance the cause of civilization. . . ." As a teacher Garfield aimed not so much to transfer professional skills as "To *inspire the men* to a lively interest in the relation which each must hold to the community, & *a desire* coupled with *fitness* to perform their part in the political life of the locality of their settlement." He drew upon Edmund Burke for his lectures in politics and called the young men to a recognition of their duties and moral responsibilities. Garfield recognized in himself the kind of institutional conservatism this implied and ruminated in his Princeton diary: "Think my natural way is to remodel, renovate, improve rather than start with new plan based on departures through legislation. We legislate too much, exchanging often the ill we have for those we know not of."[5] Garfield, like Wilson, absorbed the nineteenth-century gentry tradition, and this shared legacy helps account for the mutual respect between them. Frederic C. Howe, who had joined the Garfield brothers in their Cleveland law practice and had received their generous support despite his more advanced political views, later recalled: "They had the kind of moral distinction that the Romans described as manliness — *virtus*. It was tolerant, kindly, scrupulous."[6] Wilson evidently saw these same qualities in Harry Garfield, for as close observers noted during the war: "The President had unlimited confidence in Garfield."[7]

But Garfield, more than Wilson, also appreciated the newer strands of social thought characteristic of prewar professional groups, summed up in the phrase "the gospel of efficiency." It was an orientation that led Garfield to an early appreciation of his wartime colleague Herbert Hoover, but it was evident before that in his enormous enthusiasm for Charles Steinmetz's book, *America and the New Epoch*, published in 1916.[8] The intellectual

[4] Laurence R. Veysey provides an introduction to Wilson's thought from this perspective in "The Academic Mind of Woodrow Wilson," *Mississippi Valley Historical Review*, 49 (Mar. 1963), 613-34. See also Robert Cuff, "We Band of Brothers—Woodrow Wilson's War Managers," *Canadian Review of American Studies*, 5 (Fall 1974), 140-41.

[5] Garfield Diary, Feb. 13, 1904; February 8, 1905, emphasis in the original; Mar. 29, 1904, in the Papers of Harry A. Garfield, Library of Congress, Washington, D.C., Box 3.

[6] Frederic C. Howe, *The Confessions of a Reformer* (Chicago: Quadrangle, 1967), 198.

[7] Quoted in "Interview with Mr. Newton D. Baker, Apr. 6, 1928," in Papers of Ray Stannard Baker, Library of Congress, Washington, D.C., Box 20.

[8] Charles P. Steinmetz, *America and the New Epoch* (New York: Harper, 1916).

connection between Steinmetz — a German emigré, long-time socialist, and engineering wizard at General Electric's research laboratory — and Garfield, the patrician, is a curious one, and yet not without a certain logic. Both men embraced the wider impulse to create a consciousness appropriate to an emergent corporate society. Both men took an organic view of that society, even if Garfield drew upon an earlier, conservative tradition while Steinmetz, the engineer, embraced the promise of a scientific future. In Steinmetz, Garfield found confirmation for the general proposition that the war marked a turning point in the history of the United States and of the western world, a transformation from an age of individualism and competition to a new corporate epoch.[9]

One might have thought that as a socialist Steinmetz would turn to government control, to nationalization, as the linchpin of his new corporate order. He looked instead to the private sphere for industrial control, and in a way which a reader of Garfield's persuasion could easily identify. Steinmetz had simply tried to be realistic on this point. National control was obviously beyond the reach of the American government in its current fragmented and inefficient form. "There is no constructive supervisory power, in our country, as was represented by the central Government in Germany," he wrote; "our Governments, from the federal down to the municipal, are not organized for constructive activity, and thus their entrance in the field is largely inhibitory, liable to disorganize by interference." Nor in Steinmetz's view is this likely to change given the country's deep traditions of individualism and democratic localism.

Belief in federal ineffectiveness was only the negative side of the equation. On the positive side, Steinmetz believed he had seen the future in General Electric, and it worked. There was no need to turn to Washington for solutions because the principles of efficient national organization — "continuity, competency, and responsibility of the administrative organization" — were already embodied in the progressive industrial corporation. It was necessary simply "to extend methods of economic efficiency from the individual industrial corporation to the national organism as a whole."[10] A study of American history suggested this as the next stage in national evolution; analysis of the current war confirmed the trend on a still broader canvass. Wartime mobilization among the Allies already demonstrated both the opportunity and the necessity of corporate trends. If the United States would only combine its democratic heritage with the logic of corporate con-

[9] James Gilbert discusses the life and thought of Charles Steinmetz in *Designing the Industrial State: The Intellectual Pursuit of Collectivism in America, 1880-1940* (Chicago: Quadrangle, 1972), ch. 7.
[10] Steinmetz, *New Epoch,* 125-26, 151, 156.

solidation it could create a balance of liberty and order worthy of emulation around the world.

Steinmetz advocated a number of specific proposals common among progressive business theorists, including elimination of the antitrust laws, greater private welfare measures, more sophisticated corporate leadership, and strategems for production stability. His specific illustrations of how price and production agreements could eliminate the overproduction endemic to competitive capitalism anticipated the approach the Fuel Administration would take in the coal fields two years later.

Steinmetz's forecast for economic and political institutions under the new corporate dispensation are especially intriguing. He envisaged a form of oligopoly arising in every major industry, each with its own supervisory executive committee, with all committees presided over by a supreme governing body, an Industrial Senate, composed of competent individuals who rose to their place by a mysterious process of self-selection. Steinmetz foresaw an equivalent consolidation and centralization of political forms. A "Tribunicate" would emerge, elected at frequent intervals by majority vote, devoted to defining general industrial policy, and in possession of a veto power intended to protect the public interest against overly aggressive industrial spokesmen. Policy would originate with the "Tribunicate," but technical problem solving and effective administration would rest with the subordinate arms of the Industrial Senate. In this dual form of government, Steinmetz believed economic efficiency and democratic safeguards, technical competence and majority rule, private initiative and public interest would at last find an organizational form appropriate to the emergent corporate era.

It is tempting to draw explicit connections between a programmatic book like *America and the New Epoch* and a public figure like Garfield, but it can be very misleading. The fate of claims once made for the impact of Herbert Croly's *Promise of American Life* on Theodore Roosevelt is warning enough. Yet there can be no question of Garfield's enthusiasm for Steinmetz. Garfield is explicit on this point in private correspondence; his public speeches are redolent of the book's themes; and he eagerly forwarded a copy to Wilson himself, with the commendation, "The book is full of meat."[11] As we shall see later, moreover, a number of Garfield's postwar proposals resemble far too closely the Steinmetz approach to be regarded as merely coincidental.

[11] Harry A. Garfield to Woodrow Wilson, Jan. 16, 1916, Papers of Woodrow Wilson, Library of Congress, Washington, D.C. And see Garfield to Lucretia R. Garfield, Jan. 15, 1917, Garfield Papers, Box 29.

Garfield found Steinmetz so appealing because of his own prewar commitment to the cooperative ethic. He shunned the bellicose sentiments which swept through Eastern college campuses as the war lengthened through 1915 into 1916. And he never viewed the war as merely an opportunity for American business to press forward in the tradition of antagonistic commercial relations and displace Europe from world markets, or to build up domestic prosperity with munitions orders. Garfield defined preparedness as a search for ways the United States could perform *"useful* service to mankind,"[12] and a demonstration of the utility of cooperative attitudes both at home and abroad offered one of the best ways of all. For Garfield the war crisis illustrated "the change from competition to cooperation which is sweeping over our Western world, Europe & England, & the importance of quickly perceiving its value here in America."[13] "We have come to the parting of the ways," Garfield told the Economic Club of Boston in January 1917, "we have come to the time when the old individualistic principle of competition must be set aside and we must boldly embark upon the new principle of cooperation and combination." Such a view included a tempering of the antitrust tradition and an extension of commission government, but Garfield extended his analysis beyond economics to culture itself. He called for a new approach to education to interest students in community life and the cooperative principle in place of the current emphasis upon competition and its erroneous view of success.[14]

From Garfield's perspective war itself was a manifestation of competition and strife. He could not regard it as a solution to anything; it was part of the problem. And so through the pre-1917 period Garfield always urged caution and evenhandedness on Wilson as the president executed his foreign policy; and he greeted the final declaration of war with serious misgivings. It is remarkable that Wilson should call to Washington as an advisor a man who opposed American entry into the war to the very end. "In this crisis the President & Congress believe that the only sure way to a state of international goodwill is through war," Garfield wrote his mother in some anguish on April 6, 1917. "It is hard for me to see it, but I shall not oppose & shall do all that I ought."[15] It is indicative of Wilson's great respect for Garfield (perhaps even his emotional need for Garfield's approval) that the president should feel obliged to explain his decision four days after the declaration: "I hope with all my heart that my address to the Congress has convinced you that I had good reasons and that the course I pursued was

---

[12] From "The Attitude of the United States Toward Preparedness," an address delivered at Mount Morris Baptist Church, ibid., Box 142.

[13] Garfield to Lucretia R. Garfield, Jan. 15, 1917, Garfield Papers, Box 29.

[14] From an address to the Economic Club of Boston, Jan. 11, 1917, ibid., Box 143.

[15] Garfield to Lucretia R. Garfield, Apr. 6, 1917, ibid., Box 29.

not pursued either in haste or in vexation. I should not like to feel that I was going against the judgment of a man whose judgment I so highly and sincerely value."[16] Garfield accepted Wilson's conclusion, of course. But it is interesting that in drafting his reply he should reflect once again a theme of *America and the New Epoch.* "Too many who were war-mad," Garfield wrote, "see now that this is the last act in the drama of Democracy against Monarchy, begun by our Revolution, in which change in form of government has been the theme."[17]

Garfield first went to Washington as part of the Hoover coterie, helping to construct the Food Administration and assisting with the Administration's agricultural policies. Then in August 1917 he accepted Wilson's challenge to head the newly created Fuel Administration, and he remained with that agency until it suspended its operations in the summer of 1919.

An enormous range of problems confronted Garfield in August, problems for which his past experience afforded only meager preparation. There were the challenges of recruiting staff, establishing policy, and building an emergency field organization; of pacifying a chaotic, competitive industry still smarting from recent Administration charges of illegal price fixing; of guaranteeing the collective rights of the expanding United Mine Workers; of administering production of a commodity already largely under contract to major buyers; of countering skepticism about his own personal qualifications among Congressional spokesmen and Republican leaders. Early handling of the industry, moreover, had prejudiced the case against the Fuel Administration at the outset. The Administration stumbled badly when Wilson personally turned aside a voluntary price agreement from the industry in June 1917 and imposed a lower price instead.[18]

But relations between the agency and the industry improved dramatically in subsequent months. A steady retreat from the president's price was one of the costs Garfield incurred for industry cooperation. It was also one of the prices he paid for a series of successful wage agreements with the UMW. A steady increase in the numbers of coal industry executives in the agency also dampened early suspicions; and UMW spokesmen also found a place. The Fuel Administration cannot be counted a great success in raising coal production in 1918. But its relative success in stabilizing prices and labor—

[16] Wilson to Garfield, Apr. 11, 1917, quoted in Ray Stannard Baker, *Woodrow Wilson, Life and Letters,* Vol. 7 (Garden City, N. Y.: Doubleday, 1927-1939), 15.
[17] Garfield to Wilson, May 4, 1917, Garfield Papers, Box 29.
[18] The blow-up over the industry's early offer is described in Daniel R. Beaver, *Newton D. Baker and the American War Effort, 1917-1919* (Lincoln, Neb.: Univ. of Nebraska Press, 1966), 64-66.

management relations makes the period something of a golden age in the industry's history.[19]

It is not to be supposed that this outcome owed everything to Garfield's ideology or to his unique leadership. Both industry and labor leaders soon realized the uses of the Fuel Administration. It bolstered their position in struggles over prices with major buyers; it strengthened their hand with other segments of the administrative state, particularly the Railroad Administration; it offered a buffer against public outcries over coal shortages and promised a sympathetic spokesman in higher government circles. Excess demand over supply, a comparatively unusual occurrence in the industry, coupled with rising profits, also reduced tensions and encouraged cooperation. In sum, a variety of structural and political factors within the industry and in its evolving relationship with the Fuel Administration ensured a positive institutional setting for experiments in cooperative administration.

Still, one should not overlook Garfield's role altogether. The industry certainly recognized the personal kind of triumph his persistent tenure implied. "The United States Fuel Administrator has shown a steadfastness of purpose in moral crises," observed the *Coal Trade Journal* in August 1918, "that is reminiscent of his father's resolute spirit."[20] In this instance the *Journal* referred to Garfield's resistance against a wage hike. But it surely also had in mind such previous episodes as Garfield's firm stand against the storm of criticism occasioned by his controversial announcement of January 17, 1918, closing down all factory production east of the Mississippi for a week, and for a specified number of Mondays thereafter; and his determination to end the railroads' habit of using car supplies to play off coal producers against each other for lower prices. Garfield took this issue right to the White House and won, despite a resignation threat from the president's son-in-law, William Gibbs McAdoo, who as Railroad Administrator championed the railroad argument.[21]

The issue here, however, is not so much a question of the structural realities on which the Fuel Administration rested, or of Garfield's administrative behavior. It is rather what Garfield intended to achieve through the Fuel Administration, and what meanings he assigned to the results. One can admit, for example, that Garfield did become a spokesman for the coal

---

[19] James P. Johnson, "Rationalization Under the Fuel Administration, 1917-1918," *passim.* Production of bituminous coal rose from 551,790,563 tons in 1917 to 585,883,000 tons in 1918. Ibid., p. 35. For a sketch of the coal industry in the pre-war years see William Graebner, "Great Expectations: The Search for Order in Bituminous Coal, 1890-1917," *Business History Review,* 48 (Spring 1974), 49-72.

[20] "The State of Trade," *The Coal Trade Journal* (Aug. 28, 1918), 1037.

[21] James P. Johnson, "Rationalization Under the Fuel Administration, 1917-1918," *passim.* On the implied resignation threat see Diary of Colonel House, May 2, 17, and 19, 1918, in the Papers of Edward M. House, Yale Univ. Library.

industry in some of the interbureaucratic struggles of wartime Washington; that his administration did rest upon an intimate alliance with the industry's newly founded trade association, the National Coal Association. One can admit these things without agreeing with charges that Garfield had become the tool of the coal interests, or that he acted as he did to increase the value of his own holdings in an Ohio coal field, one of the more vicious innuendos McAdoo floated about Washington to discredit his opponent.[22] Nor in Garfield's defense is it adequate to turn to the other side of the industry–labor coin and simply underscore the good working relationship he established with the UMW leadership, or the encouragement he offered to employer–employee committees at the mines as a framework for better labor relations and increased production. This kind of response would likewise conceive too narrowly the intention which motivated Garfield's entire administration: to create a model of cooperative enterprise in the coal fields that would stand as an ideal not just for the war, but for the peace as well. This model would stand, he hoped, as an illustration of the claim that by war's end the age of competition and selfish individualism in industry would, like war itself, pass forever. It would be to miss the point that community interest, not interest group, was Garfield's guiding principle.

Liberal theorists at *The New Republic* caught the drift of Garfield's meaning. William Hard, for example, exulted in the Fuel Administration experiment just as his colleagues discovered a cooperative future in Hoover's Food Administration and Baruch's WIB.[23] Several features of the Fuel Administration excited Hard's hopes for a new kind of pluralist social order, including its decentralized administration through state fuel administrators, the labor–management committees at the mine heads, and above all, the central, voluntary role of the National Coal Association. "If one must give it a name," wrote Hard of the Fuel Administration, "one may say perhaps that it is a sort of approach within capitalism, to an idea which certain English theorists have lately popularized — the idea of Guilds. The coal industry moves toward becoming a self-conscious unit, a capitalistic Guild, discharging its responsibility to other industries through its representatives who meet The State and who cooperate with The State." From Hard's perspective, as from Garfield's, the Fuel Administration had not imposed a bureaucracy on industry. It had rather "raised the coal industry to a new dignity by imposing certain definite collective duties on it, in the name of consumers, and by then summoning it to devise and to operate the methods

[22] House Diary, May 20, 1918.
[23] Paul F. Bourke establishes the broader intellectual context for *The New Republic* response to war agencies like the Fuel Administration in "The Pluralist Reading of James Madison's Tenth Federalist," *Perspectives in American History,* 9 (1975), 177-212, esp. 187-94.

by which those duties shall be done."[24] "Dignity," "duties," "consumers," "Guild" — such words resonated with Garfield and typified the values and meanings he took to, and drew from, his wartime experience.

Garfield's intention to dramatize the utility and virtue of the cooperative approach was even more evident as the war drew to a close. President Wilson, like the American public generally, seemed anxious to end wartime controls, in part, I think, because his decision to go to Paris meant he would not be on hand to administer them. But he was not inflexible on this point. And so he acceded to Garfield's recommendation in early December to keep the Fuel Administration in place until the end of the current coal year, April 1919.[25] With the coal industry's anxious support Garfield examined other ways to extend the war-induced stability in the face of diminishing emergency government powers. Increased exports, a common theme of the period, and one which in the context of Wilsonian ideology happily combined self-interest and international service, also appealed to Garfield, but made little sense in an industry which exported virtually no production (except to Canada). The Industrial Board that Secretary Redfield established in the Commerce Department to encourage price stability appeared more promising and received Garfield's support.[26] But Garfield's mind roamed much more broadly than this. The cooperative principle, though it included a continuation of "the spirit of cooperation" in the coal fields, extended far beyond a single industry; it required in Garfield's view a complete federal reorganization to achieve.

Garfield's utopian scheme sprang in a general way from his early view that the war confronted the United states with the opportunity, even necessity, to forge a more cooperative industrial order out of the war-torn ruins of a competitive past. In April 1917 Garfield had specifically indicated to Wilson that he interpreted the war as a watershed in the evolution of institutional forms, "the last act in the drama of Democracy against Monarchy, begun by our Revolution, in which change in form of government has been the theme."[27] Garfield now intended to draw together the logical extensions of changes implicit in his wartime administration.

The wartime development that raised his hopes so high, however, was not so much the Fuel Administration as the President's War Council, or Industrial Cabinet, as Garfield called it. Wilson had been reluctant to meet

[24] William Hard, "Socialistic Coal," *New Republic,* 17 (Nov. 16, 1918) 64-66.
[25] Garfield to Wilson, Dec. 1, 1918, and Wilson to Garfield, Dec. 3, 1918, both in Garfield Papers, Box 93.
[26] Robert F. Himmelberg, "Business, Antitrust Policy, and the Industrial Board of the Department of Commerce, 1919," *Business History Review,* 42 (Spring 1968), 1-23; and Garfield to Wilson, Mar. 27, 1919, Garfield Papers, Box 93.
[27] Garfield to Wilson, May 4, 1917, ibid., Box 29.

regularly with his key economic advisors, despite the prolonged urging of Garfield and others, but he finally yielded in March 1918 in order to defuse the call by his critics for a Munitions Ministry. The Council, which met weekly thereafter, had no formal minutes or staff, but it did help Wilson develop and coordinate general economic policy. Its membership included William Gibbs McAdoo, Director of the Railroad Administration and Treasury Secretary; Josephus Daniels, Secretary of the Navy; Newton D. Baker, Secretary of War; Bernard Baruch, chairman of the War Industries Board; Herbert Hoover, head of the Food Administration; Edward N. Hurley, chairman of the Shipping Board and Emergency Fleet Corporation; Vance C. McCormick, chairman of the War Trade Board; and Garfield.[28]

For a man intrigued with the Steinmetz idea of a dual government evolving from current industrial and political forms, the Industrial Cabinet might conceivably hold the embryo of a new Industrial Senate, the directing body of the nation's political economy. Garfield certainly thought so, and in the early months of 1919 he tried to persuade the Administration to his view. His scheme would serve as the domestic analogue of Wilson's League of Nations, as he explained to Bernard Baruch in March 1919. "The cooperation which the President is aiming to secure between nations must be secured between government, representing the public, and capital and labor. The two things are part and parcel of the same great problem."[29]

The details of Garfield's plan remained in flux, but the general outline was clear. He envisaged formation of a cabinet group composed of the Secretaries of Interior, Commerce, Labor, and Agriculture, the director of the Railroad Administration, the chairman of the Shipping Board, the director of the Fuel Administration, "and such other secretaries as a thorough study of the industries supervised or controlled by the government would indicate." A complete reorganization and reclassification of the various information-gathering bureaus and regulatory commissions would follow with possible regrouping under some central body, perhaps a "Commission of Science and Statistics."[30] A later version of the plan advocated supervisory commissions for key commodities in the major economic departments. Each commission would include three representatives each from management and labor, plus a director appointed by the President. They could be formed for bituminous and anthracite coal and petroleum in the Interior Department, for example; for steel, copper, and public utilities in Commerce; for wheat, meats, lumber, cotton, and wool in Agriculture. In addition, industry repre-

[28] Robert Cuff, "Wilsonian War Managers," 136-37.
[29] Garfield to Baruch, Mar. 3, 1919, RG 67, Records of the United States Fuel Administration, Federal Government Records Center, Suitland, Md., File E-1, Box 2.
[30] Garfield to Josephus Daniels, Mar. 14, 1919, Garfield Papers, Box 129.

sentatives would have an opportunity to appear before these commissions to make their case on relevant issues. Garfield proposed, in effect, to transfer to regular government departments some of the regulatory and coordinating schemes of such agencies as the War Industries Board and the Food Administration, and to retain several emergency war boards on a permanent basis.[31]

Garfield's ideas for the postwar extension of the political side of government were less well-developed, but he clearly had the dual-government idea in mind. To parallel his "Industrial Cabinet" he proposed a "political cabinet" composed of the Secretaries of State, Treasury, War, Navy, Interior, Justice, and the Postmaster General. (He had placed the Interior Secretary in the Industrial Cabinet in another version.) The president would meet separately with each of his Cabinets but might on occasion call them together.[32] During the war Wilson had met with only his War Council, or Industrial Cabinet, though in the context of Garfield's postwar proposal the Council was really a truncated version of both political and industrial cabinets.

Wilson had not invited Garfield to Paris (possibly because of the utopian quality of his ideas) and so Garfield had to await the president's return before unveiling his scheme at the White House. In preparation for his presentation he canvassed Baker, Daniels, and Lane and claimed support from all three. In the meantime, he also won endorsement from coal industry leaders who had their own reasons for supporting any scheme which promised continuing stability.

On February 26, Garfield formally presented his scheme to the president at a War Council meeting. Wilson, as might have been expected, was not encouraging, though he did not dismiss Garfield's ideas out of hand. Legislation along such lines at the current session of Congress, however, was simply out of the question. "The President also expressed the opinion," recorded Garfield, "that even an executive order might bring down criticism from his opponents and that whatever was done should be set about quietly and be within the scope of the law, utilizing as the proposed directors and chairmen of the commissions, especially after the promulgation of peace, permanent officers of government, whose duties in that relation would have the sanction of law."[33] Wilson's response was consistent with his general opposition to new departures in emergency government in the post-

---

[31] "Further Elaboration of the Plan Submitted At The White House Meeting Feb. 26, 1919 . . . ," attached to Garfield to Wilson, Feb. 26, 1919, ibid., Box 110.

[32] Garfield to Daniels, Mar. 14, 1919, ibid., Box 129.

[33] "White House Meeting Feb. 26, 1919," a memorandum in ibid., Box 129.

Armistice period, a position which so annoyed liberal columnists and public planning enthusiasts.[34]

Garfield could hardly expect much support from Wilson. The president obviously had to avoid controversies which might further complicate his relations with Congress and inhibit his plans for the League, on which he staked so much. But Garfield persisted in subsequent months. He elaborated his plan further for colleagues; he aired the scheme once again before the coal industry, at the second annual meeting of the National Coal Association in May; and he urged the Interior Department to at least take over his coordinating activities in the coal industry and establish there his kind of industrial commission.[35] This was not an unreasonable hope, for a variety of wartime functions were finding their way into the regular government departments, including the Interior Department.

But by June 1919 this kind of modest transfer was about the most Garfield could expect. The Fuel Administration prepared to close its own doors, its records already transferred to Interior; and there was nothing more to be done for his larger scheme. Garfield's plan soon disappeared into the historical rubble of broken dreams. Even his efforts to revive the Fuel Administration and hold coal prices steady in the fall of 1919 ended in failure and in his personal resignation from the Wilson Administration in December 1919.[36]

It is remarkable that Garfield's proposal for federal reorganization received a hearing at all. It indicates the intensely fluid quality of this historical period certainly; but it indicates as well the depth of Garfield's own personal quest for the institutional forms of a more cooperative order. "Above all things," as he wrote Wilson in March 1919, Garfield feared "the return of unregulated competition. It lies at the root of industrial and international unrest, and is almost as disturbing as unbridled condemnation."[37] Garfield intended by his Industrial Cabinet and dual-government scheme to eliminate this potential on the domestic front, as he hoped Wilson's diplomacy would create a cooperative order on the international front.

It is not too much to suppose that Charles Steinmetz's *America and the New Epoch* figured in Garfield's thinking on this point. But the specific

[34] Robert D. Cuff, *The War Industries Board: Business–Government Relations during World War I* (Baltimore: Johns Hopkins Univ. Press, 1973), 242-44.
[35] "Address by Hon. Harry A. Garfield at the Second Annual Convention of the National Coal Association, Chicago, May 22, 1919," Garfield Papers, Box 143.
[36] The episode over wages and prices which eventually led to Garfield's resignation is a story in itself. For an introduction to it see Stanley Coben, *A. Mitchell Palmer: Politician* (New York: Columbia Univ. Press, 1963), 176-83.
[37] Garfield to Wilson, Mar. 3, 1919, Garfield Papers, Box 93.

nature of those interconnections is less important than our recognition of how an influential member of the Wilsonian inner circle oriented himself to the world by means of corporate values. The important point is to recognize how this strain of corporate thinking entered into and helped define the general, over-arching ideology of Wilsonian liberalism. Any discussion of what the war meant for the Wilsonians, in other words, must take this into account.

In Garfield's personal and political odyssey — from the Republicanism of his youth through Woodrow Wilson's Democracy at middle age — it is perhaps fitting that in his later years he should return to the Republican heritage of his father. It is equally appropriate that Herbert Hoover should be an instrument of this return. In any case, in 1928 Garfield, responding to an appeal for Al Smith from Franklin Roosevelt, declared firmly for Hoover.[38] Not long ago this decision by a man so obviously committed to corporatist thinking in his earlier years might have been regarded as a rather intriguing contradiction, a sign perhaps of the conservative retreat of advancing years. In light of the recent Hoover scholarship, however, it can be seen as no contradiction at all. Garfield's position is consistent with the recently uncovered tradition embodied in Hoover in which commitment to preserving individual freedom is balanced by commitment to constructing a new corporate order.

Garfield, like Hoover, was committed to the gentry tradition of the nineteenth century, yet open to the techno-corporatist thought of the twentieth. Garfield, like Hoover, was committed to a capitalist order, yet appalled by its competitive excess. Garfield, like Hoover, was committed to corporate order, yet wary of bureaucratic controls. And it is by his commitment to such values and meanings as these that Garfield, like Hoover, carried forward a central legacy of the Wilsonian mobilization during the Great War.

[38] Garfield to Roosevelt, Sept. 28, 1928, ibid., Box 89.

United States Mobilization and Railroad Transportation: Lessons in Coordination and Control, 1917–1945

☆

Robert D. Cuff

THE transportation snarl of 1917–18 holds a significant place in historical accounts of U.S. mobilization during World War I, and deservedly so. This massive paralysis of rail and port traffic in the industrial Northeast during late December 1917, touched off a firestorm of criticism of the executive branch. For U.S. citizens and allies alike, that breakdown symbolized the organizational weakness of the country's entire war effort. President Wilson's subsequent decision on 26 December to operate the railroads through a United States Railroad Administration under the direction of his son-in-law, Secretary of the Treasury William McAdoo, signalled, in turn, the beginning of a new stage in federal control of the wartime economy.

In some respects, the transportation crisis simply confronted the United States with a lesson that other belligerent states had learned years before, and that was the limits of economic competition as an instrument of organized action in wartime. Until December 1917, and notwithstanding the degree of government-sanctioned cooperation among railroads for military purposes in England, Germany, and elsewhere, both the Wilson administration and railroad managers stubbornly searched for an effective wartime rail service with a minimum change in peacetime business-government relationships. The December crisis dramatically ended that hope.

Historians have cited a number of factors to account for the tie-up.

The Journal of Military History 53 (January 1989): 33–50   © American Military Institute

They include unusually heavy snowfalls and freezing temperatures in December-January, an abnormal concentration of traffic flows to East Coast ports, unbalanced military contracting, an anarchic system of government transportation priorities, legal barriers to private pooling; and mounting labor shortages.

In addition to explanations that emphasize short-run factors, analysts have also interpreted the outcome as the logical result of an over-regulated industry that had been unfairly squeezed since at least 1915 between increases in labor and material costs on the one hand and a refusal by the Interstate Commerce Commission to raise rates on the other. Low rates of return made the industry unattractive to investors, and capital shortages in 1915 translated into car shortages in 1917.[1]

As for the meaning the wartime experiment held for federal control of industry in peacetime, contemporary commentators remained divided both during and after the war. They did generally agree, however, that federal operation, whatever its complicated and controversial causes, brought substantial improvement in transportation in 1918, and that this improvement rested heavily on technical methods and administrative arrangements that government and industry devised on behalf of more effective institutional coordination and operational control.[2]

1. For the transportation crisis and its causes, see William J. Cunningham, *American Railroads: Government Control and Reconstruction Policies* (Chicago: A. W. Shaw, 1922), chaps. 1–3; Walker D. Hines, *War History Of American Railroads* (New Haven: Yale University Press, 1928), chaps. 1–2; Ari and Olive Hoogenboom, *A History of the ICC: From Panacea to Palliative* (New York: Norton, 1976), chaps. 2–3; K. Austin Kerr, *American Railroad Politics* (Pittsburgh: University of Pittsburgh Press, 1968). chap. 3; Albro Martin. *Enterprise Denied:* Origins of the Decline of American Railroads, 1897–1917 (New York: Columbia University Press, 1971), chaps. 11–12; and Stephen Skowronek, *Building a New American State: The Expansion of National Administrative Capacities, 1877–1920* (New York: Cambridge University Press, 1982), chap. 8.

For references in a recent account to the government takeover, see Robert Higgs, *Crisis and Leviathan: Critical Episodes in the Growth of the American Government* (New York: Oxford, 1987), 144–47, 152–53. The following contain references to the close prewar relationship between railroads and military authorities in England and Germany: Susan Armitage, *The Politics of Decontrol of Industry: Britain and the United States* (London: Weidenfeld and Nicolson, 1969), chap. 2; and Gerald D. Feldman, *Army, Industry and Labor in Germany 1914–1918* (Princeton: Princeton University Press, 1966), 253–58.

2. Cunningham's *American Railroads* may be taken as representative of this centrist position. See also Lewis Sorrell, *Government Ownership and Operation of Railways for the United States* (New York: Prentice-Hall, 1937), especially 250.

The political and administrative fate of the railroads during World War II offers a striking contrast. In December 1941, President Roosevelt established an Office of Defense Transportation in his Office of Emergency Management, and this agency—which practiced administrative guidance, not federal management—retained jurisdiction for the rest of the war. After overseeing a huge peacetime expansion of government during the New Deal, and with far more personal enthusiasm for national planning than Woodrow Wilson ever possessed, Roosevelt still found no reason to emulate Wilson's wartime railroad program. In World War II there was no railroad crisis, and there was no federal take-over.

All commentators agree, moreover, that during World War II the industry turned in an outstanding performance, superior in many respects to its performance during World War I under either private or public control. As a Brookings study of 1949 noted, "The railroads handled 74 per cent more freight and 100 per cent more passenger traffic than during the First World War with one quarter fewer cars, one third fewer locomotives, and one quarter fewer men."[3] As Table I suggests, the railroad performance of 1942 surpassed the comparable railroad experience of 1918 in almost every respect.

By World War II alternative forms of transportation had come into play, and there is no question that motor transport and pipelines reduced pressure on the railroads. But it is easy to exaggerate this point. During World War II, the railroads actually increased their share of overall transport. Wartime restrictions on gasoline and rubber, coupled with a shortage of automotive replacement parts, meant a temporary resurgence in rail as compared to highway transport.

The pre–World War II percentage of ton-miles furnished by railroads peaked in 1926 at 76 percent; motor carriers in that year furnished 4 percent and grew at the expense of the railroads thereafter, as Table II indicates. The railroads furnished only 63 percent of ton-miles in 1940. In 1942, however, the load increased sharply to 71 percent and then to 73 percent in 1943, which approached the 1926 figure. So while it is true that railroads carried a smaller percentage of total transport in World War II, significant increases over peacetime brought the

---

For illustrations of improved traffic movement in 1918, and for such improved techniques in coordination and control as statistical reporting systems developed under the United States Railroad Administration, see Hines, *War History Of American Railroads,* chap. 4, and 124–25.

3. Charles L. Dearing and Wilfred Owen, *National Transportation Policy* (Washington: Brookings, 1949), 153.

Table I

Railway Performance, 1918 vs. 1942

All Railways	1918	1942	Percent 1942 over (+) or under (-) 1918
Tons of revenue freight originated (thousands)	1,376,845	1,498,477	+ 8.83
Revenue ton-miles (thousands).................	408,778,061	640,992,240	+56.81
Ton-miles of revenue freight per car-mile[1]	26.96	29.76	+10.39
Ton-miles of revenue freight per train-mile	620.68	947.87	+52.71
Average length of haul revenue freight[2]...........	296.89	427.76	+44.08
Revenue ton-miles per mile of road	1,582,796	2,638,067	+66.67
Number of revenue passengers carried (thousands)	1,122,963	672,420	−40.12
Total passenger-miles (thousands)	43,212,458	53,747,029	+24.38
Average journey per passenger (per road)	38.48	79.93	+107.72
Average revenue passenger-miles/train-mile	79	125	+58.23
Average revenue passenger-miles/car-mile(class I)	20	22	+10.00
Revenue passenger-miles/mile of road (class I)	183,066	236,400	+29.13

1. This average is obtained by dividing the revenue ton-miles by the total loaded car-miles, the latter figure including some cars loaded with nonrevenue freight.

2. All railways as a system.

Source: Interstate Commerce Commission, *57th Annual Report* (Washington: GPO, 1943), 7.

overall percentage very close to the situation in 1916, before U.S. entry into World War I.[4]

The wartime resurgence of railroads is seen more vividly in the context of passenger service, where services furnished by the railroads in World War I, when they dominated all other forms of transportation, were far less than those offered in the first full year of World War II—43,212,458,000 passenger-miles in 1918, compared to 55,073,-000,000 in 1942, and 97,704,000,000 in 1944, an all-time record.

4. Tables in the text are drawn from Joseph H. Rose, *American Wartime Transportation* (New York: Thomas Y. Crowell, 1953), 31, 33, and 34-5. On the general theme of wartime resurgence among the railroads, see also Emory R. Johnson, *The Railroads And Public Welfare: Their Problems and Policies* (New York: Simmons-Boardman, 1944), 1, 25-6, 35, and chap. 5. Railroad management predicted early the wartime decline in highway transport. See "Economic Preparation for War," *Railway Age* 107 (September 23, 1939): 429-30.

Table II

Percentage Distribution of Intercity Freight Traffic,
Public and Private, by Kinds of Transportation

Year	Railways	Highways	Inland Waterways including Great Lakes	Pipe Lines	Airways (domestic revenue services)
1916	77.2		18.4	4.4	
1926	77.6	4.	15.7	3.7	
1939	64.26	8.33	16.86	10.55	
1940	63.36	8.36	18.38	9.9	
1941	64.72	8.5	17.59	9.19	
1942	71.08	5.36	15.29	8.27	
1943	72.79	4.6	12.91	9.69	.01
1944	70.19	4.45	12.87	12.48	.01
1945	68.9	5.33	13.14	12.62	.01

Source: For data beginning with 1939, Interstate Commerce Commission, Statement No. 5046, 1950; for 1916, Annual Report to the President for the year 1942, Office of Defense Transportation, 4; for 1926, Railroad Transportation, A Statistical Record 1911-1947 (Washington: Association of American Railroads, Bureau of Railway Economics, 1948), 37.

Yearly rates of increase were equally impressive, as Table III indicates. In 1939 motor operation provided over 90 percent of intercity passenger-miles. By 1944 this portion had declined to 63.8 percent and railroad shares had risen from 8.6 percent of the total to 34.6 percent. As Table IV indicates, air transport remained insignificant for passenger service.[5]

This performance took place, moreover, in the context of overall decline in trackage and cars. In 1918 railroads operated 258,507 miles of road on 402,343 miles of track. In 1929 mileage reached 260,570 and trackage 429,055 miles. Contraction was dramatic after that point.

5. Air transportation did not become price competitive with the railroads until after World War II. See Marvin L. Fair and Ernest W. Williams, Jr., *Economics of Transportation and Logistics* (Dallas, Texas: Business Publications, Inc., 1975), 107.

21

Table III

Percentage Distribution of Intercity Passenger Traffic, Public and Private, by Kinds of Transportation on Basis of Passenger-Miles

Year	Railway	Highway	Inland Waterway including Great Lakes	Air
1939	8.6	90.6	.54	.25
1940	8.7	90.5	.46	.37
1941	9.7	89.3	.58	.44
1942	19.6	79.3	.66	.50
1943	33.1	65.5	.71	.60
1944	34.6	63.8	.78	.80
1945	30.6	67.5	.67	1.10

Source: Annual Reports of the Interstate Commerce Commission for appropriate years (Washington: GPO).

Table IV

Wartime Intercity Railway Passenger Traffic

Year	Passenger-Miles (000,000)	Percent Increase over 1940
1940	24,766	
1941	30,317	23
1942	55,073	123
1943	89,865	263
1944	97,704	295
1945	93,817	280

Source: Annual Reports of the Interstate Commerce Commission for appropriate years (Washington: GPO).

In 1939 carriers operated 246,922 miles of road and 408,350 miles of track, and by the end of 1941, just before Pearl Harbor, the figures were 244,263 and 403,625 respectively. The downward trend continued during the war; by 1945 mileage had fallen to 239,438, trackage to 398,054.

In sum, the railroads turned in an impressive performance in World War II, more impressive, in many respects, than their predecessors during World War I, and they did it without the same degree of direct, federal control. How do we explain this?

Improved operational efficiency is one key factor in understanding the performance numbers. Heavier equipment and faster speeds, more extensive electrification, and higher levels of labor productivity are all relevant to explaining gains in ton-miles, for example, despite reductions in trackage and cars.[6] Traffic flows to both Pacific and Atlantic coasts in World War II also reduced the rail congestion that had marked East Coast ports in 1917-1918. But there are more important factors to consider in explaining why a federal take-over proved unnecessary during the Second World War.

One reason for the absence of federal railroad operations during World War II was the widespread institutional learning that occurred as a result of the transportation crisis of World War I. The crisis of 1917-1918 had a dramatic impact on everyone who struggled through it, whether in industry, government, or the military. For carriers and shippers, the Great War demonstrated that government take-over would very likely follow performance failure by private management in any subsequent mobilization. As a result, the World War I experience served both as political threat and practical demonstration, an outcome that became more worrisome, of course, as entry into the second war grew more probable.

In May 1941, for example, Joseph Eastman, chairman of the Interstate Commerce Commission, warned the industry that "if any faults or deficiencies develop, I imagine the government will not long hesitate to assume control if by so doing it can see a way of correcting or averting dangerous conditions."[7] And *Traffic World,* a shipper's journal, cau-

---

6. Harold Barger, *The Transportation Industries, 1889-1946: A Study of Output, Employment, and Productivity* (New York: National Bureau of Economic Research, 1951), 102-11. See also *Recent Economic Changes in the United States* (New York: McGraw-Hill, 1929), 1: 306-8; and Johnson, *The Railroads,* 251, 275-79. The ability of the roads to increase their services without major plant expansion also indicates an oversupply of facilities—an excess capacity. See Fair and Williams, *Economics of Transportation,* 452-53.

7. Quoted in Claude M. Fuess, *Joseph B. Eastman* (New York: Columbia University Press, 1952), 271.

tioned repeatedly through 1941 that the entire industry would pay the price of government possession if carriers and shippers failed to cooperate for defense.[8]

For transportation executives—who preferred to cite governmental shortcomings in their analysis of the threat of wartime take-over of railroads—the World War I experience also demonstrated the liability to industry of a decentralized, governmental system of transportation priorities. In the future, they argued, Washington had to take a coordinated approach to rail freight, port capacity, and shipping availability,[9] since failure to align those separate functions had accounted for much of the port congestion in 1917–1918. As a result, rail executives in the interwar years, in contrast to the 1914–1916 period, began to collaborate with military officials in order to influence transportation planning and head off any potential crisis.

This increased military-industrial collaboration is the second reason why federal takeover of the railroads proved unnecessary in World War II. The military dimension of national policy shrank dramatically after World War I. In 1920, however, Congress delegated to the Office of the Assistant Secretary of War (O.A.S.W.) responsibility for mobilization and procurement planning, and that group, although very much a minority voice both in Washington and in the services themselves, led the way in thinking through the nature of wartime transportation, in cooperation with industry representatives.

Throughout these years, the Planning Branch of the Office of the Assistant Secretary of War included transportation as a subject area for specialized study, in terms of transportation needs both for specific commodities, and for devising administrative plans for national transportation control. And although army planners took into account the

8. Among various *Traffic World* editorials on this point, see July 26, 1941, 195–96; August 30, 1941, 515; and September 6, 1941, 568. Of course, shippers had every reason to worry. They had lost far more politically than either labour or management during the U.S.R.A. experiment of World War I. But shippers were not alone. *Railway Age*, the leading management journal, also argued the case against government ownership through the 1939–1941 period. See, for example, "The War and the Transportation Problem," *Railway Age* 107 (September 18, 1939): 395–97; "Economic Preparedness for War," ibid., 107 (September 23, 1939): 429–30; and "No Reason for Defeatism Regarding Railroads Now," ibid., 109 (July 6, 1940): 1–3.

9. Rose, *American Transportation*, 71, 277. According to Fair and Williams, traffic congestion at major eastern terminals in 1917–1918 created national awareness of that particular problem for the first time. They conclude that anticipation of it before World War II demonstrates that "the lessons of World War I were well learned." See *Economics of Transportation*, 474–75.

five basic transportation types—railroad, highway, waterway, airway, and pipeline—"major attention was devoted to railroads as the key transportation agency." [10] Management's leading trade association, the American Railway Association, cooperated in the process and appointed a liaison official in each of the army's fourteen procurement districts. The secretary of war noted hopefully in 1925: "This cooperation has begun now, when no major emergency is in sight. By such means it is expected that when an emergency does arise, the plans can be more easily carried into effect." [11]

In that year the War Department and Railway Association also agreed on a plan for railroad operation in event of war. The department "expressed the policy that the railroads should not be taken over by the government unless the emergency was such that in the opinion of the President such a step was necessary." [12] In the meantime, industry officials lectured at the Army Industrial College; various supply branches surveyed the likely transportation requirements of essential materials; and railroad problems found a place in industrial mobilization planning studies that culminated in the Industrial Mobilization Plan of 1930 and its successors in 1933, 1936, and 1939. [13]

10. R. Elberton Smith, *The Army and Economic Mobilization* (Washington: Department of the Army, 1959), 97. Smith notes that the Transportation Annex was one of the better developed annexes to the Industrial Mobilization Plan of 1930. Ibid., note 75.

11. *Annual Report of the Secretary of War, 1925,* 27. On the regional, decentralized approach to army procurement planning, see James W. Fesler, "Areas of Industrial Mobilization, 1917-1938," *Public Administration Review* 1 (Winter 1941): 146-66. On the general story of O.A.S.W. and interwar economic planning, see Harold W. Thatcher, "Planning For Industrial Mobilization, 1920-1940," Historical Section, General Administrative Services Division, Office of the Quartermaster General, 1943.

12. Major Edwin Kelton, "Railroad Capacity and National Defense," *Railway Age* 81 (November 8, 1926): 884. See also "What of Railroad Capacity?", ibid., 878. The full text of the plan was printed in *Railway Age,* March 7, 1925. See in praise of these developments, "Military Railroads," *New York Times,* March 5, 1925, 18.

13. See *Annual Report of the Secretary of War, 1927,* 32. See also *Annual Report of the Secretary of War, 1928,* 52. See also "Railways in a National Emergency," *Railway Age* 82 (March 26, 1927): 1007. In later plans, the army underscored its preference for private control. "They will leave them in the hands of their owners and draw in the owners to form a war service committee. It would receive orders from the government, that is, to control transportation as to what is necessary to do, It would have to go further than telling carriers what to do. Also, it will have to issue rules to shippers if we are to avoid congestion. There would have to be a licensing scheme set up whereby no shipper would be given a car unless he could

During 1939 and after, industry spokesmen trumpeted such gains to silence critics on the preparedness issue and to counter arguments for government control. In 1941, for example, the Railway Business Association assured the public: "Steps have been taken by the railways to prevent the mistakes of the first war period. New agencies have been set up, such as the Military Transportation Section, and the Manager of Port Traffic, of the Association of American Railroads. The former, with headquarters in the Quartermaster General's office in Washington, D.C., maintains close liaison with the military authorities and the railways, and the latter is delegated with the responsibility of insuring the free movement of traffic through the ports." The association had no doubt that congestion could be avoided in coming years.[14]

A third reason why a federal takeover along World War I lines proved unnecessary in World War II was that developments in policy and administration during the New Deal also strengthened the organizational potential of government and industry for managing railroad transportation in wartime. Although the railroads remained outside industrial code-making under the National Recovery Administration (1933–1935), they did share the general depression quest for economic stabilization. They were brought under the Emergency Railroad Transportation Act of 1933, which provided a Federal Emergency Coordinator of Railroad Transportation and a flexible framework for voluntary cooperation. Such activity encouraged O.A.S.W. transportation planners in the view that, "if the government continues in peacetime to set up greater control and regulation of facilities, it may be that when a time of war comes there will be sufficient permanent peacetime establishments to carry on such control as may be necessary. In that case it will not be

---

certify that he has a place to unload it at its destination." From "Conferences on the work of the Planning Branch, Office of the Assistant Secretary of War, held in Mr. Woodring's office, May 29–June 13, 1934," in Record Group 107, Records of the Assistant Secretary of War, Planning Branch, Box 7, National Archives and Records Administration, Washington, D.C. (hereafter cited as RG 107). W. W. Atterbury, president of the Pennsylvania Railroad, 1925–1935, was active in working with the military. During World War I he had gone to France as director of transportation for the American Expeditionary Forces. See Burgess and Kennedy, *Centennial History*, 567, 596.

14. P. Harvey Middleton, [Secretary, Railway Business Association], *Railways and Public Opinion; Eleven Decades* (Chicago: Railway Business Association, 1941), 143, 145, 148. See also for the same point, *Railway Age* 109 (October 5, 1940): 485. For earlier industry efforts to reassure the public, see "Railways Prepare For War Demands," *New York Times*, October 20, 1939, sec. 3, 1; and "Rails Called Ready For Defense," ibid., June 2, 1940, 14.

necessary to set up any wartime agency, as was done during the World War, and as our plan now calls for."[15] As Ellis Hawley has shown, "Under depression conditions and in view of the threat posed by newer forms of transport, the leaders of the older transportation industries had begun advocating a broad extension of the public utility approach, an extension they justified by appealing to past precedents, arguing that transportation was a 'natural monopoly,' or stressing things like public safety or national defense."[16]

New Deal transportation experiments also brought Joseph B. Eastman into the military mobilization story. Eastman, a protege of liberal Supreme Court Justice Louis Brandeis, and Roosevelt's choice for Federal Emergency Coordinator in 1933, had been on the Interstate Commerce Commission (I.C.C.) since 1919. A career public servant in the progressive tradition, Eastman represents an example of continuity in policy personnel that emerged around the railroad problem during the interwar years, a theme which his appointment as head of the Office of Defense Transportation in 1941 reinforces. His long experience in public service had given him "a thorough education in carrier problems."[17]

As Federal Coordinator between 1933 and 1936, Eastman, as his biographer writes, became an "observable symbol of a novel experiment in governmental guidance and regulation."[18] Eastman personally believed that the railroads should function as a unit, but as coordinator he found it difficult to do more than investigate means of achieving

15. From "Conferences on the work of the Planning Branch . . . , May 29–June 13, 1934," RG 107, Box 7. It is also important to note that since its establishment in 1932, the Reconstruction Finance Corporation had rescued financially troubled roads with government loans, an institution and option unavailable to industry and government in 1917.

16. Ellis W. Hawley, *The New Deal and the Problem of Monopoly: A Study in Economic Ambivalence* (Princeton: Princeton University Press, 1966), 226. For an example of the railroad argument for subsidization as part of defense preparedness, see Harry A. Wheeler, "Suggests Subsidy to Railroads," *Railway Age* 105 (November 12, 1938): 707–8. "Federal authority should not expect private ownership in a time when the return upon the investment is negligible, to maintain a defense mechanism at its own sole cost." (P. 708.) According to the president of the Lehigh Valley Railroad, "While all forms of transport have a place in war, successful military operations depend upon mass transport, a service that only the railroads can furnish." Quoted in "Rails' Prosperity Held Defense Need," *New York Times*, June 28, 1940. 33.

17. *Business Week* made the observation during its positive assessment of Eastman's appointment as O.D.T. chief. See "Eastman Rules the Roads," *Business Week*, January 3, 1942, 20.

18. Fuess, *Eastman*, 181.

economy and of improving operations.[19] As *Business Week* noted, "Tact, cajolery, and threats to use public opinion are his principal weapons."[20] But even if he had possessed more formal authority, Eastman would have shunned its use. He preferred the consultative approach.[21]

Despite its shortcomings as a coordinating instrument, however, the emergency experiment did educate industry executives to working with policy and advisory committees that negotiated between government and industry. The Emergency Railroad Transportation Act divided the nation's railroads into three regional groups, each under a coordinating committee chosen by members of carriers who, working with the federal coordinator, were to devise measures for pooling resources and for achieving more efficient service. It was exactly these features of the act that appealed to military planners. "If the office of the Federal Coordinator continues in existence and increases its control over transportation," observed one transportation specialist in 1934, "it may very well be that his office will be admirably suited to do exactly what we want done."[22]

Finally, and equally important, the industry during the interwar years developed its own coordinating mechanisms for both operations and policy. On the operational level, the roots of one experiment can be traced back to World War I when, as a result of an I.C.C. investigation, the railroads organized in February 1917 a Car Service Commission to coordinate car supply. Commission personnel were then absorbed into the U.S. Railroad Administration and empowered formally to relocate freight cars between individual railroads and regions so as to reduce back-hauling of empty cars and other wasteful practices. After the war the commission retained its functions as the Car Service Division of the Association of American Railroads. Army officials who monitored the division's work believed that in cooperation with both the I.C.C. and various advisory committees among shippers it had estab-

19. Eastman to Erwin A. Salk, January 25, 1941, Papers of Joseph B. Eastman, Amherst College Library.

20. "Railroad Bill—Orphan," *Business Week*, May 24, 1933, 22.

21. Fuess, *Eastman*, 211, and chap. 12. It should be noted that railroad unions also opposed rationalization among the railroads for fear of job losses. Management and labour united against renewal of the legislation in 1936.

22. On the experiment in federal coordination, see Earl Latham, *The Politics of Railroad Coordination, 1933–1936* (Cambridge: Harvard University Press, 1959), passim. See also "Conference on the work of the Planning Branch . . . , May 29–June 13, 1934," RG 107, Box 7.

Joseph B. Eastman: Federal Emergency Coordinator of Railroad Transportation, 1933-36; Director, Office of Defense Transportation, 1941-44. (Source: Wilson, Selected Papers and Addresses of Joseph B. Eastman, 45.)

lished effective control over the nation's freight cars, a view seconded by the industry itself. According to the Car Service Division's chairman, the division was even in times of peace "in a way . . . a war organization, experienced in dealing with the emergencies that arise from time to time in the handling of cars."[23]

23. "Railways in a National Emergency," *Railway Age* 82 (March 20, 1927): 1007. See also "What of Railroad Capacity," *Railway Age* 81 (November 6, 1926): 876; and Hines, *War History Of American Railroads*, 11-12.

On the policy level, the Association of American Railroads (A.A.R.) also enhanced wartime potential for coordination and control. The A.A.R. was established as the successor to the American Association of Railway Executives and American Railway Association in 1934 to influence the design of the Emergency Railroad Transportation Act. With a regular constitution and permanent staff, the A.A.R. aimed ultimately to displace public coordination under the Federal Emergency Coordinator with private coordination under its own auspices. It was barred from achieving tight centralization of its own organization for control purposes, however, "by the antitrust laws and by the strong individualism of the purposeful men and powerful roads they command."[24] But it did become an influential lobby group and provided a focal point for policy making within the industry. In this respect the A.A.R. provided a potential for intra-industry coordination that had no parallel before World War I.[25]

Many of the themes outlined above began to coalesce after 1939, as the economy felt the impact of the European war and such Washington initiatives as lend-lease aid to the allies. In November 1939, for example, the A.A.R. established a traffic system to prevent congestion at North Atlantic ports; in the summer of 1941 it drew up plans to head off shortages in transporting oil supplies. In the meantime, railroad executives continued to assert their determination to avoid the mistakes of 1917-1918. And *Traffic World* underscored the political need for practical action: "Those who are looking for a reason for placing the railroads in the hands of government may, we fear, find it as time goes on."[26] According to *Railway Age,* "It is a well-known fact that certain Washington bureaus are infested with socialists who are confidently hoping that something will happen to the railroads which they may plausibly—however falsely—label 'breakdown,' and thus provide an excuse for government operation."[27] Both journals agreed that carriers and shippers had to cooperate to ensure operating efficiency.

On the other hand, as a result of the factors noted above, there were

---

24. Latham, *Politics of Railroad Coordination,* 193. For greater detail on the associational networks that criss-crossed the industry during the 1930s, see 168ff.

25. The authors of the official Pennsylvania Railroad history regard the A.A.R. as "perhaps the most important outcome of the *Emergency Act of 1933,* " 662.

26. "The Car Supply Problem," *Traffic World* 68 (July 19, 1941): 122. See also *Business Week,* October 5, 1940, 50; and *New York Times,* November 8, 1939, 38; June 4, 1941, 37; June 7, 1941, 26; and June 20, 1941, 31.

27. "The Car Situation—No Cause for Panic, Nor for Complacency," *Railway Age* 110 (June 7, 1941): 1000.

good grounds for optimism. The Interstate Commerce Commission repeatedly asserted the positive case during the 1939–1941 period, citing governmental and industry gains since 1918 in policy, administration, and operational effectiveness.

In its 1939 report, for example, the commission listed six major differences between the current situation and pre–World War I days. For one thing, "It may be anticipated that as a result of the experience of the World War, the Government would be able, in the event of a similar emergency, to avoid conflicting actions of its own agencies with respect to transportation." It also suggested that the railroads had themselves become "better organized for centralized action than they were in 1917." The commission also noted how its own emergency power over traffic had increased since 1917. The Transportation Act of 1920, for example, empowered the I.C.C. to place embargoes on traffic, to determine traffic patterns, and to distribute car service upon declaration of an emergency; it was also empowered to require joint use of terminals.[28] In their annual report of 1940, the commissioners reiterated the assurances of 1939, that "the railroads are now able, because of improved methods and conditions of operation, to do materially more work per unit of equipment than was the case when they had a greater supply, and the further fact [is] that the capacity of other forms of transportation has greatly increased."[29] As the commissioners concluded in 1941, "the effort has been to avoid the mistakes which caused most of the railroad trouble at the time of the last World War."[30]

This comparatively sanguine reading of the capacity of the railroads and government to manage mobilization without a federal take-over was reflected in the Office of Defense Transportation. It was established on December 18, 1941, in the president's Office of Emergency Management under Joseph Eastman's direction, with authority for all forms of civilian transportation. But it remained a policy-making and not an operating body, in contrast to its predecessor, the United States Rail-

28. Interstate Commerce Commission, *53d Annual Report* (Washington: GPO, 1939), 22, 24.

29. Interstate Commerce Commission, *54th Annual Report* (Washington: GPO, 1940), 20–21. See also *New York Times,* June 26, 1940, 33, for industry expressions of the same point.

30. Interstate Commerce Commission, *55th Annual Report* (Washington: GPO, 1941), 4. For the same case from the perspective of railroad management, see Ralph Budd, "Transportation Is Geared To Defense," *Railway Age* 110 (January 4, 1941): 5–7; and "Freight Transportation Progress: 1917–1918 Compared with 1941," ibid., 110 (May 24, 1941): 873–76, 917.

road Administration (1917-1920). Administrative guidance, not state management was the key to its wartime activities.

The agency's founding charter captured the pervasive determination to build on the World War experience. Among other things, O.D.T. was instructed to "coordinate domestic traffic movements with ocean shipping in order to avoid congestion at port areas and to maintain a maximum flow of traffic."[31] As a close student of the subject observed:

> These responsibilities delegated to the Director of ODT constituted virtually a declaration of wartime transport policy. The policy was clearly designed to avert the evils of 1917. Thus, the emphasis on coordination was intended to prevent the confusion that had paralyzed railroad operations during World War I, and the explicit direction to "coordinate domestic traffic movement with ocean shipping" was aimed at protecting what had proved in 1917 to be the Achilles heel in the entire transport system, namely, the ports.[32]

In 1941 private and public managers alike also approached rail transportation in a policy context that *assumed* concerted action to avoid a federal take-over. By the end of 1942, the I.C.C. noted, it had become clear that "Carriers and shippers alike have sought to avoid necessity for a comprehensive and direct Federal control of transportation such as that of 1917-1920."[33] During 1917, in contrast, both industry and federal officials, for a variety of reasons—some political, some institutional—responded to mobilization in a manner so cavalier that a federal take-over seems in retrospect inevitable. If in December 1917 the I.C.C. felt compelled to consider federal control, its counterpart in 1943 felt justified in concluding that, "in the face of the situation with regard to their physical facilities, the performance of the railroads since Pearl Harbor may be regarded as extraordinary."[34]

One need not agree with the Interstate Commerce Commission's

---

31. See for the executive order, *Traffic World* 68 (December 27, 1941): 1667.

32. Quoted in Rose, *American Transportation*, 9. On the activities of O.D.T. under Eastman, see Fuess, *Eastman*, chap. 14; and Johnson, *The Railroads*, chap. 15.

33. Interstate Commerce Commission, *56th Annual Report* (Washington: GPO, 1942), 5. Throughout his tenure as O.D.T. director, Eastman emphasized that O.D.T. was "not a second United States Railroad Administration." See G. Lloyd Wilson, ed., *Selected Papers and Addresses of Joseph B. Eastman* (New York: Simmons-Boardman, 1948), 12.

34. Interstate Commerce Commission, *57th Annual Report* (Washington: GPO, 1943), 6.

fulsome praise to conclude that the railroads during World War II did turn in an impressive performance. In contrast to the earlier situation, railroad operations in the 1940s never became a focus for national controversy, nor a symbol of structural weaknesses in the nation's overall mobilization program. This was true even though by the 1930s the industry, as we can see in retrospect, had begun its inexorable downward slide as a result of changes in transportation technology. Challenged externally by the automotive industry and air transport, consistently losing mileage and cars, and hampered in adjustment by economic and labor regulations, one might have thought the industry in wartime would have collapsed gratefully into the government's arms.

Yet it managed a comparatively effective performance under private auspices, with government guidance. It did so in part because of a determination among both public and private officials to avoid past mistakes, an impulse reflected in the Office of Defense Transportation statute of December 1941; in part because of prewar gains in coordination and control. On the operating side, a variety of constraints that had barred effective response to the first mobilization had lifted prior to the second as a result of more effective means of private operations and private-public coordination. The World War II effort, indeed, appeared to vindicate private, voluntary means of mobilizing the railroads for war. But voluntarism worked in World War II because of gains industry and government had made during the interim in the means for more systematic coordination and control, gains, in other words, for administrative direction and order.

As an element of industrial mobilization, railway transportation benefitted from developments in the interwar years, as well as from the experience and example of the Great War itself. As a result, an industry which over the long-term was becoming less competitive and less significant as a component of national transportation performed comparatively more effectively in World War II than it had in World War I. For the railroads, World War II proved a positive experience, a harbinger indeed of equally prosperous if short-lived times during mobilization for the Korean War. The president of the New York Central remarked in 1958 that "since 1930 [the New York Central] has shown a profit from railroad operations in only 10 years. Seven of the ten were war years."[35]

In the context of the 1917–1945 period, the railroad crisis of 1917–1918 can be understood not only as a central episode in Wilsonian war

35. Quoted in Stephen Salsbury, *No Way To Run A Railroad: The Untold Story of the Penn Central Crisis* (New York: McGraw-Hill, 1982), 7.

33

mobilization. It can also be seen as part of a learning process that enabled government and industry to respond more effectively to transportation demands in World War II. The World War I experience taught a political lesson about consequences for failure of private sources of control in a national crisis. It also taught technical lessons for operating administration. The railroad story during two mobilizations illustrates the growth of more systematic efforts in coordination and control, and, as a consequence, the greater ability of both public and private managers to administer railroad resources more effectively during World War II than anyone might have dared to predict on the basis of their experience and performance in World War I.

Herbert Hoover, Ecologist:
The Politics of Oil Pollution Control,
1921 - 1926

All too often the history of conservation, in its overconcern with the black and white, good and bad conceptualizations of the Progressive Era, has skipped from Hetch Hetchy to the New Deal, with brief passing comments on the lack of conservation progress in the 1920's. Just as there is more to ecology than conservation, so also is there more to the decade of the 1920's. To the debates over use versus preservation must be added a very real concern for environmental *abuse*. The 1920's, then, offer clear evidence to counter the all too common assumption that our concern for environmental pollution began with Earth Day. Industrial polluters used the same arguments to postpone regulation and clean-up as they do today, and the Congress and governmental officials showed the same willingness to take the word of industry at face value. One man who did not was Herbert Hoover, who, as Secretary of Commerce under Presidents Harding and Coolidge, played a vital role in an early, abortive, effort to protect the environment.

The technological advances that developed petroleum based fuels sparked in turn a revolution in transportation capabilities that created world-wide occasions for oil pollution of the sea. Oil pollution was at best a nuisance even in that unenlightened era, and at worst a danger to health, safety, and commerce. It often stank, it irritated the skin, and it gave an oily taste to the seafood it did not kill. Fish kills of thousands were not uncommon, and it was disastrous to waterfowl and the oyster industry. A 1924 study noted that among its effects, "possibly most harmful is discouragement of water recreation." The resort owners and bathers who experienced the conditions described by Pennsylvania Congressman George Edmonds would certainly have agreed that it was discouraging: "I have known of days along that coast," said Edmonds, speaking of the New Jersey shore, "and especially at Atlantic City, when everybody who went in bathing had to use gasoline to wash off that refuse; that was the only way they could get this sticky mass of stuff off of them."[1]

---

[1] The navigation acts were sections of the Rivers and Harbors Acts of 1886 and 1888 relating to New York Harbor specifically, and the Act

The effects of oil pollution were first noted in 1902 by a biologist for the Charles River Dam Commission in Boston, but there was no official recognition of its dangers until 1916, when Dr. E. W. Nelson, Chief of the U. S. Biological Service cited it as a threat to waterfowl. Because of this late recognition, federal navigation acts directed against pollution as an impediment to navigation failed to specify the oil menace since it did not inhibit shipping in the same manner as logs and wreckage. In 1912 the Congress did authorize the Public Health Service to investigate all forms of water pollution to determine its effects on health. Like so many research programs, however, it was inadequately funded. By the early 1920's oil pollution, compounded by wartime shipping activities, had become a generally recognized problem attracting the attention of Congress and public officials. Section 5 of H. R. 16022, introduced on February 5, 1921, included oil in the list of prohibited substances enumerated in the 1899 Rivers and Harbors Act, but the amendment failed. It was a beginning, however, and during the next two Congresses, some 27 bills relating to oil pollution were introduced only to die in committee. Finally, a bill passed and was signed into law on June 7, 1924, marking the only Federal action beyond the investigative stage on water pollution until 1948. It was a weak act, to be sure, but its significance is in its existence, not its strength, for it was symbolic of the birth of the modern ecology movement.[2]

When Hoover took the oath of office as Secretary of Commerce, he found an extremely diverse department. Cheek by jowl with the Census Bureau and the Bureau of Foreign and Domestic Commerce were the Steamboat Inspection Service, the Bureau of Navigation,

---

of 1899 now being resurrected to require dumping permits for water disposal. See Marshall D. Green to Herbert Hoover, Feb. 16, 1922, Herbert Hoover Papers, Herbert Hoover Presidential Library, West Branch, Iowa, Secretary of Commerce Official File, folders marked "Pollution of Waters," hereafter cited SCOF, "Pollution"; F. W. Lane, et al, "Effect Of Oil Pollution Of Coast And Other Waters On The Public Health," Public Health Reports, 39 (July 11, 1924), 1658–1659; U. S. Congress, House Committee On Rivers And Harbors, hereafter cited HCRH, Hearings On The Pollution Of Navigable Waters, 67th Cong., 2d Sess., Oct. 25, Dec. 7–8, 1921, hereafter October and December, 1921, 134; U. S. Congress, House Committee On Foreign Affairs, hereafter HCFA, Pollution of Navigable Waters, Hearings on H. J. Res. 247, 67th Cong., 2d Sess., Feb. 15–18, 1922, hereafter February 1922, 12.

[2] Leonard B. Dworsky, ed., Pollution: A Documentary History, New York, 1971, 11, 22; George Schulz, "Stream Pollution In The United States," printed as H. Doc. 632, 69th Cong., 2d Sess., 1927, 10; G. W. Field, "Why Tar Our Feathered Friends?" Nature Magazine, 17 (January, 1931), 45; Field, "Report Of The Second Conference Of The National Coast Anti-Pollution League," reprinted in Congressional Record, 65 (January 16, 1924), 1044.

and the Bureau of Fisheries. The last three placed Hoover in the position of officially representing the interests of two conflicting parties in the oil pollution dispute: shipping and fishing. There was little doubt as to which side he would favor in the beginning. An avowed and dedicated fisherman, Hoover quite naturally sought to protect American fisheries, for both their sport and commercial value. He was also annoyed by another aspect of the issue: oil on the water meant that oil was being wasted, an affront to his whole career in attempts to eliminate wastes in industrial processing and distribution. His concern for efficiency was definitely not being served when 300 barrels of crude oil could be wasted every time an average ship pumped out ballast water.

In May, 1921, spurred by the protests of fishing interests along the Atlantic and Gulf Coasts, Hoover sent out a call for a conference of Fish Commissioners from Atlantic and Gulf states. He chaired this Conference on Pollution of Waters and Proposed Federal Control of Fisheries, which met in Washington June 16 and arrived at two significant decisions. The first was a resolution calling upon the Fish Commissioners to hold conferences in their own states, and report back to the Bureau of Fisheries by August 1. The second was the determination to introduce legislation designed to meet the problem on the national and international level.[3]

When inquiries following the conference produced the information that the Secretary of War had limited authority to act under the Rivers and Harbors Act of 1899 and the New York Harbor Act of 1888, Hoover was not satisfied. The acts had largely fallen into disuse, as an industrial nation rushed headlong into the future, using and discarding what it chose where it chose. Determined to take vigorous action, Hoover encouraged New York Congressman William Appleby to draw up legislation that could be enforced by the Commerce Department. On June 24, eight days after the Hoover Conference, Appleby introduced H. R. 7369, which prohibited oil pollution from both shipping and shore plants (refineries and factories).[4]

Appleby's bill was soon followed by others, and on October 25, the House Rivers and Harbors Committee opened hearings on these

3 Agenda for Conference On Pollution Of Waters, June 16, 1921, in SCOF, "Pollution,"; Herbert Hoover, *The Memoirs of Herbert Hoover*, 3 vols., New York, 1951–1952, II, 151; HCFA, *February, 1922*, 4.
4 E. T. Chamberlain to Hoover, June 20, 1921, in SCOF, "Pollution"; *New York Times*, June 26, 1921; *Congressional Record*, 61, 3052; HCRH, *October and December, 1921*, 5–6, 121.

anti-pollution bills. That first day quickly became a circus, as industry after industry paraded representatives into the hearing room to testify that the bills under consideration would cause them irreparable harm. For example, Van H. Manning, representing the American Petroleum Institute, which was dominated by Standard Oil interests, stated that he did not want the oil industry singled out when there were other sources of pollution. The API thus took a defensive position by attacking the legislation for its shortcomings—including all sources would have made passage almost impossible. William Gibbs, Chairman of the Technical Committee of the American Steamship Owners Association warned the Committee, "If you adopt a drastic provision denying ships the right to pump that water [bilge and ballast] overboard because it may possibly contain oil, you aim a blow directly at the privately owned merchant shipping of the United States."[5]

Despite the urgings of a New York delegation that the Appleby Bill be given immediate action, the hearings were adjourned until December 7. During the interval, and with Hoover's cooperation, Appleby acted to arouse interest in international cooperation as well as national action. On October 31, he introduced House Joint Resolution 216, calling for the United States to host an international conference on oil pollution of the sea.[6]

When the hearings resumed on December 7, Hoover testified that he viewed oil pollution as the most serious of all pollutions, and wanted immediate regulatory legislation, along with authority and appropriations to conduct an investigation into all other forms. He believed that investigation "is the method by which prevention of pollution can be accomplished and at the same time not destroy industrialism." This apparent ambivalence was just that—apparent only. Hoover argued that "as between industrial plants throwing off refuse and the fisheries, there could be no choice—the fisheries must be protected." He thus took what would later become an uncomfortable middle-of-the-road position. The fisheries must be protected, but there must be a constant concern for the perpetuation of industry.[7]

Hoover's faith in investigation came from his scientific training, and his belief that the different forms of polluton would require

    5 HCRH, *October and December, 1921*, 24, 30–2, 45.
    6 *Washington Post*, Oct. 26, 1921.
    7 *Ibid.*, Dec. 8, 1921; *New York Times*, Dec. 8, 1921; HCRH, *October and December, 1921*, 92, 94, 99–100.

different remedies. He suggested a beginning program which would sort all American streams into three categories, the unpolluted, the partially polluted, and those beyond hope. He argued that the first should be preserved, with no industries allowed unless they could prove they woud not pollute. The second category should be restored to the first, while the third could be abandoned to industrialism if they were truly beyond hope.[8]

Hoover's call for an investigation was generally supported by everyone present at the hearing. Manning, and J. H. Hays, a Standard Oil lawyer also representing the API, added their support for an investigation, but Hays could not refrain from commenting that he found it amusing to see the other industries trying to shift all the blame for pollution to the oil industry. The API's willingness to support an investigation was a strategic move to shift the glare of public opinion off of the oil industry for the moment and gain the benefit of postponing final action. Moreover, the API had had a private conference with Hoover about a week before the first hearing, and had promised to give any assistance they could in investigating the problem. The Institute's opinion of Hoover was incredibly high. Manning, for example, believed that "Mr. Hoover and nobody else, except in very isolated areas, really knows what oil is doing in navigable waters and tributaries of streams." Although Hoover did join in calling for an investigation of all pollutants, he also demanded immediate action on oil. The results of these first hearings were inconclusive. After an executive session on December 8, the chairman announced that the committee would break up into subcommittees for further study, with no more hearings to be held until the subcommittees reported.[9]

The role of the American Petroleum Institute in the politics of oil pollution control was critical. One of its chief lobbyists, Van Manning, was a former director of the Bureau of Mines, which had had a long and close association with the petroleum industry, and would play a vital role in making investigations on pollution from 1922 to 1926. Manning claimed that oil pollution had not been called to the Institute's attention until the first bills were introduced in Congress. But like many of those opposing the law, however subtly, Manning worked himself into a contradictory position by

---

[8] Hoover, *Memoirs*, II, 164; Hoover's stance on water quality was remarkably similar to that taken by the U. S. Court of Appeals on Nov. 2, 1972, regarding nondegradation of air quality standards.

[9] HCRH, *October and December, 1921*, 24–5, 95, 101, 109–10, 137–38, 141, 156, 165; HFCA, *February, 1922*, 71.

arguing that the 1899 act was adequate, and that no new legislation was needed. But then he stated that the Institute would not object to constructive legislation placing authority "in the Secretary of Commerce to apply the strict interpretation of the law." This was after he had noted that the legislation would affect thousands of industries in the United States, leaving the observer doubting whether Manning would have supported the strict interpretation of the law or any law at all.[10]

New action for legislation came late in March, 1922, when Appleby and New Jersey Senator Joseph Frelinghuysen introduced companion bills drawn after consultation with the Commerce and War Departments. Appleby also introduced an amended resolution calling for an International Conference, which ultimately passed and was signed July 1. The new bills lodged enforcement authority with the Secretary of War rather than the Secretary of Commerce. Although the reason for this change remains unknown, General Lansing Beach of the Corps of Engineers may well have made good use of the Corps' long-standing relationship with the Rivers and Harbors Committee. Certainly, this was a blow to Hoover's hopes, first because of his very real concern over the issue, and second, because it was a setback to his dream of building up a Bureau of Merchant Marine Affairs in the Department comprising all governmental activities relating to water transportation.

Despite disappointment at the compromise giving authority to the Engineers and responsibility for investigation to Commerce, Hoover urged that the legislation be passed, but repeated that he felt the Commerce Department could administer it more efficiently. Congressional action dragged, but outside pressures quickened. The Izaak Walton League, newly organized on a national basis in 1922, added support to the call for action as did the National Coast Anti-Pollution League, which was expanding its original purpose as a committee concerned with improving New York Harbor. Writing to a convention of the NCAPL which went on record favoring the Appleton Bill, Frelinghuysen stated that he believed the delay was the fault of Congress: "I am up against a deadlock between the War Department and the Senate Commerce Committee."[11]

---

10 HCFA, *February, 1922*, 67, 74.

11 Hoover to Representative S. Wallace Dempsey, June 17, 1922, in SCOF, "Pollution;" on the origins of the Izaak Walton League, see Kenneth Reid, General Manager, to Franklin D. Roosevelt, Apr. 14, 1938, reprinted in Dworsky, *Pollution*, 118; *New York Times*, Aug. 10, 12, 1922; U. S. Congress, HCRH, *Hearings On The Subject Of The Pollution Of Navigable Waters*, 68th Cong., 1st Sess., January 23–30, 1924, hereafter *January, 1924*, 57.

Frelinghuysen and Appleby tried a different tack at the end of August. While Appleby introduced a new bill calling for an amendment to Section 13 of the 1899 Act, Frelinghuysen reintroduced substantially the same bill he had entered in March. Action finally came on Frelinghuysen's. Favorably reported by the Senate Commerce Committee on August 25, the bill, S. 3968, passed the Senate August 31 and was sent to the House. At that point the action stopped, and in his annual report submitted in November, Hoover had to report that "Legislation is before Congress in this matter, and unless it is enacted great and serious damage will ensue." Hardly supporting evidence for those who claimed the situation was improving with voluntary cooperation, the matter rested there for three months.[12]

Continued prodding brought the Rivers and Harbors Committee into action and on February 9 it reported out a new version of S. 3968, which proposed to amend the 1899 law by prohibiting everything except sewage, and specifically penalized oil pollution, whether from ship or shore, with a $500 minimum fine. Following floor debate the bill was returned to committee. Reported back on February 23, the amended version proposed to set up an independent act, the Oil Pollution Act of 1923. Most significantly, it omitted land plants, and prescribed no minimum fine. The only improvement in the weakened version of the bill was clarification of the text so that there would be no need to prove that an oil discharge was an impediment to navigation before a conviction could be obtained.[13]

Despite this compromise, the House remained the stumbling block for oil pollution legislation. The Fourth Session of the Sixty-Seventh Congress ended March 4, with the Speaker *pro tempore* refusing to schedule the measure for a vote. Lame duck Representative Philip Campbell of Kansas, an important figure in Republican National Committee affairs, had filled in for the flu-stricken Speaker since February 26, three days after the bill had been favorably reported out

---

12 *Congressional Record*, 62, 12043; U. S. Congress, Senate, *Preventing The Oil Pollution Of Navigable Waters Of The United States*, S. Rept. 901 to accompany S. 3968, 67th Cong., 2d Sess., Aug. 25, 1922; U. S. Department of Commerce, hereafter DC, *Annual Report of the Secretary, 1922*, Washington, 1922, 37.
13 U. S. Congress, House, *Preventing The Pollution Of Navigable Waters Of The United States*, H. Rept. 1569 to accompany S. 3968, 67th Cong., 4th Sess., Feb. 9, 1923; U. S. Congress, House, *Oil Pollution Of Coastal Navigable Waters*, H. Rept. 1693 to accompany S. 3968, 67th Cong., 4th Sess., Feb. 23, 1923; *New York Times*, Feb. 13, 1923; *Congressional Record*, 64, 3380, 4445; U. S. Congress, Senate Commerce Committee, hereafter SCC, *Pollution Of Navigable Waters, Hearings*, before a sub-committee on S. 42, S. 936, and S. 1388, 68th Cong., 1st Sess., Jan. 9, 1924, hereafter *January, 1924*, 54.

of committee. Appleby took to the floor on March 3, to make it clear for the record where the blame lay: "As a result of the Speaker *pro tempore's* opposition and refusal to accede to the wishes of his colleagues, both in the House and the Senate, no domestic oil pollution bill can be enacted at this session."[14]

Why did Campbell refuse to allow a vote? Sedley Phinney, Executive Secretary of the NCAPL, argued that it was due to Campbell's bias as a former Standard Oil attorney. Testifying before the Senate Commerce Committee on the matter, Phinney claimed that "the bill was killed by the intervention of an oil company representative whose statement to that effect was made direct to me." Frelinghuysen named the representative in a letter to Hoover complaining of the bill's surreptitious defeat "through collusion between Campbell and Manning representing Petroleum Institute and Standard Oil."[15]

Hoover was bitter over the defeat of what he called "my pollution bill." In a conversation the next day with Will Dilg, President of the Izaak Walton League, he remarked that: "Official Washington has no knowledge that the American people give a damn about pollution, and until they do care and let their State governments and Federal Government know that they do care there will be no great advance as to pollution." Hoover's bitterness was justifiable, for when he tried to lead a movement to develop public opinion for one of the few times in his career, he had failed. Pollution control in the 1920's failed to capture the public imagination as an issue of critical importance. Hoover failed to motivate that public opinion as he had before with the war inspired crisis atmosphere surrounding the Food Administration and Belgian Relief. He had failed in a domestic arena where he would later succeed with the need inspired by the natural crisis of the Mississippi Flood of 1927. But he was leading public opinion, and leading the Federal Government full speed into a new and untried area of regulation.[16]

Congress remained out of session until December 3. In his November annual report, Hoover again urged upon Congress the necessity of enacting legislation to meet the growing problem of oil pollution. The annual report of the Chief of Engineers agreed with

[14] *New York Times,* Oct. 3, 1923, Apr. 21, 1924; *Congressional Record,* 64, 4678, 5428.
[15] New Jersey Senator Joseph Frelinghuysen to Hoover, Jan. 30, 1924, in SCOF, "Pollution"; SCC, *January, 1924,* 54.
[16] HCRH, *January, 1924,* 191.

him, labelling oil burning ships, dockyards, oil company plants, industrial plants, refueling ships and city sewers as the principal sources of oil pollution. He noted that there was no reason for this pollution. The oil companies and most industrial plants had installed separators. Salvage companies would handle the refuse oil from ships (for a price) and there was a municipal law requiring the use of oil-water separators in commercial automobile garages. Yet the problem still existed. The Bureau of Mines, in a preliminary report of a study it was conducting for the International Conference, contributed its conclusion that pollution by oil could be "virtually eliminated."[17]

The struggle for the oil pollution control legislation essentially came down to one major issue, that of the inclusion of shore plants, and two minor issues: whether the technical capacity existed to treat oil on board ship, to avoid its being pumped out with the ballast, and which administrative department would enforce the law.

Everyone, including the shipping companies, admitted that oil burning and oil carrying ships were a major source of pollution. Although the Standard Oil Company of New Jersey owned the largest fleet of tankers and oil burning ships, they did not object to legislation regulating pollution from shipping. Manning of the API admitted that oil pollution existed. "I admit it frankly," he said, "but I want to say in all seriousness that pollution is coming from floating craft and that is where your serious trouble is." David Neuberger and Phinney of the NCAPL found this stance puzzling. Phinney asked why the oil companies objected to being included in the bill if they did not pollute, and why they were willing to apply the law to ships when they claimed there were no effective devices for separation on shipboard? When Neuberger asked why no shipping men appeared at the Congressional hearings to oppose the bill when the oil companies were so well represented, he was answered by Robert Hand of the API, who also happened to be "an active member of the executive committee of the Steamship Owners Association." Hand testified for the record that the "steamship interests are not opposing this legislation for a moment."[18]

---

[17] DC, *Annual Report, 1923*, 37; U. S. War Department, hereafter WD, *Annual Report of the Chief of Engineers, 1923*, Washington, 1923, 1988; *New York Times*, Sept. 27, 1923.

[18] Van Manning, and Francis McElheny of the Sun Oil Co. and a member of the API's Pollution Committee, both agreed that the abuse was extreme. See SCC, *January, 1924*, 93, 103, and also remarks by Robert Hand and David Neuberger on 96, 106, and 109; HCRH, *January, 1924*, 46, 100–01.

Were the land plants such heavy pollutors that they preferred to offer up shipping as a sacrificial lamb, despite the financial involvement many of the oil companies had in shipping lines? The evidence does not so indicate. Hoover maintained that 90% of the oil was coming from ships. He noted that the Supervisor of New York Harbor had made an estimate of 75%, but claimed that along the coast as a whole the figure was higher. C. A. Holmquist, the Chief Engineer of the New York State Health Department had stated in 1919 that shipping was the major source of pollution, because at the refineries he had inspected, most had very effective separators, and allowed little oil to escape. However, he also reported one plant without a separator that was polluting badly. Appearing before the House Rivers and Harbors Committee on January 23, 1924, F. W. Lane, Petroleum Chemist of the Bureau of Mines was reluctant to weigh the relative importance of the various sources, but argued that although some land plants were bad, they were in general trying to do something about it, where the shipping companies were not.[19]

Why *did* Standard Oil oppose the legislation when from the evidence it could only have affected their smaller competition if they were already controlling their pollution as they claimed? One reason may have been fear of allowing precedents for control. Tied in with this was another more practical, and more likely, reason. All of the proposed legislation specifically exempted oil entering waters as a component of sewage. Evidence from New York indicates this might be one reason for Standard's position: surveys attributed oil coming out of a Brooklyn sewer pipe to garages and Standard Oil plants. A step taken to legislate against shore plants discharging directly into navigable waters might be very easily followed by another against those discharging indirectly.[20]

There was another possibility. While the larger plants, "in general" were adequately separating their oil waste water, it was possible that some were not. Lane realized this when he reported that separating devices available for land plants were adequate "when properly installed and used." Did Standard Oil always operate its separating devices? Robert Hand testified that there was no value in the oil recovered from either ship or shore separating plants "to a suffi-

---

[19] Hoover to Frelinghuysen, Jan. 30, 1924, in SCOF, "Pollution"; HCRH, *January, 1924*, 12, 17–8, 219; SCC, *January, 1924*, has a copy of the Holmquist report, 109–10; see also F. W. Lane, *et al, Typical Methods And Devices For Handling Oil Contaminated Water From Ships And Industrial Plants*, U. S. Department of Commerce, Bureau of Mines Technical Paper 385, Washington, 1926, 3, 51.
[20] *New York Times*, Sept. 9, 1921.

cient extent to pay for the operation of the plant." Even though they were nearly 100% effective, it might have been economically advantageous to *not operate* the plant when inspectors were absent.[21]

Neuberger and Phinney kept the pressure up, trying to be sure that land plants were included in the final bill. In this matter Hoover was willing to let his subordinates in the Bureau of Fisheries testify for the inclusion of land plants. Both the Commissioner and Deputy Commissioner of Fisheries called for coverage of all sources of oil. Frelinghuysen urged the inclusion of the land plants, and was joined by New Jersey Governor Silzer. The Chief of Engineers pointed out the necessity for including shore establishments, particularly gas plants, that discharge their oil refuse at night when it is extremely difficult to detect violations. As Governor Silzer noted, "No one seems to oppose such legislation but the oil interests." Hoover did not deny that the land plants were polluting. He merely believed that they contributed a small enough percentage that delay for two years while an investigation was underway would not constitute irreparable harm.[22]

The two major sources of oil from shipping were bilge water and ballast water, with the latter by far the greater source. Leaks and spills during refueling or emptying of tanks also contributed. Experiments in developing shipboard devices for separating oil from the water in ballast tanks were begun about mid-1921 by the Sharpless Manufacturing Company, working with Standard Oil. Sharpless representatives estimated then that a separator occupying about 1150 cubic feet of cargo space, could be installed for about $5000, including labor. This was not a proven machine, but a smaller, adapted version of the 300-odd separators Sharpless had in operation at various oil fields around the country.[23]

The technical innovation that was necessary to design a low-cost, high-efficiency separator that would also not take up too much cargo space was slow in developing. Manning, of the API, and Hoover, agreed that a satisfactory device did not exist, but Hoover argued that legislation would produce the necessary innovation: "I believe that drastic regulation requiring steamers to discharge their oil in receptacles while in harbor and to povide themselves at their own expense with such method of discharge will be the finest impulse

---

21 Lane, *Typical Methods*, 66; SCC, *January, 1924*, 96.
22 SCC, *January, 1924*, 7–33, 52–3, 59; Frelinghuysen to Hoover, January 30, 1924, in SCOF, "Pollution"; *New York Times*, Apr. 19, 1924; WD, *Chief of Engineers, 1925*, 1899.
23 Lane, *Typical Methods*, 5; HCFA, *February, 1922*, 45, 46, 50.

ever suggested for invention." At their own expense was a not inconsiderable penalty, for the disposal companies operating in New York were charging a dollar a barrel for the average of 300 barrels of oil in ballast water, and many industry representatives were calling for harbor disposal barges run by local or Federal authority.[24]

The technical innovation did not come quickly. In 1926, there was still disagreement between two bureaus in Hoover's Department of Commerce as to whether or not the problem had been solved. Testifying as an expert witness before the International Conference on Pollution, a Bureau of Standards representative argued that "there are separating devices now available which will give an average effluent content of not more than one-hundredth of one percent of oil on shipboard at sea under average operating conditions." But Dr. Lane, of the Bureau of Mines, disagreed. He argued that the use of barges in port was still the best method because a satisfactory mechanical separator had not yet been developed. Whether they did exist or not, the law did not make their use compulsory, and the Steamboat Inspection Service reported only 169 ships with separators by 1932, but also noted that all but three of them showed a profit on their operation.[25]

This lack of an available technological means of coping with the problem obviously would make enforcement more difficult, but the debate continued between the Commerce and War Dpartments over which of them would administer the law when it was finally passed. Hoover and the Commerce Department could argue that the War Department had not been enforcing the existing laws. The War Department could point to past practice in such cases: it already administered the 1888 and 1899 acts. However, the New York Harbor Supervisor had earlier admitted that he did not have the facilities to enforce the legislation he had, and did not expect appropriations "and until such funds are forthcoming," he wrote, "I see little use to depend on legislation putting a stop to this evil." He estimated then (1922) that it would cost the Government "millions of dollars" to properly enforce such laws.[26]

---

[24] HCRH, *January, 1924*, 9–11, 42; SCC, *January, 1924*, 104.

[25] DC, *Annual Report, 1926*, 172; United States Department of State, hereafter DS, *Minutes of the Preliminary Conference on Oil Pollution Of Navigable Waters*, June 8–16, 1926, Washington, 1926, 116; Lane, *Typical Methods*, 10, 25–9; "Investigations Into Oil Pollution," *Bird Lore*, 34 (September, 1932), 368.

[26] SCC, *January, 1924*, 109; Superintendent Hanrahan to Bancroft Hill, May 17, 1922, reprinted in H. Rept. 1569.

Essentially the struggle boiled down to each department's claim that it could administer the law with the greatest efficiency, and without any additional appropriation. Testifying on January 30 and March 17, 1924, General Beach of the Corps of Engineers argued that enforcement should lie with the Secretary of War, since the War Department already had numerous inspectors in and around harbor areas. Hoover's counterclaim was that the law should logically be enforced by the inspectors of the Bureau of Navigation and the Steamboat Inspection Service, "as making purely for economy in administration." He also claimed that "Secretary [of War] Weeks agreed with me last winter that economy required it to be administered by the Department of Commerce." If Weeks had agreed, he exercised no influence on his subordinate General Beach. The anti-pollution groups, chiefly the NCAPL, seemed content to have the law go to the War Department, even though the earlier drafts of their bills had given it to Hoover. It seemed that only the oil interests besides Hoover actively wanted enforcement of the law by the Commerce Department.[27]

These three issues, shore plants, separators, and enforcement, were central to the struggle, from the first bill introduced to deal with oil pollution in the 66th Congress, through the final enactment of the Oil Pollution Act of 1924 by the 68th Congress. During the opening session of the 68th in December, 1923, the NCAPL bill was introduced by New York Senator James Wadsworth, and was followed by several others. On January 9, the Senate Commerce Committee held hearings on Wadsworth's bill, and on two others. The result was a compromise bill, drawn and introduced by Frank Willis of Ohio. This bill, S. 1942, passed the Senate and went to the House on January 17. At this point, the forward movement stopped, as it had the year before.

The Willis Bill represented a tough stand on oil pollution by regulating both shipping and shore plants. When it arrived in the House, the Rivers and Harbors Committee was preparing to hold hearings on H. R. 612, introduced by Walter Lineberger of California. The Lineberger Bill was a compromise measure, omitting the shore plants, but calling for an investigation by the Secretary of Com-

---

[27] Frelinghuysen to Hoover, Jan. 30, 1924, in SCOF, "Pollution"; HCRH, *January, 1924,* 10, 281–82; U. S. Congress, Joint Committee On The Reorganization Of The Administrative Branch Of The Government, *Hearings On Reorganization Of Executive Departments,* January 7–16, 1924, 68th Cong., 1st Sess., 344; U. S. Congress, SCC, *Oil Pollution Of Navigable Waters, Hearings* before a subcommittee on S. 2414, Mar. 17, 1924, 68th Cong., 1st Sess., 3–4.

merce as a basis for further action two years hence. Five days of hearings produced no resolution of the differences between the two versions, and the matter was complicated by the introduction of bills to extend the prohibition from the coasts to all navigable rivers. Phinney and the anti-pollution groups realized the need for protecting the rivers as well, but objected to these bills because they would make "likely the defeat of the proper purpose of the bill," which they saw as protecting their own coastal interests.[28]

The compromise Lineberger bill was not written by the oil interests as charged by Frelinghuysen and others. Hoover favored the bill because it gave the administrative authority to the Secretary of Commerce, regulated shipping while providing for an investigation into other sources of pollution, and was written by the Department of Commerce. When the Rivers and Harbors Committee opened new hearings on January 23, Hoover's support of the Lineberger measure caused consternation in the anti-pollution ranks. When Manning of the API endorsed the measure, Lineberger interrupted to state for the record that the API had had no hand in the bill's preparation. A week later Lineberger commented that "as there has been some controversy as to the origin of this bill, I want to say that this bill was drawn in the very closest cooperation with Secretary Hoover and his Department."[29]

Except for Hoover, and his personal friend Will Dilg of the Izaak Walton League, who favored the Lineberger version with the understanding that the land plants were being given a warning to clean up at once, the support for the bill certainly did make it look suspect. F. B. Dowd, of the National Petroleum Association, a group independent of the Standard Oil dominated API, urged its passage, while denying that land plants polluted. Congressman Charles Curry, from a California oil district, also endorsed the bill asserting that the land plants in his district were not polluters: "There is no such thing as pollution from shore plants. It is absolutely negligible." A more balanced view was presented by W. H. Gartley, of the American Gas Association, who urged passage of the bill with its two year period for further study: "I do not hesitate to say that if this bill passes the gas companies will immediately start in, and at the end of two years if you can catch a gas company you are quite welcome

---

[28] SCC, *January, 1924*, 64; U. S. Congress, Senate, *Preventing The Oil Pollution Of Navigable Coastal Waters Of The United States*, S. Rept. 66 to accompany S. 1942, 68th Cong., 1st Sess., Jan. 15, 1924.

[29] HCRH, *January, 1924*, 13, 40, 249; Hoover to Frelinghuysen, Jan. 30, 1924, in SCOF, "Pollution".

to do what you want with him or with it for polluting streams."
The omission of land plants, and the study by the Commerce Department had been the industry goal all along, and with Hoover's support
success seemed likely.[30]

Consternation is a mild word to describe the attitude of the anti-
pollution forces. They had been willing to accept the compromise
bill omitting land plants that died at the last session of Congress, but
they now took up arms for a last ditch fight for the whole pie, in contrast to Hoover's willingness to go along to get some immediate action. Standard Oil's capacity for raising suspicions of corporate
duplicity also led the ecologists to forget that they themselves were
all too willing to sacrifice the principle of regulating oil in rivers to
help insure that they would be successful in winning coastal protection.

Meeting in a private conference shortly after Hoover announced
his support of the Lineberger Bill, Frelinghuysen, Neuberger, Field,
and other anti-pollution leaders decided on a course of action. They
resolved to push the Willis Bill as the best available, after criticizing
Hoover's stand for the Lineberger version "as constituting a reversal
of his attitude on previous occasions. It was the opinion that Hoover
was 100% pure, but that the wool had been pulled over his eyes by
Standard Oil in disguise." The group proposed to first try and re-
convert Hoover, and if this failed, "then to start at once a personal
attack on Hoover either before or after taking the matter up with the
President." If the attack became necessary, the group hoped to link
it with the Teapot Dome scandals.[31]

Frelinghuysen telegraphed Hoover on January 30, expressing his
regret over Hoover's stance. "I feel you have not studied carefully
both bills," he said. "We insist that failure to include land plants
makes law ineffective and ridiculous and defeats efforts to completely
stop pollution." He then charged that Hoover's support of the Lineberger draft would mean that the oil interests had won another
battle.[32]

Hoover's response was immediate and irate. "I thought I was
the arch anti-pollutionist in the country," he telegraphed back. The
situation was so bad now, he argued, that he "would be grateful for

---

30 SCC, *Jaunary, 1924*, 83–90; HCRH, *January, 1924*, 51–2, 53–4, 191,
212–13.
31 Unsigned, undated, memorandum of topics discussed at meeting can
be found in SCOF, "Pollution". Other events indicate the meeting must
have been held on the 28th or 29th of January.
32 Frelinghuysen to Hoover, Jan. 30, 1924, in SCOF, "Pollution".

even the amount of prevention that is proposed in the Lineberger bill," with its accompanying powers of investigation. "I would as before support wider authority than this," he said, "but it should also cover land pollution of all kinds." To Freylinghuysen's barb that Lineberger's version repudiated Coolidge's annual message, Hoover replied that "President Coolidge's strong recommendations which you refer to were made upon my representations." He told Frelinghuysen that he was willing to go step by step in light of the opposition, while the NCAPL wanted the whole road: "if your association can get constructive action legislation covering all forms of pollution from land sources . . . you have my blessing." Hoover followed his telegram with a letter one week later, stating again his willingness to discuss all forms of pollution, but pointing out the need to regulate such land sources as garages and sewers which the NCAPL itself had resolved to attack at its 1923 annual meeting. His back thoroughly up, Hoover wrote: "I resent the idea that because I am willing to support a major issue that I am supposed to be allied with refiners. I am prepared to make a public stand on the question as to whether responsible public officials are to be threatened and coerced, being charged with being agents of the Standard Oil Company when they want efficient and proper legislation and do not want to see the public interest divided because of demagogic stuff."[33]

There the matter rested for the time being. In March, the Senate and House favorably reported on bills intended to cover river pollution, but nothing came of them. Lineberger introduced a new version of his bill, now H. R. 9175, on May 12. This draft represented the influence of the Corps of Engineers with the Rivers and Harbors Committee, for it gave the responsibility for both enforcement and investigation to them, along with some other minor changes. When the committee finally did report out the Willis Bill, S. 1942, the last hope of the NCAPL, it was emasculated by the substitution of almost all the language from this second Lineberger draft. When the House passed this amended version on June 5, Willis reluctantly urged that his Senate colleagues concur, in order to get some action at that session. They did concur, and Coolidge signed the bill into law on June 7, 1924.[34]

The final bill was nearly identical with the one prepared for Lineberger by the Department of Commerce, with the major excep-

---

[33] *Ibid.;* Hoover to Frelinghuysen, Jan. 30, 1924, and Feb. 6, 1924, in SCOF, "Pollution".

[34] *Congressional Record,* 65, 8412, 10920, 11200; U. S. Congress, House, *Oil Pollution Of Navigable Waters,* H. Rept. 794 to accompany S. 1942, 68th Cong., 1st Sess., May 20, 1924.

tion that the Secretary of War was authorized to investigate and enforce. In his *Memoirs,* Hoover was quick to claim credit for the success, arguing that after Congress finally acted, "that particular pollution ended." More accurately, he also credited Dilg for the Izaak Walton League's efforts, and the Audubon Society claimed credit on its own as a supporter of the NCAPL, which played the major nongovernmental role in the struggle. In September, 1924, Hoover made a better assessment of the actual accomplishment than he did in his *Memoirs.* Speaking before the Sixth Annual Convention of the United State Fisheries Association, he noted that the law was "only a beginning at a solution of the pollution problem."[35]

Despite the beliefs of some that concern for oil pollution of the oceans was first met by the 1954 International Conference On Pollution Of the Sea By Oil, held under the auspices of the United Nations, this was not the case. The early efforts to cope with pollution along the American coast line led to an awareness that the problem also required international action. Hoover, and Appleby, with many others, had long urged the necessity of seeking international agreement to meet the problem of oil dumping beyond the three mile limit, knowing that the instruction to many ship captains was to dump oily ballast water outside the limit. This happened most often near New York Harbor, which was protected by law. To cope with the problem the Hoover-Appleby resolution of February 1922 was introduced and ultimately passed the House on June 5, and the Senate on June 21, 1922. This initiative in international relations met with surprisingly little resistance in a Congress that was supposedly isolationist. So, the United States took the lead in a new area, calling for action instead of waiting to be called.[36]

Two days after the resolution had cleared Capitol Hill, Hoover wrote to President Harding. "I understand Congress has passed a Resolution of which I am somewhat the father . . . looking towards a small international conference on pollution of sea water from oil and other causes." And the matter was "of eminent importance in the preservation of our fisheries and beaches." After Harding signed

---

[35] W. Snyder, a Hoover aide, "Memorandum On Oil Pollution Legislation," June 9, 1924, in SCOF, "Pollution"; Hoover to Will Dilg, June 13, 1924, in Secretary of Commerce Personal File, Herbert Hoover Papers, "Izaak Walton League"; Hoover, *Memoirs, II,* 151–52; "The New Anti-Oil Pollution Law," *Bird Lore,* 26 (July-August, 1924), 304.

[36] Dworsky, *Pollution,* 44; HCRH, *October and December, 1921,* 77; HCFA, *February, 1922,* 12; *Washington Post,* Feb. 16, 1922; U. S. Congress, House, *Preventing The Pollution Of Navigable Waters By Oil-Burning And Oil-Carrying Steamers,* H. Rept. 950, to accompany H. J. Res. 297, 67th Cong., 2d Sess., May 1, 1922.

the resolution on July 1, he immediately asked the State Department to create an interdepartmental advisory committee to make preparations for the conference of maritime nations. On August 7, representatives of the Corps of Engineers, the Navy, the Shipping Board, the Bureau of Fisheries, the Public Health Service, and the Bureau of Biological Survey met with Arthur Young, the State Department Economic Adviser, as chairman. It then broke up into two sub-committees, to investigate complaints of oil pollution, and the causes and means of prevention. When the Director of the Bureau of Mines offered to provide men to conduct technical investigations, the committee quickly accepted.[37]

The significant factor about the Bureau of Mines' investigations was two-fold. First, they were the major source of data for many of the decisions made concerning oil pollution in the decade. Secondly, they were not conducted independently by the Bureau, but by a four man technical committee, headed by Dr. Lane, with one other Bureau representative, and one representative each from the American Petroleum Institute and the American Steamship Owners Association. The first preliminary report (February 7, 1923) of the complaints sub-committee, assisted by data from Lane's group, informed the Secretary of State that the seriousness of the problem was "beyond dispute," and the sources were "oil-burning ships, oil tankers, shore refineries, and fueling stations." This report on the Atlantic and Gulf Coasts was followed by a similarly grim study of conditions along the Pacific Coast. Reports in hand, the Secretary of State informed Hoover that calling a conference would be inadvisable for the time being, but that there should be a search for a technical process or device to take care of the ship discharges, while the United States put its own house in order. On March 13, Hoover agreed to take responsibility for the technical search.[38]

As noted above, there was considerable disagreement about the existence of satisfactory technical means for shipboard separation of oil from ballast water. In their final report, January 9, 1926, the

---

[37] Hoover to President Warren Harding, June 23, 1922, in SCOF, "Pollution"; U. S., DS, Interdepartmental Committee On Oil Pollution, hereafter IDC, *Oil Pollution of Navigable Waters, A Report To The Secretary of State,* Washington, 1926, Mar. 13, 1926, 3, 5; F. W. Lane, *et al,* "Oil Pollution At Bathing Beaches," *Public Health Reports,* 39 (Dec. 19, 1924), 3195; Department of State Press Release, Apr. 9, 1926, in SCOF, "International Conference On Pollution".

[38] IDC, *Report to the Secretary,* 3, 18, 24, 57; F. W. Lane, *et al, Effect Of Oil Pollution On Marine And Wild Life,* Bureau of Fisheries Document 995, Washington, 1925, 171; "To Clean The Ocean Of Oil," *Outlook,* 143 (May 5, 1926), 16.

Bureau of Mines group continued to maintain that the means did not exist. Hoover and the Bureau of Standards believed otherwise. This matter was to remain debatable during the conference, as was the extent of protection (in terms of a 3, 25, 50, 100, or 150 mile limit) necessary to eliminate coastline pollution. In experiments conducted for the Bureau of Standards on the drift rate of oil slicks, D. V. Stroop found that oil in varying quantities could float for long distances. In one experiment using 25 barrels of oil-water mixture at an 80% water, 20% oil ratio (quite common for ballast water), there was a 90 mile drift in 72 hours before the slick broke up into unconnected blobs. The test indicated the staying power of a slick formed by the 300 barrels of oil pumped out in the ballast of the average ship. Thus, even if ship captains did follow the practice of dumping ballast water outside the harbors, it could still easily drift ashore.[39]

By March 18, 1926, the findings of the various committees were such that Secretary of State Frank Kellogg felt it was time for the conference, and he so advised President Coolidge. He suggested June 1, and reminded Coolidge to confer with Hoover on the appointment of the American personnel. The Coolidge response came from Presidential Secretary Everett Sanders on April 10, and gave Kellogg clearance to begin preparations. Correspondence between Hoover, and Arthur Young for the State Department soon produced a tentative list of 13 representatives and advisors, with ex-Senator Frelinghuysen as Hoover's choice for Chairman of the American delegation. Two of the other twelve represented the NCAPL and the National Conference on Outdoor Recreation, and others represented the Commerce, War, and Navy Departments, along with the Shipping Board. Four others represented the oil industry, a bloc of one-third of the twelve. Hoover's tentative list was identical to the final one with the single exception that California oil man, Mark Requa, could not attend. The official U. S. delegates were Frelinghuysen, Arthur Young, and Stephen Davis, Solicitor for the Department of Commerce, with the others acting as advisors.[40]

---

39 IDC, *Report To The Secretary*, 7; Lane, *Typical Methods*; DC, *Annual Report, 1926*, 192; *New York Times*, Jan. 22, 1926; D. V. Stroop, "Behavior Of Fuel Oil On The Surface Of The Sea," 1927, reprinted in HCRH, *Pollution Of Navigable Waters, Hearings* on H. R. 10625, 71st Cong., 2d Sess., May 2, 3 and 26, 1930, hereafter *May, 1930*, 42–9.
40 Frank Kellogg to President Calvin Coolidge, Mar. 18; Everett Sanders to Kellogg, Apr. 10, 1926, in Calvin Coolidge Presidential Papers, Microfilm Edition, Roll 178, File 3460. Vernon Kellogg to Hoover, Apr. 12, 1926; Hoover to A. N. Young, Apr. 13; Young to Hoover, May 1; H. P. Stokes to Young, May 4, 1926, all in SCOF, "International Conference"; DS, *Preliminary International Conference*, vi.

With a $42,000 appropriation for the expenses of the confer-
ence, Coolidge officially named Frelinghuysen to head the American
Delegation to the meeting of the ten nations on May 24. Frelinghuysen, then serving as chairman of the executive committee of the
NCAPL, joined Kellogg in expressing hopes for an international
agreement, based on the belief of the American delegation that
separators would not only work, but could also show a profit. The
importance of the conference was underscored by the report of the
Chief of Engineers on June 6, two years to the day after it had been
ordered by the passage of the Oil Pollution Act of 1924. It painted
a dismal picture, and urged that the act be extended to land plants,
and to all inland navigable waters.[41]

Running from June 8 through June 16, the conference was less
than a major success. While the United States and Great Britain
played major roles in the debates, and Frelinghuysen was elected to
chair the conference, definite resolutions were few. The controversies were familiar: How much dumping should we allow? How
close to shore? How can we enforce? Who should pay the costs?
Will the costs be prohibitive? Should separating devices be made
mandatory or voluntary? The question of dumping zones and enforcement held the conference up until Stephen Davis, Hoover's
representative, proposed a system of no-dumping zones, and agreement that a mixture of more than .05 of one per cent would be considered a nuisance. Then conferees could not agree on how far to
extend the traditional three mile limit in terms of oil discharge, with
some nations calling for 50, some 100, and some 150 miles. Finally,
the conference undertook only to recommend these measures to their
governments, and as the *New York Times* summed up, "suggested
that shipping companies be encouraged to install on vessels equipment to prevent the escape or willful discharge of oil on the waters."
In keeping with the curious posture of the shipping interests throughout the drive to control oil pollution, they again voiced no objections.
The American Steamship Owners Association even feted the British
delegates at a dinner in New York after the conclusion of the conference.[42]

---

[41] U. S. Congress, House, *Supplemental Estimates, Department of
State,* H. Doc. 387, 69th Cong., 1st Sess., May 20, 1926; *Washington Post,*
May 24, 1926, clipping in SCOF, "International Conference"; *New York
Times,* May 24, June 6, 7, 1926.
[42] *New York Times,* June 9, 19, 22, 1926; DS, *Preliminary International
Conference,* 294–96; U. S., DS, *Final Act Of The Preliminary Conference
On Oil Pollution Of Navigable Waters,* Washington, 1926; "Water Pollu-
tion From Waste Oil," *Science,* 62 (June 25, 1926), xii; "Preliminary Con-

The final result of the conference was a draft convention that required the formal adherence of the participating nations in order to legitimatize its recommendations in international law. Kellogg wanted Coolidge to have the United States begin the appropriate diplomatic action to secure adherence. Hoover urged that the Department of Commerce be allowed to act as an international clearing house for the coordination and circulation of pollution information, and Coolidge agreed. Signatures came from most nations, but not from the large merchant marine nations of Germany, Italy and Japan.[43]

Legislation, of course, varies greatly in its observance. Robert Hand of the API was probably accurate when he stated in 1930 at hearings to extend control to inland waters, that if the United States achieved full ratification of the 1926 International Convention, and got the 1924 Act enforced, much of the problem would be relieved. Standard Oil lapsed into its familiar, "let's study it" tactics. "I again wish to state," said J. C. Rohlfs, "that I believe if we take a year or two on the subject, where it affects almost the entire industry of the United States, perhaps after a year or two there would be some bird life left, and we could get at this thing properly. I suggest that that might be done, perhaps, through the American Petroleum Institute." Delay and obfuscation continued to be the main weapons of Standard Oil and the API as they confronted regulatory attempts, despite their protestations that their refineries were not polluters. They resorted to scare tactics, and warnings of industry grinding to a halt if oil pollution was regulated too strictly. James Emery, representing the National Association of Manufacturers, demonstrated industrial efforts to block regulation: "The law that we have is good enough," he stated, "but if you decide to make a new law, attack all forms of pollution, including municipal sewage." This excellent suggestion was made to a Congress whose members feared requiring cities to make "ruinous" expenditures for treatment facilities.[44]

If there was a tragedy connected with the politics of oil pollution control in the 1920's, it was one of unfulfilled potential. The 1924

ference On Oil Pollution Of Navigable Waters," *American Journal Of International Law*, 20 (July, 1926), 556; "International Conference On Oil Pollution," *Bird Lore*, 28 (July-August, 1926), 312–13.

43 Kellogg to Coolidge, Aug. 12, Coolidge to Kellogg, Sept. 2, Kellogg to Coolidge, Oct. 26, and Everett Sanders to Kellogg, Oct. 26, 1926, all in Coolidge Papers, Roll 178, File 3460.

44 HCRH, *May, 1930*, 24, 56; SCC, *January, 1924*, 45; HCRH, *October and December, 1921*, 127–28.

act in effect died on the books. It did not cover shore plants. It did not cover rivers. It ignored the Great Lakes. It provided no penalties for accidental spills, no penalties for oil pumped overboard to lighten grounded ships.

Herbert Hoover, who later took pride in being called a rugged individualist, led the fight for governmental involvement in efforts to control oil pollution in the early and middle 1920's. Like so many of us, Hoover lived in two worlds. One, the world of the present evolving into the future, was the world he had moved in while gaining fame and fortune, and therein he accepted the pace of change and the necessity for centralized coordinating action. The other world was the past, where his social values were rooted. That may explain his slackened efforts to fight pollution after 1926, when he knew that so much more was yet to be done. Perhaps, too, the long years of bumping heads with the oil lobbies had convinced him of the fruitlessness of further struggle without a more forceful public opinion behind him. Certainly his efforts failed to elicit widespread public or press support. Indeed, Hoover's role in both the Oil Pollution Act of 1924, and the 1926 Preliminary International Conference remained hidden to press commentators. Only the conservation journals gave any kind of coverage to the issue, and they gave it only scant mention.

The early, half-organized efforts of Hoover and Appleby demonstrated the futility of jousting with the highly organized oil interests without comparable organization. Even the NCAPL, with its national base, and with the support of the Izaak Walton League and the National Conference on Outdoor Recreation, along with the aid of resort and fishing interests, and with Hoover's best efforts, could only push through Congress a compromise measure. Delay and compromise were the story of the politics of oil pollution control, despite Herbert Hoover's unprecedented and unknown role in leading the government into action.

DOUGLAS C. DRAKE

Michigan State University

Defense Mobilization in the Southern Pine Industry:

The Experience of World War I

by James E. Fickle

World War I occasioned the first comprehensive mobilization of the modern American economy for military purposes. In the process the war inspired the nation's first large-scale systematized planning and bureaucratic structure for governmental coordination of the civilian economy. The wartime experience proved to be fruitful training for the business, labor, and governmental leaders who would implement the economic planning measures of the New Deal and after, as well as for planners and administrators during World War II and the Korean and Vietnam wars. The experience also raised important questions about the relationships between privately owned businesses and the public interest, about the existence of a so-called industrial-military complex, and about the efficiency and propriety of government planning and controls over the civilian economy, even during a national military emergency.[1]

Some of these questions were reflected in the wartime experience of the lumber industry, especially so the southern pine industry, located in the nation's most extensive wood-producing area. More than half of southern pine production was represented at the time by a newly formed trade organization, the New Orleans-based Southern Pine Association (SPA), which became the major force in securing and coordinating the industry's cooperation with the federal government. The story of the SPA and its industry represents a

useful case study of how the World War I mobilization effort worked — and sometimes faltered.[2]

The outbreak of war in Europe in 1914 seemed at first a serious threat to the southern pine industry's well-being. The "guns of August" struck southern lumbermen "like lightning out of a clear sky," wrote historian George B. Tindall. Dixie's lumber producers, like their agrarian neighbors of the cotton-belt South, were intensely

---

[1]There is a detailed examination of the origins and development of American war mobilization in Daniel R. Beaver, *Newton D. Baker and the American War Effort, 1917-1919* (Lincoln: University of Nebraska Press, 1966). Other studies treating various aspects of the story include Paul A. C. Koistinen, "The 'Industrial-Military Complex' in Historical Perspective: World War I," *Business History Review* 41 (Winter 1967): 378-403; Koistinen, "The 'Industrial-Military Complex' in Historical Perspective: The Interwar Years," *Journal of American History* 56 (March 1970): 819-39; Robert Sobel, *The Age of Giant Corporations: A Microeconomic History of American Business, 1914-1970* (Westport, Connecticut: Greenwood Press, 1972); and Robert D. Cuff, *The War Industries Board: Business-Government Relations during World War I* (Baltimore: Johns Hopkins University Press, 1973).

[2]"War Activities of the Southern Pine Association, An Outline of the Co-operation of the Southern Pine Lumber Industry with Various Departments of the United States Government during the War," Southern Pine Association Records (hereinafter cited as SPA Records), Box 84b, Louisiana State University Archives, Baton Rouge.

Top: Members of the Southern Pine Association assembled in New Orleans for the first annual meeting in January 1915. Bottom: Flags and posters decorated the hall for a wartime meeting in 1918. Both photos provided by the author from the SPA records, Department of Archives, Louisiana State University.

"Export" longleaf pine lumber at Gulfport, Mississippi.

concerned about the disruption of export markets.[3] The southern pine industry had not had a good year since the depression of 1907. According to a regional trade journal, 1913 had been "bad all the way through; 1914 was a little better, getting a bad start, strengthening about the middle of the year and then being smashed flat by the sudden starting of the Great War. . . ."[4]

Lumber export contracts typically contained cancellation clauses in the event of war. Soon the cables came from Europe, and export operations were immediately stopped. The export market appeared to be ruined. In the important East Texas-western Louisiana area, the curtailment directly affected some seventy sawmills representing about 4 to 5 percent of that region's production. Many ships carrying southern pine were at sea headed for Europe; those still in port and only partially filled were unloaded. On August 3 the major cotton exchanges failed to open, and that industry plunged into a deep trough, triggering a decline in all kinds of normal lumber orders by September. The downturn was also influenced by the collapse of other facets of the American export trade. The *Gulf Coast Lumberman*, a Houston trade journal, reported in September that manufacturers were being forced to curtail their output. The journal warned that scores of mills were entirely closed, that more were shutting down, and predicted that hundreds

of plants would be completely idle within a month.[5]

Early declines and dire predictions notwithstanding, the war soon caused a dramatic increase in lumber sales as the southern pine region began providing material to construct cantonments, ships, railroad cars, piers, wharves, and warehouses in the United States and France.[6] The United States as a neutral producer and carrier profited from Europe's torment. The American economy received a tremendous shot in the arm from several billion dollars borrowed in the United States by the Allies, together with the proceeds of Allied sales of American securities between January 1915 and April 1917.[7]

The efforts of producers and shippers to supply the Allies during the flush period before American entry into the war in April 1917 were not controlled or guided by any governmental machinery.

---

[3] George Brown Tindall, *The Emergence of the New South, 1913-1945* (Baton Rouge: Louisiana State University Press, 1967), p. 33.

[4] "Yellow Pine Industry of 1916," *Gulf Coast Lumberman* 4 (January 1, 1917): 4.

[5] "European War and the Lumber Situation," *Gulf Coast Lumberman* 2 (August 15, 1914): 4; Hamilton Pratt Easton, "The History of the Texas Lumbering Industry" (Ph.D. dissertation, University of Texas, 1947), p. 202; Harold Underwood Faulkner, *The Decline of Laissez Faire, 1897-1917* (New York: Holt, Rinehart and Winston, 1951), pp. 32-33; Tindall, *Emergence of the New South*, pp. 33-34; "European War and Its Results," *Gulf Coast Lumberman* 2 (September 1, 1914): 7.

[6] "War Activities of the Southern Pine Association," SPA Records, Box 84b.

[7] Faulkner, *Decline of Laissez Faire*, p. 35; George Soule, *Prosperity Decade: From War to Depression, 1917-1929* (New York: Holt, Rinehart and Winston, 1947), p. 71.

Allied purchasers had to pay whatever the traffic would bear, and their confusion and frustration were matched only by that of American businessmen, who were forced to compete for labor, raw materials, and facilities. Although the United States made some preparations for hostilities prior to 1917, not until the actual declaration of war was it possible for the government to exercise the necessary legal power to bring order, stability, and control to the American mobilization effort.[8]

The United States fought its earlier wars with only limited coordination of the military establishment and the private economic sector. Within the military there had been no systematic cooperation among the services, or even within the various bureaus of a single service, in purchases and supply matters. These traditions had to be overcome to permit concerted preparation for a modern, mechanized war. Many control agencies would be created to bring order and planning into the joint efforts of the private and public sectors; there would be many revisions before a workable situation was achieved.[9] The confusion and turmoil of the early efforts at coordination would undoubtedly contribute to some of the difficulties the SPA and its subscribers experienced during the war.

Although Congress considered coordination between the military services and the civilian economy as early as 1910, it was 1915 before the idea of industrial coordination gained currency. After President Woodrow Wilson presented Congress with a plan for national defense, on December 7, 1915, the United States began construction of "a navy second to none" and a large merchant marine. The Naval Consulting Board, headed by Thomas A. Edison, was created to coordinate the program's industrial requirements.[10]

The southern pine industry was immediately affected by the decision to construct ships. The government's shipbuilding program, begun in 1916, called for the construction of a thousand ships, each requiring at least a million board feet of lumber. Gulf Coast ports began to hum, and the industry strained to produce timbers under government regulations affecting production, prices, and shipments. Beaumont and Orange became major shipbuilding centers in Texas; by the end of 1916 in those two cities, there were eleven vessels under construction for the ocean trade. The *Gulf Coast Lumberman* reported in

November the launching of the schooner *City of Orange*, the largest ship "ever built on the Gulf of Mexico or its tributaries. . . ." The vessel was constructed entirely of longleaf pine lumber and timbers. Many lumbermen had financial ties with the construction companies, and, not surprisingly, 1916 was extremely prosperous for the southern pine industry.[11]

T he Southern Pine Association dealt with a perplexing and shifting maze of agencies that mobilized and directed economic aspects of the nation's preparedness effort. One of the most important was the Council of National Defense, created by the Army Appropriations Act of August 29, 1916. This body included a number of cabinet officers, but its work was done by the Advisory Commission, composed of civilian experts sometimes called "dollar-a-year men" for their volunteer efforts. The council's legal authority was based on the Army Appropriations Act and the National Defense Act of June 3, 1916, which gave President Wilson authority to place orders for war material directly with suppliers, to commandeer plants if necessary, and to set up an industrial mobilization board. Despite some congressional misgivings, the Advisory Commission started planning for war. Wall Street financier Bernard M. Baruch, one of the seven commissioners, was particularly concerned about shortages in raw materials and began to organize industry committees to locate resources in various areas for the preparedness effort.[12]

But when America's declaration of war came in April 1917, the nation still did not have a coordinated and centralized preparedness structure. The War Department, in despair, abandoned efforts to coordinate the various bureaus of the army and finally asked Congress for a lump sum appropriation. The Advisory Commission's efforts to coordinate munitions purchases between the military bureaus and civilian suppliers were similarly unsuccessful. Finally, on July 8, 1917, the Council of National Defense attempted to introduce centralization and systematization through the creation of the War Industries Board (WIB), which consisted of five civilians and one representative each from the army and navy. The WIB initially lacked executive authority, however, and failed to achieve the intended level of coordination in government purchases. It simply provided a mechanism for contacts between industry and government. The

[8]Soule, *Prosperity Decade*, pp. 7-8. See also the far more detailed account in Beaver, *Newton D. Baker*.

[9]Soule, *Prosperity Decade*, p. 9. See also the lengthy treatment in Sobel, *Age of Giant Corporations*, pp. 3-24.

[10]Koistinen, "World War I," pp. 378-82; Soule *Prosperity Decade*, p. 9.

[11]Easton, "Texas Lumbering Industry," pp. 201, 287-89; "Orange Will Celebrate," *Gulf Coast Lumberman* 4 (November 1, 1916): 30.

[12]Bernard M. Baruch, *American Industry in the War: A Report of the War Industries Board* (Washington: GPO, 1921), pp. 19-20; Soule, *Prosperity Decade*, pp. 10-12; Koistinen, "World War I," pp. 382-87; Koistinen, "The Interwar Years," pp. 819-23.

Wooden ship under construction in January 1918, probably by the Louisiana Shipbuilding Corporation at Slidell, Louisiana.

U. S. Army Signal Corps, National Archives

board's first two chairmen were frustrated and left because of its impotence.[13] It was not until March 1918 that President Wilson rewrote the WIB's charter to give it sweeping powers and put Baruch in overall command.

In the meantime, the Council of National Defense spawned a number of other important agencies. There were various committees treating particular problems, some of which, like the U. S. Shipping Board, War Trade Board, and the Railroad, Food, and Fuel administrations, eventually evolved into full-fledged administrative organs. There were also subordinate sections and committees of the WIB, including supervisors or commissioners of raw materials, finished products, priorities, and labor. The committees were intended to represent to the board the views of individual industries and to include experienced officials of those industries. The committees gradually grew in importance and became the chief spokesmen from industry before the divisions and agencies of government that made general policies. At first, however, the committees

had difficulty reaching or representing all members of a particular industry and thus began to depend on groups that, in Baruch's words, could "represent before the commodity sections and the functional divisions of the Board the interests of all members of the respective trades to be affected by a war regulation."[14] The SPA, of course, was such a group; it became the main channel of information from the southern pine industry to the government.

As noted earlier, there was considerable shipbuilding well before American entry into the war. Gulf Coast shipyards boomed, turning out increased tonnage in response to orders from both American and foreign governments. In September 1916 Congress passed and President Wilson signed a bill creating the U. S. Shipping Board; its function was to control shipping for the government. The bill also appropriated $50 million for a subsidiary corporation to build new ships. The subsidiary, known as the Emergency Fleet Corporation (EFC), was chartered in Washing-

---

[13]Koistinen, "World War I," pp. 387-95; Cuff, *War Industries Board*, pp. 113-47; Soule, *Prosperity Decade*, p. 12.

[14]Baruch, *American Industry in the War*, pp. 20-21, 23-24. For a description of the WIB's further development and wartime problems, see Koistinen, "World War I," pp. 395-403.

210

ton, D.C., shortly after the declaration of war. Following early quarrels between officials of the Shipping Board and EFC, the original leaders were replaced. Edward N. Hurley, a Democratic politician from Chicago, became chairman of the Shipping Board in July 1917 and remained until the end of the war. Direction of the EFC was finally taken over by steel executive Charles N. Schwab in April 1918. Both of these men, as well as their agents, were in direct contact with the Southern Pine Association and its representatives for the duration of the war.[15]

The Council of National Defense itself was involved with the SPA, particularly through the Lumber Committee of its Raw Materials Division. Lumberman R. H. Downman, who headed the committee in 1917, and Charles Edgar, who took over as lumber director in 1918, both had numerous contacts with the SPA. The Lumber Committee first approached the SPA out of a need to procure lumber for the construction of cantonments, or temporary barracks for troops. The committee organized a plan under which the government could purchase lumber directly from sawmills at reasonable prices. During the first week of the war, for example, the SPA received a request to supply 6 million feet of lumber for such construction at Camp Pike, Arkansas. Although the SPA headquarters office in New Orleans was not open for business when the request arrived, three employees worked through the weekend contacting mills and railroad shipping agents in Arkansas and northern Louisiana. On Monday lumber began rolling into Camp Pike in such quantities that a temporary halt in shipments was ordered due to shortages in storage space and railroad cars! In a subsequent emergency, 25 million feet were loaded and shipped within three days.[16]

It was concern over the shipbuilding program, however, that prompted the SPA to establish its own mobilization structure. In March 1917 the Shipping Board inquired about the southern pine industry's ability to support a wooden shipbuilding program. The SPA responded enthusiastically that both raw materials and construction facilities would be readily available. Then, just before the American war declaration, a representative of the Raw Materials Division of the Council of National Defense asked SPA President Charles S. Keith to line up the association's subscribers to negotiate agreements for delivery of lumber supplies to the government, especially for the shipbuilding program. Keith, a Kansas City lumberman, was also asked to appoint a committee with authority to represent southern pine manufacturers in establishing prices for their products and in binding the industry to furnish and deliver lumber for the war effort. Several days later, a subagent of the Shipping Board wired SPA Secretary-Manager John E. Rhodes about the possibility of forming an industry committee to fix prices and distribute orders for southern pine needed by the EFC. Keith and Rhodes gave their assurances that southern pine manufacturers would furnish every assistance. Rhodes then telegraphed SPA subscribers and asked them to authorize the Board of Directors to appoint such a committee. Within three days, more than 90 percent of the subscribers responded affirmatively.[17]

Acting quickly, the SPA Board of Directors met in Memphis on April 24, 1917, and appointed the Emergency Committee, composed of one representative from each state with association subscribers. The committee was to secure information about government lumber requirements and report to all SPA subscribers. It also was empowered to bind subscribers for the amount of lumber each should furnish, to recommend specifications and inspections, and to fix maximum prices and divide orders for all government purchases of southern pine. It was in this fashion that a subgroup of the SPA came to represent most of the southern pine industry in relations with the government.[18]

---

[15]Soule, *Prosperity Decade*, pp. 29-31.

[16]Baruch, *American Industry in the War*, p. 219; Grosvenor B. Clarkson, *Industrial America in the World War: The Strategy Behind the Lines, 1917-1918* (Boston: Houghton Mifflin Company, 1923), pp. 421, 426-27; Herbert C. Berckes, "The Pitch in Pine, A Story of the Traditions, Policies, and Activities of the Southern Pine Industry and the Men Responsible for Them," unpublished manuscript in possession of the author, p. 68. Car shortages would be a continuing problem throughout the war; see Charles S. Keith to Edward N. Hurley, December 24, 1917, and James O. Heyworth to Keith, January 3, 1918, both in Records of the United States Shipping Board, Construction Division, General File, RG 32, National Archives, Washington, D.C. (records from this file hereinafter cited as RG 32).

[17]U. S. Shipping Board to Central Coal and Coke Company, March 24, 1917, and SPA to U.S. Shipping Board, March 24, 1917, both in RG 32; U.S. Senate, Committee on Commerce, *Hearings, on S. 170, Building of Merchant Vessels under the Direction of the United States Shipping Board Emergency Fleet Corporation*, 65th Cong., 2d sess., 1918, pp. 10-11; "Report of Southern Pine Emergency Bureau," SPA Records, Box 84b; Charles S. Keith to F. A. Eustis, April 18, 1917, and J. E. Rhodes to F. A. Eustis, April 17, 1917, both RG 32; James Boyd, "It Is War!" pp 2-3. SPA Records, Box 77a; "War Activities of the Southern Pine Association," SPA Records, Box 84b.

[18]"Minutes of a Meeting of the Board of Directors of the Southern Pine Association Held at the Gayoso Hotel, Memphis, Tenn., Tuesday, April 24, 1917," pp. 2-3, SPA Records, Box 70b. For a description of the mobilization structure for the entire lumber industry, see Cuff, *War Industries Board*, pp. 75-81.

The Emergency Committee promptly traveled to Washington, where by April 30 it was conferring with the Shipping Board, the EFC, and a more formalized Lumber Committee of the Council of National Defense. Specifications and maximum prices for ship and cantonment lumber were soon established. The committee opened a Washington office and appointed an industry representative to serve as liaison officer with the several government purchasing agencies.[19] In the meantime the use of southern pine for army cantonments and wooden ships was creating a boom in lumber production. By mid-April more than 70 percent of the mills west of the Mississippi were producing exclusively for government orders. Within four months the government would purchase more than 700 million board feet of southern pine. Patriotism, morale, and business were strong.[20]

The Emergency Committee returned to Memphis, where, on May 23, the largest-ever crowd of SPA subscribers assembled to hear the committee report on its Washington activities. The southern pine manufactureres approved the price schedule and authorized the committee to distribute orders and arrange for the delivery of lumber to the government, directing it in so doing to treat non-SPA producers equitably. By action at the same meeting, the Emergency Committee became a permanent organization. It called itself the Southern Pine Emergency Bureau (SPEB), and its membership was enlarged by the addition of representatives for non-SPA producers. The SPA promised to furnish the bureau information on mill locations, production capacities, stocks on hand, shipping facilities, and freight rates. The SPA also contributed $2,000 toward the organizational expenses of the SPEB. Operating income was to be derived from assessments upon producers' sales to the government, whether or not made through the SPEB. The original assessment rate was five cents per thousand board feet. This was subsequently raised to ten, and later fifteen, cents.[21]

At first the SPEB represented no clearly defined area. As its activities developed, however, government officials outlined its territory to cover the southern pine-producing region west of the main line of the Louisville and Nashville Railroad in Alabama and south of a line drawn from Montgomery, Alabama, west to Meridian, Mississippi. It included all of the state of Mississippi south of the Alabama and Vicksburg Railroad and the entire states of Louisiana, Arkansas, Missouri, Oklahoma, and Texas. The SPEB did not represent southern pine areas along the Atlantic seaboard or elsewhere in the southeastern part of the country; these areas had their own emergency bureaus. While maintaining the office established in Washington, the SPEB opened its principal office in New Orleans, thus keeping close to SPA headquarters and to the district office of the EFC. Work of the New Orleans office was divided into five categories: 1) ship schedules for the EFC, 2) cantonment lumber requirements of the military, 3) traffic department, 4) auditing department, and 5) production department.

The SPEB's principal function was to allocate to manufacturers lumber orders from the Emergency Fleet Corporation, War Department, Railroad Administration, and Allied purchasing agents. The Washington office maintained contact with all government agencies concerned with procuring southern pine lumber. The bureau's capital personnel worked closely with the Lumber Committee of the Council of National Defense, which later became the Lumber Section of the War Industries Board. In fact, upon formation of a more powerful WIB, the SPEB, like bureaus representing other groups of lumber manufacturers, was recognized as a semigovernmental organization working under the supervision of the director of the Lumber Section, who came to be known as the national lumber director. The SPEB handled only orders of government and Allied purchasing agencies that were duly authorized and recommended by the Lumber Section. The Washington office also helped government engineers determine the specifications of lumber to be used in buildings, ships, and other projects. It kept the proper departments and agencies fully advised of orders placed with particular manufacturers, each day's shipments, and other useful information. The office also handled such problems as producers' delinquencies in filling orders and controversies over terms of settlement. Of course, it also kept in close touch with the SPEB's distribution office in New Orleans.[22]

T he complex and evolving machinery to coordinate a wartime economy had many flaws. As the war continued, and as the governmental agencies assumed larger, even dictatorial, powers, it is not surprising that disgruntlement and dissension grew. Periodically, southern pine producers were accused of profiteering and failing to supply the government's needs. Critics charged that southern pine manufacturers preferred to save their timber supplies for more

---

[19]"Report of Southern Pine Emergency Bureau," SPA Records, Box 84b.
[20]Tindall, *Emergence of the New South*, pp. 55-56.
[21]"Report of Southern Pine Emergency Bureau," SPA Records, Box 84b.

[22]*Ibid.*; "Pine and Patriotism: Official Report of the Third Annual Meeting of the Subscribers to the Southern Pine Association Held at Grunewald Hotel, New Orleans, Feb. 19, 20, 1918," p. 95, SPA Records, Box 85b.

profitable private markets. The first clash came in June 1917 when the Lumber Committee of the Raw Materials Division of the Council of National Defense called representative southern pine producers to Washington to discuss cantonment requirements. At a meeting on June 13, Lumber Committee Chairman R. H. Downman and the producers agreed upon basic southern prices, but only after lumbermen attempted to get more than the going market price. They justified their attempt to make the government pay more on the grounds that the order was of an emergency nature.[23] This was the first, but not the last, time that the facts contradicted postwar statements that lumbermen acted with "little thought of cost and profit" or that the government was "well pleased with prices."[24] Likewise, Shipping Board Chairman Hurley called a conference with southern pine producers in August 1917 to discuss prices and to persuade them to honor their commitments to produce lumber for the shipbuilding program.[25]

Controversy over prices continued between producers and the government. Prices for all government agencies, except the EFC, initially had been established by agreement between the Emergency Committee and the representatives of each agency. Later, prices were periodically adjusted by agreements between the SPEB and representatives of the EFC and the Lumber Section of the War Industries Board. In the fall of 1917, and again a short time later, the Federal Trade Commission investigated the costs of lumber production. On the basis of these inquiries, officials of the affected government agencies demanded and received price reductions.[26]

Lumbermen persisted in the belief that prices were too low — that they were not keeping pace with soaring production costs. During the winter of 1917-1918, Chicagoan Edward Hines, who had extensive interests in Mississippi, joined with other leading southern pine producers and SPA officials in efforts to increase prices through correspondence and meetings. The manufacturers clearly could get higher prices for their lumber in the civilian market, and their "often heroic" efforts in supplying the government's needs were, as one commentator noted, "not untinged with the color of human weakness and errancy." Their attitude was typified by the public statement of a Houston lumber company's sales manager: "These Government prices are so much lower than the regular commercial market, that we of course do not want to take any more than our share of the orders. . . ."[27]

Early in 1918 lumber prices in the commercial trade advanced to five to seven dollars per thousand board feet above those paid by the government. This disparity concerned government officials who, for a number of reasons, believed that

A wartime poster of the Southern Pine Association.

SPA records, Louisiana State University

---

[23]"Pine and Patriotism," p. 95, SPA Records, Box 85b.

[24]Berckes, "The Pitch in Pine," p. 68; John M. Collier, *The First Fifty Years of the Southern Pine Association, 1915-1965* (New Orleans: SPA, 1965), p. 63. For materials relating to alleged SPA price fixing and profiteering before, during, and after the war, see File 60-160-21, Records of the Justice Department, RG 60, National Archives.

[25]"Conference with Lumbermen Relative to Expediting Production of Lumber for Ships, Wednesday, August 1, 1917," typescript in RG 32.

[26]"Report of Southern Pine Emergency Bureau," SPA Records, Box 84b; "Before the Federal Trade Commission, Conference with Representatives of the Yellow Pine Lumber Industry, Federal Trade Commission Building, Washington, D.C., Oct. 30, 1917," SPA Records, Box 67a.

[27]*Report of the Federal Trade Commission on Lumber Manufacturers' Trade Associations, Incorporating Reports of January 10, 1921, February 18, 1921, June 9, 1921, February 15, 1922* (Washington: GPO, 1922), pp. 15-20; Clarkson, *Industrial America in the World War*, p. 423.

production for civilian purposes should not be stimulated by high prices. Conservation of the softwood supply was a factor, but the primary consideration was conservation of other materials and transportation needed for the war. Reducing nonmilitary production would conserve men, machinery, materials, and transportation facilities; civilian lumber needs were considered to be deferable.

The lumber industry's size and decentralized character placed it beyond the possibility of general commandeering, so the War Industries Board attacked the problem by manipulating priorities and fixing prices. The Non-War Construction Section of the WIB discouraged production beyond minimum civilian requirements by requiring lumber manufacturers and distributors to sign pledges to deliver lumber only for essential purposes or on express, written permits. Southern pine was not placed on the board's preferred list of essential war industries. It was thus deprived of any general priority classification; however, for government production the lumbermen were given top priority privileges.

The WIB concluded early in 1918 that it was necessary to fix maximum prices for all southern pine lumber. In March the producers were granted a hearing before the board's Price-Fixing Committee. No changes were made, however, until further hearings of mid-June 1918 led to a controversial agreement (soon challenged) to fix prices on the basis of figures provided by the Federal Trade Commission's cost studies. According to government officials, the manufacturers also agreed that commercial sales would be subject at any time before delivery to an option in favor of the government. The agreement further stated that lumbermen would comply with directions of the WIB concerning priorities in meeting commercial requirements. The upshot was that lumber prices were fixed at levels low enough to discourage and even curtail production. Southern pine prices were controlled from June 14 through December 23, 1918, much to the dismay of producers, as will be noted later.[28]

T he southern pine industry was concerned not alone with prices; other serious problems involved labor and transportation. Labor shortages resulted from the migration of lumber workers into southern urban centers, where more lucrative occupations were opened by wartime activities, and by the exodus of blacks to jobs in northern defense plants. The draft affected the work force everywhere. Furthermore, as noted

earlier, the government did not consider lumbering to be a "priority" industry. The Labor Priorities Section of the WIB issued its first labor priorities order on September 17, 1918, omitting lumber from the list because, according to one report, the order's "chief purpose [was] to procure an automatic flow of fuel and transportation service.... Lumber ... was not on the preference list because it was intended to discourage long hauls of that commodity for the use of civilians and to promote the use of wood as fuel."[29] Nonetheless, because there was a military need for certain kinds of lumber, some government officials viewed with alarm the loss of lumber workers to other occupations.

The industry itself seemed to have mixed opinions regarding the labor situation during the war's early stages. Those present at the SPA's annual meeting in New Orleans in late February 1918 heard a telegram from an official of the West Coast Lumbermen's Association warn that the industry in that region faced severe labor troubles because of "continued agitation on the part of official Washington, ... socialist professors, speculators in philosophy, theorists having poetical ideas of political economy, and ... walking delegates from mineworkers' unions. ..." He predicted the adoption of an eight-hour day by many operators, possibly by government order, and reported that West Coast lumber industry wages were higher than those in shipyards. SPA President Keith seemed to share the same fears for the southern pine region, conceding, "We have a labor problem to contend with." He strongly condemned any effort to establish government wage requirements, either maximum or minimum, and he bitterly attacked the eight-hour day as "seditious and treacherous."[30]

Echoing industry officials, the *Gulf Coast Lumberman* asserted in late 1917: "There is more labor trouble at the mills of the south at the present time than ever before." The trade journal ascribed the trouble to the short labor supply caused by the war and claimed that the shortage gave more than usual force to the laborers; it reported several strikes in progress and others "fomenting." In March 1918 the same journal

---

[28]Baruch, *American Industry in the War*, pp. 212-13; Clarkson, *Industrial America in the World War*, pp. 423-26; *Report of the Federal Trade Commission*, pp. 19-21; "Report of Southern Pine Emergency Bureau," SPA Records, Box 84b.

[29]Clarkson, *Industrial America in the World War*, pp. 291-92. Baruch, *American Industry in the War*, p. 90, gives essentially the same explanation for lumber's exclusion from the priority list. As early as August 1917 the SPA was complaining about labor shortages and attempting to secure exemptions from military service for sawmill workers. See SPA to F. W. Dunham, August 15, 1917; R. E. Wood Memorandum for Admiral W. L. Capps, August 16, 1917; Wood to W. C. McGowan, August 16, 1917; all in RG 32.

[30]"Pine and Patriotism," pp. 20, 139-40, SPA Records, Box 85b; "Southern Pine Meeting Breaks Attendance Record," *Southern Lumberman* 86 (February 23, 1918): 27.

Labor shortages plagued the southern pine industry during wartime. These workers handle finished short-leaf pine lumber at a plant of the J. J. Newman Lumber Company in Bude, Mississippi.

Forest History Society

turned out promptly." Kirby estimated an average labor shortage of 17 percent, noting that the draft, shipyards, and other occupations were siphoning off men. He said that southern pine mills were continuing to run on an open-shop basis and operating ten hours a day, with only a few plants maintaining night shifts. In order to meet the problem of labor shortages, lumbermen were offering increased pay and other inducements. "In some cases," Kirby noted, "negro women are being employed to do light tasks about mills." He concluded that manufacturers did not "anticipate any serious difficulties in maintaining operations during the present year" and that the territory was "practically free of any labor trouble."[32]

Evidently Kirby's opinion changed within several weeks. He and some colleagues reported in a letter to the War Industries Board in July that there was "a serious labor shortage." Constant advances in wages, reported the industry committee, were "not sufficient to overcome the effects of the draft and the competition for labor by shipyards and other war industries."[33] Labor shortages indeed remained troublesome throughout the war and into the postwar period. Some mills dealt with the situation by tapping new sources of labor, including blacks and Mexicans, and others increased wages to more competitive levels.[34] The major activity on an industry-wide basis was an SPA attempt to increase labor productivity. The extensive campaign featured speaking tours of industry officials and returning war heroes who visited the mills and labor camps to arouse the patriotism and productivity of the personnel.[35] Such efforts, however, could not overcome the effects of the labor shortages.

reported the employment of the first woman sawmill engineer in the history of the Texas lumber industry.[31]

In May 1918 Houston lumberman John Henry Kirby appraised the industry's labor situation as "fair." An enormously influential man — at the time he was president of the National Lumber Manufacturers Association (NLMA), vice-president of the SPA, and also lumber administrator in the South for the EFC — Kirby assessed the labor situation in a letter to a government official. "Though somewhat short handed in a few instances," he reported, "plants generally are running full time, and all government work is being

[31]"Labor Troubles at Saw Mills," *Gulf Coast Lumberman* 5 (October 15, 1917): 49; "Women for Sawmill Engineers," *Gulf Coast Lumberman* 5 (March 15, 1918): 40.

[32]John H. Kirby to Charles Piez, May 16, 1918, John Henry Kirby Papers (hereinafter cited as Kirby Papers), Box 144, University of Houston Library, Houston, Texas.

[33]Kirby, R. A. Long, and F. W. Stevens to Members of the War Industries Board, July 3, 1918, Kirby Papers, Box 144.

[34]A mill manager of the Sabine Tram Company in East Texas later reported that his company never employed blacks until 1917-1918, when it employed both Negroes and Mexicans because of the wartime labor shortage. Easton, "Texas Lumbering Industry," p. 268. Another student of the industry wrote that the World War I labor shortage "seems to have had little effect upon wages paid in Texas." Ruth A. Allen, *East Texas Lumber Workers: An Economic and Social Picture, 1870-1950* (Austin: University of Texas Press, 1961), p. 70.

[35]"Lumber Liquidates: Official Report of the Sixth Annual Meeting of the Subscribers to the Southern Pine Association Held at Grunewald Hotel, New Orleans, April 5, 6, 1921," p. 27, SPA Records, Box 85b. Collier, *First Fifty Years*, p. 65, writes, "A total of 164 speeches were delivered in 89 mill towns to more than 60,000 sawmill and woods workers."

A Story in a Cartoon

wartime cartoon from the HOUSTON POST lauded the patriotism of Texas lumberman John Henry Kirby.

Equally bothersome were shortages and tie-ups in the nation's transportation system. The major problem was a dearth of railroad cars that first developed nationally in 1916 and continued throughout 1917, until the creation of the Railroad Administration. The car shortage was one of the main concerns of the SPA's Transportation Committee in 1916 and after war was declared. In the interest of car conservation and transportation efficiency, the association urged its subscribers to load their cars heavily and utilize space more fully. The SPA's Traffic Department generally did yeoman service in helping the industry to secure adequate carriage.[36] Like labor, however, transportation continued to be one of the industry's nagging problems throughout the struggle to meet wartime demands.

Meeting the voracious government appetite for forest products was a supreme challenge to the southern pine industry and its foremost association — a challenge not always met and sometimes embarrassing to regional pride. The most pressing demand, as noted, was for the shipbuilding program. Inaugurated in 1916, this program called for the construction of one thousand ships, each requiring at least one million board feet of lumber. The peak need for southern pine came in October 1917 when Gulf Coast mills were instructed to hold all longleaf timbers measuring twelve by twelve inches, and twenty-four feet or longer, for the shipbuilding program. The mills were not to accept any new commercial orders for such materials and not to fill old orders. On November 2 the government extended its demand to cover all southern pine timber thicker than two inches, wider than ten inches, and longer than twenty feet. Certain other ship materials were also, in effect, commandeered. Government agents moved into the South to watch the sawmills and make sure that timbers badly needed for war use were not diverted into the domestic trade.[37]

The tremendous government demands impelled drastic efforts in the southern pine industry. To procure the extra large sizes needed for ship timbers, southern lumbermen penetrated far beyond their normal logging operations to secure specially selected trees. The manufacturers instituted a speed-up program by which they hoped to increase the daily output of ship timbers from 850,000 to 2,000,000 linear feet. They overhauled and reorganized machinery and installed new equipment, although equipment and replacement parts were often scarce. Many mills worked night and day to meet the government's demands.[38]

During the first ten months of American involvement in World War I, the southern pine industry furnished 37,803 carloads, or 756 million feet, of lumber to the military. It supplied ship timbers at the daily rate of 75 carloads, or 1.5 million feet. In addition, the industry supplied huge quantities of lumber for war industries, foreign governments, war housing, and other purposes. Despite such staggering figures, producers encountered difficulties in satiating the government's appetite for wood. By late 1917 and early 1918, the industry came under both

[36]Soule, *Prosperity Decade*, pp. 33-34; "Minutes of a Meeting of the Board of Directors of the Southern Pine Association Held at the Gayoso Hotel, Memphis, Tennessee, Tuesday, April 18th, 1916," SPA Records, Box 67a; "War Activities of the Southern Pine Association," p. 30, SPA Records, Box 84b; Berckes, "The Pitch in Pine," p. 72.

[37]Easton, "Texas Lumbering Industry," p. 287; Soule, *Prosperity Decade*, p. 31; "Government Takes All Long Leaf Timbers," *Gulf Coast Lumberman* 5 (October 15, 1917): 30; "Government Conscripts All Lumber Over 2 Inches Thick," *Gulf Coast Lumberman* 5 (November 15, 1917): 22; W. H. Sullivan to Admiral W. L. Capps, October 31, 1917, RG 32.

[38]Berckes, "The Pitch in Pine," pp. 69-70; "Forcing Ship Timber Production," *Gulf Coast Lumberman* 5 (November 15, 1917): 22.

public and internal criticism for its failure to fill government orders in quantity and price.[39]

Late in 1917 newspapers publicized the fact that large ship timbers, ordered originally from southern pine producers, had to be obtained from West Coast manufacturers in order to meet production schedules of the Shipping Board. The Senate Committee on Commerce investigated the matter in the spring of 1918. At the hearing the industry's spokesman denied that the Shipping Board had been forced to go west for timbers because of the southern producers' failure to fulfill commitments. Rather, he declared, the Shipping Board had secured the large-sized Douglas-fir timbers at the suggestion of southern pine manufacturers; the pine men ought therefore to be commended for their "pre-vision."[40]

Southern pine producers were indeed having difficulty delivering the large timbers used for keels, keelsons, ribs, and sides in the wooden ship construction program. James O. Heyworth, director of the Wooden Ship Division of the EFC, addressed the problem at the SPA's annual meeting in February 1918, stating that 100 million board feet of such timbers were required for ships then on order but that only 38 million feet had been shipped. Thus it had been necessary for the EFC, at the request of the southern pine producers, to order more than half the total requirement from West Coast manufacturers. The need for yellow pine timbers nevertheless remained great, and Heyworth exhorted the industry to redouble its efforts. If the shipbuilding program failed in the homestretch, Heyworth said, he "would not be responsible for what the people of the country will think of the lumbermen."[41]

Edward N. Hurley, chairman of the Shipping Board, also put it on the line to the SPEB: "There is a strong feeling in the country that there is only enough lumber to complete three hundred and sixty ships each year. . . . The sooner you present some facts to counteract this information, the better it will be for the lumber industry." "So far," Hurley repeated, "the southern pine people have not produced sufficient timbers of large sizes to carry out our program."[42]

SPA President Keith had already urged southern pine manufacturers to exert themselves to the limit to satisfy the needs of the ship construction program. "Any manufacturer," he wrote several months earlier, "who does not do his part by going in *advance of his logging* for the necessary timber, and who will not refuse to take orders for material which interferes with Government orders, is a *slacker* and a traitor, and is encouraging and assisting our enemies."[43]

Despite such prodding from SPA officials, the problem persisted throughout the last year of the war. The editor of the *Manufacturers' Record*, a Baltimore trade journal, wrote to powerful lumberman John Henry Kirby, seeking the Texan's reaction to charges against his industry.

> There is a feeling in Washington that the Southern pine lumber people have very badly fallen down in the promised deliveries of timber for wooden ships, and in the minds of those who have been studying the matter, there is a question as to whether this is due to the inability to get the timber specified, or whether the lumber people have been taking care of their private trade at the expense of delaying the fulfillment of their contracts to provide timbers for ships. . . . To what do you attribute the delay . . . of four to six months in the completion of ships under contract? . . . Have the lumber operators done their best to hunt out . . . trees big enough to provide the necessary lumber, or is there an actual shortage of such trees? . . .[44]

However difficult and embarrassing the situation was for the industry generally, Kirby's own operations were praised by an EFC official who reported that he had been to most of Kirby's mills and found "their managers have instructions . . . to cut every piece of timber possible that will go into ships and to spare no expenses whatever in getting these pieces." "It seems," he continued, "that the Kirby Lumber Company as a whole, are [sic] doing everything possible to increase the production over what they had been doing, and I already had evidence that they were doing that. . . ."[45]

Kirby's own prestige within the industry and

[39]Berckes, "The Pitch in Pine," pp. 69-70. For difficulties and criticism, see Directors, SPA, to Long Leaf Southern Pine Manufacturers, Members of SPA, and Those Who Are Not Members, November 3, 1917; Frank A. Brown, Memorandum for Admiral W. L. Capps, November 3, 1917; Charles Piez, Memorandum for Mr. Hurley; Edward N. Hurley to W. H. Sullivan, December 1, 1917: all in RG 32.

[40]*Hearings on Senate Resolution 170*, pp. 24-25.

[41]"Pine and Patriotism," pp. 111-12, SPA Records, Box 85b; "Southern Pine Meeting Breaks Attendance Record," *Southern Lumberman* 86 (February 23, 1918): 26. On February 1 the SPEB promised to deliver sizable quantities of timber if the western fir producers would supply some of the longer sizes. SPEB to James O. Heyworth, February 1, 1918, Records of the United States Shipping Board, Wooden Ship Division, RG 32.

[42]Berckes, "The Pitch in Pine," p. 70.

[43]Charles S. Keith to Long Leaf Yellow Pine Manufacturers, November 3, 1917, RG 32.

[44]Richard H. Edmonds to Kirby, February 25, 1918, Kirby Papers, Box 144.

[45]Frank Comstock to Wood Beal, March 9, 1918, Kirby Papers, Box 192. Another official, however, found among other firms widespread violations of the embargo on large-size timbers and many other problems as well. C. F. Holek to Mr. Haynen, January 3, 1918, RG 32.

his record of service to the government suggested that he was the man to untangle the unfortunate situation in the South. On March 13, 1918, Chairman Hurley of the Shipping Board asked Kirby to become lumber administrator for the South and to secure the timbers and other materials so badly needed for the EFC's wooden ship program.[46] Kirby was already serving, at Bernard Baruch's invitation, as a member of the Raw Materials Committee of the Council of National Defense, and he was resident in Washington, D.C. While working for the government in this capacity through most of 1917, moreover, Kirby was also president of the NLMA and vice-president of the SPA.

Kirby accepted the new position with the blessing of EFC official James O. Heyworth, who wrote, "A direct personal attention by a man like you will straighten matters out and will give to Southern Pine Producers a much better chance to deliver." The Texan moved immediately to New Orleans and, on March 20, 1918, took charge of the timber section of the EFC as lumber administrator for the South. His duties were broadly stated by the corporation's general purchasing officer as having "charge of supplying lumber for ships built on the Atlantic and Gulf Coasts and such other lumber for shipyards and other purposes as may be needed by the Emergency Fleet Corporation from time to time. . . . Use whatever new methods that may occur to you in order that lumber may be obtained at a sufficient rate that the construction of wooden ships will not be delayed." Kirby was assisted by fifteen regional industry leaders who served without pay. They included SPA subscribers, members of other organizations, and independents. Kirby's direct assistant was W. J. Haynen, the EFC's purchasing officer in New Orleans. Hurley and the EFC officials clearly expected that Kirby would bring order and increased production out of the chaotic southern pine industry.[47]

In the meantime, representatives of the southern pine industry and officials of the Shipping Board met in Washington to resolve some of the outstanding issues that had divided them in recent months. At a conference held from March 10 to 12, the Shipping Board finally adopted recommendations that had been made repeatedly by the southern pine producers. Essentially, the government agreed that it would continue to obtain large timbers from western fir forests, as it had been doing since December 1917. Moreover, the Shipping Board would permit the use of laminated or built-up materials, thus making it more realistic for the pine producers to meet the government's requirements. These and other minor modifications in wooden ship construction specifications were more in keeping with the actual limitations of southern forest stands; no longer would the government insist that lumbermen deliver timbers of a size that occurred only rarely or did not exist in the southern pine belt. The conference also spawned the idea of appointing Kirby southern lumber administrator for the EFC, and thus it ended on a hopeful note.[48] "The disagreement between the Shipping Board and the Southern Pine Association," the *Southern Lumberman* reported, "is now happily settled."[49]

T he honeymoon was brief, of course. The price-fixing issue, outlined earlier, took center stage during the spring and summer of 1918, and it would involve Kirby and other southern pine men in controversy with Baruch and the War Industries Board. Kirby by this time was enmeshed in a maze of positions and responsibilities, both public and private, that would suggest conflict of interest in a normal, peacetime situation. He was lumber administrator of the South for the EFC; he was president of a national trade association and vice-president of a regional association; he continued to head the powerful Kirby Lumber Company of Houston. Now he went to Washington to represent southern pine producers in price-fixing conferences with the WIB.

---

[46]Mary Lasswell, *John Henry Kirby, Prince of the Pines* (Austin: Encino Press, 1967), pp. 160-61. For a study of a more prominent "dollar-a-year man," see Robert D. Cuff, "A 'Dollar-a-Year Man' in Government: George N. Peek and the War Industries Board," *Business History Review* 41 (Winter 1967): 404-20. Cuff discusses the entire concept of "voluntarism" during the war in "Bernard Baruch: Symbol and Myth in Industrial Mobilization," *Business History Review* 43 (Summer 1969): 115-33, and in "Herbert Hoover, The Ideology of Voluntarism and War Organization During the Great War," *Journal of American History* 44 (September 1977): 358-72.

[47]James O. Heyworth to Kirby, March 11, 1918, Records of the United States Shipping Board, Wooden Ship Division, RG 32; Frank A. Brown to Kirby, March 15, 1918, Kirby Papers, Box 144; Lasswell, *John Henry Kirby*, p. 161; Kirby to Charles Piez, March 25, 1918, RG 32; Kirby to James O. Heyworth, March 13, 1918, Kirby Papers, Box 144.

[48]The southern pine men had requested a hearing before the Senate Commerce Committee, which at that time was investigating the controversial shipbuilding program, but, after getting matters resolved with the Shipping Board, the lumbermen simply filed a statement of record with the committee. F. L. Sanford to Duncan U. Fletcher, March 12, 1918, Kirby Papers, Box 144; L. C. Boyle, "The Southern Pine Lumbermen's Co-operation in the National Wood Ship Program, Statement on Behalf of the Southern Pine Association and Southern Pine Emergency Bureau, Before the Committee on Commerce, United States Senate, Sixty-Fifth Congress, Second Session on S. Res. 170," SPA Records, Box 143b.

[49]"Shipping Board's Wood Ship Schedule Modified; John H. Kirby Made Lumber Administrator," *Southern Lumberman* 86 (March 16, 1918): 19.

As noted earlier, WIB Chairman Baruch and Charles Edgar, acting lumber director, determined in the spring to equalize prices for lumber sold to the government with that sold on the commercial market. Wholesale and retail dealers and their associations repeatedly demanded that they be allowed to purchase lumber at the same lower price charged the government. Some manufacturers, however, preferred the double standard under which they selfishly accepted higher-priced commercial orders rather than those for the government coming through the SPEB and other regional emergency bureaus. This situation clearly affected the industry's ability to meet the government's demands for lumber, not to mention the grumbling about profiteering and patriotism.

Representatives of the highly fragmented industry, while often at odds amongst themselves over the level of prices and profits, generally opposed the principle of price fixing and, moreover, expressed little confidence in Edgar's ability to deal equitably with all aspects of the industry. R. H. Downman, Edgar's predecessor, believed that price fixing would be impossible to enforce.[50] Imperative from the WIB's point of view was the need to get industry's cooperation and agreement or at least the appearance of being full participants in the decision to set maximum prices. Kirby, already under some criticism for alleged conflicts of interest in the pricing issue, tried to play the role of statesman. As president of the NLMA, he asked his fellows for patience. "Manufacturers of lumber, in a spirit of patriotism," he wrote, "have yielded their convictions on [the] subject of price fixing [and] are attempting in good faith and in proper spirit to put into efficient action rules which government at Washington has prescribed for them."[51]

It was in this context that Kirby, Keith, R. A. Long of Kansas City, and various other southern pine men haggled with the WIB Price-Fixing Committee from June 12 to 14, hoping to reach some accord. Eventually, Dr. F. W. Taussig, acting chairman of the committee, prepared a list of maximum prices for all sales of southern pine lumber by manufacturers, whether for military or civilian use, retroactive to June 14.[52] The list was referred to Edgar and Baruch, and the lumbermen left the capital city. When the formal order was issued by President Wilson two weeks later, it stated that the prices were reached *by*

agreement. This claim shocked Kirby, Long, and Keith, who immediately protested to Taussig that they had not agreed voluntarily to the prices established, which they said were too low, nor to the idea of price fixing. "Aside from the question as to whether Southern Pine interests will accept the prices as fixed, we do want it understood at the outset that we have not agreed to the price . . . nor did we consent to administrative features covered by the order." Their telegram concluded, "We respectfully request that these errors be called to the President's attention and the order corrected to conform with the facts."[53] Baruch fired a return telegram to Kirby, expressing "surprise," "astonishment," and "regret" that the Texan had apparently changed his position on the price-fixing agreement.[54]

Southern pine manufacturers meeting in Memphis angrily denounced the government's prices for lumber and expressed dissatisfaction with its administrators, particularly Edgar and Baruch. SPA President Keith pledged that the industry would meet its commitments to the government and hoped that all parties would eventually receive fair treatment, but, he concluded, "I don't accept Mr. Baruch and Mr. Edgar as my government and I strongly favor appealing from their decision in fixing prices for our product."[55]

Kirby then went to Washington in an attempt to clear up the evident misunderstanding with Baruch and to seek redress for other grievances. Baruch kept Kirby waiting for two hours (at least, so said the Texan) and then told him that lumber prices and other terms of the order would be adjusted only if Kirby and the other industry representatives would first admit that the order of June 14 had been a matter of agreement between them and government officials. The lumbermen regarded this as "wholly indefensible" coercion (and Kirby described it as such in a letter to Keith), but they produced a rather hedging statement and then were granted a hearing before the WIB on July 9. Here the southern pine men presented a list of industry's grievances and proposed a number of adjustments. One was that a standing committee represent the southern pine industry to facilitate communication between producers and the government. Responding favorably to the proposal, the WIB recommended that producers in the territory of the Southern Pine Emergency Bureau choose a permanent committee, fully representative of all manufacturers, to serve as industrial spokesmen before the WIB. Other administrative features of

---

[50]J. E. Rhodes to Board of Directors, April 29, 1918, RG 32.
[51]"N.L.M.A. Bulletin No. 38, June 25, 1918," Kirby Papers, Box 144.
[52]"Maximum Prices for and Procedure for Distribution of Southern or Yellow Pine Lumber, June 14, 1918," RG 32.

[53]Telegram (undated copy), Kirby Papers, Box 144.
[54]B. M. Baruch to Kirby, June 28, 1918, Kirby Papers, Box 144.
[55](Memphis) *Commercial Appeal*, June 29, 1918.

the price-fixing agreement were adjusted or referred to the Price-Fixing Committee for further
consideration.[56]

Later in July the SPA's Board of Directors met
in Chicago. Kirby told the board that the WIB
wanted manufacturers in the territory of the
SPEB to select a permanent trade committee
that would be free of undue influence from any
particular association, group of mills, or faction
of the industry. Believing that action was required, the SPA board dutifully complied by
dissolving the SPEB and authorizing the SPA
president to appoint a permanent, five-man War
Service Committee of the Southern Pine Industry. The new committee was intended to
represent the SPA, its subscribers, and other
cooperating manufacturers in all matters involving the production and sale of their lumber under
conditions set by the WIB. President Keith
then appointed as committee members Kirby,
Long, F. W. Stevens of Bagdad, Florida, A. L.
Clark of Dallas, and Charles Green of Laurel,
Mississippi.[57]

The WIB, increasingly losing patience with
the southern lumbermen and their notions
of "representative," would not accept this action
by the SPA Board of Directors. In a telegram to
Long on July 30, Baruch stated that the SPA
board's Chicago action abolishing the SPEB and
setting up the new War Service Committee was
not in accord with wishes of the WIB because the
"Chicago committee was not selected by the lumber manufacturers but by [the] Board of Directors of [the] Southern Pine Association,
which association does not include a large number of independent and small mills in that territory." Baruch's disgust with leaders of the southern pine industry was further revealed by his
reference to Kirby's letters to Keith — letters
highly critical of Baruch and Edgar that had just
been published, apparently at the instigation of
the SPA, in the major lumber journals. "I am
astonished at the representations contained

therein," Baruch warned, "and advise you that
[the] War Industries Board will deal with no
committee of which those responsible for these
representations or their circulation are members."[58]

The tension had been building for at least a
month. Baruch had already expressed his out-
rage to Kirby over the Texan's apparent change
of position with regard to "agreement" on the
price-fixing measure, and a contemporary observer of the mobilization effort later noted that
Baruch's "greatest friction" with the lumbermen
was with three "obstructionist" members of the
SPA, namely, Kirby, Long, and Keith.[59]

---

[58]B. M. Baruch to R. A. Long, July 30, 1918, Kirby
Papers, Box 144.

[59]Clarkson, Industrial America in the World War,
pp. 423-24, presents an account sympathetic to Edgar
and Baruch. Edgar, according to his version, "was
a veteran in the industry and knew it from the woods
to the dry-kiln. His old associates affected to think
that he was a sort of trade traitor because he was
adamant for fair prices. They made extraordinary
efforts to get rid of him. Even Baruch thought at
first that Edgar lacked diplomacy. But these men
were not subjects for diplomacy. They drove to their
ends with the brutal energy of a donkey engine jerk-
ing a lurching log through the forest. Baruch found
that out later when they sought to batter him down.
Then, like Edgar, he tossed diplomacy out of the
window, and figuratively speaking, threw the three
obstructionists after it. He refused to have anything
to do with any bureau or committee which included
them. Whereupon the axemen were retired to ob-
scurity for the rest of the war. Thereupon the lumber sailing of the War Industries Board was smooth."

---

[56]The Washington meetings can be pieced together
in the following letters and statements, all located in
the Kirby Papers, Box 144. Kirby to Chas. S. Keith,
July 1, 1918; Kirby to Keith, July 10, 1918; Kirby,
Long, and Stevens to the War Industries Board, July
9, 1918; "Exhibit 'C' Statement Filed by the Southern
Pine Lumbermen before the War Industries Board";
"Exhibit 'D' Memorandum of Report by a Committee of the War Industries Board Appointed to Hear
the Protest Filed by the Southern Pine Lumbermen."
Some items were subsequently published in the lumber trade journals; see, for example, "Interesting
Correspondence Relating to Price-Fixing Negotiations," Southern Lumberman 89 (July 27, 1918): 26.

[57]"Minutes of a Meeting of the Board of Directors
of the Southern Pine Association Held at the Black-
stone Hotel, Chicago, Illinois, July 20, 1918," pp. 6-8,
SPA Records, Box 70b.

220

Keith said otherwise.[60]

Whether he realized it or not, Kirby was on his way out of government service — partly because of an understandable confusion of roles thrust upon him as representative of several conflicting groups, and partly because he had the temerity to tangle with and embarrass Baruch, Edgar, and other government officials. On July 16 Kirby was rather formally advised that his position of lumber administrator for the EFC in the South had been abolished, ostensibly for reasons of administrative consolidation within the agency.[61] However, he simultaneously accepted appointment as national lumber administrator for the EFC, a position of even greater power and responsibility and one that would require him to spend time at EFC headquarters in Philadelphia. This new appointment was made *after* Kirby had written to Keith, accusing Baruch and his WIB cohorts of coercion, but *before* the controversial letters were published widely in the trade press. Their publication evidently caused Baruch embarrassment with President Wilson and, thus, were the final straw in the split between two "dollar-a-year men."[62]

Several days later, on July 31, newspapers throughout the nation reported that Kirby had resigned his new position as national lumber administrator of the EFC. The Texan cited "demands of his own business" and removal of his headquarters to Philadelphia as reasons for the resignation. Insiders knew, of course, that Kirby had been forced out, and there was much speculation about the reasons. Among the unattributed stories was the long-standing complaint that the shipbuilding program was being "seriously hampered . . . because southern yellow pine interests have not met more fully and promptly the demand for heavy timbers" — this despite the fact that the problem had been officially resolved. Baruch was reported to be considering commandeering the yellow pine industry "unless the government's needs are fully supplied." The actual decision to dispense with Kirby's services was said to have been made by Director-General Schwab and Vice-President Charles Piez of the EFC, although Kirby's formal letter of dismissal subsequently came from a lower official. In a private letter to Chairman Hurley of the Shipping Board, Kirby denied all charges made against him and the industry and demanded a

Left: Charles S. Keith of Kansas City, Missouri, was president of the Southern Pine Association from 1915 to 1918. Right: John Henry Kirby, president of the National Lumber Manufacturers Association, was a controversial "dollar-a-year-man" during World War I. Later, in 1922 and 1923, he was president of the Southern Pine Association.

Forest History Society

As Baruch began pulling the strings to eliminate Kirby from the war effort, Charles Edgar moved immediately to court other prominent members of the southern pine industry. He wrote to Colonel W. H. Sullivan, manager of the Great Southern Lumber Company in Bogalusa and a sometime rival of Kirby, that the WIB still considered the SPEB, which Sullivan chaired, to be a functioning organization until such time as the industry could hold a general meeting and form a more truly representative committee. Edgar also refuted Kirby's statement about the June 14 price-fixing episode, claiming that the Texan "definitely understood the ruling was to be written by agreement." Moreover, he attached statements by two of his assistants to the effect that they had heard M. J. Scanlon, a member of the original southern pine group that met with the Price Fixing Committee, claim that prices had been fixed by "agreement" and that Scanlon could not understand why Kirby, Long, and

[60]Charles Edgar to W. H. Sullivan, July 31, 1918, Kirby Papers, Box 144. Both statements are attached to the letter.

[61]J. L. Ackerman to Kirby, July 16, 1918, RG 32.

[62]"Mr. Kirby and the Southern Pine Industry," *Gulf Coast Lumberman* 6 (August 15, 1918): 9; "John H. Kirby Appointed Lumber Administrator," *Southern Lumberman* 89 (July 20, 1918): 21; "Interesting Correspondence Relating to Price-Fixing Negotiations," *Southern Lumberman* 89 (July 27, 1918): 26.

correction. Hurley expressed his sympathy and claimed not to have made a complaint.[63]

Rumors persisted that Kirby had resigned under a cloud of dishonor, but the Texan had many loyal friends and defenders within the industry. "In times such as these," the *Southern Lumberman* editorialized, "the country can ill afford to be deprived of the services of a man of Mr. Kirby's ability merely because he excites the wrath of someone who has the power to bring about his removal." The advisory board that Kirby had selected to assist him with his duties as EFC lumber administrator in the South submitted a lengthy report on Kirby's achievements. These industrialists were extremely critical of the conditions that Kirby had inherited. They also claimed that W. J. Haynen, who preceded and succeeded Kirby, had used a staff informer to spy on the Texan and had done everything within his power to discredit Kirby and his volunteer assistants.[64]

The effort to discredit Kirby, if indeed it can be called that, was certainly not successful within the industry. When southern pine lumbermen assembled in New Orleans on August 28, 1918, to choose a "permanent" war committee, Kirby's services were lauded and he was introduced to "storms of applause." According to accounts of the meeting, "so rousing was Mr. Kirby's reception when he arose to speak that for some moments he was unable to proceed. He seemed noticeably affected by the voluntary expression of confidence and cordiality displayed by the audience." It was evident that most southern lumbermen regarded Kirby as a victim and a symbol of the charges leveled against the entire industry. The Houston lumberman then delivered a lengthy speech in defense of his record, in tribute to the patriotism and sacrifice of the industry, and, perhaps surprisingly, in generous praise of Baruch.[65]

Despite later pious tributes and expressions of gratitude from both the industry and government, the southern pine manufacturers' problems and the charges against them continued through the end of the war. As late as November 1, the War Service Committee faced allegations from Washington that the industry was dragging its feet on orders intended for railroad and car material, apparently because the orders had been placed early and thus carried lower prices than more recent ones. Although denying the charge, the committee urged industrial members to fill these orders in order to clear the industry of any suspicion of delay.[66]

W hen the armistice was signed on November 11, the government began canceling contracts and plunged headlong toward demobilization. Two days later the WIB began to remove price controls and, within approximately one month, no more priority orders were issued. The "dollar-a-year men" almost trampled one another in their haste to close down the wartime bureaucratic machinery and get back to profitable civilian life.[67] Lumber Director Edgar officially notified the SPEB on November 23 that the WIB would be making no further recommendations concerning placement of lumber orders with the various bureaus. The SPEB immediately stopped taking orders, and its Washington office was virtually closed by December 1. The New Orleans office continued to function in a restricted fashion until February 15, 1919, when the last of the government orders was filled, and the SPEB thus went out of existence.[68]

The SPEB kept careful records. By November 23, 1918, when it ceased to allocate government purchases, the SPEB had delivered a total of 1,904,308,523 board feet of lumber for the war effort. Of this vast quantity of lumber products, 295,178,221 feet went to the EFC for the construction of ships, and 1,345,648,542 feet went to the War Department for the building of cantonments and other structures for the use of the army and related service organizations, such as the YMCA and the Knights of Columbus. The Railroad Administration received 224,722,713 feet for use in the construction of railroad cars, and 38,759,047 feet were shipped to the Allies.[69] This was unquestionably a major accomplishment, one that sweetened the bad taste left in the mouths of southern lumbermen.

Even before the war ended, the SPA took positive steps to repair the industry's image. Large advertisements were placed in metropolitan newspapers to trumpet the industry's role in war mobilization. The advertising campaign also demon-

[63]"John H. Kirby Resigns," *Southern Lumberman* 89 (August 3, 1918): 23; (New York) *Globe and Commercial Advertiser*, July 31, 1918; Kirby to E. N. Hurley, August 1, 1918, RG 32. Kirby's formal notification of his dismissal came on August 9; see J. L. Ackerman to Kirby, August 9, 1918, RG 32.

[64]Editorial, "A Regrettable Resignation," *Southern Lumberman* 89 (August 17, 1918): 20; "Report of Advisory Board to the Lumber Administrator of the U.S. Shipping Board, E.F.C.," Kirby Papers, Box 144.

[65]Collier, *First Fifty Years*, p. 67; "New Committee to Represent Pine Manufacturers," *Southern Lumberman* 89 (August 31, 1918): 23-25.

[66]George R. Hicks to Southern Pine Mills, November 1, 1918, Kurth Papers, Box 489, Forest History Collections, Stephen F. Austin State University Library, Nacogdoches, Texas.

[67]Soule, *Prosperity Decade*, p. 81. For an account of the difficulties of another "dollar-a-year man" in separating private from public affairs, see Cuff, "George N. Peek," pp. 411-15.

[68]"Report of the Southern Pine Emergency Bureau," SPA Records, Box 84b.

[69]*Ibid.*

Concern for its image led the SPA to advertise widely in 1918. After the war the association launched an elaborate campaign ("Build a Home First") to end the housing shortage, create jobs for returning servicemen, and. . . sell lumber.

John M. Collier, The First Fifty Years of the Southern Pine Association, 1915-1965

strated the broad adaptability of southern pine as a construction material; returning veterans and a war-weary public soon were coached to "build a home first."[70]

In the afterglow of victory over the Central Powers, the government and the southern pine industry momentarily forgot the strife, conflict, sacrifice, and acrimony of the war years and basked in the glory of their mutual accomplishments. The SPA, the SPEB, and the southern pine industry in general received wide praise from high-ranking government officials for their wartime efforts. Among the more prized expressions of gratitude were those from the WIB's lumber director, Charles Edgar, and from its powerful chairman, Bernard Baruch. The latter wrote on December 5, 1918:

> I offer in behalf of my associates and myself a tribute of thanks to the patriotism and service shown by the entire commercial body of America. Its members have made service and not profit their rule. They have shown a desire to subordinate self and exalt public interest, and to this readiness to make sacrifice in the common cause has largely been due whatever success we may have been able to attain. I would be doing the industry of America an injustice if I did not make this acknowledgement. May I express the hope that this same spirit may continue in times of peace, so that the problems affecting all may be handled in the same spirit of helpful cooperation that had prevailed during the War. May I send this message of gratitude to the loyal co-workers in the great lumber industry which you have so ably represented.[71]

Following the war the southern pine industry, like other sectors of the economy, faced a maze of problems postponed, created, or intensified by the wartime disruptions. The southern pine industry faced reconstruction, the return to "normalcy," and the "profitless prosperity" of the postwar decade. It sought and received the assistance of a well-organized trade association that had been tempered in the fires of war. Like other associations, the SPA's service in the mobilization effort, although controversial at many points, built a reservoir of goodwill with the government that would help shape a more favorable or lenient attitude toward trade association activities during the 1920s. Business practices that were not tolerated during peacetime, such as price fixing and production controls, had proven to be essential for the defense effort and would thus seem less objectionable in the postwar period.[72] The experience of business-government cooperation, illustrated here in the case of the southern pine industry, also provided valuable knowledge and experience for future wartime mobilization, as well as for peacetime economic planning and coordination between government and business.[73] □

[70]Collier, First Fifty Years, pp. 67-73.
[71]James Boyd, "Gross Darkness — Then Comes Dawn," p. 22, SPA Records, Box 77a.

[72]Robert F. Himmelberg, "Business, Antitrust Policy, and the Industrial Board of the Department of Commerce, 1919," Business History Review 42 (Spring 1968): 1-23.
[73]The significance of World I mobilization for the National Recovery Administration of the 1930s is examined in Robert F. Himmelberg, "Business and Mobilization: WIB and NRA," Mid-America 45 (July 1963): 157-74.

Secretary Hoover and the
Quest for Broadcast Regulation

By Daniel E. Garvey

Surprisingly little has been written about the role of Herbert Hoover in formulating the regulations which control American broadcasting.

Hoover was Secretary of Commerce from 1921 to 1928. Such weak powers as the federal government had to regulate broadcasting under the Radio Act of 1912 were placed in the hands of the Secretary of Commerce. Hoover's difficulties in controlling the obstreperous young industry have been well chronicled. But when it comes to the struggle to obtain stronger federal regulation for the industry, Hoover has frequently been pictured as a reluctant supporter, if not an opponent, of greater federal control. Historian Sydney Head, for example, writes:

> Secretary of Commerce Hoover, an ardent believer in free enterprise, had hoped that the industry would be able to discipline itself without government regulation. [1]

And in an earlier edition of the same work, Head argued that the Radio Act of 1927 "...was to a large extent the product of the radio industry itself." [2]

However well this fits Hoover's oft-stated preference for a governmental philosophy of *laissez-faire*, it does not jibe with Hoover's statements and actions of the period where broadcasting was concerned. Whatever else he may have felt about government regulation of industry, Hoover was a staunch and unceasing advocate of strong federal regulation for broadcasting. Some of the powers he sought for federal regulators far exceeded the powers finally granted in the Radio Act of 1927 and reconfirmed in the Communications Act of 1934.

Many of the provisions of our present law of broadcasting were called for by Hoover years before Congress finally put them into law. Nothing in the record suggests that Hoover ever considered industrial self-regulation as anything but a stop-gap measure, useful only until strong federal legislation could be obtained.

Herbert Clark Hoover was sworn in as Secretary of Commerce of the United States on March 4, 1921. [3] Until passage of the Radio Act in February of 1927, his department exercised what little control over radio had been granted to the federal government under the Radio Act of 1912.

Daniel E. Garvey is associate professor of journalism at California State University, Long Beach.

Designed essentially to regulate ship-to-ship and ship-to-shore radio telegraphy, the Radio Act of 1912 was totally inadequate to deal with the mushrooming vehicle for entertainment, information and advertising that radio was to become in the years after World War I. During World War I, control of radio had been delegated to the U.S. Navy. When the war ended, several bills were placed before Congress which would have either retained control of broadcasting for the Navy or made the industry a government-operated service. None of these bills made it through committee to the floor of Congress; and on February 29, 1920, control of broadcast facilities not owned by the government reverted to private ownership. [4]

For the next seven years, Congress debated various bills to replace the weak Radio Act of 1912. No bill had sufficient backing to overcome the opposition of powerful members of Congress who feared placing control of the new industry in the hands of the federal government.

Meanwhile, the little authority granted to the government under the Radio Act of 1912 was eroding. The government had no power to prevent broadcasters from interfering with channels that had been allocated to others. And while Congress might take a leisurely view of this problem, the Secretary of Commerce had to cope with a situation that was rapidly reaching untenable proportions.

Before Hoover had spent a year in office, his papers indicate that he had come to recognize the need for stronger federal powers. In February, 1922, Hoover pointed out the problem to Sen. Frank B. Willis in a letter. Willis had written to Hoover, requesting that Hoover expedite the application for a radio license made by a Mr. Burkham, one of Willis's constituents. Promising to give the matter "prompt attention," Hoover launched into a lengthy description of the sad state of affairs in broadcasting:

> The whole matter of regulation of radio broadcasting is becoming of great importance. Unless we can devise a method for stopping interference there is little hope for a station such as Mr. Burkham's being much use. I believe, however, that after the Committee which is meeting here next week for a thorough investigation of the subject has made its report we can solve the problem. [5]

76

The "Committee" was the first National Radio Conference. That Hoover had issued the call for such a meeting before the end of his first year in office indicates how quickly Hoover had been forced to come to grips with the problem.

Indeed, Hoover told the first National Radio Conference, "Until the last four or five months there has been little difficulty in handling these regulations."[6] It appears that by the seventh or eighth month of Hoover's term of office (some time in the fall of 1921), the inadequacies of the Radio Act of 1912 had become obvious to him.

In his opening address to the first National Radio Conference, Hoover returned again and again to the need for federal regulation, urging, "It is one of the few instances I know of where the whole industry and country is praying for more regulation."[7] He warned the Conference "Even if we use all the ingenuity possible, I do not believe there are enough permutations [of frequency] to allow unlimited numbers of sending stations."[8]

Hoover denounced "ether hogs," and spoke of the air waves as a national resource needing public regulation:

> There is involved, however, in all of this regulation the necessity to so establish public right over the ether roads that there may be no national regret that we have parted with a great national asset into uncontrolled hands.[9]

The statement is of particular interest because of its early date, February, 1922. Historian Erik Barnouw has given credit to Congressional conservationists, led by Sen. George W. Norris, for writing into the Radio Act of 1927 the clauses which maintained "control of the United States over all channels."[10] It seems only fair to credit Hoover with having made the call for such control five years before Congress acted.

Probably the most widely quoted passage from Hoover's speech to the first National Radio Conference is this:

> It is inconceivable that we should allow so great a possibility for service, for news, for entertainment, for education and for vital commerical purposes to be drowned in advertising chatter, or for commercial purposes that can be quite well served by other means of communication.[11]

Regrettably, the sentence immediately preceding that one has been overlooked by most reseachers. In concentrating on Hoover's distaste for advertising, they have overlooked the scope of the regulatory powers he was suggesting. For the preceding sentence concludes:

> ...it becomes of primary public interest to say who is to do the broadcasting, under what circumstances, and with what type of material.[12]

Today's Federal Communications Commission may determine who does the broadcasting and under what circumstances, but it is severely circumscribed in its power to regulate content. It is specifically forbidden the power to censor programming by Section 326 of the Communications Act of 1934. It appears that in this area Hoover, rather than looking for ways to avoid regulation, was seeking stronger regulation than we have even today. More important, at this early date in 1922, he was linking

that regulation to the now familiar phrase in broadcast regulation, "public interest."

In the months after the First National Radio Conference, Hoover made frequent appeals to the public for broadcast legislation. In May, 1922, he raised the issue in an interview for the Boston *Evening Transcript.*[13] He raised it again in an article for *Scientific American* in August of the same year.[14] In September, Hoover wrote in *Radio Broadcast:*

> Bills are now before Congress which promise to provide order instead of anarchy in the ether....Accomplishment of this legislation may accordingly, be considered as the next important step in the progress of radio.[15]

Time was running out. In November, 1922, the Supreme Court of the District of Columbia issued a writ of mandamus, ordering Hoover to issue a radio license to the Intercity Radio Co. Hoover had argued that the Intercity license could not be issued without creating interference on already assigned wave lengths.[16] Hoover appealed, and followed up with another article in the January, 1923, issue of *Radio Broadcast*. The title was "The Urgent Need for Radio Legislation," and in it Hoover described the state of affairs in broadcasting as "simply intolerable."[17]

But Congress saw things differently. Hoover had actively worked with Congressman Wallace White of Maine in the quest for legislation to replace the Radio Act of 1912. Opposition came from Progressives and Democrats, mostly from the South and Midwest. Hoover was denounced as a would-be Czar, trying to set up a "big government monopoly,"[18] and Congressman Thomas Blanton of Texas voiced the states' rights argument that broadcasting was not an interstate matter.[19] The lack of a provision for judicial review in the White bill also drew opposition fire. White was unable to surmount this opposition, and the bill died.

The White bill had been debated in late January, 1923. On February 5, 1923, the Circuit Court for the District of Columbia affirmed the writ of the lower court, ordering Hoover to issue a license to the Intercity Radio Co.[20] In March, Hoover convened the Second National Radio Conference. The situation was no longer "simply intolerable." Now, Hoover told the conference, the situation had become "even worse than we could have anticipated."[21] He went on the say:

> Due to the failure of the legislation we are without the necessary authority to effectually prevent interference. In seeking authority we were supported by literally the entire radio public. They want to be regulated.[22]

During 1923, the situation continued to deteriorate. By December, Hoover found it necessary to issue a special request that all stations refrain from interfering with other stations on the same frequency long enough for the nation to hear a broadcast of the memorial services for the late President Harding.[23]

In March, 1924, Hoover was again asking the public to support legislation introduced by Congressman White. Hoover told the New York *World:*

The regulatory powers now vested in the Department of Commerce are totally inadequate and would have broken down but for the voluntary cooperation of the stations. ...The White Bill names the causes for which licenses could be revoked, and creates other powers which I am confident would enable us to keep the ether open to everybody. [24]

He voiced similar pleas to the public in a broadcast over WCAP in Washington, D.C., later the same month. [25] Later, speaking to the conservative U.S. Chamber of Commerce--after making appropriate obsequities to industrial self-regulation—Hoover said:

Even our latest great invention—radio—has brought a host of new questions. No one disputes that much of these subsidiary additions to the Ten Commandments must be made by legislation. [26]

In August, 1924, Hoover addressed the California Radio Exposition in San Francisco. The speech was a slightly revised version of the address he had given over WCAP the preceding March. He went into considerably greater detail than he had in the WCAP speech to expound on the problems of regulation and to stress the need for federal regulatory power.

There are a number of intricate problems to be solved if the art is to become the great service to the public of which it is capable. The first of these problems is regulation to prevent interference between stations. There can be no adequate development of the art unless there is very positive Federal regulation. It is the one industrial service I know of which is anxious to be regulated, for without regulation we will have absolute chaos in the ether and no adequate service can be developed. The federal law on the subject was passed a dozen years ago at the time when the telegraph was the

only radio manifestation in the field. The Department of Commerce has been unceasing for three years in endeavors to secure adequate legislation to govern the radio telephone field. Congress has been too crowded to deal adequately with so intricate a subject but it is probable that such legislation will pass in the next session. [27]

In the WCAP speech Hoover had attempted a weak joke about his inability to understand why the Secretary of Commerce had been given the burden of regulating broadcasting. The statement does not appear in the San Francisco speech. Hoover appears to have had no serious desire to see the regulatory authority taken away from his department. Later he would argue against the establishing of a new agency to regulate broadcasting.

When the Third National Radio Conference met in October, 1924, Congress still had provided no substitute for the ineffectual Radio Act of 1912. The Conference responded to Hoover's plea for self-regulation by working out a framework for self-policing by the industry.

To the Progressives in Congress, this smacked of monopoly, and Sen. Robert LaFollette branded it as such. He also accused the Conference of concocting secret agreements to keep him off the radio. [28] Hoover denied the accusations. His response gives a wryly pithy description of the state of broadcasting at the end of 1924:

Anyone who likes is free under the law and practice of the Department of Commerce to erect a broadcasting station and say anything over it that he pleases... [29]

Late in 1924, Hoover made a puzzling shift in his quest for legislation. In a letter to Congressman White, copies of

NOTES

1. Sydney W. Head. *Broadcasting in America,* 2d ed. (Boston: Houghton Mifflin Co., 1972), p. 159.

2. Head, *Broadcasting in America,* 1st ed., (1956), p. 134.

3. Harold Wolfe, *Herbert Hoover* (New York: Exposition Press, 1956), p. 90.

4. "Direct Radio Open to Wales Tonight," New York *Times,* Feb. 29, 1920, Section II, p. 1.

5. Letter to Sen. Frank B. Willis, Feb. 21, 1922, Radio Folio of Hoover Collection, Hoover Library, Stanford.

6. Speech to First National Radio Conference, Washington, D.C., Feb. 27, 1922, Document #209, Hoover Collection.

7. *Ibid.*

8. *Ibid.*

9. *Ibid.*

10. Erik Barnouw, *A Tower in Babel, A History of Broadcasting in the United States,* Vol. I, to 1933 (New York: Oxford University Press, 1966), p. 37.

11. Speech to First National Radio Conference.

12. *Ibid.*

13. "Value of Radio Phones," Boston *Evening Transcript,* May 4, 1922, p. 5; Document #221-A, Hoover Collection.

14. "Policing the Ether," *Scientific American,* CXXVII (August, 1922), p. 80; Document #252, Hoover Collection.

15. "Radio's Great Future," *Radio Broadcast,* I (September, 1922), p. 2; Document #252-A, Hoover Collection.

16. *Hoover v. Intercity Radio Co., Inc.,* 286 F. 1003 (D.C. Cir.), Feb. 5, 1923.

17. "The Urgent Need for Radio Legislation," *Radio Broadcast,* II(January, 1923), p. 211; Document #276, Hoover Collection.

18. Congressional Record, LXIV (1923) part 3, p. 2328.

19. *Ibid.,* p. 2781.

20. *Hoover v. Intercity Radio Co.*

21. Address to Second National Radio Conference, Document #297, Hoover Collection.

22. *Ibid.*

23. "Letter to All Radio Stations," Dec. 5, 1923, Radio Folio, Hoover Collection.

24. "The Government's Duty is to Keep the Ether Open and Free to All," New York *World,* March 16, 1924; Document #364, Hoover Collection.

25. Radio Broadcast from WCAP, Washington D.C., March 26, 1924, Document #382, Hoover Collection; reported in "Hoover Talks from WCAP," New York *Herald-Tribune,* March 26, 1924.

26. Address to Chamber of Commerce of the United States, Cleveland, Ohio, May 7, 1924, Document #378, Hoover Collection.

which were distributed to the press, Hoover suggested that Congress postpone action on "comprehensive" legislation for broadcasting. Instead, he urged that Congress pass a stop-gap measure which would confirm his authority to regulate wave lengths, power, emitted wave, type of apparatus and time of transmission for broadcast facilities placed under jurisdiction of the Secretary of Commerce by the Radio Act of 1912. [30]

Hoover's purpose in sending the letter is not entirely clear. No doubt he was sincere in the concern he expressed in the letter about the problems of implied censorship in setting criteria for issuing licenses. But it is doubtful that a delay would have done anything to provide a solution to the problem. At least, one can say from 50 years' hindsight that the problem is as vexing today as it was at the time of Hoover's letter.

A more plausible explanation is that Hoover feared Congress would take the regulation of broadcasting out of the hands of the Department of Commerce—as it ultimately did. The stop-gap legislation he was requesting would give him most of the powers he needed, while keeping broadcast regulation firmly under the control of the Secretary of Commerce.

Whatever Hoover's intent, the effects were disastrous. "Hoover Opposes More Radio Control," the New York Times headed its article on the letter. The Times' article predicted that Hoover's letter would kill any chance for passage of the White bill at that session of Congress. [31]

The White bill was not passed at that session—nor was

the "stop-gap" bill which Hoover had requested. Whatever its intent, the letter surely ranks as a blunder. It well may be that the White bill had little chance of passage at that time anyway; but in opting for another bill, Hoover helped defeat legislation that was desperately needed, and failed to obtain a satisfactory substitute.

Perhaps stung by this, Hoover had few public statements to make about broadcasting during the greater part of 1925. However, in September of that year, addressing the Fourth National Radio Exposition in New York City by radio from Washington, Hoover returned to the familiar theme: "This is the only industry where everybody agrees that there must be regulation....We cannot avoid Federal regulation." [32]

In November, 1925, after the meeting of the Fourth National Radio Conference, Hoover reported to the public:

> It was therefore determined that it [the conference] would ask the Congress of the United States to enact legislation in your interest....Not a dissenting voice was raised against the resolution by which they [the delegates] formally recognized that your interests are dominant.
>
> ....
> I hope that this legislation will be given us by Congress at its next session. [33]

Instead of legislation, Hoover was handed another crippling court decision. The decision in the Zenith Radio case stripped the Secretary of Commerce of anything but token authority to keep stations from broadcasting on frequencies assigned to other stations. "It is apparent," Hoover said, "..no one has the authority to protect the listening public against utter chaos." [34]

---

27. "Radio Problems," address to the California Radio Exposition, San Francisco, California, Aug. 16, 1924, Document #396, Hoover Collection.

28. "His Charge Has a Poor Basis," New York Times, Oct. 18, 1924, p. 14.

29. "Radio Monopoly and Mr. LaFollette," Press Release, Washington, D.C., Oct. 16, 1924, Document #405, Hoover Collection; reported in "No Radio Monopoly Declares Hoover," New York Times, Oct. 17, 1924, p. 3.

30. Letter to Congressman Wallace H. White, Dec. 4, 1924, Document #417-A, Hoover Collection; reported in "Hoover Opposes More Radio Controls," New York Times, Dec. 6, 1924, p. 4; and in "Hoover Wants Power Affirmed," New York Herald-Tribune Radio Magazine, Dec. 14, 1924, p. 29.

31. New York Times, Ibid.

32. Speech to Fourth American Radio Exposition, New York, Sept. 12, 1925, Document #510, Hoover Collection; reported in "Sec. Hoover Opened Radio Show from Washington With Speech," New York Herald-Tribune Magazine, Sept. 20, 1925, p. 12.

33. Broadcast on Conference Recommendations, Nov. 12, 1925, Document #522-A, Hoover Collection; reported in "Radio Problems Discussed at Captial, Sec. of Commerce Summarizes Work of Committees," New York Herald-Tribune Radio Magazine, Nov. 15, 1925, pp. 1 and 4; and in "Hoover on the Ether's 'Howls and Growls,'" Literary Digest, Dec. 19, 1925, p. 45.

34. Press Release, April 20, 1926, Document #527-A, Hoover Collection; reported in "Hoover Discusses Situation Created by Court Decision," New York Herald-Tribune Radio Magazine, April 25, 1926, p. 10.

35. Giraud Chester, Garnet R. Garrison, and Edgar E. Willis, Television and Radio, 4th ed. (New York: Appleton-Century-Crofts, 1971), p. 32.

36. Press Release, April 20, 1926.

37. Interview for Philadelphia Public Ledger, April 16, 1926, Radio Folio, Hoover Collection.

38. Ibid.

39. "Text of Ruling Denying Radio Control," New York Times, July 10, 1926, p. 5.

40. Ibid.

41. "Hoover Asks Help to Avoid Air Chaos," New York Times, July 10, 1926, pp. 1 and 5.

42. Letter to the Hon. Everette Sanders, Secretary to the President, July 27, 1926, Radio Folio, Hoover Collection.

43. Press Release, July 9, 1926, Document #604, Hoover Collection.

44. "Uncle Sam Keeping An Eye on 'Pirate' Broadcasters," New York Times, July 25, 1926.

45. Opening Speech to Fourth National Radio Conference, Washington, D.C., Nov. 9, 1925, Document #521, Hoover Collection; reported in "Hoover Urges U.S. Regulate Radio Traffic," New York Herald-Tribune, Nov. 10, 1925, pp. 1 and 8.

46. Letter to Congressman Wallace H. White.

47. Press Release, April 20, 1926.

48. Ibid.

49. Opening Speech to Fourth National Radio Conference.

Chester, Garrison and Willis have suggested that Hoover washed his hands of the broadcasting problem following the *Zenith* decision.[36] This seems doubtful. Hoover made very few public statements about broadcasting during 1926. Moreover, of those he made, some show signs of pique. Regarding the *Zenith* decision in April, 1926, Hoover said:

> So far as the Department of Commerce is concerned the extraordinary difficulties and conflicts in the situation are such that we will be well satisfied to see radio administered by any other department which can properly undertake regulation.[36]

Hoover seemed even hotter under his famous collar in an interview given to the Philadelphia *Public Ledger* the same month. He called radio a "spoiled child" which was "acting up before company."[37] Asked if he would like to see the establishment of a federal radio commission, he replied tersely, "I'd love it."[38]

However, Hoover did not give up the ship. On June 4, 1926, Hoover sent a letter to acting Atty. Gen. William J. Donovan, asking for a clarification of the scope of his power to regulate broadcasting after the *Zenith* decision. The response came on July 8, 1926. In effect, it said Hoover had no power to regulate broadcasting, except for those frequencies assigned by the Radio Act of 1912 to the federal government. Aside from this, he was obliged to issue a license when requested, and could do nothing to keep the licensee on an assigned frequency or at an assigned power.[39] The crisis transcended national import. The *Zenith* case had dealt with American broadcasters operating on frequencies assigned to Canadian stations. International relations were involved.

It seems reasonable to conjecture about what followed. It is possible that Hoover, who had been warning of "chaos" for so long, deliberately let things deteriorate, hoping that "chaos" would force Congress to act. Surely he must have had some idea of what the attorney general would rule. Donovan's ruling ended with what sounded very much like a plea for legislation:

> It is apparent from the answer contained in this opinion that the present legislation is inadequate to cover the act of broadcasting, which has been almost entirely developed since the passage of the 1912 Act. If the present situation requires control, I can only suggest that it be sought in new legislation carefully adapted to meet the needs of both the present and the future.[40]

Two days later, Maj. Gen. J.G. Harboard, the president of the Radio Corporation of America, was telling the press that the crisis "might serve to impress Congress with the great need for sound legislation."[41]

The strongest evidence that Hoover may have wanted "chaos" to force legislation lies in his reaction to a recommendation in the New York *Times* that the President personally urge all broadcasters to remain on their assigned frequencies.[42] At the same time, Hoover continued to issue press releases urging new broadcast legislation.[43] And to keep "chaos" from becoming too chaotic, he warned broadcasters that they could still be prosecuted by his office for "willful or malicious interference" with broadcasts by others.[44]

Whether Hoover schemed to create the crisis must remain conjecture. What is recorded is that in his annual message to Congress, December 7, 1926, President Coolidge asked Congress to enact new broadcast legislation. Congress, which had failed eight times in six years to enact such legislation, pushed through the Radio Act of 1927 in little more than a month.

In many ways, the law reflected the positions Hoover had espoused. In 1925, he had written, "For five years I have reiterated that these wave lengths are public property to be used by assignment of public authority."[45] This point, which Hoover returned to again and again in his speeches, was fully recognized in the new law. It was noted earlier that Hoover linked licensing with "public interest" as early as 1922. In 1924, he brought up the two well-known companions of public interest, "public convenience and necessity."

Toward these two, he was somewhat less favorably inclined. He wrote:

> ...there is growing demand for the limitation of the number of stations in a given area, and that such a limitation would be based on the service needs of the community, just as public utilities are generally limited by the rule of public convenience and necessity. Again this enters a dangerous field of recognizing monopoly and implied censorship.[46]

Hoover continually shied away from the public-utility phrasing, preferring such terms as "public service to the listener." In the end, Congress turned to the more familiar public-utility phraseology, and the law linked licensing to public interest, public convenience and public necessity— the order of the three being varied somewhat whimsically throughout the legislation. On this issue it would seem that the law did not fully meet Hoover's desires.

In another area, Hoover won only the appearance of a victory. Throughout the struggle for legislation, Hoover had sought to retain control of broadcast regulation in the Department of Commerce. True, following the *Zenith* decision he had said he would be glad to relinquish regulation to "any other department which can properly undertake regulation."[47] But no other department appears to have been seriously considered by Congress.

The struggle in Congress lay between the Republican-dominated House, which wanted to keep regulation in the hands of the Department of Commerce, and the Senate, where a coalition of Southern Democrats and Midwestern Progressives was insisting on a new independent regulatory agency for broadcasting. Hoover had been willing to relinquish the vexatious allocating of licenses to an independent board, but he insisted that all administrative duties should "rest in one of the executive departments rather than...a new and additional agency, which would imply considerable additional expense."[47]

The Radio Act of 1927 nominally left broadcast regulation in the hands of the Department of Commerce. But the powers vested in the new Federal Radio Commission made it clear from the outset that the new agency would operate independently, and that the role of the Department of Commerce in broadcast regulation was at an end. (continued on Page 85)

Hoover

(continued from Page 70)

Indeed, the new agency so quickly took on a life of its own that one other Hoover concept was swept away by actions of the agency itself, almost without notice. Hoover had once spoken of regulation of broadcasting by the "community" or the "area."[49] The Radio Act gave a sort of token recognition to this concept by dividing the nation into five zones, each to be represented by a commissioner. Whatever representative function the commissioners were to perform, the processes of administration quickly turned the tables, and the function of the commissioners became one of administering rather than representing districts.

In summary, Herbert Hoover's role in obtaining the Radio Act of 1927 was anything but passive. He campaigned actively for legislation. The legislation he got was obviously not entirely to his liking. In essence, he had wanted legislation which would have confirmed that the Secretary of Commerce had the power to regulate broadcasting through licensing—the power to assign and police frequencies, power, equipment and hours of operation.

He did not want an independent Radio Commission. He did want broadcasting to operate in the "public interest," but not particularly for "public convenience and necessity." Nevertheless, his speeches helped bring all these concepts to public attention. He showed a very solid grasp of the problem of implied censorship in licensing, and would probably be pleased that the Communications Act of 1934 still contains the sections of the Radio Act of 1927 which forbade censorship.

Whatever historians may have surmised, nothing in his acts or writings of that period shows that he was a believer in self-regulation. He played an important role in the formulation of the relationship between broadcasters and government in the United States, a role that deserves closer scrutiny by scholars.

*c*MID-*c*AMERICA

An Historical Review

APRIL 1973

VOLUME 55   NUMBER 2

The Unemployment Conference of 1921: An Experiment in National Cooperative Planning[1]

Twentieth century America was beginning its third decade in 1921. For many a New Era seemed to be arriving. The problems of the previous decade, epitomized in Theodore Roosevelt's image of "regulated monopoly" and Wilson's hope of "regulated competition," contrasted strangely with Andrew Jackson's graphic description of a nation easily managed by the average citizen. The coercive marshalling of the nation's resources for war had demonstrated the potential role that government might play and the responsibilities it might in the future assume. At the same time, however, many Americans were exhausted from the enthusiasm of the Progressive Era and the suffering of the War. They talked of a "return to normalcy," of "individualism," phrases that meant a smaller realm of government activities.

The call to action generated by the problems of the New Era and the fear of growing government bureaucracy fostered by the regulatory agencies of the Progressive Era and of the war worried equally the conscience of Herbert Hoover, the new Secretary of Commerce in Harding's Administration. There was a strong need, he felt, for a coordinated program of national reconstruction and development, one that would necessarily involve a "tempering of individualism" and a clear recognition that the "unrestricted capitalism of Adam Smith" was dead. Yet, if national progress was to continue, the methods used must preserve "individualism," maintain freedom

---

1 This is a slightly revised version of an essay that was rated second in the 1971 competition for the Organization of American Historians Pelzer Award.

83

from governmental or group "domination," and foster equality of opportunity. To bridge the gap, to build upon the sense of "service and mutuality" that had been apparent during the war and yet avoid a system of detailed regulation and incentive-destroying bureaucracy, Hoover envisioned a cooperative capitalism, one under which the duty of the federal government would be to "mobilize the intelligence of the country" through education, coordination, and occasional stimulation of the private sector, all designed to build a "cooperative system" and secure from it the actions needed to solve national problems.[2]

Hoover was not alone in holding for a cooperative approach. In 1921 he was rephrasing convictions of progressive engineers, business academics, trade association leaders, public relations experts, labor leaders, and industrialists. The Progressive Era had emphasized rationalization of government and of society according to the rules discovered by the social scientists, with attention particularly to corporate planning and on Taylorism efficiency. The War Industries Board had heightened the drive for rationalization of industry, and by 1920 over 2,000 trade associations existed among business firms to solve common problems by cooperative action.[3] Public relations experts such as George Harvey had also shown Americans that people could be manipulated to change old ways. If experts provided the "laws," government through proper education could promote cooperation and thereby ease social tensions.

One immediate problem to which Hoover sought to apply such a cooperative approach was that of unemployment during the recession of 1920–21. As a Quaker, he felt compelled to help the needy. As an engineer, he was horrified at the wastefulness of unemployment. As a recent administrator of relief in war-torn Europe, he was cognizant of the potential of massive mobilization. And, as a believer in "individualism," he feared that failure to take action would weaken the values that had made America unique. The opportunity must not be lost, he thought, to educate both private groups and government of all levels concerning their responsibilities in the New Era.

---

[2] Speech before Federated American Engineering Societies, Nov. 19, 1920, Public Statement (PS) 102; Address to Metropolitan Life Insurance Company Managers, Jan. 27, 1923; Hoover's speech to Unemployment Conference, Sept. 26, 1921, Unemployment File (UF), Box 459—President's Conference on Unemployment: Plans and Purpose, Commerce Papers—Official File (CP-OF), Herbert Hoover Papers, Hoover Presidential Library, hereinafter HHP.

[3] David A. Shannon, *Between the Wars: 1919–1941*, Boston, 1965, 42.

It should be noted, too, that the responsibilities Hoover had in mind were quite different from those prescribed by the teachings of classical economics. Where Adam Smith had argued that men are basically selfish in their actions and narrow in their outlook, Hoover maintained that a new economic leadership, tested during the war, was concerned for the welfare of others and capable of acting in terms of the happiness of society as a whole. Where Adam Smith had extolled the value of numerous independent economic units in competition with each other, Hoover envisioned a cooperative system in which information and aid flowed between businesses and governments to maximize efficiency and eliminate duplication. Where Adam Smith had postulated an "invisible hand" overseeing the economy, Hoover foresaw the quite visible activity of voluntary associations of businessmen and government officials, working together to insure full employment. Where classical economists reasoned that prosperity could be restored in a depression situation only by liquidating prices, especially wages, until balance was again restored between supply and demand, Hoover urged governmental units to expand public works and businesses to avoid wage cuts and to undertake measures which would expand rather than contract purchasing power. Philosophically, he still looked upon individual creativity as the mainspring of progress and still called for "healthy competition" within a cooperative framework, but in its main outlines, the type of system he envisioned was closer to the NRA program of the early New Deal or to corporate liberalism in general than it was to the competitive model of classical economics.[4]

The Unemployment Conference of 1921 is thus significant not only as a forerunner of the actions to be taken in 1929–32, but also as indicative of the fact that there was already in 1921 a group of men in the Harding Administration who thought in terms of national planning whose activities did generate some action. This essay will examine the Conference and the resulting efforts at relief, recovery, and reform. In doing so, it will draw upon previously unused material, and having looked at the events themselves, it will argue that they are another indication that the 1920's and 1930's should be

---

4 Herbert Hoover, *American Individualism*, Garden City, 1922; "Some Notes on Industrial Readjustment," *Saturday Evening Post*, Dec. 27, 1919, PS 39; Forward by Milton Friedman in *America and the New Era*, Feb. 4, 1920, PS 42A; Memo on Letting Highway Contracts, July 26, 1921; "Lindsay, Samuel McCune," Box 184; "Unemployment, Business Cycles," Box 304, CP-OF; HHP.

viewed as part of one evolutionary process rather than as decades with sharply contrasting ideologies and policies.

The first federally sponsored conference on unemployment in the nation's history sprang largely from Hoover's mounting concern with the problem once he had taken office. The President and Secretary of Labor Davis might believe that unemployment follows employment "just as surely as the tides ebb and flow," but Hoover could not use such rationalizations to soothe his conscience.[5] Unemployment in 1921 was severe, was nationwide, and therefore should be the concern of a federal government that several years before had been organizing the nation's resources for war. It was now time for a "war on unemployment," and as early as the summer of 1921, Hoover was taking some action.[6] He proceeded to gather a group of engineers and suggest the advantages of awarding road contracts in the fall rather than spring. Little road building, he acknowledged, could take place in the winter, but still, he reasoned, the certainty of awarded contracts would stimulate winter orders of equipment. Shortly thereafter, he advised the state governors to take a similar action.[7]

Fundamentally, Hoover hoped to tackle the problem by "organizing the areas of cooperation."[8] Accordingly, he suggested to President Harding on August 12 the appointment of a presidential commission. Its purpose, he wrote later, should be to arouse "public sentiment" and stimulate cooperative action, and to be successful it should consist primarily of men who were capable either of influencing the actions of employers or of stirring up the public.[9] On August 29 the public learned of the decision to call a federally sponsored conference. Hopefully, Harding told the nation, such a conference could determine the volume of unemployment, could offer emergency recommendations, and could study possible reforms to lessen business fluctuations in the future. It was "inconceivable,"

5 For Harding's view, see Unemployment Conference, Sept. 26, 1921, UF, Box 459—President's Conference on Unemployment: Plans and Purpose, CP-OF, HHP. For Davis' view, see Zieger, 89–90.

6 Hoover to Joseph Lee, Oct. 15, 1921, UF, Box 466—Community Service, CP-OF, HHP.

7 Hoover to President Warren G. Harding, Aug. 20, 1921, UF, Box 459—President's Conference on Unemployment: Plans and Purpose, CP-OF, HHP.

8 "The Washington Conference" by E. E. Hunt, Jan. 3, 1922, UF, Box 468—Hunt, E. E., Articles By, CP-OF, HHP.

9 Hoover to Harding, Aug. 20, 1921, UF, Box 459—President's Conference on Unemployment: Plans and Purpose, CP-OF, HHP.

he said, that a country as wealthy as the United States, "could allow any suffering amongst those of our own people who desire to work."[10]

Following the President's announcement, men cancelled trips to Europe and cut short August vacations on Cape Cod as they received calls from Hoover for assistance in making certain that this "educational" effort in cooperation would be well organized. For the names of delegates, Hoover turned to such men as Samuel Gompers of the American Federation of Labor and Joseph DeFrees of the Chamber of Commerce.[11] For the task of organizing the conference, he summoned together a group of advisers formed by expanding the Economic Committee of the Commerce Department.[12] Included, along with academic economists from Harvard, Cornell, Columbia, Johns Hopkins, the Massachusetts Institute of Technology, the New School for Social Research, and the Wharton School of Finance, were such men as Edwin Gay, former president of the National Bureau of Economic Research, Otto Mallery, originator of a controlled public works program in Pennsylvania, Bailey Burritt, director of the American Association for Improving the Condition of the Poor, and Henry Dennison, industrialist and known humanitarian. Most of these men were presumably predisposed toward aggressive governmental action, and six of them were also members of the executive board of the American Association for Labor Legislation.[13]

Hot summer weather persisted during the first two weeks of September while Hoover's "brain trust" hammered out the program which became the basis for the official recommendations adopted by the Conference. In its official report the committee divided its findings into three sections: an estimate of the extent of unemployment, suggestions for immediate relief and recovery, and recommendations for permanent reform. Concerning unemployment statistics, the group, as was customary, lamented that no reliable data

---

10 Department of Commerce Press Release, Aug. 29, 1921, Box 459—President's Conference on Unemployment: Plans and Purpose, CP-OF, HHP.

11 Hoover to Samuel Gompers, Sept. 8, 1921, and J. H, Defrees to Hoover, Sept. 1, 1921, UF, Box 471—Members Suggested: A-M, CP-OF, HHP.

12 Hoover to George Barnett, Sept. 8, 1921, UF, Box 463—Advisory Committee, CP-OF, HHP.

13 For list of members and biographical background, see UF, Box 463—Advisory Committee, CP-OF, HHP. For members of American Association for Labor Legislation, see John B. Andrews to Arthur Woods, Feb. 23, 1922, UF, Box 462—Miscellaneous: A, CP-OF, HHP.

existed, but estimated that unemployment in the early part of September stood at about 3,500,000, excluding farm laborers.[14]

In its recommendations for emergency relief, the Committee clearly reflected Hoover's concern with "cooperation" and his fear of federal dominance. Primary responsibility must rest with local governments, who should organize community employment bureaus and a vast voluntary relief association to include private citizens and organizations as well as all the resources of local governments.[15] Yet since any expansion of purchasing power promoted recovery as well as relief, the economic advisers focused on the desirability of industry's undertaking repairs and improvements and on the necessity of increasing public works on the part of governments. Unfortunately, public works required advance planning. Nevertheless, wherever possible, they should be expanded, not only for the relief provided, but also for the employment generated by the manufacture of equipment and supplies and by the spending of wages.[16]

In the area of relief and recovery, the federal government, the report urged, should publicize the type of winter work successfully managed in Canada, should complete immediately all appropriated federal public works, establish share-the-work programs among federal employees, spend the unused portion of road appropriations, and seek new appropriations for needed federal buildings. Furthermore, if these measures failed, it should issue new bonds and loan the proceeds to the states for local public works. In addition, the federal government, by advancing to the railroads the money owed them as a result of the wartime arrangements and by postponing payment of the interest on the foreign debt, could both expand domestic purchasing power and revive foreign trade by stabilizing the foreign exchange rate.[17]

In its suggestions for permanent reform, the committee touched upon such possibilities as unemployment insurance yet stressed two proposals. One was the establishment of expanded and permanent statistical services. The other was the creation of a central federal agency that could plan federal public works in advance in order to aid and supplement the private sector rather than overstimulate an already flourishing economy. The committee recognized, however, that human nature being what it was, such permanent reforms, un-

---

[14] Report of Economic Advisory Committee, Sept. 26, 1921, UF, Box 463—Advisory Committee, CP-OF, HHP.
[15] Ibid.
[16] Ibid.
[17] Ibid.

less begun during a crisis, would be "deferred, and again deferred." For this reason it urged the Conference to begin a "statesmanlike" consideration of them.[18]

With the report of the Economic Advisory Committee completed, the larger Conference began its deliberations. These, it quickly became apparent, were designed not to expand the work of the committee, but rather to mobilize public opinion along the lines indicated. Accordingly, the eighty additional delegates had been chosen primarily with reference to geographical or professional criteria. After the editor of a large Negro newspaper suggested his race should be represented, Hoover added a black delegate to the list,[19] and with the same concern for appearances Harding thought more women should be included.[20]   Indeed, several weeks before the Conference opened, Edward Hunt, former socialist and eventual executive secretary of the Conference, reported that the acceptances thus far were giving the gathering "a rather conservative look." More delegates "from left center" were needed.[21]

Influenced doubtlessly by a concern for appearances, Hoover had assigned at least one member of the Economic Advisory Committee on ten of the eleven Conference subcommittees, presumably to "guide" the subcommittee. These groups, also according to Hoover's instructions, were to report back only unanimous conclusions, the type, in other words, that presumably would have the greatest affect in swaying public opinion.[22]   While they deliberated, the press could keep the nation interested by reporting the public hearings that were started the second day.[23]   From the beginning Hoover had assumed that the experts would formulate the ideas and that the decentralized self-government would come in implementing them.[24]

To some such a conference may have appeared as a way of winning political support without doing anything meaningful.   But for

18 *Ibid.*
19 The black delegate was George E. Haynes, Ph.D., a member of the Commission on Race Relations of the Federal Council of the Churches of Christ, formerly director of the Division of Negro Economics of the U. S. Department of Labor, UF, Box 462, CP-OF, HHP.
20 George Christian Jr., secretary to the President, to Hoover, Sept. 10, 1921, UF, Box 471—Members Suggested: A-M, CP-OF, HHP.
21 Copy of radio telegram from Hunt to Hoover, Sept. 13, 1921, UF, Box 471—Members Suggested: A-M, CP-OF, HHP.
22 Unpublished editorial by H. S. Dennison, undated, UF, Box 458— Unemployment Facts, CP-OF, HHP.
23 *Ibid.*
24 Report of Economic Advisory Committee, Sept. 26, 1921, UF, Box 463—Advisory Committee, CP-OF, HHP.

Hoover, this was clearly not the case. The federal government had never previously assumed such leadership in the matter of unemployment, and conditions did not demand it at this time. Rather, the elaborate concern with the representation of the delegates and the attention given to the publicity value of the Conference were both dictated by Hoover's conception of how to use publicity as an administrative tool.[25] Unemployment, as he saw it, was a national problem requiring national planning. Accordingly, one sought the advice of experts, such as those hastily assembled to form the Economic Advisory Committee. He sought to reconcile this expertise with the need to preserve individual and local initiative. It thus became crucial that the recommendations of the experts be implemented in a decentralized way by men of influence and through the pressure of public opinion. To a man frightened by big government yet convinced that some type of collective, managed economy was needed, the elaborately publicized conference system became a key tool, that was expected to produce not obstruct the action desired.

The delegates, largely unaware of Hoover's interpretation of the conference system and of the ritualistic nature of much of their activity, approached the work seriously. John L. Lewis of the United Mine Workers, for example, arranged for a substitute when he was forced to absent himself from a portion of the proceedings. Gradually, too, they seemed to be making progress. By September 30, they had met in a second general session, agreed that there were between 3.5 and 5.5 million unemployed, and adopted emergency relief recommendations. These, like those made by the Economic Advisory Committee, assigned to the local communities the primary responsibility to organize mayor's coordinating committees, to create employment bureaus where nonexistent, and to foster civic activities such as "spruce up" campaigns. Private citizens should begin repair work. Businesses should spread work and enlarge inventories. Local governments should expand school, street, and sewage construction. The federal government should begin immediately appropriated public works, and Congress should approve additional appropriations.[26] During the next five days delegates also voiced approval for monthly

---

25 Craig Lloyd, "Aggressive Introvert: A Study of Herbert Hoover and Public Relations Management, 1919–1932," Ph.D. Dissertation, University of Iowa, 1970, 162–203.

26 General Emergency Recommendations of Unemployment Conference, Sept. 29, 1921, UF, Box 459—President's Conference on Unemployment: Plans and Purpose, CP-OF, HHP.

statistical reports,[27] for a $400,000 appropriation to the United States Employment Service to organize local emergency employment bureaus,[28] and for an immediate loan of $16,200,000 to the Reclamation Fund.[29]

On October 4 the President appealed for national cooperation with the emergency plans, and during the week that followed, the committees worked out another set of recommendations designed to promote business recovery. Formally adopted on October 11, these recognized that recovery would "be a process of gradual healing from the "great economic wounds" of the war, but still called on the government for such things as a downward readjustment of railway rates, a reduction of taxes, definite settlement of the tariff question and the financial obligations to the railroads, limitations on world armaments, steps to minimize fluctuations in world monetary rates, and programs to insure steady employment in seasonal industries such as coal.[30]

Little attention was paid to the call for a program of permanent reform. One subcommittee, however, did propose a permanent system of employment offices whose work would be coordinated by the federal government,[31] and another repeated the suggestion of the Economic Advisory Committee that more extensive action be taken in advance planning of public works.[32]

Before adjourning on October 13, the delegates selected a standing committee of fourteen to supervise the work of the emergency organization already appearing throughout the country.[33] In view of the lack of action in regard to permanent reform, they also instructed the standing committee to sponsor investigations of such

---

[27] Report of the Committee on Unemployment Statistics, Oct. 13, 1921, UF, Box 460—Reports of Committees to Unemployment Conference (3), CP-OF, HHP.

[28] Report of Committee on Employment Agencies and Registration, Oct. 10, 1921, UF, Box 460—Employment Agencies and Registration, CP-OF, HHP. This recommendation concerning the U. S. Employment Service was passed as a resolution by the Conference as a whole, Oct. 11, 1921.

[29] Report of Committee on Public Works, Oct. 13, 1921, UF, Box 460—Reports of Committees to Unemployment Conference (2), CP-OF, HHP.

[30] General Permanent Recommendations of Unemployment Conference, Oct. 11, 1921, UF, Box 459—President's Conference on Unemployment: Plans and Purpose, CP-OF, HHP.

[31] Report of Committee on Employment Agencies and Registration, Oct. 10, 1921, UF, Box 460—Reports of Committees to Unemployment Conference (2), CP-OF, HHP.

[32] Report of Committee on Permanent Public Works, Oct. 13, 1921, UF, Box 460—Reports of Committees to Unemployment Conference (2), CP-OF, HHP.

[33] "Employment and Unemployment," undated and unsigned, UF, Box 458—Unemployment Facts, CP-OF, HHP.

problems as seasonal unemployment and fluctuations of the business cycle.[34]

Judged by the anticipated goals of Secretary Hoover, the Unemployment Conference seemed a moderate success. It had made an estimate of the magnitude of the problem, had launched studies that might lead to long-range reforms, and, most importantly, had outlined an emergency program to which the nation seemed to be responding. By October 10, mayor's emergency committees had been created in thirty-one cities and were in the process of being formed in twenty others. In Washington an office had been set up for Colonel Arthur Woods, the man who would coordinate the work of national, state and city governments. By October 11, Woods had copies of the general emergency recommendations in the mail to mayors of every city over 20,000 in population.[35]

To Herbert Hoover, the Conference seemed not a moderate but an almost total success. Through it, he felt, he had used the resources and energies of the federal government to arouse public opinion and hopefully to initiate a vast cooperative program to handle the crisis. Its plan to "get through this next winter into seas less rough," he told the Conference on October 13, was a "milestone in the progress of social thought." It showed that the government while recognizing its responsibilities, could act within the framework of the "American spirit and American institutions." Instead of reaching into the "public purse," it could handle the crisis through voluntary organizations and avoid a "step backward in the progress of this country."[36]

Following the adjournment of the Conference, its Standing Committee acted quickly. Colonel Arthur Woods, a former police commissioner of New York and one-time coordinator of postwar efforts to ease service men back into civilian life, became the pivotal figure and with the assistance of other federal agencies, took the lead in stimulating local action.[37] The mayors, moreover, seemed to respond quickly to the insistent letters from him and from Secretary Hoover.

---

34 *Ibid.*
35 Report of the Executive Secretaries to the Committees of the President's Conference on Unemployment, Oct. 10, 1921, UF, Box 459—President's Conference on Unemployment: Plans and Purpose, CP-OF, HHP. Arthur Woods to Mayors, Oct. 11, 1921, UF, Box 460—Reports of Committees to Unemployment Conference (3), CP-OF, HHP.
36 Hoover's farewell address to Conference, Oct. 13, 1921, PS 177B, HHP.
37 Hoover to Governors, Oct. 11, 1921, UF, Box 452—Correspondence Regarding Highway Construction: Arthur Woods File, CP-OF, HHP.

By December, 1921, some 209 cities of the 327 cities having a population over 20,000 had established mayor's committees,[38] and by January, the figure had climbed to 225.[39]

Reports of a variety of local actions began coming in. In Portland, Oregon, the mayor's committee used vacant steel yards to house the floating unemployed.[40] In Detroit, an "odd job" campaign uncovered 500 to 1,000 jobs.[41] In Bethlehem, Pennsylvania, free stores" were established to distribute food and coal.[42] In Waterloo, Iowa, employers pressured workers into donating one percent of their monthly income for relief purposes.[43] Throughout the country, fund raises were reporting success. Buffalo, for example, had set aside $70,000 for groceries, and Kansas City reported $290,000 in its charity fund.[44]

The mayor's committees also were moving to establish free employment bureaus. In the twenty-three states where no public employment system existed[45] and in some areas where agencies were in operation, new emergency employment offices appeared, whose activities the Commerce Department followed carefully for the next nine months.[46] Nor were independent bureaus discouraged. At Philadelphia's Holy Trinity Church, an employment bureau was available to all who enrolled in the Bible class. Hearing reports that this arrangement had placed 271 applicants, Woods observed that "if a job isn't worth praying for, it isn't worth having."[47]

Expanding "necessary" public works was the third area of local activity strongly recommended by the Conference, and, according to the flood of press releases now emanating from the Commerce

---

[38] Press release, Dec. 17, 1921, UF, Box 462—Unemployment 1922, CP-OF, HHP.

[39] Press release, Jan. 3, 1922, UF, Box 462—Unemployment 1922, CP-OF, HHP.

[40] Summary of Recommendations and Plans of Portland, Oregon, Oct. 4, 1921, UF, Box 460—Employment Agencies and Registrations, CP-OF, HHP.

[41] James Couzens to Arthur Woods, Dec. 15, 1921, UF, Box 487—Detroit, Mich., CP-OF, HHP.

[42] S. A. Herrick to Woods, Jan. 31, 1922, UF, Box 468—Herrick, Mr. S. A., CP-OF, HHP.

[43] E. F. MacDonough to Hoover, Nov. 16, 1921, UF, Box 486—Waterloo, Iowa, CP-OF, HHP.

[44] Press release, Jan. 28, 1922, UF, Box 462—Unemployment 1922, CP-OF, HHP.

[45] Report of Committee on Employment Agencies and Registration, Oct. 10, 1921, UF, Box 460—Employment Agencies and Registration, CP-OF, HHP.

[46] Questionnaires filed by states, UF, Boxes 484–90, CP-OF, HHP.

[47] Press release, Jan. 21, 1922, UF, Box 462—Unemployment 1922, CP-OF, HHP.

Department, this, too, was definitely under way. Los Angeles, for example, reportedly was spending $2,000,000 on public works.[48] By February, 1922, Woods could claim that $450 million was now available in the country for local improvements, and that eighty percent of the work covered by these appropriations was in progress.[49] Just how many of the cities actually followed through with their plans is difficult to determine, but apparently quite a number did. In April, 1922, when Woods sent letters of inquiry to the mayors of the 136 cities that had supposedly expanded public works, some reacted with surprise that Washington labored under such delusions, but many did indicate a break with normal patterns. Allentown, Pennsylvania, so its mayor reported, had continued sewer construction during the winter. Baltimore was very optimistic over the relative cheapness of winter work. Buffalo reported spending $200,000 on repair work. Lynchburg, Virginia reported that more had been spent on public works in 1921 than in the previous five years combined.[50] Furthermore, the record-breaking bond sales of November and December, 1921, and of January, 1922,[51] indicate that public works were at least in the planning stages. By the close of 1921, cities had sold twice as many bonds as in any previous year, and this rate was maintained in 1922.[52]

To keep the cities active, Woods relied primarily upon exhortation, advice, and the pressure of public opinion. In an endless stream of letters, he reported on what other municipalities were doing, on the advantages of special projects like the "Give a Job for a Christmas Gift" campaign.[53] Based on information gleaned from educators, librarians, and newsmen, he asked about the progress of local projects.[54] When, for example, the Palo Alto, California, newspaper announced approval of a $40,000 bond issue for the local library, city officials soon had a letter asking for the starting date. When the president of Illinois Wesleyan University, replying to one such

---

[48] Press release, Jan. 28, 1922, UF, Box 462—Unemployment 1922, CP-OF, HHP.

[49] Press release, Feb. 5, 1922, UF, Box 462—Unemployment 1922, CP-OF, HHP.

[50] Replies to form letter, UF, Box 466—Cities, CP-OF, HHP.

[51] Otto Mallery to Hoover, Woods and Hunt, Nov. 17, 1921, UF, Box 462—Unemployment 1922, CP-OF, HHP. Mallery to Woods, Dec. 14, 1921, UF, Box 470—Mallery, Otto, CP-OF, HHP.

[52] E. Jay Howenstine, Jr., "Public Works Policy in the 20's," *Social Research*, XIII (December, 1946), 483.

[53] Woods to Mayors, Dec. 19, 1921, UF, Box 466—Community and Civic Emergency Measures, CP-OF, HHP.

[54] Letters on subject, UF, Box 452—Correspondence Regarding Library and Highway Construction, CP-OF, HHP.

letter, stated that financing was unavailable, a letter was fired off to the Illinois regional director of the Unemployment Conference asking him to "stir up" the banks in the region. If all else failed, pressure from Washington would be the "last resort."[55] In addition, press releases were issued frequently, newspapers were supplied with a booklet of twenty-five stories, to be used when they needed copy,[56] and in December, when newspaper coverage seemed to be flagging, a special publicity committee was established.[57]

Along with encouraging mayor's committees, the Conference also was trying to enlist other cooperative elements. Hoover quickly had sent "pep" letters to the state governors and had sought the aid of a number of professional and business groups.[58] In addition, the Woods' committee was trying to "touch up" the women through the National Federation of Women's Clubs[59] and to organize relief through the Federal Council of the Churches of Christ in America.[60] Hoover's activities were reminiscent of his exhortations and organizational arrangements as a war administrator, and, he frequently mentioned the success of war time voluntaryism as proof that a cooperative approach could work.

To provide coordination, the Washington committee relied partly on eighteen regional directors, partly on roving trouble-shooters. The directors functioned primarily as channels of communication, transmitting suggestions to and from Washington. The trouble-shooters, namely, Lt. Fred W. Caswell of the Army, Commander A. L. Bristol of the Navy, and S. A. Harrick, provided both detailed intelligence and on-the-spot assistance.[61] When Harrick, for example, was told in one community that construction on a new sewage system awaited only state approval, he immediately left for the state capitol.[62]

---

55 Woods to E. Sherman, Dec. 3, 1921, UF, Box 452—Correspondence Regarding Library Construction: Arthur Woods File (1), CP-OF, HHP.
56 Booklet of Press stories, undated, UF, Box 462—Unemployment 1922, CP-OF, HHP.
57 Referred to in "Publicity Reports," May 8, 1922, UF, Box 476—Unemployment Publicity, CP-OF, HHP.
58 Draft letter, Oct. 11, 1921, UF, Box 468—Governors, Communications To, CP-OF, HHP.
59 Woods' staff conference, Dec. 2, 1921, UF, Box 481—Minutes of Col. Woods' Conferences, CP-OF, HHP.
60 Woods' staff conference, Jan. 3, 1922, UF, Box 481—Minutes of Col. Woods' Conferences, CP-OF, HHP.
61 Information by reference and inference, UF, Box 464—Bristol, Comm. Arthur L., and Box 465—Caswell, Fred, 1st Lt., CP-OF, HHP.
62 Herrick to Woods, Feb. 3, 1922, UF, Box 468—Herrick, Mr. S. A., CP-OF, HHP.

The Justice Department also lent aid. Its agents interviewed mayors and submitted numerous reports on unemployment. They also attended several radical meetings in New York, where Communists were allegedly attempting to capitalize on the unemployment situation, and their reports on these sometimes were used by the visiting representatives to impress mayors with the need for local action.[63]

The chief difficulty in securing cooperation, as the reports of Bristol, Harrick, and Caswell made clear, came from the larger cities, particularly from those whose leadership, enthusiasm, and concern did not measure up to Hoover's expectations. In New York, bitterness over previous disputes between state and federal governments was very much in evidence, and the official city employment agency, known as the Industrial Aid Bureau, was anything but cooperative.[64] Caswell sat in the waiting room daily for two weeks before being allowed to speak to its chairman, Bird S. Coler.[65] A similar lack of cooperation was apparent in Chicago, where Mayor William H. Thompson, after denouncing the Unemployment Conference as a capitalistic "conspiracy to lower wages," refused at first to appoint an emergency committee, and when he did appoint one, proceeded to create, by accident or intent, a confused arrangement that no one seemed to understand.[66] In Detroit, Mayor James Couzens, who initially had been an enthusiastic delegate to the Conference, was soon complaining about decreasing cooperation.[67] In several New Jersey cities, Bristol reported, the mismanagement evident in the hastily organized emergency employment bureaus had caused both employers and the jobless to loose faith in them. The best solution for a "ticklish" situation, he thought, was to build up the state employment bureaus and discourage the creation of any new bureaus.[68]

---

[63] See example of such reports, UF, Boxes 484–6, CP-OF, HHP. See example of use of such reports: Herrick to Woods, Feb. 7, 1922, UF, Box 468—Herrick, Mr. S. A., CP-OF, HHP.

[64] Darwin J. Meserole to Woods, Apr. 28, 1922, UF, Box 488—New York City, CP-OF, HHP.

[65] Numerous irate letters by Caswell to Woods, UF, Box 465—Caswell, Fred W., CP-OF, HHP.

[66] References to attitude in newspaper clippings, notes, UF, Box 485—Chicago, Hon. W. H. Thompson, CP-OF, HHP. See also Bristol to Woods, Mar. 7, 1922, UF, Box 464—Bristol, Comm. Arthur L., CP-OF, HHP.

[67] Couzens to Woods, Nov. 29, 1921, UF, Box 487—Detroit, Mich., CP-OF, HHP.

[68] "Estimate of the Situation—New Jersey—As Regards Unemployment" by A. L. Bristol (authorship assumed with certainty), undated, UF, Box 458—Unemployment Facts, CP-OF, HHP.

A number of large cities, moreover, were soon lagging in their efforts to expand public works.[69]

As time passed, even the smaller cities seemed to become less enthusiastic. Their limited resources, Woods acknowledged, were being "squeezed dry."[70] Traditionally during depressions, governments had retrenched, and the pressure to do so again was considerable. It was also hard to point to any city where cooperation had produced dramatic improvements. In February, 1922, when Woods asked for a memo on the city benefitting most from an emergency program, he learned that "a search of our records does not reveal a single instance of a city showing sufficient contrast between bad and good...." Butte, Montana had shown great progress, "but unfortunately," this was "mainly due to a revival of the mining industry and not to this conference...."[71]

As concerned as Hoover had been with the educational possibilities of the Conference, as energetically as his staff had worked during the next six months, he was seemingly unable to instill in local governments a sustained sense of urgency or responsibility. He was far more aggressive in his desire to coordinate relief efforts than were local governments to participate.

The recommendations for federal aid to assist recovery also suffered setbacks. The recommended $400,000 appropriation for the United States Employment Service was enthusiastically endorsed by Hoover as an aid to voluntaryism and localism rather than a dole, yet Harding's new Director of the Budget Charles Dawes, anxious to curb expenditures, pared the request to $200,000,[72] and the House Appropriations Committee, in the process of cutting the First Deficiency Appropriations Bill of 1922 (H.R. 9237), dropped it altogether.[73] The Committee could find need for a $55,000 scrub kitchen in the basement of the House, but not for federal assistance to employment bureaus.[74] In the Senate Committee on Appropriations, a $100,000 appropriation was reinserted,[75] but again, in the

69 Woods to Coler, Apr. 14, 1922, UF, Box 465—Caswell, Fred W., CP-OF, HHP.
70 Woods' staff conference, Jan. 16, 1922, UF, Box 481—Minutes of Col. Woods' Conferences, CP-OF, HHP.
71 Clark to Woods, Feb. 10, 1922, UF, Box 472—Unemployment Memorandums, CP-OF, HHP.
72 Congressional Record, 67 Cong., 2 Sess., LXII, 357.
73 Congressional Record, 67 Cong., 1 Sess., LXI, 8128.
74 Congressional Record, 67 Cong., 1 Sess., LXI, 8146.
75 U. S. Senate, 67 Cong., 2 Sess., Committee on Appropriations, "First Deficiency Appropriation Bill, 1922" (Senate Report 341), Senate Reports (Public), (December, 1921), 1–2.

conference committee that met following Senate adoption, it was eliminated.[76]

In the Senate debate over accepting the conference report, six senators voiced objections to the dropping of the $100,000 appropriation, declaring, among other things, that if the Senate agreed to the report, it must assume responsibility for the men "wearing dirty and ragged fragments of uniform, soliciting aid in the city of Washington," and for "a calamity which is not far away."[77] Other senators acknowledged the obvious need, but reminded their colleagues that federal employees could not be paid tomorrow if the deficiency bill was not passed today.[78] For this reason, the report was accepted, and the payroll met, although men off the payroll were forgotten.

A week later, when a bill arrived from the House (H.R. 9548) authorizing the President to purchase $20 million in grain for the starving Russians, several senators made a final try. After Senator Henry Ashurst of Arizona observed, "How cynical, how tragic it would be to appropriate $20 million for starving Russians and then refuse to appropriate the modest... sum of $100,000," the Senate added an amendment authorizing the $100,000 for the Employment Service,[79] but again, in conference, the appropriation was eliminated.[80] Christmas was four days away, and the Senators were in a conciliatory if not a charitable mood.

Another Conference recommendation for federal action, the call for more road building, resulted in the introduction of a federal highway bill (S. 1072), appropriating $75 million for 1922. To muster support, Otto Mallery, assisted by J. B. McCord of the Bureau of Public Roads, sent letters to the state governors asking how much work they could have under contract within ninety days after the bill's passage. Some replied pessimistically, pointing out the necessities of advanced planning, the approaching winter, and the lack of funds for matching.[81] Most, however, seemed eager for all possible federal aid, and some thirty governors promised that within the allotted time they could start 6,261 miles of new roads and employ

---

[76] *Congressional Record*, 67 Cong., 2 Sess., LXII, 356.
[77] *Congressional Record*, 67 Cong., 2 Sess., LXII, 358–9.
[78] *Ibid.*
[79] *Congressional Record*, 67 Cong., 2 Sess., LXII, 575.
[80] *Congressional Record*, 67 Cong., 2 Sess., LXII, 667.
[81] Channing Cox to J. B. McCord, Oct. 24, 1921; J. J. Blaine to McCord, Oct. 18, 1921; L. J. Frazier to McCord, Oct. 18, 1921; James Hartness to McCord, Oct. 25, 1921; Gov. Nathan Miller of N. Y. to McCord, Oct. 22, 1921; UF, Box 452—Correspondence Regarding Library and Highway Construction, CP-OF, HHP.

150,000 men.[82] In November, 1921, the highway bill became law, and on the same day as its passage, new letters went out to the governors informing them of their state's share and reminding them of any promises previously made. One of the bill's main purposes, the letters stressed, was to put people to work.[83]

Neither Hoover nor his associates, however, were so unsophisticated as to believe that much road-building could be done during the winter. The chief stimulus, as they saw it, would come from the letting of contracts and the immediate ordering of equipment and supplies.[84] In practice, a number of early contracts were awarded, but the results were not striking.[85] When asked later about the impact of the program, equipment manufacturers were not enthusiastic, and some, like the Holt Manufacturing Company of Peoria, Illinois, felt that its whole effect had been cancelled out by the free distribution of surplus war equipment through the Bureau of Public Roads.[86]

In their efforts to expand other types of public works, Hoover and his aides were repeatedly blocked by an economy-minded Congress. Initially, Governor W. P. C. Harding of the Federal Reserve Board had promised that $18 million would be spent for new bank buildings, but in January, 1922, when Senator William Harris of Georgia proposed that the Federal Reserve Board be prohibited from authorizing new bank buildings without Congressional consent, Governor Harding reacted by halting all construction until the fate of the proposal was known.[87] Woods wanted to "raise . . . hell about this," but nothing happened.[88]

Hoover also found that without additional appropriations the executive departments could do little.[89] On January 26, in a letter

[82] Press release, Dec. 17, 1921, UF, Box 462—Unemployment 1922, CP-OF, HHP.

[83] McCord to Thomas Campbell, Nov. 9, 1921, UF, Box 451—Correspondence Regarding Library and Highway Construction—Ala. to Maine, CP-OF, HHP.

[84] Press release, Dec. 10, 1921, UF, Box 462—Unemployment 1922, CP-OF, HHP.

[85] McCord to E. Sherman, Nov. 16, 1921, UF, Box 451—Correspondence Regarding Library and Highway Construction—Ala. to Maine, CP-OF, HHP.

[86] George Babcock to E. E. Hunt, May 29, 1929, UF, Box 463—Conference on Unemployment: Miscellaneous B, CP-OF, HHP.

[87] McCord to Mallery, Oct. 21, 1921, UF, Box 476—Public Works: Federal Reserve Board Building, CP-OF, HHP.

[88] Clipping from "Herald" with note attached from Woods to Mallery, Jan. 6, 1922, UF, Box 476—Public Works: Federal Reserve Board Building, CP-OF, HHP.

[89] Draft of Hoover's pessimistic answer to Harding's Jan. 26 letter, undated, UF, Box 468—Harding, CP-OF, HHP.

drafted by Hoover, President Harding urged department heads to undertake "all sound repair work," but later, when Hoover asked his colleagues what they were doing, the replies were disappointing.[90] The Navy pointed to its shared work plans, but maintained its ability to assist was limited by the recent Armament Conference.[91] The Commissioner of Lighthouses in Hoover's own department concluded that due to lack of funds, little expansion was possible.[92] And the Interior Department reported that it had lost both the President's letter and the recommendations of the Unemployment Conference. New copies were requested.[93]

The recommended loan of $16.2 million for the Reclamation Service also failed in congress.[94] In this case, neither the endorsement of the Unemployment Conference, the fact that the money would be repaid, nor testimony that plans were ready and a loan would permit the immediate hiring of 16,000 men[95] were enough to prevent a proposed $20 million advance (H.R. 8719) from dying in committee.[96] At one point, Congressman A. T. Smith of Idaho, the sponsor of the bill, tried to secure a public endorsement from Hoover, but as Secretary of Commerce he was reluctant to champion specific legislation affecting the Interior Department.[97] A last try was made in the spring of 1922 to add authority for the loan to a deficiency appropriation bill, but this also was rejected.[98]

Congress similarly refused to hurry into a settlement of the federal debts to the railroads. Some three months after the Unemployment Conference had urged speedy action on this matter,[99] Arthur Woods and his staff confessed privately that the situation was "al-

---

[90] Hoover's draft of Harding's letter and final letter, Jan. 26, 1921, UF, Box 462—Unemployment 1922, CP-OF, HHP.

[91] McCord to Woods, Feb. 21, 1922, UF, Box 462—Unemployment 1922, CP-OF, HHP.

[92] G. R. Putnam to Hoover, Feb. 9, 1922, UF, Box 462—Unemployment 1922, CP-OF, HHP.

[93] McCord to Woods, Feb. 21, 1922, UF, Box 462—Unemployment 1922, CP-OF, HHP.

[94] The Reclamation Service was designed to use money from the sale of public lands and from royalties on oil and mineral lands to build irrigation projects and reclaim arid lands.

[95] Ottamar Hamaele to Mallery, Oct. 7, 1921, Congressional Record, 67 Cong., 2 Sess., LXII, 3730–1.

[96] Congressional Record, 67 Cong., 1 Sess., LXI, 6354.

[97] Mallery to Hoover, Nov. 9, 1921 and Nov. 12, 1921, UF, Box 469—Interior: Reclamation, CP-OF, HHP.

[98] Congressional Record, 67 Cong., 2 Sess., LXII, 3730–1.

[99] Report of Committee on Emergency Measures in Transportation, Oct. 12, 1921, UF, Box 467—Emergency Measures in Transportation, CP-OF, HHP.

most hopeless."[100]   Three months later in March, 1922, Woods was still providing assistance to the railroad companies with claims before the Interstate Commerce Commission and hoping settlement of their debts would result in the hiring of more men.[101] Eventually, the debts were settled, but that this was one of the successes of the Unemployment Conference, as Hoover claimed in 1924, is doubtful.[102]

At the federal level, Hoover's endeavors received the same unenthusiastic reception they had met at the hands of local governments.   In Congress, Hoover faced men who believed that nothing could or should be done, or, as in the case of opposition to the building of Federal Reserve banks, men who refused to recognize that an unemployment crisis existed.   Such men could pass a highway act because they wanted to resume the road building delayed during the war, but when appropriations were justified solely on the basis of unemployment, their reaction was different.   Even when no appropriation was needed, they seemed reluctant to act.   Thy could, for example, pass unanimous resolutions providing military cots and blankets for encampments of Civil War veterans,[103] but when it was proposed that surplus military stores be issued for the unemployed, the proposal was buried in committee.[104]   Nor did Hoover meet opposition only on Capitol Hill.   Secretary of the Treasury Andrew Mellon and Director of the Budget Charles Dawes were the most vocal expounders of a general sentiment in the Administration favoring federal budgetary retrenchment above all else.   Attorney General Harry Daugherty was suspicious of any movement sympathetic to labor.[105]   Secretary of Labor James Davis revealed little enthusiasm for any endeavor unassociated with the Loyal Order of Moose, to which he belonged.   President Harding, a supporter of the Unemployment Conference, showed no great interest in the outcome of his Secretary's experiment.   Mere callousness perhaps helps to explain such a stance, but the persistence of classical economic precepts, particularly the conviction that some suffering was necessary in

---

100 Woods' staff conference, Jan. 16, 1922, UF, Box 481—Minutes of Col. Woods' Conferences, CP-OF, HHP.
    101 Numerous letters, January-March, 1922, UF, Box 482—Miscellaneous: Railway Guaranty Claims (1), (2), and (3), CP-OF, HHP.
    102 Unsigned statement by Hoover, August, 1924, UF, Box 462—Unemployment 1923–28, CP-OF, HHP.
    103 S. J. Resolution 115 and 117, *Congressional Record*, 67 Cong., 1 Sess., LXI, 5732, 5997, 6353.
    104 S. J. Resolution 119 and H. J. Resolution 217, *Congressional Record*, 67 Cong., 1 Sess., LXI, 5788, 7215.
    105 Zieger, 13.

order to readjust high war time wages and thereby liquidate labor, was clearly another factor.[106] One thing is certain. Only a few agreed with Hoover's theories about how "progress" was to be achieved in an industrialized economy or about the role the federal government should play in the process.

The other major goals of the Conference, as envisioned by Hoover, were permanent reforms to minimize the waste and suffering produced by unemployment. One thing that would help, the Conference had decided, was the timing of public works spending so as to complement rather than compete with activities in the private sector. While the concept of deficit financing was not involved, it was argued that during periods of prosperity when public projects would only inflate costs, some "necessary" projects should be deferred and used to stimulate business during depression periods. If such a "balance wheel" had been in existence, argued Edward Hunt, many works projects, impossible in 1921 due to lack of advance planning, could be undertaken.[107]

Following the Conference, Otto Mallery drafted a bill proposing such a reserve fund of federal public works, authorizing engineering plans to be kept in readiness, and assigning to the Department of Commerce responsibility for gathering the statistics needed to forecast a coming depression.[108] The bill, introduced in the Senate by William Kenyon of Iowa, who unsuccessfully in January, 1919, had sponsored a similar measure to create an emergency board to provide jobs during War demobilization,[109] received harsh criticism from such groups as the Chicago Association of Commerce, which held that labor should be liquidated.[110] Yet, as Mallery saw it in late 1921, the measure stood a good chance of passage.[111]

In February, 1922, the bill reached the floor of the Senate and was bitterly attacked. Some charged that it gave too much power to the President, others that it assumed an unrealistic "economic and administrative perspicacity," and still others that the government, by

---

[106] For examples of classical economic viewpoint, see: *Wall Street Journal*, Nov. 22, 1920; Feb. 8, 1921; and Sept. 22, 1921; *Forbes Magazine*, Mar. 19, 1921.

[107] Hunt to R. C. Marshall Jr., Nov. 28, 1921, UF, Box 469—Kenyon Bill, CP-OF, HHP.

[108] Mallery claims authorship of the Kenyon Bill in Mallery to Hoover, Nov. 17, 1921, UF, Box 462—Unemployment 1922, CP-OF, HHP.

[109] *Congressional Record*, 65 Cong., 3 Sess., 1814.

[110] Woods' staff conference, Dec. 12, 1921, UF, Box 481—Minutes of Col. Woods' Conferences, CP-OF, HHP.

[111] Mallery to Hoover, Nov. 21, 1921, UF, Box 470—Mallery, Otto, CP-OF, HHP.

beginning to act as if a depression was coming, might precipitate one. Besides, it was said, such a "paternalistic" measure would perpetuate the growing tendency to look to Washington for help in time of trouble.[112] For men like Senator Harry New of Indiana, it seemed to flout divine law. The Bible told of seven lean years following seven fat years. Senator Kenyon replied that Joseph had set up a reserve fund against the seven lean years "just as we are trying to do . . . here in setting up a reserve unemployment fund."[113] To Senator George Norris of Nebraska, there was a considerable difference between "the prophecy of Joseph" and the "prophecies which Hoover would give us. . . ." If passed, he thought, the bill would crowd "the Lord off the throne" and put "Hoover in His place."[114] As a result of the crippling amendments, Senator Kenyon recommended that the bill be referred back to the Committee on Education and Labor.[115] It did not emerge again.

During the remainder of the decade, Otto Mallery, supported by Hoover, continued to work for a public works program. Three times he was close to success. In 1923 the Zihlman Bill (H.R. 14185), authorizing a Commission of Unemployment to prepare advance plans and secure the cooperation of city and state officials, reached the floor of the House, but was voted down.[116] By 1925, Hoover privately believed there was "still a considerable distance to go" before Congress would accept the idea of using public construction to offset unemployment,[117] yet, while cautioning the eager Mallery that he could not become involved in any legislative halocaust over the long range planning of public works,[118] he remained always willing to provide "such assistance as I can" when Mallery sought to mount another effort.[119] It was in 1926 that Mallery's labors seemed to come closest to success. Giving up on the attempt to secure passage of a specific public works bill, Mallery succeeded in getting sponsorship in the Senate of an amendment to a Public Works Bill, authorizing the Public Buildings Commission to "consider the advantage of public building" and report their findings to Congress

112 *Congressional Record*, 67 Cong., 2 Sess., LXII, 2588–97.
113 *Congressional Record*, 67 Cong., 2 Sess., LXII, 2592.
114 *Congressional Record*, 67 Cong., 2 Sess., LXII, 2649.
115 *Congressional Record*, 67 Cong., 2 Sess., LXII, 2658.
116 Howenstine, 487.
117 Hoover to James H. Brookmire, Feb. 9, 1925, Box 304—Unemployment Business Cycles, CP-OF, HHP.
118 Mentioned in Mallery to Hoover, Feb. 10, 1926, Box 191—Mallery, Otto, CP-OF, HHP.
119 Hoover to Mallery, Jan. 8, 1926, Box 191—Mallery, Otto, CP-OF, HHP.

when construction in any period fell one-third below the volume of the corresponding period of 1925.[120] After initiating a lobbying effort for the amendment on the part of engineers, the Association of General Contractors, and the American Association for Labor Legislation and after camping on "legislators' doorsteps"[121] Mallery's disappointment was considerable when the 1926 try also failed. Writing later to Hoover, Mallery explained that the "chances were hundred to one that we would get the stabilization amendment into the Public Buildings Bill, but we slipped up on the 100th chance." Mallery had gathered sufficient support for the amendment on the Senate floor to secure its passage, but "Senator Couzens, who had it in charge, forgot to be on hand at the right time and the bill passed without the stabilizing amendment." "I thought I had provided against every contingency," Mallery bemoaned, "but that of an absent-minded Senator was not one of them."[122] Several more attempts at Senate resolutions came to naught, and in 1928, the Jones-Reavis Bill (S. 2475), also a reflection of Mallery's labors and which proposed a doubling of public works when the value of awarded construction contracts for a quarter fell ten percent below normal, suffered a similar fate.[123]

Understandably, on February 10, 1931, when the then President Hoover signed the Wagner-Graham Bill providing for advance planning of construction and federal public works in preparation for future unemployment, he publicly singled out the endeavors of Otto Mallery and Edward Hunt, as the two who first advocated advance planning at the Unemployment Conference in 1921 and who had worked for its acceptance throughout the 1920's.[124] In retrospect, the rejection of such measures probably made little difference. Timing of federal public works at a time when federal employees constituted only one percent of the total work force was hardly enough to offset fluctuations in the private sector.[125] Nor were the crude statistics available likely to provide very accurate economic forecasts. At least Hoover and his aides showed an understanding of the un-

---

[120] Amendment cited in Mallery to Hoover, Feb. 10, 1926, Box 191—Mallery, Otto, CP-OF, HHP.

[121] Mallery to Hoover, Jan. 9, 1926, Box 191—Mallery, Otto, CP-OF, HHP.

[122] Mallery to Hoover, May 10, 1926, Box 191—Mallery, Otto, CP-OF, HHP.

[123] Copy of S. 2475, introduced in Senate Jan. 11, 1928, UF, Box 462—Unemployment 1923-28, CP-OF, HHP.

[124] Hoover to Press, Feb. 10, 1931, President's Personal File 1213: Mallory, Otto T., HHP.

[125] *Congressional Record*, 67 Cong., 2 Sess., LXII, 2596.

employment problem and of the responsibilities of government that was more innovative than the understanding shown by Congress.

The other major reform proposal suggested by the Conference, also basically unsuccessful, was the idea of expanding statistical services so as to facilitate planning. Hoover managed to expand the business statistical services of the Census Bureau, to provide new services through the Bureau of Foreign and Domestic Commerce, and to work out a cooperative program with the trade associations.[126] But he was unable to secure, despite repeated appeals, more reliable statistics on unemployment, as the Bureau of Labor Statistics experienced no significant expansion until 1930 and 1931.[127]

Reform required further education, and to this the studies of cyclical and seasonal unemployment that followed the Conference did make some contribution. In 1923, for example, the Committee on Business Cycles, one of the subcommittees appointed by the Standing Committee of the Conference, published an extensive and influential study. Slumps, it concluded, were caused by the waste, extravagance, speculation, inflation, and inefficiency that developed during a boom. To reduce the depth of them, businessmen must refrain from such practices, and it would also help if credit could be used to stabilize prices, if contracts could be structured to make speculation in commodities unprofitable, if public works could be timed to complement rather than compete with private construction, and if a gold reserve from America's large surplus could be set up in anticipation of foreign demands.[128] Published along with the formal report were twenty-one supporting studies made by the National Bureau of Economic Research, an organization chartered in 1920 to conduct quantitative investigations in areas affecting public welfare. These covered topics ranging from unemployment insurance and statistics gathering to methods of stabilizing production and distribution.[129]

The second major area of study, that of seasonal unemployment, was intended to encompass surveys of the transportation, bituminous

---

126 Ellis W. Hawley, "Herbert Hoover and the Expansion of the Commerce Department: The Anti-Bureaucrat as Bureaucratic Empire-Builder," Mimeographed, The University of Iowa, 1970, 7–8.
127 Carroll H. Wooddy, *The Growth of the Federal Government, 1915–1932*, New York, 1934, 364.
128 Committee on Business Cycles of the President's Conference on Unemployment, *Business Cycles and Unemployment*, New York, 1923, xix-xxxi.
129 *Ibid.*, 1–287.

coal, and construction industries.[130] The transportation study failed to materialize, and the coal study, due to its affects on the strike situation,[131] was soon diverted into other channels.[132] The committee finally appointed in July, 1923, studied seasonal operations only in the construction industry, and it was on this subject that a report, actually prepared in the Department of Commerce, was completed.[133] It concluded that custom not bad weather was the main cause of seasonal unemployment in the construction industry, and that the timing of public works could be used here to moderate seasonal as well as cyclical fluctuations.[134]

In addition to these studies, the Unemployment Conference, acting as an arm of the Commerce Department, stimulated or sponsored other research projects. Work done for it by the Russell Sage Foundation and the National Bureau of Economic Research appeared in some four published studies during the 1920's.[135] The Conference was the official sponsor of a massive analysis of American economic life since the 1920–21 recession, the multi-volume *Recent Economic Changes,* published in 1928.

For Hoover the "educational" value of such studies, particularly when well publicized and tied into a network of conferences and committees, was high. Through them it was possible to build a progressive, humane, and controlled capitalism, without resorting to the coercive government regulations that would destroy the system while trying to save it.

As prosperity returned in the 1920's, the Unemployment Conference with its employment bureaus and mayors' emergency committees was largely forgotten. Nor could it claim many practical achieve-

---

[130] Hoover to H. S. Pritchett, May 17, 1932, UF, Box 467, CP-OF, HHP.

[131] Hunt to E. F. Gay, Feb. 6, 1922, UF, Box 480—Miscellaneous: Edwin F. Gay, CP-OF, HHP.

[132] Committee on Seasonal Operations in the Construction Industry of the President's Conference on Unemployment, *Seasonal Operations in the Construction Industry,* Washington, 1924, v.

[133] Howenstine, 485.

[134] *Seasonal Operations,* vi.

[135] Hunt to Hoover, Dec. 29, 1926, UF, Box 462—Unemployment 1923–28, CP-OF, HHP. The studies are: National Bureau of Economic Research and Wilford King, *Employment, Hours, and Earnings in Prosperity and Depression, 1920–22,* New York, National Bureau of Economic Research, 1923; Russell Sage Foundation, *Burden of Unemployment: Study of Unemployment Relief Measures in 15 American Cities, 1921–22,* New York, 1923; *Regularization of Employment: A Study in Prevention of Unemployment,* New York, Harper and Brothers, 1925; Russell Sage Foundation, *Employment Statistics for the United States: A Plan for their Collection,* New York, 1926.

ments. At best it had inaugurated minor relief, a few jobs, and some studies, but studies used by academicians rather than politicians able to translate them into practical reform.

As a precedent, though, and as an indication of the new set of ideas that was emerging in the 1920's and would flower under the New Deal, the Conference was more significant. For one group of federal officials, it was apparent in 1921, that individualism needed "tempering" and capitalism needed "controlling," by a newer set of economic and political ideas. Economically, they departed from the textbooks of the classical economists and talked not of liquidation but of maintaining wage rates, expanding public works, decreasing taxes, reducing the tariff, and, in general, maintaining purchasing power. Politically, they talked of cooperation rather than individualism, of a system in which Americans were dependent upon each other and in which some degree of management was a necessity. They envisioned a managed economy presided over by public-service-minded men and based upon collective units that would preserve as much voluntaryism as possible. The differences were more matters of degree than of kind, and once this fact is accepted, it will require historians to take a fresh look both at the 1920's and at the antecedents of the New Deal.

For an understanding of Herbert Hoover, the Conference is also significant, not only as an indication of his thinking at the time and of the fact that he subscribed to a form of progressivism, but also as a force in shaping his future policies. In numerous statements throughout the 1920's, he depicted the Conference as a success, even as a "milestone in the progress of social thought." In a spirit of voluntary cooperation rather than coercion, he maintained, Americans had banded together in the fall of 1921 and by the spring the crisis was lessening. To him, this was a striking example of what could be achieved by cooperation, one that strongly reinforced his faith in it and one that provided a dress rehearsal for what he would do following the panic of 1929. If Hoover's efforts in 1921–22 were not as productive as he had hoped, it was in part because he expected more of government—at all levels—than most of his contemporaries did. If his conception of government's role in 1930–31 was more conservative than many of his fellow citizens were willing to accept, it was in part because he was convinced that voluntaryism had worked in 1921.

CAROLYN GRIN

University of Iowa

By *Ellis W. Hawley*
PROFESSOR OF HISTORY
UNIVERSITY OF IOWA

The Discovery and Study of a "Corporate Liberalism"

Once the story of modern America seemed relatively simple. On one side stood a business elite defending a market system to which it owed its power and position. On the other stood the "common man," economically weak but politically capable of forging tools that could alter the workings of market discipline. And between them, waxing and waning in response to "reform" and "counter-reform," stood the aggregation of political tools that the "common man" had been able to forge. Such was the story told in "liberal" history; and with reversed heroes and villains, the same story was told in "conservative" history. Both assumed a business-government dichotomy, and both ignored or slighted those aspects of modern America that could not be fitted into it.

In recent years, the story has become increasingly complex. Historians of modern America have not been able to ignore or slight what they once did; and the result has been an accretion of revisionist "discoveries," especially of value systems, institutions, and individuals that do not fit within the older framework and seem to require a more complex one if they are to be explained. First came the discovery of an American "consensus" shared by "common men" and elitists alike. At least a part of modern America, it seemed, had been shaped by this rather than by business-commoner conflict. Next came the discovery of other kinds of conflict, of a nation divided not only between business leaders and common people but also between new and old elites, rival ethnic and cultural groups, modernizers and anti-modernizers. Some allowance, it seemed, had to be made for the role that these kinds of conflict had played in shaping both public and private institutions. And along with these discoveries have come others, among them the preoccupation of Americans with finding "new frontiers" and the existence of a "big government" built not by mass politicians but by business

Business History Review, Vol. LII, No. 3 (Autumn, 1978). Copyright © The President and Fellows of Harvard College.

and professional elites and movements for "counter-reform." Some business leaders, it appeared, had been "statists," at least of a sort and during certain periods, and some of the opposition to "big government" had come from "common men."

All of these discoveries have complicated matters. But even greater complications have come from the recent scrutiny of organizational development in modern American history.[1] The forces behind this, so it now seems clear, have drawn only a part of their strength from business defensivism or mass-based reform initiatives, and much of the new organizational growth seems inconsistent with the assumptions of the older "liberal" or "conservative" scenarios. How, for example, can these be reconciled with a growth of organized interest groups, each headed by a specialized elite and many comprised of executive agencies and legislative committees as well as private organizations? How can they be reconciled with regulatory networks operating through business-government continuums and "enlightened partnerships" between public and private policy makers? And how can they be reconciled with the appearance of quasi-autonomous administrative and technical elites developing their own power bases and posing threats both to the older market system and to traditional forms of political action? Much of modern America, it seems, has not been organized in ways that lend credibility to the notion of a fundamental business-government dichotomy, and organizational study has been accompanied by efforts to reconceptualize business-government relations and account for the kind of organizational development that has occurred.

Most of these efforts at reconceptualization have not denied the existence of business-government conflict. Nor have they seen recent developments as representing either the business conquest of the state or the political conquest of business. What they have seen is the emergence of an "organizational sector," taking shape between the market and political ones and developing its own kind of discipline and rewards. In this sector men organized themselves by function, interest, or commodity, not by class or locality. They established new services and administrative networks to correct what were perceived as failures of the market system or of the

---

[1] For the development of the organizational school of history, see Louis Galambos, "The Emerging Organizational Synthesis in Modern American History," *Business History Review*, XLIV (Autumn 1970), 279–290, and Robert D. Cuff, "American Historians and the 'Organizational Factor'," *Canadian Review of American Studies*, IV (Spring 1973), 19–31. A recent anthology that pulls together and comments on key articles is Edwin J. Perkins, *Men and Organizations: The American Economy in the Twentieth Century* (New York, 1977).

political machinery; and seeking new sources of authority, they allowed managerial and technical elites to take over large areas of policy making and to erect and fortify their own bases of power. In this sector, moreover, private and public operations often fused into interlocked continuums. A new breed of private leaders sought to build state agencies that could render needed services without supplanting or threatening the new private institutions. And on the other side, a new breed of public officials looked to enlightened private organizations as the instrumentalities through which they could best advance the public interest. Conflict there was, but much of it was along the new lines of organization or between the new organizational order and those resisting it rather than between the antagonists featured in "liberal" or "conservative" history.[2]

This kind of reconceptualization has helped to explain much that once seemed unintelligible. Yet its central discovery, the organizational sector, has also been an area in which the locus of power and the relationships between organized units and subunits have been difficult to pin down. As perceived by some, the sector has tended toward a self-sustaining "pluralism," with power dispersed among a multiplicity of narrowly organized interests, counter-organization serving as a means of maintaining this dispersal, and coordination being achieved through the necessity for bargaining and compromise. But in the more persuasive of recent perceptions, it has vacillated between impulses toward "Balkanization" and the formation of corporative structures seeking to discipline such impulses and achieve coordination through enlightened concerts of recognized interests. As in a number of European societies, a malfunctioning pluralism has given way not to the socialist commonwealth or statist regimentation but to a degree of "corporatization," a development reflected in publicly approved or state-sponsored "private governments," advisory committee networks linking public and private action, national councils of economic coordination, and expert definers of the "enlightened" or "workable."[3] What has remained murky and in need of study is

[2] Key works on the emergence and shape of this organizational sector include Samuel P. Hays, *The Response to Industrialism, 1885–1914* (Chicago, 1957); Robert Wiebe, *The Search for Order, 1877–1920* (New York, 1967); Jerry Israel, ed., *Building the Organizational Society: Essays on Associational Activities in Modern America* (New York, 1972); Alfred D. Chandler, Jr., and Louis Galambos, "The Development of Large-Scale Organizations in Modern America," *Journal of Economic History*, XXX (March 1970), 201–217; and Thomas J. McCormick, "The State of American Diplomatic History," in Herbert J. Bass, *The State of American History* (Chicago, 1970), 119–141. For reconceptualizations of business-government relations in particular industries, see Louis Galambos, *Competition and Cooperation: The Emergence of a National Trade Association* (Baltimore, 1966) and Gerald D. Nash, *U.S. Oil Policy, 1890–1964: Business and Government in Twentieth Century America* (Pittsburgh, 1968).

[3] As used here, the term "corporative" signifies a particular kind of socio-political or-

the degree to which such institutions have appeared and taken root in American life, the men and groups that have dominated them, and the influence they have had on public and private behavior. While recent studies have added much to our knowledge of business and public administration,[4] we know relatively little about the structures through which American "corporatizers" have sought to order an unruly or badly functioning pluralism without subjecting it to a "politicization" inimical to economic and social progress.

Also in need of study is the extent to which this "corporatization" has sprung from forces other than the expressed concerns about social order, economic optimality, and containment of the state. Has it, to some extent, been an institutional expression of particular kinds of cultures or national histories? Has it been a phenomenon appearing at certain stages of economic or technological development or in response to particular kinds of economic or political crisis? Has it represented a transitional stage in state building, a phase characterized by the formation of privatized bureaucracies that tend subsequently to be transformed into governmental units? Has it been the work of particular individuals who at key junctures were in positions of power and leadership? Or has it represented the disguised efforts of one class to gain advantages over others? And if the latter, which class? Has it stemmed from the efforts of established wealth to consolidate its position, of labor to gain recognition and new tools of advancement, of a rising bureaucratic and professional class to enhance its status and prospects, or of an older middle class to protect itself from market or political mechanisms that threatened its eventual extinction? All of these ex-

---

ganization. A corporative system is one whose basic units consist of officially recognized, non-competitive, role-ordered occupational or functional groupings. It is also one with coordinating machinery designed to integrate these units into an interdependent whole and one where the state properly functions as coordinator, assistant, and midwife rather than director or regulator. In such a system there are deep interpenetrations between state and society, and enjoying a special status is an enlightened social elite, capable of perceiving social needs and imperatives and assisting social groups to meet them through enlightened concerts of interests. It is these features that distinguish corporative structures from other kinds, and it is the development of such a corporative component in a society's organization that I refer to as "corporatization." On the forms that this has taken in liberal-capitalist societies, see Theodore Lowi, *The End of Liberalism* (New York, 1969); Grant Mc-Connell, *Private Power and American Democracy* (New York, 1966); Andrew Shonfield, *Modern Capitalism: The Changing Balance of Public and Private Power* (New York, 1965); Nigel Harris, *Competition and the Corporate Society* (London, 1972); Samuel H. Beer, *British Politics in the Collectivist Age* (New York, 1965); Philippe Schmitter, "Still the Century of Corporatism," *Review of Politics*, XXXVI (January 1974), 85–131; "Collaboration between Public Authorities and Employers' and Workers' Organizations," *International Labour Review*, LXXVI (August 1957), 167–187.

[4] The story of the organizational revolution in business has been masterfully told in Alfred D. Chandler, Jr., *The Visible Hand: The Managerial Revolution in American Business* (Cambridge, Mass., 1977). For a survey and analysis of recent work on governmental regulation, see Thomas K. McCraw, "Regulation in America: A Review Article," *Business History Review*, XLIX (Summer 1975), 159–183.

planations have been advanced, and it seems clear that several impulses with differing perceptions of the ultimate goal have been at work. But the role played by each and the relationships between them are matters whose elucidation and clarification await more detailed studies of the origins and nature of the institutions involved.[5]

In need of further study as well are the relationships between institutional change and corporative pluralism as a set of ideological constructs. Among those studying institutional change, the tendency has been to see it as the work of nonideological men coping with particular situations or problems. Yet recent investigations of business, political, labor, and professional thought have uncovered a variety of individuals or groups who have articulated organizational ideals having both pluralist and corporative features. The idea of disciplining group combativeness through the introduction of a corporative as opposed to a statist component has had its American theoreticians. So has the notion of a quasi-corporative, as opposed to a governmental, welfare and planning apparatus.[6] But whether those primarily responsible for organizational development have been much influenced by such theories remains unclear. It may be that their chief use has been not as guidelines for policy making or organization building but as covers for illegitimate power or weapons in a struggle for dominance and advantage.

Still, even if the latter is the case, the discovery of this ideological dimension would appear to be an important one. Traditionally, the clash of political ideas in twentieth-century America has been conceptualized as a battle between the philosophies of laissez faire and welfare statism, with each claiming to have the prescription for realizing liberal ideals. Radicalism and authoritarian conservatism stood outside the contest, useful chiefly as demonologies to be associated with one's opponents. And the political "center," unlike its European counterparts, has been thought of not as an

[5] Recent contributions to the subject include Frederick Pike and Thomas Stritch, eds., *The New Corporatism* (Notre Dame, 1974); Robert F. Himmelberg, *The Origins of the National Recovery Administration* (New York, 1976); Charles S. Maier, *Recasting Bourgeois Europe* (Princeton, 1975); and Stuart D. Brandes, *American Welfare Capitalism, 1800–1940* (Chicago, 1976).

[6] See James Gilbert, *Designing the Industrial State* (Chicago, 1972); David Noble, *America by Design* (New York, 1977); Ellis W. Hawley, "Herbert Hoover, the Commerce Secretariat, and the Vision of an 'Associative State'," *Journal of American History*, LXI (June 1974), 116–140; Joan Hoff Wilson, *Herbert Hoover: Forgotten Progressive* (Boston, 1975); Haggai Hurvitz, "The Meaning of Industrial Conflict in Some Ideologies of the Early 1920's; The AFL, Organized Employers, and Herbert Hoover" (Ph.D. Dissertation, Columbia University, 1971); Kim McQuaid, "A Response to Industrialism: Liberal Businessmen and the Evolving Spectrum of Capitalist Reform, 1886–1960" (Ph.D. Dissertation, Northwestern University, 1975); Ronald Radosh, "Corporate Ideology of American Labor Leaders from Gompers to Hillman," *Studies on the Left*, VI (1966), 66–68; and Michael Hogan, *Informal Entente* (Columbia, Mo., 1977).

area of support for an alternative philosophy but as one where dilutions of the laissez faire creed merged with dilutions of welfare statism. What recent work seems to suggest is that the "center" has been more than this, that portions of it have embraced creeds rejecting both laissez faire and welfare statism, and that among these creeds have been systems in which a corporative pluralism became the means of realizing liberal ideals. It has been an area, in other words, in which men have expounded and responded to a "corporate liberalism." And during certain periods in American history, especially when strong concerns about market failure have been accompanied by anti-statist impulses and popular idealization of certain private elites, this kind of liberalism has been a significant force. If it has not been a major factor in institutional change, it has had its effects on political and intellectual behavior and is deserving of much closer scrutiny than it has yet received.

One difficulty in the development of such study has been the semantic one of using a label that has also acquired other meanings. As first employed, in the writings of Martin Sklar and other neo-leftist revisionists,[7] the term "corporate liberalism" meant not a particular prescription for achieving liberal ends but all reformist ideologies that accepted the large business corporation as a permanent and desirable feature of national life. In this usage, socialists and populist decentralizers were not "corporate liberals." But most welfare statists and governmental regulationists, all of America's twentieth-century reform presidents,[8] and all those muddle-headed enough to believe that they could control corporate power rather than being controlled by it did fall into this category. Subsequently, another usage has also appeared, one in which the term denotes a category of business thought rather than a kind of reformism. In this usage, it has meant an ideology in which welfare, regulatory, and full employment measures have been accepted as good for corporate business. It is only recently that the term has been used to designate a kind of liberalism standing apart from both laissez faire and welfare statism, and those who use it in this sense still risk a certain amount of confusion. If they are to stick with the label, they must take care to distinguish their use of it from other current usages.

[7] See Martin J. Sklar, "Woodrow Wilson and the Political Economy of Modern United States Liberalism," *Studies on the Left*, I (1960), 17–47. See also James Weinstein, *The Corporate Ideal in the Liberal State, 1900–1918* (Boston, 1968).
[8] For the debate on Wilsonianism and its corporate-liberal characteristics, see Alan L. Seltzer, "Woodrow Wilson as 'Corporate-Liberal': Toward a Reconsideration of Left Revisionist Historiography," *Western Political Quarterly*, XXX (June 1977), 183–212.

Posing difficulties as well has been the confusion of a type of liberalism with anti-liberal ideologies that have also looked to "corporatization" as a means of realizing their ends. In Europe the advocacy of corporative structures has been associated with anti-liberals of both the left and the right. They have been seen as steps toward or as tools for realizing the social orders envisioned by syndicalists, neo-feudalists, fascists, and technocratic authoritarians; and at times they have formed the basis for alliances in which leftists and rightists have sought to use each other.[9] Yet there has also been a corporatism of the liberal center, claiming that such structures could serve its purposes and in particular that they could, at one and the same time, enable liberal societies to meet modern social needs and save them from the evils of excessive statism, social "Balkanization," and class warfare. It is this kind of corporatism that has appeared in the centrist parties of the continent and during certain periods in Britain's Liberal and Conservative parties.[10] And what has appeared in America but only recently received much recognition is a variant of this phenomenon, an ideology, in other words, with corporative components yet also with appeal to persons of liberal values and commitments. Its rise did not necessarily signify that Americans were becoming more receptive to anti-liberal ideologies. Nor did its active promotion necessarily mean that anti-liberal conspiracies were at work to prevent truly meaningful reform.

Still, despite these semantic and conceptual difficulties, the way would now seem to be clear for a general reconceptualization of liberal thought as it has developed and exerted influence in twentieth-century America. Progressivism needs to be restudied, with particular emphasis on those formulations that looked not to an expanded state or a free market place but to private associations, economic councils, policy research institutes, and professionalized private orders as the tools really capable of maintaining both progress and liberty. The notion of a "return to laissez faire" in the 1920s needs rethinking, with particular emphasis on those formulations of anti-statism that envisioned the development of a

<hr/>

[9] See Paul Mazgaj, "The Social Revolution or the King: The Initiatives of the Action Francaise toward the Revolutionary Left, 1906–1914" (Ph.D. Dissertation, University of Iowa, 1976).
[10] See Harris, *Competition and the Corporate Society*; Matthew H. Elbow, *French Corporate Theory, 1789–1948* (New York, 1953); Richard F. Kuisel, *Ernest Mercier: French Technocrat* (Berkeley, 1967); and Ralph Bowen, *German Theories of the Corporative State* (New York, 1947). Also enlightening, especially for the British Liberal Party, is Jerry M. Calton, "Planning and Plotting: Lloyd George and the Politics of Economic Mobilization in Britain," an unpublished manuscript.

"CORPORATE LIBERALISM" 315

corporative commonwealth. The varieties of New Deal thought need reexamination, with particular emphasis on the vision of a state that would organize a concert of recognized interests and then function as a part of that concert's planning and coordinating apparatus. The neo-liberalism and "modern conservatism" of the post-1945 period need reconsideration, again with particular emphasis on their designs for indicative planning and the coordination of public and private policies. And the reformism of the 1960s needs reconceptualizing, with recognition given to those formulations calling for public-private partnerships, social contracts, and greater autonomy for responsible private orders. American liberalism has indeed had its market-oriented and statist varieties, and these have been mixed in numerous and varied ways. But developing alongside of these, competing with them and entering into many of the mixtures, has been a "corporate liberalism" seeking answers in new private orders and disciplines and claiming that it could provide a liberal but non-statist alternative to laissez-faire prescriptions.

In two major spheres then, those of organizational development and political ideology, recent research has indicated both a need to alter older historical perceptions and the presence of phenomena that would appear to be of considerable importance but about which relatively little is known. One such gap is in the knowledge of "corporatization" as an institutional development, especially in knowledge of forces, processes, and circumstances that have given rise to it, the organizational apparatus through which it has worked, and the extent to which this apparatus has supplanted the market and the state as the nation's inter-group coordinator. A second gap is in the knowledge of a "corporate liberalism" developing and being used in the political arena, sometimes to gain support for organizational innovation and sometimes to legitimize and defend existing institutions. Both gaps need filling. And each of the following articles not only makes a contribution in this regard but lends support to the reconceptualizations associated with organizational studies and closer scrutiny of liberal thought.

Indeed, in Professor Werking's article, "Bureaucrats, Businessmen, and Foreign Trade: The Origins of the U.S. Chamber of Commerce," the focus is on the establishment of a structure that was at least quasi-corporative in nature. It came into existence as a way to link the state to a sector of society, the purpose being both to provide a better coordinating apparatus for the organizations of that sector and to enable it to meet perceived challenges to the national well-being. And while the author believes that the men involved were interested chiefly in maximizing appropriations and profits, they were clearly articulating a kind of "corporate liberalism." Their solution to the perceived problems was neither a statist coordinator nor statist inaction but rather governmental action that would help an appropriate private order to emerge and serve the national interest. Revealed in the article are types of governmental and business activities largely ignored in the older versions of modern American history, and to the reconceptualization that has been under way it makes a number of contributions. In particular, it points up the linkages between pre-war policy and the responses to wartime and postwar problems, the weaknesses of a model that explains everything in terms of business pressure for a governmental connection, and the continuing strength of business particularism and business fears of an expanding public sector. Although the principals in the story seemed convinced that a new kind of state machinery could be kept responsive to business's legitimate needs, they encountered and had to overcome a good deal of skepticism about whether this could actually be done.

In the next article, Professor McQuaid's "Corporate Liberalism in the American Business Community, 1920–1940," the focus is on a group of business leaders who consciously articulated "corporate liberal" ideals and were active in campaigns to realize them. Again the solution to perceived problems was to develop appropriate private orders, with both pluralist and corporative features and with enough statist support to permit their emergence and effective operation. And while the activities described here took place in the 1920s and 1930s, periods usually thought to be quite different from the years 1907 to 1912, the kinds of actors and their relationships to each other seem remarkably similar to those in the first article. Again the principals in the story encounter the obstacles of business particularism, anti-business reformism, and deep-seated skepticism about the viability of social or public-private partnerships. Again they suffer failures and setbacks. Yet again much of the task of coordination and problem solving is eventually entrusted to private orders or to business-supported public-private partnerships. Both articles seem to confirm the existence of a larger continuity, namely the quest for inter-organization coordination that some organizational historians have seen as the central concern of both public and private policy in the years from 1905 to 1950.

Both articles are also instructive as to the forces behind the establishment of corporative structures. In them one finds little support for the view that the "corporate liberals" of the business community were men of vast sophistication and social power who, despite some obstacles and setbacks, remained in control and succeeded in molding America to fit their designs. The men studied here were acutely conscious of the power centers that lay outside their control. Their ability to influence governmental, business, and labor policy dwindled at times to virtually nil. And for Professor McQuaid, it was international conflict and militarization, not conspiratorial fulfillment of an earlier design, that allowed them and their heirs to re-emerge in positions of social and political influence. Yet the vacuum that their falls from grace created at times was never really filled by the competing designs for enforced competition, statist planning, or a return to laissez faire. On the contrary, the indications are that much of it was filled by "corporate liberals" from other social sectors. Much of the New Deal, after all, did consist of statist action designed to foster the emergence of new private orders that could function as effective members of an organizational community. If the grand design of the NRA collapsed, this was not true of the AAA, the NLRB, and the "little NRAs" set up for individual industries. And if "big business" was attacked for its irresponsibility, public policy remained receptive to the vision of a new organizational concert in which responsible and enlightened business orders would play key roles. Much of what happened in the 1930s was part of a continuing pattern, and it seems best conceptualized not as the workings of a class struggle or as the coming of "big government" but as the efforts of a pluralistic social order with liberal commitments to find private structures and elites capable of correcting perceived ills and malfunctions.

One suspects, moreover, that this belief in the possibility of finding such structures and elites was an important factor in the post-1940 rehabilitation of organized business and in the subsequent defeats suffered by statist planners, antitrust decentralizers, laborite activists, and anti-business Keynesians. Such a belief helped a regrouped corps of "corporate liberal" businessmen to devise strategies through which business managers could reestablish their social standing and turn anti-business impulses into "constructive channels." And while Professor Collins does not explore this continuing appeal of corporative solutions, his article, "Positive Business Responses to the New Deal: The Roots of the Committee for Economic Development, 1933–1942," does provide a detailed reconstruction of how the new corps of "corporate liberal" businessmen and academic allies came together and how they began to articulate a new basis for social and public-private cooperation. Revealed here are the beginnings of a story that now seems central to post-1940 American history, and Professor Collins should be congratulated for not allowing the concurrent recrudescence of old-style business fundamentalism to obscure them.

Singly and together, then, the following articles offer further evidence that the core of modern American history may consist not of class struggles, business-government conflict, and market versus statist prescriptions; that it may consist instead of an organizational pluralism in which state agencies collaborated with and became attached to private orders, of recurring crises brought on by failures of coordination and resistance to organizational values, and of persisting commitments to liberal values and the possibility of realizing them through corporative structures employing private enlighteners and disciplines. Taken together, the articles also indicate the long but largely forgotten history behind current proposals for corporative structures and attitudes as the means of coping with what appears to a new crisis of coordination and legitimacy.[11] While these proposals are offered as new departures in thought and human creativity, they can claim to be so only because those who offer and consider them know little history beyond that set forth in the older "liberal" and "conservative" scenarios. They are in reality strikingly similar to the "corporate liberalism" articulated and used, for both reform and defensive purposes, in the crises of 1916–1923, 1930–1934, and 1938–1947.

Finally, the articles suggest new avenues of research that might profitably be undertaken. As Professor Werking shows, the public sector of the pre-Wilsonian political economy is not adequately understood either as an emerging regulator or as a neutral apparatus reacting to initiatives from the private sector. It was also an apparatus generating its own initiatives for building and forging ties with private orders, and this aspect of it needs much more study. Another profitable line of inquiry might concern itself with "corporate liberalism" as a mode of social thought, especially associated with certain professions and with the political center, rather than merely a phenomenon arising in the business community. One feels the need for this in order to put Professor

[11] See especially George C. Lodge, *The New American Ideology* (New York, 1975); Walt W. Rostow, *Getting from Here to There* (New York, 1978); R. Joseph Mansen, "Social Responsibility and the Corporation," *Journal of Economic Issues*, VI (March 1972), 125–141; and Neil W. Chamberlain, *Remaking American Values: Challenge to a Business Society* (New York, 1977).

McQuaid's findings into an appropriate context. And needed, too, as Professor Collins points out, are studies that put the New Deal years in perspective and bring out the strands of continuity between New Deal action and the public policies that preceded and followed it. Along all of these lines new and significant discoveries would seem to be in prospect.

Herbert Hoover and American Corporatism, 1929–1933

ELLIS W. HAWLEY

University of Iowa

Ellis Hawley received the B.A. and M.A. degrees in the state of his birth, at the University of Wichita and the University of Kansas, respectively. In 1959 he received his Ph.D. degree from the University of Wisconsin. He has taught at North Texas State University and Ohio State University and currently is Professor of History at the University of Iowa. His interest in Herbert Hoover and the Hoover presidency stems from his profound research for his publication, The New Deal and the Problem of Monopoly *(Princeton: Princeton University Press, 1966). He has written a number of important articles including "Secretary Hoover and the Bituminous Coal Problem,"* Business History Review *(Fall, 1968) and the lead article in* Herbert Hoover and the Crisis of American Capitalism *(Cambridge: Harvard University Press, 1973). Currently he is working on a study of Hoover and associational activities, 1917–1933.*

Hawley's theory that Hoover's concept of American corporatism was prophetic arises from his considering Hoover within the framework recently developed by neoinstitutional historians and students of modernization. He argues that this presidency can be regarded as the end of an era—that by 1933 the model of informal corporatism and "cooperative competition" which Hoover and his associates developed in the twenties had been discredited. Yet, Hawley contends, the dividing line between the Hoover and Roosevelt presidencies has been exaggerated. The difference between the two consisted of different types of managements, and Hawley sees Hoover's attempt as "one of a long series of efforts to provide America with a 'middle way' between atomistic individualism, a state-directed economy, and 'new forms of the Middle Ages.'"

In recent years, a number of new perceptions have been altering older interpretations of twentieth-century American history, particularly those interpretations that have focused chiefly on liberal politics and have viewed the modern American state as a triumph of an indigenous liberal democracy. For neoinstitutionalists, neoconservatives, and neoradicals alike, the dominant theme in recent American development has been the quest for order, stability, and system, not the pursuit of liberal ideals.[1] For recent students of comparative history, the focus has shifted from the uniqueness of the American experience to its similarities with other modernizing societies.[2] And for other scholars, it has become apparent that the American version of the regulatory state was shaped not only by pragmatic tinkering within a framework of liberal-democratic ideals but also by persistent and sometimes powerful strands of what is best described as guildist or corporatist thought.[3]

This is not to say that Americans were ever much influenced by the fascist perversion of corporatist ideals or that they have ever been ready to scrap completely the ideals of the independent trader, the bourgeois republic, or the free marketplace. Nevertheless at times they have been strongly attracted to the central vision in corporatist ideology, to the notion, in other words, of a decentralized, yet harmonious, organic, interdependent social order, organized around and regulated by specialized functional groupings, which are held together and stabilized by responsible leadership, established principles of social equity and efficiency, and institutionalization of a "natural" mutuality of interests. Here, as in Europe, the late nineteenth and early twentieth-century concerns with "destructive competition" and "social anarchy" produced a burgeoning maze of private "regulators," new visions of social harmony through scientific coordination and moral regeneration, and a pervasive nostalgia for lost Edens and earlier "communities." Here, too, the experience of World War I intensified these developments, and here as in Europe, the vision of "industrial self-government" was offered as a way to provide direction and reform without sacrificing property rights or building oppressive bureaucracies.[4] In America, to be sure, there was less inclination to translate this vision into formal philosophical disquisitions. But for a time, especially in the 1920s, it was hailed as the "American way," an organic yet modern outgrowth, so it was said, of America's older traditions of voluntarism, local autonomy, and frontier neighborliness. And despite subsequent attacks on "private power," the vision has remained an influential component in the "partnership," "pluralist," and "neofederalist" formulas of recent years.[5]

Viewed in this context, then, the American regulatory system has been shaped not only by interacting pressure groups and liberal-democratic ideals but also by repeated efforts to convert private regulators" into components of a larger "community of interests," reconcile such arrangements with persisting commitments to economic and political individualism, and devise governmental machinery that could secure "constructive" private actions without creating new instruments of tyranny. In the history of such activity, so it now appears, the effort made by Herbert Hoover and his associates looms especially large.[6] And it is to the task of delineating the later phases of this effort and placing them in the larger context of corporatist thought and influence in America that the present paper is devoted. Hopefully, by focusing on the "cooperative system" that Hoover tried to build and defend, on the disillusionment with it under depression conditions, and on the alternatives that were waiting in the wings when Hoover left office, such a study can further our understanding both of the forces shaping economic policies during the Hoover administration and of the relationship between these policies and longer-range developments.

By the time Hoover entered the White House he had already become the nation's leading spokesman for what he felt to be a new and superior form of "self-government." In America's burgeoning network of self-governing associations, he had come to believe, lay the nucleus of an ideal regulatory structure, one that could bring order, efficiency, and equity without producing industrial dictatorships, closed cartels, or stultifying bureaucracies. As guildlike collectivities led by enlightened and public-spirited men, these cooperative institutions could develop codes of ethical behavior, desirable patterns of social obligation, and the harmonious productivity of which an integrated and purposeful commonwealth was capable. Yet given their dependence on moral suasion, informal pressures, and "educational" activities, they could not encroach unduly upon individual initiative, grass-roots responsibility, and self-adjusting market mechanisms. The "essential" benefits flowing from these older arrangements could be retained, and for Hoover the road to "progress" lay in developing a synthesis that would do so.[7] The task ahead, as he saw it, was to expand and coordinate this emerging "system of co-operation," guide it into "constructive" channels, and protect it from those who would either dismantle the system or turn it into an instrument of tyranny and stagnation. These had been his goals as secretary of commerce. And while critics would soon disagree, he believed that his earlier activities had done much to preserve traditional liberties yet to remedy social ills, raise living standards, and achieve "stable employment and profit." [8]

As president, moreover, Hoover quickly indicated that his goals had not changed. Just as in the 1920s, he hoped to achieve greater order, efficiency, and equity, primarily by organizing areas that were still "sick" or "chaotic," providing economic leaders with better information and advice, and bringing cooperative groups into closer and more regularized relationships. Yet at the same time, he hoped to preserve and expand the benefits flowing from individual initiative, local responsibility, and health rivalry. The right kind of organization, he believed, could achieve both ends; and while this might require some modernization of the antitrust laws, it also required that the main features of these laws be retained and enforced. They were needed both to improve the economic performance of the "cooperative system" and to prevent it from developing abuses that enemies of the system could seize upon to pervert or destroy it. [9]

From the beginning, then, the Hoover policies cut two ways, a situation that seemed to flow partly from the dialectic in the president's own thought, partly from conflicting pressures and the larger ambivalence characteristic of most New Era leaders. At times, particularly in noting the evils of economic disorder and "destructive" competition, the guiding vision seemed to be a structure of semiformal guilds or estates, each represented in a larger economic community and each having positive social obligations. Yet repeatedly, as this vision collided with the desire to preserve traditional liberties and incentives, Hoover and his lieutenants drew back, insisting that it was vital to the "American system" that market forces, individual opportunity, and existing political arrangements be retained. And repeatedly, they seemed to be saying that the evils of "big government" stemmed both from the lack of private controls and the failure to hold private power blocs within narrowly defined limits. [10]

To bring greater purpose and planning to the "cooperative system," for example, Hoover was ready to enlarge the network of expert studies, informational "clearing houses," and cooperating committees that he had helped to promote earlier. By encouraging private leaders to set up such a network, he believed, and by tying private groups into it through functional representation, the activities of the nation could be "integrated" and guided without being "regimented" or "bureaucratized." [11] Consequently, he moved quickly to expand existing activities and to add new machinery of the same sort in such fields as social reform, education, and child welfare.[12] When it came to moving beyond this, however, and creating some sort of functional representation in an established economic council, a project that some of his associates had long urged,[13] Hoover seemed of two minds. Initially, he appeared enthusiastic about a proposal advanced by his old friend Julius Barnes, one that, if adopted, would have set up a "continuing" economic directorate composed of functional group leaders, heads of the major regulatory agencies, and Cabinet members having interest-group clienteles. This, so Hoover told Robert Lamont, could serve both as an over-all economic coordinator and an informed sponsor of new "conferences or commissions for development of special subjects." Yet within a matter of weeks, he had backed away. After consulting with Senators James Watson and George Moses and being told that any such move would necessarily be interpreted as "turning Government over to big business," he dropped the idea, decided that the "American system" could function better without such a council, and developed a marked reluctance to consider it again.[14]

A similar blend of corporatist with antitrust ideals seemed to characterize Hoover's attitude toward private "stabilization" programs. On several occasions now, particularly in urging studies of how the antitrust laws could be "reoriented," conferring with proponents of "reorientation," and giving pep talks to selected trade associations, he seemed inclined to remove some of the legal checks on private power to support guildist regulations.[15] Yet at the same time, he was emerging as something of an antitruster. In April 1929, after Attorney General William Mitchell had refused to grant antitrust immunity to a plan for curbing oil production, Hoover defended the ruling and drew sharp distinctions between the proposed plan and real "conservation." [16] In August he told the new antitrust chief, John Lord O'Brian, that the law must be enforced.[17] And partly because of his own commitment to "healthy" competition, partly because it seemed that rising criticism of the anticompetitive arrangements previously encouraged by William Donovan might discredit all cooperative programs,[18] he backed the efforts of O'Brian to dismantle the semiformal cartels taking shape in a number of industries. In late 1929 the Justice Department abandoned the policy of approving cooperative schemes in advance, and in early 1930 it began moving against a series of trade association programs that Donovan had once encouraged.[19]

Under O'Brian's prodding, too, the Federal Trade Commission began changing its policies and revising the industrial codes that it had helped to formulate through its trade practice conference procedure. In the guise of eliminating "uneconomic, unmoral, or unsound practice," so it was charged now, the commission had been "fomenting conspiracies in restraint of trade." And in early 1930, after O'Brian had filed vigorous complaints and FTC Chairman William Humphrey had switched sides on the issue, a major revision of the codes got under way. Eventually, despite strong protests from the affected industries, more than sixty codes were stripped of rules considered conducive to "illegal conduct" or questionably close to the "twilight zone." [20] Hoover, moreover, seemed to approve. Although he had once hailed the trade practice conference approach as an immensely constructive procedure leading toward a new "law merchant," [21] he offered no encouragement now to those who claimed to be defending it. Spokesmen for affected industries were told that the president had neither the power nor the desire to interfere with the actions of an "independent" agency. And when former commissioner Abram Myers complained that Humphrey was tearing down the very thing that Hoover had tried to build, the president again drew sharp distinctions between the ethical practices he had hoped to encourage and the "price-fixing" that the FTC was refusing to sanction.[22]

The major area in which both Hoover and the business "stabilizers" could see far too much "destructive" and "wasteful" competition was that of the natural-resource industries, especially lumber, petroleum, and bituminous coal. In these fields, he did seem inclined to remove some of the legal checks on private power,[23] and probably, had he been able to shape matters as he desired, he would have liked to see the industries stabilized by cooperative groupings similar to those he hoped to foster in agriculture. The industries involved, however, were badly divided. In each of them, strong minorities were ready to attack almost any stabilization scheme as being "oppressive" and "monopolistic." And Hoover, caught in the crossfire and dubious about either the wisdom or legality of federal coercion, developed a marked reluctance to do much of anything until internal conflicts could be adjusted. Urged to call a coal conference, for example, he refused to do so, arguing that it had no chance to succeed and could only aid those advocating radical or political rather than "constructive" solutions.[24] Urged to organize a timber "conservation" program, he was hesitant about doing this.[25] And once the Colorado Springs Conference of June 1929 had demonstrated how badly the oil industry was divided and how unlikely it was to accept his proposal for regulation through an interstate compact, he was much more pessimistic about what could be accomplished in that field.[26]

In agriculture, on the other hand, Hoover did make a strong effort to build the type of organization that his ideology called for. Here victory at the polls had insured that his "farm plan" would be tried.[27] And here, as one historian has noted, the Agriculture Marketing Act provided an "almost perfect illustration" of Hoover's regulatory philosophy translated into practice.[28] Under it, stability, modernization, and equity were to be achieved for agriculture, not by statist controls, collective farms, or massive corporations, but rather by organizing and nourishing cooperative associations that could regulate behavior while preserving the individuality and rural virtues of their members. Viewed from one angle, the solution seemed to implement corporatist ideals. This was apparent, for example, in the carefully devised functional representation, the notion that disorder in agriculture threatened the whole social organism, and the efforts of the new Farm Board to establish one official "regulator" in each commodity.[29] Yet as Hoover saw it, there would still be room for individuals, innovators, and sturdy yeomen. "Compulsory" contracts were to be avoided. And while government might "stabilize" markets during "emergencies," it was not to set aside the "normal laws of supply and demand," convert voluntary institutions into instruments of stagnation and tyranny, or listen to those who would impose "rigid" schemes of production control. If it did so, it would destroy the very soul of a healthy system, and the "new day for agriculture" would never come.[30]

Finally, in devising a countercyclical program following the panic of 1929, Hoover tried again to translate his synthesis of corporatist and individualist ideals into practice. Acting much as he had during the recession of 1921,[31] he called the nation's economic leaders together, secured pledges of wage maintenance and expanded construction, and entrusted the implementation of these to cooperating trade bodies coordinated by the Business Survey Conference, a companion agency in the construction field, and a variety of governmental "advisers." [32] Again, there were clear elements here of a corporatist design, particularly in the "regulators" being used, the functional representation in coordinating bodies, the concern with maintaining "just" or "socially efficient" wages and prices, and the overriding notion that liquidation could and should be avoided by "responsible" decision-makers interested in preserving the social fabric and the organic unity of society. Yet again, as Hoover saw it, his approach would also preserve the flexibility and vitality of a market system. There would be no legal coercion. The program would not prevent long-range adjustments to consumer demand. And by using ad hoc coordinaters and limiting the government's role to "advice" and "assistance," the dangers of creating either a stultifying statist bureaucracy or a "superorganization" of industry would be averted.[33]

During Hoover's initial months in office, then, he tried with varying results to apply the policy guidelines that he had worked out in the 1920s and, unwisely perhaps, credited with helping to achieve the "remarkable" stability, creativity, and growth of that period.[34] His problems came when continued application of the guidelines failed to produce what it was supposed to. By mid-1930, it was becoming increasingly clear that Hoover had not found the way to maintain permanent prosperity or to provide ever-increasing benefits for all. As distress and disorder mounted, his formula for balancing the regulatory roles of the individual, the functional group, and the national state seemed increasingly inadequate. And the months that followed would bring simultaneous and ever stronger attacks from those who would increase the power and responsibilities of the state, those who would implement the corporatist vision by creating formal guilds and a "superorganization" of industry, and those who blamed the nation's difficulties on too much private or public interference with individual freedom and self-regulating market mechanisms.

From one side now, a side populated by classical economists, orthodox bankers, and antitrust traditionalists, came charges that the corporatist and statist aspects of the Hoover approach were causing the difficulties. Public and private "regulators," in other words, were holding back readjustments and blocking the competitive processes that could purge the "rottenness" from the system and restore it to economic health. And depending upon which "regulators" were seen as the primary villains, different programs were offered for dealing with them. From business quarters, for example, came a growing assault on the uneconomic" wage scales that Hoover and his allies were trying to maintain. From defenders of fiscal orthodoxy came an attack on the "wasteful" and "artificial" spending that he was encouraging. From antitrusters came charges that

Hoover-encouraged "monopolies" had destroyed purchasing power and were preventing its reestablishment. And from a variety of hard-pressed businessmen came indictments of their "monopolistic" and "prosperity-destroying" rivals, suppliers, or customers. While each group had different "restraints" or "rigidities" in mind, their general prescription was that Hoover should now permit "natural" readjustments to take place or, if necessary, help them take place by blasting away the obstacles that were preventing them from doing so.[35]

From the other side, however, came growing demands for either strengthening the "regulators" or replacing them with others that could do a better job. Economic well-being, so it was argued, had foundered on the rocks of "destructive competition" and "uncoordinated development." Its restoration required stronger or different controls than Hoover was using. And again, depending upon which regulatory weaknesses were seen as the chief villains, different programs were offered as a way to correct matters. From one set of critics came a variety of proposals for strengthening Hoover's "educational" apparatus and expanding the governmental supplements to purchasing power.[36] From another set came an increasingly powerful attack on his efforts to retain the antitrust laws and maintain "healthy" competition.[37] And from a third came proposals for replacing existing "regulators" with new ones, particularly with public and private agencies that would be less interested in "scarcity profits" and more in full employment, social justice, and the restoration of mass purchasing power.[38] Again, while different regulatory weaknesses were seen, the general idea was that Hoover should reorient his policies so as to strengthen controls over economic behavior and provide a higher degree of over-all economic coordination.

Increasingly, it seemed, Hoover's dreams of "cooperative competition" and "flexible" coordination were dissolving into a bitter struggle for contracting benefits. As in the "sick" industries earlier, a welter of conflicting groups and interests were trying to redistribute the burdens of the depression, and in pushing measures to do so, each was arguing that its preservation and prosperity were "basic" to the nation's future well-being.[39] The crying need, so growing numbers of Americans felt, was for new forms of coordination or shifts in power that could restore harmony and "progress." And among those who would strengthen or alter existing "regulators" rather than trying to revive some type of automatic economy, two broad visions of what should be done were emerging, each drawing, to some extent, on memories of the war government, the dreams associated with scientific management, and the "lessons" provided by Hoover's "failure." One would blend a statist-backed "democratization" of industrial government and social benefits with a powerful planning and disciplinary apparatus responsive both to democratic aspirations and scientific expertise. The other called for a fuller realization of the incipient corporatism that Hoover had encouraged. Voluntary associations, in other words, would become compulsory guilds; clearing houses and "educators" would give way to central coordinators, superassociations, or "integrative" arrangements backed by coercive power; and "antisocial" or "anarchic" minorities would no longer be allowed to undermine the order, security, and "scientific" direction needed for socioeconomic health.

Indicative of what one set of "coordinators" had in mind was the flurry of "national plans" that began appearing in 1931. In the spring and summer of that year, such liberal "programmers" as Stuart Chase, Charles A. Beard, and George Soule published detailed proposals, schemes that, in general, would revive the wartime apparatus, create functional syndicates representing all interests, and use them to control investment and build purchasing power.[40] Articles also appeared examining the "experiments" abroad and how they might be adapted to American needs.[41] Discussions of the broader applications of "scientific management" dominated the 1931 meeting of the Taylor Society.[42] And out of a progressive conference in March 1931 came a "stabilization" committee chaired by Robert LaFollette, Jr., further proposals for a national economic council, and, beginning in October 1931, a long series of Senate hearings focusing on a variety of planning schemes.[43] For a whole group of "neoliberals" now, some updated form of the New Nationalism, "war socialism," or Veblenian technocracy seemed desirable; and while they disagreed about how much autonomy the individual and the business group must give up, they all envisioned more power for labor and consumer groups and for a central planning and regulatory apparatus manned by disinterested experts and representatives of the "public."

What the other set of "coordinators" had in mind was also becoming increasingly clear. Throughout 1931 the attack on the antitrust laws intensified, both from groups seeking special legislative treatment and from organizations like the National Civic Federation, the American Bar Association, and the American Mining Congress, all of whom favored a system of administrative exemptions.[44] Revision became the subject of a number of business and academic conferences,[45] and in Congress bills appeared to save the trade practice codes that the FTC had been scuttling.[46] At the same time, sentiment for legal sanctions against "chiselers" was growing. Some "stabilizers" now wanted not only the right to form cartels but a law that would force all elements of their industries to join and comply.[47] And finally, disillusionment with Hoover's "coordinators" was bringing forth numerous proposals for a "superorganization" of industry, one that would be strong enough to weld these units of "self-government" into a harmonious whole, bring "responsible" group leaders into a broad "concert of interests," and thus keep statist expansion to a minimum. In essence, this was to be the function of the Peace Industries Board proposed by Bernard Baruch, the Council of Industries suggested by R. H. Whitehead, the Board of Trade advocated by Mark Requa, the Institute of Industrial Coordination urged by Benjamin Javits, the Economic Congress envisioned by Matthew Woll and James Gerard, and the less known but similar institutions projected by other corporate systematizers.[48]

As such proposals multiplied in late 1931, two particular schemes caught national attention, both, significantly perhaps, emanating from segments of the business community that Hoover had long relied on for leadership and coordination. One came from General Electric's Gerard Swope and Owen D. Young, men long regarded as prototypes of the "industrial statesman." Speaking before the National Electrical Manufacturers' Association on 16 September, Swope set forth an elaborate scheme of economic and welfare planning, one that he had worked on since May and had already discussed with a number of associates. The system, as he envisioned it, would operate through compulsory trade associations, made up of all major firms and empowered by law to regulate production, prices, and trade practices. Labor would benefit from a system of old-age, life, and unemployment insurance administered by labor-management committees in each industry, and coordination in the "public interest" would come through a supervisory agency and public representatives on the association boards.[49] The result, as some critics saw it, would be either an administrative nightmare, a closed and stagnant economy, or a "semisyndicalist" alliance of "big government" and "big business." But for Swope, Young, and their supporters, adoption of the scheme would free industry from outmoded "fetishes," revive markets and investments, and allow government and business to "cooperate" for the "benefit of the people."[50]

The other scheme was that developed under the auspices of the

United States Chamber of Commerce, chiefly by Henry Harriman, the chairman of its Committee on Continuity of Business and Employment. Set up in May 1931, this committee had studied both the proposals being made in the United States and the types of agencies being established abroad.[51] In September it turned to writing its report, and in October it released to the public a scheme calling for legalized trade-association planning, balanced by private unemployment insurance and coordinated through a "national economic council" made up of "public" men but ones chosen by the leaders of functional interest groups.[52] In essence, the plan combined the main features of Swope's proposal with a more elaborate version of what Julius Barnes had urged on Hoover in 1929. And the fact now that Chamber members approved the scheme by a majority of nearly eight to one [53] demonstrated the lengths to which a growing segment of the business community was willing to go. The "neo-liberals" on the left had their counterparts in "neocorporatists" on the right; and while these advocates of compulsory guilds and centralized "business planning" were having difficulty in capturing organizations other than the Chamber of Commerce,[54] they could no longer be dismissed as an insignificant minority.

As conditions worsened, then, growing numbers of critics could agree that Hoover's approach was a failure yet could not agree on the "lessons" to be drawn or the alternative that should take its place. Badly divided over what the new role of the individual, the private group, or the state should be, they tended for a time to cancel each other out and make innovation by anyone difficult. Yet even if change had been less difficult, it seems unlikely that Hoover would have regarded it as desirable. Ideologically committed to the guidelines he had worked out earlier and always reluctant to admit failures or "mistakes," [55] he quickly came up with his own explanation of the continued economic difficulties, blaming them not on the failure of his policies but on developments abroad over which Americans had no control.[56] And having accepted this diagnosis, he coupled continued efforts to develop and apply the "cooperative system" with an increasingly defensive campaign, one that poured more and more of his energies into answering his critics, explaining why he was promoting neither big government nor monopoly nor economic anarchy, and holding the line against the statist "short cuts" and "new forms of the Middle Ages" [57] that could put an end to the American dream.

One theme, increasingly insistent now, was the dehumanization that Americans would suffer and the libertarian institutions they must sacrifice if they turned to a system regimented, subsidized, and regulated by the state. In the summer and fall of 1930, as cooperative committees were set up to organize drought and unemployment relief, the president laid great stress upon how these agencies would preserve the roots of "self-government." [58] In 1931 the Muscle Shoals veto, the efforts to hold down federal appropriations, the launching of the President's Organization for Unemployment Relief, and the explanations of why the Farm Board should discontinue its "stabilization" activities and resist schemes to regiment agricultural production all provided opportunities for expounding on the evils of big government.[59] And in a series of formal addresses, the theme appeared again and again. Yielding to temptations of this sort, Hoover told a Lincoln Day audience in 1931, would eventually make every man a "servant of the State;" and speaking at Indianapolis four months later, he depicted the flurry of "national plans" as being an infection from Russia, argued anew that his original program would work once the shocks from abroad had been overcome, and proposed his own "Twenty Year Plan," one that would achieve its goals by giving the "American system" a chance.[60]

At the same time, despite charges that "cooperation" was being rendered impossible,[61] the Hoover administration was also resisting the notion that its informal corporatism should be converted into a formalized and compulsory system. Again, if Amerians tried to do so, the cure would be worse than the disease. It would generate pressures for elaborate regulatory bureaucracies or other anticapitalist institutions; and even if these could be resisted, it would gradually undermine progressive and creative forms of association, converting them into instruments of extortion or into closed and stagnant arrangements where men must either remain in their places or advance only at the expense of others. This, so the argument ran, had been the experience abroad.[62] And while Hoover would concede that the Sherman Act could stand some revision, especially as it applied to natural-resource industries,[63] he stubbornly refused to suspend antitrust prosecutions or to issue blanket denunciations of those who were cutting prices or selling below cost.[64] When approached by business "planners," moreover, his Commerce Department kept urging them to forget about "grandiose schemes" and concentrate on devising better "educational campaigns," improved forms of voluntary cooperation, and sounder planning by individual firms.[65]

Not surprisingly, then, the "grandiose schemes" set forth in late

1931 seemed to impress Hoover more with the evils they could bring than with any benefits that might accrue. On 11 September, after reading an advance copy of the Swope Plan, he found "only about five percent" of it to be of "some use." The rest was a scheme for "gigantic trusts such as have never been dreamed of in the history of the world." And to combat the proposal, he quickly secured an opinion that it was unconstitutional, forwarded this and other materials to Senator Felix Herbert, and persuaded the latter to issue a statement denouncing the plan and pointing out how it would destroy constitutional government, saddle the nation with inefficient and monopolistic cartels, and eventually force the creation of a vast bureaucracy.[66] Subsequently, the president also made it clear that he would have nothing to do with the Chamber of Commerce scheme. Although Julius Barnes kept supplying him with documents and pointing out how important it was to move against "destructive competition," [67] Hoover's State of the Union message merely reiterated his earlier request for a congressional investigation. Schemes for repealing the antitrust laws, he declared again, would "open wide the door to price fixing, monopoly, and destruction of healthy competition." [68]

It would be a mistake, however, to see the Hoover administration as merely holding the line against welfare statists and corporate systematizers. Although pleas of powerlessness in the face of foreign developments and domestic obstacles were now creeping into its rationale, it had not given up on its own efforts to manage economic and social behavior. The search continued for its own alternative to laissez-faire, for a regulatory structure that would remain within Hoover's guidelines and could serve both as an economic governor and a bulwark against the threats of big government or industrial dictatorship. And the result in 1930 and 1931 was a further burgeoning of Hoover's "cooperative system." There were new efforts, for example, to develop a type of "planning" compatible with "progressive" and "creative" institutions. There were new cooperative programs for some of the natural-resource industries. And much better known, there was a further proliferation of committees and governmental aids designed to secure "constructive" private and local action in providing relief, expanding credit, and solving social problems.

The first of these efforts, the campaign to develop an "American program" of planning, got underway in mid-1931, partly as an adjunct to the work of the Emergency Committee for Employment, partly in an effort to head off the agitation for coercive controls.[69]

The central idea, as developed by such Commerce Department officials as Frederick Feiker, Julius Klein, and Louis Domeratzky, was to revitalize the traditional work of trade associations and mold this into a "nationwide pattern" capable of bringing balanced and stable growth. While rejecting "centralized planning," they believed, it was possible to do much more in the way of promoting market research and cost education, setting up budgetary and investment controls, adjusting production "through statistical knowledge," and regularizing employment, trade practices, and interindustry relationships.[70] In September 1931 Feiker persuaded the American Trade Association executives to back the Commerce Department program rather than schemes for compulsory cartels, and in the months that followed he and his associates urged the approach on other groups.[71] The Cotton Textile Institute and the cement producers also received official encouragement in their efforts to curb "destructive" competitive behavior.[72] A model trade-association charter was worked out. And renewed efforts were made to publicize and expand the Department's advisory and promotional services, thus helping an "individualistic" people to "plan from the bottom up" rather than the top down.[73]

Working with established associations, the Hoover administration was also able now to set up some special "conservation" programs. In late 1930, for example, following a series of negotiations with lumber leaders, the president appointed a privately financed Timber Conservation Board, which was made up of both Cabinet members and industrial representatives and was allowed to forecast demand, suggest quotas, and recommend other remedies for economic "chaos."[74] Similar arrangements, too, were made with oil leaders. In 1930 and 1931 the Federal Oil Conservation Board, headed by Secretary of the Interior Ray Lyman Wilbur, began cooperating with the American Petroleum Institute to provide forecasts of demand, suggest quotas, and set up voluntary import controls.[75] And in June 1931, apparently under strong pressure from both the industry and interested Cabinet members, the Federal Trade Commission abandoned its efforts to revise the petroleum code and reinstated trade practice rules encouraging price maintenance.[76] In addition, plans for a coal program were repeatedly considered, and, had operators been less opposed to making labor a partner in stabilization, might have been adopted. Calls for a national coal conference continued to founder on the rock of union-management conflict, and by late 1931 the National Coal Association had turned to a plan for regional marketing cooperatives, one that O'Brian pro-

posed to contest, but which William Donovan and other association lawyers hoped to slip inside the antitrust laws as being a "reasonable" measure of "economic self-defense." [77]

Finally, the years 1930 and 1931 brought the creation of such
agencies as the National Drought Relief Committee, the Emergency
Committee for Employment, the Home Building and Child Health
Conferences, the President's Organization for Unemployment Relief, and the National Credit Association. All of these, as Hoover
saw them, were to provide a middle way, an alternative to laissez-
faire that could secure "constructive" action and relief without
resorting to big government or politicized cartels.[78] His cooperative
machinery, however inadequate his critics felt it to be, kept growing. And in such areas as resource management, construction planning, and credit relief, he seemed willing to back it with new federal
supplements. He supported legislation for a permanent Federal
Power Commission. He welcomed the creation of a Federal Employment Stabilization Board. And in December 1931, after his
National Credit Association had failed to relieve a growing credit
paralysis, he finally called for a new framework of governmental
credit and controls within which cooperative measures might be
successful.[79] His policies hardly merited the label "do-nothingism."
But in holding the line against statist regulation, federal welfare,
and formalized corporatism, he was being thrown into an increasingly negative stance.

In early 1932, moreover, Hoover continued to hold the line. In
spite of some urging from Cabinet members, he refused to endorse
the coal-stabilization or trade-practice measures being considered in
Congress.[80] In the face of new spending and relief proposals, he
continued to expound on the evils of big government, demoralized
federal credit, and "non-productive" public works.[81] And when confronted with new formulas for business planning, he continued to
see them as opening the way to "monopoly" or "socialism." In February, after meeting with a new business group put together by
Charles Abbott and Gordon Corbaley, he considered but quickly
rejected their scheme for a two-year "truce in destructive competition" so as to allow an "experiment" in production planning.[82]
Subsequently, the administration shunted aside similar proposals
advanced by such trade-association leaders as Gilbert Montague,
George Sloan, and Z. L. Potter.[83] And in June, when a group of
industrialists and American Legion officials urged revival of the
Council of National Defense as an "emergency cabinet," the presi-

dent's reaction was strongly negative. Such a body, he argued, was unneeded. It would merely add a "fifth wheel to an already much taxed coach," and if the public should become alarmed about the economic or political implications of reviving it, any effort to do so would result in far more harm than good.[84]

The difficulty, as Hoover continued to see it, was not with the regulatory structure he was trying to preserve and develop. It lay rather in the "credit paralysis" induced by shocks from abroad and irresponsible behavior at home. And to cope with this, he was not only adopting the classical prescription of budget balancing but also deploying a new array of cooperative committees and federal "supplements." New Laws in the first half of 1932 established the Reconstruction Finance Corporation and provided special credits for farm groups and holders of real-estate mortgages. A new Citizens' Reconstruction Organization conducted a campaign against hoarding:[85] And a new network of Business and Industrial Committees, set up in each Federal Reserve district and coordinated through a national conference, attempted once more to persuade businessmen that they should use the new credit facilities, expand their operations, and hire as many workers as possible.[86] In Hoover's mind, moreover, the brief upswing in the summer of 1932 became proof that his analysis was correct. For him the subsequent downturn was a politically inspired crisis, due chiefly to political uncertainties following the election and to the fears created by a new wave of irresponsible behavior on the part of Democratic politicians.[87]

Given a chance, Hoover felt, his policies could still bring economic and social well-being. And during and following the campaign of 1932, he continued to expound on the evils of "state-directed" systems and closed or politicized cartels. New governmental initiatives, as he saw it, should be limited chiefly to mobilizing additional cooperation, helping farmers to retire marginal lands, and reestablishing confidence in the financial system.[88] And to the cartelizers, his only concessions were to express further sympathy for the coal, lumber, and textile industries, suggest that test cases like the one being tried in the coal industry might provide an answer, and point out that he had urged Congress to find suitable controls for these areas where competition was truly "destructive." [89] In September 1932, when Henry Harriman threatened political retaliation unless he endorsed the Chamber of Commerce plan, Hoover heatedly declared that he would stand firm against any such attempt to "smuggle fascism into America through a back door." [90]

In October, as a new wave of business meetings and speeches attacked the antitrust laws, he refused to alter his stand; and in late 1932 and early 1933, even though some Commerce Department officials were now in close touch with those who hoped to sell some version of the Harriman plan to the incoming administration, the president himself would have nothing to do with the effort or its instigators.[91]

For a majority of Americans, though, Hoover's approach had now become either a study in weakness, an excuse for doing nothing, or a mask for economic exploitation. Demands for a "new order" had become insistent; and while Americans could still not agree upon what the proper balance between competitive rivalry, group action, and statist direction should be, they would soon have a president who was willing to give "something" to nearly everyone, institutionalize the divisions, and allow competing administrators and groups to determine where the balance should be struck. A new burst of energy and experimentation was in the making, one that would demolish the lines that Hoover had been holding but would be slow to settle on a new regulatory model. In essence, what it would provide was not a coherent alternative but a set of "economic charters" under which an alternative might take shape, frameworks, in other words, that different sets of administrators could use to build quite different versions of an "industrial democracy." And within these frameworks, sharp clashes would persist, not only between the interest groups, but also between the conflicting ideals of a corporatist order, a planning and social-service state, and a revitalized market system. Initially, policy would veer toward an approximation of what Harriman and Swope were advocating, but the resulting collision with entrepreneurial, antitrust, and welfare-statist ideals would bring a sharp reaction, forcing this version of corporatism to give ground on all sides, and postponing the emergence of a new consensus on a regulatory model until the advent of "neopluralism" in the 1940s.[92]

In some respects, then, the Hoover presidency can be regarded as the end of an era. Its governing model in economic policy, the model of informal corporatism and "cooperative competition" that Hoover and his associates had worked out in the 1920s, became during his presidency an increasingly discredited model. Under depression conditions, it seemed to block the search for order, abundance, and equity rather than promoting it, and the discrediting of the model marked the beginning of a long search for a new and presumably more satisfactory way of reconciling a modern technocorporate system with America's liberal-democratic and rural heritage. Yet the significance of this dividing line can easily be exaggerated. The shift was not from laissez-faire to a managed economy, but rather from one attempt at management, that through informal private-public cooperation, to other more formal and coercive yet also limited attempts, efforts that still made numerous concessions to individualistic and village ideals.[93] The tensions inherent in Hoover's system persisted in the vacillating policies of the New Deal and in the subsequent synthesis that "neopluralism" was supposed to provide. And the later excursions into guildist government and welfare statism built upon and were in some degree limited by the cooperative institutions that Hoover had encouraged and the federal "supplements" that he was willing to establish.[94]

Viewed in longer perspective, the Hoover years appear as a distinctive yet integral stage in the continuing process whereby twentieth-century policy-makers have tried to reconcile conflicting visions of a new order with the dreams that they inherited from nineteenth-century liberalism and agrarianism. In America, to be sure, these visions of order have frequently been disguised as "new liberalisms." But just as in Europe, they have tended to come in two varieties, one stressing statist direction and services, the other, often ignored, envisioning a regulatory system built around modern guilds and corporations. For Hoover, the latter vision was far more attractive than the former. And while his attempt to blend and balance it with "healthy competition," local communitarianism, and statist "supplements" became a casualty of economic contraction and internal tensions, it cannot be ignored by those who would understand the larger patterns of twentieth-century American development. On the contrary, it should be seen as a major attempt to work out a modern corporatist order compatible with American ideals and traditions, as a forebear of different but similar attempts in the post-World War II period, and as one of a long series of efforts to provide America with a "middle way" between atomist individualism, a state-directed economy, and "new forms of the Middle Ages."

Herbert Hoover and American Corporatism, 1929–1933
Ellis W. Hawley

1. Compare Robert Huddleston Wiebe, *The Search for Order* (New York: Macmillan Co., 1967); Rowland Berthoff, *An Unsettled People* (New York: Harper and Row, 1971); and Ronald Radosh and Murray Rothband (eds.), *A New History of Leviathan* (New York: Dutton 1972). See also Louis Galambos, "The Emerging Organizational Synthesis in Modern American History," *Business History Review* 44 (Autumn 1970): 279–90.

2. See, for example, Kenneth Barkin, "Populism in Germany and America," in Herbert Bass, ed., *The State of American History* (Chicago: Quadrangle Books, 1970), pp. 373–404; Heinrich Winkler *et al.*, *Die Grosse Krise in America* (Gottingen: Vandenhoeck and Ruprecht, 1973); and John Garraty, "The New Deal, National Socialism, and the Great Depression," *American Historical Review*, 78 (October 1973): 907–44. For broader trends in this field, see also Cyril Black, *The Dynamics of Modernization* (New York: Harper and Row, 1966), pp. 175–99.

3. See, for example, Radosh *et al.*, *Leviathan*, pp. 146–87; Grant McConnell, *Private Power and American Democracy* (New York: Alfred A. Knopf, Inc., 1966); Andrew Shonfield, *Modern Capitalism* (London: Oxford University Press,

1965), 308–14; James Weinstein, *The Corporate Ideal in the Liberal State* (Boston: Beacon Press, 1969); and William Appleman Williams, *The Contours of American History* (Cleveland: World Publishing Co., 1961).

4. One of the best short discussions of corporatism is in Eugene Golob, *The Isms* (New York: Harper, 1954), pp. 541–97. As he points out, corporatism was never necessarily linked with fascism. Nor was it, in theory anyway, incompatible with democracy. Compare also the developments described in Matthew Elbow, *French Corporative Theory* (New York: Columbia University Press, 1953), Ralph Henry Bowen, *German Theories of the Corporative State* (New York: Whittlesey House, 1947), and Robert Alexander Brady, *Business as a System of Power* (New York: Columbia University Press 1943), pp. 21–188, with those described in Wiebe, *Search for Order*, Weinstein, *Corporate Ideal*, Samuel Hays, *Response to Industrialization* (Chicago: University of Chicago Press, 1957), Louis Galambos, *Competition and Cooperation* (Baltimore: Johns Hopkins Press, 1966), and Edwin T. Layton, Jr., *The Revolt of the Engineers* (Cleveland: Press of Case Western Reserve, 1971).

5. See McConnell, *Private Power*, pp. 54–70. For American attempts to provide a philosophical base, see Herbert Hoover's Penn College Commencement Address, PS 496, HHP; Owen D. Young's "Dedication Address," in *Harvard Business Review* 5 (July 1927): 385–94; Edwin Parker's *Self-Regulation by Business* (Washington: Chamber of Commerce of the United States, 1927); and Glen Frank, "Self-Governing Industry," *Century*, 98 (June 1910): 225–36.

6. See the discussion in McConnell, *Private Power*, pp. 4–5, 64–70, 268–81, and in Peri Arnold, "Herbert Hoover and the Department of Commerce" (Ph.D. dissertation, University of Chicago, 1972), pp. 211–22.

7. See especially Herbert Hoover, *American Individualism* (Garden City, N.Y.: Doubleday, Page and Co., 1922), pp. 41–47, 54–56, 63–72; Hoover, "We Can Cooperate and Yet Compete," *Nation's Business* 14 (June 1926): 11–14; and Hoover, *The New Day: Campaign Speeches of Herbert Hoover, 1928* (Stanford: Stanford University Press 1928), pp. 9–44, 196–204.

8. Hoover, *New Day*, pp. 22–23; Hoover, *Larger Purposes of Department of Commerce* (Washington: Government Printing Office, 1928).

9. Hoover, Inaugural Address, 4 March 1929; Message to Congress, 16 April 1929; "What Business May Expect from President Hoover," 9 March 1929, PS 977, 984, 1011, HHP.

10. The tension involved in particular areas of policy is described below, but for examples of documents reflecting the dialectic see Hoover's "Address to the American Federation of Labor," 6 October 1930, PS 1385, HHP; Hoover's "Memorandum on Farm Board Organization," 13 July 1929, Farm Matters File, PSF, HHP; and Hoover's "Address to the Chamber of Commerce," 1 May 1930, PS 1279, HHP. It was also an old theme with Hoover. See, for example, *American Individualism*, pp. 41–44, and his Penn College Address, 12 June 1925, PS 496, HHP.

11. Hoover to W. O. Thompson, 30 December 1929, PS 1197, HHP; E. E. Hunt, "Looking to the Future," Box 19, E. E. Hunt Papers, HIA; Barry D. Karl, "Presidential Planning and Social Science Research," in Donald Fleming and Bernard Bailyn (eds.), *Perspectives in American History* (Cambridge, Mass.: Harvard University Press, 1969), pp. 351–52, 362–63.

12. Karl, "Presidential Planning," pp. 362–65; Alva Johnston, "Mr. Hoover's Commissions Open New Era," *New York Herald Tribune*, 30 January, 1 Febru-

ary 1930; Hoover, Press Statement, 2 July 1929, PS 1071-A, HHP. In early 1930, Hoover also planned to follow up recovery from the panic of 1929 with a full-dress study of economic stabilization. See his address to the Chamber of Commerce, 1 May 1930, PS 1279, HHP.

13. See, for example, E. E. Hunt, "National Planning Board," 2 July 1926, Box 18, Hunt Papers, HIA.

14. "Industry Conference," Commerce Dept. File, PSF, HHP; Hoover to Lamont, 17 May 1929, AFL File, PSF, HHP; Barnes, "Notes for an Autobiography," 5 January 1943, File 2, Drawer 7, Henry Elmer Barnes Papers, St. Louis County Historical Society, Duluth, Minnesota; Hunt to Arch Shaw, 17 March 1931, Box 37, Hunt Papers, HIA.

15. Hoover to J. L. O'Brian, 30 August 1929, Justice Dept. File, PSF, HHP; Rush Butler to George Akerson, 20 April 1929, Antitrust File, PSF, HHP; Galambos, *Competition and Cooperation*, pp. 143–47. B. C. Forbes of *Forbes Magazine* also believed that Hoover would take an "active part" in setting up the type of interbusiness planning agencies being advocated by such systematizers as Benjamin Javits and Manny Straus. See "Minutes of Conference on Industrial Coordination," 5 March 1929, Unemployment File, PSF, HHP.

16. Mitchell to R. L. Wilbur, 29 March 1929; Hoover, Press Statement, 2 April 1929, both in Oil File, PSF, HHP; Herbert Clark Hoover, *The Memoirs of Herbert Hoover: The Cabinet and The Presidency, 1920–1933*, Vol. II (New York: Macmillan Co., 1951), p. 238.

17. Hoover to O'Brian, 30 August 1929, Justice Dept. File, PSF, HHP; Hoover, *Memoirs*, II, p. 302.

18. Trade association lawyer Felix Levy, in particular, was threatening to turn over evidence of lax enforcement to the press, and leaders of the National Civic Federation were urging action, both to protect legitimate cooperation and with the idea of getting more groups interested in "modernizing" the law. Even before these pressures developed, however, Hoover had decided that Donovan's enforcement of the Sherman Act had been "very bad." See Hoover's "Memorandum on Reasons Why Donovan Was Not Taken into the Cabinet," Donovan File, PNF, HHP; Levy to Mitchell, 4 April 1929, File 60-o, Justice Department Archives, RG60, NA; Robert Himmelberg, "Relaxation of the Federal Anti-Trust Policy as a Goal of the Business Community, 1918–1933" (Ph.D. dissertation, Pennsylvania State University, 1963), pp. 176–81.

19. Himmelberg, "Relaxation of Anti-Trust," pp. 189–98; *Business Week* (19 February 1930): 22–24; O'Brian to Benjamin Kirsh, 22 October 1929, File 60-o, RG 60, NA. The major groups involved were the Bolt and Nut Institute, the Sugar Institute, the Wool Institute, and the Asphalt Shingle and Roofing Institute.

20. O'Brian to Mitchell, 16 January 1931, File 60-57-32, RG 60, NA; "Federal Trade Practice Conferences," 14 June 1930, FTC File, PSF, HHP; *Business Week* (16 April 1930): 25; (18 October 1930): 13–14.

21. Hoover to Coolidge, 22 September 1926, FTC File, COF, HHP; Abram Myers to Hoover, 2 May 1931, FTC File, PSF, HHP.

22. Lawrence Richey to Louis Flye, 16 September 1930; Myers to Hoover, 2 May 1931; Hoover to Myers, 4 May 1931, all in FTC File, PSF, HHP.

23. Hoover, "Address to the AFL," 6 October 1930; "State of the Union Message," 2 December 1930, PS 1385, 1429, HHP.

24. Hoover to J. J. Davis, 21 July, 13 August 1930, Coal File, PSF, HHP. For

the nature of the coal problem and Hoover's earlier struggle with it, see my "Secretary Hoover and the Bituminous Coal Problem, 1921–28," *Business History Review* 42 (Autumn 1968): 253–70.

25. Wilson Compton to Hoover, 2, 5 April 1930, National Timber Conservation Board File, PSF, HHP. For Hoover's earlier difficulties with conflicting factions in the industry, see Arnold, "Hoover and Department of Commerce," pp. 158–71.

26. Mark Requa, "Colorado Springs Petroleum Conference," 13 June 1929; Hoover to Wilbur, 15 December 1930, both in Oil File, PSF, HHP; William Olbrich, "The Hoover Administration and the Oil Crisis," unpublished ms., author's files.

27. For Hoover's plan and its origins, see James H. Shideler, "Herbert Hoover and the Federal Farm Board Project, 1921–25," *Mississippi Valley Historical Review* 42 (March 1956): 710–29.

28. Albert U. Romasco, *The Poverty of Abundance: Hoover, the Nation, the Depression* (New York: Oxford University Press, 1956), p. 23.

29. Hoover, "Memorandum on Farm Board Organization," 13 July 1929; Carl Williams to Hoover, 10 July 1930, both in Farm Matters File, PSF, HHP; Hoover, "Message to Congress," 16 April 1929, PS 1011, HHP.

30. Hoover, "Memoranda on Farm Board Organization and on Possible Procedure," 13 July 1929; Hoover to Alexander Legge, 15 March 1930; Legge to John Richardson, 1 April 1930, all in Farm Matters File, PSF, HHP.

31. The 1921 activities are described in Carolyn Grin, "The Unemployment Conference of 1921: An Experiment in National Cooperative Planning," *Mid-America* 55 (April 1973): 83–107.

32. Romasco, *Poverty*, pp. 27–31, 48–54; Press Release, 21 November 1929, Business Conference File, PSF, HHP; "Activities of the National Business Survey Conference," 23 January 1930; "The National Building Survey Conference," 21 January 1930, both in Chamber of Commerce File, PSF, HHP.

33. Hoover, "Addresses to Chamber of Commerce," 5 December 1929, 1 May 1930, PS 1178, 1279, HHP; Press Release, 22 November 1929, Business Conferences File, PSF, HHP; U.S. Chamber of Commerce, *Business Conditions and Outlook* (7 December 1929).

34. Hoover, *New Day*, pp. 22–23; Hoover to David Lawrence, 29 December 1927, American Businessman File, COF, HHP.

35. For examples of such "advice," see the *Commercial and Financial Chronicle* 132 (20 June 1931): 4524; 133 (12 September 1931): 1670–71; *New York Times*, 25 January 1931, II, p. 19; Frank A. Fetter, *The Masquerade of Monopoly* (New York: Harcourt, Brace and Co., 1931); *Barron's* 11 (29 June 1931): 3, 8; J. K. Davis to Hoover, 29 October 1930, Oil File, PSF, HHP Newton Baker, in *Review of Reviews 84* (September 1931): 57–59. For discussion of those who deplored Hoover's "artificial" intervention with "natural laws," see also Romasco, *Poverty*, pp. 79–84, and *Business Week* (13 May 1931): 56. For the antitrust view that the depression was due to "combinations," "chain organizations," and "price or cost fixing associations," see Senate Resolution 46, 72 Cong., 1 Sess., 9 December 1931, copy in Box 2, Tray 9, George Norris Papers, LC.

36. See, for example, W. H. Denney to Hoover, 25 May 1931, Business File, PSF, HHP; C. F. Abbott to Hoover, 17 October 1930, Abbott File, President's Secretary File (PSec), HHP; Gerard Swope to Hoover, 2 October 1930; Wallace

Donham, "The Unemployment Emergency," 6 February 1931; Darwin Meserole to Hoover, 24 November 1930, all in Unemployment File, PSF, HHP.

37. William Scroggs, "Anti-Trust Laws Under Fire," *Outlook and Independent* 156 (3 December 1930): 545; *Business Week* (7 May 1930): 14; (19 November 1930): 27; McGraw-Hill Co., *American Business Management Speaks Out* (1931); Philip Cabot, "Vices of Free Competition," *Yale Review* 21 (September 1931): 38–55; James H. Williams, "Reign of Error," *Atlantic Monthly* 147 (June 1931): 787–96.

38. See, for example, Oswald Garrison Villard, in *Nation* 131 (3 September 1930): 237–39; John Ryan, in *Commonweal* 12 (3 September 1930): 436–38; George Soule, in *New Republic* 56 (11 March 1931): 88–91; Rexford Tugwell, in *Political Science Quarterly* 46 (June 1931): 188–224; "Program of the Progressive Conference," 11–12 March 1931, Norris Papers, LC.

39. The arguments of cartelizers frequently stressed the notion that social health depended upon protecting capital and organizational commitments in a "basic" or "vital" industry. Labor held that all else depended upon the payment of "just" or "socially efficient" wages. Small merchants insisted that liquidating them would mean the end of "economic democracy," "local self-government," and all else that was really healthy in American society. And farm leaders argued that both economic and social well-being depended upon preserving an industry that was "fundamental" to all others and a social group that provided American society with most of its virtues. The latter two arguments, in particular, resembled the glorification of the peasant, artisan, and small shopkeeper that was characteristic of the corporatist-oriented "middle-class socialism" in Germany. See, for example, Cornelius Kelley, in New York University, *National Conference on the Relation of Law and Business* (1931), pp. 109–14; *Monthly Labor Review* 33 (November 1931): 1044–47; Frederick K. Hardy, "The Special Taxation of Chain Stores" (Ph.D. dissertation, University of Wisconsin, 1934), pp. 95–115; Louis B. Schmidt, "Role and Techniques of Agrarian Pressure Groups," *Agricultural History* 30 (April 1956): 55–57; Arthur Schweitzer, *Big Business in the Third Reich* (Bloomington: Indiana University Press, 1964), pp. 70–83, 115–17.

40. Stuart Chase, "A Ten Year Plan for America," *Harper's Magazine* 163 (June 1931): 1–10; Charles A. Beard, "A 'Five Year Plan' for America," *Forum* 86 (July 1931): 1–11; George Soule, "National Planning," *New Republic* 66 (4 March 1931): 61–65.

41. See, for example, Maurice Mendelson and Henry Baker, "The Industrialization of Russia." *Current History* 33 (January 1931): 481–92; Lewis Lorwin, in *New Republic* 66 (29 April 1931): 294–97; *Christian Century* 48 (11 March 1931): 334–36.

42. *Bulletin of the Taylor Society* 16 (April 1931): 82–83.

43. *New Republic* 69, Pt. 2 (13 January 1932); Isador Lubin, "The New Lead from Capitol Hill," *Survey* 67 (1 March 1932): 573–77; *Congressional Digest,* 11 (April 1932): 103; U.S. Senate, Committee on Manufactures, *Establishment of a National Economic Council* (72 Cong., 1 Sess., 1932).

44. Himmelberg, "Relaxation of Anti-Trust," pp. 224, 235–41; Elmer Davis, "Can Business Manage Itself?" *Harper's Magazine* 162 (March 1931): 385–96; George H. Bailey to Lamont, 14 September 1931, File 82448/48, RG 40, NA; Rush Butler, in New York University, *National Conference*, pp. 235–38.

45. Galambos, *Competition and Cooperation*, pp. 179–80; *New York Times,*

(27 October 1931): 3; (9 December 1931): 23; (11 December 1931): 29; New York University, *National Conference.*

46. *Business Week* (21 January 1931): 10.

47. Galambos, *Competition and Cooperation,* p. 177.

48. *Business Week* (14 May 1930): 22; R. H. Whitehead, "Plan for a National Industrial Council," 1 October 1931, File 83057, Commerce Dept. Archives, RG 40, NA; M. L. Requa, "Industrial Self-Regulation," Requa File, PPF, HHP; Benjamin Javits to Lamont, 15 October 1929, Box 14, Lamont Papers, RG 40, NA; Javits to Hoover, 18 December 1931, Unemployment File, PSF, HHP; Matthew Woll, Address over WOR, Business Stabilization File, PSF, HHP.

49. David Goldsmith Loth, *Swope of G. E.* (New York: Simon and Schuster, 1958), pp. 201–202; "Swope Address," reprinted in *Monthly Labor Review* 33 (November 1931): 1049–57.

50. *Literary Digest* 111 (3 October 1931): 8–9; Norman Thomas, in *Nation* 133 (7 October 1931): 357–59; H. A. Bullis to James Bell, 3 November 1931, Box 1, James Bell Papers, Minnesota Historical Society, St. Paul, Minn.; Swope, "Discussion of Stabilization of Industry," Swope File, PSec, HHP.

51. "Resolutions Adopted at Atlantic City," May 1931; Barnes to Hoover, 4 September 1931, both in Chamber of Commerce File, PSF, HHP.

52. Barnes to Hoover, 4 September 1931; "Report of the Committee on Continuity of Business and Employment," 4 October 1931, both in Chamber of Commerce File, PSF, HHP. The groups to be represented were the Chamber of Commerce, labor, agriculture, government (Department of Commerce), manufacturing, banking, railroads, utilities, distribution, law, engineering, and economics.

53. *Business Week* (30 December 1931): 14; Barnes to Hoover, 18 December 1931, Chamber of Commerce File, PSF, HHP.

54. The business community was still badly divided, and this was more apparent in other organizations than the Chamber. Large numbers of business leaders still feared that relaxing the antitrust laws would strengthen their rivals or open the way to labor "monopolies" and hostile governmental bureaucracies. See Himmelberg, "Relaxation of Anti-Trust," pp. 245–69, and A. W. Briggs, "Proposals Relating to the Antitrust Laws," 11 January 1932, Antitrust File, PSF, HHP.

55. "No President," Hoover told Barnes, "must ever admit he has been wrong." See Barnes, "Notes regarding the Panic of 1929–30," File 6, Drawer 6, Barnes Papers. For this pattern in Hoover's earlier life, see also Geoffrey Blainey, "Herbert Hoover's Forgotten Years," *Business Archives and History* 3 (February 1963): 70.

56. For the progressive development of this view, see Hoover's addresses of 2 October 1930, 2 December 1930, 15 June 1931, and 11 August 1932, PS 1382, 1429, 1587, 1939, HHP. See also Herbert Clark Hoover, *The Memoirs of Herbert Hoover: The Great Depression, 1929–1941,* Vol. III (New York: Macmillan Co.), pp. 197–202.

57. The terms appear in Hoover to Arch Shaw, 17 February 1933, Shaw File, PPF, HHP, and Hoover, "Acceptance Speech," 11 August 1932, PS 1939, HHP.

58. Hoover, Press Statements of 14, 19 August, 17 October 1930, PS 1359, 1363, 1389, HHP.

59. Hoover, "Message to Congress," 3 March 1931; Press Statements, 9 December 1930, 3 February 1931, 9 August 1931, PS 1503, 1436, 1474, HHP; Public Letter

of James C. Stone to F. J. Wilmer, 13 May 1931, Farm Matters File, PSF, HHP; U.S. Federal Farm Board, *Second Annual Report* (Washington: Government Printing Office, 1931).

60. Hoover, "Addresses," 12 February, 15 June 1931, PS 1484, 1587, HHP.

61. See, for example, R. J. Caldwell to Hoover, 30 April 1931, Box 2, Lamont Papers, RG 40, NA; J. W. Sparks to Mitchell, 9 April 1931, File 60–104–13, RG 60, NA; Oscar Sutro to Requa, 18 December 1931, Oil File, PSF, HHP; *Business Week* (9 July 1930): 12.

62. Louis Domeratzky, in *Foreign Affairs* 10 (October 1931): 34–53; William Mitchell, "Address," 16 May 1931, Justice Department File, PSF, HHP; Hoover, "Memorandum on the Swope Plan," 11 September 1931, Business Stabilization File, PSF, HHP.

63. Hoover, "State of the Union Message," 2 December 1930, PS 1429, HHP.

64. Drafts of such statements were prepared for him in late 1930, but no statements were made. See drafts dated 12 December 1930, Business File, PSF, HHP.

65. Julius Klein to Robert Blumenthal, 15 May 1931; Klein to Oscar Cooley, 7 November 1931; Lamont to John Crout, 27 May 1931, all in File 83057, RG 40, NA.

66. Hoover, "Memorandum on the Swope Plan," 11 September 1931; Hoover to Thomas Thacher, 12 September 1931; Thacher to Hoover, 1 October 1931; Hoover to Hebert, 11 September, 2 October 1931; Hebert to Hoover, 15, 18 September 1931; Hebert, "Statement on the Subject of Stabilization of Industry," all in Business Stabilization File, PSF, HHP.

67. Hoover, *Memoirs,* III, pp. 334–35; Barnes to Hoover, 10 October, 30 November, 18 December 1931, Chamber of Commerce File, PSF, HHP.

68. Hoover, "State of the Union Message," 8 December 1931, PS 1729, HHP.

69. F. C. Croxton to Heads of Trade Association, 18 July 1931; Frederick Feiker to Klein, 16 September 1931; T. R. Taylor to Feiker, 16 September 1931, all in Business Stabilization File, PSF, HHP; Feiker to Klein, 30 June 1931, Box 83, Frederick Feiker Papers, Bureau of Foreign and Domestic Commerce Archives, RG 151, NA.

70. Committee on Planning to Feiker, 22 October 1931; "Notes for Use in Asheville Speech," 19 September 1931, Boxes 81, 84, Feiker Papers, RG 151, NA.

71. Feiker, "Address before the ATAE," 24 September 1931; Feiker, "An American Economic Plan," 30 October 1931, Boxes 81, 83, Feiker Papers, RG 151, NA; American Trade Association Executives, *Listening-In,* 10 October 1931, 17 November 1931; Feiker to Lamont, 24 September 1931, Box 1, Lamont Papers, RG 40, NA; Klein to Sheldon Cary, 2 October 1931, File 81288, RG 40, NA; Himmelberg, "Relaxation of Anti-Trust," pp. 212–16.

72. Galambos, *Competition and Cooperation,* p. 156; Himmelberg, "Relaxation of Anti-Trust," pp. 209–11; Lamont, "Remarks before Conference of Textile Industry," 25 January 1932, Box 6, Lamont Papers, RG 40, NA.

73. "Accomplishments of the BFDC," Box 2, Taylor-Gates Material, HHP; "Trade Association Activities and Department of Commerce Assistance," 30 October 1931; Feiker, "An Ideal Charter for Trade Associations," Boxes 78, 94, Feiker Papers, RG 151, HHP.

74. Ripley Bowman, "The U.S. Timber Conservation Board," File 87338, RG 40, NA; Hoover to Lamont, 11 November 1930, National Timber Conservation Bd. File, PSF, HHP.

75. "Review of Efforts of FOCB and Various State Authorities to Solve Problems of Oil Industry," 13 March 1931, PS 1511, HHP; Lamont, "Address before the API," 11 November 1931, File 82272/1, RG 40, NA; E. S. Rochester to Wilbur, 1 April 1932, Box 13, Wilbur Papers, HIA.

76. "Trade Practice Conference Rules for the Petroleum Industry," 12 June 1931; Mitchell to O'Brian, 21 July 1931, both in File 60–57–32, RG 60, NA; New York Journal of Commerce, 10 August 1931.

77. W. N. Doak to Hoover, 29, 31 August 1931, Coal File, PSF, HHP; O'Brian, "Proposed Plan of Bituminous Coal Operators," 7 January 1932; O'Brian to E. L. Greever, 26 January 1932; O'Brian to Mitchell, 27 January 1932, all in File 60–187–67, RG 60, NA; National Coal Association, The Regional Sales Agency Plan (1931); Business Week (15 July 1931): 7; (16 December 1931): 18.

78. Hoover, Press Statements, 1, 14, 19, August, 17 October 1930; 19 August, 6 October 1931; "Addresses," 24 September, 19 November 1930; 2 December 1931, PS 1351, 1359, 1363, 1389, 1643, 1675-A, 1377, 1419, 1725, HHP.

79. Harris Gaylord Warren, Herbert Hoover and the Great Depression (New York: Oxford University Press, 1967 ed.), pp. 73–74; "Expression of Pleasure on Approving Wagner-Graham Act," 10 February 1931, PS 1481, HHP; James Olson, "The End of Voluntarism," Annals of Iowa 41 (Fall 1972): 1107–13.

80. Secretary of Labor Doak supported the Davis-Kelley Bill for coal stabilization and Secretary of the Interior Wilbur endorsed the Nye Bill to legalize trade practice conference agreements, but Hoover endorsed neither. See New York Times (1 April 1932): 10, and Doak to Hoover, 17 February 1932, Coal File, PSF, HHP.

81. Hoover to Crocker, 21 May 1932, Unemployment File, PSF, HHP; Hoover, Press Statements, 25 March, 6 July 1932; Message to Congress, 11 July 1932, PS 1817, 1904, 1909, HHP.

82. "Statement by 122 Industrialists," 11 February 1932; "A Plea from Representatives of Independent Industrial Units," 11 February 1932; Hoover to Malcolm Whitman, 11 February 1932; Gordon Corbaley to Richey, 22 January 1932, all in Business File, PSF, HHP; Corbaley to Richey, 7 April 1932, Corbaley File, PSec, HHP.

83. Montague to Hoover, 15 March 1932; Hoover to Montague, 16 March 1932; both in Antitrust File, PSF, HHP; Galambos, Competition and Cooperation, pp. 183–84; Z. L. Potter to Lamont, 5, 17, 27 May 1932; Lamont to Potter, 12 May, 4 June 1932, File 83057, RG 40, NA.

84. Hoover to Daniel Willard, 20 May 1932; Hoover to Albert Cox, 10 June 1932; Hoover to Howard Coffin, 13 June 1932; Cox and others to Hoover, 10 June 1932; Coffin to Hoover, 12 June 1932, all in U.S. Council for National Defense File, PSF, HHP.

85. Romasco, Poverty, pp. 189–94; Warren, Hoover, pp. 143–47, 163–66; Hoover, "Address," 6 March 1932, PS 1803, HHP.

86. "Confidential History of the National Conference of Banking and Industrial Committees," Box 59, Ogden Mills Papers, LC; Romasco, Poverty, pp. 198–199.

87. Hoover, Memoirs, III, p. 40; Hoover to Franklin D. Roosevelt, 18 February 1933, Roosevelt File, PNF, HHP.

88. Hoover, "Acceptance Speech," 11 August 1932; "State of the Union Message," 6 December 1932; "Message to Congress on Vital Measures," 29 February 1933; "Endorsement of Share-the-Work Movement," 21 November 1932, PS 1939,

2078, 2128, 2061, HHP; Hoover to Edward Butler, 3 December 1932, James Rand File, PNF, HHP; Hoover to Shaw, 17 February 1933, Shaw File, PPF, HHP.

89. Galambos, *Competition and Cooperation*, p. 184; Hoover, "Address," 28 October 1932, PS 2019-A, HHP; Hoover to R. H. Hartley and Julius Meier, 11 July 1932, Antitrust File, PSF, HHP.

90. Eugene Lyons, *Herbert Hoover: A Biography* (Garden City, N.Y.: Doubleday and Co., 1964), p. 294.

91. Taylor to Roy Chapin, 6, 7 October 1932; Silas Strawn, "Progress Report on Anti-Trust Laws," both in File 82248/48, RG 40, NA; C. J. Junkin to Chapin, 20 January 1933, Box 103, Feiker Papers, RG 151, NA; Galambos, *Competition and Cooperation*, pp. 186–90.

92. See my *The New Deal and the Problem of Monopoly* (Princeton: Princeton University Press, 1966), pp. 35–52, 472–90.

93. For political reasons, both the New Dealers and the Hooverites tended to accentuate the differences, the former applying the label of "do-nothingism," the latter seeing the New Deal as a mixture of "socialist" and "fascist" ideas. Both images rest more on political invective than on dispassionate analysis, and the time seems long since past for laying both of them aside and recognizing both Hoover's activism and the limited aims of and changes wrought by the New Deal.

94. For arguments along this line, see Galambos, *Competition and Cooperation*, pp. 199–202; Olson, "End to Voluntarism," p. 1113; Otis L. Graham, Jr., "The Planning Ideal and American Reality," unpublished ms., author's files.

Herbert Hoover, the Commerce Secretariat, and the Vision of an "Associative State," 1921-1928

ELLIS W. HAWLEY

I N recent years, the traditional image of American governmental activity in the 1920s has been substantially altered. Delving beneath the older stereotypes of "normalcy" and "retrenchment," scholars have found unsuspected survivals of progressivism, a growing federal bureaucracy that tried to use as well as serve business groups, and an incipient form of "indicative planning" based on corporatist rather than classical economics. In many respects, they have concluded, the period should be viewed as the beginnings of the "modern era," not as a reversion to past patterns or as a frivolous and wasted interlude between progressivism and the New Deal.[1] And for some, the 1920s has more current relevance than the decades that followed, particularly in efforts to balance technological needs with America's individualistic heritage, build an international community without policing the world, and work out bureaucratic arrangements that would nourish individual, community, and private effort rather than supplant them.[2]

Ellis W. Hawley is professor of history in the University of Iowa.

[1] See, for example, Arthur S. Link, "What Happened to the Progressive Movement in the 1920's?" *American Historical Review*, XLIV (July 1959), 833-51; Clarke A. Chambers, *Seedtime of Reform: American Social Service and Social Action, 1918-1933* (Minneapolis, 1963); Donald C. Swain, *Federal Conservation Policy, 1921-1933* (Berkeley, 1963); Joseph Brandes, *Herbert Hoover and Economic Diplomacy: Department of Commerce Policy 1921-1928* (Pittsburgh, 1962); and Herbert Stein, *The Fiscal Revolution in America* (Chicago, 1969), 6-24. For discussions of the revisionist literature, see also Burl Noggle, "The Twenties: A New Historiographical Frontier," *Journal of American History*, LIII (Sept. 1966), 299-314; and Joan Hoff Wilson, ed., *The Twenties: The Critical Issues* (Boston, 1972), vii-xxv, 155-63.

[2] See, for example, Carl P. Parrini, *Heir to Empire: United States Diplomacy, 1916-1923* (Pittsburgh, 1969), 248-76; Joan Hoff Wilson, *American Business & Foreign Policy, 1920-1933* (Lexington, Ky., 1971), 239-41; William A. Williams, *The Contours of American History* (Chicago, 1966), 425-50; and Bruce A. Lohoff, "Herbert Hoover, Spokesman of Humane Efficiency: The Mississippi Flood of 1927," *American Quarterly*, XXII (Fall 1970), 690-700.

Thus far, however, partly because key collections were long closed, scholars have not examined in detail the most rapidly expanding sector of New Era governmental activity, that connected with Herbert Hoover's transformation and expansion of the commerce secretariat.[3] Nor has there been much study of the goals and ideology involved in his activities, of how he could reconcile his burgeoning bureaucratic domain with his deep distrust of "big government," or of how he hoped, through grafting corporatist and technocratic visions on to a base of nineteenth-century individualism, to build a superior socioeconomic order. Fuller study of such matters seems crucial to an understanding of Hoover and the New Era, and it is now possible with the aid of recently opened materials in the Hoover Papers to shed some further light on them.

Hoover in 1921 saw himself as the protagonist of a new and superior synthesis between the old industrialism and the new, a way whereby America could benefit from scientific rationalization and social engineering without sacrificing the energy and creativity inherent in individual effort, "grassroots" involvement, and private enterprise. Such a synthesis, he argued, would make the "American system" superior to any other, particularly in its ability to raise living standards, humanize industrial relationships, and integrate conflicting social elements into a harmonious community of interests.[4] And the key to its achievement, he had concluded on the basis of his wartime, engineering, and personal experience, lay in the development and proper use of cooperative institutions, particularly trade associations, professional societies, and similar organizations among farmers and laborers. These, Hoover and other associationists believed, would form a type of private government, one that would meet the need for national reform, greater stability, and steady expansion, yet avoid the evils long associated with "capital consolidations," politicized cartels, and governmental bureaucracies. Unlike the earlier trusts, these newer institutions would preserve and work through individual units, committing them voluntarily to service, efficiency, and ethical behavior and developing for them a new and enlightened leadership capable of seeing the larger picture. And

[3] Brandes, *Herbert Hoover*, deals only with the secretary's foreign economic activities, not with his attempts at domestic reform and reconstruction.

[4] Herbert Hoover, Public Statements 45, 47, 84, 102, 128, 129, Herbert Hoover Papers (Herbert Hoover Library, West Branch, Iowa); Herbert Hoover, *American Individualism* (Garden City, 1922), 54-56, 63-72; and Herbert Hoover, "We Can Cooperate and Yet Compete," *Nation's Business*, XIV (June 5, 1926), 11-14. See also E. E. Hunt, "Reconstruction," 18-28, and E. E. Hunt, "Looking to the Future," 1-2, E. E. Hunt Papers (Hoover Institute Archives, Stanford, Cal.); and Barry D. Karl, "Presidential Planning and Social Science Research: Mr. Hoover's Experts," *Perspectives in American History*, III (1969), 351-53.

unlike governmental bureaus, they would be flexible, responsive, and productive, built on service and efficiency rather than coercion and politics, and staffed by men of expertise and vision, not by self-serving politicians or petty drudges.[5]

To some extent, too, Hoover believed that the components of this associational order were evolving naturally and had been for the past thirty years. Within the womb of the old industrialism there had developed not only the associational structures around which the new system was taking shape but also the moral awakening, the commitment to science and productivity, and the mutuality of interests that would convert such structures into instruments of social progress. As these developments continued, the new private government would take shape on its own and bring with it the superior synthesis that Hoover envisioned. Yet there was no assurance that it would do so, or that it would develop fast enough to meet national needs. There was, so Hoover also believed, a need to manage, speed up, and guide this evolutionary process, both to help realize its full potentialities and to prevent those impatient with persisting social and economic problems from turning to undesirable statist solutions.[6] And to meet this need, he envisioned an "associative state,"[7] tied to, cooperating with, and helping to develop and guide the new associational order. Paradoxically, he saw himself both as an anti-statist and as an ardent champion of one form of positive government and national planning.

For two reasons, however, Hoover did not regard these positions as being inconsistent. In the first place, the structure and methods of the associative state would be different, thus enabling it to escape the torpor and rigidity characteristic of most governmental structures. In so far as possible, it would function through promotional conferences, expert inquiries, and cooperating committees, not through public enterprise, legal coercion, or arbitrary controls; and like the private groupings to which it

[5] See especially Hoover, *American Individualism*, 41-47; Hoover, Public Statements 306, 378, 496, 579, Hoover Papers; Hoover's foreword to the commerce department manual, *Trade Association Activities* (Washington, 1923). For what Hoover's associates thought they were building, see E. E. Hunt, "The Cooperative Committee and Conference System," Dec. 14, 1926, Hunt File, Commerce Papers-Official Files (CP-OF), Hoover Papers; New York *Times*, March 21, 1926; and P. G. Agnew, "A Step Toward Industrial Self-Government," *New Republic*, XLVI (March 17, 1926), 92-95.
[6] See especially Hoover, Public Statements 128, 232, 306, 486, Hoover Papers; Hoover, *American Individualism*, 10-17, 41-45, 53-56; and William Hard, "The New Hoover," *American Review of Reviews*, LXXVI (Nov. 1927), 483.
[7] The term is the author's not Hoover's. He and his associates usually employed such labels as the "Cooperative Committee and Conference System," the "American system," or "progressive democracy."

would be tied, it would be flexible, responsive, and productive, staffed by men of talent, vision, and expertise, and committed to nourishing individualism and local initiative rather than supplanting them. In the second place, the associative state would be needed only during a transitional phase.[8] Like the Marxist state or those posited by some European corporatists,[9] it would theoretically serve as midwife to a new, non-statist commonwealth and, having performed this function, would either wither away or revert to the status of umpire, caretaker, and symbol of unity.

Hoover's New Era activities were in part efforts to implement his vision of an associative state. For him the vision defined the difference between constructive and undesirable activism. Although some of what he did can be attributed to his ambivalent personality,[10] his adjustment of an engineering approach to political realities, his recognition of new technological problems, or his accommodation of business groups desirous of governmental services but reluctant to give up their own autonomy, many of his activities flowed logically from his postwar plans for associative "reconstruction" and particularly from his conviction that the commerce department, if properly expanded and transformed, could become the central agency for implementing such plans. When offered more prestigious positions, he chose and stuck with the secretaryship of commerce, chiefly he implied, because no other department had the same potential for guiding the associational activities that were transforming American society.[11] With Harding's assurance that he could remake the department and have a voice in labor, farm, financial, and foreign policies,[12] he moved into it, as Arthur

[8] See Hoover, "Waste in Government," May 22, 1925, Reorganization of Government File (ROGF), and Harold Stokes, "Memorandum for the Chief," Dec. 3, 1924, Commerce-Achievements File, CF-OF, Hoover Papers. Stokes' memorandum attempts to sum up Hoover's thinking and policies concerning "bureaucracy." It should be noted, however, that this theme of cooperative associationism as a substitute for and supplanter of statist activities became stronger as the decade progressed. In the immediate postwar period, Hoover sometimes coupled it with arguments in which his approach became an experimental prelude to legislation, a step toward a permanent business-government partnership, or simply a practical way to get things done. See, for example, Hoover's foreword to Elisha M. Friedman and others, *America and the New Era* (New York, 1920), xxiii-xxix; and Hoover to Warren G. Harding, Feb. 23, 1921, Warren G. Harding File, Pre-Commerce Correspondence, Hoover Papers.
[9] Matthew H. Elbow, *French Corporative Theory, 1789-1948* (New York, 1953), 159-62, 200-01.
[10] Craig Lloyd, *Aggressive Introvert: A Study of Herbert Hoover and Public Relations Management* (Columbus, Ohio, 1972).
[11] See Hoover's statements rejecting offers of the interior and agriculture departments. Public Statements 134, 278, 436, Hoover Papers. See also Herbert Hoover, *Larger Purposes of the Department of Commerce* (1928), speech of March 9, 1925, Commerce-Misc. File, CP-OF, Hoover Papers; and "What Secretary Hoover Hopes to Do," *Nation's Business*, 9 (May 1921), 45-46.
[12] Hoover to Harding, Feb. 23, 1921, Harding File, Pre-Commerce Correspondence, Hoover Papers; Herbert Hoover, *The Memoirs of Herbert Hoover: The Cabinet and the*

Schlesinger, Jr., says, much "as he might have into a bankrupt mining company a decade earlier,"[13] determined to convert a collection of miscellaneous technical bureaus into the governmental apparatus needed for an assured transition to an American utopia.

Hoover must have realized at the outset that such a task was not likely to be easy. He was beginning with one of the smallest and newest of the federal departments, one whose appropriations for 1920, exclusive of those for the census, had totaled only $17,000,000.[14] He could hardly be encouraged by the inability of his predecessor, William Redfield, to salvage some of the cooperative machinery established during the war.[15] And his plans were bound to collide with the strong sentiment for governmental retrenchment, the popular disdain for overly ambitious bureaucrats, and the entrenched positions of established bureaucratic domains. Yet there was also ground for optimism. Hoover's vision was an attractive and timely one, admirably suited to make him the "old order's candidate for ushering in the new";[16] and against the obstacles in his path, he could pit his immense prestige and formidable administrative talents, his following of dedicated personal associates, and his extensive ties to like-minded men in the worlds of business, engineering, journalism, scholarship, and social uplift.[17]

Before long, too, by drawing on a variety of recommendations,[18]

Presidency, 1920-1933 (New York, 1952), 36; Robert K. Murray, "President Harding and His Cabinet," *Ohio History*, 75 (Spring-Summer 1966), 113-14.

[13] Arthur M. Schlesinger, Jr., *Crisis of the Old Order 1919-1933* (Boston, 1957), 84.

[14] Computed from data in Carroll Wooddy, *The Growth of the Federal Government, 1915-1932* (New York, 1934). See also "The Department of Commerce," *Fortune*, XIX (June 1939), 53-59, 102-04.

[15] William C. Redfield, *With Congress and Cabinet* (Garden City, 1924), 216-19; and Robert F. Himmelberg, "Business, Antitrust Policy, and the Industrial Board of the Department of Commerce, 1919," *Business History Review*, XLII (Spring 1968), 4-5.

[16] Karl, "Presidential Planning," 408.

[17] Hoover's assets and connections are apparent in the dozens of letters and memoranda in his Commerce File and its subdivisions (CP-OF, Hoover Papers). See also Lloyd, *Aggressive Introvert*, 59-96, 130-38; and Carolyn Grin, "Herbert Hoover and the Social Responsibilities of the Expert," unpublished ms. (1971) (Herbert Hoover Library, West Branch, Iowa). For the broader context and the like-mindedness of New Era leaders, see Morrell Heald, *The Social Responsibilities of Business: Company and Community, 1900-1960* (Cleveland, 1970), 83-116; Edwin T. Layton, Jr., *The Revolt of the Engineers: Social Responsibility and the American Engineering Profession* (Cleveland, 1971), 179-224; Swain, *Federal Conservation Policy*, 13-20, 160-63; Grant McConnell, *Private Power & American Democracy* (New York, 1966), 57-68; Louis Galambos, *Competition & Cooperation: The Emergence of a National Trade Association* (Baltimore, 1966), 291-95; Alan R. Raucher, *Public Relations and Business, 1900-1929* (Baltimore, 1968), 65-74, 96-106; Samuel Haber, *Efficiency and Uplift* (Chicago, 1964), 156-67; and Joseph H. Foth, *Trade Associations* (New York, 1930).

[18] George Baldwin to Hoover, April 20, 24, 1921, Commerce-Reorganization File, CP-OF, Hoover Papers; Bureau of Efficiency, "Tentative Recommendations Relating to the Statistical Work of the Government," and E. L. Jones to Hoover, March 23, 1921, ROGF, *ibid.*;

Hoover was mapping out specific plans for departmental expansion. As visualized, his agency would eventually consist of three great divisions: one for industry, one for trade, and one for transportation and communication. Into the first, in addition to his own bureaus of fisheries and standards, should go the interior department's Bureau of Mines and patent office, plus a new Bureau of Federal Statistics, formed by joining the Census Bureau with the statistical programs of several other departments. Into the trade division, as adjuncts to his Bureau of Foreign and Domestic Commerce, should go the Bureau of Markets from the agriculture department, the foreign trade service and economic consulates from the state department, the Latin-American activities of the treasury department, and the research work of the Federal Trade Commission. And into the transportation and communication division, along with the lighthouse, steamboat, and mapping services, should go a part of the Coast Guard, the navy's Observatory, Hydrographic Office, and Steamboat Movement Service, the army's Lake Survey and Harbor Supervisors, the Panama Canal, the inland waterways, the shipping subsidies, and a new Bureau of Aeronautics. In essence, the commerce department was to become a department of economic development and management; other agencies would still be responsible for special sectors of the economy, but commerce would serve as a general policy coordinator.[19] In effect, as S. Parker Gilbert once put it, Hoover would be "Under-Secretary of all other departments."[20]

Reaching out from this expanded governmental base would be an extensive net of promotional activities, cooperating committees, and other ad hoc structures, all tied to private groupings and associations and all designed to energize private or local collectivities and guide them toward constructive solutions to national problems. From Hoover's standpoint, governmental reorganization was intended not only to reduce wasteful overlap and unwise expenditures, but also to provide the necessary base on which an associative state could be built. Hand in hand with his drive

E. G. Montgomery to Hoover, Sept. 7, 1921, Guy Emerson to Hoover, March 15, 1921, E. E. Pratt to A. C. Bedford, March 14, 1921, and "Brock-Kennedy Memorandum," March 1921, Commerce-Foreign and Domestic Commerce File (C-FDCF), *ibid.*; and F. T. Miller to Hoover, May 23, 1921, Federal Trade Commission File, *ibid.*

[19] The model fluctuated somehow, but the following make it fairly clear: Hoover to Walter Brown, Dec. 8, 1921, Commerce-Misc. File, CP-OF, Hoover Papers; Hoover's handwritten memorandum on reorganization, Commerce-Reorganization File, *ibid.*; Hoover, "Problem of the Reorganization of the Federal Government," May 23, 1921, ROGF, *ibid.*; Hoover to Albert Fall, Aug. 2, 1921, Interior Department File, *ibid.*; Christian Herter to J. MacMurray, April 15, 1921, State Department File, *ibid.* See also Hoover to Harding, Feb. 23, 1921, Harding File, Pre-Commerce Correspondence, *ibid.*

[20] Quoted in Oswald Garrison Villard, *Prophets True and False* (New York, 1928), 24.

for new jurisdictional boundaries went a series of conferences, negotiations, and "missionary activities," designed to forge cooperative links with the "community at large" and develop the associational apparatus that could speed up and manage socioeconomic progress. Assuming top priority in 1921 were the problems of housing, unemployment, industrial waste, stagnating foreign trade, and inadequate business planning; and in each of these problem areas, Hoover and his deputies were soon moving to resurrect and expand the voluntaristic-cooperationist side of the war government.[21]

Initially, Hoover hoped to secure the necessary jurisdictional base through the general executive reorganization that Wilson had advocated and Harding continued to push. Such action seemed thoroughly consistent with the demands for economy and efficiency, and since Hoover was serving as advisor to Walter F. Brown, chairman of the reorganization committee, he was optimistic about getting the agencies he needed.[22] Once involved, however, he quickly learned that proposals of this sort could generate resistance of the most intense kind. Agricultural leaders were already bitter about Hoover's wartime policies and quickly expressed their determined opposition to his acquiring either the Bureau of Markets or recognized jurisdiction over the marketing of farm goods.[23] State department officials, long irritated about the pretensions of commerce, were determined to expand their jurisdiction over economic activities abroad, not see it whittled away by inexperienced rivals.[24] Labor leaders regarded Harding's proposed department of welfare as a scheme to dismantle the

[21] Operating much as he had during World War I, Hoover commissioned selected deputies to organize the necessary machinery in each problem area. Miller, for example, handled housing, Hunt industrial waste and unemployment, Julius Klein the reshaping of trade promotion, and Frederick Feiker the new standardization and statistical programs. Feiker to Hoover, July 8, 1921, Commerce-Assistants File, CP-OF, Hoover Papers; Miller to Hoover, June 6, 1921, Building and Housing File, *ibid.*, William Rossiter to Hoover, Sept. 8, 1921, Unemployment File, *ibid.*; Feiker to Klein, Sept. 18, 1921, File No. 160.2, Records of the Bureau of Foreign and Domestic Commerce, RG 151 (National Archives); Hunt to Hoover, June 20, 1921, File No. 81037, Feiker to George Babcock, July 26, 1921, File No. 81368, General Records of the Department of Commerce, RG 40 (National Archives).

[22] *National Municipal Review*, X (Aug. 1921), 436; New York *Times*, Aug. 28, 1921; Hoover to Brown, Dec. 8, 1921, Commerce-Misc. File, CP-OF, Hoover Papers.

[23] See Edward L. and Frederick H. Schapsmeier, "Disharmony in the Harding Cabinet," *Ohio History*, LXXV (Spring-Summer 1966), 127-28, 135; James H. Shideler, *Farm Crisis, 1919-1923* (Berkeley, 1957), 143-46; and Hoover's unsent letter to Milton Shreve, May 22, 1924, ROGF, CP-OF, Hoover Papers. For the earlier conflict, see Donald Winters, "The Hoover-Wallace Controversy during World War I," *Annals of Iowa*, XXXIX (Spring 1969), 586-97.

[24] Brandes, *Hoover and Economic Diplomacy*, 41-42; Herter to F. M. Dearing, May 3, 1921, C-FDCF, CP-OF, Hoover Papers. Hoover was forced to threaten resignation in order to block a measure giving the state department jurisdiction over all activities abroad.

Department of Labor and charged that Hoover's designs on the Bureau of Labor Statistics were part of this broader plot.[25] Governmental statisticians, at least in Hoover's view, reacted emotionally, turning their bureaus into virtual "hornets' nests."[26] Naval leaders, to his surprise and resentment, lobbied against turning anything over to the "politicians."[27] And conservationists, especially those attached to the Forest Service, protested strongly about the proposed transfers to Albert Fall's Department of the Interior.[28] Against the forces of scientific rationality, Hoover came to feel, had gathered an alliance of "vested officials," "paid propagandists," and selfish interest groups, and these enemies of progress had created a "confusing fog of opposition."[29]

Whether right or not, Hoover was unable to get a reorganization measure through, either by going along with interdepartmental bargaining and lowering his own sights or by urging that scientific experts hand a plan "down from on high." In the face of conflicting pressures, Congress simply refused to act.[30] And its failure to do so meant that jurisdictional expansion by the commerce secretariat would come not through some master coup, but through the slower processes of pushing established bureaus into "power vacuums," adding new structures through special laws or administrative innovations, making deals with or raids on other agencies, and carving out "spheres of influence" inhabited by cooperative satellites. By the time he had given up on general reorganization, Hoover was moving along all these lines, and as his operations gained momentum he was expanding slowly both his departmental boundaries and the network of associational activities to which the commerce department was tied.

Under his tutelage, for example, the Bureau of Foreign and Domestic Commerce was reorganized along commodity lines, staffed with men from the export industries themselves, and made the center of an associational

---

[25] *American Federationist*, XXVIII (June, Oct., Nov., Dec. 1921), 503-04, 872, 967-68, 1038; *Christian Science Monitor*, May 20, 1921; Hoover to George Huddleston, May 24, 1921, Hoover to James Davis, May 26, 1921, Labor Dept. File, CP-OF, Hoover Papers.

[26] Hoover to Roger Babson, April 19, 1922, Babson to Hoover, April 15, 1922, ROGF, CP-OF, Hoover Papers.

[27] See "Some Statements by Captain Bassett and the Answers," and Hoover to the *Scientific American*, Jan. 28, 1924, *ibid*.

[28] Clarence Stetson to Edgar Rickard, Jan. 5, 1922, *ibid*.; New York *Times*, Feb. 26, 1922; Donald L. Winters, *Henry Cantwell Wallace as Secretary of Agriculture, 1921-1924* (Urbana, Ill., 1970), 161-89.

[29] Hoover, "Waste in Government," May 22, 1925, ROGF, CP-OF, Hoover Papers.

[30] Hoover to Daniel Rogers, Feb. 3, 1922, Hoover to Brown, Jan. 24, April 7, 1924, Hoover to Calvin Coolidge, Dec. 27, 1924, Hoover, Statement before Joint Committee on Reorganization, Jan. 21, 1924, *ibid*.; Washington *Star*, Jan. 22, 1924, April 21, 1925; New York *Times*, Jan. 6, 31, Feb. 3, Aug. 30, 1925; *Congressional Digest*, IV (March 1925), 195.

system for gathering and disseminating commercial intelligence, dealing with foreign governments and cartels, and organizing trade and investment activities into a rational and integrated set of operations. Tied to and working in conjunction with each commodity division was a cooperating industrial committee, chosen typically by the trade and export associations in the field; and ideally it was these cooperating private groups that would build and develop the steadily expanding market needed for permanent prosperity. The state would act only as a clearing house, inspirational force, and protector of international rights, not as a trader, investor, or detailed regulator. And it was for the former functions that Hoover won larger and larger appropriations, set up one appendage after another, and kept expanding his network of trade commissioners, researchers, and public relations men. By 1925 the bureau's appropriations had risen 140 percent; services rendered, so it claimed, were up 600 percent; and in six months, according to its energetic director, Julius Klein, it had issued "more than enough" press releases "to put 18 columns of type up and down the Washington Monument."[31]

In attempting to expand its jurisdictional boundaries, the Bureau of Foreign and Domestic Commerce was less successful. In the areas of economic diplomacy and international finance, its role remained a limited one, thus hampering Hoover's efforts to guide overseas investment into proper channels. Nor did it ever succeed in taking over the foreign economic services of the Department of State and the Department of Agriculture. Yet its domain did expand. Its new financial division offered advice on foreign loans and investments; its research and public relations arms assumed responsibility for a new program of domestic market analysis, a massive publicity campaign against foreign "monopolies," and a world-wide search for independent sources of raw materials; and its foreign service, to the accompaniment of much friction with the state department, kept expanding and strengthening its intelligence apparatus. In 1922, in return for giving suitable credit to consular officials, it secured the right to request information from them through the diplomatic head of mission. In 1924, it secured an executive order directing all representatives abroad to meet and exchange information at least every two weeks. In 1927, it was given permanent legislative status. And repeatedly, when state department critics struck back

[31] Brandes, *Hoover and Economic Diplomacy*, 4-17; Hoover to Harding, June 15, 1923, ROGF, CP-OF, Hoover Papers; "BFDC Appropriations, 1925-26," Commerce-Appropriations File, *ibid.*; Klein to Hoover, Oct. 15, 1925, Commerce-Publicity File, *ibid.*; "Development of the BFDC," Box 6, Robert Lamont Papers, General Records of the Department of Commerce.

by charging it with wasteful duplication and diplomatic bungling, the bureau was able to defend successfully its claim to special expertise.[32]

At the same time, the Bureau of Standards was also doubling its personnel, expanding its jurisdiction, and transforming itself from a "research laboratory for governmental departments" into a sponsor of associational reform, particularly in the areas of research, housing, and industrial efficiency. By the mid-1920s, it was cooperating with some forty private associations to develop new and better products.[33] Its Building and Housing Division, launched in 1921, had become the nucleus of a network of cooperating committees and study groups, each tied to the major trade and professional associations in the housing field and each trying, through organized cooperation and educational campaigns, to overcome the "bottlenecks" that held back "modernization" and "rationalization."[34] The bureau's Division of Simplified Practice, inspired by the war experience and the *Waste in Industry* study of the Federated American Engineering Societies, was directing a similar effort to reduce industrial waste, one that functioned through standardization conferences and implemented its "simplified practice recommendations" through associational cooperation.[35] And attached to the bureau, as further agencies of what its publicists were calling the "new conservation," were such quasipublic organs as the national committees on wood and metals utilization, the one to conserve lumber and find new uses for lumber by-products, the other to reduce wastage of metals.[36] Taken together, so the Hooverites claimed, the new activities had the potentiality for raising living standards 20 to 30 percent.[37]

Similar growth and transformation also occurred in the Census Bureau,

[32] Brandes, *Hoover and Economic Diplomacy*, 43-46, 51-57, 106-28, 153-63, 171, 183, 201, 215-19; Parrini, *Heir to Empire*, 185-201; Wilson, *Business & Foreign Policy*, 107-19; Frank Surface to Hoover, July 11, 1927, Klein to Hoover, July 22, Aug. 3, 1922, Herter to Klein, Oct. 23, 1923, Exec. Order 3987, April 4, 1924, Hoover to Charles Evans Hughes, Feb. 28, 1925, Hoover to Frank Kellogg, Jan. 18, April 13, 1926, J. Marrinan to Klein, Dec. 21, 1925, C-FDCF, CP-OF, Hoover Papers.

[33] Wooddy, *Federal Government*, 479-88; "National Bureau of Standards under Hoover," Commerce-Standards File, CP-OF, Hoover Papers.

[34] Hoover to Harding, Feb. 9, 1922, "Better Homes and Decreased Costs," Jan. 11, 1928, Building and Housing File, CP-OF, Hoover Papers.

[35] "Work of the DSP, 1921-28," Commerce-Achievements File, *ibid.*; E. E. Hunt, "Elimination of Waste Program," March 18, 1925, Elimination of Waste File, *ibid.*; W. Durgin to Hoover, Nov. 1, 1922, File No. 82341, General Records of the Department of Commerce.

[36] W. C. Wetherill, "Work of the National Committee on Metals Utilization," Jan. 14, 1928, Committees-Metal Utilization File, CP-OF, Hoover Papers; E. E. Hunt, "National Committee on Wood Utilization," April 28, 1926, Conference-Wood Utilization File, *ibid.*

[37] Hunt, "Elimination of Waste Program," March 18, 1925, Elimination of Waste File, *ibid.*

which, in spite of Hoover's inability to carry out his original plans, added new services to facilitate business planning and tied these to private associational activities. In July 1921, acting in consultation with business leaders and statistical experts, the bureau launched the *Survey of Current Business*, designed to publish data on current production, prices, and inventories, most of it supplied by cooperating trade associations. In 1922, when antitrust action threatened private statistical exchanges, it sprouted a special appendage, which, for a time, mailed out data submitted by private groups. Simultaneously, it added more and more data-gathering programs for particular industries, and after 1925, when new court rulings again sanctioned private exchanges, it remained the focal point for promoting them. From a bureau expected to lapse into inactivity during intercensal periods, it had transformed itself into a dynamic sponsor of the "new competition," which, by encouraging cooperative data gathering and educating business decision makers to respond properly, was supposed to stabilize the economy without sacrificing competitive incentives and safeguards.[38]

Building on existing bureaus, Hoover was moving to implement his original designs, both of an expanded departmental jurisdiction and of an associational bureaucratic structure. And while a few critics charged that he was fostering either "big government" or "monopoly,"[39] he and his publicists were highly successful in bucking the sentiment for "economy in government" and selling their programs to the President, the budget bureau, the appropriations committees, the business community, and the general public. Their bureaucracy, they kept saying, was "different." Unlike the typical variety, with its tax eating propensities, red tape, and rigid controls, this new species paid returns on the money "invested" by generating new expansion and new revenue, delivered efficient and businesslike service, and functioned under "responsive" and competent men, who understood national needs and "cooperated" instead of "meddling." Besides, its whole purpose differed. By building industrial self-government

[38] Wooddy, *Federal Government*, 488-92; *Survey of Current Business*, July 1921; Hoover to Harding, June 9, 1921, Presidential File, CP-OF, Hoover Papers; Census Advisory Committee to Hoover, May 7, 1921, "Census Bureau Activities, 1922," Commerce-Census File, *ibid.*; David Wing, "Cooperation with Trade Associations," Commerce-Trade Association Statistics File, *ibid.*; William M. Steuart to W. Snyder, March 21, 1925, File No. 81288, General Record of the Department of Commerce.

[39] Hoover's most outspoken critics were Senators William King of Utah, Kenneth McKellar of Tennessee, and James A. Reed of Missouri. In addition, he sometimes had heated exchanges with farm leaders, rural progressives, antitrusters, and the targets of his "imperialism" in other departments. See Brandes, *Hoover and Economic Diplomacy*, 150-51; Samuel Untermyer, *Honest and Dishonest Trade Associations* (1922); and *Congressional Record*, 68 Cong., 1 Sess., LXV, 7624-7625, 69 Cong., 1 Sess., LXVII, 11859.

and thus reducing the need for governmental controls, it was actually checking the whole movement toward big government; and by fostering and nourishing the grassroots activities of private groups and local communities, it was promoting democratic decentralization rather than bureaucratic centralism.[40]

The same rationale also helped Hoover to become the administrative beneficiary of new laws. In 1924, for example, when he finally secured a measure to regulate the Alaskan salmon industry, few questioned his assumption that the Bureau of Fisheries should administer it or that cooperative arrangements with the canners' association should remain a central feature of regulatory practice.[41] In 1926, when his long campaign for aviation aids and controls led to the Air Commerce Act, he was able to add an Aeronautics Branch with its own outcropping of cooperative committees and associations.[42] And in 1927, after the courts had upset his informal controls in the radio industry, a new law was passed, creating a commission to allocate frequencies but entrusting all administration to his Radio Division and permitting private associations to implement large areas of "self-regulation."[43] In these special areas, special because of the public nature of the industries involved and the unquestioned federal jurisdiction, Hoover was ready to establish some measure of legal coercion, at least temporarily. But still, he argued, these governmental ground rules should

[40] For examples, see Hoover to Harding, June 24, 1922, J. Marrinan, "Publicity Policy," March 29, 1926, C-FDCF, CP-OF, Hoover Papers; Hoover to Charles G. Dawes, Sept. 6, 1921, Hoover to Coolidge, Nov. 5, 1923, Treasury File, *ibid.*; Klein to Hoover, Nov. 15, 1922, Commerce-Appropriations File, *ibid.*; UP Dispatch, Sept. 24, 1924, Commerce-Misc. File, *ibid.* See also Alfred Dennis' article in *Saturday Evening Post*, CXCVII (June 6, 1925), 8-9, 181-82, 184-86; and testimony in House Appropriations Committee, *Department of Commerce Bill, 1925* (Washington, 1924), 1-8, 37-49; *Appropriations, Department of Commerce, 1926* (Washington, 1925), 14-17, 214; and *Appropriations, Department of Commerce, 1927* (Washington, 1926), 2-6, 220-26.

[41] Richard A. Cooley, *Politics of Conservation: The Decline of the Alaskan Salmon* (New York, 1963), 106-27; New York *Journal of Commerce*, May 29, 1924; Hoover to Scott Bone, Feb. 14, 1923, Hoover to William Greene, Feb. 17, 1924, Hoover to Henry O'Malley, Feb. 28, 1924, Alaska File, CP-OF, Hoover Papers. Even such strong critics as Senator King and "Fighting Dan" Sutherland of Alaska, both of whom claimed that Hoover's previous reservation system had fostered a "fish trust," tried only to limit the discretionary powers to be exercised by the secretary of commerce.

[42] *Fourteenth Annual Report of the Secretary of Commerce* (Washington, 1926), 53-54; Donald Whitnah, *Safer Skyways: Federal Control of Aviation, 1926-1966* (Ames, 1966), 10-25; E. S. Gregg, "Development of Civil Aviation," Sept. 19, 1925, Commerce-Aeronautics File, CP-OF, Hoover Papers. Only a few persons seemed to agree with George Huddleston when he declared that since Hoover had "already been made dictator of the radio," he should not be made "lord of the air" as well. *Congressional Record*, 69 Cong., 1 Sess., LXVII, 7317-7319.

[43] Erik Barnouw, *A Tower in Babel* (New York, 1966), 189-201; Glenn Johnson, "Secretary of Commerce Herbert C. Hoover: The First Regulator of American Broadcasting" (doctoral dissertation, University of Iowa, 1970), 207-31.

provide the base for a developing associationalism, not a substitute for it. And this was the approach adopted by his new and rapidly expanding regulatory arms.[44]

In addition, through a process of bargaining with and pressuring other departments, Hoover was able to capture some of the agencies that he had tried but failed to capture through a general governmental reorganization. Negotiations with the treasury department brought him the Bureau of Customs Statistics, transferred in 1923, plus effective control of the Inter-American High Commission, designed to promote trade in Latin-America.[45] Negotiations with the agriculture department garnered the seismology section of the Weather Bureau, plus the statistical programs for the wool, naval stores, meat packing, and farm machinery industries.[46] And in his greatest coup, negotiations with the interior department produced executive orders in 1925 giving him the Patent Office, the Geological Survey's work in mineral statistics, and the Bureau of Mines.[47]

Most of these new accessions were tied to Hoover's associational reform efforts. Those from the treasury department became part of the Bureau of Foreign and Domestic Commerce's program of trade expansion through associational activities. The statistical programs from the agriculture department became part of the broader effort to stabilize the economy through decentralized business planning. And the mineral agencies from the interior department finally provided a departmental base for Hoover's efforts to stabilize the coal and oil industries, areas in which he had early staked a claim of special competence and received special grants of authority from Harding and Coolidge. By 1925 he and his lieutenants had been largely

[44] *Fourteenth Annual Report of the Secretary of Commerce*, 53-54, 197-98; *Fifteenth Annual Report of the Secretary of Commerce* (Washington, 1927), 44-46; Hoover to G. Lockwood, May 8, 1926, Hoover, Statement on Radio Legislation, May 1926, Radio Legislation File, CP-OF, Hoover Papers; Hoover, Statement on Commercial Aviation, Sept. 24, 1925, Commerce-Aeronautics File, *ibid.*

[45] Advisory Statistical Committee to Hoover, April 8, 1921, Hoover to Andrew Mellon, April 11, 1921, Hoover to Harding, May 17, 1922, ROGF, CP-OF, Hoover Papers; Herter to Herring, April 11, 1921, Mellon to Harding, Nov. 30, 1921, Press Release, Dec. 19, 1921, Inter-American High Commission File, *ibid.*; Wooddy, *Federal Government*, 175.

[46] Steuart to Hoover, April 6, 1922, Hoover to Wallace, April 3, 1924, Commerce-Census File, CP-OF, Hoover Papers; Hoover to Wallace, Aug. 16, 17, 1922, Wallace to Hoover, Sept. 1, 1922, Commerce-Coast and Geodetic Survey File, *ibid.*; Wooddy, *Federal Government*, 218, 490.

[47] Hoover to Hubert Work, June 3, 1925, Interior Dept. File, CP-OF, Hoover Papers; Hoover to J. Spurr, June 10, 1925, Exec. Order 4239, June 4, 1925, Commerce-Mines File, *ibid.*; Wooddy, *Federal Government*, 180, 472, 475. In return, the interior department was to acquire the Geodetic Survey; but this required legislation, which, despite Hoover's endorsement, never seemed to get through. See Work to Hoover, July 9, 1927, Hoover to Work, July 12, Oct. 26, 1927, Rickard to Hoover, Jan. 29, 1928, ROGF, CP-OF, Hoover Papers.

responsible for an associational program intended to reduce intermittent production in the coal industry, for setting up and administering an emergency distribution program during the coal strike of 1922, for directing the subsequent studies of the United States Coal Commission, and for guiding the work of the Federal Oil Conservation Board.[48] Through extradepartmental and ad hoc bodies, they had largely taken over the whole field of mineral conservation and management, relegating the established interior agencies to a secondary role; the annexations of 1925 were in part merely a recognition of this *fait accompli*.

At the same time, in further efforts to implement his original plans, Hoover was trying either to convert other departments into cooperative satellites, preempt their domains through the sponsorship of new associational bureaucracies, or fill "power vacuums" into which they had been slow to move. In his relations with the interior department, he pursued all three approaches; and once Albert Fall had been replaced by the cooperative and colorless Hubert Work, the efforts of the secretary of commerce to set up associational machinery in such areas as power and waterway development, transportation improvement, and construction planning met with little resistance.[49] In each of these areas, Hoover soon established networks of cooperating committees and allied associations, and in each of them the commerce secretariat assumed new responsibilities for making policy, stimulating "grass-roots" activity, and fostering "industrial self-government."

In the power field, Hoover tried to devise a "middle way" by seizing on the idea of "superpower," the notion of regionally coordinated and technically advanced power networks developed by a cooperative alliance of state agencies, private groups, and public-minded engineers.[50] First set

[48] Ellis W. Hawley, "Secretary Hoover and the Bituminous Coal Problem, 1921-1928," *Business History Review*, XLII (Autumn 1968), 254-64; Coal Memorandum, April 16, 1923, Hunt to Hoover, April 1, 1926, Hoover to U.S. Coal Commission, Nov. 1, 1922, Coal File, CP-OF, Hoover Papers; F. R. Wadleigh, "Herbert Hoover and the Coal Industry," *Coal Age*, 33 (April 1928), 213-14; Hoover to Work, Aug. 5, 1926, with accompanying draft of Federal Oil Conservation Board report, Oil-Federal Oil Conservation Board File, CP-OF, Hoover Papers.

[49] Henry Pringle, "Hubert Work, M.D.," *Outlook*, 150 (Sept. 5, 1928), 723-26, 754; Eugene P. Trani, "Hubert Work and the Department of the Interior, 1923-28," *Pacific Northwest Quarterly*, 61 (Jan. 1970), 37, 40.

[50] Initially, Hoover seemed to favor federally chartered regional corporations, owned and managed by private interests but operating under Interstate Commerce Commission supervision and in accordance with publicly sponsored engineering surveys. He later shifted his emphasis to "coordinated state regulation," and since he was reluctant to provide targets for the "Norrises and LaFollettes," the resulting studies always seemed to

forth in "superpower surveys" sponsored by the interior and war departments, this vision received wide publicity in the early 1920s. Beginning as a member of the interior department's Superpower Advisory Committee, Hoover quickly assumed leadership, worked with the surveyors, especially with engineer William S. Murray, to promote the idea, and began organizing the necessary cooperative alliance. The practical results of his efforts were minimal, partly because of the increasingly acrimonious polarization of power politics. But by 1924 he had set up a Northeastern Super Power Committee with himself as chairman and assistant Paul Clapp as secretary, surrounded this with an apparatus of study groups and publicity campaigns, and tied the governmental activities to interlocking private committees representing the power producers and consumers, the Chamber of Commerce, and the utility engineers.[51]

Pushing the same type of cooperative machinery, the commerce department also took the initiative in promoting waterway development and transportation reform. Around such Hoover-chaired commissions as those for the Colorado and St. Lawrence rivers, there developed an "educational campaign" to promote a national waterway plan, plus extensive ties to a web of waterway associations and reclamation groups.[52] In conjunction with Hoover-dominated presidential committees or special presidential assignments, there developed a largely unimplemented vision of how industry and government could cooperate to modernize and rationalize the railroad and shipping industries.[53] And tied to the Transportation Division

confine themselves to physical rather than structural problems. See Hoover to William S. Murray, May 31, June 9, 1921, Murray to Hoover, June 7, 29, 1921, Interior Department File, CP-OF, Hoover Papers; Advisory Board Minutes, Superpower Survey, June 23, 1921, Hoover, Statement to Superpower Conference, Oct. 13, 1923, Hoover to H. L. Stimson, Jan. 17, 1925, Superpower File, *ibid.*; Harold Stokes, "Public Relations of Superpower," July 16, 1924, Conferences-Superpower File, *ibid.*

[51] Northeastern Super Power Committee, *Super Power Studies* (1924); W. P. Lay, *Southern Super Power Zone* (1922); William Murray, *Superpower* (New York, 1925), 37-45, 68-72, 147-55; San Francisco *Chronicle*, Sept. 15, 1921; Boston *Globe*, April 8, 23, 1922; Washington *Star*, July 21, 1924; Hoover to Murray, Aug. 22, 1923, Hoover to Ezra Whitman, Oct. 20, 1923, Murray to Hoover, Sept. 30, Dec. 18, 1923, Hoover, Addresses, May 19, 1922, Oct. 13, 1923, Super Power File, CP-OF, Hoover Papers; Harold Stokes, "Public Relations of Superpower," July 16, 1924, Conferences-Superpower File, *ibid.*

[52] Swain, *Federal Conservation Policy*, 99-102; Los Angeles *Examiner*, Sept. 14, 1926; "History of the Colorado River Commission," Publicity File, Colorado River Materials, Hoover Papers; Hoover, "Organization of the Columbia Basin Irrigation Project," Sept. 4, 1926, Hoover, Statement before House Rivers and Harbors Committee, Jan. 30, 1926, Hoover to J. P. Goodrich, May 8, 1925, W. W. Morse to Hoover, May 10, 1926, Paul Clapp to E. S. Gregg, Oct. 16, 1926, St. Lawrence Commission, "Report and Recommendations," Jan. 3, 1927, Hoover, "St. Lawrence Shipway," March 12, 1927, Waterways File, CP-OF, *ibid.*; Hoover, Addresses, July 20, Aug. 21, Nov. 22, 1926, Public Statements 611, 624, 673, *ibid.*; Hunt, "Looking to the Future," 20-32, Box 19, Hunt Papers.

[53] "Report of Sub-Committee on Coordination of Rail and Steamship Activities" (1924),

of the Bureau of Foreign and Domestic Commerce was the cooperative machinery generated by a series of conferences with interested associations. From those in 1923, for instance, had come the establishment of regional shipping boards, designed to work with the railroads for purposes of eliminating periodic car shortages;[54] and from the National Conference on Street and Highway Safety, held in 1924, had come agencies for safety education and the promotion of uniform traffic control laws.[55]

Still another line of activity in which the commerce department took the initiative was that of construction planning. To Hoover and a number of his associates,[56] the development of a "balance wheel" through the proper timing of public works and new construction had long seemed highly desirable; once in office, he took the lead in organizing and directing the Unemployment Conference of September 1921, using the conference machinery to push construction activities during the recession, calling for a cutback during the subsequent boom, and urging, through such conference offshoots as the Business Cycle Committee and the Committee on Seasonal Operations, that private groups adopt regularization programs and governments set up public works reserves.[57] In this field, as in those previously noted, a commerce-dominated "adhocracy" took shape, most of it directed by Edward Eyre Hunt, the Hoover aide who served as secretary to the Unemployment Conference and its offshoots. Working in conjunction with

"Report of Committee on Matters affecting the Merchant Marine," Dec. 29, 1924, Committee File, CP-OF, Hoover Papers; Hoover to L. C. Palmer, Jan. 24, 28, 1924, Hoover, Statement before the Joint Committee on Reorganization, Jan. 24, 1924, "Memo for HH," Sept. 29, 1925, Shipping Board File, *ibid.*; Hoover, Statement before ICC, Feb. 3, 1922, Hoover to N. Gould, Feb. 24, 1922, Hoover to Ernest Lewis, June 16, 1922, Railroads File, *ibid.*; Hoover, "Railroad Reorganization," April 1923, Railroads Consolidation File, CP-Personal, *ibid.*

[54] Hoover to R. H. Aishton, April 6, 1923, Hoover to Alfred Pope, Dec. 11, 1923, M. J. Gormley to Hoover, June 11, 1923, D. Conn to Hoover, March 3, 1926, Hoover, Statement to Transportation Conference, Jan. 9, 1924, Railroads File, CP-OF, *ibid.*

[55] "Report of the National Conference on Street and Highway Safety," March 25, 1926, Press Releases, April 19, 1924, Dec. 16, 17, 1924, Oct. 15, 1926, Conference-Traffic Safety File, *ibid.*

[56] Particularly prominent in the movement were Otto T. Mallery of the Pennsylvania Industrial Board, John B. Andrews of the American Association for Labor Legislation, Joseph Defrees of the Chamber of Commerce, Samuel M. Lindsay of Columbia University, Sam Lewisohn, investment banker and spokesman for business progressivism, and Edward Eyre Hunt, Hoover's aide and trouble-shooter.

[57] Hunt, "Washington Conference on Unemployment," Jan. 3, 1922, Press Releases, Dec. 17, 1921, Feb. 5, March 8, 1922, July 21, 1924, "Business Cycles and Unemployment" (1923), Hoover to Owen Young, May 17, 1923, Unemployment File, CP-OF, Hoover Papers; Hoover to Ernest Trigg, May 28, 1923, Seasonal Industries File, *ibid.*; Hoover to Harding, March 2, 17, 1923, Hoover to John Leary, May 8, 1923, Construction File, *ibid.*; Hunt, "Business Cycles and Unemployment," Oct. 1, 1927, Box 21, Hunt Papers; Carolyn Grin, "The Unemployment Conference of 1921: An Experiment in Rational Cooperative Planning," *Mid-America*, LV (April 1973), 83-107.

Hunt and his associates was the American Construction Council, a private stabilizing agency that Hoover helped to set up in 1922. And trying to mold public opinion into a force capable of securing the desired public and private actions were such attached "missionaries" as Otto T. Mallery of Pennsylvania and John B. Andrews of the American Association for Labor Legislation.[58]

In many respects, too, Hoover functioned as the real secretary of labor and proceeded to organize associational reform efforts in that field. It was Hoover, not "Puddler Jim" Davis, who sponsored the Unemployment Conference and tried to meet the unemployment crisis through expanded construction activities. Even more indicative of his role, it was Hoover rather than Davis who took the lead in pressuring the steel industry into giving up its twelve-hour day, urging business and labor groups to develop programs of unemployment insurance, and trying to substitute cooperation for conflict in the railroad and coal industries.[59] Davis thought it more important to be at a meeting of the Loyal Order of Moose than at the Unemployment Conference. And while he sometimes complained about Hoover's expanding machinery and activities, he was usually content to echo Hoover's policies and allow what remained of the labor department to atrophy.[60]

Although the labor department retained its welfare agencies and efforts to create a new department in the welfare field had been blocked, a new welfare "adhocracy" was taking shape, attached, appropriately enough in an era of welfare capitalism, to the Department of Commerce. To deal with problems of housing, child welfare, and emergency relief, Hoover

[58] Hunt, "Business Cycles and Unemployment," Oct. 1, 1927, Box 21, Hunt Papers; John Gries to Hoover, March 9, 1922, Hoover to R. Marshall, March 10, 1922, W. S. Hays to Hoover, April 30, 1922, Hoover, Addresses, April 4, June 19, 1922, Franklin D. Roosevelt to Hoover, Jan. 13, 1928, Mallery to Hoover, Aug. 24, 1923, Jan. 7, 18, 1926, Construction File, CP-OF, Hoover Papers; Mallery to Hoover, Feb. 7, 1928, Unemployment File, *ibid.*; Hoover to Roosevelt, May 24, 1923, Building and Housing File, *ibid.*; New York *Times*, May 15, June 4, 1922, May 17, June 1, 1923; *Municipal and County Engineering*, LXIX (Dec. 1925), 295-96.

[59] Robert H. Zieger, *The Republicans and Labor, 1919-1929* (Lexington, Ky., 1969), 87-106, 123, 131-43, 199-211; Mark Hatfield, "Herbert Hoover and Labor" (master's thesis, Stanford University, 1948), 40-47, 57; Hoover to Samuel Sibley, Feb. 2, 1922, Hoover to Hale Holden, Jan. 30, 1924, Hoover to Everett Sanders, Dec. 12, 1925, Railroads File, CP-OF, Hoover Papers; Hoover to C. J. Goodyear, Jan. 26, 1924, Hoover to Julius Barnes, Jan. 28, 1924, Hoover to Coolidge, Feb. 20, 1924, Coal File, *ibid.*; Hoover to Harding, April 8, May 4, Nov. 1, 1922, June 13, 1923, Twelve-Hour Day File, *ibid.*; Hoover, Address, Jan. 27, 1923, Hoover to Samuel Gompers, Feb. 19, 1923, Unemployment Insurance File, *ibid.*

[60] Davis to Hoover, Sept. 19, Oct. 5, 1921, Unemployment File, CP-OF, Hoover Papers; Davis to Hoover, April 5, 1924, Twelve-Hour Day File, *ibid.*; Zieger, *Republicans and Labor*, 59-60.

put together associational structures similar to those used to tackle economic problems.[61] At the centers of these structures, stimulating and guiding them toward "constructive action," were men who were also serving as officials or associates of the commerce secretariat.

In the housing field, for instance, Hoover was concerned not only with stabilizing the construction industries and breaking the "blockade" against mass production but also with relieving a national housing shortage, fostering urban zoning and planning, and securing the social stability and "spiritual values" inherent in widespread home ownership.[62] John Gries, who headed the Building and Housing Division, came to think of his organization not only as a "division of construction" but also as a housing expediter, "bureau of municipalities," and social stabilizer. And to fulfill these added responsibilities, new campaigns of associational reform were constantly launched. The division was soon working with the Chamber of Commerce to devise community housing plans, with the American Institute of Architects to set up small house service bureaus, with a network of expert committees and cooperating interest groups to develop model building codes and model zoning and planning laws, and with realtors, loan associations, and interested philanthropists to educate prospective home owners and develop better methods of mortgage and construction financing.[63]

In addition, Hoover utilized an organization known as Better Homes in America to carry on a massive educational campaign, one that reached out through some 3,600 local committees and a host of affiliated groups to provide exhibits of model homes, foster better "household management," promote research in the housing field, and generate a "greater, steadier, and more discriminating demand for improved dwellings," especially for families with "small incomes." Originally founded by Marie Meloney of the *Delineator*, Better Homes had first operated independently. But in late 1923, seeing the potentialities in the organization and taking advantage

[61] See Hoover's statement for the *Christian Science Monitor*, March 25, 1925, Building and Housing File, CP-OF, Hoover Papers.
[62] Social and spiritual values of home ownership were especially common themes with Hoover. For examples, see his statement for *Liberty Magazine*, May 11, 1926, Building and Housing File, CP-OF, Hoover Papers; and his foreword to Better Homes in America, *Guidebook for Better Homes Campaign* (1924), 5-6.
[63] Gries to Hoover, Aug. 24, 1921, Feb. 16, 1922, Nov. 28, 1924, Gries to Stokes, Feb. 11, 1926, F. T. Miller to Hoover, April 1, 1921, Hoover to Defrees, April 19, 1921, Hoover to Harding, Feb. 9, 1922, Hoover to Irving Hiett, May 1, 1922, Hoover to Edwin Brown, April 9, 1924, Hoover to Willoughby Walling, March 5, 14, 21, 1925, "Better Homes and Decreased Costs," Jan. 11, 1928, "Federal Activity in Promotion of Better Housing Conditions and Home Ownership" (1923), Walling to Julius Rosenwald, Jan. 6, 1927, Building and Housing File, CP-OF, Hoover Papers.

of Meloney's desire to reduce her own role and to keep what she had started from being "commercialized," Hoover reorganized it as a public service corporation with himself as president, thus converting it, in his words, into a "collateral arm" of the commerce department. He then secured operating funds from private foundations, persuaded James Ford, a professor of social ethics at Harvard, to serve as executive director, and tied the whole apparatus to his Housing Division by having the directors of that agency serve as officers in the new corporation.[64] Again, by building another dependent "adhocracy" that could stimulate and work through private groups, he was able to reconcile his conflicting roles as a bureaucratic expansionist who was also a declared foe of "big government."

Similar, too, were the secretary's operations along a second welfare front, that of improving child health and well being. Here the major vehicle, analogous to Better Homes, was the American Child Health Association, formed in 1922 when Hoover arranged a merger between the American Child Hygiene Association and the Child Health Organization of America, installed himself as president of the new body, and brought in his lieutenants from the American Relief Administration to direct it.[65] After a fund raising campaign failed, financing was also arranged through the A.R.A. Children's Fund.[66] And since Hoover and his lieutenants, at the expense of some internal friction and several reorganizations, managed to impose their program and priorities on the association,[67] it too became a "collateral arm" of the commerce secretariat, filling another "vacuum" and

[64] "Better Homes and Decreased Costs," Jan. 11, 1928, Better Homes in America (BHA), Executive Director's Report, March 5, 1928, Hoover to Coolidge, Jan. 9, 1924, Hoover to Local BHA chairmen, Jan. 28, 1924, Hoover to George Wilder, June 14, Oct. 6, Dec. 22, 1923, Hoover to A. L. Lowell, Dec. 28, 1923, Hoover to Beardsley Ruml, Dec. 15, 1923, Hoover to BHA directors, Jan. 16, 1924, Hoover to Arthur Woods, Nov. 21, 1923, Hoover to E. Goodwin, March 28, 1923, Hoover to Hiett, Sept. 13, 1922, Hoover to George Christian, July 12, 1922, Hoover to Marie Meloney, Jan. 26, 1926, Meloney to Hoover, March 5, 1923, Jan. 17, 1924, Wilder to Hoover, July 20, Nov. 1, 1923, Rickard to Hoover, May 16, 1923, *ibid.*; Hoover to Meloney, March 15, 1923, *Delineator* File, CP-Personal, *ibid.* In the early years, Hoover was constantly troubled by efforts of realtors, builders, and furniture dealers to turn the movement into an "advertising game." By 1926, however, he believed that he had this problem under control.
[65] Minutes of Amalgamation Committee Meeting, Oct. 24, 1922, American Child Hygiene Association (ACHA) File, American Child Health Association Papers (ACHAP) (Herbert Hoover Library, West Branch, Iowa). Hoover to Philip Van Ingen, Dec. 18, 1922, George Baker, "ACHA and ARA," Nov. 28, 1922, ACHA-American Relief Association (ARA) File, *ibid.*; Minutes of ACHA Board of Directors, Dec. 29, 1922, Reports File, *ibid.*
[66] Frank Page to Hoover, March 19, 1923, Child Health Appeals File, *ibid.*; E. M. Flesh to Hoover, Dec. 3, 1924, Feb. 8, 1926, Jan. 30, 1928, ARA Children's Fund File, *ibid.*
[67] Page to Herter, Jan. 17, 1923, Amalgamation File, *ibid.*; Page to William Mullendore, June 8, 1923, Financial Assistance File, *ibid.*; Page to Rickard, Nov. 19, 1923, Page Memoranda re ACHA, Dec. 13, 26, 1923, Memoranda File, *ibid.*; Memorandum for Hoover, Oct. 5, 1926, Policy File, *ibid.*

in the process colliding at times with the Children's Bureau of the labor department and the treasury department's Public Health Service.[68] By 1927 the American Child Health Association was working to survey, rate, and upgrade municipal health services, to assist and coordinate local health programs, to promote health education, both in the schools and through demonstration and publication projects, and to secure comprehensive birth registration, cleaner milk, improved prenatal care, and better control of communicable diseases.[69]

Given Hoover's previous experience, it seemed logical for him and his department to handle federal relief activities and thus to broaden still further their responsibilities in the welfare field. The Unemployment Conference was largely a Hoover production, and its subsequent Committee on Civic and Emergency Measures, which tried to provide unemployment relief during the winter of 1921 and 1922, functioned essentially as a departmental appendage and model of how an associative state should function. Its approach was not to provide jobs or funds but to organize, coordinate, and inform a "cooperative" effort, thus enabling a grassroots network of mayors' emergency committees, public-minded business groups, concerned social organizations, and ad hoc employment bureaus to meet the needs of the jobless.[70] And similarly in 1927, during the decade's greatest natural disaster, it was the secretary of commerce who took charge of a special Mississippi Flood Committee and drew on both personal and departmental resources to construct another special bureaucratic apparatus, one that worked with and through a network of local citizens' committees, Red Cross chapters, and cooperating private organizations and public agencies to provide systematic coordination, make available the needed refugee centers and rehabilitation credits, and consider future flood prevention and social "reconstruction."[71]

[68] In the early 1920s, for example, plans for a child conservation conference collided with activities being pushed by the Children's Bureau and were eventually dropped, and in 1923, when the Public Health Service refused to follow Hoover's lead in surveying municipal health activities, friction also developed with that agency. See Sophie Loeb to Hoover, July 12, 1921, Hoover to Loeb, Nov. 4, 1921, March 7, 1922, Herter to Grace Abbott, March 1, 1922, Abbott to Herter, March 4, 1922, Conference File, ibid.; Hoover to Hugh Cumming, Dec. 11, 1923, Hoover to Mellon, Dec. 20, 1923, Cumming to Hoover, Dec. 14, 1923, Public Health Service File, ibid.
[69] "Report to the ARA Children's Fund" (1927), Reports File, ibid.; "Five Years of the ACHA" (1927), Report-Five Years of ACHA File, ibid.
[70] Press Releases, Dec. 17, 31, 1921, Jan. 21, March 10, 17, 20, 1922, Minutes of Colonel Woods' Conferences, Dec. 1, 2, 12, 21, 23, 1921, Jan. 3, 16, 1922, Unemployment File, CP-OF, Hoover Papers; McKenzie, "Organizing Communities through Mayors' Emergency Committees," Unemployment Reports File, ibid.; Grin, "Unemployment Conference of 1921"; Lloyd, Aggressive Introvert, 134-40.
[71] Lohoff, "Herbert Hoover," 691-97; Bruce A. Lohoff, "Hoover and the Mississippi

While constructing new bureaucracies in areas that might more logically have been left to the secretaries of labor or interior, Hoover was also trying, with somewhat greater difficulty, to convert other departments into cooperative satellites or friendly allies. In the antitrust realm, for example, where "outmoded" interpretations of the law threatened to wreck Hoover's cooperative machinery and undermine his vision of an associational order, the commerce department appeared at first to be losing the battle but by the mid-1920s had emerged victorious. Initially, efforts to secure a new interpretation of antitrust regulations through proposed amendments, expanded governmental cooperation, clarifying letters, and "friendly criticism" from sympathetic Federal Trade Commissioners all seemed ineffective.[72] But after Harry Daugherty's resignation in 1924, the picture changed rapidly. The new attorneys general, first Harlan Stone and later John Sargent, were more sympathetic. The Supreme Court in June 1925 sanctioned the associational activities of the maple flooring and cement industries. And following the reorganization of the Federal Trade Commission and the appointment of William Donovan to head the Antitrust Division, these agencies became friendly allies. The former, through its trade practice conferences, was soon promoting numerous codes of ethical behavior, devices that Hoover regarded as highly "constructive," and Donovan was ready to give friendly advice to business cooperators on how to stay within the law.[73]

By the mid-1920s, too, another Hoover protégé, William Jardine, had succeeded Henry C. Wallace as secretary of agriculture and was trying, although only with limited success, to win support for Hoover's associational approach to the farm problem. Initially, attempts to expand in this direction met with stiff resistance, resulting in bitter jurisdictional conflicts

Valley Flood of 1927" (doctoral dissertation, Syracuse University, 1968), 255-74; Hoover's memoranda of May 12, 16, 19, 1927, Hoover, "Credit Arrangements," Mississippi Valley Flood-Relief Work-Reports File, CP-OF, Hoover Papers.

[72] For Hoover's efforts, see Hoover to Harry Daugherty, Feb. 3, 1922, Dec. 11, 1923, Daugherty to Hoover, Feb. 8, 1922, Jan. 10, 1924, Trade Associations File, CP-OF, Hoover Papers; David Wing, "Cooperation Work for Distribution of Association Statistics," Aug. 5, 1922, Commerce-Trade Association Statistics File, ibid.; Hoover to Walter Edge, June 12, 1922, Edge to Hoover, June 14, 1922, Senate File, ibid.; Hoover, Memoirs: The Cabinet and the Presidency, 168-70; Robert Himmelberg, "Relaxation of the Federal Anti-Trust Policy as a Goal of the Business Community, 1918-1933" (doctoral dissertation, Pennsylvania State University, 1963), 104-23.

[73] Himmelberg, "Relaxation of Federal Anti-Trust Policy," 126-33; Department of Commerce, Trade Association Activities (Washington, 1927), 344; William Shepherd, "Today's Trust Buster's," Collier's, LXXXIII (Feb. 23, 1929), 8-9, 44; Hoover to Coolidge, Sept. 22, 1926, FTC File, CP-OF, Hoover Papers; G. Cullom Davis, "Transformation of the Federal Trade Commission, 1914-1929," Mississippi Valley Historical Review, XLIX (Dec. 1962), 446-55.

over export promotion, lumber standards, and farm processing statistics, and in heated policy debates, with each side impugning the motives of the other.[74] As Hoover saw it, he was fighting socialists and petty bureaucrats, men who could see nothing but the pernicious McNary-Haugen bill and the preservation of their own domains and men who were ready to use "smear tactics" to achieve their ends.[75] To Wallace, the struggle was a defensive battle against business aggression, particularly against a cooperative marketing plan intended to cripple genuine cooperatives, divert attention from real relief measures, and shift marketing activities to a farm board dominated by the commerce department.[76] For a time, Hoover's offensive scored few gains, but with the death of Wallace in 1924 he was able to select the new secretary, shape the recommendations of Coolidge's Agricultural Conference, secure a "purge" of the "petty bureaucrats," and bring the Department of Agriculture into alignment with his vision of agricultural self-government through cooperative marketing associations.[77] Given the new relationship, he was even ready to establish sharp boundaries between forestry activities and his own wood utilization program, conceding while doing so that his Lumber Standards Committee had "embarrassed" him by trying to move into areas which did not "rightfully belong in the Department of Commerce."[78]

Hoover had less success in his efforts to influence the state department, the treasury department, and the Federal Reserve Board, partly because in these areas he came into conflict with powerful men. He was forced to

[74] See, for example, Steuart to Hoover, April 6, 1922, Commerce-Census File, CP-OF, Hoover Papers; Hoover to C. B. Slemp, Feb. 25, 1924, C-FDCF, ibid.; Hoover to Dawes, Nov. 26, 1921, Treasury File, ibid.; Hoover to Wallace, Feb. 8, March 7, 1922, Agriculture Department File, ibid.; Hoover to C. C. Teague, Dec. 1, 1924, Agriculture-Cooperative Marketing File, ibid. See also James H. Shideler, "Herbert Hoover and the Federal Farm Board Project, 1921-1925," Mississippi Valley Historical Review, XLII (March 1956), 711-16, 720-29; Russell Lord, The Wallaces of Iowa (Boston, 1947), 259-62; Winters, Wallace, 217-42.

[75] Hoover was particularly perturbed when Louis Michael of the Bureau of Agricultural Economics prepared a detailed memorandum tracing the alleged "encroachment" of the commerce department on the agriculture department and turned it over to the American Council of Agriculture for publication. See Hoover to George Peek, Dec. 19, 1924, Hoover to Howard Gore, Nov. 24, 1924, Max Pam to Hoover, May 21, 1925, Agriculture File, CP-OF, Hoover Papers; Winters, Wallace, 241-42.

[76] Winters, Wallace, 226, 245, 275-77; Wallace to Coolidge, April 18, 1924, Agriculture File, CP-OF, Hoover Papers; Annual Report of the Secretary of Agriculture (Washington, 1924), 44.

[77] Winters, Wallace, 243-44; Hoover to William Jardine, April 1, 1926, Jardine to Hoover, Feb. 16, 1925, Agriculture Department File, CP-OF, Hoover Papers; Hoover to Jardine, April 24, 1925, Hoover to H. C. Smither, May 23, 1925, Jardine to Hoover, April 29, 1925, Committees-Agriculture and Commerce File, ibid.; Hoover to Ralph Merritt, April 4, 1925, Agriculture File, ibid.

[78] Hoover to Gore, Nov. 24, 1924, Hoover to Coolidge, Nov. 28, 1924, Coolidge to J. Blodgett, Dec. 1, 1924, Conferences-Wood Utilization File, CP-OF, Hoover Papers.

accept a continued division of foreign economic activities, and in the face of strong opposition from the treasury department, state department, and banking leaders, he was unable to establish the qualitative standards and purposeful controls that he hoped to use in guiding American investments abroad.[79] He was also reluctant to challenge Andrew Mellon's dismantling of the progressive tax system.[80] He was unable to do much about the "pro-British," "easy money" policy of the Federal Reserve Board.[81] And although his role in the making of foreign policy was far from insignificant, he was frequently unable to move the diplomatic establishment in directions he felt desirable.[82]

In later years, Hoover would attribute some of the difficulties after 1929 to the resistance that he had encountered from financial and foreign policy makers.[83] But at the time he did not seem to regard his failures in these fields as constituting major threats to the continued development of a superior socioeconomic order. Although some of his initial plans had miscarried, he had succeeded in raising the commerce department to the "first rank" and transforming a collection of technical bureaus into a unified, purposeful, and rapidly expanding organization, with a strong sense of esprit de corps and with a far-flung apparatus that was attempting to guide socioeconomic development as well as serve business groups. Essentially, he believed, he had created the type of governmental tool that he had envisioned in 1921, one that functioned as an economic "general staff," business "correspondence school," and national coordinator, all rolled into one, yet preserved the essentials of American individualism by avoiding bureaucratic dictation and legal coercion, implementing its plans through nearly 400 cooperating committees and scores of private associations, and relying upon appeals to science, community, and morality to bridge the gap between the public interest and private ones.[84] It was a tool, moreover,

[79] Brandes, *Hoover and Economic Diplomacy*, 153-55, 201; Parrini, *Heir to Empire*, 185-201.

[80] Hoover to Lindsay, April 4, 1924, Lindsay File, CP-OF, Hoover Papers.

[81] Brandes, *Hoover and Economic Diplomacy*, 156-57; Lester Chandler, *Benjamin Strong, Central Banker* (Washington, 1958), 254-55; William Starr Myers and Walter H. Newton, *The Hoover Administration: A Documentary Narrative* (New York, 1936), 9-10.

[82] For his inability to secure fully the type of economic diplomacy that he had in mind for Latin America, see Brandes, *Hoover and Economic Diplomacy*, 192-203.

[83] Herbert Hoover, *The Memoirs of Herbert Hoover: The Great Depression, 1929-1941* (New York, 1952), 5, 13.

[84] "Hoover as Secretary of Commerce," Commerce-Achievements File, CP-OF, Hoover Papers; New York *Times*, Feb. 19, 1928; Hard, "The New Hoover," 483-84; Herbert Hoover, *The New Day: Campaign Speeches of Herbert Hoover 1928* (Stanford, Cal., 1928), 22-23; "Department of Commerce," *Fortune*, XIX (June 1939), 102; Harris Gaylord Warren, *Herbert Hoover and the Great Depression* (New York, 1967), 26-29. Between 1921 and 1928 the commerce department had increased its personnel by more than 50 per-

whose use was hastening the day when "functional self-government" through a "cooperative system" of self-regulating "organisms" would meet the needs of industrial democracy without statist interference.[85] Like the war to end all wars, it was the bureaucratic empire to end future bureaucratic empires; and in theory at least it was supposed to wither away once the new order was built.

As Hoover surveyed the state of associational development in the late 1920s, he was also optimistic about the progress that had been made toward his ultimate goal. The number of national associations had multiplied from approximately 700 in 1919 to over 2,000 by 1929. Inspired and coordinated by the right kind of governmental structures—those fostering "associational activities" imbued with "high public purposes"—these associations had in Hoover's eyes become "legitimate" and "constructive" instruments for advancing the "public interest" and ushering in a "fundamentally new" phase in the nation's economic evolution.[86] The dream of an associational order, it seemed, was on the way to realization; and as if to symbolize the role of the commerce secretariat in making such a superior system possible, a new "temple of commerce" was under construction, which, except for the Capitol, would be the largest building in Washington.[87]

The next few years, of course, would demonstrate that Hoover's utopia was not to be. Viewed from the altered perspective that took shape after 1929, his emerging private government seemed increasingly undemocratic, oppressive, and unresponsive. Associationalism, once widely accepted as a new and superior formulation of the "American way," became for many a mere facade behind which "selfish monopolists" had abused their power and plunged the nation into depression. And the leaders of his new order, revealed now to be far less altruistic and far less prescient than Hoover had hoped they would be, seemed unable either to sustain expansion, solve festering social problems, or check the greatest economic contraction in the nation's history. As conflict mounted, moreover, demands for more effective "coordination" were soon transforming Hoover's efforts at associational direction and reform into programs and agencies he had never

cent and nearly doubled its appropriations. The notion of its three-fold function as adviser, educator, and coordinator had been publicized in John Burnham, "What Hoover is Doing," *Nation's Business*, 10 (Feb. 1922), 16-17.

[85] The phrases are from Hunt, "Cooperative Committee and Conference System," Dec. 14, 1926, Hunt File, CP-OF, Hoover Papers.

[86] Hoover, *New Day*, 196-98; Department of Commerce, *Trade Association Activities* (1927), viii; Commerce Department Press Release, June 24, 1929, Official File 3, Presidential Papers, Hoover Papers.

[87] The new building had been authorized in 1926. Washington *Star*, June 30, 1926.

intended. Ironically, by demonstrating that they could not achieve the sustained expansion, rising living standards, and decentralized, non-coercive planning that they were supposed to achieve, he helped open the way for "big government" and state-enforced market controls in the 1930s.[88]

Viewed in terms of its utopian goals and assumptions, Hoover's approach can only be adjudged a tragic failure. Yet this should not obscure the fact that he and his New Era associates, far from being mere tools of rapacious business interests or unimaginative proponents of laissez-faire, drift, and governmental inaction, were groping their way toward a form of American corporatism and indicative planning, were engaged in imaginative processes of state building and bureaucratic expansion, and were wrestling actively with the still unsolved problem of reconciling techno-corporate organization with America's liberal-democratic heritage. If historians are to understand either the men involved or the era in which they operated, it seems imperative that their associational structures and activities be explored in greater depth. And viewed from the perspective of the 1970s, from a time of disenchantment with the solutions flowing from the 1930s and of a search by "neo-federalists," "new radicals," and "post-liberals" for new organizational arrangements that will liberate and humanize rather than mechanize and oppress, such explorations may be more relevant and more instructive than most historians have previously assumed.

[88] See Albert Romasco, *Poverty of Abundance: Hoover, the Nation, the Depression* (New York, 1965), 65, 233-34; Roy Lubove, *Struggle for Social Security 1900-1935* (Cambridge, Mass., 1968), 8-9, 116; Zieger, *Republicans and Labor*, 107-08.

Ellis W. Hawley
Herbert Hoover and Economic
Stabilization, 1921–22

Editor's Introductory Note

My study of Herbert Hoover began in 1950, when Professor James C. Malin of the University of Kansas suggested that I write a master's thesis that was subsequently entitled "The Relation of Hoover's Policies to the National Industrial Recovery Act." I later turned my attention to the New Deal's business policies. But with the opening of Hoover's papers in 1966, I again became interested in his efforts to build trade associations and commit them to larger social ends. I began what I initially thought of as a study of federal trade association policy, and it was only as I became immersed in the new collections that I began to realize the extent to which Hoover's actions in this sphere had parallels in numerous other policy areas. Not only was he seeking to apply the association idea to other functional groupings but also to develop integrating institutions through which it could be applied to society as a whole. At work, it seemed, was a vision of social order resembling that being articulated by managerial corporatists in Europe. And gradually, I shifted my research focus away from industrial interest groups and toward the origins, nature, and workings of this managerial vision.

The following paper is one product of this changed focus. It examines the economic stabilization program that Hoover sought to implement during his first two years as secretary of commerce, seeking to understand both the organizational ideals involved and the difficulties encountered in realizing them. The program, I argue, was not an economic success. Recovery would probably have come without it, and the new institutions that it fostered were unable to control the forces leading to the economic debacle of 1929. But this failure, I also argue, should not be allowed to obscure the historical importance of the program. It is in 1921 and 1922, not in the 1930s, that federal officials first attempt to create tools for managing a peacetime economy. It is this experience, not the traditions of a more remote past, that serves as the model for public policy during Hoover's presidency. And it is in the development and advocacy of such a program, more perhaps than anywhere else, that Hoover and his associates stand revealed as men who have broken with and largely abandoned the laissez-faire notions of the "invisible hand." They are best seen not as champions of traditional market ideals but as articulators of an associational progressivism, developers of an Americanized variant of the neo-corporative ideal, and foreshadowers of much that would become part of the American system in the 1930s, 1940s, and 1950s.

The paper published here is essentially the one that I presented to the Hoover Seminar in 1974. I have made only a few stylistic revisions and a few changes in the footnotes. In the intervening years, however, I have become more aware of how much of the program of 1921 was anticipated by failed initiatives in 1919 and hence more inclined to view Hoover's contribution as a reassembling of these initiatives rather than a pioneering exploit. I am also less convinced than I once was that Hoover had reconciled in his own mind the tensions between individualistic and techno-corporative ideals. He had gone farther toward this than most other figures in public life, and the result was an ideology that shaped and constrained his activities. But I would now concede a residue of confusion and ambivalence, which may account in part for the fuzziness in portions of the organizational ideal, the hyper-sensitivity with which Hoover reacted to criticism, and his efforts at times to unify by proclamation rather than logic. Still, I would stand by the central arguments in the paper and its general reassessment of the stabilization program of 1921-22.

Herbert Hoover and Economic Stabilization, 1921-22

In recent scholarship the cleavage that American historians once drew between the New Deal's "managerial state" and an earlier "negativism" has seemed less and less sharp. In the new studies of progressive reform, the managerial impulse has been much in evidence, and upon re-examining the New Era, scholars have discovered a number of its leaders to be thinking in terms of macroeconomic management rather than particularistic reform or mere regulation of the money supply.[1] Like the New Dealers, such men were strongly influenced by the experiences of World War I.[2] And the more their actions are studied, the clearer it has become that New Deal interventionism had significant precedents, not only in the Hoover program of 1929 but in an earlier Hoover program, launched during the recession of 1921 and carried on under the auspices of an administration commonly associated with "normalcy" and "reaction."[3]

This is not to say, of course, that these managers of the Harding era favored the expanded public sector associated with the war government and the New Deal. Like their more conservative colleagues in 1921, they blamed a part of the nation's economic difficulties on an over-grown government and burdensome taxes; and for the most part, they went along with the type of economy measures, tax revision, and governmental retrenchment urged by business conservatives and Andrew Mellon's Treasury Department.[4] For them, however, much of the difficulty also lay in defective business organization, ill-informed decision-making, and improper uses of private power. And while they agreed that the economy must be purged of its wastes, inefficiencies, and uneconomic price-cost relationships, they believed that this could be done without putting it through the wringer of liquidation or running the social and economic risks of mass wage cuts, prolonged unemployment, and acute agricultural distress. Given the right kind of coordination and cooperative action, they argued, such painful purges were neither necessary nor inevitable. And acting on this belief, they developed a program that would foreshadow the analysis and remedies adopted after 1929.[5]

It is upon these stabilization actions, then, especially those undertaken by Herbert Hoover's Department of Commerce, that the present paper will focus. It will look, in particular, at the context in which the Hoover programs took shape, the goals and methods of the men involved, and the activities and agencies through which they hoped to short-circuit the liquidation phase of the business cycle and regularize future growth. It will also attempt to assess the significance of these actions, both in terms of their immediate impact and their influence on future governmental policy. And hopefully, by pulling together and adding to the recent scholarship on these matters,[6] it will contribute to a growing understanding of Hoover's approach to economic management, the policies of the Harding administration, and the paths along which the American version of the "managerial state" developed.

II

To understand the impulses behind Hoover's activities and the constraints within which his programs took shape, one must recognize the conflicting forces at work in the immediate postwar period. For a variety of "progressive" businessmen and their allies in the professions and social sciences, the wartime experience had strengthened an earlier vision of managerial progress through scientific inquiry, expert administration, and coordinated group action. Along this path, they had come to believe, lay the nation's hope for ever increasing efficiency, harmony, and material abundance, and at war's end a number of them had hoped to adapt the wartime machinery to this type of peacetime development.[7] Even under war conditions, however, the powerful traditions of anti-statism, anti-monopoly, and anti-collectivism, all deeply embedded in America's institutional and legal structure, had forced would-be systematizers to make numerous compromises.[8] And in the postwar period, as these traditions became rallying cries for groups seeking redistributions of power or blaming their difficulties on departures from the "American way," the result was an incoherent mixture of the war-fostered initiatives with drives for governmental retrenchment, campaigns of antitrust action, and orgies of union-busting and red-baiting.[9] If scientific managers and enlightened capitalists were to act as agents of progress, it appeared, they would have to do so while making proper obeisance to these older traditions. Under the circumstances of 1920 and 1921, it had become all but impossible to install any system managed by a "peace industries board," a set of formalized cartels, or the type of syndicalist arrangements envisioned by some reformers.

As these political constraints took shape, moreover, the notion had reasserted itself that an approach blending the managerial vision with inherited American traditions was not only possible but clearly superior to anything being advocated by un-American "collectivists." If properly preserved, the envisioners of this "American system" argued, the older individualistic traditions could still contribute to national progress. And building now on a set of ideas developed by pre-war advocates of "cooperative competition,"[10] they insisted that the economy could be ordered and stabilized without creating harmful state bureaucracies, repressive monopolies, or some type of American "soviet." The answer lay in the nation's growing network of cooperative institutions, especially its trade and professional associations, its socially-minded corporations, and its efficiency-minded labor and farm groups. With proper assistance, coordination, and delimitation, so the argument ran, these institutions could provide a new and superior type of economic system—a way whereby America could have intelligent planning and scientific rationalization without sacrificing the energy and creativity inherent in individual effort and private enterprise.[11]

Taking shape, too, particularly in the engineering societies, trade association movement, and postwar inheritors of the earlier efficiency movement, were a number of specific proposals whose implementation would allegedly help to build the new economic order. The nation, so it was argued, needed cooperative programs that would help to reduce industrial costs, allocate resources to their most productive uses, and iron out harmful fluctuations in employment, output, and demand. And government, so the argument continued, could and should play a limited role in launching and nourishing such programs. There was a need for some postwar equivalent of the wartime Conservation Division, for an expanded commercial intelligence service, for statistical assistance of the type provided during the war period, and for other agencies that could help the leaders of cooperative institutions to coordinate their activities, mobilize their constituencies, and act in the public interest. If only such agencies had been in existence and functioning, so the lament frequently ran, much of the postwar economic gyration, with its accompanying wastes and acerbation of economic and social conflict, could have been avoided.[12]

With this ideology and program, moreover, Herbert Hoover had become increasingly associated. In the postwar clashes between free-market advocates and proponents of statist direction, he had consistently sought a "middle way," a program of action that could draw on the energy and resources of private enterprise yet deploy these within the context of purposeful planning and coordination. Such had been the nature of his plans for European reconstruction and postwar trade revival.[13] And subsequently, as he concerned himself with labor conflict, agricultural adjustment, and the performance of the coal, housing, and transportation industries, he consistently called for governmental agencies that would provide "illumination, guidance, and cooperation" rather than dictation or coercive controls.[14] Clearly, he argued, there was a need for collective initiative, overall coordination, and national planning. Left to "haphazard development" and the workings of unrestrained competition, modern economies functioned badly. Yet when "politicized," they performed in even worse fashion. If their potential was ever to be fully realized, it could be done only through organizing cooperation in "the community as a whole," providing the cooperative groups with a "national conception" of what could and should be done, and supplementing their efforts with informational aids and supportive governmental actions.[15]

As the emerging spokesman for managerial cooperativism, Hoover was also setting forth a theory of recovery and prosperity that diverged markedly from classical prescriptions. In late 1920 and early 1921, in what amounted to an early version of the New Era's high-wage doctrine and the New Deal's purchasing-power theory, he was already arguing that maintenance of labor and farm income would help to check the economic downturn and stimulate new expansion. And this, he maintained, was not inconsistent with lowering business costs and restoring profit incentives. The latter could be achieved through organized campaigns of waste elimination, market expansion, and counter-cyclical investment; and in each of these areas, he was already moving to construct appropriate machinery. In November 1920, after meetings with Samuel Gompers and the industrial engineer Robert Wolf, he used his position as head of the Federated American Engineering Societies to launch a "survey of waste" that could provide a blueprint for managerial action.[16] In December, he endorsed the newly launched Foreign Trade Financing Corporation as the key to trade revival.[17] And throughout the period, he was considering what could be done, especially through statistics, education, and cooperative mobilization, to encourage counter-cyclical construction and business planning that would serve the interests of overall stability.[18]

By early 1921 Hoover had also decided that the Department of Commerce could be used to implement this recovery and stabilization program. Its enabling act, he found, provided a broad charter under which new programs could be developed. And once this realization had dawned, he had moved away from earlier plans for private orchestration,[19] set aside his fears that Harding was trying to use him, and negotiated an arrangement that would give him a free hand in departmental reorganization and a voice in financial, foreign, labor, and farm as well as business policies. In particular, he told the in-coming president, he wanted to strengthen the department by adding bureaus "properly belonging in the field," establish close teamwork with the government's other economic agencies, and use the resulting structure to build cooperative programs of waste reduction, market expansion, and labor reform. These things, he was assured, would have presidential support. And having received such assurances, he joined the Harding cabinet as secretary of commerce.[20]

III

By March of 1921, then, Secretary Hoover had given some thought both to the program he hoped to implement and the role that his agency should play in the process. The task ahead was one of building the private and public institutions that could implement what he had in mind; and within days of assuming office, he was moving vigorously to bring the appropriate bureaus under his jurisdiction, staff them with men who shared his vision, and forge "a wider and better organized co-operation" with the private sector.[21] Almost immediately, claims were staked out to the statistical, marketing, transportation, and development agencies in other departments. Just as quickly, men were put to work on plans for restructuring and expanding such bureaus as Standards, the Census, and Foreign and Domestic Commerce.[22] And on March 9, in the hope of creating an advisory agency that would unify and coordinate private leadership, Hoover began consultation with some twenty-five trade and industrial associations.[23]

Despite vigorous action, however, the contemplated agencies of recovery and stabilization did not spring magically into life. On the contrary, Hoover's initiatives quickly ran into three major obstacles, all of which would continue to plague him throughout his tenure in office. One was strong resistance from established agencies who did not share his vision, had no desire to be transferred or "coordinated," and interpreted his activities as those of a bureaucratic empire-builder.[24] The second was the difficulty of fitting cooperative "stabilization" inside the framework of the antitrust laws, especially since the Department of Justice and the Federal Trade Commission seemed inclined to interpret these strictly and not to give advisory opinions on what might be prosecuted.[25] And the third was sharp criticism from business groups who were not being consulted or represented and who looked upon Hoover's scheme of public-private cooperation as amounting to an informal version of recognizing and using monopolistic chosen instruments. So sharp did such protests become that Hoover quickly backed away from the idea of a formalized economic advisory council and announced that he would work instead through monthly conferences with different business, labor, and farm leaders participating.[26]

Nevertheless, even as these obstacles took shape, some progress was being made in forging what Hoover would later call the "three legs" of his recovery and reconstruction program.[27] In Washington, one conference followed another, particularly with engineering leaders, statistical advisers, and export groups. In the confines of the Commerce Department, new desks and operations kept appearing, manned by the coordinators and trouble-shooters that the secretary had assigned to ride herd on the emerging programs. And through the swirl of activity, the outlines of the waste reduction, statistical dissemination, and trade expansion programs were taking shape, generating new institutional structures, and being sold both as recovery measures and pathways to permanent economic and social progress.[28] To support them, moreover, Hoover was lining up an impressive array of the private sector's "progressive-minded" leaders. While backing away from the idea of a permanent advisory council, he had drawn in a number of his closest associates in the earlier war government, set up both a Reorganization Committee and an Industrial Group, and was making use of these bodies to further the "upbuilding of the Department."[29]

In constructing the first "leg," that of organized waste reduction, the blueprint was still to come from the "survey of waste" being conducted by the Federated American Engineering Societies. Since January, its seventeen-man Industrial Waste Committee had been organizing and directing "assays" of six representative industries and a variety of labor, educational, health, and management factors. Riding herd on the operation was Edward Eyre Hunt, a former radical who had been caught up in the scientific-management mystique and attached himself to Hoover during the war period. And hoping now to get the "findings" into the hands of people who could act on them, Hunt arranged for preliminary summaries to be released at a meeting of the American Engineering Council in St. Louis. There on June 3, 1921, the country was told that it was suffering from immense wastes in the use of its resources—wastes that derived partly from faulty management, partly from short-sighted production restraints, partly from the failure to conserve human resources and bring harmful economic fluctuations under control. In the Waste Committee's view, moreover, more than fifty percent of these wastes were due to poor management, and this being the case, it seemed possible to organize economic recovery without liquidating labor and running the risks inherent in mass suffering.[30]

In business and engineering circles, the reaction was not entirely favorable, particularly to the notion that management was chiefly responsible for the nation's economic difficulties. Hoover and the "Taylorites," so it was charged, were trying to stir up "class antagonism." And instead of joining them in their war on waste, such groups as the National Industrial Conference Board and the American Institute of Electrical Engineers reacted with campaigns designed to discredit the blueprint.[31] Such reactions, however, were insufficient to derail plans for a new "waste elimination division" or for turning the Bureau of Standards into a "super-consultant" on research and standardization problems.[32] In May, Hoover had assigned the implementation of such plans to Frederick Feiker, an engineer and publicist long associated with the Arch Shaw and McGraw-Hill trade publications.[33] Shortly thereafter, he had persuaded a Conference of Business Paper Editors, convened by Feiker, to conduct a survey of standardization work. And by August, armed both with the Industrial Waste report and material gathered by the business editors, Feiker was mapping out programs of standardization and simplification, contemplating the creation of a new agency to handle them, and negotiating with the National Paving Brick Manufacturers for what would become the first of the department's simplified practice conferences.[34]

By August, too, some progress was being made in forging the second "leg" of Hoover's program, that designed to generate statistical information and improve overall stability through statistically-informed production planning. The possibilities here had been explored by economists such as Allyn Young, Edwin Gay, and Wesley Mitchell, all serving now on Hoover's reconvened version of the Advisory Committee on the Census.[35] These possibilities had then been discussed in a series of conferences, both with individual industries and with such groups as the Chamber of Commerce, the Business Paper Editors, and the National Association of Manufacturers.[36] And while some businessmen seemed disinclined to share their "secrets" or put up with more questionnaires and more "meddling,"[37] enough support had developed to set up a new government service and tie it into the informational activities of cooperating trade associations. In July 1921, the Census Bureau launched its *Survey of Current Business,* making available on a monthly basis the production, sales, and inventory data supplied by cooperating industries and technical periodicals. It was a "little service," Hoover told Frank Taussig. But he planned to build upon it. And eventually, he hoped, the statistical program could provide the knowledge and foresight necessary to combat panic or speculative conditions, prevent the development of diseased industries, and guide decision-making so as to iron out rather than accentuate the business cycle.[38]

In addition, the Commerce Department was making some slight progress in its drives to take over other statistical agencies and secure protection of the program from "unreasonable" antitrust action. Along the first line, Hoover was in the process of acquiring the Treasury Department's Bureau of Customs Statistics.[39] And along the second, he and departmental solicitor William Lamb were engaged in a series of conferences with the Justice Department, seeking to define which statistical activities were desirable and which might be used to further improper restraints of trade.[40] Along both fronts, however, resistance remained stiff. Most of the departments, Hoover lamented, were hanging on to their statistical activities like "grim death," unable, it seemed, to rise above petty bureaucratic jealousies or see how centralization in the Commerce Department could serve national interests.[41] And despite his willingness to steer clear of "open price" exchanges and condemn the type of "stabilization" that would protect inefficiencies and accentuate economic fluctuations, the Justice Department remained reluctant to spell out permissible activities. Nor was it receptive to pleas that businessmen were only doing what the Department of Commerce was urging them to do or to calls for quashing actions already begun against the activities of building-materials associations.[42]

In forging the third or trade-expansion "leg" of his program, Hoover was also encountering somewhat similar obstacles, particularly from the marketing information services in the State and Agriculture Departments and from Federal Trade Commissioners inclined toward a strict interpretation of the Webb-Pomerene Act.[43] Yet here, too, new structures and activities were taking shape. In Julius Klein, the new head of the Bureau of Foreign and Domestic Commerce, Hoover had found another energetic organizer and missionary.[44] And in well-publicized speeches, he was spelling out how a properly designed trade program could act both as a stimulant to recovery and as a permanent "balance wheel and stabilizer" yet not require such counterproductive measures as wage cuts, tariff abolition, or statist enterprise. As with the domestic economy, he argued, the answer lay in waste elimination and better marketing to reduce costs, cooperative mobilization and guidance of the needed credits, and the eventual transformation of the world economy into one producing for properly protected but ever-expanding mass markets.[45]

To help in building such a program, moreover, Hoover was moving rapidly to reorganize the Bureau of Foreign and Domestic Commerce, tie it into a network of cooperating associations, and use the resulting machinery to achieve his goals. In March and early April, he had considered a variety of plans for new commodity divisions and technical services,[46] all allegedly designed to help exporters eliminate waste and rationalize their operations. In late April, he had called the customary conference, bringing together business and academic advisers and using them to mobilize support for the bureau's expansion. And by early September, he had begun the reorganization that would eventually produce some seventeen new commodity divisions, staff them with "experts" drawn from the export industries, and regularize cooperation through parallel industrial advisory committees. "I see in my own mind," said Frederick Feiker, "a wall chart at the top of which is a horizontal list of manufacturing associations interested in export leading down through committees" and functioning "with different commodities in our own organization."[47]

As the national "exporting and selling scheme" was reorganized,[48] Hoover was also considering what could be done to provide needed credits and bring about needed adjustments in tariff rates, international debts, and foreign practices. Such actions, he had hoped initially, could be handled by special export credit corporations,[49] the transfer of tariff and debt adjustment to qualified "experts," and a properly delimited participation of the United States in the League of Nations. Efforts to secure such measures, however, had been disillusioning. The nation's banks had been reluctant to subscribe to the Hoover-endorsed Foreign Trade Financing Corporation, and its congressmen seemed bent upon collecting the war debts, retaining the traditional methods of tariff-making, and saving America from League "entanglement." Hence, by the summer of 1921, Hoover was thinking more in terms of some type of informal financial concert, linking governmental policy-makers with financial leaders at home and central bankers abroad, and using the resulting alliance to encourage American investors, press for needed reforms abroad, and reduce political irrationality to a minimum. As yet, this line of thinking had not produced specific programs, but within a few months it would begin to do so.[50]

As the summer drew to a close, then, Hoover was making progress in implementing the proposals of late 1920 and early 1921. Waste elimination, statistical dissemination, and trade expansion programs were all taking shape, and these, as Hoover visualized them, were to be the keys to a relatively painless recovery and a new era of managed and stable prosperity. Nor was this all that he had been doing. From the beginning, he had also concerned himself with a number of "problem" areas where economic "sickness" seemed to be holding back recovery and progress in the rest of the economy. And out of this concern had come special programs and plans for restoring economic health to such areas as housing, coal mining, agriculture, and the railroads.

IV

The "housing problem," as Hoover perceived it at the time, was essentially one of a backward and disorganized field of endeavor, unable to meet its obligations to the society as a whole and seemingly committed to patterns of operation that destabilized the overall economic system. Over the years, this backwardness and disorganization had left the nation with a shortage of "a million homes," blocked the modernization that could make it a "nation of homeowners," and repeatedly thrown the national economy "out of step" by subjecting it to a succession of building booms and slumps. Yet here as elsewhere, Hoover had decided, excursions into statist enterprise, detailed controls, or organized campaigns of wage reduction were likely to make things worse instead of better. The answer, he argued, lay in cooperative programs of modernization and construction planning, designed to lower costs, regularize employment, and build up construction "reserves" that could be expanded during slack periods of economic activity.[51] And shortly after assuming office, he had secured the services of housing specialist Franklin T. Miller,[52] put him to work organizing the necessary cooperative machinery, and won presidential backing for a $50,000 appropriation to support these activities. The result, when the funds became available on July 1, 1921, was a new Division of Building and Housing in the Bureau of Standards.[53]

To head the new division Hoover appointed John M. Gries, a housing specialist from the Harvard Business School.[54] And in the summer of 1921, while Hoover continued to publicize what he had in mind,

Gries moved energetically to expand upon Miller's earlier activities. On one front, the Housing Division worked with the Chamber of Commerce and the National Federation of Construction Industries to organize "community action programs," some of which quickly went "upon the rocks" over labor matters, but others of which did have some initial success in adjusting the conflicts that were paralyzing construction activities. On a second front, it worked with other Commerce officials and allies to interest the construction industries in the emerging programs of waste elimination and statistical dissemination. On a third, it proceeded to organize special advisory committees designed to work out and publicize model building codes, better zoning laws, and standardized contract specifications. And on a fourth, it began considering the problems of home financing, seasonal fluctuations, and future construction planning.[55] In each of these areas, it was hoped, some part of the "housing problem" could be solved; and once this was done, the construction field could lead the way to general recovery and contribute to future progress and stability.

Another problem area to which Hoover hoped to apply somewhat similar solutions was that of bituminous coal. Here again, as he saw it, the "problem" was essentially one of a backward and disorganized industry trapped into patterns of intermittent operation and labor turmoil that disrupted the whole economy. And again, he believed, the answer lay not in nationalization, detailed controls, or the type of union-busting that one wing of the industry was pushing. It lay rather in cooperative modernization and regularization, especially in cooperative action to reduce marketing wastes, encourage the storage of coal during slack periods, and provide the market information and statistical data needed to rationalize production, puchasing, and investment decisions. Such an approach, he had declared repeatedly, could work to the benefit of all parties concerned. And to provide the necessary stimulation and assistance, he had hoped to create a Coal Division, endow it with fact-gathering powers, and use it to organize programs similar to those being sponsored by the new Housing Division.[56]

In the case of coal, however, these plans ran into stronger obstacles and were slow to materialize. As embodied in the Frelinghuysen Bill of April 1921,[57] for example, they ran into strong opposition from the southern coal operators and their supporters in Congress. Fact-gathering and statistical dissemination, so the argument ran, was the entering wedge for government control, unionization, and removal of the South's competitive advantages. And once the southern operators had captured control of the National Coal Association's executive board the chances that Hoover could secure passage of the bill dwindled to virtually nil.[58] Nor was he able as yet to compensate for this setback by taking over existing bureaus and converting them into the agency he had in mind. Those in charge of the Interior Department's Bureau of Mines and Geological Survey were not enthusiastic about being transferred and were putting up stiff resistance to all such designs.[59]

During the same period, similar difficulties had also sidetracked Hoover's efforts to deal with another "problem" area, namely that of a depressed railroad industry unable to attract new capital and seemingly committed to rate structures that compounded the problems in housing, coal, and agriculture. The best treatment here, he felt, was one that combined cooperative efficiency measures with selective rate revision for industries that were in trouble and prompt settlement of the claims arising out of government operation during the war. This was the program that he urged upon all concerned, especially in a series of summer conferences with industry leaders, Treasury officials, and railroad regulators. Yet in implementing the program, one setback seemed to follow another. The railroads, rejecting his version of their long-range interests and social obligations, refused to consider special rate structures for coal or building materials. Anti-railroad elements in Congress blocked the bill for claim settlement. And the wage and rate cuts imposed by the Railway Labor Board and the Interstate Commerce Commission seemed designed chiefly to generate new labor turmoil and make the problem worse instead of better.[60] For railroads as for coal, it seemed, an extraordinary effort would be required to get the right kind of machinery established and operating.

Finally, as still another impetus to recovery and future progress, Hoover hoped to restore the prosperity and purchasing power of American agriculture. Like many of his contemporaries, he tended to go along with a type of agrarian corporatist thinking which looked upon farming not only as the nation's "fundamental" industry but also as basic to the general health of the whole social or national organism. And while he did not believe that extensive governmental controls could cure agricultural ills, he did see their cure as being vital and as requiring some type of remedial action along collective lines.[61] In August, in a move designed to substitute a "constructive" alternative for Senator George Norris's export subsidy bill, he helped to draft and put through the Emergency Agricultural Credits Act, authorizing the War Finance Corporation to extend credit to farm cooperatives, foreign purchasers, and rural banks.[62] And as early as April, he began advocating the creation of "a national food-marketing board" that could help farmers organize themselves into cooperative associations, provide them with "outlook" and planning data, and work with organizations of middlemen to improve marketing efficiency. This, he thought, was the "major answer," and by the fall of 1921 he had come to believe that most of this contemplated machinery belonged in the Department of Commerce rather than in Agriculture. Against strong resistance, he was trying to capture the Bureau of Markets and use it to develop the needed programs.[63]

V

Hoover's first months in office, then, had produced a variety of efforts to "organize" recovery and progress. Yet for all the activity, the economy was still shrinking and popular distress growing. More, it seemed, would be necessary to check and reverse the downward cycle; and by early August, Hoover had decided upon another major experiment in government-stimulated cooperative action. The need now, he told the president, was for new machinery that could mobilize leadership in the "community," meet the need for temporary unemployment relief, and stimulate new consumer and investment spending. And on August 29, two days after issuing a plea for autumn letting of highway contracts, his department joined with the White House in announcing that the president would call an Unemployment Conference, both to secure emergency recommendations and to study ways of lessening business fluctuations in the future.[64]

As the preliminaries unfolded, moreover, it became clear that this new initiative would reflect Hoover's thinking and build on his earlier activities. It was he who selected the conferees and arranged for preliminary study committees. And with the assistance of Edward Eyre Hunt and an enlarged version of the earlier statistical advisory committee,[65] a program was worked out well in advance of the formal meeting. As set forth in preliminary recommendations, it would reject anything approaching a federal dole or governmental works projects, ignore those calling for union-busting and wage cuts, and concentrate on organizing a cooperative relief and recovery system working through private groups and local communities. In particular, relief should come through a network of emergency committees drawing upon both private and local governmental resources and sponsoring such things as community employment bureaus, give-a-job campaigns, and share-the-work programs. Spending should be revived by encouraging industry to undertake capital improvements and governments to build needed public works. And future stability should be enhanced by educating businessmen to avoid speculative booms, providing them with improved statistical services, and establishing planning agencies that could build up construction "reserves" for the next slack period. In these proposals for long-range stabilization, the whole program was remarkably similar to the "practical measures" that the American Association for Labor Legislation had been advocating since 1914.[66]

The conference itself convened on September 26 and occasionally gave signs of getting out of hand. In the corridors, Jacob Coxey and other "ghosts of the nineties" put in an appearance, and in the closed committee meetings, unsympathetic champions of "natural law" and the "open shop" occasionally spoke out. For the most part, however, the conferees behaved according to plan, produced the unanimous committee reports that Hoover had insisted upon, and adopted a set of general recommendations that deviated only slightly from those made by the preliminary advisory group. Before adjourning on October 13, moreover, they entrusted the implementation of the program to the secretary of commerce and his lieutenants. Supervising the operation would be a Committee of Fourteen made up of the same officials and advisers who had planned and guided the conference proceedings.[67]

To head the emergency relief effort, Hoover had already enlisted the services of Arthur Woods, a former police commissioner of New York with experience in postwar demobilization activities. And during the weeks that followed, in what amounted to the most ambitious program of organized voluntarism since the war period, Woods's Committee on Civic and Emergency Measures became the coordinator, "clearing-house," and cheer leader for the charitable and job-expansion activities of some 225 local committees and a variety of cooperating organizations. At the same time, it called upon local governments and industrial groups to cooperate by undertaking needed capital improvements and public works.[68] And in the federal sphere, Hoover and his organization took the lead in urging prompt spending of appropriated funds and prompt congressional action on measures to expand road-building and reclamation work, settle the railroad claims against the government, and enlarge the work of the United States Employment Service. Through such actions, the argument ran, the pressures for liquidation could be turned into pressures for sustained expansion, and the whole matter could be accomplished without undermining America's spiritual and institutional heritage.[69]

It was only logical, too, that these new stimulants to construction should be tied into and used to reinforce Hoover's earlier activities. Special emphasis was now put on the value of statistical programs for the building and construction industries. Simplification, coordinated now by a new Division of Simplified Practice under William Durgin, focused its primary attention on the chaotic diversity of construction materials and practices.[70] And working with and through the Unemployment Conference machinery, Gries's Housing Division became the vehicle for new efforts to revise building codes, encourage home ownership, and organize the construction field for cooperative endeavor.[71] In early 1922, it lent its support to plans for a new national organization, which, as Hoover saw it, could end the "antagonism" between manufacturers, builders, and workers, unite them in an effort to "lower the cost of homes," and thus create more business and more employment.[72] The eventual result, in June 1922, would be the formation of the American Construction Council under the direction of Franklin D. Roosevelt.[73]

While mounting these new attacks on the construction problem, Hoover was also continuing to wrestle with the difficulties of agriculture, coal, and the railroads. In the first field, he was having little success in winning jurisdictional control of agricultural marketing. But he did take a keen interest in the Agricultural Conference of January 1922, strongly supported the Capper-Volstead Act of the following month, and continued to push cooperative marketing as the major solution.[74] In the second field, he used the Unemployment Conference machinery to put Frederick Tyron and a staff of twenty-five to work on a "coal stabilization" study, one that he was temporarily keeping "under cover" but hoped to "stage" later with "great effect."[75] And in the third, he continued to push for claim settlement and selective rate revision, worked out a new scheme to encourage investment through government guarantees to railroad equipment trusts, and took charge of contingency planning for and efforts to head off a national railroad strike. In October 1921, such a strike was averted when the Railway Labor Board announced that it would consider no further wage cuts for six months, and in early 1922 Hoover hoped that his action in persuading railroad and union leaders to set up regional negotiating conferences could transform the pattern of conflict into one of efficiency-minded cooperation.[76]

Trade revival, too, continued to be offered as a major facet of the recovery and reemployment drive. And here, so Hoover believed, substantial progress was being made, both in providing a "correspondence school" and "general staff" for American traders and in removing the obstacles blocking European revival and beneficial flows of credit. As reorganized, he assured Harding, the Bureau of Foreign and Domestic Commerce was becoming a highly effective instrument for generating commercial intelligence and formulating constructive trade strategies.[77] And on other fronts, the disarmament negotiations, the setting up of the debt-funding commission, the insertion of a flexible provision in the tariff, and the establishment of a loan consultation procedure designed to steer American capital into "reproductive" channels were at least partially in line with Hoover's prescriptions.[78] The task ahead was one of using such instruments effectively, and at the time he seemed optimistic about the chances of doing so.

In addition, Hoover was lending his support to programs for developing the aviation, radio, and electrical power industries, trying in each area to work out some form of public-private cooperation that could reduce investment hazards, open up large markets, and guide the development process along "constructive" lines. By early 1922, he had held conferences with both the radio and aviation industries, endorsed their efforts to set up industrial codes, and started pushing for new bureaus that could establish necessary ground rules and work with private developers.[79] And in the power field, he was now emerging as the chief spokesman for interconnected "superpower" networks, hailing these as offering an advance comparable to the first transcontinental railroad, and laying plans for regional conferences that could remove the regulatory, technical, and financial obstacles in the way of their development.[80]

Finally, as he worked to get the economy expanding again, Hoover was also following up on the suggestions for moderating future booms and slumps. In Congress, the Kenyon Bill for public works planning had his endorsement.[81] And amidst much talk of a "business service division" or "advisory planning board" to foster more and better business planning,[82] he had arranged for a quasi-public study of business fluctuations, to be conducted as an offshoot of the Unemployment Conference, but with private funds and research facilities,[83] with the results to be distributed through a prestigious private committee headed by Owen D. Young. In formal terms, this was not a planning agency, but the build-up it received, the careful coordination of its work with national trade associations, and the results expected all make it clear that Hoover and his aides hoped to use such "studies" as key tools in the future management of economic prosperity.[14]

As Hoover's first year in office drew to a close, then, his department had become the center of a complex effort to forge new tools of economic management. It was the Food Administration all over again, remarked Raymond Pearl. And the ironic thing about it, he thought, was that an administration elected to get government out of business was now "doing more interfering with business than any other administration that we have had in peace times."[15] Yet judged either in terms of economic recovery or in terms of the blueprints with which Hoover began, the effort was still far from being an unqualified success. The recession persisted, and in the process of accommodation to political realities and economic conflicts, much of the original vision had proved as yet unrealizable. Emergency relief activities were also beginning to flag as the winter wore on.[16] And of prime significance now, two major crises—one engendered by the antitrust authorities, the other by labor difficulties—were threatening to undermine the whole approach and undo what had been achieved.

VI

From the beginning, Hoover had conceded that the tools through which he hoped to improve the economy's performance could sometimes be converted into instruments of exploitation or blockades against needed readjustment. Yet given the present stage of business evolution, he insisted, this problem was marginal. Scrapping the tools because of it was like prohibiting brick houses because people were sometimes murdered with "brickbats." And it was with general consternation that he realized that the antitrust authorities and the courts seemed to be fashioning just such a prohibition. In the Hardwood Lumber Case *(American Column and Lumber Company v. U.S.)*, decided in December 1921, the Supreme Court held that the statistical program of the Hardwood Manufacturers Association amounted to a price-fixing conspiracy and, in doing so, seemed to be saying that all similar activities were *per se* illegal.[17] "The result," noted George McIlvaine of the American Trade Association Executives, "has been a 'panicky feeling' among thousands of members of national trade organizations and in many lines general demoralization."[18]

Hoover's initial response was an effort to minimize the impact of the ruling, primarily by distinguishing his programs from those of the hardwood manufacturers and urging the Justice Department to endorse these distinctions. The latter, however, remained wary of making specific commitments; and while it did agree to a public exchange of "clarifying letters,"[89] its insistence upon defining illegality in terms of economic intent and effect rather than types of activities left large areas of the Hoover program under a continuing cloud.[90] In Congress, Senator Walter Edge now agreed to sponsor "clarifying" legislation, both to define the limits of associational activities and to protect government-approved programs from prosecution.[91] And in early April, partly to mobilize support behind such legislation, Hoover called some 500 trade association representatives into conference, re-emphasized the distinctions he was making between beneficial cooperation and undesirable "price-fixing," and suggested that a revised statistical program with more of the data distributed through public channels could serve the purposes intended without running afoul of the law.[92]

In the legislative arena, opposition from antitrusters, dissident businessmen, and conservatives fearful of opening the path to new governmental controls prevented passage of either the Edge bills or the new substitutes drafted in the Commerce Department.[93] Yet as spring gave way to summer, other activities did seem to be repairing the damage done by the Hardwood ruling. To provide further "clarification," Hoover was taking two sorts of actions, one involving friendly advice to association leaders from such accommodating Federal Trade Commissioners as Nelson Gaskill, the other involving a new committee to study the subject and produce a "trade association manual."[94] In addition, he had been able to persuade those cooperating in the waste-elimination program that their activities would not be affected, particularly if they stayed within the indicated guidelines in regard to voluntarism and individual adherence to government-endorsed "recommendations."[95] And finally, he had followed up the trade association conference by commissioning David L. Wing to organize and direct a new statistical program. Under it, information that lent itself "readily" to "illegal use" was to be excluded, and associations likely to become targets of legal attack were not to participate. But with these exceptions, cooperating groups could now file their data with a special appendage of the Census Bureau and have it distributed through public channels to all who wished to receive it.[96]

If the antitrust threat had diminished, however, the one posed by labor difficulties had now burgeoned into a major crisis that threatened either to bring the economy to a standstill, force the undesirable liquidation that Hoover had hoped to avoid, or drive the public toward statist measures that, in his view, could undermine the whole basis of future progress. In April 1922, the refusal of coal operators to renew wage contracts at existing levels led the United Mine Workers to call a national coal strike, and on July 1, after the Railway Labor Board had announced further wage cuts, the walkout of the railroad shopmen produced the first nationwide rail strike since 1894. Failure to solve the coal and railroad "problems," it seemed, was about to result in national economic disaster.[97]

In the spring and summer of 1922, then, even as the Woods Committee was winding down and terminating its operations,[98] the Department of Commerce was sprouting new appendages to manage another crisis. From May through August, while Congress was considering the establishment of an emergency distribution system for coal, Hoover was organizing and operating a voluntary structure built around transportation priorities and seeking, through national and district committees, to commit the non-union operators to "fair" prices and responsible behavior.[99] At the same time, he was doing his best to set up machinery that could settle the strikes and handle future disputes.[100] And with the crisis creating a new sense of urgency, he was again working on longer-range proposals that could "solve" the coal and railroad problems. In May, he began circulating a long memorandum on coal reform, proposing now an elaborate stabilization plan featuring district cooperatives, joint-sales agencies, unemployment insurance programs, and action that would retire marginal mines and put them in a "coal reserve."[101] And in June, he began work on a railroad plan that would combine scientific rate rationalization and cooperative modernization with financial incentives to induce voluntary consolidation. The latter, he told Ernest Lewis of the Interstate Commerce Commission, was urgently needed if the railroads were to achieve "constructive leadership" and if "the almost hopeless drifting toward nationalization" was to be checked.[102]

In the railroad field, the Hoover effort to save the shopmen's union and forge a new basis for labor-management cooperation was thrown into disarray by the strike-breaking injunction that Attorney General Daugherty secured on September 1, 1922. It was not until later, with the passage of the Railway Labor Act of 1926 and the adoption of "efficiency plans" by some of the leading railroads, that elements of what Hoover had urged were adopted.[103] But in coal, the secretary of commerce was more influential, and here the settlement that emerged in August and September did bear the hallmarks of his handiwork.

Under it, union operators would maintain existing wage levels for another year; emergency controls would ease the transition from strike-induced shortages to full production; and a newly created United States Coal Commission, with Edward Eyre Hunt as secretary, would complete the "stabilization study" begun by the Unemployment Conference and hopefully lay the basis for implementing something similar to Hoover's reform plan.[104]

By late 1922, then, the two crises that had occupied most of Hoover's energies during the spring and summer months had seemingly been weathered. Although efforts to "modernize" the antitrust laws had failed, he had been successful in stemming the panic engendered by the Hardwood decision and devising strategies that kept his "stabilization" programs operating and flourishing. And while the coal and railroad problems had not been solved to his satisfaction, the threats that they had posed to national well-being had now abated and solutions, at least in the coal field, seemed closer than before. Economic activity, moreover, was picking up. It could be measured in new building starts, an expanding job market, and a rising volume of trade.[105] And like other would-be controllers of economic forces, then and since, Hoover was soon crediting his activities with having checked the forces of contraction, produced recovery along the lines desired, and provided tools that could be used to secure permanent prosperity and perpetual progress.[106]

VII

Whether Hoover's activities really had the effects with which he later credited them is at least questionable. Despite his efforts, such things as public works planning, counter-cyclical investment, balanced world recovery, and the transformation of housing into a modernized mass-production industry never really materialized in the 1920s. In all probability, too, he overestimated the effects that the new statistics and simplification programs were having on economic behavior.[107] And in the post-1922 period, the difficulties in coal, agriculture, and the railroad industry would remain as persistent "problems."[108] Recovery had come. But it was a much less balanced and stable recovery than Hoover had envisioned; and the chief forces behind it, according to economists who have studied the period, were not the Hoover activities but the liquidation of earlier inventories, the new wave of investment in the automobile and other durable consumer-goods industries, and the accumulation of enough savings to finance another burst of construction.[109] It is arguable, perhaps, that Hoover's activities contributed to these developments, or that in helping to sustain the purchasing power of labor he helped to provide the mass markets upon which the new industries would depend. But it also seems arguable that his contributions here were not such as to be crucial, that without them the course of events would have been much the same.

Nevertheless, Hoover and his associates were firmly convinced that the actions taken in 1921 and 1922 had been a great success. As they saw it, these efforts had not only vindicated the purchasing-power theory[110] but helped to shape the tools needed to optimize performance in a modern economy and save the nation from some regressive excursion into radical foolishness or bureaucratic tyranny. The whole experience, so Hoover told Will Payne in 1923, demonstrated that prosperity could be "organized" at home, even in the face of lagging exports and a persisting farm problem. It was all a matter of "organization," "intelligent cooperative effort," and "national industrial planning."[111]

These convictions, moreover, did have significant implications for the future. In the post-1922 period, Hoover would continue to build upon and utilize the tools that had allegedly brought recovery, extol them as the keys to a new and superior "American system," and take substantial credit for what he believed to be an era of unprecedented advance and remarkable stability.[112] And in the wake of a new slump in 1929, he would turn again to the strategies followed by the Unemployment Conference; organize new programs of wage-maintenance, counter-cyclical investment, and emergency relief; and tenaciously defend the notion that his type of "cooperative system" could save the nation from the triple evils of economic disorder, political radicalism, and statist regimentation.[113] In part, of course, these post-1922 policies constituted responses to new developments and pressures, but it is difficult to understand the pattern they took without taking into account the perceptions and convictions formed during Hoover's first two years as secretary of commerce.

Viewed in longer perspective, too, this period can no longer be dismissed as a time when progressive ideas went into hibernation and the country returned to "normalcy" and "laissez-faire." Intermixed with the drives for reinstating nineteenth-century Republicanism was a new vision born of the organizational revolution and the progressive and war experiences, a vision of an ordered economy guided by scientific and service-minded managers and acting collectively to translate the wonders of modern technology into ever higher levels of material abundance and social well-being. And intermixed with the policies of Mellon and Daugherty were a set of activities that did try to implement this vision and develop tools of macroeconomic management. Federal responsibilities in this field, so it now seems, began not in 1933 or 1929 but in 1921.

Again, this is not to say that Hoover and his associates were early-day New Dealers or early exponents of a formalized corporate state. Through the magic of education, voluntarism, and cooperativism, they hoped to avoid the type of statist bureaucracies, make-work endeavors, and government-backed cartelization that would later become significant features of America's "managerial state." And later, when pressures for these kinds of institutions became intense, Hoover would strongly resist them.

Yet if the Hooverites were not New Dealers or corporate statists, neither were they advocates of laissez-faire or classical economic prescriptions. In their conception of how a modern economy worked and what needed to be done to improve its performance, one can find early versions of the purchasing-power and corporatist notions that would dominate later reform thinking. And in the techniques used—especially the bringing together of established interest-group leaders for higher ends, the effort to institutionalize this through functional representation on advisory bodies, and the tendency to equate democratic progress with the participation of these private organizations in policy-making and public management—one can find an early version of the type of "corporate pluralism" that would be idealized in the 1950s and would come under attack in the 1960s.[114] In these respects, the Hoover programs of 1921 and 1922 constitute important precursors of things to come, and if one is to understand the path along which the American quest for a managed prosperity moved, it seems imperative that they receive greater emphasis and more study than they once did.

NOTES

1 Compare Richard Hofstadter, *The Age of Reform* (New York, 1955), pp. 272-328, or Carl Degler, *Out of Our Past* (New York, 1959), pp. 379-416, with Robert Wiebe, *The Search for Order, 1877-1920* (New York, 1967), pp. 111-302, James Weinstein, *The Corporate Ideal in the Liberal State* (Boston, 1968), pp. ix-xiii, 252-54,

Herbert Stein, *The Fiscal Revolution in America* (Chicago, 1969), pp. 6-38; Evan Metcalf, "Secretary Hoover and the Emergence of Macroeconomic Management," *Business History Review,* 49 (Spring 1975), 60-80, and Peri Arnold, "Herbert Hoover and the Continuity of American Policy," *Public Policy,* 20 (Fall 1972), 525-44.

2   Compare William Leuchtenburg, "The New Deal and the Analogue of War," in John Braeman and others, eds., *Change and Continuity in Twentieth Century America* (Columbus, 1964), pp. 81-143, with James Olson, "Herbert Hoover and 'War' on the Depression," *Palimpsest,* 54 (July-August 1973), 26-31.

3   See Albert Romasco, *Poverty of Abundance* (New York, 1965), pp. 24-38, 230-34; Carolyn Grin, "The Unemployment Conference of 1921," *Mid-America,* 54 (April 1973), 83-107; Robert Zieger, *Republicans and Labor* (Lexington, 1969), pp. 87-97; and Robert Murray, *The Harding Era* (Minneapolis, 1969), pp. 195-98, 231-34.

4   Murray, *Harding Era,* pp. 172-92, 381. For Hoover's praise of these policies, see his addresses of July 15, 1921, and October 17, 1922, Herbert C. Hoover Papers (Herbert Hoover Presidential Library, West Branch, Iowa), Public Statements, Nos. 164 and 264. Hoover's chief disagreement with Mellon was over the type of tax that would be most helpful. He favored lower rates on "earned income," high rates on inheritances and "unearned income."

5   Edward Eyre Hunt, "Reconstruction," 13-15, 24-25, Hunt Papers (Hoover Institution Archives, Stanford, California), Box 19; Stein, *Fiscal Revolution,* pp. 6-12. See also Hoover's addresses of February 14 and July 15, 1921, Hoover Papers, Public Statements, Nos. 128 and 164.

6   In addition to the previously cited works by Grin, Stein, Metcalf, and Arnold, see Edwin Layton, *Revolt of the Engineers* (Cleveland, 1971), pp. 189-204, Daniel Nelson, *Unemployment Insurance, 1915-35* (Madison, 1969), pp. 28-40, and Peri Arnold, "Herbert Hoover and the Department of Commerce," Ph.D. Diss. (U. of Chicago, 1972), 63-101.

7   See Robert Himmelberg, "The War Industries Board and the Antitrust Question in November, 1918," *Journal of American History,* 52 (June 1965), 59-74, and Samuel Haber, *Efficiency and Uplift* (Chicago, 1964), pp. 122-24.

8   Robert Cuff, *The War Industries Board* (Baltimore, 1973), pp. 148-90, 273-76.

9   William Moore, "Dissolution of the War Industries Board," and "Post-Armistice Industrial Developments," both in Hunt Papers, Box 10; Robert Himmelberg, "Relaxation of the Federal Antitrust Policy as a Goal of the Business Community during the Period, 1918-1933," Ph.D.Diss. (Penn. State U., 1963), 19-82; John Hanrahan, "The High Cost of Living Controversy, 1919-20," Ph.D. Diss (Fordham U., 1969).

10   See, for example, such works as Arthur Eddy, *The New Competition* (New York, 1912); E. H. Gaunt, *Co-operative Competition* (Providence, 1917); Forrest Crissey, *Teamwork in Trade Building* (1914); and Edward Hurley, *Awakening of Business* (Garden City, 1917).

11   See, for example, Glenn Frank, "Self-Governing Industry" and "The Tide of Affairs," in *Century Magazine,* 98 (June 1919), 225-36, and 102 (June 1921), 311-15; Emmett Naylor, *Trade Associations* (New York, 1921), pp. 15-31; and William Allen White to Hoover, October 18, 1920, Hoover Papers, Pre-Commerce Section, White File. These notions of "cooperative collectivism" were part of a larger postwar consid-

68 *ECONOMIC STABILIZATION, 1921-22*

eration of how cooperative and "integrative" institutions could usher in a new order without sacrificing the essentials of the old. In Europe, various forms of neo-corporatism, neo-guildism, and neo-pluralism were flourishing. And in America, the proposals ranged from syndicalist designs on the left through Mary Follett's "new state" to the corporate communities envisioned by John Leitch and John D. Rockefeller, Jr. In the centrist proposals, like those of Follett, functional associations would be joined by neighborhood units and factory communities as the key regulators of the new order. See Haber, *Efficiency and Uplift*, pp. 124-27; Layton, *Revolt of the Engineers*, pp. 147-48, 179-80; and Charles Maier, "Between Taylorism and Technocracy," *Journal of Contemporary History*, 5 (April 1970), 33-46.

12 The Commerce Department under William Redfield had tried to establish such agencies, but had been largely unsuccessful in doing so. See Redfield, *With Congress and Cabinet* (Garden City, 1924), pp. 216-19. By 1921 agitation for them centered in such groups as the American Association for Labor Legislation, the American Statistical Association, the Taylor Society, the American Management Association, the National Foreign Trade Council, the Chamber of Commerce of the United States, and the American Engineering Council. See, for example, the *American Labor Legislation Review*, 10 (December 1920), 233-39, and 11 (March 1921), 47-58; the *Journal of the American Statistical Association*, 15 (March 1920), 67-75; the *Bulletin of the Taylor Society*, 5 (February 1920), 8; *Nation's Business*, 9 (June 1921), 48-52; *Industrial Management*, 61 (January 1921), 67-68; *Scientific American*, 123 (August 1920), 176.

13 See Robert Van Meter, "The United States and European Recovery, 1918-1923," Ph. D. Diss. (U. of Wisconsin, 1971), 130-31.

14 Hoover, in Senate Committee on Education and Labor, *Industrial Conference* (1920), pp. 26-38, and Senate Commitee on Reconstruction, *Reconstruction and Production* (1921), pp. 617-27; Hoover's Statement to the Kansas Board of Agriculture, James Bell Papers (Minnesota Historical Society), Box 1; Hoover, in *Mining and Metallurgy*, 159 (March 1920), 1-2; Hoover's addresses of February 17, April 10, August 27, October 12, November 19, 1920, and February 14, 1921, Hoover Papers, Public Statements, Nos. 45, 59, 84, 94, 102, 128. See also E. E. Hunt, "Notes on the Hoover Creed," Hunt Papers, Box 20, and Barry Karl, "Presidential Planning and Social Science Research," in *Perspectives in American History* (1969), pp. 351-58.

15 Hoover, in Senate Reconstruction Committee, *Reconstruction*, pp. 625-26; Hoover's addresses of August 27, 1920, and February 14, 1921, Hoover Papers, Public Statements, Nos. 84 and 128.

16 Hoover's address of February 14, 1921, Hoover Papers, Public Statements, No. 128; Hunt, "Reconstruction," 11-15, 24-25; Layton, *Revolt of the Engineers*, pp. 190-94; Metcalf, "Hoover and Emergence of Macroeconomic Management," 61-66.

17 Van Meter, "U.S. and European Recovery," 205-11.

18 Hoover to Harding, September 8, 1920, and February 23, 1921, Hoover Papers, Pre-Commerce Section, Harding File; Metcalf, "Hoover and Emergence of Macroeconomic Management," 66-69.

19 In 1919 he had felt that "a few strong men" could exert greater influence from outside the government than from within. Hoover to William Glasgow, April 12, 1919, Hoover Papers, Pre-Commerce Section, Glasgow File.

20 Hoover to Harding, February 23, 1921, Hoover Papers, Pre-Commerce Section, Harding File; E. E. Hunt, "Interview with Hoover," January 16, 1935, Hunt Papers, Box 20; Hoover, *Memoirs,* (New York, 1951), 2:36.

21 *New York Times,* March 11, 1921; Hoover's statement of March 11, 1921, Hoover Papers, Public Statements, No. 134.

22 Hoover, "Memorandum on Reorganization," and George Baldwin to Hoover, April 24, 1921, Hoover Papers, Commerce Section, Reorganization File; Hoover, "The Problem of Reorganization," May 23, 1921, Hoover Papers, Commerce Section, Reorganization of Government Departments File; "Departmental Reorganization" and "Suggestions for Expansion along Domestic Lines," Bureau of Foreign and Domestic Commerce Records (National Archives), File 160; "How the Department of Commerce Should Be Reorganized and Should Function," Hoover Papers, Commerce Section, General Government Reorganization File.

23 "List of National Organizations Prepared for Hoover," March 9, 1921, Hoover Papers, Commerce Section, Recommendations for Advisory Board File.

24 See Edward and Frederick Schapsmeier, "Disharmony in the Harding Cabinet," *Ohio History,* 75 (Spring-Summer 1966), 127–28; Joseph Brandes, *Herbert Hoover and Economic Diplomacy* (Pittsburgh, 1962), pp. 41–42; *American Federationist,* 28 (June 1921), 503–04; and Hoover to Harding, December 31, 1921, Hoover Papers, Commerce Section, Reorganization of Government Departments File.

25 Hoover, "Trade Organizations and the Law," *American Machinist,* 54 (June 30, 1921), 1147; Himmelberg, "Relaxation of Antitrust," 100–01; G. D. Goff to Hoover, March 28, 1921, and Harry Daugherty to Hoover, May 16, 1921, Hoover Papers, Commerce Section, Justice Department File.

26 Arnold, "Hoover and Department of Commerce," 86–87; *Women's Wear,* April 26, 1921.

27 Donald Wilhelm, "Mr. Hoover as Secretary of Commerce," *World's Work,* 43 (February 1922), 409.

28 Arnold, "Hoover and Department of Commerce," 121–22; *New York Times,* March 11, 15, 20, April 17, 23, 29, 1921.

29 J. W. Drake to Hoover, June 9 and 24 and July 5, 1921, Hoover to Drake, June 4, 1921, Hoover to Arch Shaw, June 29, 1921, Hoover to Charles Piez, June 4, 1921, Hoover Papers, Commerce Section, Commerce—Industrial Group File; Commerce Department Press Release, April 29, 1921, Hoover Papers, Commerce Section, Commerce—First Conference File; Hoover to Walter Tower and others, April 25, 1921, Hoover Papers, Commerce Section, Commerce—Foreign and Domestic Commerce File.

30 Federated American Engineering Societies, *Waste in Industry* (1921), pp. v, 8–16, 24–30; Layton, *Revolt of the Engineers,* pp. 201–03; Hunt, "Reconstruction," 17–21; "Purpose and Plan," February 16, 1921, Hoover Papers, Pre-Commerce Section, Industrial Waste Committee File.

31 Haber, *Efficiency and Uplift,* p. 159; Layton, *Revolt of the Engineers,* pp. 203–04. Of the groups making up the Federated American Engineering Societies, only the American Society of Mechanical Engineers endorsed the report.

32 Typical of what was being proposed and considered were George Dickson, "A Suggestion," March 21, 1921, Hoover Papers, Commerce Section, Suggestions File, and Calvin Rice to Hoover, July 26, 1921, Hoover Papers, Commerce Section, Reorganization File.

33 Craig Lloyd, *Aggressive Introvert* (Columbus, 1972), pp. 62–63. Shaw had

headed the wartime conservation agency and was now offered the post of assistant secretary of commerce. He refused, but arranged for Feiker to become Hoover's assistant.

34 Lloyd, *Aggressive Introvert,* p. 63; Conference of Business Paper Editors, "Standardization Survey," Feiker to George Babcock, July 26, 1921, Feiker to Maurice Greenough, August 8, 1921, Commerce Department Records (National Archives), File 81368.

35 Herbert Heaton, *Scholar in Action* (Cambridge, 1952), pp. 189-91; William Rossiter to Hoover, March 12, 1921, and Advisory Committee on the Census to Hoover, May 7, 1921, Hoover Papers, Commerce Section, Commerce—Bureau of the Census File. The committee had been appointed originally as an advisory body on the Census of 1920. It was chaired by the publisher William S. Rossiter.

36 Hoover's address of April 28, 1921, Hoover Papers, Public Statements, No. 149; Hoover to J. Jackson, June 1, 1921, Commerce Department Records, File 76850/1; Hoover to Harding, June 9, 1921, Hoover Papers, Commerce Section, Presidential File; Feiker to Hoover, July 8, 1921, Hoover Papers, Commerce Section, Commerce Assistants File; Nathan Williams, "Conversation with Hoover," July 7, 1921, Hoover Papers, Commerce Section, Feiker File.

37 Such opposition is discussed in the *New York Journal of Commerce,* July 2, 1921.

38 Secretary of Commerce, *Annual Report* (1922), pp. 88-89; Hoover to Frank Taussig, July 2, 1921, Hoover Papers, Commerce Section, Taussig File; Hoover to Harding, June 9, 1921, Hoover Papers, Commerce Section, Presidential File.

39 See Hoover to Mellon, April 11, 1921, Hoover Papers, Commerce Section, Reorganization of Government Departments File. The transfer finally took place in 1923.

40 *New York Times,* June 3, 1921; William Lamb to Hoover, July 11, 1921, Commerce Department Records, File 81288.

41 Nathan Williams, "Conversation with Hoover," July 7, 1921, Hoover Papers, Commerce Section, Feiker File; Hoover to George Huddleston, May 24, 1921, Hoover Papers, Commerce Section, Labor Department File; Hoover to Harding, June 9, 1921, Hoover Papers, Commerce Section, Presidential File.

42 *New York World,* June 11, 1921; Hoover to Daugherty, June 13, 1921, Hoover Papers, Commerce Section, Justice Department File; Hoover to William Jennett, September 24, 1921, and E. H. Naylor to Feiker, October 18, 1921, Commerce Department Records, File 81288; William Lamb to Feiker, August 31, 1921, Hoover Papers, Commerce Section, Feiker File.

43 Brandes, *Hoover and Economic Diplomacy,* pp. 40-42; Donald Winters, *Henry Cantwell Wallace as Secretary of Agriculture* (Urbana, 1970), pp. 222-27; A. J. Wolfe to Louis Domeratzky, March 25, 1922, and Duncan Fletcher to C. R. Snow, March 9, 1922, Bureau of Foreign and Domestic Commerce Records, File 033.

44 R. L. MacElwee, the bureau chief when Hoover took over, was dismissed for lying about material that he had fed to the press. See Hoover to Harding, March 17, 1921, Hoover Papers, Commerce Section, Commerce—Foreign and Domestic Commerce File. Klein, a protegé of Edwin Gay, had headed the Latin American division of the bureau during the war and later served as a commercial attache in Argentina. For his background, ideas, and activities, see Robert Seidel, "Progressive Pan Americanism," Ph.D. Diss. (Cornell U., 1973).

45   See especially Hoover's address before the National Shoe and Leather Exposition, July 12, 1921, Hoover Papers, Commerce Section, Feiker File.

46   See, for example, Guy Emerson to Hoover, March 15, 1921, Hoover Papers, Commerce Section, Reorganization File. See also Louis Domeratzky's "Plan for Commodity Divisions" and C. E. Herring to Hoover, April 20, 1921, Bureau of Foreign and Domestic Commerce Records, File 160.

47   Hoover to Walter Tower and others, April 25, 1921, Hoover Papers, Commerce Section, Commerce—Foreign and Domestic Commerce File; Feiker to Klein, September 18, 1921, Bureau of Foreign and Domestic Commerce Records, File 160.2; Secretary of Commerce, *Annual Report* (1922), p. 4; "Development of the Bureau of Foreign and Domestic Commerce," Commerce Department Records, Robert Lamont Collection, Box 6.

48   The phrase is used by Donald Wilhelm in *World's Work,* 43 (February 1922), 408. For a detailed discussion of the completed reorganization and the men in charge of each commodity division, see Will Kennedy, "Business Experts Make Sacrifices to Help Put the Hoover Plan Across," *Washington Star,* December 25, 1921.

49   The Edge Act of 1919 had authorized the chartering of such corporations, and Hoover had taken part in the most ambitious effort to organize one, namely the launching of the Foreign Trade Financing Corporation in December 1920. See Van Meter, "U.S. and European Recovery," 121-23, 205-11.

50   Van Meter, "U.S. and European Recovery," 212-17, 293, 317-30; Michael J. Hogan, "The United States and the Problem of International Economic Control, 1918-1928," Ph.D. Diss. (U. of Iowa, 1974), 96-99; Murray, *Harding Era,* pp. 271-74; Melvyn Leffler, "Origins of Republican War Debt Policy, 1921-1923," *Journal of American History,* 59 (December 1972), 591-96.

51   Hoover, "The Housing Problem," *Industrial Management,* 60 (December 1920), 424a-24b; Hoover to Ernest Trigg, May 16, 1921, Hoover to Harding, February 9, 1922, and "Better Homes and Decreased Costs Through Elimination of Waste in Construction," January 11, 1928, Hoover Papers, Commerce Section, Building and Housing File; Hunt, "Reconstruction," 57-62.

52   Hoover to Harding, March 16, 1921, Harding Papers (Ohio Historical Society), Box 5. Miller had directed the Senate inquiry into housing in 1919 and 1920. According to Hoover, he had "a larger knowledge of the building trades and labor conditions than anyone in the country."

53   "Better Homes and Decreased Costs Through Elimination of Waste in Construction," January 11, 1928, and Miller to Hoover, April 22, 1921, Hoover Papers, Commerce Section, Building and Housing File; Secretary of Commerce, *Annual Report* (1922), p. 7.

54   Miller to Hoover, June 7, 1921, and Hoover to Miller, July 18, 1921, Hoover Papers, Commerce Section, Building and Housing File. Gries had been in the pre-1914 Bureau of Corporations and in the wartime Division of Planning and Statistics. Since 1914 he had held the Chair of Lumber at Harvard.

55   "Better Homes and Decreased Costs Through Elimination of Waste in Construction," January 11, 1928, "Federal Activity in Promotion of Better Housing Conditions and Home Ownership" [1923], Gries to Hoover, August 16 and 24, 1921, Hoover to Joseph DeFrees, April 19, 1921, Hoover to William Calder, August 12, 1921,

and Hoover to Harding, February 9, 1922, Hoover Papers, Commerce Section, Building and Housing File; Hoover's addresses of May 12 and July 15, 1921, Hoover Papers, Public Statements, Nos. 152 and 164.

56   Hoover, in *Mining and Metallurgy,* 159 (March 1920), 1–2; Hoover to D. B. Wentz, May 18, 1921, Hoover to Joseph Frelinghuysen, June 18, 1921, Hoover to H. E. Loomis, June 27, 1921, and Miller to Hoover, May 13, 1921, Hoover Papers, Commerce Section, Coal File.

57   The original bill called for an independent coal commission to gather and publish statistics. As revised, it would authorize the Commerce Department to do so. Succeeding drafts of the bill are in the Hoover Papers, Commerce Section, Coal File.

58   "Description of Coal Conferences of June 7–8, 1921," and Hoover to Walter Smith, January 16, 1922, Hoover Papers, Commerce Section, Coal File; T. O. Busbee to C. H. Huston, May 11, 1921, W. J. Willits to Morrow Chamberlain, June 21, 1921, and E. McAuliffe to C. P. White, July 10, 1921, Commerce Department Records, File 80769. See also Ellis Hawley, "Secretary Hoover and the Bituminous Coal Problem," *Business History Review,* 42 (Autumn 1968), 255.

59   Albert Fall to Harding, November 28, 1921, and Hoover to Harding, December 31, 1921, Hoover Papers, Commerce Section, Reorganization of Government Departments File. It was not until 1925 that the Bureau of Mines and portions of the Geological Survey were finally transferred to the Commerce Department.

60   Murray, *Harding Era,* pp. 221–23; Miller to Hoover, June 8, 1921, Hoover Papers, Commerce Section, Building and Housing File; Hoover to Ernest Lewis, June 15, 1921, and Lewis's "Conference Memorandum No. 1," June 15, 1921, Hoover Papers, Commerce Section, Interstate Commerce Commission File; Hoover's memorandum of July 13, 1921, Hoover to Mark Potter, June 29, 1921, Hoover to Andrew Mellon, June 27, 1921, and Hoover to Harding, July 21, 1921, Hoover Papers, Commerce Section, Railroads File.

61   Hoover's statement before the Kansas Board of Agriculture [1920], Bell Papers, Box 1; Hunt, "Reconstruction," 66–67.

62   Murray, *Harding Era,* pp. 208–10; Winters, *Wallace,* pp. 82–86; Hoover to Harding, August 18, 1921, Hoover Papers, Commerce Section, Agriculture File; Gary Koerselman, "Herbert Hoover and the Farm Crisis of the Twenties," Ph.D. Diss. (Northern Illinois U., 1971), 130–36.

63   Hoover to Arthur Capper, April 23, 1921, Henry C. Wallace Papers (U. of Iowa), Box 2, Folder 10; Winters, *Wallace,* pp. 225–29.

64   Grin, "Unemployment Conference," 86–87; *New York Times,* August 29, 30, 1921; Hoover's letter on fall letting of highway contracts, August 27, 1921, Hoover Papers, Commerce Section, Construction File; E. E. Hunt, "From 1921 Forward," *Survey,* 62 (April 1, 1929), 6.

65   The committee was enlarged from seven to twenty members, and three subcommittees were set up, one on unemployment statistics, one on temporary relief, and one on permanent prevention of unemployment. Among the new members were Otto Mallery, Sam Lewisohn, Henry Seager, Leo Wolman, John Andrews, Samuel Lindsay, and Henry Dennison, all prominent in the development of the unemployment stabilization program being urged by the American Association for Labor Legislation. See Grin, "Unemployment Conference," 87; Metcalf, "Hoover and the Emergence of Macro-

economic Management," 62–64, 71–73; Nelson, *Unemployment Insurance,* pp. 37–38; and William Rossiter to Hoover, September 8, 1921, Hoover Papers, Commerce Section, Unemployment Advisory Committee File.

66 Economic Advisory Committee Report, September 26, 1921, Hoover Papers, Commerce Section, Unemployment Advisory Committee File. An advance summary of the report was made available on September 22. For the similarities with the earlier AALL program, compare the report with John B. Andrews, "A Practical Program for the Prevention of Unemployment in America," *American Labor Legislation Review,* 5 (June 1915), 173–92.

67 William Chenery, "Mr. Hoover's Hand," *Survey,* 47 (October 22, 1921), 107; Grin, "Unemployment Conference," 90–92; Hunt, "Reconstruction," 32–40; President's Conference on Unemployment, "General Recommendations," October 11, 1921, Hoover Papers, Commerce Section, Unemployment Conference File.

68 Grin, "Unemployment Conference," 92–96; E. E. Hunt, "Washington Conference on Unemployment," Hoover Papers, Commerce Section, Unemployment Conference File; Commerce Department Press Release, December 17, 1921, Hoover Papers, Commerce Section, Unemployment Press Releases File.

69 Hunt, "Reconstruction," 44–47; Grin, "Unemployment Conference," 97–102. Congress passed the Federal Highway Act, but delayed action on the railroad claims bill and rejected the reclamation and employment service measures.

70 Following their success in reducing the varieties of paving brick from 66 to 7, the simplifiers concentrated their attention on the face brick, refractories, building hardware, plumbing, paint, and lumber industries. Feiker to E. W. McCullough, November 19, 1921, Commerce Department Records, File 81368; Hoover to Feiker, December 9, 1921, Hoover Papers, Commerce Section, Commerce Assistants File; Secretary of Commerce, *Annual Report* (1922), pp. 138–40. Durgin, an electrical engineer from Commonwealth Edison, took charge of the program in November 1921. It was organized as a new division in January 1922.

71 Gries, "Standardization in the Building Industry," February 22, 1922, Gries to Hoover, February 16, 1922, and Hoover to Harding, February 9, 1922, Hoover Papers, Commerce Section, Building and Housing File; Gries to Hoover, March 8, 1922, Hoover Papers, Commerce Section, Construction Industries File.

72 Gries to Hoover, March 9, 1922, Hoover to R. C. Marshall, March 10, 1922, and Hoover's address to the Construction Industries Meeting, Chicago, April 4, 1922, Hoover Papers, Commerce Section, Construction Industries File.

73 Rose C. Field, "Industry's New Doctors," in *New York Times,* June 4, 1922; Frank Freidel, *Franklin D. Roosevelt: The Ordeal* (Boston, 1954), pp. 153–55; Hoover's address of June 19, 1922, Hoover Papers, Public Statements, No. 243. The new council was to bring together the leaders of ten functional groups, namely the architects, engineers, contractors, workers, materials manufacturers, financiers, retailers, government builders, utilities, and local communities (as represented by the chambers of commerce). Its job, as Roosevelt saw it, was to harmonize their work, raise their ethical standards, and commit them to "intensive national planning" in the public interest.

74 Murray, *Harding Era,* pp. 213–14, 218–20; Koerselman, "Hoover and Farm Crisis," 259–61, 309–16.

75   Hunt to Paul Kellogg, February 28 and March 24, 1922, and February 6, 1923, Survey Associates Papers (Social Welfare History Archives, U. of Minnesota), Folder 622.

76   Murray, *Harding Era*, pp. 240-42; Hoover's statements to the Railway Conference and the Interstate Commerce Commission, January 16 and February 3, 1922, Hoover to Eugene Black, February 10, 1922, Hoover to Norman Gould, February 24, 1922, Daniel Willard to Hoover, January 26, 1922, and "Federal Emergency Organization for the Movement of Necessities in Case of a Railway Strike," Hoover Papers, Commerce Section, Railroads File.

77   John Burnam, "What Hoover Is Doing," *Nation's Business*, 10 (February 1922), 16-17; Hoover to Harding, June 24, 1922, Hoover Papers, Commerce Section, Commerce—Foreign and Domestic Commerce File.

78   Hoover to Harding, January 4, 1922, Harding Papers, Box 5; Murray, *Harding Era*, 274-76, 355, 361-62; Hogan, "U.S. and International Economic Control," 97-99; Carl Parrini, *Heir to Empire* (Pittsburgh, 1969), pp. 186-88.

79   Murray, *Harding Era*, 410-11; Secretary of Commerce, *Annual Report* (1922), pp. 13-14; Glenn Johnson, "Secretary of Commerce Herbert Hoover: The First Regulator of American Broadcasting," Ph.D. Diss. (U. of Iowa, 1970), 82-88.

80   See his remarks as reported in the *San Francisco Chronicle*, September 15, 1921, and the *Boston Globe*, April 8 and 23, 1922. See also his address to the National Electric Light Association, May 19, 1922, Hoover Papers, Commerce Section, Superpower File. As part of the new development, Hoover hoped to see coal transformed into electricity at the mines and "shipped" over the wires.

81   The bill, however, failed to pass. Conservatives argued against interference with "natural law," and others opposed it because it was "fathered by big business," might be used for partisan purposes, or would give undue power to Hoover. Senator George Norris thought "we had better let God run it as in the past, and not take the power away from Him and give it to Hoover." Hunt, "Reconstruction," 46-47; President's Conference on Unemployment, *Business Cycles and Unemployment* (1923), pp. 247-48; Grin, "Unemployment Conference," 102-03.

82   See, for example, Otto Mallery to Hoover, May 5, 1922, Hoover Papers, Commerce Section, Reorganization File, and E. E. Hunt to Philip Cabot, September 13, 1922, Hunt Papers, Box 18. Symptomatic of the period was a proposal by Roger Babson in January 1922. He would eliminate "abnormal fluctuations and thus solve the problem of unemployment and social conflict" by bringing the representatives of the "great national associations" together in an "industrial capital" and having them serve as an economic council on the "nation's problems." Secretary of Labor James Davis was much taken with the idea, but Hoover did not respond. See the *New York Times*, January 23, 1922, and Davis to Harding, January 25, 1922, Harding Papers, Box 32.

83   The funds came from the Carnegie Foundation, the research staff from the National Bureau of Economic Research. Wesley Mitchell served as research director. Hunt, "Business Cycles and Unemployment," October 1, 1927, Hunt Papers, Box 28.

84   Hunt, "Business Cycles and Unemployment," October 1, 1927, Hunt Papers, Box 28; Hunt to Hoover, April 6, 1922, Hoover Papers, Commerce Section, Hunt File; Metcalf, "Hoover and the Emergence of Macroeconomic Management," 74-77.

85   Raymond Pearl to John Ford Bell, October 29, 1921, Bell Papers, Box 1.

86 Grin, "Unemployment Conference," 96–97.

87 257 *U.S.* 377; Himmelberg, "Relaxation of Antitrust," 101–02, 116; *New York Times,* June 3, 1921, and April 13 and 14, 1922.

88 McIlvaine to Hoover, February 4, 1922, Hoover Papers, Commerce Section, Trade Associations File.

89 Daugherty to Hoover, January 3, 1922, Hoover Papers, Commerce Section, Justice Department File; William Lamb to Hoover, January 16, 1922, Hoover to Daugherty, February 3, 1922, and Daugherty to Hoover, February 8, 1922, Hoover Papers, Commerce Section, Trade Associations File.

90 As trade association official Charles White put it, "Mr. Daugherty's opinion or answer to Mr. Hoover's letter has practically said nothing, and until and unless we can have some more definite statement . . . then we are just as much in the dark as ever we were, and our own people . . . will certainly not feel justified in beginning any such trade activities as are outlined in Mr. Hoover's letter." White to Hoover, February 13, 1922, Hoover Papers, Commerce Section, Trade Associations File.

91 S.J.Res. 188 and S. 3385, 67 Cong., 2 Sess., April 3, 1922, copies in Hoover Papers, Commerce Section, Trade Associations File.

92 Himmelberg, "Relaxation of Antitrust," 118–19; Conference of Trade Associations Proceedings, April 12, 1922, Lamb to Hoover, April 1, 1922, and Commerce Department Press Releases, March 17 and April 1, 1922, Hoover Papers, Commerce Section, Trade Associations File.

93 For the critique from the antitrust camp, see the exchange with Samuel Untermyer, *New York Times,* April 17, 1922. For that from the right, see the *Manufacturers' News,* April 20, 1922. For legislative action, see Edge to Hoover, April 22 and May 5, 1922, and Hoover to Edge, June 12, 1922, Hoover Papers, Commerce Section, Trade Associations File; Edge to Hoover, June 14, 1922, Hoover Papers, Commerce Section, Senate File, and David Wing to Richard Emmet, June 19, 1922, Hoover Papers, Commerce Section, Commerce—Trade Association Statistics File.

94 David Wing, Report on Cooperation Work, August 5, 1922, Hoover Papers, Commerce Section, Commerce—Trade Association Statistics File; "General Committee Cooperating on Trade Association Activities," Hoover Papers, Commerce Section, Trade Association Activities File; Feiker to Klein, December 8, 1922, Bureau of Foreign and Domestic Commerce Records, File 712.1.

95 "Report on Cooperation between Department of Commerce and the American Engineering Standards Committee," March 9, 1922, Hoover Papers, Commerce Section, Construction File; Durgin to Hoover, November 1, 1922, Commerce Department Records, File 82341; *New York Times,* May 23, 1922.

96 Wing, Reports on Cooperation Work, May 13, 23, and 27, June 19, and August 5, 1922, Wing's "Methods of Cooperation with Associations in Distributing Trade Information," and Wing to Emmet, June 7, 1922, Hoover Papers, Commerce Section, Commerce—Trade Association Statistics File; "Department's Cooperation for Distribution of Trade Statistics Gathered by Trade Associations," Hoover Papers, Commerce Section, Trade Associations File.

97 Zieger, *Republicans and Labor,* pp. 114–17; Murray, *Harding Era,* pp. 225, 243–44.

98   The Woods operation came to an end in May 1922. Harding to Hoover, May 22, 1922, Hoover Papers, Commerce Section, Unemployment File.

99   "Coal," April 16, 1922, Hoover to James Goodrich, August 26, 1922, and Hoover to Harding, August 23, 1922, Hoover Papers, Commerce Section, Coal File; Hawley, "Hoover and Bituminous Coal," 257–58.

100   Zieger, Republicans and Labor, pp. 123–25, 131–34; Murray, Harding Era, pp. 245–46, 249–50; Hoover's memorandum of July 23, 1922, Hoover Papers, Commerce Section, Railroads File; Ronald Radosh, "Labor and the Economy," in Jerry Israel, ed., Building the Organizational Society (New York, 1972), pp. 76–78.

101   Hawley, "Hoover and Bituminous Coal," 259–62; Hoover, "A Plan to Secure Continuous Employment and Greater Stability in the Bituminous Coal Industry," and Hoover to Julius Barnes, July 22, 1922, Hoover Papers, Commerce Section, Coal File.

102   Hoover to Ernest Lewis, June 16, 1922, Hoover Papers, Commerce Section, Railroads File; Hoover, "Railroad Reorganization" [April 1923], Hoover Papers, Commerce Section, Railroad Consolidation File; Hoover, "The Railways," November 7, 1922, Harding Papers, Box 5.

103   Zieger, Republicans and Labor, pp. 138–40, 202–12; Radosh, "Labor and the American Economy," 78–81; Murray, Harding Era, pp. 254–57, 261.

104   Hawley, "Hoover and Bituminous Coal," 258–59, 262–63; Murray, Harding Era, pp. 258–59; Federal Fuel Distributor's Report, December 27, 1922, Hoover to the U.S. Coal Commission, November 1, 1922, and Commerce Department Press Release, September 16, 1922, Hoover Papers, Commerce Section, Coal File.

105   Department of Commerce, "Review of Business in 1922," reprinted in Commercial and Financial Chronicle, 115 (December 30, 1922), 2860–61.

106   Hoover's addresses of October 17, 1922, and October 25, 1924, Hoover Papers, Public Statements, Nos. 264 and 406; Hoover, The New Day (Stanford, 1928), pp. 66–83.

107   For the meagerness of results in these areas, see Grin, "Unemployment Conference," 97–107; Zieger, Republicans and Labor, p. 96; Parrini, Heir to Empire, pp. 268–76; George Soule, Prosperity Decade (New York, 1947), pp. 172–74; and Metcalf, "Hoover and the Emergence of Macroeconomic Management," 77–79.

108   Soule, Prosperity Decade, pp. 160–62, 176–78, 229–34. In November 1923, Hoover still regarded coal and railroads as the "two most pressing economic problems." Hoover to Coolidge, November 22, 1923, Hoover Papers, Commerce Section, Presidential File.

109   Soule, Prosperity Decade, pp. 110–20.

110   "Within sixty days," Hoover noted in 1923, the "forced temporary employment" undertaken in the wake of the Unemployment Conference became "permanent employment." "The wages that the men earned on a temporary footing went into consumption and helped to make the employment permanent." Quoted in Will Payne, "Income Tax Dividends," Saturday Evening Post, 196 (September 1, 1923), 122.

111   Ibid. See also Grin, "Unemployment Conference," 92, 106–07, and Hunt, "Business Cycles and Unemployment," October 1, 1927, Hunt Papers, Box 28.

112 William Hard, "The New Hoover," *Review of Reviews,* 86 (November 1927), 478–84; Hoover to David Lawrence, December 29, 1927, Hoover Papers, Commerce Section, American Businessman File; Hoover, "The Department of Commerce" [1926], Hoover Papers, Commerce Section, Commerce Department Achievements File; Hoover, *New Day,* pp. 22–23.

113 Romasco, *Poverty of Abundance,* pp. 24–65.

114 See Arnold, "Hoover and the Department of Commerce," 217–22, and "Hoover and the Continuity of American Public Policy," 526–44. The corollary of these conclusions, of course, is that the New Deal period was far less innovative or revolutionary than once depicted. And while recent scholarship has disagreed about whether this was good or bad, it had tended to agree that such was the case.

SUMMARY OF COMMENTARY BY DISCUSSANTS AND CONFEREES

Discussion of the paper began with formal commentaries by Professors Peri Arnold of the University of Notre Dame and Alan Seltzer of the University of Maryland, Baltimore. Both expressed fundamental agreement with the central arguments, but each called for more discussion and analysis at key points. Arnold urged fuller recognition of defects in the Hooverian ideal, especially its lack of mechanisms for dealing with inequity, irrationality, and irresponsibility in the private sector and its assumption that organizations committed to conflict and clientelism could become vehicles for cooperative stabilization. He also noted how Hoover's philosophy cut across the traditional divisions between left and right, and he wondered how Hoover could fail to see that his actions were paving the way for big government. Seltzer urged further elucidation of Hoover's views on antitrust. These should be distinguished, he thought, not only from the views of Daugherty's antitrust division, the New Nationalists of 1912, and the later supporters of the NRA but also from those held by Arthur Jerome Eddy and other proponents of open price plans. In addition, he called for fuller recognition of Hoover's "naive optimism." The secretary, he noted, had once expressed strong doubts about business altruism, especially in peacetime. Yet in 1921 he relied upon the very thing he had once portrayed as weak, acted as if businessmen were or would become statesmen, and seemed willing to accept any progress as an indication that things were going well.

In a brief response to the commentaries, Hawley made several points. In Hoover's mind, he thought, there had been no contradiction between departmental expansionism and opposition to big government. The expansionism was for the purpose of erecting institutions that would save us from creeping statism; and once these were erected, governmental controls and services would tend to wither away. Hoover seemed not to doubt that they could be erected, that potentially the private sector was capable of far greater rationality, responsibility, and equity than statist institutions ever could be. Nor was this because he saw no defects in the private bodies to which he would delegate power and responsibility. It was more a matter of the greater defects he perceived in other schemes for securing economic order. As for his illusions about the effectiveness of his program, he was not much different in this regard from other men who have taken action and then witnessed the improvement of the economy. Both the New Dealers of 1936 and the New Frontiersmen of the mid-1960s fell victim to similar illusions. And as for antitrust, Hoover did not stay put to the extent that he did on most other aspects of his organizational ideal. He tried to distinguish between those statistical exchanges that contributed to general economic stability and the kind used to protect exploitive or inefficient industries. But at one time he had looked upon open price plans as belonging in the first category rather than the second, and he did support legislation widely regarded as weakening the legal barriers against open price systems and related market restraints.

The discussion following the formal commentaries revolved mostly around three aspects of Hoover's thought. One was his vision of a new business management, divorced from ownership and operating in a new institutional context as enlightened social trustees. Further comments on this were made by Peri Arnold, Robert Wood, Ellis Hawley, Robert Zieger, and Alan Seltzer, with some noting the parallels between Hoover's ideas and later managerial thought, and with others focusing on his failure to see the need for external checks and new mechanisms of social accountability. The second topic of discussion, commented on by Melvyn Leffler, Joseph Brandes, and Alan Seltzer, was Hoover's prescriptions for international stability, especially in regard to combatting radicalism and statism and developing transnational cooperation between enlightened business groups. And the third subject discussed was Hoover's "apoliticalism," a quality reflected particularly in his efforts to shift decision making into an allegedly more rational syndicalist arena where it would be less influenced by mass, interest-group, and partisan impulses. Those commenting on this agreed that Hoover had made such efforts and had called them "apolitical." But some pointed out that the actual effect was to enhance the importance of a kind of bureaucratic politics at which Hoover excelled; and others thought that "apoliticalism" was itself a political strategy, designed to strengthen a political position by insisting that it was a non-negotiable technological necessity. One commentator compared it to "solidarism" in France.

In addition, two other lines of discussion developed. One arose from Francis O'Brien's questions concerning the economic and political effects of Hoover's programs. The treatment of these, he thought, had been a bit deflating; and at his request, Hawley restated and elaborated upon the arguments as to what had brought economic recovery and how the experience of the early 1920s had shaped future policy decisions. The other line of discussion revolved around a continued debate concerning Hoover's attitudes toward open price plans. Peri Arnold argued that Hoover's renunciation of them was based on legal rather than economic considerations. Had they remained legal, they would have remained one of the mechanisms through which he was attempting to manage and stabilize market behavior. But with this view, Alan Seltzer strongly disagreed. Hoover, he insisted, came to see open price plans as being among those restraints that were contrary to the public interest, and his post-1929 position remained consistent with this perception.

Finally, as the session drew to a close, Hawley was asked to compare his interpretation of Hoover with that set forth by William Appleman Williams. In doing so, he argued that Williams had made Hoover into too much of a corporate syndicalist and had failed to bring out how corporative institutions would, in theory, work in tandem with healthy competition and individual initiative.

Three Facets of Hooverian Associationalism: Lumber, Aviation, and Movies, 1921–1930

ELLIS HAWLEY

University of Iowa

•

I

Writing in 1927 to Edward Eyre Hunt, Herbert Hoover's principal aide and handyman, paper manufacturer Henry S. Dennison deplored both the workings of uncontrolled markets and those of governmental regulation. The public, he conceded, was entitled to industrial efficiency, reasonable prices, and rising standards of living, but the way to secure these was not through the recipes put forth by laissez faire ideologues, archaic antitrusters, or utility-type regulationists. It was through a "scientific regulation" built "from the inside" through structures "controlled by the laws of Scientific Management." And the government needed was not a "political government" operating through antitrust bureaus or regulatory commissions. It was an "economic government" resting on socially responsible economic institutions and processes and operating through enlightened economic councils and authorities.[1]

What Dennison was expressing, although he would not have used the term, was an American variant of the neo-corporatism then appearing in most of the world's advanced industrial societies.[2] Underlying his prescription for meeting public needs was the

95

213

notion that the disinterested "public man" envisioned in earlier regulationist theory[3] could be found not in a civil service or a political elite but rather in enlightened areas of the private sector, and that, consequently, the essence of good public policy was to fashion a form of regulation that made use of this social resource. For America it was a notion that lost much of its credibility during the 1930s. But in a variety of ways it has continued to influence regulatory policy, and during the years from 1916 to 1934 it was a prime influence, not only on the shape that publicly approved regulation took but on the support that antitrust and utility-type regulationists could muster. It deserves study as a factor shaping a whole era of the nation's regulatory history, one that influenced in particular the histories of those industries that became that era's "national problems." And at a time having striking parallels with this earlier era—a time when concern with market failures is again combined with a turning away from governmental regulation and a search for alternatives that can make use of regulatory resources in the private sector—a fuller knowledge of this historical experience seems especially relevant.[4]

My purpose, then, in what follows is to examine and analyze selected aspects of this earlier search for a corporative as opposed to a governmental form of "regulation." I propose, first of all, to sketch briefly the general nature of this search, noting the context in which it emerged, the forms that it took, and the central role of Herbert Hoover and his associates, especially in the years from 1921 to 1930. Secondly, with this as background, I want to move from generalities to particulars and examine three of the corporative mechanisms created during these years, namely the Central Committee on Lumber Standards and its offshoots and successors as lumber "regulators," the union of Aeronautical Chamber of Commerce and Aeronautics Branch as aviation "regulators," and the Hays Office with its extensions into government as the "regulators" of motion picture production and distribution. Each of these reflects action in an industry whose competitive behavior had made it a "national problem," and each stands as an attempt to realize the sort of regulation envisioned in Dennison's letter. Yet the three also illustrate, I shall argue, differing kinds of in-

96

dustrial situations posing different problems for those who would make use of the private sector's regulatory resources.

II

The immediate roots of what was attempted during the 1920s reach back to the perceptions of a "new associationalism" that became especially prominent in the years from 1910 to 1917. Appearing primarily in the literature that accompanied a massive wave of associational formation, these perceptions drew qualitative distinctions between an older impetus toward organization and the one currently at work. The older impetus, it was argued, had come from the desire to monopolize markets, exploit the unorganized, or protect inefficient and backward industries. It had been a force working against social and economic progress, and it was therefore appropriate that a progressive people should use their government to keep this organizational activity to a minimum. The new organization, on the other hand, came mostly from the progressive and dynamic elements in society, who were seeking better instruments with which to meet modern needs. It could mean greater efficiency, more orderly growth, better social integration, higher degrees of national competitiveness in international markets, more rational rewards for the meritorious—all of the things, in other words, that American intellectual and political leaders were holding up as the ideals for which a progressive people should be striving. Given the change in the nature of organization, so the argument continued, the antitrust system had become outmoded and antiprogressive. It was not only keeping America backward in an organizational sense. It was also forcing the demand for better organization to be met through governmental expansion or through the creation of giant corporate consolidations, both of which involved dangers and evils that could and should be avoided; beyond this, it was weakening America's competitive position in the increasingly important international economy, especially in relation to countries like Germany that did encourage progressive forms of organization.[5]

In this prewar period such perceptions did not lead to an aban-

97

donment of antitrust action, much less to a strong associational network taking over the regulatory function. But public policy did move away from the antitrust ideal. From the Supreme Court came a "rule of reason" narrowing the coverage of the Sherman Act. From Congress came antitrust exemptions and a monetary regulation heavily reliant on enlightened uses of private power. From executive agencies came efforts to build and cooperate with associational partners in the private sector, efforts that succeeded in producing a network of farm bureaus, a variety of resource users' associations, and in 1912 the Chamber of Commerce of the United States.[6] Following the establishment of the Federal Trade Commission in 1914 there was constant pressure to make it a sponsor of associational activities and industrial self-government.[7] Increasingly, as the war approached, the notions of what constituted progressive policy were changing in the direction of organizational promotion rather than suppression.

The second major step toward the policies of the 1920s was, of course, the system used to mobilize national resources for war purposes. For these ends, so it was said and believed, the market system and its regulatory supplements were hopelessly inadequate. The need was for an administrative network with unifying, planning and directive capabilities; in a society lacking well-developed governmental or party bureaucracies this need was met through the creation of a quasi-corporative bureaucracy, part private and part public, yet with its public side substantially distinct from the regular agencies of government. On this public side the characteristic organization was the commodity division, technically a governmental agency but staffed mostly with people who were on temporary leave from positions in the private sector. On the other side the characteristic organization was the industrial authority or war service committee, chosen typically through the industry's associational machinery, yet endowed with allocative and regulatory powers delegated to it by the corresponding commodity division. In this structure such peak associations as the Chamber of Commerce and the American Federation of Labor also assumed governmental duties, primarily as certifiers and coordinators of private governmental units or as representatives of functional

98

blocs in the new war "councils." And moving into another kind of coordinating role, one calling for official generators of the system's information, were a number of technical, scientific, and professional associations.[8]

The system was sometimes referred to as "war socialism." But the more appropriate label was something like "war guildism" or "war corporatism," and out of this organizational experience, both here and abroad, came movements to shift policy-making power from parliamentary institutions and governmental regulators to associational networks and corporative bodies arising out of the private sector. This, so it was said, was the path to a higher and more efficient form of democracy, one that would allow liberal societies to overcome social fragmentation and realize their ideals without undergoing either socialist revolutions or some kind of statist regimentation.[9]

In America this postwar movement produced a variety of designs for regulatory reform, and it was during the debate over these, in 1919 and 1920, that Herbert Hoover first outlined the approach to regulation that he would attempt to implement between 1921 and 1930. Unlike some of the would-be "corporatizers," he insisted that governmental or monopolistic encroachments on economic liberty must be rolled back and held in check. Liberal societies did need firm restraints on the abuse of both public and private power. Yet they also needed, so Hoover insisted, new mechanisms for dealing with social fragmentation, market failures, and economic disorder. And to provide these he envisioned both a new kind of societal "regulation" and a new kind of government. Within society a systematized network of cooperative associations and councils would provide the ordered freedom needed for continued economic and social progress; and government, as Hoover proposed to use it, would function not as a regulator but as an aide in developing and operating these societal mechanisms. It would recognize what the war had demonstrated, namely, that the resources for meeting new regulatory needs were to be found mostly in the private rather than the public sector, and would act accordingly.[10]

It was Hoover and others with similar views, moreover, who

moved into the policy vacuums opened by Warren Harding's willingness to recruit and defer to the nation's "best minds." Of this a number of congressmen were critical, sensing that in effect it meant the generation of public standards by corporative rather than parliamentary institutions. But this criticism was insufficient to prevent a partial replication of what had happened in 1917 and 1918. While there was no war, there were new economic and social difficulties that the market system and its regulatory supplements seemed incapable of resolving. And while there was no grant of emergency power to the president, there were expandable agency charters under which the "best minds" from the private sector could reestablish the parallel structures of the war period, defend them as instruments of a more efficient democracy, and use them to promote a societal regulation allegedly superior to any that could emerge from legislative debate or governmental bureaucracies. This happened especially under Hoover's charter to promote commerce. But there were also operations of a similar sort under charters to promote agriculture, mining, and better resource usage, and by mid-decade there was a new set of federal trade commissioners intent less upon policing trade than upon building a new form of "self-regulation." If the decade was one of meager federal budgets, it was not one of inactive federal administrators or of a return to laissez faire assumptions. Coming into existence, as the means through which national goals were now to be attained, was a new network of nongovernmental or quasi-governmental mechanisms that were supposed to perform regulatory functions.[11]

In part the proclaimed goals were macroeconomic. From the workings of the structure, in theory anyway, would come a "cooperative competition," a more enlightened monetary management, and a new set of counter-cyclical spending mechanisms, all serving to improve the performance of the economy as a whole.[12] But also involved was the notion of industrial "problems" or "market failures" that could not be dealt with through action at the macroeconomic level. The remedy for these was a set of industry-specific "regulators," and public policy, as it developed under the administrative charters of the period, did make a place

100

for such "regulators" and extend something approaching official recognition to a number of them. In this sense, if not in the sense of a national plan, there was an "industrial policy."

Within this category of problem industries the most prominent, or at least the most studied, were those caught between receding demands and productive capacities resistant to downward adjustments. In the terminology of the time, these were the "sick" industries, and much effort was spent in trying to devise organizational machinery to facilitate the needed adjustments.[13] Such industries, however, did not exhaust the "problem" category; nor were all those that remained in it perceived as inherently monopolistic. Included as well were industrial situations where the chief problems were resource depletion, underdevelopment, or the production of socially harmful goods, all situations that in other times and places might have led to governmental regulation or operation. For these, too, there was to be a new kind of societal regulation, making use of the superior regulatory resources that had allegedly developed in the private sector; and it is upon three bits of the resulting experience, bits that constitute parts of a larger regulatory pattern yet also illuminate differing manifestations of it, that I want now to concentrate.

III

Prior to 1921 Herbert Hoover had not concerned himself with the malfunctioning of America's lumber industry, and as secretary of commerce he might have limited this concern to a few export aids and technical services. This was not in keeping, however, with his image of himself as the nation's trouble shooter and organizational engineer, and within months of taking office he had been drawn into a controversy that had its roots in the prewar concern with resource depletion and the high costs of basic raw materials. Lumber, so a variety of people had then argued and were now continuing to argue, was an industry in which unregulated competition could not secure what its defenders claimed that it could. In theory it should have produced an efficient and technically progressive plant making available a renewable re-

101

source at constantly decreasing costs. But what had emerged instead, constituting clear evidence of market failure, was an immensely wasteful plant resistant to technological advance and operated in ways that must eventually mean lower rather than higher living standards.[14]

With these perceptions of the industry Hoover found himself in substantial agreement. Too many lumbermen, as he came to see it, were engaged in forest wrecking rather than forestry, and in almost all phases of the industry enormous wastes were keeping productivity low, returns meager, and prices higher than they should be. The public was not getting efficient and responsible management of a basic resource, nor was it getting the cheaper building materials that could help to improve housing conditions and allow more Americans to become homeowners. Yet the poor performance of the industry, in Hoover's eyes, could not be corrected through regulatory legislation or some form of governmental production. The answer, so he was arguing by 1922, was to foster internal mechanisms capable of redirecting the quest for profits into socially constructive channels. What was needed, in particular, was organizational machinery that could break the traditional barriers to technological advance and reduce the kinds of social support that permitted those engaged in destructive forms of profit seeking to remain in business.[15]

In believing that such mechanisms could be developed in the lumber industry, Hoover was engaging in a considerable act of faith. The industry, after all, was a highly fragmented one, made up of thousands of enterprises, torn by regional and product rivalries, and fiercely resistant to the designs of production engineers and scientific rationalizers.[16] Historically, such organization as had appeared at the industry level had been concerned primarily with protecting existing forms of production and profit making rather than with enhancing productivity, and among those engaged in the lumber trade ethical standards had been notoriously low.[17] Yet here, as elsewhere, the war experience was supposed to have left an expanding nucleus of "industrial statesmanship" out of which the new societal regulation could now emerge. From it, in theory anyway, had come a more "public-spirited" and

102

technically progressive leadership, a new capacity for enlightened forms of associational action, and new perceptions of an industrial future that could be both profitable and socially constructive. And all of this, taken in conjunction with changes in public attitudes, had allegedly created institutional or organizational gaps that could be filled with the mechanisms that Hoover had in mind.[18]

It was to create this "internal machinery," then, that Hoover moved into the ongoing debate, aligning himself, in particular, with men who had administered the wartime system and who had been trying, since the end of the war, to reestablish a public-private partnership in which the National Lumber Manufacturers Association and its constituent groups would play a central role. This had been one objective of an American Lumber Congress in 1919, the idea at that time being an associational partnership with sympathetic administrators in the Forest Service. Interest had then turned to the establishment of such a relationship with Hoover's Commerce Department; and following a series of exploratory conversations, particularly between Hoover and Michigan lumberman John W. Blodgett, the secretary had asserted his jurisdiction over the lumber problem and called an organizational conference. Raising productivity in the manufacture and distribution of lumber, so Hoover told Secretary of Agriculture Henry C. Wallace, should be undertaken by the Bureau of Standards rather than the Forest Service; and while Wallace disagreed, the result was a Hoover conference rather than one at Agriculture.[19]

Convened in Washington on May 22, 1922, Hoover's first lumber conference produced a plan for a quasi-public agency, made up of functional representatives from the private sector yet having access to Commerce Department facilities and theoretically engaged in providing a superior substitute for public regulation. Bureaucracy, so Hoover told the conferees, was often incompetent, grabbing, and inefficient. But through public-private cooperation it was possible to develop "internal machinery" that could correct industrial malfunctions. In lumber such "machinery" could establish grades, standards, and guarantees, which, once established, could alter the pattern of demand in ways that would encourage a less wasteful production and a more scientific for-

103

estry. It could, in short, meet public needs while rendering governmental policing unnecessary, and it was to this dual task that the new Central Committee on Lumber Standards was officially committed. Worked out in more detail at a subsequent conference in Chicago, it consisted of John W. Blodgett, filling, so it seemed, the dual role of "industry leader" and "public man," plus functional representatives from the manufacturers, whole-salers, retailers, architects, railroads, and wood users.[20]

In operation the CCLS tended to think of itself as an indicative planner, generating, through committee action and consultation with advisory bodies, a design for standardization that would then be implemented through the actions of its constituent associations. It also hoped to establish a private inspection service to ensure that standards agreed to were being observed. But initially the gap between aspiration and achievement remained large. The hardwood manufacturers, in particular, refused to abandon the standards of their association for those to be set by the CCLS. They were joined by other groups in opposing a central inspection service. And when subjected to pressure, primarily through critical statements issued by Hoover aide William Durgin, they reacted with countercharges—"rotten" countercharges, as Hoover saw them—alleging misrepresentation, bureaucratic arrogance and intrusion, and gross misuse of the term "scientific."[21] Not until December of 1923, at another lumber conference in Washington, was a design for standard sizes, terms, and grades adopted; and this came only after decisions to leave hardwoods outside the system, lodge inspection responsibilities at the association level, and establish both a standard and an extra-standard thickness for one-inch lumber.[22]

Still, as the industry entered 1924, Hoover remained highly optimistic about the potentialities of its new "internal machinery." At last, so he told William Durgin, the "stupendous problem of standardization" was being tackled in a constructive fashion; and this, when taken in conjunction with improved statistical exchanges, better export promotion, and informed study of building needs, was pointing the way to a new era in organizational development, a time when regulation would become internal yet

104

would be directed for the "combined interest of the manufacturer, [the] distributor, and the public." If it could be done in an industry "so complex and difficult" as lumber, then this very fact would open the way for its adoption in dealing with other industries that had become "national problems."[23]

Far from being discouraged, then, Hoover now moved to supplement the design for standardization with one prescribing fuller utilization of wood products, not only to make them go further but also to bring existing wastes into productive use and thus allow both a cheapening of building materials and an expansion of timber growing. Action along these lines had been under discussion since early 1923. It had been explored both by a Wood Waste Committee, composed of Hoover aides and trade association officials, and through industrial surveys jointly financed by the CCLS and the Commerce Department. The surveyors had thought it eminently feasible, and it was with these perceptions in mind that Hoover and his lieutenants accepted invitations to attend and address a forest products conference scheduled to meet under the auspices of the Department of Agriculture on November 19, 1924. In calling it, Secretary Wallace had combined a justification for Forest Service action with a plea for interdepartmental cooperation, and in a subsequent letter Chief Forester William B. Greeley had reemphasized the importance of working together to realize common aims.[24]

By the time the conference met, Wallace was dead,[25] and by the time it had adjourned it was clear that wood utilization work, like lumber standardization, would be in Hoover's province rather than that of the Forest Service. Following addresses by Coolidge, Hoover, Greeley, Blodgett, and others, the conferees agreed that governmental aids for private forestry, recently expanded under the Clark-McNary Act, must be coupled with an organized effort to reduce wastage of the forest cut. It was only by working from "both ends" that the ominous gap between consumption of forest products and their renewal could be narrowed and eventually closed.[26] But having agreed on this, the conference then decided that the machinery needed was not an extension of the Forest Service, but rather an expanded version of the CCLS. In the

105

organizational design finally approved, this expanded CCLS, to be renamed the Central Committee on Utilization of Forest Products, was to become not only a standardizer and waste eliminator but the central coordinating agency for all lumber and forestry programs involving public-private cooperation. To the apparent dismay of those who had initially convened the conference, it had become the means for moving new pieces of bureaucratic territory into Hoover's expanding empire.[27]

In the days that followed, to be sure, both Hoover and Blodgett backed away from the conference recommendations. The CCLS, they decided, should not attempt to become a "superorganization." Nor should it get involved in such areas as reforestation, fire prevention, forest insects, timber surveys, or forest laboratories. But in "clearing up the situation," Hoover did secure a presidential letter specifying that all organizations concerned with wood utilization or with the manufacture, transportation, and distribution of lumber should be under the jurisdiction of the Commerce Department. This, as he saw it, cleared the way for constructive action, and the result, by May of 1925, was the formation of a National Committee on Wood Utilization (NCWU) designed to work in tandem with the Central Committee on Lumber Standards.[28]

Brought together again were functional representatives from the private sector, who, in theory, could generate designs for improved utilization and secure their implementation through associational action. Representatives of the paper makers, mining engineers, commercial buyers, contractors, and agricultural users served on the committee, as well as representatives of the groups previously involved in the CCLS.[29] In addition, the committee and its secretariat included several individuals who also held public office. Partly, it seems, because Hoover could not find another Blodgett to serve as both "industrial leader" and "public man," he decided to make himself chairman and William Greeley vice-chairman, to install Edward Eyre Hunt as committee secretary, and to designate the chief of his lumber division, Axel Oxholm, as committee director. As finally constituted, the NCWU reflected

106

both a "corporatization" of the policy-making process and a virtual disappearance of the line between public and private administration. Commingled in its operations were both public and private monies, public and private officials, and public and private facilities.[30]

In its efforts to alter industrial and consumer practice, the NCWU undertook a variety of surveys, issued a series of bulletins, and spun off ancillary organizations concerned with specific lines of action. It concentrated, in particular, on reducing the wastage involved in logging, seasoning, milling, and handling operations; on reducing the raw material needs of the paper and wood chemical industries; and on promoting increased usage and hence a larger demand for sawdust, underutilized woods, and short-length lumber. In addition, it studied and urged changes in carpentry practice, wood preservation techniques, container usage, and waste disposal.[31] But in all of these areas it encountered considerable resistance, and the changes actually taking place seem to have been considerably less than those for which the agency and its sponsors had hoped. In any event, this was the view of critics in the forestry profession, the conservation societies, and dissident economic and political circles. While acknowledging some changes, they noted the general persistence of a shrinking timber stand, destructive logging practices, wasteful production and usage methods, and hidden but high social costs.[32]

Some critics also insisted that it was paradoxical to advocate the conservation of forest products while at the same time seeking to create larger markets for them. Real conservation, so it was said, should have a place for nonuse and nonexport as well as more efficient use, and from those seeking to take advantage of these sentiments came such advertising slogans as "Use Brick and Save the Forest." To Hoover, Oxholm, and Greeley, however, this alleged paradox was not a real one. The national interest, they argued, was best served by encouraging timber growing and reforestation rather than hoarding the timber on hand, and the basic prerequisite for this was an adequate, stable, and properly developed market. In their minds the people most likely to bring on a

107

timber "famine" were not the marketers and users of timber but rather those who would undercut the needed market with substitutes, imports, and constraints.[33]

Such criticism, moreover, did not shake Hoover's faith in the kind of "internal machinery" that he had been able to establish in the lumber industry. For him it was "Exhibit A of government by co-operation," and as such was to be kept "at the head of all other industries in the hope that some of them will come into the path of righteousness that are not now in." There would, so he was predicting by the late 1920s, be no more serious proposals for setting up regulatory commissions and subjecting the industry to the control of statist bureaucracies.[34]

Hoover, of course, was wrong. Whatever the accomplishments of his "machinery" in the 1920s, it could not prevent an industry subjected to severe depression conditions from reverting to the behavior that had initially made it a "national problem." As in other natural resource industries, the struggle for survival meant increased wastage and heightened social costs. While Hoover reacted with the creation of a National Timber Conservation Board, another quasi-corporative body intended to check and reverse these developments,[35] the eventual result would be a general discrediting of the "Hoover idea" and the emergence of attitudes that would open the way to the market controls of the NRA period and, following their failure, to new stabilizing roles for the Forest Service.[36] For a time the idea of moving beyond "monopolistic" and "statist" solutions to a system-conscious "internalism" and "government by cooperation" had seemed promising if problematic. But the failure of Hooverism at the macroeconomic level would prevent the realization of what promise there was.

IV

As an industry, air transportation in the 1920s was markedly different from lumbering. It was an infant industry offering a new service, not a mature one providing a basic raw material, and it had become a "national problem" not because of resource depletion and wastage but because of its "underdevelopment" when

108

measured against perceived national needs and potentialities.[37] America, so the argument ran, was in urgent need of a service essential to economic progress and national defense. It was also potentially capable of supporting this service through private market transactions; the gap between potentiality and actuality, a gap held open by barriers that existing market forces seemed unable to overcome, constituted the problem to be resolved through regulatory intervention.[38] In essence, the perceived market failure was of the kind causing stunted growth in essential infrastructure rather than potential resource famines.

Such differences also made for marked dissimilarities in the detailed concerns of aviation and lumber policy during the 1920s. The kinds of standardization, waste elimination, and economic direction envisioned for lumber were different from those envisioned for aviation, and the technical and political problems encountered were not the same. Yet the two stories, dissimilar as they were in detail, are best seen not as discrete responses to unrelated problems but as variations on a common theme. Both were manifestations of the period's willingness to credit the theorists of a new societal regulation, allegedly more effective, more scientific, and more American than controls imposed through governmental action. Both were parts of a more general effort to transfer the generation of public standards from parliamentary to techno-corporative processes. Both reflected the period's discovery of market irrationalities and technical backwardness as major causes of industrial malfunctioning. And at the core of both, acting as prime movers in making things happen, were similar alliances of industrial and Hooverian "statesmen" working together on mechanisms that would allegedly achieve the ends set forth in federal administrative charters. Perhaps the chief difference in this respect was in aviation's emphasis on broadening existing charters and creating a new body of administrative law.

As with the lumber industry, the aviation story had its origins in the immediate postwar period. Aircraft manufacturers, anxious to find a substitute for military markets, believed that a federal administrative apparatus, modeled on the war system, could help them to develop one. The initial idea, as set forth in the report of an American Aviation Mission in 1919, was to create a new aeronautics department under which the wartime machinery could be reassembled. But this had proved politically unfeasible, and by 1921 the Manufacturers Aircraft Association was urging that a new bureau of civil aviation be established in the Commerce Department. Bills for this, introduced in Congress, had been endorsed by the Aero Club of America and the quasi-public National Advisory Committee on Aeronautics. In the press a campaign was underway stressing the benefits that could flow from navigational aids and safety regulations. With them, so it was being argued, air transportation could become an important "medium of commerce" enhancing both economic development and national security. Without them it would remain stunted and retarded, held back by high accident rates, irresponsible adventurism, and public misperceptions of its potential.[39]

As with lumber, too, Hoover had remained essentially uninvolved prior to his becoming secretary of commerce. A bureau of civil aviation was not something that he had seen as a major national priority, and partly perhaps because the aircraft manufacturers were being investigated for wartime profiteering he continued through the early months of his tenure to keep his distance from them. When asked to call a conference, he suggested that they take their problems directly to Congress.[40] By July of 1921, however, the connection that the manufacturers were seeking had been established. Hoover had proved receptive to the arguments of industry spokesmen, especially those of Lester D. Gardner, publisher of the *Aviation and Aircraft Journal.* He had seemingly been persuaded that at least some of the aircraft manufacturers and the engineering leaders affiliated with them were public-spirited individuals, who would respond to his leadership and help to resolve what an interdepartmental committee and a subsequent presidential message had identified as a "national problem." And the result, on July 18, was a conference to discuss legislative, administrative, and organizational action. Represented were not only the manufacturers but the insurance underwriters, the engineers, and the Aero Club of America—the latter, so it seems, as a proxy for the nation's air-minded public.[41]

110

In the wake of the conference three lines of action were apparent. One consisted of surveys and data gathering, done mostly by the manufacturers' association but with some aid from the Commerce Department. The second was the organization of an Aeronautical Chamber of Commerce, bringing in other groups besides the manufacturers and claiming therefore to be a fit representative of the "new associationalism" and a suitable instrument for implementing the "Hoover idea."[42] The third was intensive legislative lobbying, which did produce passage of an administrative charter, the Wadsworth bill, in the Senate, but failed to get action in the House of Representatives. There Congressman Samuel Winslow, chairman of the House Commerce Committee, had to be enlisted as a sponsor; and Winslow was not only unsure about a bureau in the Commerce Department but unwilling to ignore the viewpoints of states' righters, defenders of congressional prerogatives, and legal experts in aviation law. Eventually a bill did emerge from consultations between these groups and Hoover's representatives. But it was slow to do so, was not ready for congressional action in 1922, and was less than satisfactory to Hoover's industrial allies.[43]

In 1923 and 1924 legislation also failed to pass. Constantly revised, Winslow's bill became increasingly detailed and increasingly unsatisfactory to those seeking a charter to be implemented by administrators. Technically, it still had Hoover's support. But he seemed to agree with criticisms of its complexity and rigidity. While he continued to make a case for legislative action, arguing that the best system was one that combined the practicality and progressiveness of private initiative with a foundation of constructive regulatory law, he was now putting more emphasis on things that could be done without legislation. Close linkages were established between industrial committees and departmental bureaus, and the result was joint preparation and promulgation of an aeronautical safety code, joint development of standardization agreements, and joint action to demonstrate and publicize the usefulness of air transportation.[44]

In 1925 the only legislation to pass was the Kelly Air Mail Act, authorizing the Post Office to contract with private carriers for

111

airmail delivery. By the end of the year, however, a series of developments had opened the way for the kind of legislation initially envisioned at the 1921 conference. One was the decision of Henry Ford to enter the airline business and bid for an airmail contract, a decision that helped to bring other investors into the field. A second was the highly publicized formation of the National Air Transport Company, with Howard Coffin as president, former postal official Paul Henderson as general manager, and movie "czar" Will Hays as chairman of its public relations committee. A third was a new and larger survey, jointly conducted by the Commerce Department and the American Engineering Council, and finding, as one might have predicted, that the potential for commercial aviation in the United States was greater than anywhere else in the world.[45] And finally, there were General William Mitchell's charges of incompetence and negligence in developing aviation for defense. To investigate these and review national aviation policy, Coolidge appointed a President's Aircraft Board with Dwight Morrow as chairman, Howard Coffin as a leading member, and Herbert Hoover as stage manager and star witness.[46]

By late 1925 it had become clear that the Winslow bill would be shoved aside and its place taken by a more discretionary measure under which regulatory law could emerge from "experience" and from "sincere cooperation" between the public and private sectors. This, so Hoover assured Iowa lawyer Clarence Young, was the intent of the bill being prepared by the Aircraft Board's two congressional members, Senator Hiram Bingham of Connecticut and Congressman James S. Parker of New York.[47] Once completed, with substantial assistance from Commerce Department solicitor Stephen Davis, this bill did move through Congress with relative ease. In May of 1926 it became the Air Commerce Act, creating a new assistant secretary of commerce for aeronautics and authorizing the Commerce Department to promote air commerce, provide aids and facilities for air navigation, establish traffic and safety rules, and license aircraft and airmen.[48]

Under the new charter, hailed in some quarters as the Bill of Rights of the aviation industry, Hoover now proceeded to develop

112

a public-private apparatus resembling the "regulators" that he had helped to create for other problem industries. On the public side this consisted of an aeronautics branch, pulling together all air work whether done by the regular bureaus or specially created divisions.[49] On the private side it consisted of industrial committees and the offices and agencies of the Aeronautical Chamber of Commerce. Linking the two were collaborative committees and a kind of revolving door through which officials passed from the private sector to public work and then back to private positions again. William P. MacCracken, the man finally selected to head the new system, had been a governor of the National Aeronautic Association, a participant in drafting the aviation bills, and legal counsel for the National Air Transport Company. In 1929 he would return to the private sector as a lawyer and lobbyist for the major airlines.[50]

Public policy, moreover, as embodied in rules and allocative decisions, was intended to emerge not from adversary proceedings and judicial-like decrees but from consensus-building conferences and consultations. The major body of air regulations, for example, as promulgated in late 1926, was the work not only of a private law-making apparatus on loan to the government but also of a series of consensus-building conferences, bringing together interested government agencies, aircraft and engine manufacturers, aircraft operators, insurance companies, editors of aircraft publications, and the leaders of the Aeronautical Chamber of Commerce. In all, some eight conferences were convened, and what emerged was law that the leadership of the industry wanted and would use its power and influence to help enforce.[51] In theory, of course, it was law that would help to achieve national goals as well.

In addition to a new body of law, the apparatus also produced a new structure of improved airways, licensed planes and pilots, and local commitments to building and developing airports. By 1928 it had licensed over 2,000 planes and 3,000 pilots, designated and improved 7,500 miles of national airways, helped to open a good portion of the nation's 207 municipal airports, and eliminated, as MacCracken put it, the "competition from patched-

113

up war surplus." In Hoover's mind it had become a "great economic and human agency," attuned to American ideals and conditions and acting to implement a "distinctly American plan" under which constructive cooperation was building a better service than the Europeans had developed with their statism and direct subsidies.[52]

What the apparatus did not produce, however, was clear foresight concerning market conditions. Great expectations brought an investment boom in 1927 and 1928. But in 1929 it became clear that the expected demand for air transportation services was not materializing, and under the impact of the stock market crash the aviation boom turned into an industrial "bust." The mission of the apparatus now became a salvage rather than a developmental one. The industry had to be saved, it was argued, if public investments in its support system were not to be lost.[53] And Congress did respond with the Watres Act of 1930, authorizing the postmaster general to use the airmail contracts as an instrument of industrial rationalization. These could now be awarded or extended on the basis of public interest rather than competitive bidding, and the result was the so-called spoils conferences of 1930, in which administration and industry representatives decided which airlines were to be saved and what routes they were to have. In theory "public men" on both sides of the apparatus were still acting to advance the public interest, and the very persistence of the design adopted suggests that it did have a degree of economic rationality.[54] But with the discrediting of the "Hoover idea," the design would be subjected to a long period of political attack. It would have to weather the cancellation of the contracts, the reopening of the routes to competitive bidding, and a series of hostile congressional investigations before something approaching it would again achieve legitimacy under the Civil Aeronautics Act of 1938.[55]

In aviation, then, the apparatus that Hoover helped to create between 1921 and 1930 proved more enduring than the mechanisms through which he tackled the lumber problem. It was, in the end, less vulnerable to political attack, chiefly perhaps because of the differing structure and function of the industry. But as with

114

lumber, the apparatus rested on an ideological foundation that would subsequently lose much of its credibility, partly because of flawed assumptions but also because of the failure of the design at the macroeconomic level.

V

Still another of the decade's new industrial "regulators," differing from yet also bearing marked resemblances to the "regulators" for lumber and aviation, was the Hays Office, established in 1922 by the Motion Picture Producers and Distributors of America (MPPDA). Technically an executive agency for a trade association, the office actually functioned as a quasi-governmental body, both in the sense that it became America's central mechanism for dealing with a public policy problem and in the sense that some of its branches were also federal administrative units. Unlike the offices of most trade associations, moreover, the organization had machinery that was supposed to integrate functional groupings into a harmonious whole and make it capable of acting in the broader social interest.[56] Its appearance and operation was another reflection of the kind of neocorporatism being hailed during the period as America's answer to creeping statism.

The office's primary developer, of course, was Will H. Hays, not Herbert Hoover. Yet from the agency's beginnings, Hoover viewed its machinery as the kind best equipped to protect social interests while preserving essential liberties. It was the kind that government should encourage, the kind that public agencies should cooperate or merge with, and the kind that he was working to establish in other areas of market failure. It was, in short, recognized and treated as a comrade in industrial Hooverization, and on the industry's side the value of such a connection was early appreciated. There had been some discussion in 1921 of luring Hoover into the position that Hays eventually filled, and in that position Hays took pains to relate his version of societal regulation and government by cooperation to what was being attempted in other problem industries.[57]

From the industry's standpoint the need for a Hays Office

115

stemmed from two major problems that had brought it to public attention and generated hostile criticism and political attack. One was its inability to contain an ongoing battle over control of exhibition, a battle that was perceived in some quarters as a new attack by would-be monopolists on independent entrepreneurs. The other was its failure to find ways of exploiting the "new morality" without arousing the fear and anger of those determined to uphold and protect the old. This failure, in particular, had produced an array of "reform groups" agitating for censorship boards or regulatory commissions; and it was at the height of this agitation, with the industry's position further weakened by scandals in Hollywood, that the Motion Picture Producers and Distributors of America was formed and the Hays Office created.[58] The latter's power rested in part on the industry's fear of punitive or restrictive legislation. But contributing to it also was the hope that a man of Hays's stature and organizational talents could find acceptable solutions to the industry's two major problems.[59] Outside the industry the Hays Office was able to enlist and maintain support among those who viewed the situation as a national problem requiring remedial action yet were anxious to avoid the evils that they associated with legal censorship and governmental controls.[60]

In operation the Hays Office proceeded to create a variety of new mechanisms and to argue that they constituted the practical, effective, and "American" way of dealing with the situation. There was machinery now for screening extras and getting rid of "immoral" players, machinery that would presumably prevent future scandals. There were organized linkages to community and civic groups, linkages that in theory could identify and build support for pictures that were both profitable to make and "wholesome" in content.[61] There was a Studio Relations Committee, the purpose of which was to weed out unsuitable scripts, review pictures before their release, and limit the showing of those produced outside the system.[62] There was contract standardization with arbitration machinery to resolve disputes, the hope being that this would reduce exhibitor discontent and cut down on expensive litigation. And in a studied effort to avoid antitrust prosecution,

116

there was a kind of conscious parallelism in organizational design. Some of the new agencies were technically independent of the Hays Office, and from 1924 on there were two associations rather than one. Interlocked with the MPPDA but legally separate from it was the Association of Motion Picture Producers, commonly called the California or West Coast Association.[63]

While engaged in the creation of this apparatus, the Hays Office also developed a special branch for dealing with international aspects of the movie problem. This was the "foreign department," which, in Hays's own words, became "almost an adjunct of our State Department." In effect it operated as a quasi-diplomatic agency, making foreign policy through officially supported negotiations with foreign governments and organizations.[64] In addition, with Hoover's support and collaboration, Hays secured legislation under which the Bureau of Foreign and Domestic Commerce created a motion pictures unit staffed with individuals selected by the office and used as a part of its data-gathering and publicity apparatus. Formally established in 1926, the unit proceeded to issue numerous bulletins and reports, conduct a variety of surveys and special studies, monitor through a special trade commissioner any "agitation or legislation" against American films, and put out press releases giving the industry's perspective on foreign disputes.[65] Like the lumber division and the aeronautics branch, it was part of an industrial government whose functioning was supposed to be the best means of achieving national goals, the goals in this case being open markets exploited to give positive impressions of the American people and their character.

As in lumber and aviation, moreover, the creators and operators of the new machinery were not timid about presenting themselves as regulatory pioneers opening the way to a new and higher stage of institutional development. Their mechanisms, they insisted, were true regulatory mechanisms, not merely agencies for altering public images or enhancing group bargaining power. They were serving society through their activities as "harmonizers," "moral engineers," and builders of responsible "home rule." And they were, so Hays kept saying, getting at the fundamental causes of the movie problem, not through prohibitions and crackdowns but through actions that filled institutional gaps through the building of an internal "policyship" to become the basis of a "responsible self-direction, considerate of the public good as well as the box office." [66] Such were the claims being made by the late 1920s, and those making policy for the Coolidge presidency seemed to assume that national ends were indeed being served by the expansion and functioning of the Hays Office. Asked to participate in industry convocations, Hoover appeared with words of encouragement and praise for the contributions being made to the nation's economic progress and "cultural advance." [67]

Hoover's own files, however, indicated that the principal successes of the Hays Office had been in blocking censorship legislation, holding foreign markets, and turning out public relations material. Its efforts to harmonize the decisions produced by moral, artistic, and marketing judgments had not succeeded, and the result in 1928 and 1929 was not only growing friction between the office and uncooperative producers but a resurgent agitation for "reform." On one side were civil and artistic libertarians calling for greater freedom and arguing that internal controls of the Hays type were just as pernicious as police censorship. On the other were the champions of "clean," "wholesome," and "decent" movies, who, for some reason, seemed to feel that Hoover should be supportive of their cause. Even as he continued to work with Hays, he was receiving much of the literature generated by such anti-Hays groups as the International Reform Federation, the Citizens League for Better Pictures, and the Federal Motion Picture Council. They complained that the "real business" of the Hays Office was "whitewashing" rather than regulating the movie makers, that the nation was paying an enormous price for the continuation of their "suggestiveness, indecency, and criminality," and that only a "centralized authority" at the national level could "effectively regulate the centralized motion picture industry." [68]

If "harmonization" had failed on the moral issue, it had also failed on issues dividing the major producers and rebellious groups of exhibitors. Protests about the arbitration system and trade practices, especially block booking, had persisted.[69] Efforts to achieve harmony through a trade practice conference at the

118

Federal Trade Commission had not been successful,[70] and by 1929 a new exhibitors' group, the Allied States Association of Motion Picture Exhibitors, had mobilized considerable support for legislative and antitrust action. Headed by Abram F. Myers, a former federal trade commissioner who had worked with Hoover on trade practice codification, the organization looked upon the Hays Office as camouflage for a sellers' cartel, insisted that what Hays called "bulk selling" was really monopolistic exploitation, and demanded that the voice of the exhibitors be heard in the formation of "industrial policy." It had, moreover, formed a loose alliance with those concerned about "immoral" pictures. If the exhibitors could take only the pictures they wanted, it argued, they could function as protectors of their communities from "filth" and "indecency."[71]

As the decade ended, then, the machinery that was supposed to solve the movie problem was under increasing attack, and in the 1930s the problems inherent in it would intensify. Faced with depression conditions, some movie makers tried to save themselves through additions of "spice" or further exactions from exhibitors. As Hays himself noted, calls for morality and cooperation in the "cataclysm" of 1931 and 1932 were like voices "crying in the wilderness."[72] Nor was such behavior conducive to keeping legislators and antitrust officials quiescent. Regulatory proposals won new support in Congress, and antitrust action, despite Hays's efforts to keep it in "constructive" channels, finally forced an abandonment of the industry's arbitration system. In Hays's view the new antitrust chief, John Lord O'Brian, was "absolutely impossible." He was "doing more harm" than "a dozen Walshes or Brookharts or such," largely, so Hays thought, because he had been "poisoned" by Abram Myers, whose wife was on O'Brian's staff. Protests, however, to Hoover and to Attorney General William Mitchell brought little more than advice on how the industry's "internal machinery" might be revamped. They did not put an end to O'Brian's activities.[73]

Still, in the face of these difficulties, the Hays Office proved remarkably resilient and adaptive. It was eventually successful in saving, strengthening, and putting teeth into its production code.

119

It emerged at the center of the industry's NRA machinery; and while court decisions would finally force the withdrawal of producers from the exhibition end of the industry, the office itself weathered the political storms of the late 1930s, regained quasi-official status during World War II, and continued, after 1945, to function as America's central mechanism for dealing with the kind of market failures that made motion picture production and distribution a public policy problem.[74] In this respect its post-1930 history more nearly resembled that of the aviation mechanisms than of those developed for lumber.

VI

What, then, can be said about these "industrial policies" of the 1920s and more particularly about the mechanisms entrusted with meeting perceived regulatory needs in three of the period's problem industries? What explains these? In what contexts are they best understood? And of what significance were they? In attempting to answer such questions, one must, of course, be cautious about generalizing from a sample of three. But the regulatory experiences studied here, when taken in conjunction with what is now known about other developments during the period, do suggest the need for rethinking some of the central propositions that have governed previous work on the nation's regulatory and public policy history. They tend, at the very least, to call some of these into question and suggest alternatives that may get us closer to historical reality.

In the first place, the stories reconstructed here suggest that ideas and ideology have been important determinants in shaping national regulatory policy and the mechanisms for supplementing it. In part, of course, these took the form that they did because of the peculiar structure, position, and politics of each industry involved. Nor can one rule out the influence of general prosperity and Republican political dominance. Yet in three widely different industries, each a public policy problem for different reasons, one finds variations on a regulatory model that seems to have been adopted for ideological reasons or because certain ideas had

120

gained credibility and could be used to advance particular interests. Without this ideological dimension it is difficult to explain the mechanisms that emerged or what happened to them later.

Secondly, the stories reconstructed here point up the importance of a set of ideas often assumed to be alien to and largely absent from American political culture. They suggest that the regulatory history of the period is best understood not as a return to laissez faire, a foundation for the regulatory state, or a prelude to democratic pluralism, but rather as an effort to realize or make use of a set of techno-corporate ideals that had gained credence and power as a result of the war experience. At work was an American expression of a larger corporative impulse apparent in most industrial societies, one that had its adherents in both public and private bureaucracies. And it is only by ignoring or misinterpreting these developments of the 1920s that current advocates and critics of corporative formulas can claim to be debating a new American ideology.

Thirdly, the stories reconstructed here suggest that some of the mechanisms developed under the influence of this ideology were able to survive the loss of its credibility, adapt themselves to new conditions, and remain parts of the nation's regulatory system. The lumber mechanisms did not do so, reflecting perhaps their weaknesses in terms of industry support, industry power, and rivalry with the older Forest Service complex. But those in aviation and motion pictures did survive and remain important factors in shaping subsequent regulation in these industries. While subjected to attack and stripped for a time of their status as performers of public or social duties, they had developed in the kind of industries and with the degree of industrial support that enabled them to resist attacks and adapt themselves to new social and political roles. Also significant perhaps was the fact that they had no older rivals comparable to the Forest Service complex in lumber. They had taken shape in new regulatory territory where the claims of other would-be regulators had not yet been established.

As to the workability and effectiveness of this New Era regulation, it is more difficult to come to any definite conclusions. In lumber, changes in the plant and in economic behavior seem to have been far less than were claimed in self-congratulatory statements of the Hooverites and their allies in the lumber associations, whereas in movies and aviation they were more substantial. But in each case they were not changes that brought the kind of markets and development that the "regulators" were trying to engineer. In all three cases, moreover, assessment is complicated by the advent of depression conditions that altered the pattern of regulatory support and concern and tended to turn the mechanisms into instruments of salvage rather than development. Given proper action at the macroeconomic level, it might be argued, such "regulators" could have evolved into more effective tools for changing behavior and realizing the proclaimed goals. In other societies similar tools have been used to improve economic performance.

Still, it should be recognized that such societies have had to find ways of dealing with a series of political problems that seem to be inherent in this form of "regulation." They have had to develop institutional arrangements for bringing in or neutralizing the social constituencies that have idealized small business or consumer sovereignty, for giving industrial labor and its associations a satisfactory role in the apparatus, for dealing with tensions between the bureaucracies at the firm level and those at the industrial level, for bringing law made in other quarters into line with that made through the corporative structure, and for maintaining the competence and reputation of the central core of public and private administrators.[75] Experience suggests that these problems have been very difficult to deal with in societies and cultures resembling those of the United States. And while the machinery of the 1920s seemed to be working toward solutions, one wonders whether continued growth alone would have allowed these to be achieved. The possibility exists that it would have strengthened the critics of the mechanisms and created an environment increasingly hostile to their operation.

Finally, it should also be recognized that solving such problems meant, to some degree at least, a movement away from the institutions that had emerged in the democratic revolutions of the eighteenth and nineteenth centuries. To the extent that they were

122

solved, the chances of realizing the dreams of the Jacksonians, the populists, and the new economic and political pluralists were reduced, an argument perhaps for not seeking to solve them or for being glad that those who were developing the corporative regulation of the 1920s suffered major setbacks in the decade that followed.

THREE FACETS OF HOOVERIAN ASSOCIATIONALISM   Ellis Hawley

1. Henry S. Dennison to Edward Eyre Hunt, April 14, 1927, with enclosed memorandum, Hunt Papers, Springfield, Ohio, copy made available by Neil Basen.

221

Regulation in Perspective

2. See the essays in the *Revue Recherches*, special issue on "Guerre, Fascisme, et Taylorisme," September 1978. See also Charles S. Maier, *Recasting Bourgeois Europe: Stabilization in France, Germany, and Italy in the Decade After World War I* (Princeton: Princeton University Press, 1975). "Corporatism" as used in this paper is a designation for an ideal socio-political type in which (a) the basic units are functional groupings, (b) institutions recognize and integrate the units into an interdependent whole, (c) there are deep interpenetrations between state and society, (d) the state functions chiefly as midwife and partner rather than director or regulator, and (e) an enlightened social elite identifies social needs and provides leadership for concerted social action. Movement toward this ideal type constitutes "corporatization."

3. For a discussion of this see Robert H. Wiebe, *The Search for Order, 1877–1920* (New York: Hill and Wang, 1967), pp. 159–63.

4. Indicative of this, I would argue, are such works as Bruce L. R. Smith, ed., *The New Political Economy: The Public Use of the Private Sector* (New York: Wiley, 1975); George C. Lodge, *The New American Ideology* (New York: Knopf, 1975); Neil W. Chamberlain, *Remaking American Values: Challenge to a Business Society* (New York: Basic Books, 1977); and Ezra F. Vogel, *Japan as Number One* (Cambridge, Mass.: Harvard University Press, 1979). Smith's argument that the attainment of national goals requires "the partnership effort of industry, universities, not-for-profit laboratories, and government agencies" and that "the kinds of talent needed, and the professional administrative structures required to integrate the effort, have not been available within the formal government hierarchy" is much like the argument of the 1920s.

5. See, for example, Arthur J. Eddy, *The New Competition* (New York: Appleton, 1912); E. H. Gaunt, *Co-operative Competition* (Providence: Stevens Press, 1917); Forrest Crissey, *Teamwork in Trade-Building* (New York: Association Bureau, 1914); Edward Hurley, *The Awakening of Business* (Garden City: Doubleday, Page, 1917); Ida Tarbell, "The Golden Rule in Business," *American Magazine* 78 (1914); and Gilbert H. Montague, "Business and Politics at Home and Abroad," *Annals of the American Academy of Political and Social Science* 42 (July 1912): 156–71. See also the discussion in Burton Kaufman's *Efficiency and Expansion: Foreign Trade Organization in the Wilson Administration, 1913–1921* (Westport, Conn.: Greenwood, 1974), pp. 32–47, and in the introductory sections of David Horowitz's "Visions of Harmonious Abundance: Corporate Ideology in the 1920s" (Ph.D diss., University of Minnesota, 1971).

6. Various aspects of this movement away from the antitrust ideal are discussed in A. Jerome Clifford, *The Independence of the Federal Reserve System* (Philadelphia: University of Pennsylvania Press, 1965); Grant McConnell, *The Decline of Agrarian Democracy* (Berkeley: University of California Press, 1953); Melvin Urofsky, *Big Steel and the Wilson Administration* (Columbus: Ohio State University Press, 1969), pp. 51–83; James Weinstein, *The Corporate Ideal in the Liberal State, 1900–1918* (Boston: Beacon Press, 1968), pp. 82–91; Richard Hume Werking, "Bureaucrats, Businessmen, and Foreign Trade: The Origins of the United States Chamber of Commerce," *Business History Review* 52 (Autumn 1978): 321–41; and Samuel P. Hays, *Conservation and the Gospel of Efficiency* (Cambridge, Mass.: Harvard University Press, 1959), pp. 272–76.

222

7. Kaufman, *Efficiency and Expansion*, pp. 153–59; Urofsky, *Big Steel*, pp. 73–78.

8. On the war system, see Robert D. Cuff, *The War Industries Board* (Baltimore: Johns Hopkins Press, 1973); Kaufman, *Efficiency and Expansion*; and Frederick Paxson, "American War Government," *American Historical Review* 26 (October 1920): 57–76. See also Murray Rothbard's provocative "War Collectivism in World War I," in Ronald Radosh and Murray N. Rothbard, eds., *A New History of Leviathan* (New York: Dutton, 1972).

9. See again the references in note 2. See also Robert D. Cuff, "Harry Garfield, the Fuel Administration, and the Search for a Cooperative Order during World War I," *American Quarterly* 30 (Spring 1978): 39–53; Kim McQuaid, "Corporate Liberalism in the Business Community," *Business History Review* 52 (Autumn 1978): 342–46; and Haggai Hurvitz, "Ideology and Industrial Conflict: President Wilson's First Industrial Conference of October 1919," *Labor History* 18 (Fall 1977): 509–24.

10. See especially his "engineering speeches," February 17, August 26, November 19, 1920 and February 14, 1921, all in Public Statements file, Hoover Papers, Hoover Presidential Library, West Branch, Iowa (hereinafter cited as Hoover Papers). See also his testimony in U.S., Senate, Select Committee on Reconstruction and Production, *Reconstruction and Production, Hearings Pursuant to S. Res. 350*, 66th Cong., 2nd sess., 1920 (Washington, D.C.: Government Printing Office, 1921), pp. 609–27, and U.S., Senate, Committee on Education and Labor, *Industrial Conference, Hearing on Report of Industrial Conference*, 66th Cong., 2nd sess. (Washington, D.C.: Government Printing Office, 1920), pp. 26–38. Glenn Frank associated Hoover with "a new kind of creative regulation" capable of avoiding both "the sins of an anarchic business freedom and the sins of an ineffective and suicidal political control of business." See Frank, in *Century Magazine* 52 (June 1921): 312. William Allen White saw him as the proponent of an "extra government life, quite apart from the government, somewhat regulated by the government, but upon the whole a distinct institutional life" that could "solve a good many problems." See White to Hoover, October 18, 1920, White folder, Pre-Commerce files, Hoover Papers.

11. On the expansion of these administrative domains, see Donald L. Winters, *Henry Cantwell Wallace as Secretary of Agriculture* (Urbana: University of Illinois Press, 1970); Donald C. Swain, *Federal Conservation Policy, 1921–1933* (Berkeley: University of California Press, 1963); Craig Lloyd, *Aggressive Introvert: Herbert Hoover and Public Relations Management* (Columbus: Ohio State University Press, 1972); and Ellis Hawley, "Herbert Hoover, the Commerce Secretariat, and the Vision of an Associative State," *Journal of American History* 61 (June 1974): 116–40. On the changes in the Federal Trade Commission, see G. Cullom Davis, "The Transformation of the Federal Trade Commission, 1914–1929," *Mississippi Valley Historical Review* 49 (December 1962): 437–55. For Hoover's initial perceptions of what could be done and what would justify his leaving the private sector, see Hoover to Harding, February 23, 1921, Harding file, Pre-Commerce files, Hoover Papers.

12. On this macroeconomic dimension see Evan Metcalf, "Secretary Hoover and the Emergence of Macroeconomic Management," *Business History Review* 59 (Spring 1975): 60–80; Carolyn Grin, "The Unemployment Conference of

223

1921: An Experiment in Cooperative Planning," *Mid-America* 55 (April 1973): 83–107; and Ellis Hawley, "Herbert Hoover and Economic Stabilization, 1921–22," in Hawley, ed., *Herbert Hoover as Secretary of Commerce: Studies in New Era Thought and Practice* (Iowa City: University of Iowa Press, 1981), pp. 43–79. See also Edward Eyre Hunt, "Recent Economic Changes in the United States" (1929), Hunt Papers, Springfield, Ohio.

13. Two of the "sickest" areas were bituminous coal and agriculture. On the efforts to equip them with adjustment machinery see Ellis Hawley, "Secretary Hoover and the Bituminous Coal Problem," *Business History Review* 42 (Autumn 1968): 253–70, and Joan Hoff Wilson, "Hoover's Agricultural Policies, 1921–1928," *Agricultural History* 51 (April 1977): 335–61.

14. For the postwar concern with the industry's misbehavior and a possible timber "famine," see Lawrence Hamilton, "The Federal Forest Regulation Issue," *Journal of Forest History* 9 (April 1965): 2–11; William Robbins, "Voluntary Cooperation and the Search for Stability: The Lumber Industry in the 1920s," NEH Seminar Papers, Hoover Presidential Library; and George T. Morgan, *William B. Greeley: A Practical Forester* (St. Paul: Forest History Society, 1961), pp. 39–52. Much of the debate revolved around Gifford Pinchot's report to the Society of American Foresters in late 1919. In it he called for a federal commission to make rules for private forestry, the rules to be enforced through a licensing system to be administered by the Forest Service.

15. See Hoover's addresses on the problem, May 22, 1922, December 12, 1923, November 19, 1924, and May 2, 1925, Public Statements file, Hoover Papers. See also Hoover to William Durgin, April 15, 1924, National Lumber Manufacturers Association file, Commerce files, Hoover Papers.

16. The manufacturing census of 1919 counted 35,872 manufacturing firms. In addition, there were approximately 5,000 wholesalers and 30,000 retailers. On the structure of the industry, its technical backwardness, and its labor intensiveness, see Joseph Zarema, *Economics of the American Lumber Industry* (New York: Speller, 1963), pp. 1–18, 45, 218. See also Nelson C. Brown, *The American Lumber Industry* (New York: Wiley, 1923).

17. John Ise, *The United States Forest Policy* (New Haven: Yale University Press, 1920), pp. 338–53; Federal Trade Commission, *Report on Lumber Manufacturers Trade Associations* (Washington, D.C.: Government Printing Office, 1922).

18. Robbins, "Lumber Industry in the 1920s," pp. 4–6; National Lumber Manufacturers Association, *Highlights of a Decade of Achievement* (1929), pp. 8–12; Hoover to Durgin, April 15, 1924, NLMA file, Commerce files, Hoover Papers.

19. Department of Commerce, *Elimination of Waste: Lumber* (1924), p. 2; Hoover to Wallace, February 8, March 7, 1922, Agriculture Dept. file, Commerce files, Hoover Papers; Emmet to William Mullendore, March 23, 1922, Lumber Grading Simplification file, Commerce files, Hoover Papers; Hoover to Walter Drake, June 15, 1923, National Hardwood Lumber Association file, Commerce files, Hoover Papers. In the Forest Service there was the continuing conflict between Pinchot's "regulationism" and William B. Greeley's "cooperationism." Greeley eventually won out, but his program at this stage stressed the

224

need for cooperative fire protection rather than organization for greater productivity. See Morgan, *Greeley*, pp. 48–56.

20. Department of Commerce, *Elimination of Waste: Lumber*, pp. 2–3; Hoover, Address of May 22, 1922, NLMA file, Commerce files, Hoover Papers; *New York Times*, May 23, 1922 and October 8, 1922; *Public Ledger*, October 4, 1922; "Action of General Lumber Conference, Chicago, July 22," Lumber file, Commerce files, Hoover Papers. The functional representatives on the original committee were John E. Lloyd (retailers), Dwight Hinckley (wholesalers), John H. Kirby and Charles A. Goodman (manufacturers), Emory S. Hall (architects), and W. E. Hawley (railroads). Later added was E. E. Parsonage (wood users). R. G. Merritt became executive secretary. Attached to the Central Committee there was also a consulting committee, made up of 31 members chosen for their positions or expertise.

21. John McClure to National Hardwood Lumber Association members, September 13, 1922; AP Bulletin, Chicago, June 15, 1923; Hoover to Walter Drake, June 15, 1923; Hoover Statement to AP, June 16, 1923; Drake to Hoover, June 18, 1923, all in National Hardwood Lumber Association file, Commerce files, Hoover Papers; Peri Arnold, "Herbert Hoover and the Department of Commerce" (Ph.D. diss., University of Chicago, 1971), pp. 162–71.

22. Department of Commerce, *Elimination of Waste: Lumber*, pp. 3–4; "Minutes of General Standardization Conference on Lumber," December 12–13, 1923, Conferences, Lumber file, Commerce files, Hoover Papers.

23. Hoover to Durgin, April 15, 1924, NLMA file, Commerce files, Hoover Papers. There had also been cooperation with a number of lumber associations in developing and defending statistical programs, studying building codes, and gathering information on foreign markets. See F. T. Miller, "Building Codes," Building and Housing file, Commerce files, Hoover Papers; Wilson Compton to Stephen Davis, January 21, 1924, NLMA file, Commerce files, Hoover Papers; "U.S. Foreign Trade in Lumber for 1924," Lumber file, Commerce files, Hoover Papers.

24. Axel Oxholm to Julius Klein, February 15, 1923, Commerce Dept., BFDC, Lumber Division file, Commerce files, Hoover Papers; Klein to Hoover, March 6, 1923, File 82219/27, Commerce Dept. Records (RG 40), National Archives; J. C. Nellis to John W. Blodgett, October 28, 1924, Lumber file, Commerce files, Hoover Papers; Wallace to Hoover, October 8, 1924; William Greeley to Hoover, October 13, 1924; Hudson to Stokes, October 15, 1924; Greeley to Walter Drake, November 11, 1924, all in Conferences, Wood Utilization file, Commerce files, Hoover papers.

25. Wallace died on October 25, 1924, of complications following an operation to remove his gall bladder and appendix.

26. "National Conference on Utilization of Forest Products," Conferences, Wood Utilization file, Commerce files, Hoover Papers; National Conference on Utilization of Forest Products, *Report* (1925); Remarks by Secretary Hoover, November 19, 1924; Address by President Coolidge, November 19, 1924, both in Conferences, Wood Utilization file, Commerce files, Hoover Papers; *American Lumberman*, November 22, 1924.

27. National Conference on Utilization of Forest Products, *Report*, pp. 69–

225

72; *American Lumberman*, November 22, 1924. The Clark-McNary Act had provided funds for developing a number of cooperative activities, especially in fire protection, tax studies, forestry experimentation, and timberland surveys.

28. John H. Blodgett to Coolidge, November 22, 1924; Hoover to Howard Gore, November 24, 1924; Hoover to Coolidge, November 28, 1924; Coolidge to Blodgett, December 1, 1924; Hoover to Blodgett, December 4, 1924; Commerce Dept. press release, April 30, 1925, all in Conferences, Wood Utilization file, Commerce files, Hoover Papers.

29. Commerce Department press releases, April 30, May 2, 1925. As initially established, the committee had 21 members representing 12 functional groups. Later, it was expanded to include more specialized groups who desired representation, such groups, for example, as the plywood manufacturers, shipbuilders, cooperage industries, and wood turners. By June of 1926 it had 98 members, but policy making by 1926 had been largely concentrated in an executive committee that subsequently varied from 9 to 14 members. The changing membership and organization can be followed in "Status of the Work of the NCWU, 1926"; Commerce Dept. press release, January, 11, 1927; Oxholm to Hoover, October 17, 1927, all in Conferences, Wood Utilization file, Commerce files, Hoover Papers.

30. Hoover to Blodgett, March 2, 1925; Hoover to Walter Poleman, March 2, 1925; Press release, May 2, 1925; Hoover to James L. Kilpatrick, September 26, 1925; Daily Bulletin, December 4, 1925, all in Conferences, Wood Utilization file, Commerce files, Hoover Papers; Edward Eyre Hunt to Robert Lamont, October 16, 1929, Box 30, Hunt Papers, Hoover Institution Archives, Stanford University, Palo Alto, Calif.

31. "Status of the Work of the National Committee on Wood Utilization," 1926; Axel Oxholm to Hoover, January 6, 1926, January 11, June 16, October 17, 1927; Press release, November 5, 1926, all in Conferences, Wood Utilization file, Commerce files, Hoover Papers; Hunt to Lamont, October 16, 1929, Box 30, Hunt Papers, Hoover Institution; "Accomplishments of the Department of Commerce," Commerce, Accomplishments file, Commerce files, Hoover Papers.

32. Robbins, "Lumber Industry in the 1920s," pp. 25–29; Ward Shepard and John B. Woods, in *Journal of Forestry* 25 (January 1927) and 28 (November 1930). A subsequent study concluded that there were no major advances in productivity during the 1920s, nor for that matter during the whole period between 1899 and 1953. There were some technological advances, but the effect of these was more than offset by such factors as declining tree size, the lower quality of the timber being cut, and the greater distances that lumber had to be transported. Lumber prices kept rising relative to all-commodity prices. See Zaremba, *Economics of the American Lumber Industry*, pp. 1–3, 222. Interestingly, Zaremba, writing in 1963, still saw the establishment and enforcement of standards and grades as the industry's central problem, one whose solution "would revolutionize lumber manufacture, distribution and use." And like Hoover in the 1920s, he saw its solution coming through "strong industry organization and close cooperation of allied groups."

33. Oxholm to Anderson, January 4, 1928; Oxholm to Greeley, January 20, 1928; Greeley to Oxholm, January 25, 1928, all in Conferences, Wood Utili-

226

zation file, Commerce files, Hoover Papers; *Engineering News-Record*, December 15, 1927, p. 979.

34. National Lumber Manufacturers Association press release, May 10, 1927, Lumber file, Commerce files, Hoover Papers.

35. Leighton H. Peebles to James S. Taylor, November 17, 1931, reporting on a trip to district offices in the lumber areas, Box 92, Frederick Feiker Papers, Records of the Bureau of Foreign and Domestic Commerce (RG 151), National Archives. The National Timber Conservation Board was structured along lines similar to the CCLS and the NCWU. It brought together industrial, public, and governmental representatives, commingled private and public support, and had a mixed secretariat. Its chief concerns were with surplus inventories, over-production, and disorderly marketing. See Ripley Bowman, in *Southern Lumberman*, December 15, 1931; Wilson Compton, in *American Economic Review Supplement* 22 (March 1932): 101–4; and Robert Lamont to Hoover, June 18, 1932, National Timber Conservation Board file, Presidential Subject files, Hoover Papers.

36. On the NRA experience see Peter A. Stone and others, *Economic Problems of the Lumber and Timber Products Industry*, NRA Work Materials #79, 1936, pp. 103–10, and A. C. Dixon and others, "The Lumber Code," NRA Code History #9, Code Histories file, NRA Records, National Archives. On what followed see the relevant sections of Harold K. Steen, *The U.S. Forest Service* (Seattle: University of Washington Press, 1976).

37. For general accounts of the industry during this period, see Henry Ladd Smith, *Airways: The History of Commercial Aviation in the United States* (New York: Knopf, 1942); Elsbeth S. Freudenthal, *The Aviation Business from Kitty Hawk to Wall Street* (New York: Vanguard, 1940); John H. Frederick, *Commercial Air Transportation* (Chicago: Irwin, 1946); Gene R. Simons, ed., *The History of the American Aircraft Industry* (Cambridge, Mass.: MIT Press, 1968); and Thomas W. Walterman, "Airpower and Private Enterprise: Federal-Industrial Relations in the Aeronautics Field, 1918–1926" (Ph.D. diss., Washington University, 1970).

38. For expositions of this view, see "Notes for a Meeting of the Aircraft Men," July 16, 1921; Press release, November 5, 1925; Hoover's Address to the San Francisco Chamber of Commerce, September 2, 1926, all in Aviation file, Commerce files, Hoover Papers; "Memorandum for Hoover on Proposed Bureau of Aeronautics"; Hoover's Statement before the President's Aircraft Board, September 24, 1925; Press release, January 24, 1926, all in Commerce Dept., Bureau of Aeronautics file, Commerce files, Hoover Papers; "Report of the Joint Committee on Civil Aviation" (1926), Aviation file, Commerce files, Hoover Papers.

39. Charles D. Walcott to Hoover, March 23, 1921, Aviation file, Commerce files, Hoover Papers; clippings from *Buffalo News*, July 21, 1921, *Philadelphia Inquirer*, October 12, 1921, and *Philadelphia Inquirer*, September 3, 1921, in Commerce Dept., Bureau of Aeronautics file, Commerce files, Hoover Papers; "Notes for Meeting of the Aircraft Men," July 16, 1921, Aviation file, Commerce files, Hoover Papers.

40. Hoover to L. D. Gardner, June 14, 1921, Aviation file, Commerce files,

227

Regulation in Perspective

Hoover Papers; David D. Lee, "Herbert Hoover and the Development of Commercial Aviation, 1921–1926," NEH Seminar Papers, Hoover Presidential Library.

41. L. D. Gardner to Hoover, June 18, 1921; Hoover to Gardner, June 23, 1921; Luther Bell to Clarence Stetson, July 11, 1921; "Notes for Meeting of the Aircraft Men," July 16, 1921; Hoover to Maurice Cleary, June 25, 1921; "Aviation Conference," July 18, 1921, all in Aviation file, Commerce files, Hoover Papers; Charles T. Menoher to Secretary of War, April 1, 1921, National Advisory Committee for Aeronautics file, Commerce files, Hoover Papers; Robert Murray, *The Harding Era: Warren G. Harding and His Administration* (Minneapolis: University of Minnesota Press, 1969), pp. 410–11.

42. Samuel Bradley to Hoover, April 11, August 24, 1922; Howard Coffin to Hoover, April 18, 1922, all in Commerce Dept., Bureau of Aeronautics file, Commerce Files, Hoover Papers; *New York Times,* September 20, 1921; Lee, "Hoover and Commercial Aviation," pp. 12–14, 23–24; Howard Mingos, in Simons, ed., *Aircraft Industry,* pp. 55–57; *Aviation,* January 2, 1922. As originally established, the Aeronautical Chamber of Commerce included 26 manufacturing and engineering companies, 31 operators and distributors, 29 manufacturers of accessories, 8 trade publications, and the insurance writers association. The Manufacturers Aircraft Association remained in existence and was closely linked with the ACC. They shared offices and facilities, and Samuel Bradley served as general manager of both associations. Also organized in 1922, largely through the efforts of Howard Coffin, was the National Aeronautics Association. It replaced the earlier Aero Club of America.

43. Hoover to Samuel E. Winslow, December 19, 1921; Hoover to James Wadsworth, December 20, 1921; Hoover to William MacCracken, February 15, 1922; Hoover to Theodore Roosevelt, Jr., April 11, 1922; William Lamb to Emmet, April 15, 1922; Hoover to Howard Coffin, April 21, 1922; Julius Klein to Emmet, May 25, 1922; Hoover to Lamb, June 2, 1922; Hoover to Winslow, June 12, 13, 19, 1922; James O'Hara to Emmet, August 7, 1922; Winslow to Hoover, September 15, 1922, all in Commerce Dept., Bureau of Aeronautics file, Commerce files, Hoover Papers.

44. Christian Herter to Julius Klein, September 28, 1923; Earl Osborn to Hoover, January 9, 1925; R. H. Fleet to Hoover, January 10, 1925; Hoover to Hiram Bingham, September 23, 1925; Clarence Young to Hoover, December 7, 1925; Hoover to Young, December 14, 1925, all in Commerce Dept., Bureau of Aeronautics file, Commerce files, Hoover Papers; Hoover interview, in *Boston American,* October 13, 1924; Press release, November 13, 1924, Aviation file, Commerce files, Hoover Papers; Lee, "Hoover and Civil Aviation," pp. 24–25; *Aviation,* February 19, 1923, June 1, 1925.

45. *New York Times,* May 22, 1925; National Air Transport, Inc., "Public Relations Committee," Aviation file, Commerce files, Hoover Papers; Press releases, November 5, 1925, January 24, 1926; "Recommendations and Summarized Findings of the Committee on Civil Aviation," October 21, 1925; E. S. Gregg, "The Development of Civil Aviation," September 19, 1925, all in Commerce Dept., Bureau of Aeronautics file, Commerce files, Hoover Papers; Will H. Hays, *The Memoirs of Will H. Hays* (Garden City: Doubleday, 1955), pp. 312–17; Lee, "Hoover and Civil Aviation," pp. 28–31; Allan Nevins and Frank

Hill, *Ford: Expansion and Challenge* (New York: Scribner's, 1957), pp. 238–45.

46. Lee, "Hoover and Civil Aviation," pp. 31–33; Alfred F. Hurley, *Billy Mitchell: Crusader for Air Power* (Bloomington: Indiana University Press ed., 1975), pp. 100–101; President's Aircraft Board, *Report* (Washington, D.C.: Government Printing Office, 1925); "Statement of Hoover on Civil Aviation," September 24, 1925, Commerce Dept., Bureau of Aeronautics file, Commerce files, Hoover Papers.

47. Clarence Young to Hoover, December 7, 1925; Hoover to Young, December 14, 1925; Wadsworth to Hoover, December 5, 1925; Hoover to Wesley L. Jones, December 9, 1925, all in Commerce Dept., Bureau of Aeronautics file, Commerce files, Hoover Papers. Young would become the first chief of the air regulations division and would subsequently be appointed director of the Aeronautics Branch.

48. Lee, "Hoover and Civil Aviation," pp. 33–35; 44 *U.S. Statutes* 568.

49. As finally established, the Aeronautics Branch consisted of the new assistant secretary's office, a directorship working in conjunction with the office, a division each from the Lighthouse Service and the Bureau of Standards, a section from the Coast and Geodetic Survey, and newly created special divisions for air regulations and air information. See Laurence F. Schmeckebier, *The Aeronautics Branch, Department of Commerce* (Washington, D.C.: Brookings Institution, 1930), pp. 13–14; Lester D. Gardner, "Development of Civil Aeronautics in America," October 1, 1927, Aviation file, Commerce files, Hoover Papers; *Aviation*, July 13, 1929.

50. Hoover to Coolidge, August 3, 1926, with attached statement; Hoover to Hiram Bingham, July 30, 1926; Hoover to George W. Pepper, June 23, 1926, all in Commerce Dept., Bureau of Aeronautics file, Commerce files, Hoover Papers; William MacCracken, "Re Herbert Hoover," August 1, 1968, Hoover Oral History Program file, Box 13, MacCracken Papers, Hoover Presidential Library. MacCracken was not Hoover's first choice. The position was offered to Paul Henderson, the general manager of National Air Transport, and to Hollinshead N. Taylor, a Philadelphia business executive active in the National Aeronautic Association and in Hoover's programs for standardizing building codes. Both declined because of business responsibilities.

51. Gardner, "Development of Civil Aeronautics in America," October 1, 1927, Aviation file, Commerce files, Hoover Papers; testimony of MacCracken and Hoover before U.S. Senate Committee on Appropriations, *Departments of State, Justice, Commerce and Labor Appropriations Bill, 1928: Hearings on H.R. 16576,* 69th Cong., 2nd sess., 1927 (Washington, D.C.: Government Printing Office, 1927), pp. 10–26; Department of Commerce, *Air Commerce Regulations* (Washington, D.C.: Government Printing Office, 1926).

52. Hoover, "Progress in Commercial Aviation," [1928], Aviation file, Commerce files, Hoover Papers; Clarence Young to George Akerson, July 10, 1929, Aeronautics file, Presidential Subject files, Hoover Papers; MacCracken, in Senate Appropriations Committee, *Hearings: Appropriations Bill, 1928,* pp. 19–20.

53. Clippings from *Boston Herald,* October 10, 1929, and *Commerce and Finance,* November 6, 1929; Fairfax Naulty to Hoover, November 18, 1929; William McAdoo to Hoover, November 21, 1929; Clarence Young to Hoover,

229

August 22, 1930, all in Aeronautics file, Presidential Subject files, Hoover Papers; Walter Brown, Address to the Cleveland Chamber of Commerce, January 14, 1930, Post Office file, Presidential Subject files, Hoover Papers.

54. *U.S. Daily,* February 4, April 3, April 30, May 3, 1930; clipping of an article by David Rotroff [1930], Airmail file, Box 9, MacCracken Papers; U.S., Congress, House, Antitrust Subcommittee of the Committee on the Judiciary, *The Airlines Industry, Report No. 1328 pursuant to H. Res. 107,* 85th Cong., 1st sess., 1957 (Washington, D.C.: Government Printing Office, 1958), pp. 10–12, 19.

55. For the evolution of New Deal policy in regard to aviation, see Ellis Hawley, *The New Deal and the Problem of Monopoly* (Princeton: Princeton University Press, 1966), pp. 240–44, and Francis A. Spencer, *Air Mail Payment and the Government* (Washington, D.C.: Brookings Institution, 1941). See also House Antitrust Subcommittee, *Airlines Industry,* pp. 12–17.

56. See, for example, Will H. Hays, "The Motion Picture Industry," *Review of Reviews* (January 1923), pp. 65–80, and Hays, "Motion Pictures and the Public," April 20, 1925, Hays file, Commerce files, Hoover Papers. The most corporatively organized portions of the apparatus were (1) the machinery for "harmonizing" producer-exhibitor relations and (2) the public relations committee (later department) with its mixture of industrial, consumer, and "public" representatives. For general accounts of the Hays Office, see Raymond Moley, *The Hays Office* (Indianapolis: Bobbs-Merrill, 1945); Ruth A. Inglis, *Freedom of the Movies* (Chicago: University of Chicago Press, 1947); Mae D. Huettig, *Economic Control of the Motion Picture Industry: A Study in Economic Organization* (Philadelphia: University of Pennsylvania Press, 1944); Louis Nizer, *New Courts of Industry* (New York: Longacre, 1935); and "The Hays Office," *Fortune,* December 1938, pp. 68–72.

57. Hoover to Hays, March 7, May 8, 1922; Hoover to Walter S. Tower, June 7, 1923; Emmet to Hays, July 26, 1923; Hoover to Julius Barnes, August 14, 1922, all in Hays file, Commerce files, Hoover Papers; Hoover to Grace Harriman, December 19, 1921; Emmet to Mrs. M. B. Dean, February 10, 1922, both in Motion Pictures file, Commerce files, Hoover Papers; "Hays Office," *Fortune,* December 1938, p. 139; Hays, *Memoirs,* pp. 356, 510. Officially, however, especially in correspondence with groups seeking governmental regulation, Hoover took the position that the movie "question" was not before his department except in connection with export trade.

58. Moley, *Hays Office,* pp. 27–32; Inglis, *Freedom of Movies,* pp. 62–96; Henry F. Pringle, "Will Hays—Supervisor of Morals," *Outlook,* April 11, 1928, pp. 576–78. As Pringle puts it, Hays was "hired—hokum aside—to block additional Government supervision, to tame radical spirits among the producers, to prevent trade practices which cause expensive litigation, to use his influence as an important politician of the party in power." The most notorious of the scandals were those involving the murder of William Desmond Taylor, the trial of Roscoe "Fatty" Arbuckle, and the political activities of William A. Brady of the National Association of the Motion Picture Industry. In view of these the industry was looking for respectability, much as baseball had done following the "Black Sox" scandal of 1919.

59. Hays was noted chiefly for his feats as a political organizer and conductor

230

of public relations campaigns. Before entering Harding's cabinet as postmaster general, he had for three years headed the Republican National Committee. His approach to administrative and organizational problems was much like Hoover's, and the two had been associated during the war when Hays was chairman of the Indiana State Council of Defense.

60. See Inglis, *Freedom of Movies*, pp. 73–74, 88–90.

61. *Ibid.*, pp. 97–111; Moley, *Hays Office*, pp. 132–39, 213–19; Hays, "Motion Picture Industry," *Review of Reviews*, January 1923, pp. 74–79. The machinery linking the office to community and civic groups was known as the Committee on Public Relations. Set up in 1922 following a conference in New York, it consisted of representatives from about 80 civic, fraternal, welfare, religious, and professional organizations, each serving in theory to bring the thinking of the movie makers and that of groups making up the "public" closer together. At the heart of the apparatus was a group of administrators functioning both as a unit of the Hays Office and as the executive secretariat for the group representatives. In 1925 the committee as such dissolved itself and the apparatus was absorbed into a Department of Public Relations. There were also cooperating organizations set up by the participating groups, and after 1929 there was a staff position held by a "representative in the industry of organized women."

62. Moley, *Hays Office*, pp. 57–64; Inglis, *Freedom of Movies*, pp. 111–16. The machinery here began with informal consultation and evolved through a formula for identifying and securing industry-wide rejection of unsuitable scripts, an advisory system on pictures to be released, and promulgation of a list of "don'ts" and "be carefuls." Not until 1930 was there a formal production code. Movies were made outside the system, and some were even advertised as "banned by Will Hays." But these could not be shown in theatres owned or controlled by MPPDA members.

63. Moley, *Hays Office*, pp. 50–51, 90–97; Hays, *Memoirs*, pp. 338–39, 355–56, 433; Inglis, *Freedom of the Movies*, pp. 90–91; *System*, September 1926, pp. 277–80.

64. Hays, *Memoirs*, pp. 333–34, 505–10; Moley, *Hays Office*, pp. 169–76.

65. Hoover to Julius Klein, March 5, 1925, Commerce Dept., BFDC file, Commerce files, Hoover Papers; "Accomplishments of the Department of Commerce," Commerce, Accomplishments file, Commerce files, Hoover Papers; Bureau of Foreign and Domestic Commerce, *Annual Reports*: 1926, pp. 13, 45–46; 1927, pp. 41–42; 1928, p. 34; 1929, p. 39; C. J. North, "Our Foreign Trade in Motion Pictures," *Annals of the American Academy of Political and Social Science* 128 (November 1926): 100–108.

66. Will H. Hays, "The Motion Picture Industry," *Review of Reviews*, January 1923, pp. 65–80; Hays, "Motion Pictures and the Public," Hays file, Commerce files, Hoover Papers; Hays, *The Motion Picture and the Public* (New York: MPPDA, 1925); C. C. Pettijohn, "How the Motion Picture Industry Governs Itself," *Annals of the American Academy of Political and Social Science* 128 (November 1926): 158–62; Hays, *Memoirs*, pp. 327–31, 377.

67. Hoover, Address at dinner of MPPDA, New York, April 2, 1927; Hoover to Hays, April 20, 1926; George Canty to Motion Picture Section, BFDC, April 2, 1928, all in Hays file, Commerce files, Hoover Papers.

68. Ernest I. Lewis to Hoover, May 16, 1925; International Reform Federa-

231

tion to Hoover, January 29, 1927; Mrs. R. M. Gibbs to Hoover, with attached article, July 22, 1927, all in Motion Pictures file, Commerce files, Hoover Papers; William S. Chase to Hoover, May 4, 1929, with attached memorandum by William Seabury; Fred Eastman, "The Menace of the Movies" (reprinted from *Christian Century*, 1930), all in Motion Pictures file, Presidential Subject files, Hoover Papers; Grant M. Hudson and Burt New, "Should the Government Control Motion Pictures?" *Congressional Digest* 7 (November 1928): 314–15; Hays, *Memoirs*, pp. 389–96; Moley, *Hays Office*, pp. 61–67. Under the regulatory proposals being debated, the Upshaw and Hudson bills, a federal commission would be established in the Bureau of Education and would be empowered to censor movies being released, license those operating in the industry, supervise production and distribution, and, if necessary, take over and operate the distribution system. An alternative proposal, by 1929, called for a Film Inspection Bureau in the Commerce Department. This was also sponsored by Congressman Grant M. Hudson.

69. Block booking was the practice of requiring an exhibitor to take all or a certain percentage of a group of films, sometimes all of a company's annual production, in order to obtain any film in the group. The producers called it "selling in bulk" and insisted that the security thus provided was essential to the industry's operation. The exhibitors saw it as an effort to make them shoulder an unfair portion of the risks involved in marketing pictures.

70. The conference produced a fifteen-rule trade practice agreement. But the arbitration provisions of this were quickly challenged, and in the courts the producers continued to defend block booking. They were unwilling to accept an FTC order against it. Federal Trade Commission, *Trade Practice Conferences* (Washington: Government Printing Office, 1929), pp. 83–93, 99; Abram F. Myers, "Fair Methods of Competition in the Motion Picture Industry," October 10, 1927, Motion Pictures file, Commerce files, Hoover Papers.

71. Abram F. Myers to Hoover, March 27, June 18, 1929, Motion Pictures file, Presidential Subject files, Hoover Papers; Moley, *Hays Office*, p. 200.

72. Hays, *Memoirs*, p. 438; "Hays Office," *Fortune*, December 1938, p. 140.

73. Memorandum of a phone call from Will Hays, March 17, 1930, Motion Pictures file, Presidential Subject files, Hoover Papers; Moley, *Hays Office*, pp. 199–202; "Activities and Accomplishments of the Antitrust Division during the Hoover Administration," Box 1, Taylor-Gates material, Hoover Presidential Library. Apparently O'Brian's activities stemmed from a 1929 conference between Hays and Hoover, in which it was agreed that the industry would cooperate in an equity suit designed to clear up the legality of its trade practices, get them established in a consent decree, and thus remove any potential embarrassments for the new administration. See Hays to Hoover, August 28, 1929, Antitrust Laws file, Presidential Subject files, Hoover Papers, and Hoover to Richey, March 17, 1930, Motion Pictures file, Presidential Subject files, Hoover Papers.

74. Moley, *Hays Office*, pp. 74–99, 201–12; "Hays Office," *Fortune*, December 1938, pp. 70, 142–44; Hays, *Memoirs*, pp. 444–504, 526–58, 569–72; Hawley, *New Deal and Monopoly*, pp. 365–68, 451–52. Hays retired in 1945, but the basic mechanisms of the office remained. Hays was replaced by Eric Johnston.

232

75. See, for example, G. Lehmbruch, "Liberal Corporatism and Party Government," *Comparative Political Studies* 10 (1977): 91–126; Frederick Pike and Thomas Stritch, eds., *The New Corporatism* (Notre Dame: University of Notre Dame Press, 1974); Andrew Shonfield, *Modern Capitalism* (New York: Oxford University Press, 1965); and Vogel, *Japan as Number One.*

American Businessmen and
Foreign Policy: The Recognition
of Mexico, 1920-1923

N. STEPHEN KANE

Historians and political scientists have recently shown an increasing interest in the interrelationship between business and government in the field of foreign policy during the twentieth century. While few of them would accept uncritically the radical revisionist contention that the relationship between businessmen and policy makers is virtually collusive, even fewer would deny that business groups exert significant influence on the formulation and implementation of foreign policy. Despite mounting evidence to the contrary, many scholars continue to attribute to individual businessmen and business-interest groups power over policy far greater than they actually possess.

Although much of the scholarship dealing with the subject is impressionistic,[1] studies by Tansill, Beard, Campbell, and Vevier,[2] for ex-

[1] See, for example, Scott Nearing and Joseph Freeman, *Dollar Diplomacy: A Study in American Imperialism* (New York, 1925); Leland H. Jenks, *Our Cuban Colony: A Study in Sugar* (New York, 1928); C. Hartley Grattan, *Why We Fought* (New York, 1929); J. Fred Rippy, *The Capitalists and Colombia* (New York, 1931); and Carleton Beals, *The Crime of Cuba* (Philadelphia, 1934).

[2] Charles C. Tansill, *America Goes to War* (Boston, 1938), especially chap. III; Charles A. Beard, *America in Mid-Passage* (New York, 1939); Charles S. Campbell, *Special Business Interests and the Open Door Policy* (New Haven, Conn., 1951); and Charles Vevier, *The United States and China, 1906–1913: A Study in Finance and Diplomacy* (New Brunswick, N. J., 1955).

N. STEPHEN KANE is an historian at the U.S. Department of State and a member of the editorial board of *Societas: A Review of Social History.* A contributor to scholarly journals, he is currently at work on a book dealing with business influence and United States policy toward Latin America.

Political Science Quarterly Volume 90 Number 2 Summer 1975

293

ample, cannot be dismissed in the same way. They are not only sophisticated pieces of research, but they rest on certain common assumptions:
that patterns of influence are an integral part of the political process, affecting foreign policy as well as domestic issues; that financial power
and social prestige enable business leaders to gain easy access to policy
makers; and that of all interest groups within the political system businessmen are the most effective because they can readily claim economic
injury and because they can afford the expensive and time-consuming
participation necessary to manipulate the legislative process. But these
same studies also contain a common flaw; their authors tended to regard
the holding of similar positions by businessmen and policy makers as
evidence of influence. Moreover, they made little effort to dissect the decision-making process in order to determine precisely the flow of influence in specific situations. As a result, they generally failed to prove a
direct connection between business pressure and actual policy decisions.

Recently radical revisionist scholars have developed a different set of
assumptions concerning the interrelationship between business and
government in the field of foreign policy.[3] Radical revisionists such
as Williams, Kolko, Magdoff, Horowitz, Gardner, and Paterson[4] evidently assume that the policy-making structure is controlled by an elite,
consisting primarily of corporate leaders and their political-military al-

[3] As used here, the term "radical revisionist" applies to those scholars who believe
that United States foreign policy is the result primarily of forces generated by the domestic institutions of American capitalism, and that its alleged counterrevolutionary
orientation will not change until a basic political-economic transformation occurs
in American society. For a critique of radical revisionist scholarship which addresses
itself in part to this point of view, see Robert W. Tucker, The Radical Left and American Foreign Policy (Baltimore, 1971).

[4] William Appleman Williams, The Tragedy of American Diplomacy (Cleveland,
1959), The Contours of American History (Cleveland, 1961), and The Roots of the
Modern American Empire (New York, 1969); Gabriel Kolko, The Politics of War: The
World and United States Foreign Policy, 1943–1945 (New York, 1969), The Roots of
American Foreign Policy: An Analysis of Power and Purpose (Boston, 1969), and
Gabriel Kolko and Joyce Kolko, The Limits of Power: The World and United States
Foreign Policy, 1945-1954 (New York, 1972); Harry Magdoff, The Age of Imperial-
ism: The Economics of American Foreign Policy (New York, 1969); David Horowitz,
The Free World Colossus: A Critique of American Foreign Policy in the Cold War (New
York, 1965); Lloyd Gardner, Economic Aspects of New Deal Diplomacy (Madison,
Wis., 1964), and Architects and Illusion: Men and Ideas in American Foreign Policy,
1941–1949 (Chicago, 1970); Thomas G. Paterson, "The Quest for Peace and Prosperity: International Trade, Communism, and the Marshall Plan, in Barton J. Bernstein
(ed.), Politics and Policies of the Truman Administration (Chicago, 1970), pp. 78–
112. See also David Horowitz (ed.), Corporations and the Cold War (New York, 1969),
which contains essays by Williams, Gardner, G. William Domhoff, David W. Eakins,
Joseph D. Phillips, and Charles W. Nathanson.

lies, which possesses sufficient power to shape national decisions.[5] They concede that businessmen often disagree over policy questions, but they regard such disagreements as merely tactical, and therefore of no real consequence. From the revisionist perspective, the roles of business leader and policy maker are virtually interchangeable; the common denominator is their firm belief in the imperative need to expand the American capitalist system—a belief which transcends all competitive differences between business groups and which ultimately renders irrelevant any question concerning the role of influence or the impact of group conflict in the pursuit of policy preference. On the surface, this interpretation is attractive, but it vastly oversimplifies the nature of decision making, in part by reducing motivation to a single impulse and in part by failing to appreciate the way noneconomic factors link together with economic ones to form the options from which policy makers have to choose.[6]

Despite the currency of radical revisionist assumptions, the available empirical evidence does not appear to sustain the view that businessmen have a major influence on policy decisions. Case studies of business efforts to exert pressure on the policy process, in fact, substantially point to the opposite conclusion. For example, Wilson has disproved the widely held view that business pressure was responsible for inducing the Roosevelt administration to recognize the Soviet Union in 1933; Wilkins has found, contrary to the assumptions of previous scholars, that businessmen had little impact on the course of United States relations with Japan from 1931 to 1941; Cohen has demonstrated that business interests were generally unable to obtain their objectives in the formation of the Japanese Peace Treaty in 1951; and Bauer, de Sola Pool, and Dexter have

[5] The radical revisionists' intellectual debt to C. Wright Mills, *The Power Elite* (New York, 1956), is quite apparent. For a trenchant analysis of Mills's concept of "the power elite" and an instructive discussion of the very limited circumstances under which it can be subjected to empirical verification, see Robert A. Dahl, "A Critique of the Ruling Elite Model," *American Political Science Review*, LII (June 1958), 463–469.

[6] This is not to suggest, of course, that only radical revisionists currently assume a vital connection between businessmen and policy makers. Many scholars would probably agree with the statement in Carl Parrini, *Heir to Empire: United States Economic Diplomacy, 1916–1923* (Pittsburgh, 1969), p. x: "that while business interests do not dictate to the political leadership the policies they pursue, they do establish an economic reality within which the alternatives available to the politician are rather sharply circumscribed." But this view raises two immediate questions, not answered by Parrini: (1) precisely how are differing perceptions of economic reality reconciled in policy decisions, and (2) how is the significance of the economic reality calculated when it is merely one of several "realities" impinging on the decision-making process at any given time?

demolished the idea that business influence is the primary force in shaping tariff policy.[7]

In considering the role of influence in the relationship between businessmen and policy makers, there are at least three distinct possibilities. Businessmen may try to influence policy makers to adopt certain policies beneficial to business interests; policy makers may try to influence businessmen to undertake tasks conceived as vital to the nation's interests which the latter would ordinarily be reluctant to pursue; and the objectives of the two groups may be sufficiently congruent to permit effective cooperation without involving an effort by either to exert influence on the other. This article deals with the first of these possibilities.

The case of American businessmen and the recognition of the regime of Álvaro Obregón in Mexico provides an excellent opportunity to assess business response to a particular policy.[8] From 1920 to mid-1923, the State Department withheld recognition from Obregón as part of an effort to compel him to sign a treaty guaranteeing protection for American property rights threatened by the potentially confiscatory provisions of Article 27 of the Constitution of 1917. Those businessmen concerned

---

[7] The works referred to in this paragraph are as follows: Joan Hoff Wilson, "American Business and the Recognition of the Soviet Union," *Social Science Quarterly*, LII (September 1971), 349–368; Mira Wilkins, "The Role of U.S. Business," in Dorothy Borg and Shumpei Okamoto (eds.), *Pearl Harbor as History: Japanese-American Relations, 1931–1941* (New York, 1973), pp. 341–376; Bernard C. Cohen, *The Political Process and Foreign Policy: The Making of the Japanese Peace Settlement* (Princeton, N. J., 1957); and Raymond A. Bauer, Ithiel de Sola Pool, and Lewis Anthony Dexter, *American Business and Public Policy: The Politics of Foreign Trade* (Englewood Cliffs, N. J., 1964). For a broader study which reaches somewhat similar conclusions about the impact of business pressure on major foreign policy decisions, see Joan Hoff Wilson, *American Business and Foreign Policy, 1920–1933* (Lexington, Ky., 1971).

[8] Recent scholarship dealing with United States-Mexican relations during the Harding period has emphasized the importance of business pressure in bringing about the recognition of Obregón. Both Eugene P. Traini, "Harding Administration and Recognition of Mexico," *Ohio History*, LXXV (Spring–Summer 1966), 145, and Robert K. Murray, *The Harding Era: Warren G. Harding and His Administration* (Minneapolis, Minn., 1969), p. 330, note the intense public and business pressure which they believe helped to facilitate recognition, but neither adduces sufficient evidence to support his view; C. Dennis Ignasias, "Propaganda and Public Opinion in Harding's Foreign Affairs: the Case for Mexican Recognition," *Journalism Quarterly*, XLVIII (Spring 1971), 41–52, contends rather implausibly, that the Mexican government's active propaganda campaign in the United States stimulated public opinion in favor of recognition to the extent that President Harding, motivated "by the voluminous written and spoken word of the 'popular will,'" "pressured" Secretary of State Charles Evans Hughes to reformulate the department's position; Robert Freeman Smith, *The United States and Revolutionary Nationalism in Mexico, 1916–1932* (Chicago, 1972), pp. 213–220, strongly implies that a single businessman—Thomas W. Lamont—was responsible for bringing about recognition.

with the status of relations between the two countries divided into pro-recognitionists, consisting predominantly of manufacturers and exporters of consumer goods, and antirecognitionists, including mostly investors in Mexican petroleum and agrarian properties. Despite widespread and growing pressure for recognition within the business community, the State Department refused to alter its policy. When recognition finally was extended, it was clearly the result of concessions by Mexico rather than business pressure in the United States.

This study confirms the findings of scholars such as Bernard C. Cohen, Raymond Bauer, and Lester Milbrath,[9] who have concluded that business-interest groups have little effective influence on foreign policy, and it also suggests that the collusion between businessmen and policy makers stressed by radical revisionists is more hypothetical than real.

THE BASIS FOR NONRECOGNITION

The status of United States relations with Mexico between 1920 and 1923 is generally well known and requires no extensive treatment here. Suffice it to say that one of the fundamental aims of United States policy was to preserve the economic position of American citizens in Mexico, which was threatened by Article 27 of the Constitution of 1917. That article contained provisions calling for the nationalization of the subsoil and outlining an ambitious program of agrarian redistribution. Although these provisions were not immediately implemented, they were clearly directed against the foreign investor. They not only endangered American control of the Mexican petroleum industry and the titles secured by American landowners under laws in force prior to the promulgation of the new constitution, but they also challenged prevailing conceptions of international law that were beneficial to capital-exporting nations.[10]

In responding to the surge of economic nationalism in Mexico, the United States relied upon two principal weapons—the withholding of

[9] Bernard C. Cohen, *The Influence of Non-Governmental Groups on Foreign Policy-Making* (Boston, 1959); Lester W. Milbrath, "Interest Groups and Foreign Policy," in James A. Rosenau (ed.), *Domestic Sources of Foreign Policy* (New York, 1967), pp. 231–251.

[10] The following works are instructive on the origin and impact of Article 27, as well as the broader implications of the controversy over property rights in Mexico: Pastor Rouáix, *Genesis de los artículos 27 y 123 de la Constitución Política de 1917* (México, 1959); Oscar Morineau, *Los derechos reales y el subsuelo en México* (México, 1948), pp. 197–245; Wendell C. Gordon, *The Expropriation of Foreign Owned Property in Mexico* (New York, 1941); John P. Bullington, "Problems of International Law in the Mexican Constitution of 1917," *American Journal of International Law,* XXI (October 1927), 685–705.

recognition from the Adolfo de la Huerta/Álvaro Obregón regime, which had come into power in the spring of 1920, and the application of financial pressure in the form of a loan ban. The Department of State refused to extend recognition until Mexican leaders signed a treaty containing stipulations designed to nullify the potentially confiscatory provisions of Article 27. Moreover, until recognition was granted, the capital markets of the United States were to remain closed to Mexico. Secretary of State Charles Evans Hughes defended this policy as necessary in order to safeguard legitimate American property rights against confiscation, and to eliminate conditions destructive to international trade. "A confiscatory policy strikes out not only at the interests of particular individuals," he stated in a press release of June 7, 1921, "but at the foundation of international intercourse, for it is only on the basis of the security of property validly possessed under laws existing at the time of its acquisition that commercial transaction between the peoples of two countries . . . is possible."[11]

In 1920, Mexico was not altogether unattractive as a trade area for the United States, despite the destructive and disorganizing impact of ten years of intermittent revolution. The Mexican economy had reached its nadir in 1915–1916, but the demands created by the European war had halted the downward trend. Between 1916 and 1920 the economy steadily recovered. Various statistical indicators confirm the upward swing: increases in the production of minerals, petroleum, hemp, and textiles, the sale of light and power, and railroad traffic; and a shift from a net-importing to a net-exporting basis for cattle and rice. After 1921, oil production declined, as American petroleum interests began to concentrate on developing new fields in other countries, but the general level of raw material and agricultural exports continued to rise.[12] Perceptive American businessmen interested in the Mexican market could thus discern a country undergoing a process of economic recovery, in which there was no shortage of foreign exchange—in short, a country offering prospects for profitable trade.

Economic recovery in Mexico coincided in part with the postwar economic depression in the United States. The collapse of wartime demand, the reentry of industrialized countries into the peacetime trade, rapid credit deflation in the United States, and the termination of public loans to European governments combined to produce a severe dislocation in the

[11] *New York Times,* June 8, 1921.
[12] Joseph E. Sterrett and Joseph S. Davis, *The Fiscal and Economic Condition of Mexico. A Report Submitted to the International Committee of Bankers on Mexico* (New York, 1928), pp. 213, 227–230; Clark W. Reynolds, *The Mexican Economy: Twentieth-Century Structure and Growth* (New Haven, Conn., 1970), pp. 26–31.

American economy. The volume of business declined steadily during the last quarter of 1920, and it hit bottom in 1921, when wholesale prices dropped as much as one-third. Although manufacturers curtailed production in order to meet the crisis, many of them had built up surplus stocks during the preceding years, and these could not be sold until viable markets were found. Under such conditions, Latin America in general, and Mexico in particular, assumed an increasing importance in the calculations of American businessmen.[13]

DIVISION WITHIN THE BUSINESS COMMUNITY

It is against this background that business opinion toward the Department of State's Mexican policy must be assessed. On the whole, those businessmen and business groups concerned about conditions in Mexico and the fate of the Obregón regime divided into prorecognition and anti-recognition camps on the basis of their individual or group self-interest.

Small and medium-sized firms with established business ties in Mexico were among the first to complain that the government's Mexican policy was injurious to American commercial interests. In most cases, they had been compelled to stop shipments below the border during the revolution, while maintaining agents on salary in the country and incurring other business-related expenses there.[14] Although these firms may not have felt the pinch during the war, by 1920 they were ready once again to begin exporting to Mexico. Lack of recognition, they believed, hampered the full restoration of commercial activity, and prevented them from recouping their losses. In letters to the State Department, Commerce Department, and their representatives in Washington, they claimed that conditions in Mexico were sufficiently stable to warrant recognition, and that the absence of normal relations was "strangling" opportunities for American businessmen in Mexico. A typical communication to

---

[13] The state of the economy in 1920–1921 is described in John D. Hicks, *Republican Ascendancy, 1921–1933* (New York, 1960), pp. 21–22, and George Soule, *Prosperity Decade, From War to Depression: 1917–1929* (New York, 1947), pp. 81–86. For an indication of business optimism concerning trade with Latin America, see the address entitled "South American Business," by F. De St. Phalle (Baldwin Locomotive Works) to the Foreign Trade Convention, 1922, printed in National Foreign Trade Council, *Official Report of the Ninth National Foreign Trade Convention, Held at Philadelphia, Pa., May 10, 11, 12, 1922* (New York, 1922), pp. 342–352.

[14] In a paper entitled "Trade Notes," prepared February 21, 1923, Consul Thomas D. Bowman at Mexico City, reported that 172 American firms were represented in Mexico City by local agents, while 21 branch firms of American enterprises were located there; a copy of the paper is in National Archives, Record Group 84, Records of the Foreign Service Posts of the United States: United States Embassy, Mexico City, 1923, File 610 (hereafter cited as Embassy, Mexico City, with file number).

Secretary Hughes came from Sheldon B. Cary, president of the Browning Company in Cleveland, which produced locomotive cranes:

Talking yesterday with our representative, who travels for us and several other concerns through Mexico, I was impressed with the fact that recognition of the present government of Mexico by our government would release about one hundred thousand dollars of business for our little concern and would be an item in getting our property on to a paying basis and increasing certainty of continued employment of our present force through the Fall and Winter.[15]

Those businessmen who visited Mexico during the early 1920s were enthusiastic about the direction of Mexico's economic future and trade opportunities for American products. Numerous delegations representing local chambers of commerce and merchants' organizations in the United States made excursions to Mexico in order to observe conditions there at first hand. When they returned, they consistently reported their belief that Obregón was a competent leader who understood the "practical" needs of business and who was doing his utmost to put Mexico on the road to full economic recovery. They usually noted that because of depleted warehouse stocks Mexican importers were prepared to purchase large amounts of consumer goods, and they expressed considerable concern that prospective purchasers might turn to the exports of those countries which had already extended recognition, particularly Japan and Germany.[16] They urged early recognition in part because they believed

[15] Sheldon B. Cary (president, The Browning Company, Cleveland) to Hughes, September 16, 1922, National Archives, Record Group 59, General Records of the Department of State, File number 612.1115/29 (hereafter cited as NA with file number). See also H. L. Stevenson (general manager, Motor Supply Company, Phoenix, Ariz.) to Carl Hayden (U.S. Congress, Arizona), November 18, 1921, enclosed in Hayden to Hughes, November 25, 1921, Howard Whittemore (vice-president, Parsons & Whittemore, Exporters and Importers, New York) to Senator William M. Calder, August 11, 1921, NA612.1115/11, 9; J. J. Charles (president, Hibbard, Spencer, Bartlett & Company, Chicago) to Hughes, April 26, 1922, W. M. Sinclair (manager, Export Department, The Rubberoid Company, New York) to Hughes, April 27, 1922, G. A. Ricker (treasurer, Walworth Manufacturing Company, Boston) to Hughes, May 11, 1922, NA711.12/430, 431, 435; Caleb R. Layton (U.S. Congress, Delaware) to Hughes, May 3, 1922, enclosing quotations from the president of Hilles & Jones Manufacturing Company (Delaware), F. B. Downs (Detroit) to Hughes, September 13, 1922, Austin S. Kibbee (Lewis S. Crossett Shoe Company, North Abington, Mass.) to Hughes, September 28, 1922, NA812.00/25558, 25908, 25947; C. H. Cochrane (president, Utility Heater Company, New York) to Hughes, July 16, 1921, T. F. Doyle (vice-president, Babbitt-Doyle Cattle Company, Litchton, Ariz.) to Hughes, July 21, 1921, Papers of Charles Evans Hughes, Manuscript Division, Library of Congress, Containers 15, 18 (hereafter cited as Hughes Papers).

[16] Increased commercial activity throughout Mexico of German firms, which were allegedly offering lower prices and more generous credit terms than their American

that it would put American manufacturers and exporters in a much stronger competitive position to capture Mexican trade.[17]

A number of industrialists representing large manufacturing firms, especially those producing capital equipment which a recovering economy would need, added their voices to the demand for recognition. Two of the most notable examples were Judge Elbert H. Gary of the United States Steel Corporation and Samuel M. Vauclain, president of Baldwin Locomotive Works, both of whom were no doubt aware that the revolution had virtually destroyed Mexico's internal railway system. After a two-week tour of Mexico in August 1921, Vauclain announced that business opportunities were plentiful there for "real Americans," but not "profiteers, speculators or confidence men . . . ," and that Obregón was sincere in his intention to protect legitimate foreign investments. As a result of his visit, he signed a contract with the Mexican government whereby his firm agreed to extend a $2,500,000 revolving credit to allow Mexico to purchase sixty-five locomotives. In this way, Vauclain not only confirmed his faith in Obregón, but he also circumvented the intended effect of the State Department's loan ban on Mexico by financing his own exports.[18]

While businessmen were most directly interested in the potential profits of the Mexican market, they were also aware of the tie between domestic politics in Mexico and commercial traffic. They believed that recognition would strengthen Obregón against his political enemies and promote the stability of his regime, and they regarded a stable government as a prerequisite to profitable trade. Many of them appreciated the

---

competitors, was frequently reported by American consuls. See, for example, the reports of Consul Francis J. Dyer, Nogales, Sonora, November 27, 1920; Consul Cornelius J. Ferris, February 13 and 23, 1921; Consul A. J. McConnico, Guadalajara, March 11, 1921; and Vice-Consul Jack D. Hickerson, Tampico, November 7, 1921; all in Embassy, Mexico City, File 610.

[17] C. B. Yandell, (general manager, Chamber of Commerce, San Antonio, Tex.) to Senator William E. Borah, May 28, 1921, Papers of William E. Borah, Manuscript Division, Library of Congress, Container 207; Robert J. O'Connor (manager, O'Connor Furniture Company, Santa Rosa, Calif.) to Congressman Clarence Lea (California), August 10, 1921, enclosed in Lea to Hughes, August 15, 1921, NA612.1115/8; James Z. George (vice-president, Chamber of Commerce, Dallas, Tex.) to Hughes, April 22, 1922, NA711.12/427; W. F. Carter (president, Chamber of Commerce, St. Louis, Mo.) to President Harding, April 30, 1921, NA812.00/24968; "Report on San Francisco Excursion of Businessmen, sponsored by the San Francisco Chamber of Commerce," New York Times, January 10, 1921; press release, Los Angeles Chamber of Commerce, Los Angeles Times, March 11, 1921.

[18] Commercial and Financial Chronicle, CXII (August 27, 1921), 899. Similar expressions of support can be found in Henry Woodhouse, "The New Understanding with Mexico," Current History, XVI (September 1922), 1012–1014.

dilemma Hughes's policy created for Obregón, and they feared that if he was not recognized his regime would eventually collapse and lead to another period of disruptive anarchy. John B. Glenn, Mexican representative for the Equitable Trust Company, expressed sentiments commonly held by many business leaders when he publicly declared that Obregón wanted to comply with the intent of the treaty proposed by Hughes, but that his signature on such a document prior to recognition would constitute a humiliating act, thereby destroying his stature as a patriot, and encouraging rebellions against his authority.[19]

On the other hand, prorecognition businessmen showed no ideological concern about the alleged "bolshevism," "communism," or "radicalism" of either the Constitution of 1917 or the members of Obregón's administration. In fact, they were impressed by the "rugged individualism" reflected in his rise to prominence and his middle-class appearance. They regarded him as politically and economically moderate, an image which Obregón cultivated, and they believed that recognition would obviate any necessity for him to introduce "Bolshevik schemes" in order to gain local support. Thomas W. Lamont, senior partner in J. P. Morgan Company, for example, told a group of businessmen early in 1922 that he had found Mexican leaders "not at all bolshevistic or anarchistic" and that the Constitution of 1917 was subject to criticism "not so much on the ground of its radicalism, as upon its unworkableness."[20]

Lamont's attitude was no doubt influenced by the fact that he was chairman of the International Committee of Bankers on Mexico, which had been organized in 1918 and currently was engaged in a series of negotiations with the Mexican government aimed at the resumption of payments on its defaulted external debt. American financiers who were members of the committee scrupulously avoided public statements about the issue of recognition both before and after the signature of the so-called Lamont-De la Huerta Agreement in June 1922, but almost as soon as the agreement was signed, Lamont began to apply subtle pressure upon Hughes to assume a less rigid position toward Mexico. Because of the

[19] Glenn's statement is in *New York Times*, August 7, 1921. See also George H. Eichelberger (Harvey Fisk and Sons) to President Harding, October 8, 1921, Papers of Warren G. Harding, Ohio Historical Society, Columbus, Ohio, Box 167; W. M. James to Albert B. Fall (secretary of the interior), May 27, 1921, Papers of Albert B. Fall (microcopy), "Mexican Affairs," Case 2, item 1726; J. J. Charles (Chicago) to Hughes, April 26, 1922, NA711.12/430; "Memorandum of a Conversation between Mr. George Young, of the Cananea Consolidated Copper Company, and the Under Secretary of State (Fletcher)," June 21, 1921, Hughes Papers, Container 176.

[20] Lamont, "Remarks Before the Dutch Treat Club Luncheon held at the Martinique Hotel (Lincoln)," March 14, 1922, Thomas W. Lamont Papers, Baker Library, Harvard University, Box 201.

financial agreement, Lamont wanted the Obregón government to survive, and he believed that recognition was essential to its survival.[21]

The opponents of recognition were less numerous but better organized than the prorecognitionists. Representing almost exclusively large firms or individuals with direct investments in Mexican petroleum and agrarian properties, the antirecognitionists depended upon formal pressure groups to spread their message to the American public and government officials. The most important of these groups was the National Association for the Protection of American Rights in Mexico (NAPARM). Organized in 1919 through the initiative of the powerful American oil companies in Mexico, NAPARM conducted an extensive propaganda campaign which stressed the themes of a rising tide of Bolshevism in Mexico, the incompetence of Mexican leaders, and the insecurity of American lives and properties. Although at its inception NAPARM had implicitly advocated intervention as the best solution to Mexico's problems, by 1921 the tone of its propaganda moderated, and it became a solid supporter of Hughes's policy of conditional recognition.[22] NAPARM's effectiveness was impaired, however, by several factors. After 1920 the association could not obscure the fact that general stability had returned to Mexico under Obregón, nor could it prove that any American-owned properties had actually been confiscated. Moreover, its image suffered a serious blow in 1922 because of revelations connecting the association's executive director, Thomas F. Lee, with an attempt to encourage Mexican émigrés in Texas to lead a revolt against Obregón's government.[23] Finally, NAPARM was rent by internal dissension which culminated in the resignation of a sizable group of independent investors led by William F. Buckley, who publicly charged that NAPARM was a tool of the oil companies, and who proceeded to organize the American Association of Mexico (AAM).[24]

The AAM was the most persistent and militant opponent of recogni-

[21] The relationship between the bankers and the State Department is analyzed in the author's "Bankers and Diplomats: The Diplomacy of the Dollar in Mexico, 1921–1924," Business History Review, XLVII (Autumn 1973), 335–352.

[22] The best source for background material on NAPARM is United States Senate, "Investigation of Mexican Affairs; Preliminary report and hearings of the Committee on Foreign Relations," Senate Document No. 285, 2 vols., Series 7665–7666, 66th Congress, 2nd Session, passim. See also Clifford W. Trow, "Woodrow Wilson and the Mexican Interventionist Movement of 1919," Journal of American History, LVIII (June 1971), 46–72.

[23] Chester T. Crowell (NAPARM) to Henry P. Fletcher, January 20, 1922, NA 812.6363/1070; New York Times, January 20, 1922; The Nation, CXIV (February 1 and March 1, 1922), 110, 236.

[24] William F. Buckley, Paul Hudson, and Sidney A. Smith (Provisional Executive Committee, AAM) to Fall, January 31, Ira Jewell Williams (NAPARM) to Buckley,

tion. In public addresses, a series of bulletins, and private letters to government officials, Buckley and his colleagues charged that the Constitution of 1917 had been inspired by Bolshevik ideas and was designed purposely to drive American property owners out of Mexico. They described Obregón's regime as illegal and usurpative, and they claimed that the revolution did not represent the will of the Mexican people. They insisted that conditional recognition was completely in order, since it was much wiser to extract promises before rather than to try to do so after recognition had been extended.[25] In line with their position, the leaders of the AAM made an effort to dissuade other businessmen from visiting Mexico, and to prevent direct negotiations between American investors, particularly the oil interests, and the Mexican government.[26]

The division of the business community over the question of recognition was most clearly evident among the oil interests. The larger American petroleum companies with vested interests in Mexico naturally supported the State Department's policy, but more significantly, they tried to wage a widespread publicity campaign, which they aimed at other businessmen, as well as the general public. Companies such as Standard Oil of New Jersey and Edward L. Doheny's Mexican Petroleum Company distributed their "educational" material through the Association of Petroleum Producers in Mexico (APPM),[27] an affiliate of NAPARM. They were largely responsible for financing the activities of NAPARM, and they exerted considerable influence in certain trade associations, such as the American Petroleum Institute.

The director of the institute, Van H. Manning, a former government employee, never tired of pointing out that the consumption of petroleum

---

February 14, and Buckley to Williams, February 17, 1921, Fall Papers, Case 1, items 540, 1896, 1897; AAM press release, *New York Times*, February 14, 1921.

[26] Buckley, "Some Aspects of the Problem of Recognizing the Present Government of Mexico," a paper read at the Mississippi Valley Historical Association, May 12, 1922, AAM, "Protection for American Citizens Abroad," *Bulletin 2*, May 15, 1921, and "Essentials of a Just Policy Toward Mexico," *Bulletin 3*, June 20, 1921, Fall Papers, Case 1, items 2010, 563, 566; Sidney A. Smith to Hughes, June 14, 1921, NA 711.12/338; Buckley to Representative Tom Connally (Texas), April 15, 1922, enclosed in Buckley to Hanna, April 17, 1922, NA 812.00/25535.

[26] See, for example, Buckley to Seattle Chamber of Commerce, March 16, 1921, enclosed in Milton E. McIntosh (director, Foreign Trade Bureau, Seattle Chamber of Commerce) to Ben G. Davis (chief clerk, State Department), March 26, 1921, NA 711.12/322; AAM press release, *New York Times*, August 24, 1921; AAM, "Result of the Oil Committee's Visit to Mexico City," *Bulletin 7*, September 26, 1921, NA 812.6363/1270.

[27] Numerous samples of NAPARM's publicity campaign—pamphlets, special bulletins, flyers, and newsletters—may be found in the Fall Papers, Cases 1 and 2.

in the United States outran production, and that consequently the United States had to depend on foreign sources of supply. It was vitally necessary, he insisted, because of the needs of American industry and defense to maintain an uninterrupted supply of oil. Therefore, he urged the government to protect the petroleum rights acquired by American citizens in Mexico and elsewhere against retroactive legislation, "empirical regulation," and confiscatory taxation.[28]

Small, independent companies drilling in Mexico saw matters in a different light. They believed that they were more threatened by their larger competitors, who controlled the pipelines in Mexico and the marketing facilities outside of Mexico, than by the Mexican government. They cooperated with the government as a means of improving their competitive position. Companies such as Mid-Continental, AGWI, Pierce Oil, and the Norman Oil Corporation accepted the government's claim to ownership of the subsoil, complied with existing laws, and paid their taxes without complaint. On the other hand, they frequently raised questions about the legality of titles held by the larger companies, and they openly supported recognition. For instance, M. N. Bensabat, vice-president of the Norman Oil Corporation and one of Obregón's staunchest defenders, declared that the Mexican president had no intention of depriving American investors of their legitimate rights, and that recognition should be extended to him quickly and unconditionally.[29]

Independent continental producers also favored recognition, but their motives were slightly different and their approach was less direct. They were motivated almost exclusively by a desire to reduce the privileged status of Mexican crude oil imported into the United States by their primary competitors, the large petroleum companies. Among other things, they demanded a tariff on Mexican crude oil, and they vigorously opposed any form of "aid" given to members of the APPM by the State Department. From their perspective, any policy which benefited their rivals constituted such aid, and this included the withholding of recognition from Obregón. The most vociferous complaints along this line came from the Independent American Oil Producers Association, which report-

[28] Van H. Manning, "An Oil Entente," *Bulletin of the Pan American Union*, LII (June 1921), 560–566.

[29] Bensabat, "Taking Obregón's Side," in *New York Times*, July 10, 1921. See also Eben Richards (vice-president, Pierce Oil Company) to Joseph W. Folk, September 28, 1920, enclosed in Folk to Secretary of State Bainbridge Colby, September 30, 1920, NA711.12/324; statements of E. W. Marland (Marland Oil Company), enclosed in George T. Summerlin (Chargé, Mexico City) to Hughes, August 18, 1920, Arthur Williams (Atlantic Lobos Oil Company) to Hanna, December 9, 1922, NA812.6363/717, 1307 1/2; interview with Joseph Guffey (AGWI), published in *El Excelsior*, February 5, 1920, and statements of Guffey, in *New York Times*, December 27, 1920.

edly represented about 60 percent of petroleum production in the United States.[30]

Although the prorecognitionists were less organized than their opponents, their ranks continued to swell during 1922, and by early 1923 they began to unite behind a demand for the appointment of a joint commission to discuss United States-Mexican problems as the most preferable means of reaching an early agreement and renewal of relations. The idea was promoted most actively by the Tri-State Association of Credit Men, representing local credit unions in Texas, New Mexico, and Arizona,[31] and its appeal found a receptive audience among businessmen not only in the Southwest, but elsewhere in the nation as well.[32]

DEPARTMENT OF STATE RESPONSE TO ADVOCATES OF RECOGNITION

There is little doubt that prorecognition sentiment in the business community increased during the period from 1920 to 1923, and that the State Department was aware of the trend. In November 1921 President Harding wrote to Undersecretary Henry P. Fletcher that he had noticed "a change of front on the part of many interests which heretofore strongly opposed recognizing Mexico. . . . "[33] Early in April 1922 Matthew E. Hanna, chief of the Division of Mexican Affairs, carefully described the extent of pro-Mexican feeling in the United States in a memorandum for

[30] C. J. Wrightsman (Independent American Oil Producers Association) to Hughes, June 19, 1921, NA 600.127/185. For similar sentiments expressed by other independent producers, see A. B. Butler (vice-president, National Oil and Development Company, Oklahoma City) to Hughes, August 26, 1921, Gulf Coast Oil Producers Association of Louisiana and Texas, North Texas Oil and Gas Producers Associaton, Oil Men's Protective Association of Oklahoma and Kansas, Kansas Oil and Gas Association to Hughes, June 10, 1921, NA600.127/241, 177.

[31] The association distributed pamphlets soliciting support from local affiliates of the National Association of Credit Men, other business organizations, and prominent political figures in the Southwest. For an idea of its activities, see T. E. Blanchard (secretary, Tri-State Association of Credit Men, El Paso, Texas) to Hughes, February 24, March 10, 1922, both with enclosures, NA711.12/393, 401.

[32] The impact of the Tri-State Association's campaign can be gleaned from Governor Thomas E. Campbell (Arizona) to President Harding, February 28, 1922, Arthur W. Parry (secretary, Association of Credit Men, Fort Wayne, Ind.) to Harding, March 22, 1922, E. R. Leonard (secretary, Northern Montana Association of Credit Men) to Hughes, March 25, 1922, James Z. George (vice-president, Chamber of Commerce, Dallas, Tex.) to Hughes, April 21, 1922, C. A. Daniels (president, Quaker City Rubber Company, Philadelphia) to Harding, April 25, 1922, George P. Miller (secretary, American Vulcanized Fibre Company, Wilmington) to Hughes, May 3, 1922, and G. A. Ricker (treasurer, Walworth Manufacturing Company, Boston) to Hughes, May 11, 1922, NA711.12/401, 414, 416, 427, 428, 433, 435.

[33] Harding to Fletcher, November 19, 1921, Harding Papers, Box 167.

the secretary.[34] Two months later in a letter to Fletcher, who had been appointed ambassador to Belgium on March 6, 1922, Hanna prophesied that efforts to induce the administration to change its Mexican policy would continue with "increasing force."[35] From his listening post at Tampico, Consul Claude I. Dawson, early in January 1923 reported an unusually high degree of sympathy for recognition among American businessmen who visited Mexico as well as those with firms established there.[36] Dawson's reports were corroborated by similar information filtering into the State Department from private individuals such as John Barrett, former director of the Pan American Union.[37]

The State Department responded to business demands for recognition in several ways. First, department officials attempted to persuade individual businessmen that recognition without adequate safeguards for American property rights would be distinctly detrimental to the national interests. When an executive from the Underwood Typewriter Company called at the department in July 1921, for example, to inquire about the delay in recognition, Undersecretary Fletcher "definitely and emphatically" explained the department's position.[38] And Secretary Hughes told Thomas W. Lamont that the immediate advantages to investors of recognition would "hardly outweigh long run policy," a message Hughes evidently hoped that Lamont would convey to other businessmen.[39] Second, the department took steps to counter the "optimistic" propaganda emanating from Mexico and prorecognition business groups in the United States by encouraging the Department of Commerce to publish a "true statement" of the business situation in Mexico.[40]

Finally, Hughes tried to neutralize criticism of his policy directly. On May 10, 1922, he addressed the national convention of the United States Chamber of Commerce in Washington, D. C. He insisted that if countries refused to recognize valid titles acquired in accordance with existing laws, international intercourse would collapse because the rules under which commercial exchange proceeded would become meaningless. Firm-

---

[34] "Memorandum for Secretary Hughes," April 6–7, 1922, by Hanna, NA812.00/26097.

[35] Hanna to Fletcher (in Brussels), June 21, 1922, Papers of Henry P. Fletcher, Manuscript Division, Library of Congress, Container 9.

[36] Dawson to Hughes, January 29, 1923, NA812.202/1/2.

[37] Barrett to President Harding, March 20, 1922, enclosed in Harding to Hughes, March 21, 1922, NA812.00/25494.

[38] Fletcher to Summerlin, July 19, 1921, NA812.00/25084 1/2.

[39] Hughes to Lamont, June 17, 1921, NA812.51/725.

[40] Ralph H. Ackerman (chief, Latin American Division, Bureau of Foreign and Domestic Commerce) to M. R. Emmett (BFDC), with enclosures, February 16, 1922, Herbert Hoover Papers (Commerce, Official), Herbert Hoover Library, West Branch, Iowa.

ly denying that the administration favored one set of businessmen over another, he stated that the primary object of the administration toward business was "to keep open the course of fair and equal opportunity."[41]

While these efforts by State Department officials to "educate" businessmen toward a proper understanding and appreciation of the department's Mexican policy may indicate a concern about the status of business opinion, they certainly did not reflect any change of attitude within the department. Hughes's principal advisers on Mexican affairs—Undersecretary Fletcher (until his appointment as ambassador to Belgium), Hanna, and Summerlin—all of whom had served in Mexico under President Wilson and had come to oppose what they regarded as Wilson's "soft" policy by 1919–1920,[42] continued to view the Constitution of 1917 as representing a distinct threat to American investments in Mexico, and to characterize the Obregón administration as one that was contaminated with bolshevism. All three shared a conviction that the best means of obtaining protection for American rights in Mexico, given the fact that armed intervention had for all practical purposes been rejected as a policy alternative, was through the signature of a formal treaty containing clear and explicit guarantees. They did not believe that an internal Mexican program consisting of legislative enactments, executive decrees, and Supreme Court decisions could provide a satisfactory substitute for a treaty, and they counseled Secretary Hughes accordingly.[43] Hughes, who had entrusted the day-to-day implementation of Mexican policy to them, readily accepted their advice.

By the fall of 1922, however, it was becoming increasingly difficult for Hanna and Summerlin to justify an inflexible stance toward Mexico, particularly after Hughes stated in a speech in Boston on October 30 that the United States was "not insistent on the form of any particular assurance to American citizens against confiscation."[44] By the time

[41] "Some Aspects of the Work of the Department of State," address reprinted in *American Journal of International Law*, XVI (July 1922), 355–364.

[42] Fletcher had been appointed ambassador to Mexico in February 1916; he resigned his post in early 1920. Both Hanna and Summerlin served at the Embassy during Fletcher's tenure as ambassador. For an indication of Fletcher's attitude, see, for example, "Memorandum for President Wilson," August 18, 1919, NA711.1211/187; Fletcher to Secretary of State Robert Lansing, December 11, 1919, and Fletcher to Wilson, January 3, 1920, Fletcher Papers, Containers 7, 8.

[43] Fletcher to Summerlin, September 9, 1921, memoranda for Secretary Hughes, by Hanna, April 11, 24, May 10, 1922, NA812.00/25169A, 26097; Summerlin to Hanna, October 6, 1922, NA812.6363/1219; Hanna to Hughes, May 12, June 19, 1922, NA 711.1211/52, 36; Summerlin to Hanna, April 8, May 5, June 8, 1922, Embassy, Mexico City, File 710; Hanna to Fletcher, June 21, 1922, and Summerlin to Fletcher, July 10, 1922, Fletcher Papers, Container 9; Fletcher to Harding, November 14, 1921, Harding Papers, Box 167.

[44] Hughes's speech was printed in the *New York Times*, October 31, 1922.

the secretary delivered his speech, it had become clear to many observers that conditions within Mexico had definitely improved, and that the Mexican government had taken a series of steps in the interests of American investors. These included the signing of the Lamont-De la Huerta Financial Agreement on June 16, 1922 (ratified in September 1922), which provided for the resumption of payments on the defaulted Mexican external debt;[45] the adjustment of a bitter tax controversy between the government and American petroleum firms in the fall of that year;[46] and, also in the fall, the establishment of a legal precedent by the Mexican Supreme Court protecting petroleum properties on which some development had occurred prior to the promulgation of the Constitution of 1917 from the application of Article 27.[47]

As a result of these developments officials in the State Department revised their original estimates of Obregón and his administration. They now began to view the Mexican leader as the strongest available bulwark against radicalism in Mexico, and to believe that an accord with him was the best means of encouraging stability in that country. In late January 1923 Hanna reevaluated United States relations with Mexico in a lengthy memorandum for the secretary which stressed the Obregón regime's domestic accomplishments, and its efforts to meet its international obligations.[48] The following March, when Hughes was already weighing the possibility of a joint commission to discuss the outstanding problems between the two countries, Hanna urged him to abandon the treaty demand altogether and to accept a written statement from Obregón assuring that American property rights would be fully respected.[49] "The great advance which Mexico has made under General Obregón," Hanna wrote, "towards stable and efficient self-government (employing the adjectives in a comparative sense and with a sympathetic understanding of the difficult conditions surrounding him) would appear not only to jus-

[45] For information on the financial agreement, see Jan Bazant, *Historia de la dueda exterior de México (1923–1946)* (México, 1968), pp. 186–193.

[46] On the negotiations concerning oil taxes, consult Lorenzo Meyer, *México y el Estados Unidos en el conflicto petrolero, 1917–1942* (México, 1968), chaps. 4–5.

[47] Translations of the Supreme Court decisions are enclosed in Summerlin to Hughes, July 17, 1922, NA812.6363/1160.

[48] "Memorandum for Secretary Hughes," by Hanna, January 26, 1923, enclosed in Hanna to Summerlin, January 27, 1923, Embassy, Mexico City, File 710.

[49] It is interesting to note that early in the Harding administration Secretary of Commerce Hoover had advocated precisely this method of dealing with Mexico. Motivated by a desire to remove all unnecessary obstacles from the export markets of the United States, he was the only important figure in the administration to question the wisdom of withholding recognition from Obregón. His efforts to press his view were rebuffed by Hughes. See Hoover to Hughes, April 15, May 27, and Hughes to Hoover, May 28, 1921, NA812.00/24978, 25010 1/2.

tify this Government in accepting much that it could not accept two years ago but compel it in justice to do so."[50]

In presenting his case for a change in policy, Hanna cited as an incidental benefit the generally positive effect a settlement would have on public opinion in the United States. All those miscellaneous American interests whose prosperity were tied to conditions in Mexico, he asserted, would welcome the resumption of relations. At the same time, Hanna professed that he could see "no good reason why the American owners of petroleum interests and large landed estates should complain when they understand that the Department is improving its position for their protection."[51]

The petroleum interests, however, found it difficult to understand precisely how the department was "improving its position for their protection," especially after they learned about the terms of the so-called Bucareli Agreements, which became the basis for recognition.[52] At first, they tried to persuade Hughes to hold out for a treaty as the only means of adequately protecting their interests. When Hughes proved unresponsive, they tried to exert pressure on him indirectly through Secretary of the Treasury Andrew W. Mellon, who agreed to intercede in their behalf. But Hughes wanted a settlement with Mexico, and he was no more inclined to heed an appeal from Mellon than he was from the oil men directly. Thereafter the oil men, unhappily to be sure, resigned themselves to accepting the secretary's position.[53] Recognition was extended to Obregón on August 31, 1923, and the public announcement was fol-

[50] Hanna to Hughes, March 23, 1923, NA711.12/541.

[51] Ibid.

[52] The Bucareli Agreements contained three instruments: (1) a general claims convention covering mutual claims originating since July 4, 1868; (2) a special claims convention covering claims of United States citizens against Mexico for revolutionary damages suffered between November 1910 to May 1920; and (3) a set of official minutes embodying certain "understandings" reached on the controversial agrarian and petroleum issues. Briefly stated, on the agrarian question, the United States surrendered its insistence on immediate cash payment to its nationals in Mexico for lands expropriated for *ejidos* (communal lands) and agreed to accept instead federal bonds as adequate compensation, while the Mexican government agreed that such payment would not constitute a precedent for future expropriations of any kind of property and also agreed to limit the size of *ejidos*. On the subsoil issue, the Mexican commissioners pledged that the Mexican government would respect the Supreme Court decisions declaring that Article 27 of the Mexican Constitution of 1917 was inapplicable to American-owned oil properties acquired prior to May 1, 1917, on which some "positive act" of exploitation had been performed, and they broadly defined such acts.

[53] See Guy Stevens (APPM) to Hughes, August 13, 24, 1923, NA812.6363/1438; Hanna to William Phillips (undersecretary of state), August 27, 1923, NA812.6363/1440.

lowed by many statements in the press heralding a new dawn of commercial prosperity for Mexico and the United States.[54]

CONCLUSION

It is difficult to measure precisely the impact of prorecognition pressure on the State Department. Public-opinion studies indicate that organized business groups have a better chance than any other interest groups of influencing foreign policy, especially when they can show that a particular policy decision has caused or will potentially cause a clear economic injury, and the issue involved has a low crisis level.[55] The recognition question certainly was not a crisis issue, but prorecognition businessmen were generally unorganized, and consequently their pressure was diffuse. Moreover, their requests were screened by officials who were distinctly indisposed to listen, and who tended in any case to interpret selectively incoming expressions of opinion.

The State Department's decision to extend recognition to Obregón in August 1923 clearly resulted more from concessions made by Mexico than from business pressure in the United States. In a sense the policy was changed because it had achieved a measure of success, and because officials in the State Department perceived in this case the limitations of nonrecognition and financial pressure as diplomatic weapons. It would have been fruitless for Hughes to continue to insist upon the signing of a treaty, and probably counterproductive as well, given the fact that Obregón had proved his ability to survive without recognition, and that he had demonstrated his willingness to reach reasonable compromises with the United States.

In a more general sense, the controversy among businessmen over the recognition of Obregón vividly demonstrates one of the major problems encountered by policy makers when they attempt to justify a particular policy in terms of the "national interest." No matter how the national interest is conceived, policies designed to serve it will benefit some economic interest groups and harm others. In the Mexican case, the long-

---

[54] "Mexican Recognition as a Spur to Business," *Literary Digest*, LXXVIII (September 15, 1923), 13.

[55] For an instructive specific example, see the discussion of the impact of the West Coast tuna fishing interests on the negotiations during 1951 leading to the North Pacific Fisheries Convention in Cohen, *The Political Process and Foreign Policy*, pp. 253–277. Consult also Lester W. Milbrath, *The Washington Lobbyists* (Chicago, 1963), Part IV, and Theodore J. Lowi, "Making Democracy Safe for the World: National Politics and Foreign Policy," in Rosenau (ed.), *Domestic Sources of Foreign Policy*, pp. 295–331.

range goals pursued by Secretary Hughes coincided with the self-interest of the oil men and the landowners and conflicted with those of the manufacturers and exporters. Consequently, after Hughes formulated the nonrecognition policy, he found himself in the rather awkward position of apparently denying support to some sectors of the business community when he seemed to be providing it for others. When the policy was altered in the spring of 1923, policy makers within the department rationalized the change in part on the basis that it would satisfy all those interests desiring a change and not injure those which had been opposed to a change.

This study also underscores the fact that the business community is not internally cohesive. Functional, organizational, dimensional, geographical, and other differences between firms create competing sets of interests, and these in turn often stimulate still other interests outside of the business community. Within a framework of conflicting demands, the policy maker is virtually free from all demands. This is particularly true in cases such as those involving the recognition of new governments, where the individuals responsible for the policy decisions normally do not have to share the selection of alternatives with the legislative branch or other officials in the executive branch. As Lester Milbrath has pointed out, the narrower the decisional system, the less susceptible it is to external pressure.[56]

Another important implication arises here. While many historians and political scientists equate access with influence, it is apparent that the two are not equivalent. Simply because businessmen maintain friendly relations with certain policy makers and are received cordially at the State Department does not in itself constitute proof that business opinions influence policy decisions. Although it is quite true that influence cannot be exerted without access of some kind, scholars frequently overlook the fact that open doors at the Department of State also give policy makers opportunities to present their side of any particular issue directly to representatives of the business community.

In the final analysis, it would appear that some of the assumptions commonly made by historians and political scientists about business influence on foreign policy do not survive empirical tests. Perhaps Bernard C. Cohen was correct when he wrote a decade and a half ago that "while business groups seem to be the most effective of the various types of interest groups, they are nevertheless only mildly influential and then only with respect to a rather narrow range of economic issues which comprise only a small proportion of the fundamental issues of American

[56] Milbrath, "Interest Groups and Foreign Policy," pp. 235–237.

foreign policy."[57] But we will not be able to prove this with any degree of certainty until we have many more case studies of business efforts to influence specific policy decisions, particularly with respect to the executive branch.*

[57] Cohen, The Influence of Non-Governmental Groups on Foreign Policy-Making, p. 20.

* This is a revised version of a paper delivered at the Missouri Valley History Conference in Omaha, Nebraska, March 8, 1973.

Jeı *JOURNAL OF ECONOMIC ISSUES*
Vol. XVI   No. 3   September 1982

Supply-Side Economic Policies during the Coolidge-Mellon Era

Robert R. Keller

President Ronald Reagan's Program for Economic Recovery includes policies such as government spending cuts, tax rate reduction, and deregulation of government controls over business.[1] These policies are viewed by proponents as the embodiment of "supply-side" solutions to the problems of sluggish economic growth, inflation, and budget deficits. Reagan's program has, in part, been justified by connecting it with the economic policies and prosperity of the twenties.[2] Jude Wanniski, an ardent popularizer of supply-side economics, maintains that the twenties contain a relevant lesson for today: "Because Mellon was successful in persuading Republican Presidents—first Warren G. Harding and then Calvin Coolidge—of the truth of his ideas the high wartime tax rates were steadily cut back .... As a result, the period 1919–29 was one of phenomenal economic expansion."[3]

The parallels between Reagan's program and the supply-side economic policies of the twenties go beyond tax rate reductions. Economic policies in the twenties were founded on a conservative Republican ideology of business-government relations. These views and the implementation of supply-side economic policies reached their zenith during the administration of Calvin Coolidge and his Secretary of the Treasury, Andrew Mellon.

The author is Professor of Economics, Colorado State University, Ft. Collins. He wishes to acknowledge the constructive comments of Marc R. Tool and anonymous referees on an earlier draft.

The Coolidge-Mellon policies not only included deregulation of government controls over business, they also incorporated an integrated fiscal program of government spending cuts, debt reduction, and tax cuts.

It is instructive to interpret Reagan's economic proposals as resurrecting the ideology of 1920s conservative Republicanism, which in turn explains the strong parallels in the economic policies of the two periods. At the same time, we must be cautious and recognize the fact that the Coolidge-Mellon supply-side economic policies differ in three substantive ways from Reagan's program. First, the Coolidge-Mellon policies corresponded very closely to the policy recommendations expressed by leaders of business organizations such as the National Association of Manufacturers and the Chamber of Commerce; part of Reagan's program, although generally supported, has been attacked by influential business leaders. Second, Coolidge and Mellon's supply-side policies made government spending cuts and public debt reduction (budget surpluses) a prerequisite for a reduction in tax rates; Reagan's administration did not. Third, the national economy of the 1920s was better able than that of the 1980s to accommodate government spending cuts and tax rate reduction.

A closer examination of supply-side economic policies in the Coolidge-Mellon era provides us with a powerful framework for understanding the pro-business ideological underpinnings of Reagan's economic program. At the same time, comparing Coolidge and Mellon's supply-side economic policies with Reagan's uncovers significant differences that invalidate the simplistic lessons of history intimated by some of the proponents of supply-side economics.

Business Ideology and the Supply-Side Economic Policies of Coolidge and Mellon

Frederick Lewis Allen describes the 1920s as an era when "the great god business was supreme in the land, and Calvin Coolidge was fortunate enough to become almost a demi-god by doing discreet obeisance at the altar."[4] Business ideas in the realm of government spending, taxation, and regulation were articulated by leaders of such organizations as the National Association of Manufacturers and the Chamber of Commerce. The supply-side views of these business leaders show a virtual one-to-one correspondence to the ideas of Coolidge and Mellon. As we shall see, Coolidge and Mellon and other conservative Republicans were effective spokesmen and policy makers for the business view of supply-side economics.

Business Ideology

The business ideology of the twenties in the areas of spending, taxation, and regulation was well expressed by spokesmen for the two dominant business organizations of the day, the National Association of Manufacturers (NAM) and the Chamber of Commerce (CC).[5] At minimum, these leaders reflected the views of an important element of the business community. However, Coolidge believed the views of one of the organizations reflected a broader constituency. "I have been greatly pleased," he said, "to observe the many evidences which come here, indicating that the attitude of the Chamber of Commerce very accurately reflects that of public opinion generally."[6]

Charles N. Fay, Vice President of the NAM, defined the appropriate role of government as the principle of "Least Government, with its companion principle of Least Taxation."[7] The minimum and primary role for government was defined to include only national defense, a judicial system, police protection, and tax gathering. Fay reluctantly admitted that the government had a role to play in secondary activities: "Such are for state and local government, in the order of their importance, water-supply, good-roads, sanitation, education, care of the sick and defective, and the poor; and for national government good money, weights and measures, and the fostering of agriculture, trade, science, and art."[8] When in doubt, government functions were to be reduced. "The simple and logical way to minimize American discontent with the shortcomings of American government most obviously is to minimize government itself."[9]

A minimal role for government was thought to promote maximum individual freedom, which in turn would unleash productive entrepreneurial and innovational activities, to the advantage of all. John E. Edgerton, president of the NAM, believed that opportunities for unfettered individualism in the twenties were unprecedented. "There is not now nor has there ever been a country in which it was so easy as in this one for a little business to grow into a big one or for a little person to become as great as his mental and spiritual boundaries permit."[10]

When government programs and costs are pared to a minimum, the principle of Least Taxation can be implemented. The tax burden is distributed according to the view that taxpayers should feel that they have a stake in society and that the imposition of taxes should not dampen incentives to produce. James A. Emery, general counsel of the NAM, believed that "as you remove man from the necessity of paying taxes, you remove any interest in the character of the tax policy adopted."[11] During the twenties, the NAM and the CC endorsed the imposition of some form of a gross sales tax because it was felt that existing taxes on property, income, and imports were hidden. A sales tax would make the tax burden more visible to the bulk of the population (including the poor).[12] In addition, it was felt that the sales tax would discourage consumption and encourage saving, and by substituting for an income or profits tax it would not dampen the incentive to produce. If incentives to produce were preserved by the tax structure, the benefits would trickle down to all people.

> As for what each saves, and puts to work, . . .—though he is purely selfish, and saves for himself, not for the community—nevertheless, *the more there is of such working-capital*, rolled up but not enjoyed by him and thousands of his kind, to grow larger and larger in active production, *the better for us all! Let its ownership remain with those who saved it— for they will use it wisely.* But the real blessing of it, the support of great masses of men and women in honest and well paid toil; and the abundant output of the necessaries and luxuries of life—*that blessing goes to the people.* (Emphasis added.)[13]

To summarize, taxes should be visible and reflect the cost of government programs, and the tax structure should encourage saving and productivity, which in turn benefits all of society. However, as James Warren Prothro concludes, the ideological view of business toward taxation "calls with equal clarity for an increase of taxes on the masses and a decrease of taxes on the elite."[14]

There are three dimensions of the business view toward the regulatory role of government. First, natural economic laws make government regulation of business unnecessary. Fay believed that "if business grows so big that it challenges the jealousy of the collectivist, its very size proves *that it has already voluntarily done for the public*, especially the working-folk, *precisely what collectivist government would force it to do!* 'Regulation' could not possibly do more; but would be pretty sure to do less." (Emphasis added.)[15]

Second, government must understand that business knows best. Julius H. Barnes, President of the CC, said that "government must learn that business conviction, matured after careful study, observation and experience, must be respected in policies of government."[16]

Third, government has a responsibility to regulate labor organizations because they constitute a threat to society. George E. Roberts, vice-president of National City Bank, claimed that " *'labor' is organized to hold up the public*—not merely an employer here or there—and is as pitiless of public suffering as it is defiant of private right."[17] Fay went so far as to say that the time had come to *"suppress by law all wholesale organization of labor."* (Emphasis added.)[18]

Finally, the ideology of business in the twenties stated that business success demonstrated worth and competence in all areas. Business success was specifically equated with expertise in the field of public affairs. Thus, insofar as possible, public servants should be selected from the business community.

Coolidge's Supply-Side Economic Policies

In discussing supply-side economic views of conservative Republicanism, the names of Calvin Coolidge and Andrew Mellon are inseparable. Mellon was Secretary of the Treasury under Harding, Coolidge, and Hoover. It was during Coolidge's presidency, however, that William Allen White claims that Mellon's power and policies reached their apogee: "Indeed, so completely did Andrew Mellon dominate the White House in the days when the Coolidge administration was at its zenith that it would be fair to call the administration the reign of Coolidge and Mellon."[19]

Coolidge believed that the voters gave him a clear mandate in the election of 1924. "This administration has come into power with a very clear and definite mandate from the people .... When we turn from what was rejected to inquire what was accepted, the policy that stands out with the greatest clearness is that of economy in public expenditure with reduction and reform of taxation."[20]

Coolidge's views on spending, taxation, and regulation closely corresponded to the ideas expressed by business leaders. Business was of paramount importance and had a revered position in society: "The man who builds a factory builds a temple, the man who works there worships there, and to each is due not scorn and blame, but reverence and praise."[21] The ideology of government-business relations was clearly stated by Coolidge in his inaugural address: "It is the important and righteous position that business holds in relation to life which gives warrant to the great interest which the National Government constantly exercises for the promotion of its success."[22] Coolidge's infatuation with the hallowed position of business led him to believe that business was an exemplary model for government. "This is a business country ... and it wants a business government."[23]

Coolidge's pro-business ideology was the foundation for his supply-side economic policies. Coolidge used the phrase "constructive economy" to explain government's role in supply-side policies; it refers to establishing a more efficient government while at the same time reducing the amount of government spending. Coolidge was so enamored with the idea of constructive economy that he called it "idealism in its most practical form."[24]

Reducing government spending permitted a reduction in the national debt and its associated fixed interest obligations. Thus the idea of constructive economy applies not only to short-run spending but also to reducing long-run contractual government financing commitments. The pre-eminence of debt reduction and fixed interest payments provided a rationale for constraining government spending on national defense. Coolidge said that "while I am in favor of very generous provisions for national defense, the weakest place in the line of national defense is at present the large debt of the country. So that I am trying to indicate that in my view the necessity of retiring that debt is the predominant necessity of the country, in an orderly way of course, and with a reasonable rate of taxation."[25]

To limit defense spending, Coolidge recognized the importance of arms control "to eliminate competition in armaments," which would "afford great financial relief."[26]

> I think the practical policy to pursue at this time is not to enter into a competitive method of arming ourselves. As I have already indicated, they have staggering expenses abroad. I don't like to refer to it too often— they owe us money over there. I should very much prefer that they should take their money and pay us, than on account of any action we took over here feel that they should take their money and build battleships. I think it would be very much better for all concerned to adopt a policy of that kind.[27]

The reduction in government spending, the national debt, and fixed interest payments also provided an opportunity to cut taxes: "The immediate fruit of economy and the retirement of the public debt is tax reduction. The annual saving in interest between 1925 and 1929 is $212,000,000. Without this no bill to relieve taxpayers would be worth proposing."[28] In fact, Coolidge emphatically stated that tax reduction should only be implemented in the presence of spending cuts, "but this always has to be borne in mind—that tax reduction is to be secured only as the result of economy."[29]

Coolidge identified the advantages of tax rate reduction as added production incentives, more tax revenues, and expansion of economic activity for the benefit of all. "I am opposed to extremely high rates, because they produce little or no revenue, because they are bad for the country, and, finally, because they are wrong. We can not finance the country, we can not improve social conditions, through any system of injustice, even if we attempt to inflict it upon the rich. Those who suffer the most harm will be the poor."[30]

In his 1928 message to Congress, Coolidge noted that a tax rate cut would stimulate business production to the extent that total tax revenues would increase: "Four times we have made a drastic revision of our internal revenue system, abolishing many taxes and substantially reducing almost all others. Each time the resulting stimulation to business has so increased taxable incomes and profits that a surplus has been produced."[31]

In his address to the Chamber of Commerce in New York in 1925, Coolidge stated his views on the regulation of business by government. "Regulation has often become restriction, and inspection has too frequently been little less than obstruction."[32] As a response, pro-business personnel were appointed to regulatory commissions. The commissions moved away from progressive regulation and moved toward promoting and cooperating with business.

G. Cullom Davis's history of the Federal Trade Commission (FTC) provides an instructive, and perhaps the most dramatic, case study of the transformation of regulatory commissions. "It would probably be accurate to say that before 1925 a majority of the commissioners desired to execute a strict regulatory policy in accordance with the progressive ideals of economic reform . . . . It was not until 1925 that the remaining Wilson appointees faced a majority selected by Warren G. Harding and Calvin Coolidge."[33]

In 1925, William E. Humphrey was appointed to the FTC. Humphrey was an active Republican party regular, one of Coolidge's campaign managers, and had close connections with northwestern lumber interests, which had been investigated by the FTC. Prior to his appointment, he had been a bitter foe of the FTC. Humphrey viewed the agency as "an instrument of oppression and disturbance and injury instead of a help to business."[34] He also accused the FTC of being a "publicity bureau to spread socialistic propaganda."[35] As chairman of the FTC, Humphrey encouraged the commission to satisfy one of the goals of an influential segment of the business community, which was "nothing less than self-regulation with governmental approbation."[36]

Mellon's Views on Taxation

As Secretary of the Treasury under three presidents, Andrew Mellon clearly articulated the tax policy component of conservative Republican supply-side economic policies. By way of background, it is important to note that financing requirements for World War I bequeathed a legacy of unprecedentedly high rates of taxation. The structure of taxes included a personal income tax that reached a maximum of 77 percent, a corporate income tax, an excess-profits tax, estate and gift taxes, and excise taxes. A series of four tax cuts between 1921 and 1928 significantly reduced the wartime level of taxation. By 1928, the maximum tax rate on personal income was down to 25 percent, corporate income and excise taxes were reduced, and the excess-profits and gift taxes were repealed.[37]

Mellon's views on taxation were consistent with the ideas of constructive economy: lower tax rates generating higher total tax revenues; the trickle-down theory of tax rate reductions for upper income groups; and the stake-in-society principle of imposing taxes.

Mellon emphasized the importance of constructive economy because a reduction in government spending serves to increase a budget surplus that then forms the basis for tax reduction. He insisted that "tax reduction must come out of surplus revenue."[38]

Mellon believed that higher rates of income taxation would result in lower total tax revenues. "The history of taxation shows that taxes which are inherently excessive are not paid. The high rates inevitably put pressure upon the taxpayer to withdraw his capital from productive business and invest it in tax-exempt securities or to find other lawful methods of avoiding the realization of taxable income."[39]

Mellon thought that a reduction in income tax rates would increase total tax revenues not only because it would reduce the incentive to avoid taxes, but also because it would increase production incentives and taxable income. In this respect, Mellon noted the problem with existing high rates of taxation: "The vital defect in our present system is that the tax burden is borne by wealth in the making, not by capital already in existence. We place a tax on energy and initiative; and at the same time provide a refuge in the form of tax-exempt securities, into which wealth that has been accumulated or inherited can retire and defy the tax collector."[40]

Mellon underscored the importance of tax rate reduction on incentives to produce: "But where the Government takes away an unreasonable share of his earnings, the incentive to work is no longer there and a slackening of effort is the result."[41]

The overall effect of tax reduction and government economy would trickle down to benefit all of the people through general prosperity and more jobs. "If a sound system of taxation is adopted and the present policy of economy in government is continued, the country may look forward during the present generation not only to a decrease in the tax burden but to increased prosperity in which everyone will share."[42]

Finally, Mellon, like Coolidge and the business leaders of the NAM and

CC, believed in the stake-in-society view of taxation, that "nothing so brings home to a man the feeling that he personally has an interest in seeing that Government revenues are not squandered, but intelligently expended, as the fact that he contributes individually a direct tax, no matter how small, to his Government."[43]

Summary

Coolidge was an effective spokesman for the business view of government spending, taxation, and regulation. Mellon clearly articulated the case for lowering tax rates. Supply-side policies in the Coolidge-Mellon era emphasized constructive economy, tax rate reduction, budget surpluses, and deregulation of government controls over business. Supply-side fiscal policies rested on the foundation of constructive economy and reductions in the national debt. Budget surpluses, in turn, provided the basis for reducing tax rates. Tax rate reduction, given the legacy of high wartime taxes, would provide production incentives, increase total tax revenues, and trickle down to benefit the entire population through increased prosperity.

Deregulation would eliminate costly restrictions of business activity, and if existing regulatory institutions were administered by enlightened people, they could promote business activity. Thus, deregulation would enlarge the sphere for efficient resource allocation in the market sector through unfettered business activity.

A Comparative Economic History

A cursory comparison of Coolidge-Mellon supply-side economic policies with Reagan's suggests an uncanny parallelism. The fiscal component of both supply-side policies emphasizes spending cuts and tax rate reduction. In both periods, tax rate reduction was expected to increase production incentives, taxable income, and total tax revenues.[44] Moreover, tax cuts were to generate prosperity that would trickle down to benefit the entire population. Furthermore, policies in both periods emphasize deregulating government controls over business, and apply the same strategy for appointing administrators to regulatory agencies. In the Coolidge-Mellon era, and in the first stage of Reagan's term, appointments for major posts were dominated by people from the business sector, or by individuals critical of the policies of the very agency they administer.[45] Senator Robert M. LaFollette's concern over the pro-business orientation of the Federal Trade Commission expresses current fears about some of Reagan's appointees to regulatory bodies: "The last of the Commissions at Washington to be taken over by the forces it was intended to regulate, the Federal Trade Commission has been packed with its worst enemies, its rules have been perverted, the law under which it was created has been emasculated, and its usefulness has been destroyed."[46] In this general sense, Reagan appears to be resurrecting the pro-business ideology and the supply-side economic policies of conservative Republicanism in the Coolidge-Mellon era.[47]

The pro-business ideological parallels notwithstanding, a closer examination of supply-side economic policies in both periods reveals distinct and substantive differences. First, Reagan's policies reduce the rate of increase, not the level, of government spending and include a significant increase in defense spending.[48] Second, Reagan's program is expected to generate budget deficits beyond 1984.[49] Thus, the conceptualization and implementation of supply-side economic policies differ in the two periods. The Coolidge-Mellon program rested on constructive economy, including the realization of armaments control and reductions in defense spending, and reductions in the national debt. Government spending declined from $5.1 billion in 1921 to $3.1 billion in 1929, and the defense spending component decreased from $2.6 billion to $0.7 billion in the same period.[50] The federal budget, beginning in 1920, ran continuous surpluses throughout the 1920s.[51] Thus, government spending cuts and budget surpluses existed prior to the implementation of tax cuts in the twenties. Conversely, under Reagan's program, increases in defense spending and decreases in tax rates are causing a federal budget deficit. Current and expected budget deficits appear to be the Achilles heel of Reagan's program. Business and financial leaders, as well as financial markets, have identified budget deficits as the culprit behind high interest rates.[52] High interest rates are antithetical to supply-side policies because they choke off investment and capital accumulation. Thus, at this early stage of Reagan's program, his policies are not consonant with the views of a significant segment of the business and financial community.[53] In fact, the magnitude of the rift has resulted in insinuations by the administration that the business and financial community is sabotaging Reagan's program. According to Secretary of Commerce Malcolm Baldridge, the problem is that "if business waits to take action until every last shred of evidence is in on the effectiveness of our economic policy, that inaction will clearly hurt the success of the program."[54]

Finally, is there a relationship between supply-side economic policies and economic performance in the twenties, and are there lessons for today? Wanniski claims that supply-side tax policies caused "phenomenal economic expansion" and the "great Coolidge bull market" in stock prices.[55] There are a number of reasons why Wanniski's response is overly simplistic and shallow. In the early twenties, reductions in government spending and taxation reflected a "natural" winding down as the economy adjusted to peacetime after World War I. Also, the revenue acts of 1924 and 1926 were enacted in the context of full employment and price stability.[56] The rapid expansion of economic growth in the twenties has been explained by "pent up" demand and the unleashing of a Schumpeterian growth process, rather than by policy actions.[57] This perspective argues that a number of sectors, most notably automobiles, chemicals, housing, and electricity, were in position for growth after World War I. Thus, it may have been the return to peacetime and the strong performance of the economy that explained the simultaneous realization of tax rate cuts, increased tax revenues, and budget surpluses.

In contrast, the Reagan program was formulated, in part, to attack the complex problem of stagflation. Tax and spending cuts are more difficult to implement when they are not accompanied by a "natural" winding down of the government sector. In fact, entitlement programs, interest payment on the national debt, and increases in defense spending constitute a formidable barrier to cutting government spending.[58] The state of the economy and the difficulty of cutting government spending are background conditions that place an enormous obstacle in the path of implementing a twenties-type supply-side economic policy package. The economic history of the 1920s suggests that a strong economy may be a prerequisite to implementing and achieving the objectives of a supply-side economic package.

Replicating the prosperity that the United States enjoyed in the twenties would not be an unmitigated blessing. The distribution of income was dramatically skewed toward capital and upper income groups during the 1920s.[59] Holt claims that the lower 93 percent of the nonfarm population experienced a 4-percent decline in real disposable per capita income between 1923 and 1929.[60] Lastly, a number of economic historians believe that the seeds of the Great Depression were sown in the prosperity of the 1920s.[61]

An Institutional Appraisal

Institutional thought provides an analytical perspective that permits a deeper appraisal of conservative Republican supply-side economic policies.[62] A comprehensive evaluation is beyond the scope of this article; however, elements of institutional thought are used to develop a brief critique of supply-side policies.

Thorstein Veblen, in his critique of orthodox economics, issued the following challenge: "There is the economic life process still in great measure awaiting theoretical formulation."[63] Conservative Republican supply-side policies ignore Veblen's contention and implicitly resurrect the very orthodoxy that Veblen excoriated. The conservative Republican policy package is mandated by a doctrinaire pro-business ideology and relies on natural market forces for its success. As a result, these policy packages should be identified as ceremonial institutions that create and maintain status, power, rank, and privilege. Indeed, the Coolidge-Mellon proposals were in large part rationalized, albeit in a different language, on this basis ("The business of America is business").[64] The Reagan administration takes the justification for its policies one step further by asserting that they will cure existing macroeconomic problems. This assertion is evaluated below.

Veblen described orthodox economics as being flawed because it exhibits hedonistic, taxonomic, tautological, teleological, and non-evolutionary features.[65] For the sake of brevity, only three problems associated with these flaws will be examined.

First, the reliance of orthodox theory on a Newtonian concept of change leads to the belief in the reversability of processes.[66] This view neglects the evolutionary process of cumulative change in economic life and institutions. Reagan's proud acknowledgement of using policies more than a half-century old to solve new economic problems is a prime example of his belief in the reversability of processes. Reagan's policy approach ignores the evolution of the economic structure and the new problems of stagflation, which Marc Tool claims has caused, in part, the "compulsive shift to institutional analysis."[67] Reagan's supply-side economic policies completely neglect important institutional facts of life in 1981, such as the pervasiveness of economic power and cost-oriented administered prices, that make the present situation significantly different from that of the twenties.[68] Moreover, because of its ideological blinders, the Reagan administration recognizes the pervasiveness of government controls as the only important institutional problem. The administration's solution to this problem is to simply reverse the process through deregulation. Larry Reynolds is critical of this solution because explicit government controls change "individuals' perceptions of economic activity and the philosophical foundations of implicit regulations."[69] Thus, removal of explicit government regulations does not guarantee the same outcome as in the twenties because ethics, values, and attitudes that undergird implicit regulations have changed. Furthermore, Reynolds argues that orthodoxy emphasizes efficiency at the expense of equity and other objectives of government regulation.[70] Even if the removal of government regulations improves efficiency, it does so at the expense of other regulatory objectives. Aspects of government regulation certainly qualify as "imbecile institutions." However, the solution is not simply one of eliminating regulations, but rather a complex one of changing explicit *and* implicit regulations by an evolution from below.[71]

Second, orthodox economic theory and business ideology employ a social value theory that emphasizes pecuniary gain, especially profits, as the dominant indicator of success. As pointed out by many institutionalists and summarized by Tool, the attribution of real worth to pecuniary gain is wholly conjectural.[72] Moreover, Veblen clearly underscored the fundamental dichotomy between pecuniary and industrial activities, and also between business and industry, and business prosperity and industrial efficiency.[73] At minimum, Veblen's dichotomy should alert us to the misconceptions of those who would tautologically connect profits, capital accumulation, and productive efficiency. In the place of pecuniary gain, institutionalists have offered a criterion of social value that is captured in the phrase, "the continuity and instrumental effectiveness of recreating community non-invidiously."[74] This social value criterion recognizes the importance of, among others, the continuity of human life, the evolution of culture, the use of reliable knowledge to resolve economic problems, and the character of community. Reagan's supply-side proposals fail miserably with respect to the institutionalists' criterion of social value. Reagan's proposed solutions are founded on (1) a pro-business ideology rather than instrumental logic and reliable knowledge, (2) creating a recession to solve inflation rather than attempting to minimize disruption,[75] (3) transferring wealth and power to the few rather than dispersing them more equitably, and (4) denigrating the environment and casually transferring natural resource wealth from the public to the private sector rather than attempting to preserve the continuity of the life process.

Third, supply-side policies are based to a large extent on a "savings-centered" theory of capital accumulation and productive efficiency. Louis Junker, using Veblen's dichotomy between pecuniary and real (industrial) capital, has constructed a telling critique of the savings-centered theory.[76] He questions the causal connection between savings, capital accumulation, and macroeconomic performance, and argues that the saving rate is a reflection rather than a determinant of economic expansion: "Saving 'makes possible' capital development not positively and dynamically, as does the technological process, but *permissively* in terms of a set of institutional arrangements which may or may not be flexible enough to allow technology to proceed."[77]

Conclusion

A historical comparison of the supply-side economic policies of the Coolidge-Mellon era with those of today reveals strong parallels in their pro-business ideological foundations. Their dissimilarities stem from their different historical settings; the legitimacy of the role of the federal government especially differed from era to era. From an institutional perspective, conservative Republican supply-side economic policies are seriously flawed because they are founded on the misconceptions of orthodox theory.

Our current macroeconomic problems reflect a breakdown of institutions. If the administration is serious about solving macroeconomic problems, and not simply using the sick state of the economy as a means to establish ceremonial institutions, then the administration's supply-side policies are ill-conceived. The policies fail to address fundamental questions, raised by comparative economic history and institutional analysis, about the transformation and evolution of the economic process. This neglect of an evolutionary and historical perspective increases the chance of severe dislocations and policy failure.

Notes

1. See White House Report, "Program for Economic Recovery," *Presidential Documents* (23 February 1981). To guard against over-simplification, it is important to remember that the administration not only includes supply-siders, but also includes balanced-budgeteers, monetarists, and gold standard advocates. For an interesting and detailed account of conflict, the role of ideology, and compromises based on political power, see William Greider, "The Education of David Stockman," *The Atlantic* 248 (December 1981): 27–54.

2. ʼeagan himself has made this connection: see Allan J. Lichtman, "Back ɔ the Coolidge Era," Christian Science Monitor News Service, *Rocky 1ountain News*, 22 August 1981, p. 61.

3. ɪde Wanniski, "Taxes, Revenues, and the 'Laffer Curve,'" *The Public ɪterest* 50 (Winter 1978): 14.

4. rederick Lewis Allen, *Only Yesterday* (New York: Harper & Row, 931), p. 154.

5. This section relies on the excellent study by James Warren Prothro, *The Dollar Decade: Business Ideas in the 1920s* (Baton Rouge: Louisiana State University Press, 1954).
6. Ibid., p. 224.
7. Ibid., p. 118.
8. Ibid., p. 116.
9. Ibid., p. 119.
10. Ibid., p. 28.
11. Ibid., p. 121.
12. Ibid., pp. 124–27.
13. Ibid., p. 133.
14. Ibid., p. 136.
15. Ibid., pp. 145–46.
16. Ibid., p. 138.
17. Ibid., p. 150.
18. Ibid., p. 152.
19. William Allen White, *A Puritan in Babylon* (New York: MacMillan, 1940), p. 251.
20. Calvin Coolidge, "Inaugural Address," March 4, 1925. See Calvin Coolidge, *Foundations of the Republic* (New York: Books for Libraries Press, 1926), p. 200.
21. Prothro, *Dollar Decade*, p. 224.
22. Coolidge, *Foundations*, p. 320.
23. Arthur M. Schlesinger, Jr., *The Crisis of the Old Order, 1919–1933* (Boston: Houghton Mifflin, 1957), p. 61.
24. Coolidge, *Foundations*, p. 201.
25. Robert H. Ferrell and Howard H. Quint, *The Talkative President: The Off-the-Record Press Conferences of Calvin Coolidge* (New York: Garland Press, 1979), p. 109.
26. Coolidge, *Foundations*, pp. 357–58.
27. Ferrell and Quint, *The Talkative President*, pp. 151–52.
28. Calvin Coolidge in Donald R. McCoy, *Calvin Coolidge: The Quiet President* (New York: MacMillan, 1967), p. 334.
29. Ferrell and Quint, *The Talkative President*, p. 110.
30. Coolidge, *Foundations*, p. 202.
31. John D. Hicks, *Republican Ascendency, 1921–1933* (New York: Harper Brothers, 1960), p. 107.
32. Coolidge, *Foundations*, p. 322.
33. G. Cullom Davis, "The Transformation of the Federal Trade Commission, 1914–1929," *Mississippi Valley Historical Review* 49 (December 1962): 440.
34. Ibid., p. 445.
35. Ibid., p. 448.
36. Joan Hoff Wilson, *The Twenties: The Critical Issues* (Boston: Little, Brown, 1972) p. xvii. Humphrey proudly proclaimed the FTC's revolutionary change in direction. "If it was going east before, it is going west now." See Davis, "The Transformation," p. 449.

37. Sidney Ratner, *American Taxation* (New York: W. W. Norton, 1942), pp. 384–443.

38. Andrew W. Mellon, *Taxation: The People's Business* (New York: Mac-Millan, 1924), p. 20.

39. Ibid., p. 13.

40. Ibid., p. 94.

41. Ibid., p. 95.

42. Ibid., p. 138.

43. David A. Shannon, *Twentieth Century America*, vol. 2, *The Twenties and Thirties* (Chicago: Rand McNally College Publishing, 1977), p. 63.

44. For details of Reagan's economic program refer to White House Report, "Program." Jude Wanniski and Arthur Laffer have popularized these tax relationships through the concept of the Laffer Curve in Figure I, Appendix. They argue that the economy is operating with a tax rate like A, and therefore a reduction in the tax rate toward B will increase total tax revenues. The concept of the Laffer curve was clearly articulated by Mellon and Coolidge.

45. A few examples include Donald Regan, Secretary of the Treasury; Malcolm Baldridge, Secretary of Commerce; James Watt, Secretary of the Interior; and Ray Donovan, Secretary of Labor.

46. LaFollete cited in Davis, "The Transformation," p. 452.

47. The parallel may extend to other areas as well. Preliminary observation suggests similarities with respect to anti-unionism, trade protection, and anti-trust laxity.

48. White House Report, "Program."

49. Walter S. Mossberg and Timothy D. Schellhardt, "Modest Cut in Pentagon Spending Is Seen Drawing Fire from Congress, Wall Street," *The Wall Street Journal*, 14 September 1981, p. 3.

50. U.S. Bureau of the Census, *Historical Statistics of the United States: From Colonial Times to 1970*, Bicentennial Edition (Washington, D.C.: U.S. Government Printing Office, 1975), p. 1115.

51. Ibid., p. 1104.

52. Kenneth H. Bacon, "Despite Market Fears, President Holds Firm on Economic Policies," *The Wall Street Journal*, 17 September 1981, p. 1.

53. Ibid.

54. Ibid.

55. Jude Wanniski, *The Way the World Works* (New York: Simon and Schuster, 1978), pp. 121–22.

56. Unemployment was down to 2.4 percent in 1923 (Stanley Lebergott, *Manpower in Economic Growth* [New York: McGraw Hill, 1964], p. 512); and the Consumer Price Index was 50.2 in 1922, 51.1 in 1923, and 51.2 in 1924 (U.S. Bureau of the Census, *Historical Statistics*, p. 211).

57. Robert A. Gordon, *Economic Instability & Growth: The American Record* (New York: Harper & Row, 1974), p. 27. Joseph Schumpeter, "The Decade of the Twenties," *American Economic Review* 36 (May 1946): 1–100.

58. Bacon, "Despite Market Fears."

59. See Robert R. Keller, "Factor Income Distribution in the United States

During the 1920s: A Re-examination of Fact and Theory," *The Journal of Economic History* 33 (March 1973): 252–73; and Charles F. Holt, "Who Benefited from the Prosperity of the Twenties?" *Explorations in Economic History* 14 (July 1977): 277–89.

60. Holt, "Who Benefited," p. 286.
61. See James M. Potter, *The American Economy Between the World Wars,* (New York: John Wiley and Sons, 1974); George Soule, *Prosperity Decade: From War to Depression, 1917–1929* (New York: Harper & Row, 1947); and Schlesinger, Jr., *The Crisis.* Prosperity in the twenties was accompanied by increased income inequality, which in turn was viewed as a primary determinant of underconsumption and the collapse of investment spending.
62. It is important to separate conservative Republican supply-side policies from a general supply-side approach. This section criticizes the former and not the latter. Institutional and comparative historical analysis suggests that many of our current problems emanate from the supply-side and necessitate institutional adjustment.
63. Thorstein Veblen, *The Place of Science in Modern Civilization* (New York: Russell and Russell, 1961 [1919]), p. 70.
64. Calvin Coolidge, cited in Shannon, *The Twenties and the Thirties,* p. 49.
65. Veblen, *The Place of Science.*
66. David Hamilton, *Evolutionary Economics: A Study of Change in Economic Thought* (Albuquerque: University of New Mexico Press, 1970), pp. 18–28.
67. Marc R. Tool, "The Compulsive Shift to Institutional Analysis," *Journal of Economic Issues* 15 (September 1981): 569–92.
68. See John Kenneth Galbraith, "Power and the Useful Economist," *American Economic Review* 63 (March 1973): 1–11; Tool, "The Compulsive Shift"; and Mark A. Lutz, "Stagflation as an Institutional Problem," *Journal of Economic Issues* 15 (September 1981): 745–68.
69. Larry Reynolds, "Foundations of an Institutional Theory of Regulation," *Journal of Economic Issues* 15 (September 1981): 654.
70. Ibid., pp. 641–42.
71. Reynolds, "Foundations," p. 654; and Marc R. Tool, "A Social Value Theory in Neoinstitutional Economics," *Journal of Economic Issues* (December 1971): 839.
72. Tool, "A Social Value Theory," p. 833.
73. For an extensive listing of dichotomies, see Tool, "A Social Value Theory," p. 827.
74. Ibid., p. 841.
75. The recession reflects the impact of supply-side policies *and* contractionary monetary policy.
76. Louis Junker, "Capital Accumulation, Savings-Centered Theory, and Economic Development," *Journal of Economic Issues* 1 (June 1967): 25–43.
77. Ibid., p. 34. Keynes also viewed saving as a passive element—a residual. John Maynard Keynes, *The General Theory of Employment, Interest, and Money* (New York: Harcourt, Brace & World, 1964 [1936]), p. 183.

APPENDIX

Figure I

The Laffer Curve

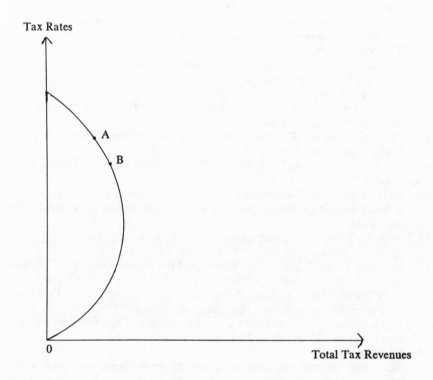

The "Industrial-Military Complex" in Historical Perspective: The InterWar Years

PAUL A. C. KOISTINEN

SCHOLARS and journalists have limited their analyses of the "industrial-military complex" to the years of World War II and the Cold War.[1] This focus is quite natural, for it is during this period that the multibillion-dollar war and defense budgets have had the most dramatic effects upon the nation's institutional structure. Nevertheless, to neglect the years prior to 1940 greatly limits an understanding of the "complex" which has resulted from the military's expanded role in the federal government and its elaborate ties with the industrial community.

The "industrial-military complex" of World War II and after is an outgrowth of economic mobilization for World War I, of interwar planning by the armed forces and the business community for future emergencies, and of defense spending during the 1920s and 1930s. Almost all practices currently ascribed to the "complex" arose before 1940.

During World War I, as during World War II, federal agencies, largely controlled by industry and the military, regulated the economy. World War I differed from World War II, however, in that the army, the largest wartime military service, was a reluctant participant in the civilian mobilization agencies. Relatively isolated within the federal government and the nation before hostilities, the army was suspicious of, and hostile toward, civilian institutions. It was also unprepared for the enormous wartime responsibilities. Congress and the Wilson administration had to force the army to integrate its personnel into the War Industries Board (WIB). This integration was essential for coordinating army procurement with the Board's regulatory functions in order to maintain a stable economy.

Mr. Koistinen is associate professor of history in San Fernando Valley State College.

[1] For example, see C. Wright Mills, *The Power Elite* (New York, 1956), 212; Walter Millis, *Arms and Men: A Study in American Military History* (New York, 1956), 306-07; Fred J. Cook, *The Warfare State* (New York, 1962), 41-65; Jack Raymond, *Power at the Pentagon* (New York, 1964), 167; H. L. Nieburg, *In the Name of Science* (Chicago, 1966), vii-viii, 184-85.

After the war, Congress authorized the army to plan for procurement and economic mobilization in order to insure its preparation for future hostilities. The navy also joined the planning process. The interwar planning was guided by thousands of industrialists, and by the late 1930s the armed services were not only prepared for wartime operations but also in full agreement with prominent industrial elements on plans for economic mobilization. Those plans, based on World War I mobilization, provided the guidelines for regulating the World War II economy.

Interwar planning was inseparable from defense spending. Many of the businessmen who participated in the planning were associated with firms that were actual or potential military contractors. Despite the relatively small defense budgets of the 1920s and 1930s, the pattern of industrial-military relations during those years foreshadows in many striking ways what developed after World War II.

The American economy was mobilized for World War I by federal agencies devised and staffed primarily by businessmen.[2] In the Army Appropriations Act of August 1916, Congress provided for a Council of National Defense, which consisted of six cabinet members, to serve as the President's advisory body on industrial mobilization. It was assisted by a National Defense Advisory Commission (NDAC), composed largely of businessmen serving for a dollar-a-year or without compensation; most of the members surrendered neither their positions nor incomes as private citizens. When the nation declared war, NDAC assumed responsibility for mobilizing the economy. In July 1917 a more effective mobilization agency, WIB, took over NDAC functions; the former agency, like the latter, was controlled by business elements. Until March 1918, neither NDAC nor WIB had legal authority to enforce its decisions; both were subordinate to the Council of National Defense, and it could only advise the President.

During 1917, businessmen perfected the mobilization agencies and devised the means for curtailing civilian production and converting industry to meet governmental needs. In addition, they developed price, priority, allocation, and other economic controls. By the end of the year, WIB had created the organization and the controls essential for regulating a wartime economy.

Through WIB, industry largely regulated itself during World War I. Key to WIB's operations were major subdivisions called commodity com-

[2] Paul A. C. Koistinen, "The 'Industrial-Military Complex' in Historical Perspective: World War I," *Business History Review*, XLI (Winter 1967), 378-403. Further research by the author in the papers of Woodrow Wilson, Newton D. Baker, James W. Wadsworth, Jr., George W. Goethals, and Bernard M. Baruch and in commerce department records has not significantly modified the conclusions reached in the essay on World War I.

mittees, which served under the chairman and his lieutenants. These committees, which made policy for and administered the various industries, were staffed by businessmen who often came from the industries they directed. Assisting the commodity committees were war service committees which were trade associations or councils elected by the national industries. Since the war service committees were neither organized nor financed by the government, they officially only "advised" the commodity committees. But in practice the commodity committees relied heavily upon industry representatives to formulate and execute all policy decisions.

Even without legal authority to enforce its decisions, WIB had industry's cooperation because businessmen dominated it. Industry's cooperation, however, was not enough to maintain a stable wartime economy. WIB required some control over procurement by the war and navy departments and other agencies. Throughout 1917 it attempted to coordinate procurement with its own operations in order to prevent the various departments and agencies from competing among themselves and to insure uniform prices and the distribution of contracts according to availability of facilities, resources, and transportation. Economic stability depended upon such coordination, since wartime demand always exceeded supply. With only advisory powers, WIB relied upon the procurement agencies' voluntary cooperation. While most of these proved to be reasonably cooperative, the war department—the largest, most powerful procurement agency—undermined WIB's regulatory efforts by acting independently and purchasing billions of dollars worth of munitions. As a result, industrial plants in the Northeast were overloaded with contracts; prices skyrocketed; critical shortages of fuel, power, and raw materials developed; and the railway and shipping systems became hopelessly congested.

The war department was both unwilling and unable to cooperate with WIB—unwilling, because it feared that the civilian agency would try to take over army procurement functions; unable, because the department could not control its own supply operations, let alone coordinate them with WIB. As many as eight supply bureaus, such as the Quartermaster Corps and the Ordnance Department, purchased independently for the army. Competing with one another and other purchasing agencies, the bureaus let contracts indiscriminately, commandeered facilities without plan, and hoarded supplies. Cooperation between WIB and the war department was also thwarted by the fact that WIB was organized along commodity lines while the army's supply network was structured by function (such as ordnance and quartermaster). Before army procurement could be coordinated with WIB, the war department had first to accept the need for cooperating with the civilian mobilization agency and then to centralize its supply network along commodity lines. For months, the department would do neither, not only because it was suspicious of WIB but also because it was torn by internal dissension.

In theory, the war department was under the centralized control of the chief of staff, aided by the General Staff. Serving as the secretary of war's principal military adviser, the chief of staff supervised the entire army, including the supply bureaus as well as the combat troops. This system never worked in practice. The bureaus resisted control by the chief of staff. Conflict between the General Staff and the bureaus rent the war department before the war; it paralyzed the department during hostilities.

Unable to regulate the economy without war department cooperation, WIB during 1917 sought the authority to impose its will on the department. But Secretary of War Newton D. Baker, reflecting army suspicion of the Board, squelched the efforts to give it more than advisory powers. He managed to do so because he served as chairman of the Council of National Defense, under which WIB functioned, and as Woodrow Wilson's chief adviser on industrial mobilization.

By the winter of 1917-1918, with WIB stalemated by the war department and the latter virtually collapsing under burgeoning munitions requirements, the economy had become critically dislocated. The business community and Congress demanded that the crisis should be resolved by placing military procurement under a civilian munitions ministry. Adamantly opposed to such a drastic remedy, Wilson headed off the critics in March 1918 by separating WIB from the Council of National Defense and placing it directly under his control. He granted it broad powers for regulating the economy, including a measure of authority over the procurement agencies. To avoid losing control of procurement and to facilitate coordination with WIB, the war department also began reforming its supply system. In December 1917, the department began to consolidate the bureaus into one agency under General Staff control. The new organization was structured to match WIB's commodity committee system.

From March 1918, the strengthened WIB, under the chairmanship of Bernard M. Baruch, effectively used the organization and economic controls developed over the past year to regulate the economy. Procurement was coordinated with WIB activities by integrating war department representatives and those of the other purchasing agencies into WIB. Once the department reorganized its system and adopted a cooperative attitude, members of the army commodity committees joined WIB committees and shared equally in making decisions. Working together, industrial and military personnel learned that WIB could function for their mutual interests. Through WIB's operations, the foundation for the "industrial-military complex" was laid.

The collaboration of industry and the military continued during the 1920s and 1930s and took the form of procurement and economic planning for future wars. This planning was authorized by Congress in the National Defense Act of 1920, which reorganized the war department's system of supply and procurement. To insure that the army did not disrupt economic mobilization in a future emergency, the act placed the supply bureaus under an assistant secretary of war. It was assumed that he would be an industrialist. The assistant secretary would supervise the bureaus and, through planning, prepare them for wartime procurement. Since the assistant secretary was made the chief of staff's equal, the secretary of war had two principal advisers instead of one, as had been the case before 1920.[3]

Congress based the legislation upon the recommendations of Assistant Secretary of War Benedict Crowell, various industrial consultants, several bureau chiefs, and other military personnel. Crowell, a Cleveland businessman who had been involved in military procurement since 1916, believed that World War I demonstrated that industrial production was as important to military success as were tactics and strategy. He felt that supply and procurement must receive the same emphasis in war department affairs as did the traditional military functions. That would not take place, he maintained, under the old system in which the chief of staff, aided by the General Staff, served as the secretary of war's principal adviser. The General Staff would neglect supply and procurement because it knew little about those subjects. Only by placing the bureaus under a qualified civilian who was equal to the chief of staff, he argued, would the army be prepared for future hostilities.[4] Crowell and his associates intended that the assistant secretary of war should plan only for army procurement. Congress went fur-

[3] U. S. Statutes at Large, XLI (1921), Part 1, pp. 762-65.

[4] "Reorganization of the Army," Senate, Hearings before the Subcommittee of the Committee on Military Affairs, 66 Cong., 2 Sess., 1919, pp. 1760-77; "Army Reorganization," House, Hearings before the Committee on Military Affairs, 66 Cong., 1 Sess., 1919-1920, pp. 1801-35; Charles Saltzman, "Reminiscences of the Battle of Washington," Nov. 26, 1935, File No. 020/2/113.1, Planning Branch (PB), Assistant Secretary of War (ASW), Office of the Secretary of War, RG 107 (National Archives); Benedict Crowell and Robert F. Wilson, The Armies of Industry (New Haven, 1921), 8-19. See also E. O. Saunders, "National Defense Act—Legislative History of Industrial Mobilization Clauses," Oct. 11, 1923, File No. 628, PB ASW Office of the Secretary of War; A. H. Moran, "Legislative History of the General Staff Corps and the Assistant Secretary of War," Feb. 14, 1928, File No. 46, ibid.; Troyer S. Anderson, "Introduction to the History of the Under Secretary of War's Office," 1947, Office of the Chief of Military History, Washington, D. C.; Harry B. Yoshpe, "Economic Mobilization Planning Between Two World Wars," Military Affairs, XV (Winter 1951), 199-204, XVI (Summer 1952), 71-83.

ther. The National Defense Act empowered the assistant secretary, though in an ambiguous way, to plan for an entire wartime economy. Why Congress authorized the more comprehensive planning is obscure.

J. Mayhew Wainwright, the first assistant secretary of war under the act, set up an Office of the Assistant Secretary of War (OASW) with personnel drawn from the bureaus. In 1922 an Army-Navy Munitions Board was created in order to include the navy in the planning and to coordinate the supply systems of the two services. And, in 1924 the war department supply planners organized an Army Industrial College to facilitate their work.[5]

At first, OASW concentrated upon wartime military procurement, but it soon became obvious that this planning was futile without also planning for economic mobilization.[6] Though authorized to draft such plans, war department officials, civilian and military alike, hesitated to assume what they considered to be civilian responsibilities. It took the influence of Baruch to convince the war department that economic planning was not exclusively a civilian matter. After World War I, he and other architects of wartime mobilization insisted that the nation's security depended upon constant preparation for war. They favored joint industry-military planning for economic mobilization in order to avoid confusion and delay.[7] Baruch pleaded with the department to draw up full-scale plans for mobilization based on World War I.[8] After years of hesitation, OASW began to plan for eco-

[5] Harold W. Thatcher, *Planning for Industrial Mobilization, 1920-1940* (Washington, D. C., 1943), 16, 24-25, 42-43.

[6] J. Mayhew Wainwright to President, Aug. 29, 1940, PPF 1678, Franklin D. Roosevelt Papers (Franklin D. Roosevelt Library, Hyde Park, N.Y.); War Department, *Report of the Secretary of War to the President, 1925* (Washington, 1925), 27-28; War Department, *Report of the Secretary of War to the President, 1926* (Washington, 1926), 30-31; War Department, *Report of the Secretary of War to the President, 1927* (Washington, 1927), 25, 27, 29-35; War Department, *Report of the Secretary of War to the President, 1928* (Washington, 1928), 16-18, 50-58. See also Marvin A. Kreidberg and Merton G. Henry, *History of Military Mobilization in the United States Army, 1775-1945* (Washington, 1955), 502-07; Erna Risch, *The Quartermaster Corps: Organization, Supply, and Services* (2 vols., Washington, 1953), I, 56-57, 208-10, 243-52, 323-29.

[7] Bernard M. Baruch, *American Industry in the War: A Report of the War Industries Board (March 1921)* (New York, 1941), 7-8, 36, 102-04; Crowell and Wilson, *Armies of Industry*, 18-19; Grosvenor B. Clarkson, *Industrial America in the World War: The Strategy Behind the Lines, 1917-1918* (New York, 1923), 483-84; "Final Report of the Chairman of the United States War Industries Board to the President of the United States, February, 1919," Senate, Special Committee Investigating the Munitions Industry, *Senate Committee Print No. 3*, 74 Cong., 1 Sess., 1935, pp. 44-52; "Reorganization of the Army," 371-72, 432-41; United States Council of National Defense, *Third Annual Report, Fiscal Year Ended June 30, 1919* (Washington, D.C., 1919), 16-17; United States Council of National Defense, *Fourth Annual Report, Fiscal Year Ended June 30, 1920* (Washington, D.C., 1920), 3-108.

[8] Bernard M. Baruch, Speeches Delivered at the Army War College, Jan. 15, Dec. 2, 1925, Dec. 14, 1926, File No. 011.2, Records of the War Production Board, RG 179 (National Archives); John W. Weeks to Chairman, House Military Affairs Committee, Feb. 9, 1923, File No. 374, PB ASW Office of the Secretary of War; Baruch to Dwight

nomic mobilization as well as procurement. Under Baruch's critical eye, the supply planners between 1929 and 1931 drafted the first official economic blueprint for war—the "Industrial Mobilization Plan" of 1930.[9]

This plan amounted to little more than a proposal for using the methods of World War I to regulate a wartime economy. The key to OASW's blueprint was a War Resources Administration. Comparable to the War Industries Board, the War Resources Administration would rely upon a commodity committee-war service committee system for economic control. The military services would also organize their procurement networks along commodity lines and integrate their personnel into the War Resources Administration. In a future war, the economy would be mobilized by new federal agencies largely dominated by industrial and military personnel.[10] In 1933, 1936, and 1939, the war department published revised editions of the plan. With each revision, the proposed mobilization apparatus was simplified and patterned more explicitly after the World War I model.[11]

The fact that the war department wrote the 1930 plan is of the greatest significance. After ten years of planning, OASW recognized that modern warfare required a totally planned economy; the armed services would have to adapt themselves to the civilian mobilization agencies during hostilities. The Industrial Mobilization Plan did not mean, however, that the army as a whole had accepted the new conditions of warfare. Before that could take place, the supply planners had to convert the chief of staff and the General Staff to their point of view. Throughout the 1920s and into the 1930s, the army's command structure refused to recognize that supply and procurement set limits for tactics and strategy; and the General Staff's war plans provided for raising and fielding an army at rates that exceeded the economy's capacity. The General Staff insisted that supply had to adjust to strategy. OASW and the supply bureaus adamantly opposed such thinking. Both the economy and the military mission, they argued, would be threatened.[12] The admonition went unheeded for years.

F. Davis, March 6, 1923, Dec. 11, 1924, June 6, 1925; Baruch to Weeks, Jan. 22, 1923; Baruch to H. E. Ely, Feb. 20, Oct. 29, 1925; Ely to Baruch, Oct. 30, 1925, Bernard M. Baruch Papers (Princeton University Library). Harry B. Yoshpe, "Bernard Baruch: Civilian Godfather of the Military M-Day Plan," *Military Affairs*, XXX (Spring 1965), 1-15.

[9] "Plan for Governmental Organization For War," Nov. 12, 1929, File No. 109, PB ASW Office of the Secretary of War (Baruch's comments are written on the Plan); George Van Horn Mosely to Baruch, Jan. 9, Feb. 1, 13, 1930; Baruch to Moseley, Feb. 4, 18, 1930, Baruch Papers.

[10] "Industrial Mobilization Plan," 1930 ("IMP"), File No. 110, PB ASW Office of the Secretary of War. In "IMP," 1939, the major mobilization agency was called the War Resources Administration.

[11] "IMP," 1933, File No. 112, PB ASW Office of the Secretary of War; "IMP," 1936, File No. 120, *ibid.*; "IMP," 1939, File No. 334/117.3, *ibid.*

[12] Kreidberg and Henry, *History of Military Mobilization*, 382-461, 502-03; War De-

The General Staff turned a deaf ear to OASW because, knowing little about procurement, it could not gauge the effects of industrialized warfare on the army or the economy and, therefore, continued to view civilian and military responsibilities as if they were unrelated. In addition, the General Staff and OASW were rivals for power. The General Staff resented the 1920 reorganization which deprived it of control of the bureaus. It was intent upon keeping the supply side of the department subordinate to itself. If the General Staff granted the importance of supply and procurement in military affairs, it would strengthen the hand of its rival. Relations between the two groups in the war department became so embittered in the 1920s that communication broke down almost completely. In the 1930s, however, the strife began to wane. As relations improved, the General Staff gradually became more receptive to OASW ideas.[13]

A major turning point occurred in 1935-1936, when General Malin Craig became chief of staff and Harry W. Woodring, secretary of war. Woodring, who had served as assistant secretary of war from 1933 to 1936, was convinced of the need for practical war plans. Craig agreed. Under their combined influence, the General Staff's Mobilization Plan of 1933 was scrapped and the Protective Mobilization Plan drawn up and perfected between 1936 and 1939. It was the first war plan based on the nation's industrial potential.[14] A radical change had taken place in the thinking of the army's command structure. It had finally accepted army dependence on the civilian economy in order to fulfill the military mission. Woodring observed: "I believe the reduction of our mobilization program to sensible workable proportions to be one of the highest attainments of the War Department since the World War."[15]

OASW planning naturally led to numerous war department contacts with the business community. Thousands of industrialists, most of whom had participated in wartime mobilization, guided and assisted the depart-

partment, *Report of the Secretary* . . . *1928*, pp. 56-57; War Department, *Report of the Secretary of War to the President, 1935* (Washington, 1935), 36; Constance McLaughlin Green, Harry C. Thomson, and Peter C. Roots, *The Ordnance Department: Planning Munitions for War* (Washington, 1955), 51-54.

[13] Paul A. C. Koistinen, "The Hammer and the Sword: Labor, the Military, and Industrial Mobilization, 1920-1945" (doctoral dissertation, University of California, Berkeley, 1964), 15-16, 24-27; War Department, *Report of the Secretary* . . . *1927*, p. 38; War Department, *Report of the Secretary* . . . *1928*, p. 58; Kreidberg and Henry, *History of Military Mobilization*, 382-461, 502-03.

[14] Kreidberg and Henry, *History of Military Mobilization*, 382-461, 466-92, 502-03; Otto L. Nelson, Jr., *National Security And The General Staff* (Washington, 1946), 303-07; Mark S. Watson, *Chief of Staff: Prewar Plans and Preparations* (Washington, 1950), 78, 81-84.

[15] War Department, *Report of the Secretary of War to the President, 1938* (Washington, 1938), 1.

ment's efforts in various ways. When the Army Industrial College was organized, it had an Advisory Board graced with such prominent business figures as Baruch, Elbert H. Gary, and Walter Gifford. The various procurement districts also set up civilian advisory boards composed of army contractors to review the department's supply operations. In 1925 the department organized a Business Council, which included members from the nation's largest corporations, to help introduce modern business techniques into army operations and to familiarize the industralists with army procurement and planning methods.[16]

Most contacts between the war department and industry involved representatives from trade associations and interested corporation executives. Often these men were or became reserve officers assigned to OASW. By 1931 about 14,000 individuals served in such a capacity. They aided in the drafting of procurement and mobilization plans and sought to further cooperative relations between the military and business.[17]

Mixed motives explain industry's participation in war department planning.[18] Firms contracting with the army obviously welcomed the opportunity of working closely with OASW in order to secure or advance their special interests. Some business elements assisted the army so that they could identify their products or materials with national defense in order to

[16] War Department, *Report of the Secretary* . . . *1925*, p. 27; War Department, *Report of the Secretary* . . . *1926*, pp. 30-31; War Department, *Report of the Secretary* . . . *1927*, pp. 28, 34, 39; War Department, *Report of the Secretary of War to the President, 1929* (Washington, 1929), 35-65; Senate, *Hearings Before the Special Committee Investigating the Munitions Industry*, 73-74 Congs. (40 parts, Washington, 1934-1943), Part 15, pp. 3623-26, Part 16, pp. 3996-4022; Thatcher, *Planning for Industrial Mobilization*, 26; Green, Thomson, and Roots, *Ordnance Department*, 26-27, 36-37, 54-55; Harry C. Thomson and Lida Mayo, *The Ordnance Department: Procurement and Supply* (Washington, 1960), 13.

[17] EFK memo, [circa] Feb. 1922, File No. 46, H. B. Ferguson to Planning Branch, Dec. 12, 1924, File No. 44, PB ASW Office of the Secretary of War; War Department, *Report of the Secretary* . . . *1925*, p. 27; War Department, *Report of the Secretary* . . . *1927*, pp. 31-33; War Department, *Report of the Secretary* . . . *1928*, p. 53; War Department, *Report of the Secretary of War to the President, 1932* (Washington, 1932), 34-35; U. S. War Policies Commission, "Hearings," *House Doc.*, 72 Cong., 1 Sess., No. 163 (Serial 9538), 188.

[18] War Department, *Report of the Secretary* . . . *1926*, p. 30; War Department, *Report of the Secretary* . . . *1927*, pp. 28, 38; War Department, *Report of the Secretary* . . . *1928*, pp. 15, 51, 57; War Department, *Report of the Secretary* . . . *1929*, pp. 35-65; War Department, *Report of the Secretary of War to the President, 1931* (Washington, 1931), 26; War Department, *Report of the Secretary* . . . *1932*, p. 32; War Department, *Report of the Secretary of War to the President, 1934* (Washington, 1934), 31; War Department, *Report of the Secretary* . . . *1938*, p. 21; Koistinen, "Hammer and the Sword," 16, 19-21, 29-30, 58-59, 61-62, 71-77; War Policies Commission, "Hearings," 258-65; Thatcher, *Planning for Industrial Mobilization*, 128-29; Green, Thomson, and Roots, *Ordnance Department*, 54-57; Thomson and Mayo, *Ordnance Department*, 22; Dulany Terrett, *The Signal Corps: The Emergency (To December 1941)* (Washington, 1956), 58-69.

enhance their chances for tariff protection, government assistance, or other special privileges. Also, their firms received free publicity of a "patriotic" nature. But reasons other than immediate economic concerns must be considered in assessing industry's role in army planning. Industrial preparedness became almost an ideological crusade for some business executives after the war. That was the case with Baruch and his coterie; with Howard E. Coffin, a prominent industrialist and leading participant in wartime mobilization; and with businessmen associated with the American Legion.[19] They participated in army planning as a means of preparing the nation for war. The business community in general was not so disposed. Without being committed to industrial preparedness *per se*, many businessmen were willing to assist in the planning at the war department's request because it helped the department to adjust its structure and thinking to modern warfare.

The general trend of the interwar political economy is also significant for measuring the response of business to army planning. World War I greatly strengthened the cooperative ethic within the business community and between it and the government. Before World War II, both business and the government experimented with official and unofficial attempts at economic control through industrial cooperation. The National Recovery Administration was only the most formal example. The army's economic planning accurately reflected this cooperative trend.[20] For that reason, among others, the planning received the endorsement of interested businessmen.

OASW did not confine itself simply to planning for industrial mobilization. It also sought legislative authority for implementing the "Industrial Mobilization Plan" in an emergency.

During the 1920s the department's drive for industrial preparedness was carried on in conjunction with the American Legion. The Legion rank and file seethed with resentment about alleged wartime profiteering and the unequal burden shouldered by the fighting forces. In order to remove the promise of riches as an inducement to war and to distribute the burdens of warfare more equitably, the returning veterans demanded a total draft of manpower and capital in any future emergency. Ironically, the Legion's peace movement, which originated in dissent over the economics of World War I, was ultimately converted into support for the "Industrial Mobilization

---

[19] Concerning Howard E. Coffin, see Koistinen, " 'Industrial-Military Complex,' " 381-82, and Coffin's correspondence with the Hoover and Roosevelt administrations, File No. 92819, General Correspondence, Office of the Secretary of Commerce, RG 40 (National Archives). Coffin to Stephen Early, Dec. 21, 1936, OF 172, Roosevelt Papers.

[20] The War Department's participation in NRA resulted directly from ASW planning. See Senate, *Hearings Before the Special Committee Investigating the Munitions Industry*, Part 17, pp. 4292-93, 4319-20, 4444-45.

Plan" based on the wartime model. Legion leadership and its special relationship with the war department explains why. Substantial business elements and former military officers dominated Legion affairs; throughout the 1920s the secretaries and assistant secretaries of war were usually active Legionnaires. When acting on the proposal for a total draft that was favored by the rank and file, the Legion leaders turned to the war department for assistance. In 1922, OASW drafted for the Legion a bill that in general terms would have granted the President almost unlimited authority over the nation's human and economic resources in the event of war.[21] The Legion consistently referred to the bill as a "universal draft," as a measure for promoting peace, and as a proposal for "equalizing wartime burdens." That was scarcely the case. The bill was so vague that it could be used for many different purposes. Its grant of authority was so great and its power so general that it could sanction a presidential dictatorship. Once the economic planning of OASW was fully underway, the war department and the Legion leadership clearly intended the bill to be a general grant of authority for implementing the "Industrial Mobilization Plan."

Beginning in 1922, the Legion-sponsored bill was repeatedly introduced in Congress. Despite Legion lobbying and war department support, each Congress sidetracked the proposed legislation. Unable to get its bill through Congress, the Legion asked for a bipartisan commission to study and recommend policies for industrial mobilization. An active campaign by congressmen who were also Legionnaires soon led to action. By a joint resolution in June 1930, Congress created the War Policies Commission (WPC), which consisted of eight congressmen and six cabinet members. Six of the fourteen commissioners were Legionnaires. The Commission was to study and make recommendations for equalizing war burdens and preventing war profiteering, and it was to formulate "policies to be pursued in event of war."[22]

WPC, like the Legion's drive for a "universal draft," quickly became a means for furthering military preparation.[23] Because the war department

[21] D. John Markey to Weeks, Feb. 1, 1922, File No. 62, PB ASW Office of the Secretary of War; correspondence concerning the Legion-war department bill, File No. 560, *ibid.*; "Mobilization of Manpower and Industrial Resources, Legislative History," Feb. 18, 1937, File No. 010/178, *ibid.*; Thatcher, *Planning for Industrial Mobilization*, 100-09; Marcus Duffield, *King Legion* (New York, 1931), 4-12, 109-15, 129-45; Justin Gray with Victor H. Bernstein, *The Inside Story of the Legion* (New York, 1948), 44-70, 87-92. See also Roscoe Baker, *The American Legion and American Foreign Policy* (New York, 1954); Richard Seelye Jones, *A History of the American Legion* (Indianapolis, 1946). The Legion affiliations of the war department officials can be traced through the above volumes.
[22] War Policies Commission, "Report to the President," *House Doc.*, 72 Cong., 1 Sess., No. 163 (Serial 9538), vi.
[23] In addition to the hearings and reports of the War Policies Commission collection, see War Policies Commission Files No. 1-211, PB ASW Office of the Secretary of War.

dominated the proceedings, WPC emphasized how to mobilize the economy for war and not how to equalize war burdens and eliminate war profits. Secretary of War Patrick J. Hurley, an active Legionnaire, served as WPC's chairman. WPC's staff came almost exclusively from the war department. The department's presentation of its 1930 "Industrial Mobilization Plan" and Baruch's testimony on the economics of World War I were the highlights of WPC's public hearings. After extended deliberations, WPC, with only one dissenting vote, directly endorsed the department's planning and indirectly endorsed the "Industrial Mobilization Plan."[24] WPC efforts were more impressive as an attempt to popularize and legitimize department planning than as a serious study of wartime economics.

Despite a friendly Commission, the department was unable to drum up much overt support for its plans. In addition to the department itself, the principal advocates of the planning before WPC were the American Legion and some wartime mobilization leaders like Baruch, Gifford, and Coffin.[25] The business community in general was either unconcerned about or unwilling to commit itself publicly on issues involving economic mobilization. Of the thousands of businessmen participating in the army planning, only a few came forward to testify.

Although support for department planning was weak, the opposition was vociferous. Witnesses like Norman Thomas, several congressmen, and spokesmen for some peace societies and humanitarian groups were hostile to WPC and the department's plans. Some advocates of peace detected inherent dangers in the department's work. According to their analyses, the promise of wartime riches, while not a major cause of war, was a contributing one that had to be eliminated. The army's plans would not do this. Moreover, the opponents feared that the industrial-military ties resulting from department planning could endanger the nation's future.[26] But the critics—among them a member of WPC, Representative Ross A. Collins of Mississippi—were weak on analysis. Their critique of the department's plans and planning was often nebulous, contradictory, or incomplete. Seymour Waldman, a journalist covering the hearings, articulated more clearly and precisely what appeared to alarm Collins and some witnesses before WPC:

[24] "Message from the President . . . Transmitting . . . the Final Recommendation of the Commission," *House Doc.*, 72 Cong., 1 Sess., No. 264 (Serial 9549), 2-5. See also War Policies Commission, "Documents by War Policies Commission," *House Doc.*, 72 Cong., 1 Sess., No. 271 (Serial 9549), 1-71.

[25] War Policies Commission, "Hearings," 7-72, 85-113, 121-44, 169-90, 218-21, 252-65, 288-323, 481-88, 776-90, 794-836, 854-75.

[26] *Ibid.*, 20-24, 66-71, 73-85, 93-94, 119-21, 136-40, 186-89, 258-65, 272-73, 279-80, 323-50, 380-85, 489-502, 535-687, 722-76, 850-54; Seymour Waldman, *Death and Profits: A Study of the War Policies Commission* (New York, 1932), 91, 131-34.

The hearings revealed a gigantic machine, whose intricate parts touch the entire nation, which is being constructed by the War Department and industrial magnates for use in the event of war . . . . They reveal the dangers inherent in a militarization of industry, an industrialization of the military forces, or a combination of the two. . . .

I would feel rewarded and gratified if this book should be the precursor of a much needed diagnosis of the whole problem, a study of the interlocking of our war mechanism and our economic system. . . . Such a work . . . is imperative if we are to be effective in preventing more national and international bloodshed.[27]

Opposition to the department's plans and proposed legislation for implementing them increased after WPC's hearings as the peace and isolationist movement gained in strength.[28] The most formidable challenge came from the Senate's so-called Nye Committee. In addition to the munitions makers, the Nye Committee's purview included economic mobilization for World War I, interwar military procurement policies, and the "Industrial Mobilization Plan." In a fragmentary manner, the Committee disclosed the dynamics of an emerging "industrial-military complex." The elements were presented in the Committee hearings and reports, but they were not fitted together. Senator Gerald P. Nye and his colleagues still saw only through a glass darkly.[29]

The Nye Committee clearly perceived that industrialized warfare created qualitatively new and ominous problems for the nation. To fight a modern war, even to prepare for one, eroded the barriers between private and public, civilian and military institutions. The Committee observed that during hostilities "[p]ractically every important industry in the country is necessary for the supply of the armed forces." "[E]ven in time of peace," the Committee reported, "the line of demarcation between the munitions industry and other industries is not clear and fixed."[30]

From its investigation of interwar defense spending, the Committee established that various industries depended upon military contracts for profitable operations and that the military services depended upon them for developing and producing weapons. There were many prime examples. Shipbuilding indirectly included "the steel companies, the electrical manufactur-

---

[27] Waldman, *Death and Profits*, v-vii. See also *ibid.*, 71, 147-56.
[28] File No. 049.12/175, 381/116.4b, PB ASW Office of the Secretary of War; Kreidberg and Henry, *History of Military Mobilization*, 516, 518, 529-31, 538-40; Rose M. Stein, *M-Day: The First Day of War* (New York, 1936).
[29] The Nye Committee findings, although not all of its recommendations, received the unanimous endorsement of all members.
[30] "Report on War Department Bills S.1716-S.1722 Relating to Industrial Mobilization in Wartime," *Senate Report*, 74 Cong., 2 Sess., No. 944, Part 4 (Serial 9884), 7. See also "Report of the Special Committee on Investigation of the Munitions Industry," *Senate Report*, 74 Cong., 2 Sess., No. 944, Part 3 (Serial 9983), 3.

ing groups, the boiler producers, the instrument people," and "the biggest banking interests in the Nation." Du Pont and other munitions producers were virtual adjuncts of the war department. Industrialists and military leaders regarded their interests as mutual. Industry favored and worked for increased military appropriations; the armed services granted industry special favors, encouraged monopoly where it served their interests, financed research, and, despite legislation to the contrary, displayed little concern about profit restraints.[31] Committee members were shocked to find that the war and navy departments, and even the commerce and state departments at times, cooperated with munitions firms in a manner that compromised national policies for disarmament, arms limitation, arms sales, and arms embargoes.[32] The fact that Public Works Administration funds, intended to stimulate industrial recovery, went to the armed services and that some businessmen favored defense spending as an antidote to the depression also disturbed Nye and his colleagues.[33]

The Nye Committee found a web of personal as well as contractual ties binding industrial-military elements. Retired army and navy officers often joined firms contracting with the services. Frequently, officials of corporations supplying the armed services became reserve officers. A society like the Army Ordnance Association, organized in 1919, combined in its membership actual or potential military contractors and retired and active army officers. The Association lobbied for the army, participated in the industrial mobilization planning, and attempted to influence war department policies and the selection and promotion of personnel.[34]

[31] "Preliminary Report of the Special Committee on Investigation of the Munitions Industry," *Senate Report*, 74 Cong., 1 Sess., No. 944, Part 1 (Serial 9881) 1-8, 15-343, 384-89; "Report . . . on Investigation of the Munitions Industry," No. 944, Part 3, 159-204; "Report on Government Manufacture of Munitions by the Special Committee on Investigation of the Munitions Industry," *Senate Report*, 74 Cong., 2 Sess., No. 944, Part 7 (Serial 9987), 1-13.

[32] "Report . . . on Investigation of the Munitions Industry," No. 944, Part 3, pp. 3-12, 15-17, 159-204; Wayne S. Cole, *Senator Gerald P. Nye and American Foreign Relations* (Minneapolis, 1962), 76, 79-81; John E. Wiltz, *In Search of Peace: The Senate Munitions Inquiry, 1934-36* (Baton Rouge, 1963), 81.

[33] Senate, *Hearings Before the Special Committee Investigating the Munitions Industry*, Part 37, pp. 12409-37, 12502-26, 12766; "Report . . . on Investigation of the Munitions Industry," No. 944, Part 3, pp. 204-07; Wiltz, *In Search of Peace*, 116.

[34] "Preliminary Report . . . on Investigation of the Munitions Industry," No. 944, Part 1, pp. 220-21; "Report . . . on Investigation of the Munitions Industry," No. 944, Part 3, pp. 10-11, 159-217; Senate, *Hearings Before the Special Committee Investigating the Munitions Industry*, Part 36, pp. 11972-12043; Part 37, pp. 12399-443, 12501-28, 12766. Concern existed about military contractors employing retired officers before World War I. "To Increase the Efficiency of the Military Establishment of the United States," House, *Hearings before the Committee on Military Affairs*, 64 Cong., 1 Sess., 1916, pp. 540-42, 1147-48, 1153-55; "Army Appropriations Bill, [Fiscal] 1917," House, *Hearings before the Committee on Military Affairs*, 64 Cong., 1 Sess., 1916, pp. 848-50.

The Nye Committee carefully avoided charges of conspiracy. It pointed out that plausible reasons existed for what was done and stated that it was not drawing a one-to-one correlation between expenditures for defense and the causation of war.[35] Nevertheless, argued the Committee,

any close associations between munitions and supply companies . . . and the service departments . . . , of the kind that existed in Germany before the World War, constitutes an unhealthy alliance in that it brings into being a self-interested political power which operates in the name of patriotism and satisfies interests which are, in large part, purely selfish, and that such associations are an inevitable part of militarism, and are to be avoided in peacetime at all costs.[36]

In order to check the growth of an "unhealthy alliance," a majority of the Committee favored nationalizing the munitions facilities. Congress never seriously considered the proposal. Upon the advice of the Roosevelt administration, Congress even refused to strengthen regulations governing military procurement as the Committee minority recommended.[37]

The army's economic planning for war also disturbed the Nye Committee. The planning, argued the Committee, assured that industry and the military would function more effectively as a team than they had in World War I; but, because the "Industrial Mobilization Plan" was patterned after wartime methods, it would not eliminate the "economic evils of war." According to the Committee's analysis, World War I mobilization was accompanied by "shameless profiteering" and extravagant waste. The war left a legacy of inflation, debt, and increased concentration of economic power. Similar results would occur in a future war if industry, in conjunction with the armed services, virtually regulated itself.[38]

In order to secure the nation's economic future and to remove the promise of riches as an inducement to war, the Nye Committee maintained that

[35] "Preliminary Report . . . on Investigation of the Munitions Industry," No. 944, Part 1, p. 222; "Report . . . on Investigation of the Munitions Industry," No. 944, Part 3, p. 8; Cole, *Senator Gerald P. Nye*, 95-96; Wiltz, *In Search of Peace*, 224-27.

[36] "Report . . . on Investigation of the Munitions Industry," No. 944, Part 3, p. 12.

[37] *Ibid.*, 15-17; "Preliminary Report . . . on Investigation of the Munitions Industry," No. 944, Part 1, pp. 11-14; "Report on Government Manufacture of Munitions . . . ," No. 944, Part 7, pp. 1-123; Wiltz, *In Search of Peace*, 91-98, 115-16.

[38] "Preliminary Report . . . on Investigation of the Munitions Industry," No. 944, Part 1, pp. 345-89; "Report on War Department Bills S.1716-S.1722 . . . ," 74 Cong., 2 Sess., No. 944, Part 4, p. 1-46 (direct quotations, 7, 11), 57-61; "Report on Government Manufacture of Munitions . . . ," No. 944, Part 7, pp. 3-64; "To Prevent Profiteering in War," *Senate Report*, 74 Cong., 1 Sess., No. 577 (Serial 9879), 9-20. See also Senate, *Hearings Before the Special Committee Investigating the Munitions Industry*, Parts 13, 14, 15, 16, 17, 21, 22, 24, 36, 37. The Nye Committee was less critical of World War I military procurement practices than an earlier investigation by the so-called Graham Committee. See "War Expenditures," House, *Hearings before the Select Committee on Expenditure in the War Department*, 66 Cong., 1 Sess., Vol. 3, 1921 (Serial 1), [Reports of Committee]; *ibid.*, Vol. 1, 1921 (Serial 1); *ibid.*, 1920 (Serial 3).

wartime "economic evils" had to be eliminated. That required radical changes in the economic system during hostilities, not the preservation of the status quo as proposed by the "Industrial Mobilization Plan." The profit motive and the prerogatives of private property would have to be modified. To accomplish that purpose, the Committee supported legislation drafted under the direction of John T. Flynn. In an emergency, profits would be limited to 3 percent and personal annual income to $10,000. No individual with direct or indirect interests in an industry could serve in a government capacity involving that industry. Moreover, the President would be granted vast authority over the economy to the point of conscripting capital and management if necessary.[39] Although vague at many points, the Flynn legislation amounted to a proposal for state capitalism during wartime with the industrial managers removed from the seats of power.

The war department opposed the Committee's major recommendations. It viewed with alarm any taxation proposals that threatened production. It maintained that conscripting management would not work and insisted that economic mobilization was impossible without the assistance of managers of the industries to be regulated.[40] Baruch responded to the proposed bill with undisguised hostility. Attempting to change the economic system during a war, he argued, was an invitation to disaster.[41]

In its most impressive reports, the Nye Committee curiously agreed with both the war department and Baruch. The Committee's support of the Flynn proposals ignored its own findings. Without constitutional amendments that could be "far worse than the situation of profiteering in a national emergency," the Flynn legislation could not be enforced. The Committee recognized that, even if the bill and the necessary amendments were adopted, they would probably be repealed or ignored in an emergency. The only men qualified to administer a wartime economy were industrialists themselves. It was inconceivable that they would attempt to enforce laws they considered detrimental to the economy and to the war effort.[42]

The Flynn bill was introduced into Congress in 1935. For a time, Franklin D. Roosevelt seemed disposed toward the bill. Ultimately, he joined

[39] "To Prevent Profiteering in War," No. 577, pp. 1-9, 20-35. See also Senate, *Hearings Before the Special Committee Investigating the Munitions Industry*, Part 22, pp. 6179-257. 6425-29, 6643-48, Part 24, pp. 7087-7112.

[40] Memo on conference on HR 5529, May 24, 1935, File No. 1401, PB ASW Office of the Secretary of War; Planning Branch Orientation Conference, Oct. 27, 1936, pp. 11-12, File No. 010/178.1A, *ibid.*; "IMP," 1936, pp. 99-113, File No. 120, *ibid.*

[41] Senate, *Hearings Before the Special Committee Investigating the Munitions Industry*, Part 22, pp. 6623-43. See also *ibid.*, 6259-423.

[42] "Preliminary Report on Wartime Taxation and Price Control," *Senate Report*, 74 Cong., 1 Sess., No. 944, Part 2 (Serial 9882), 1-164 (direct quotation, 3); "Report on War Department Bills S.1716-S.1722 . . . ," No. 944, Part 4, pp. 1-46.

Baruch, the war department, and, with reservations, the Legion in backing competing legislation that would have granted the President authority for mobilizing the economy, but with few safeguards against abuse. That bill would have sanctioned what the "Industrial Mobilization Plan" proposed. The administration let it be known that it, too, believed that curtailing the profit motive during a war would jeopardize any mobilization program. No legislation was passed.[43]

After the Nye Committee investigation, the nation knew more about the political economy of warfare; but short of avoiding war and excessive spending for defense, there was no viable way to prevent close and compromising relations between business and the armed services. Military spending in the American industrial system inevitably drew industrial and military elements together, and the threat of an "unhealthy alliance" was always present.

War department planning entered its final and most important phase after the Nye Committee investigation. With the approach of war and the growing American preparedness movement, the department launched a drive for the appointment of a joint industry-military board to review and ultimately to implement the "Industrial Mobilization Plan."

The proposal for a joint board originated with civilians who were concerned about a major flaw in the "Industrial Mobilization Plan." Because of a continuing distrust of civilian institutions, the army determined to dominate the wartime mobilization agencies. To insure that OASW plans were realistic and to keep the nation ready for war, Baruch and others repeatedly recommended that industrialists officially meet each year with the war department. They would review the department's plans and prepare themselves for the eventuality of official duty.[44]

The war department resisted suggestions for officially sharing its planning authority with industrialists until Louis Johnson, a past American Legion commander, became assistant secretary of war in June 1937. With in-

[43] Wiltz, *In Search of Peace*, 119-22, 131-46. For some relevant data on the administration and the Nye Committee, see OF 178, 1934-1935, OF 1672, PPF 1820, Roosevelt Papers.
[44] "Plan for Governmental Organization for War," Nov. 12, 1929, File No. 109, PB ASW Office of the Secretary of War; "IMP," 1936, pp. 14-21, 34-35, File No. 120, *ibid.*; Assistant Secretary of War and Navy to Joint Board and memo of C. T. Harris and W. S. Farber, July 19, 1934, File No. 112, *ibid.*; W. A. Buck to Harry B. Jordan, April 4, 1936, File No. 1401, *ibid.*; H. K. Rutherford at John Hancock Lecture, "Mobilization of Industry," May 27, 1938, File No. 352/109.1, *ibid.*; War Policy Commission, "Hearings," 38, 55-56, 169-90, 288-309, 481-88, 776-90, 854-56; Senate, *Hearings Before the Special Committee Investigating the Munitions Industry*, Part 22, pp. 6281-82; Thatcher, *Planning for Industrial Mobilization*, 84-91; Kreidberg and Henry, *History of Military Mobilization*, 507-08, 530.

ternational relations deteriorating, Johnson was determined to prepare both the army and the nation for war. He arranged for Baruch, some former WIB members, and younger talent to serve as an advisory board to OASW.[45] For Johnson, that was the first essential step for instituting the "Industrial Mobilization Plan." But the President refused to sanction the scheme.[46] Despite the setback, Johnson was determined to create an advisory board. He was stealthily maneuvering to achieve that end in mid-1939,[47] when Roosevelt, fearing that war was imminent and that the nation might become involved,[48] authorized Johnson to set up a mobilization advisory group called the War Resources Board (WRB). Roosevelt chose Edward R. Stettinius, Jr., of the United States Steel Corporation as chairman and left the selection of other members to the war department. With Stettinius serving as an intermediary, Johnson, Acting Secretary of the Navy Charles Edison, Army Chief of Staff George Marshall, and two senior members of OASW selected the others. In addition to Stettinius, WRB included Gifford, president of American Telephone and Telegraph; John Lee Pratt of General Motors Corporation; Robert E. Wood, chairman of Sears, Roebuck, and Company; Karl T. Compton of the Massachusetts Institute of Technology; and Harold G. Moulton, president of the Brookings Institute. The membership was cleared with the President.[49] Why Baruch was excluded is still unclear. He was described as being "sore as hell" about being passed over.[50] WRB did not get his blessing until his close associate, John Hancock, was appointed to it in September. Hancock played a prominent role in WRB proceedings.

Assistant Secretary of War Johnson announced to the nation that WRB would review the "Industrial Mobilization Plan" of 1939, revise it if neces-

---

[45] Louis Johnson to Baruch, Sept. 19, 1937, File No. 381/116.4b, PB ASW Office of the Secretary of War; War Department, *Report of the Secretary of War to the President, 1937* (Washington, 1937), 21-25; War Department, *Report of the Secretary . . . 1938*, pp. 19-25; War Department, *Report of the Secretary of War to the President, 1939* (Washington, 1939), 15-20.

[46] Roosevelt to Johnson in Johnson to Roosevelt, Oct. 23, 1937, OF 813, Roosevelt Papers.

[47] Johnson to Roosevelt, Aug. 9, 1939, OF 25, *ibid.*; Charles Hines to John Hancock, July 1, Aug. 11, 1939, Hancock to Hines, July 7, 1939, File No. MB-223-23.1, Records of the Joint Army and Navy Boards and Committees, RG 225 (National Archives); Johnson to Crowell, Aug. 9, 1939, File No. 011/27c, Records of the War Production Board.

[48] Charles W. Wiltse to James W. Fesler, July 19, 1946, File No. 011.2, Records of the War Production Board; "Industrial Mobilization Plan," Senate, *Hearings Before the Special Committee Investigating the National Defense Program*, 80 Cong., 1 Sess., 1948, Part 42, pp. 25662-69.

[49] War Resources Board (WRB) Minutes, Aug. 17, 1939, pp. 1-2, File No. 011.25, Records of the War Production Board; Wiltse to Fesler, July 19, 1946, File No. 011/2, *ibid.*

[50] Memo. Re: "War Industries [sic] Board," undated, PPF 702, Roosevelt Papers.

sary, and implement it in an emergency.[51] Key to the plan was the War Resources Administration, organized along commodity committee-war service committee lines with military representatives integrated into it. Unlike earlier plans, the 1939 edition moderated proposed military influence in the civilian agencies.[52]

Working hand in hand with the armed services, WRB, while still reviewing the "Industrial Mobilization Plan," began preparing to institute it. In sharp contrast to its attitude toward WPC, the business community was eager to cooperate with WRB. The National Association of Manufacturers and the United States Chamber of Commerce rushed forward to volunteer their services. Through conferences with these organizations, former WIB members, the commerce department, and other private and public sources, WRB drew up an industrial who's who to staff the War Resources Administration and also made provisions for the use of war service committees.[53] The most daring move was a memorandum drafted for the President's signature that would have granted the WRB and the Army-Navy Munitions Board authority to mobilize the economy and that instructed all government agencies to cooperate with those two boards.[54]

Roosevelt suddenly cut the ground from under WRB shortly after its creation because the war scare had waned and because of widespread opposition within the administration and the nation to it. Liberal Democrats were aghast at the dominant position held by the major banking and industrial interests in WRB. They identified Stettinius, Gifford, and Pratt with J. P. Morgan. The anti-Morgan banking elements on Wall Street who were sympathetic to the administration were bitterly disappointed. Labor and agriculture were irate over their exclusion.[55]

[51] Joint Release, war and navy departments, Aug. 17, 1939, WRB Minutes, File No. 011.25, Records of the War Production Board.
[52] "IMP," 1939, File No. 334/117.3, PB ASW Office of the Secretary of War.
[53] WRB Minutes, Aug. 17, 1939, p. 2, Aug. 23-25, 1939, pp. 1, 3-4, Aug. 29-31, 1939, pp. 1-3, Sept. 9, '1939, pp. 1-2, Sept. 13-14, 1939, pp. 1-4, File No. 011.25, Records of the War Production Board; Memo of A. B. Anderson, Sept. 1, 1939, ibid.; Rutherford to Edward R. Stettinius, Jr., Sept. 4, 1939, ibid.; Wiltse to Fesler, July 19, 1939, File No. 011.2, ibid. For the fourteen-page list of the names of individuals selected to staff the mobilization agencies, see File No. 011.27c, ibid.
[54] WRB Minutes, Sept. 6, 1939, p. 1, File No. 011.25, Records of the War Production Board. Memo, acting secretary of war and navy to President, Sept. 6, 1939; "Memorandum for Departments and Executive Agencies, Federal Government," from the President, File No. 334/117.3, PB ASW Office of the Secretary of War. These documents were never sent out.
[55] WRB Minutes, Aug. 29-31, 1939, pp. 1-2, Sept. 13-14, 1939, p. 3, File No. 001.25, Records of the War Production Board; Memo. Re: "War Industries [sic] Board," PPF 702, Roosevelt Papers. See also OF 3759, 1939, PPF 5344, PPF 702-H, OF 200XXX, Roosevelt Papers; File No. 011.25, File No. 011.27c, Records of the War Production

The President waited until WRB had completed reviewing the "Industrial Mobilization Plan" and had submitted a final report in November 1939 before dismissing it. In its final report, WRB indirectly endorsed the war department plan and fully accepted its basic assumptions. A wartime economy should be regulated by federal agencies largely controlled by industry and the military services. In circumscribed terms, WRB recommended the suspension of the antitrust laws and also suggested that domestic reform would be a casualty of a mobilized economy. It further proposed that the Army-Navy Munitions Board, through consultation with industry, continue to explore the yet unresolved issues of industrial mobilization. It concluded by offering its advisory services for the future.[56] Roosevelt thanked WRB members and never called on them again.[57]

WRB's fate did not negate the years of planning. Because of this planning, the war department adjusted to emergency conditions during World War II with relative ease. In the late 1930s the department began a gradual transition from planning for, to participating in, a mobilization program. Starting in 1937-1938, Congress, after years of departmental advocacy, authorized educational orders and the stockpiling of essential and strategic raw materials and slowly modified peacetime restraints on military contracting.[58] As the army and military budgets grew, OASW expanded its

---

Board. See also Harold L. Ickes, *The Secret Diary of Harold L. Ickes* (3 vols., New York, 1953-1954), II, 710, 716-20; Albert A. Blum, "Birth and Death of the M-Day Plan," Harold Stein, ed., *American Civil-Military Decisions: A Book of Case Studies* (University, Ala., 1963), 61-96; Eliot Janeway, *The Struggle for Survival: A Chronicle of Economic Mobilization in World War II* (New Haven, 1951), 47-71.

[56] "Report of the War Resources Board," Oct. 13, 1939, File No. 334.117.3, PB ASW Office of the Secretary of War. The Army-Navy Munitions Board (ANMB) was reorganized and strengthened in 1931-1932, and the "IMP" was published by ANMB even though OASW continued to do most of the work.

[57] President to Stettinius and others, Nov. 24, 1939, File No. 370.26/110.B, *ibid.*

[58] Educational orders were intended to help industry and the army through the transitional phase from planning to mobilizing for war. Without the restrictions of competitive bidding, the army could award contracts to selected firms for the limited production of various munitions items. In that way, industry accumulated the tools and worked out the techniques for quantity production and the army tested its munitions designs and procurement plans. Educational orders were first introduced before World War I at the instigation of businessmen and public officials striving to prepare the nation for hostilities. For years after the war, Congress rejected bills authorizing educational orders. Before such legislation was passed in the late 1930s, however, the army interpreted the laws and regulations governing procurement in a way that allowed it to grant some educational orders to selected firms. During the 1930s, the businessmen in the Army Ordnance Association launched a drive for educational orders to help stimulate industrial recovery. See "Investigation of the War Department," Senate, *Hearings Before the Committee on Military Affairs*, 65 Cong., 2 Sess., 1917-1918, pp. 2268-71; War Department, *Report of the Secretary* . . . *1927*, pp. 36-38; War Department, *Report of the Secretary* . . . *1928*, p. 57; War Department, *Report of the Secretary* . . . *1929*, pp. 47-49, 53-65; War Department, *Report of the Secretary* . . . *1932*, pp. 32-34; War Department, *Report of the Secretary* . . . *1935*, pp. 34-35; War Department, *Report of the Secretary of War* . . .

staff and activities proportionately until the mobilization stage was reached in 1940-1941. Writing in mid-1940, Assistant Secretary of War Johnson observed: "Without the benefit of plans perfected by 20 years of study the successful and timely execution of this [expanded munitions] program would have been virtually impossible."[59]

When the war department began the transition to mobilization in 1937-1938, it also launched the drive for implementing the "Industrial Mobilization Plan"; it had been convinced by the years of planning that civilian mobilization agencies were essential for fulfilling the military mission. During 1940-1941, the Army-Navy Munitions Board played a more active role in mobilizing the economy than the army plans had envisaged. But that was the case principally because the civilian agencies were weak. After WRB's demise, the Roosevelt administration relied upon the resuscitated NDAC and other agencies that were totally inadequate for mobilization. War department officials were in the vanguard of those working for more effective civilian agencies until the creation in early 1942 of the War Production Board.

Throughout the years 1940-1941, the war department, and the navy department as well, sided with industry on most major policies involving economic mobilization. After war was declared, the nation's largest corporations and the armed forces ultimately dominated the War Production Board through an alliance of mutual interests.[60] Though officially rejected in 1939, the principal proposals concurred in by WRB and the military were adopted during World War II. As foreseen by the Nye Committee and others, relations between the business community and the armed services during World War I and the interwar period prepared the way for the full-blown "industrial-military complex" of World War II and the Cold War years.

1938, pp. 21-25; War Department, *Report of the Secretary . . . 1939*, pp. 15-22; War Department, *Report of the Secretary of War to the President, 1940* (Washington, 1940), 1-10; War Department, *Report of the Secretary of War to the President, 1941* (Washington, 1941), 21-46; Senate, *Hearings Before the Special Committee Investigating the Munitions Industry*, Part 37, pp. 12409-37, 12502-26, 12766; "Report . . . on Investigation of the Munitions Industry," No. 944, Part 3, pp. 204-07. See also R. Elberton Smith, *The Army and Economic Mobilization* (Washington, 1959), 61-65; Irvin Brinton Holley, Jr., *Buying Aircraft: Matériel Procurement for the Army Air Forces* (Washington, 1964), 6-193, Edwin H. Rutkowski, *The Politics of Military Aviation Procurement, 1926-1934: A Study in the Political Assertion of Consensual Values* (Columbus, 1966).
[59] War Department, *Report of the Secretary . . . 1940*, p. 10.
[60] Economic mobilization for World War II is treated extensively in Koistinen, "Hammer and the Sword," 553-831.

Young, Swope and General Electric's 'New Capitalism':

A Study in Corporate Liberalism, 1920-33

By KIM MCQUAID

ABSTRACT. During the decade following World War I, a *"New Capitalism"* impulse enjoyed strong support on the U.S. corporate scene. Most *businessmen* merely propagandized. But others—among them the leaders of the *General Electric Company* figured prominently—attempted ambitious *programs of employee "welfare work," company unionism,* and *industrial "self regulation"* under federal auspices. In an era when conservative instincts dominated *labor, government,* and *academic councils,* such corporate initiatives conditioned public debate. But businessmen, too, were faced with problems of comprehending how to "cooperate" with governmental and labor *agencies* in a *"private enterprise" system.* This discussion of the genesis, rationale, and limitations of G.E.'s New Capitalist approach clarifies the patterns-of-power and perception formulated before the onset of the Great Depression forced expanded corporate definitions of capitalist normalcy.

DURING THE PAST DECADE, Neo-Marxist and liberal scholars have formulated markedly different analyses of the historical equations between American business and social reform. In the Neo-Marxist schema, U.S. corporate leaders appear as gray eminences who have consistently and effectively controlled the wellsprings of Twentieth Century political and economic life. To mainstream commentators, on the other hand, the "anti-business" aspects of American reform serve to define the very concept of liberalism itself. The nation's industrial and financial elites often assume the characteristics of frustrated Babbitts mouthing the slogans of the Gilded Age (1).

In the following essay, an attempt is made to delineate the interplay of personality and program among America's industrial elite; measure the effect of corporate interests upon governmental policy; and gauge the extent to which liberalism has remained independent of entrepeneurial-managerial control. Its focus is the leadership of one large corporation prominently mentioned in the Neo-Marxist critique of American reform.

I

DURING THE FIRST TWO DECADES of its corporate existence, the General Electric Company, founded under House of Morgan auspices in 1892, was administered along absolutist lines sanctified by Gilded Age prece-

American Journal of Economics and Sociology, Vol. 36, No. 3 (July, 1977).

dent.   Charles A. Coffin, G.E.'s first chairman, issued occasional mollifying statements regarding "pure and simple" trades unionism in elite Progressive Era business associations like the National Civic Federation.   But diplomatic utterance did not often extend into the realm of practical tolerance.   Unions might be acceptable in decentralized industries like construction, coal, and clothing manufacturing.   But organized labor fared well at none of G.E.'s plants. After 1906, the corporation instituted a series of piecemeal "welfare work" programs in some of its factories.   Health, safety, and industrial education standards were improved.   Some service pensions were presented to particularly loyal personnel.   But workers were allowed no significant participation in the creation or administration of such programs.   No well-considered approach existed for dealing with the employees' collective concerns (2).

In 1911, however, the situation began to change.   Thirty union locals in Schenectady, New York, focal point of G.E.'s production empire, formed an "Electrical Industry Trades Alliance" and began to organize the corporation's skilled employees.   Three years later, the American Federation of Labor cautiously took the E.I.T.A. under its wing.   The onset of war in Europe led to a rash of highly profitable war orders, labor scarcity, and a heightening of worker demands. G.E.'s directors tried to guarantee uninterrupted production by ameliorating grievances sufficiently to avoid rapid labor turnover and strikes (3).

Following the entrance of the United States into the world conflict, the federal government embarked upon an unprecedented effort to arbitrate worsening employer/employee relations.   "Czar" Bernard Baruch of the War Industries Board sponsored trade associations and apportioned contracts and materiél.   A companion organization, the War Labor Board, was created to protect worker interests.   By early 1918, the W.L.B. was pressuring strategic employers—G.E. included— to institute collective bargaining through the medium of firm-specific "works councils."   Despite the resistance of anti-union employers, the War Labor Board enforced significant measures of compliance (4).

The Armistice all-too-speedily brought an end to the existence of Wilsonian industrial and labor mediation agencies.   But G.E.'s problems were not thereby relieved.   Labor unrest continued at important corporate facilities in Lynn and Pittsfield, Massachusetts, Erie, Pennsylvania, and Schenectady.   The activities were part of a wave of post-war strikes aimed at preserving wage gains or forcing union recognition (5). Uncertain how to proceed, G.E.'s governing directorate, acting on the advice of their legal counsel, Owen D. Young, sponsored an ambitious investigation of industrial relations within the company.

The report they obtained alerted G.E.'s leaders to the magnitude of the problems they faced. After noting the growth of syndicalist and socialist ideas among corporation employees, the report concluded that a well organized labor relations policy must be created. As a necessary first step in forwarding the work, G.E. administrators must learn to cooperate with freely-elected employee representatives to reformulate work rules and employment practices. In order to ensure that the large majority of quiescent and conservative workers would never be dominated by numerically small "Red" elements, local leaders of the A. F. of L. should occupy a prominent place in labor/management relations (6).

After this confidential report circulated, Coffin and his aides engaged in a slow and fitful process of administrative evolution during the five years from 1919 to 1924. G.E.'s post-war labor relations approach, while "enlightened" by contemporary business standards, did not envision the creation of independent agencies to preserve employee interests. Shop committees were created for the express purpose of settling disputes *within* the firm. Managers were willing to explain their actions to workers and provide appeal from the decisions of foremen and lower level administrators. But they did not thereby intend to diminish the range of their own powers and perquisites (7).

New men, however, were needed to carry through these conservative innovations. Most high G.E. administrators were in no mood to countenance "experiments." C. A. Coffin, then almost eighty, selected a more diplomatic manager to fulfill these changed corporate requirements: Owen D. Young.

II

YOUNG, A FARM BOY from upstate New York, was a relative new-comer to the G.E. organization. Born in modest circumstances in 1874, he had attended a local college, then gone on to receive a law degree from Boston University in 1896. During his first decade of legal practice, Young came in contact with the directors of many fast growing public utilities and electrical manufacturing companies, G.E. among them. Young liked what he saw. More importantly, G.E. leaders marked him as a man to watch. In 1912, Young was recruited to head G.E.'s legal department and given the title of "Vice President in Charge of Policy." Finally, in May of 1922, Young became Chairman of the Board (8). Lawyer Young possessed no flair for technical decision-making. Financial and public relations were his elements. An "expediter," Young's task in life seemed not so much to make decisions as to help others to do so. Understanding his ignorance of production, Young helped select a company president to supervise manufacturing, research, and marketing aspects of the firm's operations: Gerard Swope, another late-comer to G.E.'s organization.

Unlike Young, Swope began life in relatively affluent surroundings. Eldest son of a German-Jewish watch case manufacturer in St. Louis, Swope early evinced a penchant for basement tinkering. After attending the Massachusetts Institute of Technology from 1891 to 1895, Swope went to Chicago to become a laborer in the machine shops of the Western Electric Company. Straitened family circumstances initially left Swope little time for consideration of any human problems other than his own. But after "some little time" in Chicago, Swope was asked to teach night classes in algebra and electricity at Jane Addams' Hull House. Once acclimatized, Swope took up residence at the settlement and was thoroughly exposed to the massive problems of poverty and corruption incident in depression-ridden *fin de siecle* America. Swope's Hull House years never made him a reformer. But he did form lasting personal attachments to settlement personnel, particularly fellow-resident Mary Hill, who became Swope's wife in 1901.

The fifteen years following Swope's departure from Hull House in 1899 saw him rise steadily through the managerial hierarchy at Western Electric. G.E. was soon out to hire him away from their competitors. In 1918, they finally succeeded, installing Swope as president of G.E.'s international sales subsidiary. Shortly thereafter, Swope's combination of Prussian efficiency and merchandising know-how made him a logical candidate for president of the parent corporation.

The Young/Swope style emphasized corporation public and social relations. Young quickly assumed a high profile on the post-war business and political scene, most notably in President Woodrow Wilson's abortive "National Industrial Conferences" of 1919 and 1920. During his tenure as an alternate to the first conference and employer representative at the second, Young emerged as a spokesman for a policy of labor conciliation. No advocate of militant unionism, Young argued that capitalists must provide alternate avenues of worker/ management cooperation if they wished to avoid strikes and radical agitations. The War Labor Board had, for the first time in American history, actively guaranteed labor's right to industrial representation of some kind. Rather than ignoring this fact, employers must modify their opposition to collective bargaining, set up "company unions," and, thus, provide a necessary escape valve for industrial discontent (9).

Slowly, such viewpoints had an effect. A severe post-war strike wave led more and more businessmen to see the logic of company unionism. By 1927, approximately 430 firms had non-union works council plans which covered almost 1.5 million workers. Second generation managers of the nation's largest corporations proved less inclined than their predecessors had been to comprehend employees as a collection of atomized individuals. "Labor" was defined in a collective fashion: becoming a phenomenon of mass psychology to be analyzed or a factor of production to be efficiently administered by the group-conscious behavior of managerial capitalists (10). At large firms like Eastman-Kodak, National Cash Register, Standard Oil of New Jersey, U.S. Rubber, and General Electric, the fledgling vocabularies of "human engineering" and industrial psychology began to replace Social Darwinian usages (11).

At G.E., works councils were followed by life insurance and pension programs. Workers were allowed to buy company stock at preferred rates. Company-guaranteed mortgages enabled higher-paid personnel to obtain homes. The firm agreed to match funds that workers contributed to an employee relief and loan society. And, finally, abortive attempts were made to set up an unemployment insurance plan acceptable to both managers and employees (12). Relatively stable employment and wage levels and the demonstrated unwillingness of the crafts-dominated A.F. of L. to essay serious organizing drives in the mass production industries led large numbers of workers to acquiesce in—or actively support—these managerial welfare policies (13).

III

IN NEW POST-WAR CIRCUMSTANCES, ideals were increasingly replaced by interests. The bloody futilities of world conflict weakened the ranks of labor, religious, radical, and reform organizations and allowed businessmen to assume an increased ascendancy in the political affairs and ideological opinion molding of the nation. To many ambitious commentators, a hardheaded "New Capitalism" seemed emergent through the "enlightened selfishness" of an entrepeneurial elite. The venality of Harding-era Normalcy and widespread fears of national contamination by Old World revolutionary movements further undermined Progressive Era liberal trends. Businessmen, in contrast, depicted a reassuring era of boundless economic opportunity through mass production, invention, and industrial "self regulation" under governmental auspices.

Owen D. Young figured prominently among the spokesmen for the New Capitalist era. He maintained working contacts with a wide spectrum of influential government, financial, and business leaders, balancing political loyalties with a sure sense of the necessary and the expedient. Though a registered Democrat all his life, Young's relations with Republican party leaders were amicable. Secretary of Commerce Herbert C. Hoover was an especial favorite. Young's and Hoover's views on economic requirements were often similar. Both opposed any efforts to impede U.S. commercial expansion in world markets. Neither desired a draconian approach in the settlement of war debts and reparations, Young going so far as to regret the very existence of such impediments to world trade. A trusted Coolidge-era advisor on international banking questions, Young several times acted as an unofficial U.S. representative at European reparations conferences. The Dawes Plan of 1924 and the Young Plan of 1929 were the main results of these endeavors. But American unwillingness to countenance cancellation or drastic reduction of war-related debts hampered Young's efforts. Public opinon remained confused or apathetic. Contractural tinkering was substituted for necessary popular clarification of the political and economic issues involved (14).

In the midst of these activities, Young also retained close connection with opposition party opinionmakers. Smarting from many years in the presidential wilderness, Democratic stalwarts sought legitimization in the eyes of a powerful business community and wealthy contributors like Young, Bernard Baruch, Jesse Jones, and John W. Davis to fill campaign coffers. Among those who solicited Young's influence were ambitious New York State politicians Al Smith and Franklin Delano Roosevelt. By 1926, Young was firmly enough established in F.D.R.'s political estimation that Eleanor Roosevelt publicly announced a preference for G.E.'s chairman over liberal Robert F. Wagner in that year's U.S. senatorial primaries (15).

Swope's political relations also reached to influential levels. Gerard's brother, Herbert Bayard Swope, was a crack reporter for the liberal *New York World* and a prominent partisan of Al Smith. Using Herbert's good offices, Swope made his opinions known to the New York Democratic party. Though extremely close-mouthed about his political life, Swope stated on at least one occasion that Al Smith had used himself, Robert Moses, and Belle Moskowitz as advisors on many important occasions (16).

By the mid-1920s, the new corporate style of G.E.'s leaders was reaping rich dividends. Liberal businessmen Edward A. Filene and Henry S. Dennison and former Muckrakers Ida M. Tarbell and Lincoln Steffens saw Young as a New Capitalist of the first order. Conservative businessmen generally agreed with such gracious estimations. The *New York Times* suggested Young as a Democratic presidential nominee. All the while, G.E. plants, assets, profits, and dividends expanded. Occasional anti-trust suits were brushed aside or avoided by corporate divestiture of affected properties (17).

As G.E.'s fortunes rose, Young sought to elaborate his version of a New Capitalist ethic, most notably in an address at Harvard University in 1927. Young envisioned a steadily expanding domestic and international economy whose rewards would gradually become more equitably distributed. As members of the middle and "responsible" laboring classes bought into the business system through stock purchases, their desires for stability would spur the growth of a "new management" free of buccaneering proclivities. Through a growing voluntaristic network of industrial trade associations fostered by Secretary of Commerce Hoover, a true "Government of Business" was fulfilling the ideal of providing the masses with adequate opportunity (18). In line with such a trickle-down approach to social change, Young and Swope made G.E. a pace-setter in the "self regulation" drive in the public utilities industry (19).

In 1927, few prominent political or business leaders gainsaid such ideals or actions. But even as Young spoke, the New Capitalist economic system was crumbling. The half-enunciated Manchester Liberalism which underlay Young's thinking became increasingly ineffective. More international cartels did not necessarily result in closer

political or social understanding. Underdeveloped regions continued
to suffer the imperialistic corollaries of "free trade" (20). On the
domestic scene, efficiency-oriented "human engineering" approaches
were also faltering. Doctrines of high wages and shorter hours supposedly popularized by entrepeneurs like Henry Ford did not gain
more than a verbal application in many industrial quarters. Industrial "self government" likewise proved abortive, as dominant enter-
prisers in oligopolistic or capital intensive industries proved unable to
transcend industry or firm-specific matrices. Developments at G.E.
signalled the need for elaborated welfare capitalist strategies. A 1921
employee stock purchase plan foundered when workers sold their shares
to obtain capital gains. The scheme was patched up by creating a
securities corporation which held stock in trust for worker-owners.
But, plainly, laborers were not going to automatically evolve into
stockholding capitalists. Subsequent frustrating attempts at instituting an unemployment insurance plan demonstrated failures of communication and concept among both administrators and employees.
Further guarantees of effective worker self-regulation and good behavior seemed necessary, and Swope investigated trades unionism as
an organizational tool to achieve this end.

IV

IN 1926, SWOPE CONTACTED A.F. of L. president William Green. At
a subsequent meeting, Swope told Green that he could expect covert
support from G.E. if the A.F. of L. attempted to create a *single* union
in the electrical industry. Green, a lackluster conservative, evinced
no interest in the proposal. But Swope kept investigating the possibilities of organizing G.E. workers on industrial lines. G.E., he stated,
had "no objection to a trade union if (it) could have one trade union.
But the company simply could not deal with twenty different crafts
unions and have jurisdictional disputes between them." Impressed
by Swope's arguments, New York's Governor Roosevelt advised state
labor leaders to institute industrial union drives—without discernable
result. Swope continued to devote attention to settlement and public
health work. But his efforts at collaboration with the organized labor
movement ground to a temporary halt (21).

The awakening to the failures of New Capitalism was neither expected nor pleasant. Tariff walls rose as world trade and stock markets plummeted. For three frustrating years, powerful corporate

leaders like Young and Swope labored to halt the slide into fearsome depression. Long an advocate of holding companies, Young served as mediator in ultimately abortive negotiations between New York bankers and the tottering Insull utilities empire. He attended meetings of *ad hoc* "committees on industrial cooperation" staffed by capitalists like Walter C. Teagle (Standard Oil of New Jersey), Alfred P. Sloan (General Motors), Henry I. Harriman (U.S. Chamber of Commerce), and William Green and Matthew Woll of the A.F. of L.

To banking and political friends Melvin Traylor and Jouett Shouse, Young argued for lower tariffs to relieve the agricultural depression which was a basic cause of the worsening economic situation. Unless economic isolationsm was halted, he affirmed, the U.S. would "retain the surpluses that we might otherwise market to the world and which, so long as they stay with us, destroy our own prosperity." Until the severe banking crisis of early 1933, Young arranged numerous covert salvage operations of bankrupt financial institutions, including a "Federation Bank" set up by A.F. of L. unions in New York City.

By mid-1932, however, Young knew that business alone was incapable of dealing with massive economic dislocations. In a well-publicized address at Notre Dame University, Young called for government leadership in stabilizing the banking system, restoring agricultural buying power, and underwriting enhanced social welfare measures. A highly technological society, he concluded, was too complex to be allowed to "bottom out" in a manner foreseen by the large majority of contemporary economists (22).

Such opinions drew an enthusiastic audience among what the *Nation* termed "the usual quota of dilettante liberals" ready to discover messianic traits in big business leaders. Young's careful strictures of contemporary capitalism offered to many a conscientious "moderate" alternative. Early in 1931, journals like *Fortune, Collier's, The Review of Reviews* and the *New York Times* launched another unsolicited Young-for-President boom that gained substantial support among Southern Democratic party spokesmen. Young, however, expressed no desire for public office and became one of a small group of business advisors attached to Franklin Delano Roosevelt's campaign organization (23).

Young's cooperative relations with Roosevelt did not, however, long outlast the election of 1932. In May of 1933, Young's name was included on a sensational list of "favored subscribers" obtained from the offices of J. P. Morgan Company by a Senate committee investigating lawbreaking among prominent New York financiers. One month later, Young was warning of the dangers of New Deal "collectivism." The bribery scandal soon blew over, not least because influential Democrats like Secretary of the Treasury William Woodin and Senator William G. McAdoo were involved. But Young's heretofore enviable reputation had received a severe public buffetting.

Throughout the following five years, Young maintained an increasingly icy neutrality towards the New Deal. Government, he concluded, must set minimum economic and accountancy standards and then allow business to govern itself. Opposed to regulatory commissions like the Securities and Exchange Commission and large public works projects like the Tennessee Valley Authority, Young feared that "Franklin" was creating class consciousness and prejudice in America by singling out business for draconian treatment. "Readjustments" were necessary. But government should not "guarantee economic security in any substantial measure to the individual." All people, Young believed, *could* succeed as he and his group themselves had. The fact that most did not, convinced him that the vast majority of human-kind valued "comfort above progress" (24). Therefore, government interference with the affairs of the talented minority of industrial leaders threatened economic and social stagnation: the death of the American Dream (25).

Lake Erie College
Painesville, O. 44077

1. New Left historiographical opinion is well represented in William Appleman Williams, *The Contours of American History* (Chicago: Quadrangle, 1966), pp. 345–488; Gabriel Kolko, *The Triumph of Conservatism* (Chicago: Quadrangle, 1963); James Weinstein, *The Corporate Ideal in the Liberal State* (Boston: Beacon Press, 1968); Barton J. Bernstein, ed., *Towards a New Past* (New York: Knopf, 1969), pp. 263–88; Ronald Radosh and M. N. Rothbard, *A New History of Leviathan* (New York: Dutton, 1972), pp. 111–88. Major liberal works are: Arthur M. Schlesinger Jr., *The Age of Roosevelt* (Boston: Houghton-Miflin, 1957–1960) 3 vols.; James MacGregor Burns, *Roosevelt, the Lion and the Fox* (New York: Harcourt-Brace, 1956); William E. Leuchtenburg, *Franklin D. Roosevelt and the New Deal* (New York: Harper, 1963).

2. Charles M. Ripley, *Life in a Large Manufacturing Plant* (Schenectady, N.Y.: General Electric, 1919), *passim*.

3. H. A. Millis, *et al.*, *How Collective Bargaining Works* (New York: Twentieth Century Fund, 1942), pp. 744–50.

4. Henry F. Pringle, *The Life and Times of William Howard Taft* (New York: 1939), Vol. 2, pp. 915–19; Henry Pelling, *American Labor* (Chicago: Univ. of Chicago Press, 1960), pp. 134–35.

5. Millis, *et al.*, *op. cit.*, pp. 744ff.

6. (Anonymous), "General Electric Industrial Relations," bound typescript

circa: 1919, pp. 4–5, 47, Owen D. Young Collection, Van Hornesville, New York (hereafter designated ODYC); Ida M. Tarbell, *Owen D. Young: A New Type of Industrial Leader* (New York: Scribner's 1932), pp. 125–26. (Mr. and Mrs. Everett Case of Van Hornesville, New York are currently at work on a new biography of Owen D. Young. My own efforts were greatly aided by their kind cooperation.)

7. Owen D. Young to W. W. Trench, 10/22/1920, ODYC; R. H. Rice to E. W. Rice, 5/16/1920, ODYC; C. M. Ripley to Young, 10/28/1920, ODYC; Young to W. H. Johnson, 1/4/1922, ODYC; "General Electric Industrial Relations" (bound typescript circa: 1919), pp. 2; Cyrus S. Ching, *Review and Reflection* (New York: Forbes, 1953), pp. 28–29.

8. Tarbell, *op. cit.*, pp. 89*ff*; (Anonymous), "Life of Owen D. Young," *Fortune*, 3 (January, February, and March, 1931), pp. 95–98 (January) and 46–48 (February).

9. Gerard Swope, "Oral History Memoir" at Columbia University, Oral History Project Archives, New York City (bound typescript), pp. 1–35; David Loth, *Swope of G.E.* (New York: Simon and Schuster, 1958), pp. 1–39; David Lawrence, "Owen D. Young Speaks His Mind," *Review of Reviews*, 82 (August, 1930), p. 129; Haggai Hurvitz, "The Meaning of Industrial Conflict in Some Ideologies of the Early 1920's: The A.F.L., Organized Employers, and Herbert Hoover," (unpublished Ph.D. thesis, Columbia University, 1971), pp. 31–33.

10. Robert W. Dunn, *The Americanization of Labor* (New York: International Publishers, 1927), p. 129; Irving Bernstein, *The Lean Years: A History of the American Worker, 1920–1933* (Baltimore: Penguin Books, 1966), pp. 144–89; Hurvitz, *op. cit., passim.*

11. J. T. Broderick, *40 Years With General Electric* (Albany, N.Y.: 1929), pp. 134–44; Charles A. Coffin, "Employer-Employee Counsel in Industry," *Electrical World*, May 24, 1924, pp. 1082–83.

12. Gerard Swope, "Management Cooperation with Workers for Economic Welfare," *Annals of the American Academy of Political and Social Science*, 154 (March, 1931), pp. 131–35; S. Northrup, *Boulwarism* (Ann Arbor: Univ. of Michigan Press, 1964), pp. 11–12.

13. Welfare capitalist approaches are covered in: D. Lescohier and E. Brandeis, *History of Labor in the United States* (New York: Macmillan, 1935) Vol. 3; David Brody, "The Rise and Decline of Welfare Capitalism," in John Braeman, *et al., Change and Continuity in Twentieth Century America: The 1920's* (Columbus: Ohio Univ. Press, 1968), pp. 147–78.

14. F. W. Stearns to Young, 3/25/1919; Young to F. W. Stearns, 10/18/1920; Young to Calvin Coolidge, 3/5/1925, Box 7, ODYC. (Young advised Herbert Hoover on personal investment policies, supported Hoover's presidential ambitions in 1920 and 1928 and dispatched high G. E. administrators to assist in the postwar reorganization of the Department of Commerce); Joan Hoff Wilson, *American Business and Foreign Policy, 1920–1933* (Lexington, University Press of Kentucky, 1971), pp. 123–56; B.S. Beach to Young, 3/25/1921; H. Hoover to Young, 3/23/1920; Young to Hoover, 1/5/1926; Young to C. F. Smith, 5/8/1920, Box 9, ODYC.

15. Kenneth Davis, *F.D.R.: The Beckoning of Destiny* (New York, 1972), pp. 629, 689, 801, 833.

16. Harold Ickes, *The Secret Diaries of Harold Ickes* (New York: Simon and Schuster, 1954), 3 vols., Vol. 1, pp. 690; Young to Hoover, 8/10/1928, Box 9, ODYC; H. B. Swope Jr. to author, 12/6/1973.

17. Tarbell, *op. cit.*, pp. 208–209; Lincoln Steffens, *The Autobiography of Lincoln Steffens* (New York: Literary Guild, 1931), pp. 851*ff*.; E. A. Filene to Young, 7/3/1922, Box 300, ODYC; *New York Times*, August 9, 1929, p. 2.

18. Owen D. Young, "Dedication Address," *Harvard Business Review*, July, 1927, pp. 390–92; Tarbell, *op. cit.*, pp. 267–68; R. G. McCloskey, *American Conservatism in the Age of Enterprise, 1865–1910* (Cambridge: Harvard Univ. Press, 1951), pp. 173–74.

19. Loth, *op. cit.*, pp. 163–64.

20. Owen D. Young, "The Future of International Trade," *Queen's Quarterly*, 41 (Spring, 1934), pp. 21–22.

21. Loth, *op. cit.*, pp. 162–72; Frances Perkins, *The Roosevelt I Knew* (New York: Viking Press, 1946), p. 309; Gerard Swope, "The Engineer's Place in Society," *Survey*, Vol. 51, pp. 635–36; M. K. Simkovitch, *Neighborhood: The Story of Greenwich House* (New York: 1938), p. 224; *New York Times*, October 29, 1955, p. 19. (Mrs. Gerard Swope joined her husband in his social settlement work. And, late in the 1930s, she became a prominent member of the pacifist Women's International League for Peace and Freedom.)

22. Forrest Macdonald, *Insull* (Chicago: Univ. of Chicago Press, 1962), pp. 299–300; Young to Samuel Insull, 10/30/1927, Box 14, ODYC; Young to Melvin Traylor, 5/6/1930, ODYC; O. P. White, "Doubts of Owen D. Young," *Collier's*, July 9, 1932, p. 42. (For Young's attendance at "industrial cooperation" conferences, see letters in Box 200, ODYC. For the salvage of the A.F.L.-backed "Federation Bank," in which Young helped raise over $1 million in donations from firms like I.B.M., Standard Oil of N.J., General Motors, American Radiator, American Locomotive, Chrysler, General Foods, Westinghouse, and DuPont, see Box 49, ODYC—folders no. 5–18; For Young's growing disenchantment with "brains of the industry" consultations, see Young to Bruce Barton, 11/25/1932, Box 19, ODYC.)

23. P. Y. Anderson, "Young for President?", *Nation*, February 25, 1931, p. 207; *Literary Digest*, March 7, 1931, p. 12; Tarbell, *op. cit., passim.;* Charles Merz, "If Owen D. Young Were Nominated," *Harper's*, August, 1931 pp. 275–83; F.D.R. to Young, 8/30/1932, Young to F.D.R., 7/28/1939, Box 27, ODYC; Raymond Moley, *After Seven Years* (New York: Harper's, 1939), pp. 45–46, 111–113; "Life of Owen D. Young," *Fortune, op. cit.*

24. "The Loss of Owen D. Young," *Nation*, January 4, 1933, p. 4; Norman Thomas, "Owen D. Young and Samuel Insull," *Nation*, January 11, 1933, p. 1; *New York Times*, June 22, 1933; March 22, 1934, p. 17; May 25, 1933, p. 35; Young to W. Williams, 12/28/1933, Box 627, ODYC; J. P. Morgan to Young, 4/16/1937, Box 27, ODYC; Young to Senator G. L. Radcliffe, 10/14/1936, Box 27, ODYC; Owen D. Young, "Courage for the Future," *Vital Speeches*, April 22, 1935, pp. 459–60; Owen D. Young, "The Nation's Sounding Board," *Vital Speeches*, March 9, 1936, pp. 366–67; Owen D. Young, "The Science of Better Living," *Vital Speeches*, August 15, 1937, pp. 657–59; *American Magazine*, July, 1930, p. 136; Twentieth Century Fund file, Box 487, ODYC.

25. Others of the 'New Capitalist' group managed to adjust to the New Deal and played an important role in influencing its development. See my "Competition Cartellization and the Corporate Ethic: General Electric's Leadership During the New Deal Era, 1933–40," forthcoming in this *Journal*.

ANGLO-AMERICAN CORPORATISM AND THE ECONOMIC DIPLOMACY OF STABILIZATION IN THE 1920S

Carl Parrini

Michael J. Hogan. *Informal Entente: The Private Structure of Cooperation in Anglo-American Economic Diplomacy, 1918-1928.* Columbia: University of Missouri Press, 1977. ix + 245 pp. Bibliography and index. $12.50.

Michael Hogan's *Informal Entente: The Private Structure of Cooperation in Anglo-American Economic Diplomacy, 1918-1928* is one of the half-dozen or so major books dealing with economic diplomacy in the 1920s. Because it is significant it deserves to be examined critically and its contributions and weaknesses carefully analyzed. Hogan does several things which are entirely or almost entirely new: first of all, he extensively researched both public and private manuscripts in Britain and America which might shed some light on United States economic diplomacy from 1918 to 1928, and in the process he was able to correct, modify, or sustain accounts of the epic contained in the work of Burton Kauffman, Joan Hoff Wilson, and the partly unpublished but very important work of Robert Van Meter, Frank Costigliola, and Melvin Leffler.[1]

Indeed the most questionable part of Hogan's study is the odd set of conclusions he reaches. He generalizes that "the outcome of American policy was the creation of multi-national monopolies dominated by British and American interests—monopolies that helped to reduce Anglo-American conflict but at the same time destroyed the broad equality of opportunity that was believed [by whom?] to be essential for economic peace" (p. 217). When one examines exactly what it is Hogan has done one must realize that his conclusions are not completely borne out by his research. I believe that this is due to two basic methodological weaknesses: his failure to develop completely the implications of his assumptions into a clear research model, and his failure to periodize and so clarify what he regards as cause-and-effect relationships.

Hogan's theory of causation is based on some minimal assumptions. He argues that American foreign policy is an external continuation of the development of its internal policy—corporatism. He assumes that the

0048-7511/78/0063-0379 $01.00
Copyright © 1978 by The Johns Hopkins University Press

American variant of corporatism is the product of the trend in American business and government away from laissez faire and toward a third alternative between Adam Smith's (competitive) capitalism and the socialism of Karl Marx. From 1918 onward Herbert Hoover "became the philosopher of this kind of 'cooperative competition,'" so helping to rationalize America's political economy. Hogan argues that United States corporatism differs from the European variety in that it rejects state management and control because they would interfere with individual intitiative, local control, voluntary cooperation, and economic efficiency.

Under these assumptions about the nature of reality, corporate leaders were supposed to fulfill a triple "trusteeship to owners, workers and the community at large" (p. 41). Hogan takes this model largely from Ellis Hawley's article, "Herbert Hoover, the Commerce Secretariat, and the Vision of an Associative State 1921-1928" (*Journal of American History* 61 [June 1974]), and uses it to explain that when Hoover argued that the objectives of American foreign economic policy ought to be "'a cooperative effort among nations to secure the greatest total output and total consumption'" (p. 42), this was simply an extension of American domestic corporatist conceptions (as analyzed by Hawley) to America's foreign policy. To obtain this greatest total output, European recovery and economic growth had to be structured, and this in turn could only be done if interstate debts were settled, German reparations were reduced, nations reduced inflation by balancing their budgets, commercial discrimination were excluded from world markets, and the state were taken out of the international marketplace. The key to bringing all this about was an agreement between British and American governments (as well as private corporations) on a "common strategy that linked reparations and war debts," yielding joint leverage to obtain "allied cooperation on the German problem" (p. 59).

Using these sometimes ambiguous assumptions Hogan is able to accomplish a great deal both in terms of correcting interpretive weaknesses in the existing literature and in telling parts of the historical tale not heretofore told. Hogan claims that he has sharply modified Joan Hoff Wilson's assertion that there was not enough business-government coordination to carry out an effective foreign economic policy when he maintains that "American leaders considered excessive state intervention to be wasteful and inefficient, incompatible with the private character of the American political economy, and a threat to world peace" (p. 9). But he has not fully succeeded in that endeavor, for if "excessive" state intervention (which Hogan does not explicitly define, but by which he means the practice of Germany up to November of 1918) is inherently more wasteful and inefficient than the category "less than excessive state intervention" there would be no threat to world peace. The point is that such excessive state intervention is extremely successful for the nation-state (Germany then, Japan now) practicing it, and that this success or "efficiency" did stimulate the kind of conflicts that threatened world peace. The issue between Hogan and Wilson, an issue which I believe is not yet resolved, is the degree to which a system of market organization, development, and apportionment without "excessive" state intervention yields enough economic opportunities to allow for the stability of all the major nation-state participants in the market place. Wilson says the degree is insufficient. Hogan has not refuted that argument.

Hogan does modify the account of business-government relationships contained in Burton Kauffman's *Efficiency and Expansion* (1974), which maintains that existing scholarship places too much emphasis on business-government tensions, whereas in reality, Kauffman argues, beginning with the Wilson administration there was really a business-government partnership in which "business has appeared more and more as a distinctively senior partner in formulating and carrying out public policy." In general, Kauffman's orientation is rooted in assumptions about American society which are "structural" and issue from the work of Louis Galambos. In contrast to Hogan, this leads Kauffman into an overly determinist stance which tends to minimize the very sharp differences between the essentially non-"state capitalist" American corporatism and the extremely "state capitalist" German corporatism. For instance, Kauffman argues that the effect of the Edge Act "was to involve the government still further in postwar economic development" (p. 233). Kauffman's evidence for this is of two types: he argues that the U.S. Treasury was prepared to purchase obligations of the War Finance Corporation in 1919 and that the act provided for Federal Reserve Board "supervision" of the Edge corporation, both of which demonstrate partnership, with business the senior partner.[2] It seems to me he is wrong in interpreting both pieces of evidence: Treasury purchases of War Finance Corporation and/or Edge Corporation obligations were not envisaged as normal precedents for future action but simply as emergency measures; beyond marketing grain surpluses already in Europe the Treasury did not merge public funds with corporations making private marketing efforts; and Federal Reserve Board supervision of the Edge Corporation was no more of a "qualitative" departure in business-government relations than was the practice of the controller of the currency of examining domestic banks under the National Banking Act of 1862. Hogan's assumptions tend to make such distinctions among categories clearer than Kauffman's.

One cannot quarrel, per se, with the web of assumptions composing this model; they are necessary but not sufficient. Some things are missing from the model. As a starting point it is adequate to assume that a nation does abroad approximately what it does at home. But then it is necessary to ask "why" the United States is doing what it does at home, and subsequently attempting to do abroad. Asserting the domestic-foreign analog cannot substitute for a theory of causation, but merely pushes it one step backward. The question of "why" still remains. It is true that there are implicit assumptions about "why" in Hogan's book, but they are never made explicit and can confuse the unwary reader. What Hawley is analyzing at home and what Hogan is analyzing abroad are what came to be called, in the years subsequent to World War I, "stabilization policies" for the industrial-capitalist system as a global phenomenon. Once that is acknowledged then it becomes clear that additional explicit assumptions are needed to make the model more "explanatory," that is, to suggest questions to be put to documents which will tell us more about "why" the United States is doing what it is doing.

To put it a bit differently—just why does the United States seek the "greatest total output and total consumption among nations"? There are a number of possibilities—that the United States does what it does abroad because it is innately "good" (some version of special selection or "manifest destiny"), or that there are structural reasons for the adoption of such external policies. In an offhand way Hogan acknowledges the structural aspect of causation when he explains that "American leaders were anxious to use their surplus capital to stimulate world development and to promote the export trade" (p. 79). But the relationship of that assumption to the problem of causation is not further developed.

In addition it seems to me that what is missing from the model is a definition of the "open door" which is consistent with the vision of American leaders that certain steps had to be taken to prevent a new world war from breaking out due to the concurrent pressure of the multinational flaw of surplus capital appearing in a majority of industrial nations concurrently, so increasing the war danger. In general, two separate explanations of the "open door" are current in the literature of American diplomatic history, one by George F. Kennan and the other by William A. Williams. Unfortunately Hogan chose to use that "popularized" by Kennan rather than the sharper tool which Williams developed.[3]

In the first part of chapter 5 Hogan demonstrates that the United States was instrumental in the construction of the second consortium which was to eliminate conflict among the major powers over the right to develop Chinese resources and to divide China into separate preferential spheres and to protect United States economic interest "without risking dangerous governmental conflicts" (p. 95). But then this intepretive stance is altered to argue that the United States consortium construction was a reversal of the open door because it was "actually designed to eliminate the economic and political conflicts that *could result* from the kind of wide open competition inherent in that concept" (p. 96; italics mine). Hogan is wrong here. First his definition of the open door, as it developed historically under American policy in China, is wrong. From the time of John Hay's service as secretary of state the United States defined the open door to mean equal access to markets; tariffs were perfectly permissible so long as they were not preferential, that is, did not discriminate against one state in favor of another. In relation to what we now call "third world states" (which were called "third markets" prior to World War II) the American definition was that access to third world sales and investment markets be equal for all competitors. Prior to the second consortium most large capitalist powers other than the United States maintained monopolistic investment outlets in China. These took shape formally in 1898 with the secret agreement between British and German governments delineating and agreeing mutually to respect the Shantung Peninsula and the Yangtse Valley as the investment monopoly spheres of Germany and Britain, respectively. Other powers followed suit. When the United States constructed the second consortium between 1917 and 1920 it obtained a "recession" by the European powers, and to some extent by Japan, of their monopolistic investment spheres to China, under consortium regulation. This was the establishment of an investment open door, the opposite of an investment monopoly and the political sphere of influence issuing therefrom. The consortium form was the only logical tactical form for an investment open door to take in China, in view of its history up to that time. It effectively prevented nation-states and their banking and industrial corporations from uniting to seek of the Chinese government "closed door" investment outlets which excluded the capital of all other powers. The consortium was not a closed door because it included virtually all the nations with capital surpluses and interest in investment in China (except Germany and Russia for special reasons). Had Hogan not mistakenly taken his definition of the "open door" from Kennan (who in turn derived it from A. E. Hippisley) and instead used that definition which Williams developed (by observing John Hay's practice) he would have avoided this interpretive confusion.

Chapter 6, on "Cable Policy in the Postwar Decade," is entirely new, and goes beyond the accounts in Joseph Tulchin's *The Aftermath of War: World War I and U.S. Policy Toward Latin America* (1971) and in Brady A. Hughes's dissertation, "Owen D. Young and American Foreign Policy, 1919-1929" (University of Wisconsin, 1969). Hogan's analysis of the involved conflict between those American political leaders who wanted an independently United States-controlled worldwide cable communications system and the executives of the private corporations who wanted to cooperate with their British rivals is convincing and makes the best case for his argument that the United States had to recede from extreme open door demands and accept British proposals for a sharing of cable control, a sharing which left the British in a more dominant position. The analysis of radio communications rivalries in chapter 7 also sustains Hogan's thesis that multinational cooperation, especially Anglo-American cooperation, was the key to stability.

In the first part of chapter 8 Hogan makes a convincing case on how Anglo-American cooperation was arranged in Middle East petroleum affairs. Hogan argues that American leaders redefined "traditional principles, especially the Open Door, in order to reconcile their competitive implications with the private vision of constructive development through multinational management" (p. 160). Modified in this way Hogan's argument is more tenable, but he still tends to see the open door as dangerously competitive, whereas the consortium approach was multinational cooperation. But insofar as I know, the consortium approach to oil in the Middle East did not amount to a politically structured contractual monopoly over investment in the development of resources, among which petroleum was the most important resource. In brief, even with respect to petroleum, which is a very special resource because it forms the basis for shipping, petrochemicals, commercial and recreational road transport, and naval defense, Hogan submits no evidence that the Middle East consortium agreements on petroleum closed any resource doors. That is to say the consortium approach, which had been attempted first in China, was applied to the Middle East, and the door which had until then been shut by the British was forced open to American capital. In this connection the open door *via* consortium leaves open the possibility that in the future other powers, as they produce capital surpluses and need petroleum, may seek concessions (as Japanese capital now does) precisely because the United States government and chosen instrument petroleum corporations opened the door and thus eliminated a political monopoly over resources theretofore held by British interests as spoils of war. In effect Hogan says since we did not obtain full equality of access for our own capital in the Middle East petroleum lands by 1923, that we must have given up the open door. But that is wrong because it conceives the open door as an all-or-nothing proposition at a given moment. American leaders did not so conceive the open door.

The best illustration that American leaders thought of the open door as a process rests in an analysis of how and why American leaders picked which monopolistic investment doors to be pried open. China was the first experiment. The reasons for experiment there were simple; although investment spheres were being established after the Treaty of Shiminosekei,

China was still juridically sovereign, so spheres could be technically reversed when the specific opportunity arose in connection with America's gradual assertion of leadership over the first and especially the second consortiums. This opportunity arose mainly out of the war-induced weakness of the Europeans. The second opportunity arose indirectly out of European weakness also. When the Allies sought Liberty Loans, the United States made it a condition of those loans that areas "changing hands as a result of the war or the Peace Treaty" be administered on open door terms. These included the former German, Austrian, Turkish, and Russian empires, among which was included the Shantung Peninsula, which was part of the former German empire (as an investment sphere). A third area was contemplated, the empires of the victors! When the American delegation to Versailles was preparing its position for negotiation, Walter Lippmann suggested that the open door be demanded in connection with the empires of the victors. The Wilson administration decided not to make that demand. In abstract "moral" terms Indians, or Moroccans, or Vietnamese had as much "right" to self-determination as did the Czechs, Slovaks, Poles, Finns, or Syrians. But a demand for a "general" open door at that time (1919) would have been defined as overly aggressive by our co-belligerents, and probably resisted with considerable strength. That third step in generalization of the open door to the empires of West European imperial states was taken during and after World War II by Franklin D. Roosevelt, and it met little successful resistance. The 1920s is the middle of an ongoing process which began in the 1890s and came to completion in the 1950s.

On raw materials (outside petroleum) Hogan argues that there was a "retreat from cooperation" because the "aspirations for independent sources of supply were particularly strong" on the part of Americans and "British authorities [were unwilling] to abandon restrictionist schemes in favor of an Anglo-American understanding" (p. 186). But this interpretation contradicts that which Hogan made in the case of petroleum. America wanted to have adequate supplies of tin, rubber, and potash, but no less did they want adequate supplies of petroleum. Hogan must ask himself why the British government and private interests were willing to abandon efforts to monopolize petroleum resources which fell into their hands in the Middle East and eastern Europe, as well as areas of the old Russian empire, including a distribution monopoly on Soviet Oil. The answer is that the United States defeated British efforts to obtain control of the development of Russian resources including oil at Genoa and the Hague (nowhere mentioned in Hogan's analysis). In analogous fashion the British tried to maintain restrictionist schemes on such other raw materials as rubber and tin because they were able to maintain a level of monopoly (70 percent in the case of rubber sufficient to affect the world market price of those materials. It is not that American aspirations for independent supply were particularly strong; in the case of rubber and tin the United States could not break that measure of control allowing the British to rig prices, whereas in petroleum the British never controlled enough of the supply to rig the price.

In discussing the division on raw materials other than petroleum, Hogan quotes the British colonial secretary, Winston Churchill, in September or October of 1922 (one cannot tell from p. 192n15) that in addition to saving the rubber planters from bankruptcy the rubber restriction scheme, "by making the Americans pay more for rubber," would also "contribute materially to stabilizing the dollar exchange" (p. 192). That is true. But Hogan ought to translate it into something more meaningful to the average educated reader and connect it to petroleum and raw materials generally. If the British had kept Middle Eastern oil under closed door-British control, and if they had won the diplomatic duel at Genoa over the development of Russian resources (wheat, cotton, meat, timber, etc.), they would not have had to import such large quantities of these materials from the United States and pay dollars for them.

Hogan adds to our knowledge of the Genoa conference when he describes British proposals to organize a British-controlled system of inter-European currency parities which would give an inflationary bias to the international monetary system. But Hogan does not mention that had the United States government consented to such a structure Britain could have used such paper-based currencies as a means of relieving itself of its war debts to the United States and so retained closed door monopolies which it had obtained from World War I. British failure in this effort represented a victory for the American open door approach. The year 1922 marked British defeat, and the cooperation which took place between the two nations subsequently was on a United States-defined set of rules.

Hogan does not discuss tariff making and international commercial policy generally. Nowhere in the book is there any mention of the structure of international commercial treaties. The whole question of the impact of the preferential investment and trading systems of the British, French, Japanese, Dutch, and Belgians on investment outlets, and on the pace of world market expansion, is not discussed. Equally important the 1920s version of the General Agreement on Trade and Tariffs (GATT), the 1927 International Economic Conference at Geneva, is not discussed, even though it was, like the Dawes meetings, a conference at which private businessmen controlled by the Commerce, Treasury, and State Departments, and so acting as "private cooperators" under public control, represented the United States. Hogan does not really discuss the interaction between domestic "politics" and the structure of private cooperation which he otherwise so ably sketches.

Next to his questionable conclusions the greatest weakness of Hogan's very important and serious contribution to our knowledge of United States foreign economic policy in the 1920s is its lack of some definite statements about the relationship of that policy to the economic crisis of 1929. İt is true that the book's limits are set by the dates 1918 and 1928, whereas the crisis appears in 1929. But that is not a legitimate explanation of the evasion of the crisis as an interpretive problem. Historians believe in "process" and development. What happened in 1929 must have been maturing, that is to say "developing," prior to 1929. Herbert Hoover is the key personality in terms of giving direction to the development of the United States variant of corporatism, and it was Hoover's essential view that the economic crisis came out of international factors. It seems to me that all those who research and write on Hoover and foreign economic policy in the 1920s cannot evade the need to test Hoover's hypothesis, at least in some tentative way. Perhaps Hogan's next book will do this.

Despite these serious reservations, Hogan's book remains a thoughtful and informative contribution which scholars and public policy makers interested in the 1920s must read, understand, and think about in the interest of the further development of scholarship and public policy.

Professor Parrini, Department of History, Northern Illinois University, is the author of Heir to Empire: United States Economic Diplomacy, 1916-1923 *(1969).*

1. Burton I. Kauffman, *Efficiency and Expansion: Foreign Trade Organization in the Wilson Administration, 1913-1921* (Westport, Conn.: Greenwood Press, 1974); Joan Hoff Wilson, *American Business & Foreign Policy, 1920-1933* (Lexington: University Press of Kentucky, 1971); Frank C. Costigliola, "The Politics of Financial Stabilization: American Reconstruction Policy in Europe, 1924-1930" (Ph.D. diss., Cornell University, 1972); Melvin P. Leffler, "The Struggle for Stability: American Policy Toward France, 1921-1933" (Ph.D. diss., Ohio State University, 1972); Robert H. Van Meter, Jr., "The United States and European Recovery, 1918-1923: A Study of Public Policy and Private Finance" (Ph.D. diss., University of Wisconsin, 1971).

2. Kauffman, *Efficiency and Expansion*, pp. xiv, 233; the best example of Louis Galambos is his "The Emerging Organizational Synthesis in American History," *Business History* 45 (Autumn 1970): 279-90.

3. George F. Kennan's *American Diplomacy 1900-1950* (New York: Mentor, 1951), ought to be read in its entirety to understand clearly Kennan's view about why American leaders do what they do, but his view of the open door and its development can be obtained from pp. 24-32, 35-36; Williams's developmental view of the open door is best obtained in his *Tragedy of American Diplomacy* (New York: Delta, 1972), esp. pp. 48-57, but the whole book must be read to understand the open door as a process from 1898 to virtually the present.

MID-AMERICA
An Historical Review

From Depression to Depression: Hooverian National Planning, 1921-1933

Patrick D. Reagan
Tennessee Technological University

Traditionally, scholars assume that American national planning emerged under the aegis of the federal government via the New Deal's reaction to the Great

* *The author would like to thank William J. Brinker, Ellis W. Hawley, and K. Austin Kerr for comments on an earlier version of the article. Research was made possible through a National Endowment for the Humanities stipend to attend a seminar at the University of Iowa and through a grant for archival research from the Faculty Research Committee of Tennessee Technological University.*

Depression of 1929-1941.[1] However, recent studies of Secretary of Commerce Herbert Hoover during the New Era suggest that Hoover set pre-New Deal precedents for American planning in the 1920's.[2] Drawing on his experiences from the wartime mobilization of 1917-1918, Hoover set the pace for planning in reaction to the depression following World War I. Yet Hoover did not act alone; he served as symbolic leader in an evolving, yet fragile network of planning institutions overlooked by scholars. Acting through ad hoc institutional mechanisms created directly in response to the depression of 1920-1921, Hooverian planners laid the groundwork for a distinctly American form of voluntary national planning that would be used throughout the New Era of managerial capitalism in the 1920s. Between 1921 and

---

[1]Ellis Hawley, *The New Deal and the Problem of Monopoly* (Princeton, 1966); Richard S. Kirkendall, *Social Scientists and Farm Politics in the Age of Roosevelt* (Columbia, Mo., 1966); Otis L. Graham, Jr., "The Planning Ideal and American Reality: The 1930s," *The Hofstadter Aegis,* eds. Stanley Elkins and Eric McKitrick (New York, 1974); Otis L. Graham, Jr., *Toward a Planned Society: From Roosevelt to Nixon* (New York, 1976); Philip W. Warken, *A History of the National Resources Planning Board: 1933-1943* (New York, 1979); Marion Clawson, *New Deal Planning* (Baltimore, 1981). For purposes of brevity the following abbreviations are used to identify sources in the Herbert Hoover Papers, Herbert Hoover Presidential Library, West Branch, Iowa: Commerce Papers (CP); Unemployment File, CP (UF); UF-individual file by name, CP.

[2]For a review of the recent literature on Hoover see Joan Hoff Wilson, *Herbert Hoover: Forgotten Progressive* (Boston, 1975); David Burner, *Herbert Hoover: A Public Life* (New York, 1979); U.S. Congress, Senate, *Herbert Hoover Reassessed: Essays Commemorating the Fiftieth Anniversary of the Inauguration of Our Thirty-First President,* S. Doc. 96-63, 96th Cong., 2nd sess., 1981 (Washington, D.C., 1981); Patrick G. O'Brien and Philip T. Rosen, "Hoover and the Historians: The Resurrection of a President, Parts 1 and 2," *Annals of Iowa,* 46 (1982): 25-42 and 83-99; *Herbert Hoover and the Republican Era: A Reconsideration,* eds. Carl E. Krog and William R. Tanner (Lanham, Md., 1984). For key works see Peri Ethan Arnold, "Herbert Hoover and the Continuity of American Public Policy," *Public Policy,* 20 (1972): 522-544; *Herbert Hoover and the Crisis of American Capitalism,* eds. J. Joseph Hutchmacher and Warren Susman (Cambridge, Mass., 1973); *The Hoover Presidency: A Re-Appraisal,* eds. Martin L. Fausold and George T. Mazuzan (Albany, 1974); *Herbert Hoover: The Great War and Its Aftermath, 1914-1923,* ed. Lawrence Gelfand (Iowa City, 1979); Ellis W. Hawley, *The Great War and the Search for a Modern Order* (New York, 1979); and *Herbert Hoover as Secretary of Commerce,* ed. Ellis W. Hawley (Iowa City, 1981). For works which specifically identify Hoover as a planner see Clifford J. Hynning, "Administrative Evolution of National Planning in the United States in the Pre-New Deal Era," *Plan Age,* 5 (June 1939): 157-189; Carolyn Grin, "The Unemployment Conference of 1921: An Experiment in National Cooperative Planning," *Mid-America,* 55 (1973): 83-107; Ross Thomas Runfola, "Herbert C. Hoover as Secretary of Commerce, 1921-1923: Domestic Planning in the Harding Years" (Ph.D. diss., State University of New York, Buffalo, 1973); Ellis W. Hawley, "Techno-Corporatist Formulas in the Liberal State, 1920-1960: A Neglected Aspect of America's Search for a New Order," unpublished 1974 paper in the author's files; Ellis W. Hawley, "Herbert Hoover, the Commerce Secretariat, and the Vision of an 'Associative State,' 1921-1928," *Journal of American History,* 61 (June 1974): 116-140; Evan B. Metcalf, "Secretary Hoover and the Emergence of Macroeconomic Management," *Business History Review,* 49 (1975): 60-80; Ellis W. Hawley, "Herbert Hoover and Economic Stabilization, 1921-22," in *Herbert Hoover as Secretary of Commerce,* 43-77; Guy Alchon, *The Invisible Hand of Planning: Capitalism, Social Science, and the State in the 1920s* (Princeton, 1985).

1933 representatives of the state, corporate business, philanthropic foundations, and social science research organizations cooperated to form this planning network.[3] By 1927, Hoover and a close aide referred to these planning projects as the "committee and conference system." With the onslaught of a new and far more devastating depression in the 1930s, Hooverian planning faltered. Yet certain of the Hooverian planners were appointed to President Franklin D. Roosevelt's planning board in 1933. Hooverian initiatives of the 1920's took American national planning from depression to Depression.

Recent scholars interested in understanding, rather than reviling, the Hoover legacy show that as Secretary of Commerce, and later as President, Hoover served as midwife to national planning. As head of the Department of Commerce from 1921 to 1929, Hoover presided over piecemeal planning for economic standardization and rationalization, stabilization of the "sick" economic sectors, promotion of emerging economic sectors, and the search for a voluntarist conception of national planning. The rediscovery of Hooverian attempts to build what Ellis Hawley has termed the "associative state" reveals a picture at odds with traditional understanding of the relationship among the planning ideal, the institutional capacity for planning, and the people who planned. Contrary to the view that, by definition, national planning must inherently stem from the coercive efforts of a farseeing state working through clearly defined public sector institutions, scholars of Hooverian planning indicate the need for a more complex--and ambiguous--view of American planning.[4]

---

[3]Alchon, *The Invisible Hand of Planning.* The present essay differs in interpretive focus from Alchon's work in noting the importance of Hooverian reaction to the depression of 1920-1921. Alchon posits the existence of a "legitimation crisis as noted in the work of Max Weber and Jurgen Habermas. Alchon argues that the developments of the 1920s called forth a "technocratic bargain" among leaders of the state, corporate capital, and professional social science. As such, Hooverian planning efforts involved an exchange of power among these three groups aimed at achieving legitimacy. Social science researchers received professional and scientific credibility in exchange for assisting the state which, under Hoover's leadership, sought to resolve the legitimation crisis of corporate capital's authority in the 1920s. The present essay forgoes generalization in order to identify the historical specifics of Hooverian national planning as stemming from the concerns of the postwar depression of 1920-1921..

[4]Hawley, "Herbert Hoover, the Commerce Secretariat, and the Vision of an Associative State"; Ellis W. Hawley, "Secretary Hoover and the Bituminous Coal Problem, 1921-1928," *Business History Review,* 42 (1968): 247-270; Ellis W. Hawley, "Three Facets of Hooverian Associationalism: Lumber, Aviation, and Movies, 1921-1930," *Regulation in Perspective,* ed. Thomas K. McCraw (Cambridge, Mass., 1981), 95-123; James Johnson, *The Politics of Soft Coal* (Urbana, 1979); Philip T. Rosen, *The Modern Stentors* (Westport, Ct., 1980); the special issue on Hoover's agricultural policies in *Agricultural History,* 51 (April 1977); William G. Robbins, "Voluntary Cooperation vs. Regulatory Paternalism: The Lumber Trade in the 1920s," *Business History Review,* 56 (1982): 358-79; and Kendrick A. Clements, "Herbert Hoover and Conservation, 1921-33," *American Historical Review,* 89 (1984): 67-88. On the importance of state institutional capacity for planning see Stephen Skowronek, *Building a New American State* (New York, 1982) and Theda Skocpol and Kenneth Finegold, "State Capacity and Economic Intervention in the Early New Deal," *Political Science Quarterly,* 97 (1982): 255-278.

Hoover hoped to bridge the increasing gap between nineteenth-century liberal values and the realities of the twentieth-century corporatist society. The Hooverian vision of American society saw the atomistic, self-interested individuals of Adam Smith's self-regulating world struggling to survive in the organizational hothouse of group power permeated by the corporate model of the hierarchical, functionally-oriented, administrative structure first established by national business corporations in the late nineteenth century. Hoping to preserve the liberal values of republican America--individual liberty, private property, the work ethic, socioeconomic mobility, and a stable economy dominated by private sector activity--Hoover sought to create new institutional avenues of opportunity through the transformation of the ideal and institutional representations of voluntary association. Hooverian loyalists, businessmen, social science research experts, and philanthropic managers cooperated to build the Hooverian planning network. In emphasizing a new role for organized group knowledge, power, and influence in policymaking, Hoover and his supporters built what can be termed "associative national planning." Never intending to create permanent public sector bases to institute planning, the Hooverians nevertheless brought together a congeries of public, public-private, and private sector planning groups that confound much of the scholarly literature on national planning in the United States. By its intertwining of public and private sector activity, Hooverian national planning looms larger than scholars previously have thought.[5]

Hoover, his loyal aides, corporate managers, and a growing corps of social scientists acted within the historical context of American mobilization for the Great War of 1914-1918 and the postwar reconstruction debate which followed. In the work of the war mobilization agencies--the Commission for Relief in Belgium, the War Industries Board, the Food and Fuel Administrations, and the War Labor Board--these managers quo mobilization planners sought to find hints of things to come.[6] Having erected temporary planning structures, some of Wilson's war man-

---

[5]The author is indebted to Ellis W. Hawley for clarifying this point in discussions at the National Endowment for the Humanities' seminar, "The New Rationality: Politicians and Planners in Wartime and Interwar America, 1917-1945," University of Iowa, summer 1984. On the continuing tension between nineteenth-century liberal republican values and the twentieth century state see the works of Ellis W. Hawley cited above and the incisive comments in Barry D. Karl, *The Uneasy States* (Chicago, 1983).

[6]On mobilization for the Great War see Paul A. C. Koistinen, "The 'Industrial-Military Complex' in Historical Perspective: World War I," *Business History Review*, 41 (1967): 367-403; Murray N. Rothbard, "War Collectivism in World War I, "*A New History of Leviathan*, eds. Murray N. Rothbard and Ronald Radosh (New York, 1972), 66-110; Robert D. Cuff, "Business, the State, and World War I: The American Experience," *War and Society in North America,* eds. Robert D. Cuff and J.L. Granastein (Toronto, 1971), 1-19; Robert D. Cuff, *The War Industries Board* (Baltimore, 1973); Robert D. Cuff, "We Band of Brothers--Woodrow Wilson's War Managers," *Canadian Review of American Studies,* 5 (Fall 1974): 135-148; Robert D. Cuff, "Herbert Hoover, the Ideology of Voluntarism, and War Organization During the Great War," *Journal of American History,* 64 (September 1977): 358-372; Hawley, *The Great War;* David M. Kennedy, *Over Here: The First World War and American Society* (New York, 1980), esp. Cs. 2 and 6; Valerie Jean Conner, *The National War Labor Board* (Chapel Hill, 1983); the important essay by Ellis W. Hawley, "The Great War and Organizational Innovation: The American Case," unpublished 1984 paper in the author's files.

agers tried to carry over the lessons into the period of postwar demobilization and reconstruction. Failing at that by the spring of 1919, the planners looked on as the boom of 1919-1920 seemed to belie their arguments as to the need for national coordination and planning for the economic and social future of postwar America.[7]

Nevertheless, the postwar reconstruction period raised key issues for debate regarding control of the business cycle and relief of unemployment that would take on increased importance following the boom and collapse of 1919-1921. Between mid-July 1919 and early January 1920, the Senate Select Committee on Reconstruction and Production held hearings to determine the extent of economic dislocation in the coal and housing industries. By March of 1921 the Committee presented a series of recommendations to the Senate that presaged the planning efforts about to begin under Hoover's tutelage. Even before his appointment as Secretary of Commerce in March 1921, Hoover had begun to address the problem of what he termed "industrial waste." As head of the Federated American Engineering Societies, Hoover instigated the economic investigation published as *Waste in Industry* on October 29, 1921. Edward Eyre Hunt, secretary of the committee which conducted the study, wrote to Hoover that the cooperative voluntary spirit among members of the committee and use of the knowledge of engineering experts "mark an epoch." Such committee work, Hunt argued, would further the standardization drive directed by the Department of Commerce's Bureau of Standards and lay the basis for cooperation between labor and management. As a newly appointed member of the Harding Cabinet, Hoover reorganized the Department of Commerce to promote economic rationalization and stabilization. By reordering old or creating new bureaus within the Department with the help of a group of aides who had followed him from war and postwar work, Hoover hoped to play a central role in building what later became known as New Era Capitalism. The emerging economic order depended on the interaction of high production, high consumption, and high wages.[8]

---

[7]On demobilization and reconstruction see Frederic L. Paxson's Presidential address to the American Historical Association of December 29, 1938 in "The Great Demobilization," *American Historical Review*, 44 (1939): 237-351; Robert F. Himmelberg, "Business, Antitrust Policy, and the Industrial Board of the Department of Commerce, 1919," *Business History Review*, 42 (1968): 1-23; Burl Noggle, *Into the Twenties* (Urbana, 1974); Robert D. Cuff, "Harry Garfield, the Fuel Administration, and the Search for a Cooperative Order During World War I," *American Quarterly*, 30 (1978): 39-53; for a contemporary view see *America and the New Era*, ed. Elisha M. Friedman (New York, 1920).

[8]U.S. Congress, Senate, Select Committee on Reconstruction and Production, *Reconstruction and Production, Hearings Pursuant to S. Res. 350*, 66th Cong., 2nd sess., 1920 and *Reconstruction and Production*, S. Rept. No. 829 Pursuant to S. Res. 350, 66th Cong., 3rd sess, 1921; E. Jay Howenstine, "Public Works After World War I," *Journal of Political Economy*, 51 (1943): 523-547; Craig Lloyd, *Aggressive Introvert: Herbert Hoover and Public Relations Management, 1912-1932* (Columbus, 1972), 59-72, 123-142; Hawley, "Herbert Hoover, the Commerce Secretariat, and the Vision of an 'Associative State'"; American Engineering Council, Committee on Elimination of Waste in Industry, Federated American Engineering Societies, *Waste in Industry* (New York, 1921); Alchon, *The Invisible Hand of Planning*, 63-67 for an analysis of the Waste in Industry study; W. Elliot Brownlee, *Dynamics of Ascent* (New York, 1979), second ed., 384-405 for a good analysis of New Era capitalism.

But before that work could start, Hoover faced the crisis of the postwar depression of 1920-1921. Economic collapse in the wake of the boom of 1919-1920 proved to be one of the most severe and rapid downturns of the business cycle in American economic history. From the zenith of February 1920 to its nadir in April 1921, industrial production fell thirty-four per cent. Between July 1920 and August 1921, the wholesale price index fell forty-five per cent. The Bureau of Labor Statistics index of factory employment decreased thirty-one per cent between March 1920 and July 1921. The money supply declined by nine per cent over the course of the cyclical downturn. The average annual unemployment rate increased from the postwar low of 1.4 per cent in 1919 to 5.2 per cent in 1920 and hit the depression peak of 11.7 per cent in 1921. By 1921, almost five million people in the civilian labor force were unemployed. As business cycle economist Wesley C. Mitchell noted at the 1921 meeting of the American Economic Association, the problem of fluctuations in the business cycle and the resulting shifts in unemployment as seen in the depression of 1920-1921 called for national action.[9]

In his post-presidential memoirs Hoover drew attention to the depression in noting that "the postwar slump had deepened, and unemployment had seriously increased." In the summer of 1921, after the reorganization of the Department of Commerce had begun, Hoover conferred with key leaders in the business community about calling a conference sponsored by the President and directed by Hoover to deal with the issue of unemployment. The resulting President's Conference on Unemployment brought together a limited number of leaders of the business community in Washington, D.C. in the fall of 1921 to study "the unemployment situation." In a telegram to the presidents of the United States Chamber of Commerce, the National Association of Manufacturers, the National Federation of Construction Industries, and the Association of Railway Executives, Hoover explained that the Conference would

> endeavor to make such constructive suggestions as may assist [the depression's] amelioration during the winter and as would tend to give

---

[9]On the importance of industrial depressions see David P. Thelen, "Social Tensions and the Origins of Progressivism," *Journal of American History*, 56 (1969): 323-341. On the boom and collapse of 1919-1921 see Paul A. Samuelson and Everett E. Hagen, *After the War--1918-1920* (Washington, D.C., 1943); George Soule, *Prosperity Decade* (New York, 1947), 81-106; John D. Hicks, *Rehearsal for Disaster: The Boom and Collapse of 1919-1920* (Gainesville, Fla., 1961); and John D. Pilgrim, "The Upper Turning Point of 1920: A Reappraisal," *Explorations in Economic History*, 11 (1974): 271-298. For sources indicating that those close to Hoover saw the issue in terms of the memories of the depressions of 1893-1897, 1908, and 1914 see Hoover's speech to the Engineers Club of San Francisco, December 24, 1921, Economic Situation in the U.S., 1921-1924, CP; Edward Eyre Hunt press release dated [1922?], UF; John B. Andrews to Hoover, 2 September 1921, UF-John B. Andrews; and Wesley C. Mitchell's address to the American Economic Association, Pittsburgh, December 21, 1921, "The Crisis of 1920 and the Problem of Controlling Business Cycles," *American Economic Review*, 12 Supplement (March 1922): 20-32. The statistics are from Pilgrim, "The Upper Turning Point of 1920," 276 and *Historical Statistics of the United States: Colonial Times to 1970* (Washington, D.C., 1975), Part 1, Series D 85-86, 135.

confidence to the business community...We will need to have some flexibility in choice [of members] so as to round out the whole conference geographically and represent the most important sectors of the community.[10]

Drawing on the staff of the Department of Commerce, representatives of the business community, and experts from the reformist American Association for Labor Legislation, the Taylor Society, and the National Bureau of Economic Research, Hoover set up an Economic Advisory Committee to plan the agenda of the Unemployment Conference. Memories of the failure of President Wilson's two industrial conferences in late 1919 and early 1920 in the wake of the steel strike of 1919 haunted Hoover, who had served as chairman of the second conference. While the Advisory Committee gathered, Hoover carefully selected the delegates to the Conference proper so as to avoid the conflicts reflected in President Wilson's two earlier industrial conferences.[11]

In organizing the Unemployment Conference, Hoover brought together representatives from functional sectors of the economy, professional economists, various other experts, token leaders of organized labor, and "neutrals" representing the public. Yet the real work of the Conference proved virtually complete even before the delegates met in the nation's capital city. In early September 1921, Hoover consulted with a small group of economists from Columbia, Harvard, M.I.T., Cornell, and other prominent universities to determine the technical program for the public conference. The two most important of the economists were Edwin F. Gay and Wesley C. Mitchell, co-founders of the National Bureau of Economic Research (NBER), a private research organization established in 1920 to study scientifically the composition and distribution of national income and wealth of the United States. The NBER would prove to be a long-running player in Hooverian

---

[10]*The Memoirs of Herbert Hoover,* Vol. II (New York, 1952), 44; *Report of the President's Conference on Unemployment* (Washington, D.C., 1921), 15-16; the quote is from Hoover telegram to J.H. Defrees, J.E. Edgerton, Ernest T. Trigg, T. DeWitt Cuyler, 27 August 1921, UF-Conference Members Suggested.

[11]*Report of the President's Conference,* 7-14; Chairman, Advisory Committee to Secretary of Commerce, 8 September 1921, UF-Advisory Committee-Organization, Lists; and material in UF-Conference-Members and – Members Suggested. On Wilson's industrial conferences see Henry S. Dennison and Ida Tarbell, "The President's Industrial Conference of October 1919," *Bulletin of the Taylor Society,* 5 (April 1920); 79-92; David Brody, *Labor in Crisis: The Steel Strike of 1919* (Philadelphia, 1965), 105, 115-128; Haggai Hurvitz, "Ideology and Industrial Conflict: President Wilson's First Industrial Conference of October 1919," *Labor History,* 18 (1977): 509-524; Wilson to Hoover, 19 November 1919, CP-Industrial Conference of March 6, 1920; and Gary Dean Best, "President Wilson's Second Industrial Conference, 1919-1920," *Labor History,* 16 (1975): 505-520.

planning.[12]

Cooperating with the economists, the Economic Advisory Committee set the deliberative direction for the Conference by calling for expert investigation and delegate discussion in committee of four major issues. What was the extent of unemployment? How could the Conference encourage voluntary cooperation at the local level to provide relief for the unemployed? Would increasing public and private works expenditures during this and future depressions help to stabilize the business cycle? How well did economists and businessmen understand the workings of the business cycle and could that understanding lead to control of the cycle in some way? The Unemployment Conference's consideration of these questions established the framework for later national planning efforts from 1922 through 1933. Hoover hoped to use advice from business leaders and social science experts cooperating through the medium of government sponsorship. Private sector voluntary activity with the help of the emerging social sciences could lead via public encouragement by the state to collection of accurate, scientific statistics regarding employment and unemployment. Such voluntary associative planning for immediate unemployment relief would give experience in planning for future unemployment relief. Hooverian planning also advocated the use of public works spending as a countercyclical balancing tool to even out the peaks and valleys in the business cycle. All of these efforts in turn would promote long-range economic stablization. The planning effort focused on the need for using voluntary associational groups at the core of the planning process in order to avoid a coercive, bureaucratic state. Hooverian planners sought to employ corporatist institutions in the private sector as a means to engage in macroeconomic national planning. The role of the federal government lay in

---

[12]Herbert Heaton, *A Scholar in Action: Edwin F. Gay* (Cambridge, Mass., 1952); Hoover to Gay, 29 August 1921, UF-Edwin F. Gay; Steuart to various economists, 3 September 1921, UF-Conference-Members; *Memoirs of Herbert Hoover* II, 44; and Edgar Rickard to C.C. Stetson, 2 September 1921 and lists for Conference members dated 2 and 3 September 1921, UF-Conference-Members Suggested Misc. On the emergence of professional economics in the United States see David W. Eakins, "The Development of Corporate Liberal Policy Research in the United States, 1885-1965" (Ph.D. diss., University of Wisconsin, 1966); Robert L. Church, "Economists as Experts: The Rise of an Academic Profession in the United States, 1870-1920," *The University in Society* ed. Lawrence Stone (Princeton, 1974), Vol. II, 571-609; and David M. Grossman, "American Foundations and the Support of Economic Research, 1913-29," *20 (1982); 59-82*. On Mitchell and the NBER see Joseph Dorfman, "Wesley C. Mitchell (1874-1948)," *Economic Journal* 59, (September 1959): 448-458; Alvin H. Hansen, "Wesley Mitchell, Social Scientist and Social Counselor," *Review of Economics and Statistics* 31 (1949): 245-255; Arthur F. Burns, "Wesley Mitchell and the National Bureau," National Bureau of Economic Research, *Twenty-Ninth Annual Report* (New York, 1949), 3-55; Guy Alchon, "Building a Technocratic Social Science: The National Bureau of Economic Research and the 'New Capitalism', 1917-1929," unpublished paper delivered at the Social Science History Association convention, Washington, D.C., October 1983, in the author's files.

promoting these private efforts through the committee and conference system.[13]

Functional representation of economic leaders served as the organizing principle for selection of public delegates to the Conference. Hoover noted in his memoirs that "We had selected some three hundred leaders from production, distribution, banking, construction, labor and agriculture" as delegates to the Unemployment Conference which met in Washington, D.C. between September 26 and October 13, 1921. The Economic Advisory Committee had determined in large part the deliberative results. Delegates accepted the experts' findings as to the extent of unemployment stemming from the downturn of the business cycle, rather than from seasonal unemployment, and that most of the jobless had worked in the industrial sectors of the economy. The problem of cyclical unemployment seemed one of real concern for future investigation and planning. In regard to immediate relief, one committee wrote that "as winter approaches every community ought to be prepared and whatever agencies-public or private-that are willing to cooperate in the relief of unemployment, should unite in a common program." That program, the recommendations continued, should

> consist of plans for advancing and increasing public works, of stimulating wise programs by public and private charitable and civic agencies, of strengthening family welfare agencies, of creating and directing special community and municipal activities. Most important of all is the consideration of what private employers are doing to spread employment, to undertake repairs and improvements, to manufacture wherever possible for replenishing stocks. Even the Federal Government can help in emergency measures not only through public works but in its fiscal policies in their effect upon the stimulation and revival of industry.[14]

The Conference drew on the Hooverian ideal of voluntary association among representatives of the corporate and competitive business community, economic experts, and Hoover's veterans of the war and postwar mobilization and reconversion experience. In its final report, the Conference included more extended analyses of the issues that had been posed by the Economic Advisory Committee. By September 1921, the delegates found, around three and a half million people in the nonfarm labor force were unemployed. Working from the business cycle theory developed by such economists as Wesley C. Mitchell, the delegates pointed to the need for scientific collection and analysis of both cyclical and seasonal business data in order

---

13"Advance Summary of Report of Economic Advisory Committee to the President's Unemployment Conference," 22 September 1921, UF-Advisory Committee Reports; Advisory Committee Reports and "Report of the Economic Advisory Committee to the Unemployment Conference," 26 September 1921, UF-Conference Plans and Programs; *Report of the President's Conference* 47-58,66-69,99-106,161-167.
14*Memoirs of Herbert Hoover* II, 44 and "Advance Summary of Report of Economic Advisory Committee," 1-2.

to discover ways to control or flatten out the cycle. The Committee on Public Works drew on the ideas of its chairman, Otto T. Mallery, who had developed the theory that increased public and private works spending during economic declines in the key construction industries could help to even out the fluctuations in the business cycle.[15]

To raise immediate unemployment relief, the Conference established the Civic and Emergency Measures Committee. Committee Chairman Arthur Woods had worked as a businessman, the police commissioner of New York City, member of the Committee on Public Information, head of the Aviation Section of the American Expeditionary Force, and as special assistant to Secretary of War Newton D. Baker in 1919 to find jobs for returning veterans.[16] The Woods Committee acted as a clearinghouse for information gathering and distribution at the state and local levels. While claiming that voluntary relief planning helped to meet the crisis of unemployment in the winter of 1921-1922, the Committee overlooked the facts collected by its own roving investigators. Most unemployment occurred in the industrialized cities of the Northeast, the Central Atlantic, and the Midwest. By way of President Harding's encouragement to state governors and local communities to set up governors' and mayors' committees to register the unemployed and help them find private sector jobs, the Woods Committee hoped to avoid the European dole, reinvigorate the spirit of wartime cooperation, and preserve the national tradition of voluntary action. Though the Committee's public releases seemed to indicate widespread success of the relief effort, its internal records told another story. Political resistance from the mayors of New York City, Chicago, and Boston prevented relief efforts in those key cities from effectively responding to the plight of the unemployed. In December 1921, Mary Van Kleeck, head of the Department of Industrial Studies of the Russell Sage Foundation and delegate to the Unemployment Conference, wrote Woods that local mayors failed to make the voluntary committees "truly representative. They are appointing business men and leaving out both labor and the social workers." The Foundation sponsored a study of relief efforts in fifteen cities over the winter of 1921-1922 which found that local committees lacked continuity, finances, and effective relief coordination.[17]

---

[15] *Report of the President's Conference* passim and Otto T. Mallery, "Draft Report of Sub-Committee No. 3 of the Advisory Committee to the Unemployment Conference, on Public Works," UF-Advisory Committee Reports. Mallery had served on the Industrial Board of Pennsylvania during the Great War which developed a public works program that served as a model for later programs. Mallery was chairman of the Public Works Committee at the Unemployment Conference, drafted several public works bills stemming from the work of the Conference, and became the leading advocate of advance public works planning throughout the 1920s. See materials in UF-Mallery and E. Jay Howenstine, "Public Works Policy in the Twenties," *Social Research* 13 (1946): 479-500.

[16] Arthur Woods, "Putting the Servicemen Back to Work," *World's Work,* 38 (August 1919): 396-399 and E. Jay Howenstine, "Lessons of World War I," *Annals* 238 (March 1945): 180-187.

[17] *Report of the President's Conference* 60-63; Woods to Mary Van Kleeck, 9 November 1921, UF-Mary Van Kleeck; Minutes of Woods' Committee Meetings in UF-Public Works-Misc.; Colonel

By late May 1922, Hoover concluded that "the business tide has turned," that a permanent relief administrative structure appeared to be off to a good start, and that the work of the Unemployment Conference "should all give continuing results of constructive character in dealing with these problems of the future." In the aftermath of the Conference, Hoover conducted a large-scale publicity campaign modeled on that of his wartime work that ignored the flaws in the committee and conference system. Yet Hoover took the Unemployment Conference as the starting point in his plan for "reconstruction and development" which continued throughout the New Era. The Conference originally had been intended as a long-range look into the American future, but had added the short-range planning perspective in response to the depression of 1920-1921.[18]

Scholars have noted Hoover's piecemeal, short-range planning aimed at stabilizing "sick" industries--such as coal and lumber--and promoting newly emerging industries--such as aviation, motion picture, and radio. These actions eventually encouraged the trade association antitrust revision movement that culminated in the New Deal's National Recovery Administration. Hoover's New Era long-range planning began in 1921. In its genesis, organization, structure, deliberations, publicity, and results, the Unemployment Conference of 1921 laid the groundwork for Hooverian national planning.[19] Hoover drew a number of lessons from the planning experience of the Unemployment Conference. It confirmed his own vision of associative national planning bringing together public, public-private and private sector

---

Arthur Woods, "Unemployment and You," typescript marked "for Sat. Evening Post," UF-Publicity-1922; Woods, "Unemployment Emergency," *North American Review*, 215 (April 1922): 449-458; and materials in UF-Arthur Woods. For Hoover's aides' reactions see Hunt memo to Hoover, 22 May 1923, Hunt draft of letter to John M. Glenn, 22 May 1923, and [R.S. Emmet] memo to Hunt, 28 May 1923 all in UF-Civic and Emergency Relief Commissions 1921-1923. On the problems in New York, Chicago, and Boston see the appropriate sections in UF-Cities. For Van Kleeck's criticisms and the Russell Sage Foundation study see Van Kleeck to Woods, 1 and 6 December 1921, UF-Van Kleeck and Philip Klein, *The Burden of Unemployment: A Study of Unemployment Relief in Fifteen American Cities, 1921-22* (New York, 1923). Hoover admitted indirectly the limitations of the voluntary relief efforts in New York and Chicago in Hoover to the President, 20 May 1922, UF-1922 though that perspective changed by the time Hoover wrote about it in *Memoirs of Herbert Hoover*, II, 46.

18Hoover to the President, 20 May 1922, while the quote is from Hoover to Hunt, 5 June 1922, UF. On the publicity for the Conference and the Woods' Committee see Edward Eyre Hunt, "Action: An Account of the Measures That Have Arisen Out of the President's Conference on Unemployment," *The Survey*, 17 December 1921, 427-427; newspaper clippings in UF-Unemployment Facts; and Major R.L. Foster, "Publicity Report: The President's Conference on Unemployment," typescript dated 8 May 1922, UF-Publicity Report 1922. For Hoover's use of public relations techniques throughout this period see Lloyd, *Aggressive Introvert*.

19On Hoover's piecemeal planning efforts see references in Note 4; Robert F. Himmelberg, *The Origins of the National Recovery Administration: Business, Government, and the Trade Association Issue, 1921-1933* (New York, 1976) and Himmelberg, "Government and Business, 1917-1932: The Triumph of 'Corporate Liberalism'?," *Business and Government: Essays in 20th-Century Cooperation and Confrontation*, eds. Joseph R. Frese and Jacob Judd (Tarrytown, New York, 1985), 1-23; cf. Robert B. Reich, *The Next American Frontier* (New York, 1983), C.V.

organizations in the corporatist mode, assistance from social science experts in the universities and private research agencies, and the help of Hooverian loyalists in using publicity to promote voluntary cooperation rather than forcing a turn to direct coercion by the state. This vision gave birth to what Hoover and his close aide, Edward Eyre Hunt, called "the committee and conference system."

The Economic Advisory Committee assured the continuation of Hooverian planning when Conference delegates accepted its resolution providing for establishment of a Standing Committee headed by Hoover. The Standing Committee received authority to appoint special committees to plan investigations of the business cycle, remedies for unemployment in seasonal industries, possibilities for unemployment insurance, and economic revival of the construction industries. Of these four potential committees, two grew to fruition--the Business Cycle Committee and the Committee on Seasonal Operation. Creation of these committees in the wake of the Unemployment Conference of 1921 engendered a full-blown emergence of the committee and conference system which Hoover and his key aide, Edward Eyre Hunt, used throughout the remainder of the New Era.[20]

For Hooverian associative national planning to work effectively, Hoover had to combine a number of disparate components. He needed a superb organizer loyal to his vision of cooperative planning in order to coordinate the activities of the people and organizations involved in each of the specialized planning studies. Hoover refused to seek financial support from the Congress; however, he insisted on sponsorship by the Executive branch via the President, himself as Secretary of Commerce, or one of the newly-organized divisions within the Department of Commerce. To finance the studies, Hoover turned to a burgeoning network of philanthropic foundations managed by a second generation of managerial trustees and directors. As the plans shaped up, Hoover had to consider the relationship between social science expertise and policy implementation of knowledge in practical, useable form. He chose to organize each of the studies around a carefully-picked coterie of loyalists who made up the sponsoring committee which directed the study, managed the policy recommendations through the deliberative process, and wrote the final report. Invariably, this committee consisted primarily of representatives of the business community which Hoover usually equated with "the public." Under the sponsoring committee, social science experts from private sector research organizations conducted the technical investigations upon which the business delegates and the Hooverian loyalists would draw for final recommendations for inclusion in

---

[20]Economic Advisory Committee resolution [15-19?] September 1921, UF-Advisory Committee-Organization, Lists; E.E. Hunt to Mortimer Fleishhacker, 29 October 1921 and resolutions in UF-Standing Committee, 1921; Hoover to James M. Lee, 3 November 1921, UF-Advisory Committee-Corres.; Minutes of Standing Committee, 7 November 1921, UF-Business Cycles-1921. For a rather unconvincing view of Hoover's planning for unemployment relief see Vaughn Davis Bornet, "Herbert Hoover's Planning for Unemployment and Old Age Insurance Coverage, 1921 to 1933," *The Quest for Security*, ed. John N. Schacht (Iowa City, 1982), 35-71. For a more thoroughly researched and argued view see Daniel Nelson, *Unemployment Insurance: The American Experience, 1915-1935* (Madison, 1969).

the committee report. To promulgate information about both the investigations and the findings published in the final report, Hoover relied on extensive public relations campaigns orchestrated by veterans of the Commission for Relief in Belgium, the Food Administration, the American Relief Administration, and the divisional staffers and privately-hired assistants in the Department of Commerce. For implementation of the recommendations, Hoover depended upon voluntary cooperation among private sector businessmen, corporate managers, heads of local and state Chambers of Commerce, trade association representatives, and past and present presidents of the United States Chamber of Commerce and the National Association of Manufacturers. Cooperation would be elicited through personal contacts and public relations techniques.[21]

First use of this systematic approach to planning came with the Business Cycle Committee of 1921-1923. Edward Eyre Hunt, a true Hoover loyalist, coordinated the actions. An ex-socialist from the Harvard class of 1910 which had included Walter Lippmann and John Reed, Hunt had gone to work for Hoover with the Commission for Relief in Belgium during the Great War. By 1921, he served as secretary of the Waste in Industry study, from which position he moved on to become secretary of the Unemployment Conference of 1921. Since the Conference technically continued through the work of the committees appointed by the Standing Committee, Hunt acted as the secretary of the Business Cycle Committee. Over the course of the New Era decade, Hunt saw the work of these Hooverian committees as all of a piece in the progression toward national planning. By the end of the 1920s, Hunt consciously referred to the committee and conference system as "national planning" in correspondence with his chief, Herbert Hoover.[22] Shortly after

---

[21]The description of the Hooverian committee and conference system in the text is drawn as a composite picture based upon study of the specialized investigations discussed below in the text. On the emergence of the philanthropic foundations see Barry K. Karl, "The Power of Intellect and the Politics of Ideas," *Daedalus*, 97 (1968): 1002-1035; Barry D. Karl, "Philanthropy, Policy Planning, and the Bureaucratization of the Democratic Idea," *Daedalus*, 105 (Fall 1976): 129-149; and Barry D. Karl and Stanley N. Katz, "The American Private Philanthropic Foundations and the Public Sphere, 1890-1930," *Minerva*, 19 (Summer 1981): 236-270. On the connections between organized philanthropy, social science research, and policy analysis in this period see Gene M. Lyons, *The Uneasy Partnership: Social Science and the Federal Government in the Twentieth Century* (New York, 1969), 1-49; Eakins, "The Development of Corporate Liberal Policy Research," passim; David W. Eakins, "Policy Planning for the Establishment," *A New History of Leviathan*, 188-205; David W. Eakins, "The Origins of Corporate Liberal Policy Research, 1916-1922: The Political Economic Expert and the Decline of Public Debate," *Building the Organizational Society*, ed. Jerry Israel (New York, 1972), 163-179; articles by Ellis Hawley and Kim McQuaid in special issue on "Corporate Liberalism" in *Business History Review*, 52 (Autumn 1978); Martin Bulmer and Joan Bulmer, "Beardsley Ruml and the Laura Spelman Rockefeller Memorial, 1922-29," *Minerva*, 19 (1981): 347-407; Grossman, "American Foundations and the Support of Economic Research"; Alchon, *The Invisible Hand of Planning*; Patrick D. Reagan, "The Architects of Modern American National Planning," Ph.D. diss., Ohio State University, 1982, passim.

[22]Lloyd, *Aggressive Introvert*, 61-62; Hunt files in Pre-Commerce Papers, Hoover Papers; F.M. Feiker to James H. McGraw, 14 March 1925 attached to Feiker to Hunt, 25 March 1925, E.E. Hunt Collection, Hoover Library; and Hunt's drafts of articles in UF-Hunt. Biographical detail on Hunt can be found in the Hunt Collection.

the end of the Unemployment Conference in mid-October 1921, Hunt wrote Hoover about the purposes of the Business Cycle study. He emphasized that the work should be practical in aiming at economic stability and growth, should use the expertise of researchers in business and the social sciences, and should deal with the question of control of the cycle via dissection by economists. Hunt wrote the proposal sent to the philanthropic foundations to fund the Business Cycle investigation using the earlier model of the Waste in Industry proposal that had been submitted successfully to the Russell Sage Foundation. At key points in the negotiations between Hoover, his philanthropic contact man, Edgar Rickard, and the philanthropic managers, Hunt stepped in to iron out any difficulties.[23]

To fund the Business Cycle study, Hoover turned to the Commonwealth Fund, the Carnegie Corporation, and the Russell Sage Foundation. Following his usual technique of staying quietly out of sight, Hoover had Julius Barnes--former head of the wartime Grain Corporation, organizer and member of the Unemployment Conference, and a member of the Standing Committee--consult with Edgar Rickard. Rickard, a publisher of mining journals, had befriended Hoover in London in 1914, served on the executive committee of the American Relief Administration's European Children's Fund, and became Hoover's longest-tenured publicist. Rickard contacted the heads of the Commonwealth Fund and the Carnegie Corporation, sent them Hunt's memo about the study over Hoover's signature, and, after denial of funding from the Commonwealth Fund, also turned to the Russell Sage Foundation. The result of these complicated maneuverings brought $50,000 for the Business Cycle investigation from the Carnegie Corporation by February 1922.[24] In the midst of the negotiations, Hoover wrote Rickard about his perception of the aims of the study, perhaps unaware that his remarks would be passed on to philanthropic managers:

> It is extremely critical that the matter should be carried out as a private undertaking under the guidance of such leading manufacturers and industrial leaders as the above mentioned. Even were it possible to obtain an appropriation from Congress for such a purpose, the character of the result would not have the weight that they will have under a committee such as this.

---

[23]"Seasons and Business Cycles as Causes of Unemployment," UF-Advisory Committee Reports: "Unemployment and Business Cycles: Recommendation on Need for Cycle Study," memo marked "confidential--for conference members only," UF-Business Cycles-1921; Hunt to Hoover, 21 October 1921, UF-Business Cycles; and Hoover to Joseph Defrees, 5 November 1921 and Hunt to W.J. Myers, 26 October 1921, UF for the model from Waste in Industry.

[24]Lloyd, *Aggressive Introvert*, 12, 53; Julius Barnes to Rickard, 12 October 1921; Rickard to Barry Smith, 14 October 1921; Rickard to R.A. Franks, 14 October 1921; Rickard to Christian Herter, 16 November 1921; Rickard to John M. Glenn, 16 November 1921; Hunt to Henry S. Pritchett, 21 December 1921; all in UF. For the Carnegie Corporation grant see Pritchett to Hoover, 14 February 1922, UF-National Bureau of Economic Research.

The object of such a study is to clarify the atmosphere in the United States. There is a great under current of demand for governmental action in the matter of unemployment of the type of European countries and I believe that a careful investigation will demonstrate that such methods are not applicable nor desirable to American life but that there are constructive suggestions consonant with our own economic system that can be outlined.[25]

Clearly Hoover sought to find an "American" middle way to achieve economic stabilization, ironically, by way of a government-sponsored study aimed at promoting macroeconomic policy through private sector businessmen, corporate firms, and trade associations--means well in tune with the precepts of New Era Capitalism.[26]

Hoover appointed "such leading manufacturers and industrial leaders" to the sponsoring committee on November 7, 1921 in the middle of the negotiations for financing. Owen D. Young, President of General Electric, served as chairman due to his intervention with philanthropic managers at a key point in the campaign to win support for funding the Business Cycle study. The other members of the Committee included Joseph H. Defrees, President of the U.S. Chamber of Commerce; Clarence M. Woolley, Chairman of the Amerian Radiator Company; Mary Van Kleeck, Director of the Department of Industrial Studies of the Russell Sage Foundation; the token labor representative, Matthew Woll of the Executive Council of the American Federation of Labor; and E.E. Hunt as secretary. All of them had been delegates to the Unemployment Conference except Young. Hoover put the direction of the Business Cycle study under this committee in order to ensure that "practical" use would be made of the technical study conducted by the National Bureau of Economic Research.[27]

While financing and committee organization proceeded, Hunt approached Edwin F. Gay and Wesley C. Mitchell of the National Bureau of Economic Research (NBER) about their organization's preparing the economic studies that would address the statistical problem of how to determine the extent and numbers of the unemployed, the relationship of unemployment to the changes in the business cycle, and surveying of methods to prevent or dampen extreme fluctuations in the business

---

[25]Hoover to Rickard, 14 November 1921, UF.

[26]Metcalf, "Secretary Hoover and the Emergence of Macroeconomic Management" and Alchon, *The Invisible Hand of Planning.*

[27]Hoover to Rickard, 18 November 1921; Hunt to Defrees, Van Kleeck, and Woll, 5 November 1921; and Hoover to Defrees, 5 November 1921 all in UF. For background on Young see Kim McQuaid, "Young, Swope, and General Electric's 'New Capitalism': A Study in Corporate Liberalism," *American Journal of Economics and Sociology,* 36 (1977): 323-334; Kim McQuaid, "Corporate Liberalism in the American Business Community, 1920-1940," *Business History Review,* 52 (1978): 342-368; Josephine Young Case and Everett Needham Case, *Owen D. Young and American Enterprise* (Boston, 1982), esp. 244, 266-268. On the concern for practical use see Hunt to Young, 13 February 1922, UF-Business Cycles.

cycle. Using a draft outline proposal written by Hunt, Mitchell worked up the final proposal which was submitted to the philanthropic foundations and used by the NBER staffers to guide research for the technical studies. Mitchell, the acknowledged national expert on business cycle theory and statistical series, pointed to such possible methods of prevention as efforts by individual firms, stabilization efforts across whole industries by trade associations, legislative proposals including monetary and banking reforms, advance planning of public works, a new system of public employment offices, forms of unemployment insurance, and upgrading of statistical services by the Department of Commerce. Not surprisingly, despite tensions between the NBER and the sponsoring committee between the spring and fall of 1922, the final recommentions listed by the committee in its report came very close to the ideas listed by Mitchell in the initial proposal. Hoover and Hunt were quite pleased with the work of the Business Cycle Committee as reflected in its public report.[28]

Long before public release of the final report on April 2, 1923, coordinator Hunt worked at publicizing the Committee's work and the value of the NBER's technical investigations. He had reason for concern. John B. Andrews, long-time secretary of the American Association for Labor Legislation, had advocated passage of unemployment compensation legislation at the state level since 1914. In the midst of the Business Cycle Committee's deliberations, Andrews wrote Hunt that only through direct state action could "the financial burden [be placed] upon the business managers and thereby keep them thinking about this problem in good times as well as in times of business depression." Shortly after publication and release of the final report, the president of the National Unemployment League wrote Hunt that

> the Report is a very great disappointment to me, as it does not seem to deal so much with the suffering and plight of the unemployed and with remedial measures for their relief in times of business depression, as it does with regulating business conditions and attempting to do away with the losses there.[29]

Hunt had corresponded with Frederick M. Feiker, Vice President of McGraw-Hill Book Company, who was responsible for that firm's network of trade and profes-

---

[28]Mitchell to Hunt, 20 October 1921; Hunt to Hoover, 21 October 1921; Gay to Hoover, 25 October 1921; Hunt, "Plan of Follow-Up of Work of the President's Conference on Unemployment," 2 November 1921 all in UF-Business Cycles; Gay to Hoover, 22 October 1921, UF-National Bureau of Economic Research; Gay to Hunt, 21 October 1921, Hunt to Gay, 27 October 1921, Hunt memo to Hoover, 13 February 1922 all in UF; minutes of committee meetings and correspondence in UF-National Bureau of Economic Research for NBER-committee tensions; and for the final recommendations see President's Conference on Unemployment, Committee on Business Cycles and Unemployment, *Business Cycles and Unemployment* (New York, 1923).
[29]Andrews to Hunt, 26 July 1922, UF-National Bureau of Economic Research and Darwin J. Meserole to Hunt, 24 April 1923, UF-Business Cycles Report-Comments.

sional journals about publication of articles promoting the Committee's work. Hunt also arranged with Ordway Tead of the same firm's Business Publications division to publish the final report as part of the educational and publicity campaign. In late summer 1922, Chairman Owen D. Young proposed taking a referendum among trade associations, the Chambers of Commerce, unions, the American Banking Association, and other organizations as a way to keep discussion and action about business cycle information alive after completion of the report. Hoover aides in the Department of Commerce worked at placing articles and editorials in newspapers across the country as well as features in trade and technical journals in hopes of making the publicity campaign a success.[30]

Thinking of writing a book on the theme of unemployment in response to the increasing criticisms raised by Mary Van Kleeck and John B. Andrews, Hunt canvassed his friend and colleague, Wesley Mitchell, about the idea. Mitchell wrote back:

> I really don't see much in the idea of arguing the merits of any given social philosophy. You could do a most attractive and persuasive presentation of voluntary individual action; but after you had gotten done and lost the glow of the moment, you would be quite as capable, doing an equally charming and persuasive account, the rising tide of cooperative action through government. We don't know enough yet to know which philosophy is the more effective in the long run. My guess is that each is better in certain fields, and that in many fields both can be used to better effect than either alone. Anyway, that kind of discussion would run out into dialectic and you have too clear and too modern a head to feel content with the kind of writing that would have suited the generations between Bentham and Darwin. Indeed you would sink to the level, Mr. Gladstone and be praised so widely as to become a misanthrope [sic].
>
> It's a big task and a hard one--the kind that is really worth doing and that leaves you a stronger man for all your future years for doing it. Most people won't understand what you have in mind until you have done it. And then people will see a good deal more in your results after ten years than within the months during which the book reviews often [sic].[31]

---

[30]Feiker to Hunt, 4 May 1922; UF-Feiker; Hunt, "How Industry Can Avoid Summer Depression," *Printer's Ink*, May 18, 1922, copy in reprint file, Hoover Library; Tead to Hunt, 30 June 1922 and committee resolution of 18 July 1922, UF-Business Cycle-Report-Publication of; Committee minutes of meeting, 18 July 1922, UF-Business Cycles-1923-May-November; Hunt to Hoover, 18 August and publicity release dated 2 April 1923, UF; and Hunt, "The Long Look Ahead," *The Survey*, 1 July 1923, 400-401.
[31]Mitchell to Hunt, 17 September 1922, UF-Mitchell.

Hunt--and Hoover--must not have thought much of the commentary. When Young suggested that the Cycle Committee meet after release of the report to consider its impact and ways to recruit converts, Hoover noted it was a "splendid idea as it will keep the pot boiling. I am rather astonished at the result the report is actually having in the conduct of business already." Hunt kept faith as well. At the end of 1926, he sent Hoover a list of all the investigatory reports "directly attributable to the [Unemployment] Conference." Prominently displayed on the list was *Business Cycles and Unemployment*, the title of the Committee's final report.[32]

The pattern of Hooverian associative planning continued in the other committee investigation stemming from the Unemployment Conference. As secretary of the Committee on Seasonal Operation, Hunt coordinated the program by obtaining financial support and suggesting ideas for the publicity campaign. Hunt first discussed the possibility of monetary support with Mary Van Kleeck of the Russell Sage Foundation for a study of seasonal operation and unemployment intended to complement the Business Cycle study of cyclical operation and unemployment. After Van Kleeck indicated that the Foundation already had committed monies to the NBER for the Business Cycle technical study, Hunt contacted President Henry S. Pritchett of the Carnegie Corporation to request a grant for $25,000. Ultimately, the Committee on Seasonal Operation garnered $13,000 from the Carnegie Corporation contingent on obtaining another $5,200 from other sources which included American Telephone & Telegraph Co., six trade associations in the construction industries, and the American Federation of Labor which gave a small contribution. While Hunt put together the financial package, Hoover selected members of the sponsoring committee. He appointed Ernest T. Trigg, former head of the National Federation of Construction Industries and president of a Philadelphia lumber company, as chairman along with presidents of two other national trade associations, presidents of two construction companies, two token labor representatives, one banker, two experts, his public works planning specialist--Otto T. Mallery, and John M. Gries, Chief of the Division of Building and Housing in the Department of Commerce.[33]

Hunt approached Harold G. Moulton of the Institute of Economics about conducting the technical study, while Hunt's boss, Hoover, raised the same point with Moulton's boss, Robert S. Brookings. After consulting with Wesley C. Mitchell of the NBER, Hunt decided that Brookings' Institute of Economics did not have

---

[32]Hoover to Young, 17 May 1923, UF-Business Cycles and Hunt to Hoover, 29 December 1926, UF.
[33]Hunt to Mitchell, 7 November 1921, Mitchell to Hunt 10 November 1921 and attached memo to Hoover, all in UF-Mitchell; Hunt to General R.C. Marshall, 5 December 1921, UF-Marshall; Hunt to Edwin F. Gay, 25 January 1922 and Gay to Hunt, 1 February 1922, UF-Gay; Hunt to Pritchett, 17 May 1923 and Pritchett to Hoover, 22 May 1923, UF-Financing and Expenses of Conference; Hoover to Trigg, 28 May 1923, CP-Seasonal Industries Investigation; and U.S. Department of Commerce, Elmination of Waste Series, *Seasonal Operation in the Construction Industries* (Washington, D.C., 1924), v.

the requisite influence with important businessmen. John Gries and his assistant, James Taylor, both of the Division of Building and Housing in Hoover's Department of Commerce, were given the job of conducting the technical study for the Committee. Originally the investigation included plans to examine seasonal unemployment in the bituminous coal, construction, transportation, banking, credit, and other industries. But Hoover decided to concentrate research on construction industries which he argued were of "strategic importance...as a balance wheel, and these industries are notoriously seasonal." After completing its deliberations on March 5, 1924, the Committee on Seasonal Operation in the Construction Industries presented its recommendations. Standardization of contracts and building materials should continue. Statistical collection by the Division of Building and Housing should be upgraded. Outmoded custom regarding cutbacks during the winter season should be overturned. Voluntary associations should accept the idea of long-range planning of public works during boom times to prepare for depression periods. Hunt arranged for publication of the final report in book form with McGraw-Hill and in shortened pamphlet form in the Department of Commerce's Elimination of Waste Series.[34]

Even though John M. Gries of the Division of Building and Housing in the Department of Commerce saw the report as having a decided impact via increases in winter construction, Hoover and his aides might have taken a closer look. Otto T. Mallery, chief proponent of legislative enactment of long-range planning of public works projects, had argued for this form of countercyclical (and counterseasonal) economic policy since his work for the Unemployment Conference and the Business Cycle Committee. Bills for direct action on this issue to promote stabilization in the key construction industries or creation of government committees to at least consider the policy had been introduced in Congress in 1922, 1923, and 1924. Similar bills were introduced in 1927 and 1928--the one in the latter year taking the title of a "Prosperity Reserve" plan. Not one of the bills passed both houses.[35]

To follow up on the work of the Unemployment Conference, the Business Cycle Committee, and the Seasonal Operation Committee, Hunt and Hoover next

---

[34]Hunt to Mitchell, 7 May 1923 and Mitchell to Hunt, 8 May 1923, UF-Mitchell; Hoover to Brookings, 9 May 1923, UF-Seasonal Stabilization; Hoover to H.S. Pritchett, 12 June 1923, UF-Financing and Expenses of Conference for the quote; material in UF-Committee on Seasonal Operation in the Construction Industries-1923-1924 for deliberations; Ernest T. Trigg to Hoover, 6 March 1924, CP-Seasonal Industries Investigation for completion of the report; *Seasonal Operation in the Construction Industries--Report and Recommendations of a Committee of the President's Conference on Unemployment* (New York, 1924) and U.S. Department of Commerce, Elimination of Waste Series, *Seasonal Operation* for the published reports.

[35]Gries to Hoover, 16 October 1924, UF-Seasonal Stabilization; Hoover speech before Associated General Contractors of America, 12 January 1925, Speech File, Hoover Library; Gries to Hoover, 14 November 1925, CP-Seasonal Industries Investigation; Howenstine, "Public Works Policy in the Twenties"; and materials in UF-Mallery, UF-Public Works-Bills-1921-1923, and UF-Prosperity Reserve.

tried to put together a study on the bases of adjustment of industrial disputes. Obviously worried about another outbreak of industrial conflict like that of 1919, they sought to use the associative planning network to arrive at a conception of peaceful adjustment of labor-management conflict through social science expertise. Between late October 1923 and mid-February 1925, Hunt and Hoover contacted Arthur Woods, now a close adviser to the Rockefeller Foundation and President of the Laura Spelman Rockefeller Memorial (LSRM), and Beardsley Ruml, Director of the LSRM, to ask for a grant of $100,000. The study would be conducted by Professor Joseph Willits of the Wharton School of Business at the University of Pennsylvania. Both John D. Rockefeller, Jr. and philanthropic manager Ruml proved reluctant to fund the investigation. In reporting his telephone conversation with Ruml to Hoover, Hunt noted Ruml's pronouncement of what proved to be the death knell of the study:

> Mr. Rockefeller had advised [Ruml] yesterday that he is much interested in the proposed study of Bases of Adjustment in Industrial Disputes but feels that it would be unwise for him to give the entire amount or to take any action that would seem to imply his initiative in the matter. [He is willing to give twenty-five per cent of the amount needed up to $25,000 if balance can be raised from other sources.] He wishes you to consider this as an anonymous proposition until the necessary sum is in hand.

Despite their efforts to procure the "necessary sum," neither Hunt nor Hoover was ever able to get this planning effort implemented.[36]

With completion of the projected economic planning from the Unemployment Conference of 1921 by 1924, Hooverian associative national planning entered a hiatus. Hoover already had begun to carry out his system of voluntary cooperation by reorganizing the Department of Commerce and institutionalizing that organization's simplification, standardization, and stabilization plans. In the construction industries, Hoover encouraged the work of the American Construction Council, founded in June 1922, under the leadership of Franklin D. Roosevelt. Both Hoover and Roosevelt hoped that the Council would promote upgraded collection of statistics in the key construction industries while simultaneously enacting from the private sector a countercyclical policy of increased building during cyclical downturns with

---

[36]Hunt to Mitchell, 26 October 1923, UF-Mitchell; Hoover to Woods, 26 September 1924, CP-Rockefeller Foundation; Hunt, "Bases of Agreement in Industrial Disputes," memo, 8 October 1924 and Hunt to Willits, 26 October 1924, CP-Hunt; Hunt to Hoover, 28 October 1924 and Hoover to Woods, 28 October 1924, UF-Bases of Agreement in Industrial Disputes; Hunt to Ruml, 31 October 1924, CP-Hunt; Hoover to Woods, 14 January 1925, for the quote see Hunt memo to Hoover, 14 February 1925, for Hunt's last effort see Hunt memo to Hoover, 14 May 1926, CP-Rockefeller Foundation.

complementary cutbacks in periods of growth. After 1925, Secretary of Commerce Hoover broke free of the restraining influence of other Cabinet departments to promote a wide range of industrial conferecnes at which representatives of the trade association movement voiced their desires for antitrust revision. This movement toward industrial self-government under government encouragement eventually would culminate in partial victory through the New Deal's National Recovery Administration.[37]

While Hoover acted, Hunt drew back to think through the implications of the committee and conference system. In 1925, Hunt published *Conferences, Committees, Conventions and How to Run Them,* a comparative study of private, private-public, and public sector conferences based on his own experience and reading. In private correspondence and memoranda, Hunt wrote even more openly about what he unabashedly termed "national planning." Writing to journalist Frederick Lewis Allen, Hunt noted that American national planning such as evidenced in the work of Hoover's Department of Commerce would simultaneously preserve private sector incentive. Hunt now saw the Hooverian committee and conference system built since 1921 as worthy of institutionalization in the form of national planning. As he thought about the subject, Hunt expanded his ideal of planning to include government cooperation with large corporations, national business organizations such as the Chamber of Commerce, national trade associations, state and local business groups; use of social scientific surveys; and, as a "leavening," work with some representatives of organized labor. He pointed to investigations sponsored by the American Engineering Council (a private body), the Unemployment Conference of 1921 (a private-public body), and the U.S. Coal Commission (a federal public body) to buttress his argument.[38]

---

[37]Hawley, "Herbert Hoover, the Commerce Secretariat, and the Vision of an 'Associative State'"; on the American Construction Council see "Industry's New Doctors," *New York Times,* 4 June 1922; Hoover to President Harding, 17 March 1923, copy from holdings in the Franklin D. Roosevelt Library, Hyde Park, New York in the Franklin D. Roosevelt Collection, Hoover Library; "Meeting of the Board of Governors of the American Construction Council," 16 May 1923, American Construction Council file, Record Group 14, National Archives, Washington, D.C., copy in ibid.; Hoover to Roosevelt, 12 June 1923, from holdings in the Roosevelt Library, copy in Roosevelt Collection, Hoover Library. On the trade association movement and antitrust revision see Himmelberg, *Origins of the National Recovery Administration,* esp. 75-109.

[38]Hunt, "Stabilizing Employment--The National Point of View," address to the Young Men's Christian Association, 31 August 1923 at Silver Bay Conference in Reprint File, Hoover Library; Hunt, "Conference," mimeographed typescript dated December 1924, CP-Conferences; Hunt, *Conferences, Committees, Conventions and How to Run Them* (New York, 1925); Hunt, "The Cooperative Committee and Conference System," memorandum to Hoover, 14 December 1926, CP-Hunt; Planning," address before North Carolina Conference for Social Service, Raleigh, North Carolina, 10 February 1927 and Hunt, "Economic Investigations," 19 May 1927, memorandum for use of Sir Arthur Salter attached to memorandum to Mrs. Goodwin, 17 June 1927, Hunt Collection; and Hunt, "Notes on Economic and Social Surveys," *Bulletin of the Taylor Society,* 13 (February 1928); 3-11.

As Hunt and Hoover understood the term, "national planning" involved a cooperative effort among enlightened federal officials in the Executive Branch, business-oriented national organizations, philanthropic managers and social science experts. The culmination of Hooverian associative planning occurred with two landmark investigations. The National Bureau of Economic Research assisted in the case of the Committee on Recent Economic Changes (1927-1929), while the Social Science Research Council (SSRC) served a similar function for the President's Research Committee on Social Trends (1929-1933). Ironically, at the very time that Hooverian planning reached its zenith, New Era Capitalism collapsed.[39]

In March 1927, Hoover decided to reactivate the study of business cycles in order to consider fundamental changes over the long run history of the business cycle, how far the cycle's peaks and valleys had been "mitigated," where the economy stood in the current cycle, and what statistical services could be used or begun to "more clearly give warnings or indications of the position." Hunt approached managers of the Carnegie Corporation and the Laura Spelman Rockefeller Memorial about funding--he obtained $75,000 from each foundation by early 1928. Once again, Hoover carefully selected the sponsoring committee and turned to the National Bureau of Economic Research to conduct the technical studies. McGraw-Hill again published the resulting report, the two – volume study, *Recent Economic Changes in the United States.* (1929).[40]

The Committee on Recent Economic Changes presented a generally optimistic outlook for the nation's economic future in the summary sections written by the sponsoring committee. The NBER's special investigations and some additional ones were included in chapters written by businessmen and social science experts in the fields of industry, construction, transportation, marketing, labor, management, agriculture, price movements, money and credit, foreign markets and credit, and the national income and its distribution. Wesley C. Mitchell, research director of the NBER and the Committee, wrote the lengthy final review chapter. Hunt published short articles and later a two-hundred page popular summary of the Committee's findings in hopes of publicizing the work and sparking cooperative voluntary action. The ideological basis of the report paralleled that of New Era capitalism's triad--high production, high consumption, and high wages. These legs of economic growth

---

[39]Committee on Recent Economic Changes of the President's Conference on Unemployment, *Recent Economic Changes in the United States* 2 vols. (New York, 1929) and President's Research Committee on Social Trends, *Recent Social Trends in the United States* 2 vols. (New York, 1933).

[40]*The Memoirs of Herbert Hoover*, Vol. II, 176 and Vol. III, 14-15; Hoover memo to Dr. Gries et al., 17 March 1927, UF; Hunt memo to Hoover, 15 September 1927 and Hoover to F.P. Keppel, 26 October 1927, UF-Business Cycles; Hoover to Henry M. Robinson, 7 January 1928, CP; Hunt memo to Hoover, 17 December 1927, Hoover to Woods, 23 December 1927, Ruml telegram to Hoover, 29 December 1927, and Hoover letters of invitation to serve on committee, 6-7 January 1928 all in CP-Committees-Economic Study-1927-1928; and Hunt to Paul Devinat, 26 April 1928, Hunt collection.

could be maintained through what the Committee called "the technique of economic balance." The ideas behind Hooverian planning permeated the final report--the belief that the business cycle could be understood and controlled scientifically, seasonal unemployment could be overcome easily, advance public works planning could be an effective countercyclical tool, and ultimately, reliance on voluntary cooperation among organized economic interests would preserve the traditional American system.[41]

The President's Research Committee on Social Trends (1929-1933) varied the pattern of Hooverian planning by going beyond economic planning into the wider arena of social welfare. President Hoover cooperated with his close friend, Ray Lyman Wilbur, Secretary of the Interior. Wilber and Hoover hoped to reorganize Interior just as Hoover had Commerce. They saw Interior as expanding to two divisions, one for public works, the other for education, health, and recreation. In September 1929, presidential aide Edgar French Strother brought social scientists from the Social Science Research Council to the White House to discuss with Hoover plans for the first national inventory of the nation's physical, biological, and social resources. Sociologists William Ogburn and Howard Odum, political scientist Charles E. Merriam, and economist Wesley Clair Mitchell agreed to take part in the study. Merriam and Director Beardsley Ruml of the Laura Spelman Rockefeller Memorial had co-founded the SSRC in early 1923 with LSRM financial support in order to create a national research network for social science paralleling that of the American Council of Learned Societies for the humanities and the war-generated National Research Council for the physical sciences. Ruml worked to expand this social science research network to include private research bodies such at the National Bureau of Economic Research, policy analysis organizations that blurred the lines between public and private sector work such as the Brookings Institution, and cooperative federal agencies interested in promoting data collection and distribution. Through this complicated organizational nexus built up since 1921, these associational planners brought forth the country's first planned social resources inventory. A massive grant of $560,000 from the newly-created Social Science Division of the Rockefeller Foundation, which had taken up the Ruml-directed LSRM's work, made the two and one half year investigation possible.[42]

But this time, the Hooverian associative planning process revealed its flaws. As President, Hoover clearly indicated at the inception of the study that he intended

---

[41] *Recent Economic Changes;* Hunt, "America's Increasing Economic Stability," *Current History,* 30 (August 1929): 811-816; Hunt, *An Audit of America: A Summary of Recent Economic Changes in the United States* (New York, 1930). For analysis of the Committee see Alchon, "Technocratic Social Science," 208-232. For one of the first scholarly analyses of Hoover's economic policies see Herbert Stein, *From New Era to New Deal: Herbert Hoover, the Economists, and American Economic Policy, 1921-1933* (Cambridge, Eng. and New York, 1985).

[42] Reagan, "The Architects," esp. 122-130; Barry D. Karl, "Presidential Planning and Social Science Research: Mr. Hoover's Experts," *Perspectives in American History,* 3 (1969): 347-409; Barry D. Karl, *Charles E. Merriam and the Study of Politics* (Chicago, 1974), 118-139, 201-225.

to use advance copies of the Committee's reports as guides for action. In the midst of the election year of 1932, that intention created tensions both within the Committee proper--between the research purists and those who argued for policy application of research findings--and between Hoover's liaison, Strother, and the Committee members. Though the two-volume summary report, *Recent Social Trends in the United States,* appeared in January 1933--published by McGraw-Hill--changing external conditions buried publicity about the report.[43]

New Era capitalism proved fundamentally flawed. Underconsumption by those with the money to spend and maldistribution of income and wealth so that many consumers did not have enough to spend brought the dream of a New Era crashing down. The Great Depression struck with gale force, a "slowly sucking maelstrom," as one Boston businessman put it. The closer the social scientists got to the political and social arena, the more controversial their ideas and actions became. The pattern would recur in the course of New Deal planning from 1933 through 1943. Never completely institutionalized due to Hoover's overweening fear of the managerial state, the Hooverian administrative planning mechanisms proved ill-fated. Governmental sponsorship, financing through managerial philanthropists, deliberation by organized businessmen and Hooverian loyalists on the sponsoring committee, research by private sector organizations of experts such as the National Bureau of Economic Research and the Social Science Research Council, and, ultimately, an overabundance of faith in their own publicity contributed to the failure of Hooverian national planning.[44]

Yet external events clearly delivered the death blow. The onset of the Great Depression of 1929-1941 meant that the earlier depression of 1920-1921 paled in comparison--it became "the forgotten depression." Herbert Hoover--once the American hero, now the American goat--fell victim to his own vision and experience of national planning. Turning to the planning experience stemming from the response to the earlier depression by the Unemployment Conference of 1921 and its offshoots, Hoover set up voluntary cooperative efforts in a variety of areas. One-by-one, the committees and conferences of industrialists, builders, and bankers fell apart from 1930 through 1932. Perhaps the ultimate irony came with Hoover's calling Arthur Woods back to national service to rerun the work of the Civic and Emergency

---

[43]Karl, "Presidential Planning" emphasizes the tensions within the Committee.

[44]Economists, economic historians, and other scholars still have not solved the riddle of what "caused" the Great Depression. But clearly maldistribution of income and wealth in the 1920s was in large part the difficulty which led to what some analysts refer to as "underconsumption." For recent efforts to clarify the issues see Charles Holt, "Who Benefitted From the Prosperity of the 1920s?," *Explorations in Economic History,* 14 (July 1977): 277-289 and Frank Stricker, "Affluence for Whom?--Another Look at Prosperity and the Working Classes in the 1920s," *Labor History,* 24 (1983): 5-33. For a thought-provoking view of the subject within a broader context see Robert S. McElvaine, *The Great Depression: America, 1929-1941* (New York, 1984). "Slowly sucking maelstrom" comes from Henry S. Dennison, "Our Captains," an unpublished 1936 poem in possession of Elizabeth Dunker of Cambridge, Massachusetts.

Measures Committee of 1921-1922. It had not really worked then--Woods and Hoover did not see that though--and it did not work now. Between October 17, 1930 and August 19, 1931, as head of the President's Emergency Committee for Employment, Woods invoked the once-tried publicity campaign for voluntary relief of unemployment at the state and local levels. The system failed.[45]

Hooverian national planning shriveled in the wake of national catastrophe; however, associative planning, like the phoenix rising from the ashes, arose reborn to pave the way to the future. Included among the array of Hooverian associationalists were President Franklin D. Roosevelt's New Deal planners. Frederic A. Delano, uncle to FDR, had used associational planning techniques to establish and then head the National Capital Park and Planning Commission in the 1920s. Both Hoover and Roosevelt renewed his appointment. Charles E. Merriam, chairman of the Department of Political Science at the University of Chicago, co-founded the Social Science Research Council which sponsored the work of President Hoover's Research Committee on Social Trends. As Vice-Chairman of that Committee, Merriam wrote the original draft of the "Review of Findings" which called for creation of a national planning board by the federal government. Roosevelt appointed Delano and Merriam to just such a board in July 1933. Wesley Clair Mitchell, co-founder of the National Bureau of Economic Research which served Hoover so well, succeeded Merriam as head of the SSRC and followed him to the planning board during the period 1933-1935. Henry S. Dennison, Boston welfare capitalist, delegate to the Unemployment Conference of 1921, author of the key "Management" chapter in *Recent Economic Changes,* joined Roosevelt's planners in late 1935 after service on the

---

[45]Hoover's response to the Great Depression is discussed in Harris Gaylord Warren, *Herbert Hoover and the Great Depression* (New York, 1959), Albert U. Romasco, *The Poverty of Abundance: Hoover, the Nation, the Depression* (New York, 1966), Hawley, *The Great War,* 173-229. On the PECE see William Hard, "Our Doctor of Unemployment," *Review of Reviews,* 82 (December 1930): 42-43; E[rving] P[aul] Hayes, *Activities of the President's Emergency Committee for Employment* (Concord, N.H., 1936), Irving Bernstein, *The Lean Years* (Boston, 1960), 262-311; Romasco, *The Poverty of Abundance,* 55-56, 143 ff.; Richard Earl Edwards, "Herbert Hoover and the Public Relations Approach to Recovery, 1930-1932" (Ph.D. diss., University of Iowa, 1976), esp. 103-106 on the PECE's publicity staff. Case studies of the PECE's state and local committees' failure include Bonnie R. Fox, "Unemployment Relief in Philadelphia, 1930-1932: A Study of the Depression's Impact on Voluntarism," *Pennsylvania Magazine of History and Biography,* 93 (1969): 86-108; Richard T. Ortquist, "Unemployment and Relief: Michigan's Response to the Depression During the Hoover Years," *Michigan History,* 57 (1973): 209-236; Charles M. Kimberly, "The Depression in Maryland: The Failure of Voluntarism," *Maryland History Magazine,* 70 (1975): 189-202; Ronald L. Nye, "The Challenge to Philanthropy: Unemployment Relief in Santa Barbara, 1930-1932," *California Historical Quarterly,* 56 (1977-78): 310-327; William H. Mullins, "Self-Help in Seattle, 1931-1932: Herbert Hoover's Concept of Cooperative Individualism and the Unemployed Citizens' League," *Pacific Northwest Quarterly,* 72 (1981): 11-19. Cf. William W. Bremer, "Along the 'American Way': The New Deal's Work Relief Programs for the Unemployed," *Journal of American History,* 62 (December 1975): 636-652 and Bonnie Fox Schwartz, *The Civil Works Administration, 1933-1934: The Business of Emergency Employment in the New Deal* (Princeton, 1984).

Industrial Advisory Board of the National Recovery Administration. Jovial, elusive, and powerful Beardsley Ruml, manager of the Laura Spelman Rockefeller Memorial, had channeled philanthropic monies to most of Hoover's planning committees and conferences. He joined the New Deal planners in 1935 making possible private sector financial support for establishment of state planning boards under the auspices of the New Deal planning agency.[46]

In July 1933 President Roosevelt chose five experienced Hooverian planners to sit on the New Deal planning board. Between 1921 and 1933, public and private sector organizations forged associational linkages that created a distinctly Hooverian style of voluntary national planning. Government officials, businessmen, social scientific experts, and philanthropic managers came together in an attempt to respond to the concerns raised by the depression of 1920-1921. Veterans of the wartime mobilization agencies and members of Hoover's reorganized Department of Commerce moved into the Unemployment Conference of 1921 and its followup committees. Each of these conferences and committees was staffed by managers of business corporations, representatives of trade associations, and leaders of such business groups as the U.S. Chamber of Commerce. Social scientists from the National Bureau of Economic Research and the various professional organizations associated with the Social Science Research Council provided the expertise that undergirded Hooverian planning efforts. Yet rather than seeking funding from the federal government, planners sought the aid of private philanthropic managers heading such voluntary philanthropies as the Russell Sage Foundation, the Commonwealth Fund, the Carnegie Corporation, and the Laura Spelman Rockefeller Memorial. Among these Hooverian planners were Delano, Merriam, Mitchell, Dennison, and Ruml--the people who became New Deal planners trying to come to grips with the depression of the 1930s. Though transformed by the catalyst of the Great Depression, Hooverian planning experienced a rebirth under the auspices of Franklin D. Roosevelt's New Deal. Associative national planning died, only to be reborn to face another depression. Between 1921 and 1933, Hooverian national planning moved from depression to Depression.

---

[46]Reagan, "The Architects." For two thought-provoking works on the larger implications of Hooverian national planning see Barry D. Karl, "Herbert Hoover and the Progressive Myth of the Presidency," address at the Herbert Hoover Seminar, Hoover Library, August 1974, copy on file at the Hoover Library and Karl, *The Uneasy State.*

By William G. Robbins
ASSOCIATE PROFESSOR OF HISTORY
OREGON STATE UNIVERSITY

Voluntary Cooperation vs. Regulatory Paternalism: The Lumber Trade in the 1920s

¶*In the 1920s, leaders of the lumber business tried to bring stability to their industry through vigorous trade association activity conducted with the encouragement of then Commerce Secretary Herbert Hoover. Despite the optimism of association spokespeople and publicists, the hoped for stability was not attained because the associations were incapable of relieving the intra- and inter-industry competition lumbermen confronted. Nevertheless, the efforts of those involved threw into sharp relief attitudes in business and government about the nature of the political economy of the "New Era."*

The movement west and south of the logging frontier from its origin in Maine is one of the most striking aspects of the lumber industry in the pre-twentieth century United States. Optimistic and reckless exploitation, economic boom and then disaster, characterized this outward push. When the timber resources in one region were spent, there were bigger and taller trees just beyond the ring of the woodsman's axe — in the Great Lakes states beginning in the 1840s and 1850s, the extensive pine forests of the southeast in the last quarter of the nineteenth century, and then on to the last great stand, the Douglas fir forests of the North Pacific slope in the early twentieth century.[1]

The growth of the lumber and wood products business in the United States was always closely linked to the requirements of westward expansion and to the development of the nation's expanding industrial economy. To meet these needs, industry groups sought political solutions to the persisting problems of unregulated competition and cyclical instability. And in the process they were able to influence the ideological and political nature of the emerging regulatory and legislative mechanisms and to direct and shape policy to suit their perceived needs. In the case of the lumber enterprise (and other resource industries like oil and coal), periodic overproduction and unrestrained competition contributed to instability and glutted markets.[2]

Business History Review, Vol. LVI, No. 3 (Autumn, 1982). Copyright © The President and Fellows of Harvard College.

[1] For an informal, yet informative history of the North American lumber industry, see Stewart Holbrook, *Holy Old Mackinaw: A Natural History of the American Lumberjack* (New York, 1938).

[2] Revisionist studies that address these issues, either directly or indirectly, are Samuel P. Hays, *Conserva-*

To alleviate these tensions, spokesmen for these dynamic and sometimes volatile business enterprises sought institutional and cooperative adjustments to conform with changing industrial and economic circumstances. Lumbermen who understood these conditions attempted to link proposals for conserving the forests to the specific economic requirements for stabilizing and rationalizing business activity. They argued that material conditions should define legislative and regulatory programs for conservation.[3]

The lumber industry achieved part of its legislative program in 1924 with congressional passage of the Clarke-McNary Act. This measure offered expanded federal assistance to states for fire protection, an objective that lumbermen had sought for at least twenty years. This act can be viewed as the industry's supreme effort to effect more rational and stable modes of business operation independently of federal regulation. Consistent with the growing influence of business in government, Clarke-McNary did not restrict silvicultural practices on private timberland, nor did it limit lumber business activity.[4]

The purpose of this study is to look beyond legislation and to examine the various cooperative efforts between government agencies and the lumber industry in the 1920s to attain economic stability. That these voluntary attempts failed to resolve the lumberman's persisting economic difficulties suggests the limitations of voluntarism in intensely competitive industries. Morever, because the larger companies dominated most of the lumber associations, trade policy often placed smaller operators at a competitive disadvantage. This underscores again the true impact of association activity.

The National Lumber Manufacturers Association

Legislative efforts at the federal and state level represent only part of the business community's attempt to control the destablizing influences of an overly competitive situation. During the first quarter of the

tion and the Gospel of Efficiency: The Progressive Conservation Movement, 1890–1920 (Cambridge, Mass., 1959); Elmo Richardson, The Politics of Conservation: Crusades and Controversies, 1897–1913 (Berkeley) 1962); Gabriel Kolko, The Triumph of Conservatism: A Reinterpretation of American History, 1900–1916 (New York, 1963); Robert H. Wiebe, The Search For Order, 1877–1920 (New York, 1967); James Weinstein, The Corporate Ideal in the Liberal State (Boston, 1968); Ellis W. Hawley, The Great War and the Search for a Modern Order, A History of the American People and Their Institutions (New York, 1979).

[3] I am indebted to Professor Ellis W. Hawley, University of Iowa, for clarifying many of these issues. Also see Weinstein, The Corporate Ideal, x; Louis Galambos, Competition and Cooperation: The Emergence of a National Trade Association (Baltimore, 1966), 3, 10; Robert F. Himmelberg, The Origins of the National Recovery Administration: Business, Government, and the Trade Association Issue, 1921–1933 (New York, 1976), 1–2; Peri Ethan Arnold, "Herbert Hoover and the Continuity of American Public Policy," Public Policy, 20 (Fall 1972), 528–529.

[4] For the conventional view of the Clarke-McNary legislation, see William B. Greeley, Forests and Men (New York, 1951), 103–114; Samuel Trask Dana, Forest and Range Policy (New York, 1956), 216–217; George T. Morgan, Jr., William B. Greeley, A Practical Forester (St. Paul, 1961), 45–58; Harold K. Steen, The U. S. Forest Service: A History (Seattle, 1976), 185–195.

twentieth century, government officials and industrial modernists believed that the federal government could make an active and positive contribution toward achieving economic stability and maintaining the hegemony of dominant economic groups. This period marked the intensification of business efforts to forge cooperative trade associations as a way to a rationalized political economy. The expanding trade association movement was the institutional expression of cooperative business activity designed to avoid the problems posed by an excessively competitive market system. In effect, the associations were part of a maturing capitalist order that found expression in the pool, the trust, the holding company and, of course, the large corporation. And like other forms of business consolidation, trade associations raised questions about monopoly and restraint of trade, issues that were partly resolved when the Supreme Court in the mid-1920s (e.g., the Maple-Flooring Case) declared most forms of associational activity to be legitimate.[5]

The intense competitiveness of the lumber enterprise and its inherent tendency to over-production prompted lumbermen at a very early period to attempt to control the market; the industry made cooperative efforts to contend with industrial problems, railroad rates, and uniform grading. It also proposed various designs to plan and control production. But the easy availability of timber across the continent and the ready access to capital multiplied the number of competitors and worsened the situation. Despite the vigorous work of industry modernists to cope with these tendencies, the maladjustments persisted until World War II, when competitive conditions began to change.

Beginning in the 1890s in the midst of depression and demoralized markets, a small group of prominent lumbermen sought to resolve the perplexing issue of overproduction and instability through cooperative activity. These early lumber trade associations achieved a few limited successes when business conditions were favorable but proved ineffectual during periods of depression and contracting markets. Although competitive conditions had forced the search for relief through trade agreements, Wilson Compton, who was to become a trade association leader, noted in 1917 that the quest was "comparatively fruitless and was discouraged from within and repressed from without."[6]

---

[5] Weinstein, *The Corporate Ideal*, 252. Louis Galambos, *Competition and Cooperation*, is a study of the cotton textile industry but with broader implications. John H. Cox, "Trade Associations in the Lumber Industry of the Pacific Northwest, 1899–1914," *Pacific Northwest Quarterly*, 41 (1950), 285. The best general discussion of the relation between trade associations and the antitrust issue is in Himmelberg, *Origins of the National Recovery Administration*. The antitrust issue in the lumber industry is treated in Cox, "Trade Associations in the Lumber Industry," 294–296.

[6] Cox, "Trade Associations in the Lumber Industry," 285, 288–289; Wilson Compton. "The Price Problem in the Lumber Industry," *American Economic Review*, 7 (1917), 583. An excellent discussion of lumber trade association activity on the Pacific Coast in the nineteenth century is in Thomas R. Cox, *Mills and Markets: A History of the Pacific Coast Lumber Industry to 1900* (Seattle, 1974), 255–283. For other accounts of early

Wilson M. Compton

As Secretary-Manager of the National Lumber Manufacturers Association from 1916 to 1944, Compton advocated close cooperation between the Association and the Department of Commerce.

But changing circumstances and the experiences of the United States in World War I contributed to a favorable environment for associational activity. The war effort gave the lumber business an economic boost and accelerated the move toward cooperative activity at all levels. David T. Mason, a consultant forester with close ties to the lumber trade, observed that sharp competition and lack of cooperation were the most noticeable features of lumbering before the war. "What is needed in the lumber industry," Mason noted, "is the modern spirit of cooperation rather than the extreme spirit of individualism which now exists." Like others who promoted trade association activity after the war, Mason proposed a relaxation of the anti-trust laws so that lumbermen could legally regulate prices and lumber production.[7]

lumber trade association activity, see Nelson Courtlandt Brown, *The American Lumber Industry, Embracing the Principal Features of the Resources, Production, Distribution and Utilization of Lumber in the United States* (New York, 1923), 232–254, and Charles A. Gillett, "Citizen and Trade Associatons Dealing with Forestry," in Robert K. Winters, ed., *Fifty Years of Forestry* (Washington, D.C., 1950), 285–298.

[7] U. S. Forest Service, *Timber Depletion, Lumber Prices, and Concentration of Timber Ownership* (Washington, D. C., 1920), 66; David T. Mason, *Timber Ownership and Lumber Production in the Inland Empire* (Portland, 1920), 13, 76, 79. For an account of the postwar efforts to repeal antitrust legislation, see Himmelberg, *Origins of the National Recovery Administration*, Chapter One.

The bitter rivalries among various lumber organizations and different producing regions in the prewar years, coupled with the positive experience with the federal government during the war, led directly to the reorganization and revitalization of the largest lumber trade group, the National Lumber Manufacturers Association. The reorganized association placed greater authority and responsibility in its newly created Secretary-Manager, and Wilson Compton, a trained economist and lawyer, was the first appointee to the position. The organization revamped and standardized its procedures for collecting fees and dues, took steps to promote a more positive image of lumbermen, and initiated a rapprochement among professional and academic foresters, an alarmed public, and the wood producing industry.[8]

The restructured National Lumber Manufacturers Association pursued its legislative and regulatory objectives vigorously in the next few years. It attempted to rationalize and stabilize conditions in the lumber industry and to integrate real and potential opponents within its broader political framework. The association's effectiveness in achieving its peculiar brand of legislative and regulatory policy in the 1920s is testimony to a successful public relations program that identified the needs of the lumber industry with the national interest. This included a regulatory program predicated on voluntary private initiative, and the whole-hearted cooperation of two vital government agencies — the United States Forest Service and the Department of Commerce.

The Department of Commerce best expressed the prevailing philosophy of government-industry cooperation in the 1920s. Moreover, lumber trade associations, in addition to their intimate working relationship with the Forest Service and Chief Forester William B. Greeley, also established positive ties with the Department of Commerce and its dynamic Secretary Herbert C. Hoover. The relationship was a reciprocal one, because no other individual articulated the idea of government-industry cooperation more forcefully than Hoover. He repeatedly emphasized the need for friendly cooperation between government and industry and believed that the substantive interests of industry and the public were identical. Hoover's policies struck responsive chords throughout the trade association world, and his dramatic expansion of Commerce Department activities excited the imaginations of industrial spokesmen who wanted to achieve a more stable and efficient economic order. Hoover's version of New Era industrialism emphasized the standardization and simplification of production, the elimination of waste, and the exchange of statistical information.[9]

[8] *Highlights of a Decade of Achievement* (n.p., 1929), 8–12, 30, 41.
[9] The expanded activities of the Department of Commerce under Herbert Hoover are reviewed in Ellis W.

Barely had Hoover taken over at Commerce when friendly and enthusiastic reports began flooding the office in response to his call for a close working relationship between his department and trade associations. Lumber trade people like W. W. Schupner, of the National Wholesale Lumber Dealers Association, were prominent among those who assured Hoover that they would "be glad to cooperate in any way possible so far as the lumber industry is concerned." In similar fashion George Sisson, president of the influential American Paper and Pulp Association, supported Hoover's plan for trade association cooperation with the Department of Commerce "with the idea of aiding in the revival of business." In an address to the annual meeting of the American Paper and Pulp Association in April 1921, Sisson called for "more business in government" and suggested that the government continue to encourage industrial associations as it did during the Great War, because "costly competition is not conducive to the general welfare." Sisson noted that Hoover had struck "a refreshing note" and "has a high conception of the duties and relations of his department toward industry."[10]

Secretary Hoover moved quickly and aggressively to promote lumber trade association activity as an aid to stabilizing the industry. Two months after Hoover's confirmation as Commerce Secretary, and at his suggestion, regional trade leaders agreed to turn over to the Department of Commerce monthly reports on production, orders, shipments, and stocks on hand as part of a plan of cooperation with the government agency. Commerce, in return, would make this information available on a monthly basis thereby providing lumbermen with the knowledge necessary to make intelligent production decisions. If this statistical service had been available during the previous year, Hoover believed, production would have slowed down and "minimized the depth of [the] present slump."[11]

The trade journal, *Lumber,* a market service paper published in St. Louis, called the Hoover proposals "A 'Constructive Revolution.'" It noted that his suggestions were "revolutionary — even sensational — when compared with other emanations from Government sources in all matters concerning the lumber industry." Hoover's proposal for compiling statistics on production and consumption, the paper observed, was a

Hawley, "Herbert Hoover, the Commerce Secretariat, and the Vision of an 'Associative State,' 1921–1928," *Journal of American History,* 61 (June 1974), 116–140.

[10] W. W. Schupner to Hoover, March 24, 1921, "National Wholesale Lumber Dealers Association, 1921–1922," Commerce Papers, Hoover Papers (hereafter CPHP), Herbert Hoover Presidential Library. Sisson to Hoover, April 5, 1921, "Paper and Pulpwood, 1920–1925," Ibid.; Annual Address of the President, American Paper and Pulpwood Association, in *The Paper and Pulp Industry,* Bulletin No. 11 (April 1921), filed in "Paper and Pulpwood, 1920–1925," Ibid.

[11] *Lumber,* 67 (May 27, 1921), 23.

"startling suggestion" and well in advance of the Forest Service, which had compiled yearly statistics of production but published these only once each year, long after the data were gathered. The Forest Service work was "of considerable interest, but [its] value is historical rather than commercial." Hoover, *Lumber* observed, put forth "the most constructive suggestion that has ever come to the industry from the government." The *Southern Lumberman* also praised the Hoover proposals, especially in view of the lawsuits and rumors directed at the lumber industry over the previous eighteen months "for doing the very things which Mr. Hoover now proposes to do with the co-operation of the lumbermen."[12]

Although the legal relationship between trade associations and the antitrust laws puzzled Hoover, he viewed the work of the majority of trade groups as "a constructive contribution of public welfare." He praised the organizations for collecting information on raw material and stocks on hand and commended the high percentage of manufacturers who were actively cooperating — "all of which . . . contribute to stability and the increasing efficiency of industry and to the protection both of the smaller manufacturers and the consumer." Hoover believed that the association movement had its greatest potential in promoting voluntary cooperation and in avoiding regulatory legislation.[13]

TRADE ASSOCIATIONS AND THE SUPREME COURT

Trade association cooperation with the Department of Commerce received a legal setback in December 1921 when the Supreme Court in the Hardwood case declared certain kinds of association activity illegal. The *Southern Lumberman* called the Hardwood decision "a stunning blow" and said that the "chaos and demoralization" that would accompany application of the legal principle "staggers the imagination." The southern trade paper thought that the issue could be resolved only through legislative enactment: "Clearly the Sherman Act has outlived its usefulness." Other trade journals were less harsh in their criticism, and some, like *Lumber,* thought that the publication of prices for the use of buyers and sellers alike was not a restriction of competition and therefore not proscribed by the court.[14]

Doubt about the effects of the Hardwood decision confused trade association leaders and Commerce officials, and Hoover had to defend

[12] Ibid. (June 3, 1921), 11; *Southern Lumberman*, 99 (May 28, 1921), 28.
[13] Department of Commerce memo, June 2, and Nathan B. Williams, President, National Association of Manufacturers, memorandum of a conversation with Hoover, July 7, 1921, "Trade Associations — 1921," *CPHP.*
[14] *Southern Lumberman*, 104 (December 24, 1921), 36; *Lumber*, 68 (December 30, 1921), 13.

his department from accusations that it acted in collusion with private businesses. He argued that making statistical information public "acts alike to protect legitimate business enterprise and the public interest" and that in the long run the Hardwood case would have a bearing on only a small number of trade associations.[15]

The Supreme Court did not actually make a clear-cut decision against trade associations in its opinion. The Hardwood Manufacturers Association was somewhat unusual because it had limited the circulation of price listings to its own members and then had added personal interpretations and predictions of future activity about the hardwood sector of the industry. Well before the court handed down its findings, one trade journal warned the Hardwood Manufacturers Association that it was in violation of the law. The circulation of price information to association members only, the paper charged, was illegal and contrary to public policy because it meant withholding it from the general population.[16]

The Harding Administration's initial response to the Hardwood decision was equivocal. Secretary of Commerce Hoover exerted his considerable influence to gain a more moderate interpretation of the case, while Attorney General Harry Daugherty apparently wanted stricter enforcement. Hoover and Daugherty resolved the issue to some extent early in 1922 when they reached a compromise; in an exchange of correspondence Daugherty agreed with Hoover that it was not illegal for associations to collect statistics on prices, to average them, and to circulate the results through the Commerce Department. The *American Lumberman* observed that publication of the Hoover-Daugherty correspondence offered "a few notes of encouragement" for trade association activity and that Daugherty had recognized the legality "of most ordinary activity of such associations."[17]

The exchange between the Secretary of Commerce and the Attorney General seems to have cleared the air for the more confident believers in organized trade activity. Gilbert Montague, a prominent New York corporation lawyer with close ties to trade associations, told Hoover that his compromise with Daugherty "was the most important step forward in Governmental assistance to business that has been taken in our time. You . . . deserve the thanks of every business man for the persistence and courage that you have shown in working out this matter with the Attorney General." In a subsequent news release Montague praised the Commerce Secretary's willingness to use the department's facilities to collect, digest, and distribute trade information. He looked forward to

[15] *Lumber*, 69 (January 6, 1922), 21.
[16] Ibid. 65 (February 23, 1920), 17.
[17] Himmelberg, *Origins of the National Recovery Administration*, 16–21; Correspondence Between Department of Commerce and Department of Justice Upon Activities of Trade Associations, February 3, 1922, "Trade Associations," CPHP; *American Lumberman* (February 18, 1922), 36, 40.

the trade movement's entering "a new era of voluntary cooperation with the Government, which will open up possibilities of almost limitless benefit to industry and to the public." The president of the American Trade Association Executives, George D. McIlvaine, also defended Hoover and noted that trade associations derived "great satisfaction from the fact that in you, a Cabinet officer and representative of all that is best in American business, they have a friend and advocate."[18]

The Hardwood decision apparently did not deter most lumber trade associations from cooperating with the Department of Commerce, which continued to publish, on an expanded scale, its *Survey of Current Business*. By June 1922, the *Survey* included statistics from seventy different trade groups. Trade organizations praised the Commerce Department for providing commercial organizations with information about the legality of various kinds of statistical data, and the *American Lumberman* called Hoover "a champion of the rights of industry and a believer in the merits of organized activity of the right kind." The Forest Service added its support for association work when Assistant Forester Earle H. Clapp inquired about the "desirability and practicability of compilation and dissemination of lumber price information by the Government." Clapp argued that the Forest Service could provide a public service "by the collection and dissemination of lumber prices," which, in turn, would "serve the greatest public interest, considering lumber manufacturers and distributors as well as consumers."[19]

In 1925, the National Industrial Conference Board, a cooperative industrial research agency, published a lengthy study, *Trade Associations: Their Economic Significance and Legal Status*. The Conference Board's report found the facts in the Hardwood case to be relatively simple and undisputed — the Hardwood people had used a scheme of cooperation called the "Open Competition Plan," which required each member to submit daily reports of sales and shipping, monthly production reports, stocks on hand, and monthly price lists. The association compiled and interpreted this information and then communicated it to members in the form of weekly summaries that included editorial comment about the evils of overproduction and urged members to restrict supply to maintain prices. The "Open Competition Plan," the Conference Board suggested, provided intimate and detailed disclosures on a confidential basis. The Supreme Court had declared the secretive nature of the shared information to be in restraint of trade and therefore

    [18] Montague to Hoover, February 15, 1922, "Trade Associations, Correspondence on Press Releases and Proceedings, Daugherty-Hoover Correspondence, February, 1922," Montague News-Release, February 16, 1922, McIlvaine to Hoover, February 27, 1922, "Trade Associations-1922," CPHP.
    [19] Himmelberg, *Origins of the National Recovery Administration*, 17, 21, 26; *American Lumberman* (March 3, 1923), 31; Clapp is quoted in the *National Lumber Bulletin*, 2 (March 5, 1922), 5.

unconstitutional. This, the National Industrial Conference Board pointed out, had spread doubt and indecision throughout the trade association world.[20]

The board had made an accurate assessment. The absence of a clear and definitive legal statement about appropriate trade activity continued to disturb proponents of associational work. Federal Trade Commission investigations, the Justice Department's threats, and occasional prosecution of antitrust suits kept lumber trade officials on the alert. A good example was the Federal Trade Commission's investigation of the Douglas Fir Exploitation and Export Company formed by lumbermen in the Pacific Northwest. The *American Lumberman* said that the commission's inquiry threatened the export company with dissolution and implied that lumbermen were "undesireable [sic] citizens." The commission persisted in its inquiry, the trade paper claimed, despite the fact that the export company would help to restore prosperity to the industry. By contrast, its dissolution would be disastrous for business conditions in Oregon and Washington.[21]

In May 1923, the Justice Department filed suit against the Western Pine Manufacturers Association for acting in restraint of interstate trade and commerce. The Justice Department based its suit on a Federal Trade Commission investigation conducted at the behest of the Attorney General's office. The *American Lumberman* again ridiculed talk "about collusion in fixing prices of lumber or combining to control markets." Despite the alleged absurdity of the charge, the government was going ahead with the suit and accusing the association of conspiracy to control prices "and asking the courts to restrain them from doing some of the things that another department of Government is urging the lumbermen to do." The journal blamed the Federal Trade Commission for spending the people's money to harrass "the lumber industry, just as it now is doing on the Pacific Coast." These activities, it noted, would harm the industry and remove the incentive to cooperate in the "splendid work" of the Department of Commerce. In response to the Justice Department suit, one western pine lumberman emphasized the competitive nature of his association: "There is no commodity . . . that is subject to such violent competition at the present moment as lumber." An official of the West Coast Lumbermens Association also protested that the Federal Trade Commission had constituted "itself complaining witness, prosecuting attorney, jury and judge."[22]

[20] National Industrial Conference Board, *Trade Associations: Their Economic Significance and Legal Status* (New York), 1925), 89, 115.

[21] *American Lumberman* (March 31, 1923), 52.

[22] Ibid. (May 5, 1923), 38, 42–43; Robert B. Allen to National Association of Cost Accountants, February 8, 1924, Box 94, National Forest Products Association Records (hereafter NFPA Records), Forest History Society, Santa Cruz, California.

During this period of uncertainty, Wilson Compton continued to speak and write enthusiastically about the benefits of trade association cooperation which, he suggested, would bring higher living standards, the elimination of waste, the promotion of conservation, lower lumber prices, and commercial stability. Compton urged executives of the regional association to cooperate with the Department of Commerce and to keep their statistical work in accord with Supreme Court decisions. Compton's advice puzzled the skeptical Secretary-Manager of the Western Pine Manufacturers Association who wondered "to what decision you refer, as I am not familiar with any decisions that shed any ray of light on the subject of statistical activities."[23]

Most trade association leaders did not share Compton's view that the legal principles "in Federal Court decisions are sufficiently clear as a guide to the practice of trade associations." Because he realized "that great uncertainty" prevailed, Compton proposed a general conference of trade associations to discuss the confusion over the compilation and publication of statistics "and to consider suitable action." In the midst of doubt and recrimination in the association world, Compton counselled lumbermen to be conciliatory and cooperative, especially with the Department of Commerce. Early in 1924, he advised the West Coast Lumbermens Association to work with the Department of Commerce in its statistical gathering. Such cooperation, he advised, had strategic value "regardless" of its questionable legality, because the Secretary of Commerce considered it constructive and "helpful both to the industry in question and to the general public. . . . Irrespective, therefore, of the future policy of the Department of Commerce, it is my judgement that it is to the advantage of the lumber manufacturers associations, to formulate specifically in writing a program of statistical compilation, exchange and publication in accord with the principles of this plan, [and] make it operative promptly."[24]

Under Compton's legal advice the National Lumber Manufacturers Association cooperated fully and worked hard to compile statistical information for Hoover's department. Compton told Hoover early in 1924 that the national association was forming "statistic exchanges in accord with your recommendations," and he advised the North Carolina Pine Association to maintain a "constructive" relationship with the Department of Commerce even though it was not extending its cooperative plan "in light of recent developments."[25]

[23] Compton to Stephen B. Davis, Solicitor, Department of Commerce, January 21, 1924, "National Lumber Manufacturers Association, 1921–1927," CPHP; Compton to A. W. Cooper, July 11, 1923, Box 94, NFPA Records.

[24] Compton to Earl Constantine, January 24, 1924, and Compton to J. N. Teal, January 16, 1924, Box 94, NFPA Records.

[25] Compton to Hoover, January 19, 1924, and Compton to North Carolina Pine Association, January 19, 1924, Ibid.

The most puzzling problem for Compton and for most officials of trade associations was the equivocal position of the Justice Department. Compton accused the Attorney General's office of failing to cooperate because it passed the question back to the Department of Commerce when Hoover requested an opinion regarding statistical compilations.[26]

Hoover added to the sense of uneasiness in his annual report for 1924 when he complained that the antitrust issue "is not today clearly defined whether by law or by court decision and in consequence we are losing the value of much admirable activity." His report called for further elucidation of the antitrust situation so that "assurance of legality or proper conduct can be had." The West Coast Lumbermens Association gave practical expression to the same fears in its own report for 1924, complaining that "prospective members" were inhibited from joining "by reason of the present administration's seeming inclination to regard all associations as illegal combinations."[27]

Lumber executives vigorously denied the allegations of the Federal Trade Commission and the Justice Department that trade groups acted in monopolistic fashion. In their defense Hoover argued that trade associations provided a means to resolve national problems "without creating dominations of groups that would stifle equality of opportunity" and chiefly benefited smaller establishments that lacked the size and capital resources of big business. Wilson Compton of the national association concurred; cooperation through industrial organizations "can improve competition by making . . . available current statistics and trade information." In short, trade associations, it was claimed, promoted competition.[28]

Robert B. Allen, the veteran secretary-manager of the West Coast Lumbermens Association, contended that trade associations fostered rather than retarded competition because they enabled men with limited capital to conduct intelligent business activity. Without the information that associations provide, he noted, "the little fellow, operating without definite trade facts would be lucky to survive," while the larger operators possessed the facilities and financing "to secure this service without association aid." Allen thought that the application of the antitrust laws was contradictory and was being used against trade associations that provided services to small operators, which services actually had the effect of preserving competition.[29]

[26] Compton to Stephen B. Davis, January 21, 1924, "National Lumber Manufacturers Association, 1921–1927," CPHP.

[27] U. S. Department of Commerce, Annual Report (1924), 16–18; West Coast Lumbermens Associations, Annual Report (1924), 2, filed in folder 23, Box 1, West Coast Lumbermens Associations Records (hereafter WCLA Records), Oregon Historical Society, Portland, Oregon.

[28] Statement by Herbert Hoover to Chamber of Commerce of the United States, April 12, 1922. Box 94, NFPA Records; Wilson Compton, "How Competition Can Be Improved Through Association," Proceedings of the Academy of Political Science, 11 (January 1926), 32.

[29] West Coast Lumbermens Association, Annual Report (1924), filed in folder 23, Box 1, WCLA Records.

The Commerce Department's report for 1924, likewise, praised "legitimate" trade associations for providing small businesses with facilities equivalent to those that big business could afford independently. This system, the Commerce report indicated, would prove a strong force for maintaining a competitive system if properly directed. "There is a vast difference between the whole social conception of capital combinations against public interest and cooperative organization profoundly in the public interest. The former extinguishes individualism, legitimizes and fosters monopoly, dams up our channels — all of which penalizes the consumer and make for less efficiency in production. The latter encourages individualism, fosters competition and initiative resulting in efficient service and reasonable prices to the consumer."[30]

The persisting threat of prosecution by the Justice Department caused uneasiness in the Commerce Department and throughout the lumber industry. Much of this anxiety undoubtedly reflected the Justice Department's equivocation on the antitrust issue through 1923. Although lumber associations feared that a renewed antitrust campaign would severely restrict trade organizations, that danger never materialized. Attorney General Daugherty, one of the chief proponents of restricted trade cooperation, was coming under increasing congressional criticism for corruption and mismanagement. One senses an element of glee in Wilson Compton's letter to Robert Allen in February 1924, in which he remarked that the Department of Justice was "absorbed somewhat in other directions right now." Finally, with Daugherty's exit from the Attorney General's office in late March 1924 and the Supreme Court's less restrictive decision in the Maple Flooring case in June 1925, Hoover's more liberal version of trade association activity emerged triumphant.[31]

The Supreme Court's Maple Flooring opinion cleared the way for most forms of lumber trade cooperation. The Court, which divided six to three on behalf of a more liberal interpretation of the antitrust laws, declared legal the gathering and dissemination of statistics on costs, sale prices, production, and stocks on hand. The decision, according to the *American Lumberman*, marked "a victory of very real importance to trade associations" and was "a bright beacon light on the highway of progress . . . a new magna charta of legitimate organized business." Moreover, the Court's opinion delineated the precise conduct that associations might pursue and cleared away the confusion surrounding the statistical work of the Department of Commerce.[32]

Allen to National Association of Cost Accountants, February 8, 1924, Box 94, NFPA Records.

[30] U. S. Department of Commerce, *Annual Report* (1924), 18.

[31] Himmelberg, *Origins of the National Recovery Administration*, 33–34, 43–47; Compton to Allen, February 28, 1924, Box 94, NFPA Records.

[32] *United States Supreme Court Sanctions Collection and Dissemination of Lumber Statistics* (Chicago: Reprinted from *American Lumberman*, June 6, 1925), 37–38.

Joseph N. Teal, legal counsel for the West Coast Lumbermens Association, contended that the Maple Flooring decision removed "the prohibition of the law from intelligent cooperation in the compilation of business information," recognized the nature of "economic law," and adjusted the Sherman Act to conform wth changing circumstances. The court, he said, put its "stamp of approval" upon the work of the Department of Commerce. Charles S. Keith of the Southern Pine Association thought that the Maple Flooring opinion vindicated the statistical activities of his association and provided a vehicle for the "rational control of production and distribution," and the National Industrial Conference Board declared that Maple Flooring "upheld trade associational statistical services of an elaborate nature." O. T. Swan of the Northern Hemlock and Hardwood Manufacturers Association put the case succinctly: "The logical thing happens if you wait long enough."[33]

ATTEMPTS TO STANDARDIZE LUMBER

Most lumber trade associations applauded Herbert Hoover's wide-ranging commitment to voluntary industrial cooperation. Wilson Compton told an annual meeting of the National Lumber Manufacturers Association that "the constructive activity of the Department of Commerce" was commonly acknowledged in the lumber trade, and lumbermen should "take full advantage of the opportunity" to demonstrate their ability to conduct their "own business economically and without waste." Self discipline and honesty, he observed, would effectively end "wasteful experiments of Government control and regulation."[34]

Secretary Hoover reciprocated these expressions of good will. During the legal confusion over trade group activity in 1924, Hoover congratulated the membership of the National Lumber Manufacturers Association for its leadership in "the great national values of trade association work," which brought "greater stability to business, greater economies in production and distribution — greater conservation of our natural resources." The heart of association work, he noted, was the efficient production and distribution of goods and the elimination of waste. The participation of the National Lumber Manufacturers Association with Hoover and the Department of Commerce to promote the standardization and simplification of lumber products enhanced this sense of mutual respect and good will.[35]

The adoption of uniform and standardized grades and cuts of lumber was an early objective of most lumber trade associations. The industry's leaders associated standardization with conservation and the more effi-

[33] *Lumber World Review,* 48 (June 10, 1925), 33–34; *Trade Associations,* 115.
[34] Compton, "National Lumber Problems and Prospects," in National Lumber Manufacturers Association, *Annual Report* (1923), 12.
[35] Hoover is quoted in National Lumber Manufacturers Association, *Annual Report* (1924), 46–47.

cient utilization of lumber and argued that its adoption would bring greater marketing efficiency and stability. Trade spokesmen argued that manufacturers, wholesalers, retailers, and consumers all were interested in standardization because it promised increased profits, stability, and more efficient and economic service to the public. The adoption of national standards would further rationalize the system of production and distribution. The Forest Service, through its Forest Products Laboratory in Madison, Wisconsin, had been studying and recommending the adoption of national standards for many years, and by the early 1920s many of the larger lumber trade groups had joined the campaign. They found their champion in the person of the dynamic Commerce Secretary.[36]

At the request of the National Lumber Manufacturers Association, representatives from all phases of the trade met in May 1922 in a series of conferences to formulate common lumber standards and to decide on methods to interpret and enforce their recommendations. Secretary Hoover advised the industry to "develop these things from the internal machinery of the trade," rather than establish government inspection mechanisms for grading lumber. The national trade organization subsequently appointed a Central Committee on Lumber Standards, which acted as the clearing house for establishing regularized grades and cuts of lumber. The committee completed its work after a lengthy series of meetings in late 1923.[37]

To allay the fears of some association members, Wilson Compton issued a ringing defense of the cooperation between the lumber trade organizations and the Department of Commerce. There was no more positive demonstration of Hoover's high purpose, Compton insisted, than the Commerce Secretary's desire "to keep the wasteful hand of the Government out of the affairs of ordinary business enterprise." Lumbermen, he said, were cognizant of the public's interest in the "efficient, stable and honest conduct of the lumber industry," but the associations wanted to do their own regulating. Compton noted that recommendations for government grading had been offered for at least twenty-five years and lumber trade groups had sponsored some of the proposals. The industry's present need, he contended, was to "develop these things through the internal machinery of the trade itself as a matter of self-government."[38]

[36] For industry leaders views on standardization, see the testimony of Everett Griggs in *Proceedings of the Fourth National Conservation Congress* (Indianapolis, 1912), 187. Circular Distributed to Organized Consumers, Technical Experts, Distributors, and Manufacturers Interested in Lumber, December 23, 1923, "Conferences — Lumber," CPHP.

[37] Ibid.; Hoover's Address to the National Lumber Manufacturers Association, May 22, 1922, "National Lumber Manufacturers Association, 1921, 1927," Memo on the Central Committee on Lumber Standards, July 22, 1922, "Lumber, 1921–1924," Ibid.

[38] Press Release, "Keeping the Government out of the Lumber Business," July 12, 1922, Box 144, NFPA Records.

Hauling Logs in Minnesota in the Late 1920s.

The life and work of these men in the forests seemed far removed from the negotiations between Wilson M. Compton, Herbert Hoover, and other officials of business and government.

At its concluding session in December 1923, the Central Committee on Lumber Standards indicated that a standardized lumber product would bring a roseate future for the lumber industry. It meant "large direct savings" and "a direct contribution to the sound, honest and efficient conduct of the lumber trade on the highest plane of integrity, economy and service. . . . It has been characterized as a vital aid to the orderliness, stability and profitability of the lumber business. Furthermore, the nationally organized standardization effort of the lumber trade is a direct test of the capacity of the lumber industry for self-government . . . in such manner as to secure . . . orderly, efficient and profitable business for those engaged in the industry itself."[39]

Secretary of Commerce Hoover echoed the Central Committee's sentiments. He praised it for representing one of the greatest industries in the United States and for its effort to forestall government regulation through voluntary action. Hoover reminded the committee that the government's role was one of cooperation and assistance, because "the original demands for this service came from the industry itself." He applauded the Central Committee for its contribution to the "improve-

[39] Minutes of the General Standardization Conference on Lumber, December 12–13, 1923, "Conferences-Lumber, 1923–1928," CPHP.

ment of the whole production and distribution machinery in the United States . . . , out of [which] . . . we shall have raised the standard of living of the American people." William Greeley, speaking for the Forest Service, also commended the standardization movement. The adoption of uniform standards, he told the gathering of lumber trade leaders, would stabilize the industry, bring order, efficiency, and economy to the use of forest products, and assist "the growing of timber as part of a general conservation program."[40]

The task of implementing lumber standards on a voluntary basis proved difficult, especially during periods of overproduction and in depressed regions like the South and the Far West. Trade officials complained to the Commerce Department that the adoption of lumber standards was moving slowly, and occasionaly an association executive asked Hoover to use his influence to bring recalcitrants into line. And there were problems in the southern lumber region, where the larger lumbermen viewed the implementation of grading standards as an opportunity to improve their competitive situation against the smaller, "peckerwood" mills. To make matters more difficult for the small scale units, the large operators who dominated the Southern Pine Association determined standardization policy. By the mid-1920s the secretary-manager of the Southern Pine Association noted that "the competition of these small mills must be met," and the vehicle to accomplish this "will be grade-marking." John W. Blodgett, chairman of the Central Committee on Lumber Standards, added to this sentiment when he told a correspondent that standardization offered protection for large efficient mills that "are now competing directly with the portable mills cutting only second growth stumpage."[41]

But the most important aspect of the effort to standardize lumber was the fact that spokesmen for the trade association and the Secretary of Commerce shared ideological perceptions about its effects on the lumber industry. Both contended that common standards would contribute to a more stable and orderly lumber economy. Lumbermen found the appeals of the Commerce Department attractive, because it had proposed measures that avoided the hoary specter of federal regulation but, at the same time, would help achieve a rationally ordered industry. On the eve of Hoover's resignation as Commerce Secretary to take up presidential politics, Frederick K. Weyerhaeuser, vice-

[40] Ibid.

[41] J. F. Martin, Secretary, Pennsylvania Lumbermens Association, to Hoover, September 8, 1924, "Lumber, 1921-1924," John W. Blodgett, Chairman, Central Committee on Lumber Standards, to Hoover, April 23, 1925, "Lumber, 1925," CPHP. Herbert C. Berckes, "Association Activities," in the Report of the Ninth Annual Meeting of the Subscribers to the Southern Pine Association, March 11-12, 1924, pp. 25-26, quoted in James C. Fickle, "Origins and Development of the Southern Pine Association," chapter 6, p. 2 (manuscript in the Forest History Society); Blodgett to A. C. Goodyear, December 1, 1924, Box 74, NFPA Records.

president of the Weyerhaeuser Company, thanked him for "the splendid contribution you have . . . made in the interest of standardization in the lumber industry."[42]

Weyerhaeuser and the leaders of the southern trade association expressed the view of the larger operators on the issue of standardization. Moreover, the numerous complaints from lumber officials about small millmen who refused to comply make it clear that there was no community of interest between large and small operators when it came to implementing standardization. In this instance it is evident that the trade association's attempt to institute efficient and rationalized marketing practices was not working in the interests of the smaller business units. This same type of resistance ultimately undermined the work of the Lumber Code Authority under the National Recovery Administration.

MORE EFFICIENT UTILIZATION OF WOOD

As an adjunct to the standardization effort and as part of a move to improve the efficient use of the timber resource, Secretary of Agriculture Henry C. Wallace in the fall of 1924 called for a conference on the utilization of forest products. Its objective was to urge the lumber and wood manufacturing industries "to adopt improved methods of manufacturing and using wood and thus to greatly cut down our enormous drain and lessen the severity of the timber shortage." Wallace requested the cooperation of the Commerce Secretary, because he had "done so much to stimulate the interest of industry and of the public in problems of industrial waste" and in conserving natural resources. When Wallace died in October 1924, Herbert Hoover became the moving force behind the officially designated National Conference on the Utilization of Forest Products. President Coolidge set the tone at the November conference when he told the forest industry representatives that their survival depended on "economic fitness" which could be achieved through "good management and good technical processes," the tools of industrial progress.[43]

Coolidge and Hoover made brief inspirational speeches to the initial wood utilization conference. Chief Forester William B. Greeley, however, delivered a lengthy address in which he provided lumbermen with an ideological synthesis that tied the conservation of resources to the elimination of waste and the industry's need for order, stability, and

---

[42] Weyerhaeuser to Hoover, May 25, 1928, "Lumber, 1926–1928," CPHP.

[43] Wallace to Hoover, October 8, 1924, "Conferences — Wood Utilization, 1924–1925," CPHP; Donald L. Winters, *Henry Cantwell Wallace as Secretary of Agriculture* (Chicago, 1970), 291; Coolidge's Address to the National Conference on Utilization of Forest Products, November 19, 1924, "Conferences — Wood Utilization, 1924–1925," CPHP.

improved profit margins. "Waste," he observed, "is a problem for which we are all responsible" and whose roots lie in an historically overabundant resource. Changing economic circumstances and new commercial incentives were inducing lumbermen to utilize waste materials, and, he insisted, an industry operating free from government controls would be the best means to eliminate waste and achieve the conservation of timber resources. "In the last analysis," Greeley argued, "the commercial incentive of more profitable business will be the driving power behind the whole movement." Profit-making, he intimated, was both compatible and necessary to effective conservation.[44]

Secretary of Commerce Hoover appointed a quasi-permanent National Committee on Wood Utilization in May 1925. The leadership of the cooperative government-industry undertaking was vested in the National Lumber Manufacturers Association. Axel Oxholm, Chief of the Lumber Division in the Department of Commerce, served as chairman and worked closely with the committee to find markets for otherwise wasted materials. Such markets, according to Oxholm, would bridge the gap in a predicted timber shortage until second growth stands were harvestable. Even more important, efficient wood utilization would raise timber values and stimulate commercial reforestation. Like Chief Forester William Greeley, Oxholm believed that the market system would lead to efficiency, the elimination of waste, and the achievement of resource conservation. Trade spokesmen responded favorably to Hoover's proposals. The *American Lumberman* remarked that the industry was fortunate in having "an able and sympathetic collaborator in Herbert Hoover," and urged its readers to "treat seriously Hoover's warnings about the dangers of bureaucratic control of business. Business ought to rejoice that there is still in Washington an important servant of the government who holds and on every proper occasion expressed such views. But, they ought not to overlook the implication of Secretary Hoover's statement, which is that, if industry does not want the government to interfere in its affairs and undertake its control, businessmen must get together and themselves solve the problems that vitally affect the public interest."[45]

Most lumber trade officials were as enthusiastic in their praise of Hoover's wood utilization program as they were for lumber standardization. E. C. Hole, manager of the *American Lumberman*, told Hoover: "The Department of Commerce . . . is one of the educational institutions in the United States for business men." Moreover, he noted,

[44] *American Lumberman* (November 22, 1924), 45–47.
[45] Hoover to John W. Blodgett, March 28, 1925, "Conferences — Wood Utilization, 1925," CPHP; U. S. Bureau of Foreign and Domestic Commerce, *Services Available to the Lumber Industry Through the Department of Commerce* (Washington, D. C., 1930), 14. *American Lumberman* (May 1, 1926), 42.

Hoover was showing lumbermen how better to serve both their government and themselves. The *Southern Lumberman* called the wood utilization effort, "A Promising Movement," because lumbermen were cooperating "so heartily" in one of the most extraordinary efforts ever attempted in the country. William Nichols, a southern lumber manufacturer, told Axel Oxholm that traditionally suspicious lumbermen from his region were gradually overcoming their prejudice and suspicions about the federal government. "This is a perfectly natural feeling in view of the happenings in the past," Nichols remarked, "but I think they are making progress in showing the manufacturers that your Department is a help."[46]

Through the remainder of his appointment as Secretary of Commerce, Hoover persisted in his unstinting praise for the wood utilization program. In April 1927 Hoover informed the annual meeting of the National Lumber Manufacturers Association that the industry's prosperity depended on efficient wood utilization and converting a maximum of the tree into marketable wood products. Maximum use was necessary, he said, to enable successful commercial reforestation and "to give greater stability to the industry" and more profits to lumbermen. One month later, Hoover told the National Wood Utilization Committee: "You are Exhibit A of government by cooperation. We have never sought to impose anything upon this industry. . . . The work has been cooperative action in the highest sense." The success of voluntarism, he observed, made the threat of congressional regulation a creature of the past, because the public now realized that lumber operators were responsible citizens. He doubted that there would be further sentiment for regulation.[47]

Just before his resignation as chief forester in 1928, William Greeley reiterated his views on the integral and important relation between effective timber growing, the economic requirements of the lumber industry, and the efficient use of forest products. Forests "cannot be widely and generally produced," he noted, unless there was "an adequate market for forest products" and closer utilization of the forest crop to increase its value and enhance production. Although this was an industrial problem, the chief forester urged public agencies to help through research "and by the promotion of more effective utilization through such admirable work as that of the National Committee on Wood Utilization."[48]

[46] E. C. Hole to Hoover, November 22, 1924, "Conferences — Wood Utilizatiion, 1924–1925," CPHP; *Southern Lumberman* 122 (May 1, 1926), 20; William Nichols to Oxholm, July 13, 1927, "Lumber, 1926–1928," CPHP.

[47] Hoover to Frank Wisner, April 6, 1927, "Conferences — Wood Utilization, 1927," National Lumber Manufacturers Association, News Release, May 7, 1927, "Lumber, 1926–1928," CPHP.

[48] Greeley to Axel Oxholm, January 25, 1928, "Conferences — Wood Utilization, 1928," CPHP.

Toward the end of the 1928 presidential campaign, candidate Hoover told a St. Louis audience that the voluntary initiatives of lumbermen had eliminated abuses "without resorting to legislation and regulation." The effusive candidate recalled that in 1923, "We created a series of committees . . . [and] perfected a system for the grading of lumber," and because individual operators cooperated in this effort and a subsequent one to eliminate waste, "there has been no . . . [call] for legislation from congress." One trade journal carrying Hoover's speech remarked that "progressive element[s] in the lumber industry won the fight for unquestioned fair dealings." If they had not pursued this objective, the journal feared, the federal government would have instituted "onerous regulations of its own."[49]

Herbert Hoover's ideas and ambitions for a smoothly functioning business and industrial order were broad, systematic, and theoretically designed to embrace all major elements of the American political economy. In a long letter to the young journalist David Lawrence in late 1927, Hoover called for a determination of production, consumption, stocks of goods, and business trends, which, he believed, would enable individual businessmen to erect a strong barrier against booms and slumps. These rationally motivated individuals, he suggested, would then take safeguards against speculative periods or the approach of depression, and "the total effect of such action would tend to mitigate these disastrous swings in business." The Department of Commerce, he told Lawrence, had cooperated with trade associations and expanded its informational services and otherwise made a prodigious effort to comply with demands from the business world. The results were obvious, because "the remarkable period of stablity which we have enjoyed for the past six years has been to some extent contributed to by these services." Furthermore, the ambitious Commerce Secretary argued, government cooperation with the private sector had accomplished this remarkable feat and not "regulatory paternalism."[50]

CONCLUSION

Although lumber trade association officials were optimistic about the benefits to be derived through the standardization and utilization programs, in the actual conduct of the lumber business this enthusiasm was unwarranted and misleading. Hoover, and, to a lesser degree Greeley, based their optimism on the mistaken assumption that the open cooperation of the Commerce Department and the Forest Service

[49] Hoover's speech was published after the election in the *Lumber Manufacturer and Dealer*, 81 (December 1928), 39.

[50] Hoover to Lawrence, December 29, 1927, "Commerce, American Business Men," CPHP.

with the lumber trade associations would usher in a stable and orderly industrial world. By the end of the decade, as the lumber industry foundered in a sea of overproduction, the realities of contracting markets eroded the bright hope that New Era politics had brought an end to the business cycle. The problems were partly the traditional ones of excessive mill capacity and the rapid liquidation of timber stands to meet carrying charges, which combined to contribute to overproduction and glutted markets. The impressive increases in the manufacture of non-lumber building materials in the 1920s (cement, steel, and cellulose products) worsened even further the industry's dilemma. These substitute construction materials induced greater instability in the lumber market and inspired lumbermen to combat the new commodities through better advertising and merchandising, through more closely integrated trade organizations, and through a program of public education in the uses of wood products.[51]

Despite the aggressive propaganda efforts of the National Lumber Manufacturers Association, despite the editorializing of the trade press, and despite the over-weening optimism of the Commerce Secretary, economic conditions in the lumber trade worsened as the decade advanced. In the midst of what association officials defined as great successes — the achievements in national lumber standards beginning in 1922, the passage of the much-heralded Clarke-McNary Act in 1924, and the inception of the wood utilization effort later the same year — the industry's troubles persisted. Even the Commerce Department's enterprising promotion of foreign trade did little to halt the continuing decline in lumber consumption after 1925.[52]

At the end of the decade, a plunging stock market heralded a general contraction in virtually every sector of the American economy. The optimistic and energetic Hoover, now in the presidency, initiated a wide-ranging series of government-sponsored voluntary and cooperative programs to slow economic decline and to restore industrial growth. All to no avail because conditions continued to worsen. Lumbermen, of course, like their brethren in agriculture, understood well the problems of a contracting economy, because total lumber production and consumption had been declining steadily since 1925. The experiences of the early depression years simply magnified their perennial difficulties a hundred-fold.[53]

---

[51] Orion Howard Cheney, "The New Competition in the Lumber Industry," in National Lumber Manufacturers Association, *Annual Report* (1927), 3.

[52] For the Commerce Department's promotion of foreign trade, see *Services Available to the Lumber Industry*, 7–12.

[53] For a discussion of Hoover's economic recovery initiatives, see David Burner, *Herbert Hoover: The Public Life* (New York, 1978), 245–283; Hawley, *The Great War and the Search for a Modern Order*, 192–205; Joan Hoff Wilson, *Herbert Hoover, Forgotten Progressive* (Boston, 1975), 122–167; John D. Hicks, *Republican Ascendancy, 1921–1933* (New York, 1960), 260–280.

THE LUMBER TRADE IN THE 1920s   379

EXPLORATIONS IN ECONOMIC HISTORY **26,** 453–476 (1989)

The Strategy, Effectiveness, and Consistency of Federal Reserve Monetary Policy 1924–1933

DAVID C. WHEELOCK*

Department of Economics University of Texas at Austin

This paper presents new empirical tests of alternative hypotheses of Federal Reserve behavior from 1924 to 1933. The Fed used open-market operations in government securities to smooth economic fluctuations, to limit stock market speculation, and to assist Great Britain to return to the gold standard. However, this study finds that during the 1920s open-market operations did not affect the volume of Federal Reserve Credit outstanding. The Fed seems to have continued to use this ineffective strategy during the depression, which can account for its failure to respond vigorously to the economic downturn. © 1989 Academic Press, Inc.

INTRODUCTION

This paper presents new empirical evidence about the strategy of Federal Reserve monetary policy from 1924 to 1933. There has been considerable debate about the objectives of Fed policy during this period, but it is now widely accepted that "inept" monetary policy exacerbated the Great Depression.[1] However, there has been little effort to study the Fed's behavior econometrically, particularly within the framework of the strategy actually used by the System. Such an analysis would help identify the reasons for the Fed's mistakes during the depression. This paper seeks to test alternative hypotheses of Fed behavior within that framework, and to suggest new insights about the failures of policy during the Great Depression.

First, I outline the Fed's policy strategy and describe the relationship between System open-market operations and total Federal Reserve Credit outstanding. Reaction function estimates of open-market policy from 1924 to 1929 support the view of Friedman and Schwartz (1963)

* The comments on earlier drafts by Larry Neal, Jeremy Atack, Michael Bordo, Donald Hodgman, and an anonymous referee are gratefully acknowledged.
[1] Field (1984a, 1984b), Miron (1986), and Hamilton (1987) are recent studies adding new support to the conclusion of Friedman and Schwartz (1963) that monetary policy was mishandled terribly during the depression.

that the Fed responded to fluctuations in economic activity and sought to limit stock market speculation. But Wicker's (1966) claim that the Fed desired to assist Great Britain's return to the gold standard is also supported.

The Fed believed that open-market operations worked through their influence on the demands of banks for discount loans. Since banks were thought to be reluctant to borrow from the Fed, they would attempt to minimize their discount borrowing by calling loans and selling securities when open-market sales produced a reserve shortage. Thus, open-market sales would lead to higher interest rates and generally firmer credit conditions. Similarly, open-market purchases eased credit conditions by reducing the need of banks to borrow reserves.

Toma (1989) has recently questioned the effectiveness of open-market operations during the 1920s, rejecting implicitly the Fed view of how open-market operations worked. His analysis shows that open-market operations were offset exactly by changes in discount loan volume, implying that they had no effect on total Federal Reserve Credit outstanding, bank reserves, or the money supply. The econometric analysis of this paper illustrates further that the Fed's response to its various policy goals was not reflected in the behavior of Federal Reserve Credit outstanding. Nevertheless, the Fed believed that its operations had been successful, particularly in 1924 and 1927 when its purchases had apparently led to lower interest rates and economic growth. I argue that the Fed's perception that these operations had been successful led it to use the same open-market policy strategy during the early 1930s. And I argue this strategy can account for the failure of the System to pursue a vigorous countercyclical policy in the depression.

THE BEHAVIOR OF FEDERAL RESERVE CREDIT

Federal Reserve Credit (FRC) deserves special attention because it reflects the contribution of monetary policy to banking system reserves and the money supply. It consists of the Fed's government security holdings, its bankers acceptance holdings, and discount loans to member banks.[2] Benjamin Strong, Governor of the Federal Reserve Bank of New York and the dominant figure within the System until his death in 1928, testified to the importance of FRC:

> The experience of the past few years seems to indicate that the conduct of the normal volume of business now being transacted in this country, at the present level of prices, requires the use of about a minimum of a billion dollars of Federal reserve credit in order to provide the reserves . . . for the amount of credit and currency required by the banking system to conduct that business.[3]

---

[2] In addition, there is a small miscellaneous component, comprised mainly of float.

[3] United States House of Representatives (1926, p. 438).

The behavior of FRC has received considerable attention in the debate over the consistency of Fed policy between the 1920s and early 1930s. Friedman and Schwartz (1963) argue that there was a dramatic deterioration in the quality of Fed policy making with the death of Benjamin Strong and loss of influence of the Federal Reserve Bank of New York. But, based on the behavior of FRC, Brunner and Meltzer (1968) argue that there was no change in Federal Reserve performance. They point out that FRC fell during the recessions of 1924 and 1927, as it did from 1930 to 1931, suggesting that there was no inconsistency in Fed policy. However, Miron (1986) has concluded recently that there was a change in the seasonal behavior of FRC with the onset of the depression, and he contends that the Fed was less accommodative of seasonal credit demands after 1928 than before.[4] Despite this considerable attention there has been little econometric analysis of the behavior of Federal Reserve Credit, or of the specific means by which the Fed responded to various policy objectives.

The supply of banking system reserves is often analyzed in terms of the sources and uses of reserve funds. Federal Reserve Credit is one source of banking system reserves; the monetary gold stock and Treasury currency are other principal sources. An increase in any of them will lead to an increase in bank reserves, currency in circulation, or some other use of reserve funds.[5] During the 1920s and early 1930s, the principal determinants of changes in the stock of bank reserves were gold and currency flows and changes in Federal Reserve Credit outstanding.[6] Gold inflows (outflows) tended to increase (decrease) reserves. Increased currency held by the public tended to reduce bank reserves, while a reduction in currency held by the public tended to increase them. Friedman and Schwartz (1963) show that changes in the volume of FRC outstanding tended to offset gold and currency flows, and thus stabilized bank reserves.[7] In other words, through changes in FRC outstanding, the Fed limited the effects of gold and currency flows on the money supply.

The Fed's role in offsetting gold and currency flows was generally passive. As described by Riefler (1930), a gold or currency outflow created a reserve need which member banks could meet by borrowing from the Fed or by selling bankers acceptances to the Fed. The Reserve Banks did not initiate these operations. Each bank set a discount rate and

---

[4] Miron does not test explicitly whether there was a change in Fed accommodation, and such tests do not confirm his claim. See Wheelock (1988b).

[5] See Goldfeld and Chandler (1986, pp. 286–290) for a discussion of the sources and uses of reserve funds.

[6] Treasury currency changed very little during the period examined here. See Riefler (1930, Chap. 7) for further detail.

[7] Friedman and Schwartz (1963, pp. 279–287).

acceptance buying rate schedule, and it was up to member banks and bill dealers to determine the quantity of discount loans and acceptances offered. Only in the case of open-market operations in government securities did the Fed determine the volume of its operations. But despite its passive role in offsetting gold and currency flows, it was System policy that they be offset.[8]

Beyond simply offsetting the effects of gold and currency flows on bank reserves, the Fed developed a strategy for achieving other policy objectives. Chandler (1958), Friedman and Schwartz (1963), and Wicker (1966) all argue that by 1924 at the latest the Fed had developed a systematic monetary policy, although they disagree about the specific objectives of policy. Friedman and Schwartz argue the Fed focused primarily on domestic goals: limiting fluctuations in economic activity, preventing financial crises, and checking speculation.[9] Wicker (1966) contends the Fed's primary objective during the 1920s was the reestablishment of the international gold standard.[10] And Chandler (1958) argues:

> By 1924 Federal Reserve officials had developed three major objectives or considerations that were to shape their policies for about a decade. These were: 1) Promotion of high and stable levels of business activity and employment and stability of price levels, 2) curbing excessive use of credit for stock market speculation, and 3) assistance to monetary reconstruction and stability abroad.[11]

Given that the Fed did have specific policy goals, how did it attempt to achieve these goals, and how did Fed actions affect FRC? By the early 1920s the Fed had observed that its open-market operations in government securities appeared to produce predictable and desirable changes in interest rates. The System established an Open Market Investment Committee in 1923, and by the end of that year had begun to employ open-market operations to achieve certain policy objectives.[12] In Congressional testimony in 1926, Benjamin Strong described how he believed open-market operations affected Federal Reserve Credit. Referring to previous operations, Strong stated:

> Changes in holdings of government securities were almost exactly offset by changes in discounts and bill (Federal Reserve acceptance) holdings. These changes are an important influence on the credit situation but they are quite distinct from increasing or diminishing directly the volume of reserve bank credit (FRC)

---

[8] See Strong's testimony in U.S. House of Representatives (1926, pp. 442, 454).

[9] Friedman and Schwartz (1963, pp. 249–270).

[10] Wicker (1966, especially Chaps. 6 and 8).

[11] Chandler (1958, p. 199).

[12] See Chandler (1958, Chap. 6) for an extensive description of the discovery of open-market operations and the emergence of open-market operations as the dominant tool of policy.

in use. The effect of open-market operations is to increase or decrease the extent to which the member banks must of their own initiative call on the reserve banks for credit. . . . The influence of the reserve banks upon the volume of credit is thus felt not directly, but indirectly through the member banks. The reserve banks do not "push" credit into use.[13]

In the Fed view, open-market operations in government securities, combined with gold and currency flows, determined the extent to which member banks had to borrow reserves from the Fed. By influencing the extent of such borrowing, Fed officials believed they could affect the cost and availability of commercial bank credit. Central to their theory was the view that banks are reluctant to borrow from the Fed, and will seek to minimize that borrowing by calling loans and raising interest rates. Similarly, to ease credit conditions, the Fed believed that open-market purchases provided reserves with which banks would reduce their borrowing and extend new credit to their customers at lower rates.[14]

OPEN-MARKET POLICY

This section presents a regression analysis of Federal Reserve open-market operations in government securities. I attempt to test the alternative hypotheses about the Fed's policy objectives of Chandler (1958), Friedman and Schwartz (1963), and Wicker (1966). I demonstrate also that the variables which seem to explain open-market policy from 1924 to 1929 cannot explain the behavior of total Federal Reserve Credit. As Toma (1989) implies, the Fed's policy intent was not reflected in total Federal Reserve Credit outstanding.

The Fed had three policy tools: open-market operations in government securities, the discount rate, and the acceptance buying rate. In general, the three tools were used consistently with one another, i.e., open-market purchases (sales) were made in conjunction with discount and acceptance buying rate reductions (increases).[15]

In Congressional testimony in 1926, Benjamin Strong outlined the general considerations which guided monetary policy. He stated that the price level, the extent of speculation, business inventories, credit conditions in general, the international flow of gold and a desire for a "uniform" flow of business all were considerations.[16] Moreover, he stressed

---

[13] U.S. House of Representatives (1926, p. 468).

[14] See Riefler (1930) or Burgess (1946) for a full description of the Fed theory and operating strategy.

[15] A notable exception occurred in August 1929 when the Fed increased the discount rate, lowered the acceptance buying rate, and undertook no open-market operation. For a discussion of this episode, see Chandler (1971, pp. 71–76).

[16] U.S. House of Representatives (1926, p. 329). See also his description of the specific objectives of the Fed's open-market purchase program in 1924 (pp. 335–336).

the advantage of coordinating discount rate changes with open-market operations:

> If speculation arises, prices are rising, and possibly other considerations move the reserve banks to tighten up a bit on the use of their credit . . . it is a more effective program . . . to begin to sell government securities. It lays a foundation for an advance in our discount rate. If the reverse conditions appear, . . . as we thought were developing in late 1923, then the purchase of securities eases the money market and permits the reduction of our discount rate.[17]

The Fed's third tool, the buying rate on bankers acceptances, appears to have been used less for general policy purposes than were open-market operations and the discount rate. Burgess (1946) writes, "the fixing of the rate for buying bills (acceptances) is less a matter of policy than the fixing of the discount rate for loans. The buying rate for bills ordinarily follows closely changes in the open market rates for bills."[18]

Trescott (1982) and Epstein and Ferguson (1984) treat the Fed's operations in government securities and its operations in bankers acceptances as substitutes in their econometric models of Fed behavior. However, I believe the distinction between them is important. The Fed initiated operations in government securities only; it was up to banks and bill dealers to offer acceptances to the Fed at the System's buying rates. Moreover, the Fed never sold acceptances.[19] But, beyond these institutional differences, Friedman and Schwartz (1963) and Wicker (1966) note that some Fed officials did not view operations in government securities and bankers acceptances as substitutes. These officials believed that the use of reserves provided by an open-market purchase depended upon the type of paper purchased, and that the Fed had less control over the reserves supplied by a purchase of government securities than by a purchase of acceptances.[20] Chandler (1971) identifies occasions during the depression when the Fed considered buying government securities, but opted instead for reducing its acceptance buying rate. The Fed preferred to extend credit by purchasing these real bills, rather than by purchasing government securities.[21] Nevertheless, the Fed probably had

---

[17] U.S. House of Representatives (1926, pp. 332–333).

[18] Burgess (1946, p. 234).

[19] Burgess (1946, pp. 172–173).

[20] Friedman and Schwartz (1963, pp. 266–268) and Wicker (1966, pp. 127–128). Friedman and Schwartz cite a diary entry by Charles Hamlin, a Reserve Board member, which illustrates the point: "There was a fundamental difference between putting money into circulation by a) Buying government securities and b) Bills; . . . . Money put out for b) went primarily to aid a genuine business transaction, while in the case of a) no one could tell where it might go, e.g., to be loaned on Wall Street, etc." (p. 266).

[21] For example, at its April 29, 1931, meeting, the Open Market Committee approved the purchase of government securities, but felt it should attempt to meet its objectives "first, through (lower) bill rates, second, through the reduction of discount rates, and then, if necessary, to resort to the purchase of government securities" (Chandler, 1971, p. 156).

a great deal of influence over the volume of acceptances offered to it. And while not perfect substitutes, the Fed did view operations in government securities and acceptances as somewhat interchangeable. Thus, in the econometric analysis I estimate separate regressions for open-market operations in government securities alone and for the sum of changes in the Fed's government security and acceptance portfolios.

In contrast to modern operating procedures, during the interwar era the Open Market Committee determined the specific quantities of government securities to buy and sell. Today that job is left to the trading desk at the Federal Reserve Bank of New York. The Open Market Committee issues a directive to the desk specifying target ranges for certain variables, such as the Fed funds rate, and the desk then buys and sells securities as necessary to achieve the targets. During the 1920s the Fed's proximate policy objective was the cost and availability of bank credit, as indicated by interest rates and discount loan volume. But most often the Fed's directives did not specify specific targets for interest rates or discount loans. At most, the Fed used these variables as "indicators" of credit conditions, rather than as "targets."[22] Moreover, market forces probably limited the extent to which the Fed could control these variables. Hence, it would be an error to use discount loans or some market interest rate as the measure of the Fed's policy intent, i.e., as the dependent variable in a model of the Fed's reaction function. Nevertheless, because the Fed viewed these variables as important indicators of credit conditions, it is necessary to consider their behavior when analyzing monetary policy.

As a starting point, it seems that open-market operations in government securities probably indicate best the Fed's response to specific policy objectives. I use the 1-month first-difference of Federal Reserve government security holdings (ΔGS) as the dependent variable in a regression model of open-market policy. Chandler (1958) and Friedman and Schwartz (1963) contend that the Fed sought to smooth economic fluctuations and to limit the use of credit for stock market speculation. To test their hypotheses, I use the Fed's Index of Industrial Production (AIP),[23] All Commodities Price Index (PRI), and a Standard and Poor's index of stock prices (STK) as explanatory variables in the open-market policy reaction function. I use an average of the monthly changes in each index over the 3 months prior to the Fed's open-market operations.[24]

---

[22] An indicator is used to judge the ease or tightness of monetary policy, while a specific quantity objective is set for a target variable.

[23] The Index of Industrial Production was first available in 1927, and then constructed back in time. Thus, the Fed did not have access to this index when policy decisions were made in 1924–1926. However, the index is a composite of several indices which were available when actual decisions were made. Nevertheless, the index can only be considered a proxy for the various economic data which may have guided policy makers.

[24] For example, for the January 1925, ΔGS observation, the observations of the ex-

The coefficient on each is expected to be negative, indicating that the Fed made countercyclical open-market operations and sought to limit stock market speculation.

Wicker (1966) argues that the Fed's main policy objective, at least from 1924 to 1927, was to assist Great Britain's return to the gold standard. To do so, the Fed sought to reverse the flow of gold to the United States by reducing U.S. interest rates relative to those in England. Wicker asserts, "the desire of the Federal Reserve Bank of New York to establish a rate spread between New York and London to encourage capital outflows and reduce gold imports was indeed the chief determinant of policy (in 1924 and 1927)."[25] Even when international objectives were perhaps not paramount, as in 1925–1926 and 1928–1929, they were not discarded altogether. Of the tight money policy adopted in 1928–1929 to check stock market speculation, Wicker writes, "The (Open Market) committee was . . . not unmindful of the international consequences of rising market rates in the U.S. *vis a vis* Europe."[26]

Friedman and Schwartz (1963) illustrate that Federal Reserve Credit varied to offset the effects of gold flows on bank reserves. But the Fed did not see this sterilization as incompatible with assistance to Britain. A gold inflow, for example, tended to produce a reduction in discount loans and acceptance sales to the Fed. Total reserves changed little, if at all, because an increase in one source of reserves (the gold stock) led to a decrease in another (FRC). But the Fed believed that the decline in discount loans would lead to a decline in market interest rates and discourage further gold inflows. Open-market purchases could reinforce this process, and Wicker argues that in 1924 and 1927 the Fed bought securities in response to gold inflows with the aim of reducing discount loans and interest rates sharply.

To test Wicker's hypothesis, I include the lagged 3-month average bankers acceptance interest rate in New York (RUS) and the similar rate in London (RUK) as regressors. The differential (RR) between New York and London rates is included in an alternative specification.[27] The coefficient on the New York rate is expected to be positive, indicating that the Fed sought to stabilize interest rates with open-market opera-

---

planatory variables are the average changes in each index from September to November 1924.

[25] Wicker (1966, p. 77).

[26] Wicker (1966, p. 131). For this reason, I chose to model the Fed's response to international goals using the rate differential (see below), rather than simply using dummy variables for the 1924 and 1927 episodes.

[27] As might be expected, the two rates were highly correlated. For January 1924– September 1929 the correlation coefficient between RUS and RUK is 0.55, significant at the 0.01 level.

tions.[28] The coefficient on the London rate is expected to be negative. And the coefficient on the differential is expected to be positive, indicating that, as the U.S. rate rose relative to that in England, the Fed bought government securities.

The lagged, 3-month average net gold inflow (ΔG) is included as an independent variable in one specification of the model. If the Fed sought to reinforce gold flows, as described above, its coefficient should be positive. Of course, gold flows were undoubtedly related to the interest rate differential.[29] No attempt is made here to model the determinants of gold flows. The purpose of including them is to judge whether there is quantitative support for Wicker's hypothesis, and whether they may have exerted an independent influence on open-market policy.

As a final addition to the model, I include the lagged 3-month average change in the currency stock (ΔC). It was Fed policy to prevent currency flows from affecting bank reserves.[30] Thus, the coefficient on ΔC indicates the extent to which open-market operations were used for this purpose. A positive coefficient is expected. An increase in currency held by the public tended to reduce bank reserves; an open-market purchase would offset this effect. Although currency flows were quite seasonal, seasonal dummy variables also are included in each regression. Miron (1986) argues that open-market operations were used to meet seasonal fluctuations in credit, and hence reserve demands. Thus including ΔC tests whether the Fed responded to nonseasonal currency flows.

Table 1 presents regression estimates for January 1924–September 1929. This period was selected to omit the possibly anomalous open-market purchases in the wake of the stock market crash in October 1929.[31] Equation (1.1) supports the hypothesis that the Fed used open-market operations countercyclically and to check stock market speculation.[32] Since the Durbin–Watson (DW) statistic indicates the possibility

---

[28] Because interest rates tend to be related positively to economic activity, a positive coefficient on RUS may simply reflect a desire to stabilize economic activity. However, the correlation coefficients between RUS and AIP, PRI, and STK are 0.01, −0.25 and 0.34. The first is not statistically significant; the second is, but one would expect a positive correlation; and the third is significant at the 0.01 level.

[29] The correlation coefficients between ΔG and RUS, RUK, and RR from January 1924 to September 1929 are 0.27, −0.04, and 0.36. The first and third are significant at the 0.05 level, while the second is not significant.

[30] See Friedman and Schwartz (1963, pp. 292–296).

[31] The Open Market Investment Committee was established in 1923, and in December 1923 a Special Investment Account was set up for its operations at the Federal Reserve Bank of New York. Chandler (1958, pp. 221–233) describes the Committee's struggle for autonomy from the Reserve Board and Treasury during 1923. Benjamin Strong was on leave of absence from March to October, and Chandler reports that within 2 months of his return in November procedural matters had been settled and the Fed had begun open-market operations in pursuit of its general policy objectives.

[32] By their nature, reaction functions assume that policy makers follow a rigid feedback

TABLE 1
ΔGS Reaction Functions January 1924–September 1929

Variable	Equation 1.1	Equation 1.2	Equation 1.3	Equation 1.4
Intercept	30.75	32.70	−10.17	36.61
	(35.57)	(43.42)	(15.31)	(38.26)
ΔAIP_{-1}	−8.30	−6.66	−7.40	−8.37
	(2.90)**	(3.41)*	(3.33)*	(2.70)**
ΔPRI_{-1}	−3.95	−3.80	−1.61	3.26
	(6.78)	(7.78)	(7.59)	(6.73)
ΔSTK_{-1}	−3.59	−3.38	−4.24	−3.24
	(1.96)*	(2.20)	(2.05)*	(1.82)*
RUS_{-1}	21.86	21.77		15.43
	(6.91)**	(8.63)**		(6.88)*
RUK_{-1}	−32.58	−33.34		−25.63
	(9.59)**	(12.11)**		(9.23)**
RR_{-1}			24.26	
			(8.48)**	
ΔG_{-1}				0.48
				(0.15)**
ΔC_{-1}				−0.15
				(0.32)
ρ		−0.25	−0.26	
		(0.14)*	(0.14)*	
AR^2	.46	.48	.48	.54
DW	1.55	2.02	2.04	1.79

Note. Equations (1.1) and (1.4) were estimated using ordinary least squares (OLS). Equations (1.2) and (1.3) were estimated using maximum likelihood (ML). Each regression included seasonal dummy variables. Standard errors are in parentheses. For data sources and variable definitions, see Appendix.

 * Significant at the 0.05 level (one-tail test).
 ** Significant at the 0.01 level (one-tail test).

rule. Since the Fed has always allowed discretion to affect its decisions, it is unlikely that the estimated coefficients of reaction functions are stable over time. Indeed, as illustrated below, the models estimated from 1924 to 1929 seriously overpredict Fed open-market holdings from 1930 to 1933. And, even within 1924–1929, it is unlikely that the estimated coefficients were perfectly stable. A referee noted that the controversy among policy makers over how to limit stock market speculation in 1928–1929 may have this implication. And, despite indications of earlier concern with speculation, it is possible that the Fed did not respond to stock market activity before 1928. To test this possibility, I multiplied the stock index variable by a dummy which took the value 1 from January 1928 to September 1929, and 0 in all other months, and reestimated the regression. The coefficient on the new stock index is not statistically different from the original coefficient (−4.41 with a standard error of 1.85).

of serially correlated errors, the equation was reestimated using maximum likelihood with an AR(1) error process (Eq. (1.2)). The coefficients on the Index of Industrial Production and stock price index are smaller in this equation, and their statistical significance less strong, but they still offer support for the hypotheses.

The coefficients on the lagged U.S. and U.K. interest rates have the anticipated signs and are statistically significant. Higher U.S. rates apparently led to open-market purchases, while higher U.K. rates led to sales. Equation (1.3) was estimated using the rate differential as an independent variable, and its coefficient also has correct sign and is significant. These results support Wicker's hypothesis that international objectives did influence Fed policy.

I include both gold flows (ΔG) and changes in the public's currency holdings (ΔC) as independent variables in Eq. (1.4). The gold flows coefficient estimate is positive, suggesting the Fed used open-market operations to reinforce, not to offset, their effects on bank reserves. Wicker argues that the Fed bought securities in response to gold inflows in an effort to reduce interest rates and check future inflows. Open-market purchases added to the reduction in discount loans (and acceptance sales to the Fed) produced by the gold inflows. The Fed believed that the reduction in discount loans would lead to lower domestic interest rates and thus limit future gold inflows.

Finally, the coefficient on ΔC is not statistically significant. However, this probably does not imply that the Fed was unconcerned with currency flows. These flows were particularly seasonal, and most of the seasonal variation in FRC was accomplished through discount loans and acceptance operations. Moreover, since seasonal dummies are included in the regressions, including the highly seasonal ΔC is largely superfluous.

The open-market policy regressions reported in Table 1 suggest clearly the Fed's response to both domestic and international objectives. However, it may be more correct to judge the Fed's policy intent by the sum of its operations in government securities and in bankers acceptances, as done by Trescott (1982) and Epstein and Ferguson (1984). This is true if the Fed viewed open-market operations in government securities and in bankers acceptances as close substitutes, and if the Fed was able to control accurately the volume of acceptances offered to it by banks and bill dealers.

Still another possible measure of the Fed's policy intent is the flow of unborrowed reserves. Fed officials knew that open-market operations were not unique in their effects on discount loan volume and market interest rates. Any cause of a reserve flow into or out of the banking system would produce the same results. A gold inflow, for example, would have the same effect as an open-market purchase of similar size.

In the Fed view, it was the net change in unborrowed reserves which determined the change in discount loans (borrowed reserves). Thus open-market operations might be unnecessary if reserve flows from other sources produced the desired effects on discount loans and interest rates. For this reason, open-market operations may have reinforced gold and currency flows at times, and offset them at other times. And it suggests that changes in unborrowed reserves might indicate better the Fed's responsiveness to its policy goals.

Unborrowed reserves is the difference between total reserves and borrowed reserves (discount loans). Gold inflows, a reduction in currency held by the public, and open-market purchases of government securities or acceptances add to the stock of unborrowed reserves. The change in unborrowed reserves accurately measures the Fed's policy intent if open-market operations were used to offset *undesired* changes in the gold and currency stocks and in acceptance sales to the Fed.[33] And to achieve some policy goal, the Fed would use open-market operations to produce a desired change in unborrowed reserves. Conceivably, an apparently perverse operation may have taken place. For example, the Fed might have sold securities during a recession if other reserve sources were adding sufficiently to the stock of unborrowed reserves. Thus it may be that open-market operations did not reflect the Fed's policy intent as well as the flow of unborrowed reserves. Certainly this possibility merits further investigation.

Regressions of the sum of open-market operations in government securities and in bankers acceptances (ΔFOM) and of the flow of unborrowed reserves (ΔUR) are presented in Table 2. Although the coefficients of the ΔFOM regressions have the anticipated signs, few are precisely estimated. The same is true of the ΔUR models. At least some Fed officials recognized that a gold flow, or any other source of a change in unborrowed reserves, had the same effect on discount loans and interest rates as an open-market operation. But, as noted above, the Open Market Investment Committee generally set only the specific volume of open-market operations, and thus operations in government securities alone probably gives the best measure of the Fed's policy intent during this period. Nevertheless, the results in Table 2 are qualitatively similar to those of the government security operations regressions reported in Table 1, and offer further support for the hypotheses that the Fed sought to smooth economic fluctuations, to limit speculation, and to respond to interest rate differences between New York and London.

---

[33] And in the minor reserve sources, such as Treasury currency.

TABLE 2
ΔFOM and ΔUR Reaction Functions January 1924–September 1929

Variable	Equation			
	2.1^a	2.2^a	2.3^b	2.4^b
Intercept	−26.78	−16.14	167.68	190.78
	(71.65)	(73.63)	(89.72)*	(26.56)*
ΔAIP_{-1}	−2.75	−3.27	−9.30	−9.02
	(4.71)	(4.53)	(5.75)	(5.59)
ΔPRI_{-1}	−2.61	3.89	−16.19	−16.89
	(11.01)	(11.12)	(13.51)	(13.11)
ΔSTK_{-1}	−6.61	−6.32	−7.79	−7.48
	(3.14)*	(3.03)*	(3.67)*	(3.43)*
RUS_{-1}	17.20	8.60	35.72	
	(15.01)	(14.24)	(18.79)*	
RUK_{-1}	−19.50	−12.04	−29.64	
	(19.41)	(18.48)	(24.54)	
RR_{-1}				34.46
				(17.56)*
ΔG_{-1}		0.61		
		(0.28)*		
ΔC_{-1}		−0.13		
		(0.55)		
ρ	−0.45	−0.41	−0.49	−0.48
	(.15)**	(0.15)**	(0.14)**	(0.14)*
AR^2	.66	.68	.69	.69
DW	1.89	1.88	1.86	1.85

Note. Each equation was estimated using maximum likelihood. Each regression included seasonal dummy variables. Standard errors are in parentheses.
  ^{a} ΔFOM: Eq. (2.1) and (2.2).
  ^{b} ΔUR: Eq. (2.3) and (2.4).
  * Significance at the 0.05 level (one-tail test).
  ** Significance at the 0.01 level (one-tail test).

THE EFFECTIVENESS OF OPEN-MARKET OPERATIONS

The evidence presented in the previous section illustrates that the Fed used open-market operations systematically in response to various policy goals. And, it is widely accepted that the Fed achieved its objectives.[34] But Toma (1989) challenges this view. Toma contends that open-market operations were ineffective because they produced opposite changes in the volume of discount loans. His analysis shows that changes in discount loan volume offset open-market operations dollar for dollar and thus had

[34] See Chandler (1958), Friedman and Schwartz (1963), and Wicker (1966). Although they disagree about the specific objectives of policy, they all seem to believe that at least from 1924 to 1927 the Fed's operations were effective.

no effect on the total volume of Federal Reserve Credit outstanding. This implies that FRC did not reflect the Fed's response to its policy goals. In this section, I analyze the behavior of total FRC and show that indeed it did not reflect the Fed's open-market policy response.

Again, Federal Reserve Credit is the sum of Fed government security and bankers acceptance holdings and discount loans to member banks. The Fed believed that the volume of FRC outstanding was determined largely by the demand for it, and Toma's study seems to confirm this. Open-market operations, gold flows, changes in the public's currency holdings, and other causes of reserve flows affected the extent to which banks turned to the Fed for credit, either in the form of discount loans or through acceptance sales to the Reserve Banks. A gold or currency flow produced a change in the volume of FRC outstanding, but an open-market purchase did not since, for example, an increase in the Fed's government security holdings of $1 led to a decrease in discount loans of $1.

Table 3 presents a set of regression estimates for ΔFRC. Equation (3.1) includes non-lagged gold and currency flows as the only independent variables. The immediate impact of these flows was to affect bank demands for discount loans and their sales of acceptances to the Fed. For example, given a relatively constant demand for reserves, a $1 gold inflow would lead to a $1 reduction in the sum of discount loans and acceptance sales to the Fed, and total FRC would decline by $1. Regardless whether the Fed made a simultaneous open-market operation, the impact on total FRC would be the same. A Fed sale of $1 of securities would offset the impact of the gold inflow on bank reserves, and total FRC would decline by $1. A Fed purchase of $1 of securities would augment the impact of the gold inflow, causing discount loans and acceptance sales to decline by $2, but the net change in FRC would still be a $1 decline. Moreover, Toma's study indicates that open-market operations made in response to previous gold flows had no effect on total FRC since they were offset exactly by changes in the other forms of FRC outstanding. Thus only contemporaneous gold and currency flows had an impact on total FRC.

Gold and currency flows can account for much of the monthly variation in FRC. The coefficient on ΔG is close to -1.0, although the hypothesis that it equals -1.0 can be rejected at the 0.05 level. The sterilization of gold flows was thus virtually, but not entirely, complete. The coefficient on ΔC is not significantly different from 1.0, suggesting that currency flows led to a dollar for dollar offsetting change in FRC. Equation (3.2) includes seasonal dummy variables. An F-test indicates that they add significant explanatory power.[35] However, currency flows were quite seasonal and thus ΔC is highly correlated with the seasonal dummies.

[35] $F = 3.364$, significant at the 0.01 level.

TABLE 3
ΔFRC Functions January 1924–September 1929

Variable	Equation		
	3.1	3.2	3.3
Intercept	7.58	−16.30	59.15
	(3.23)*	(36.55)	(49.39)
ΔG^a	−0.88	−0.81	−0.83
	(0.10)**	(0.09)**	(0.11)**
ΔC^a	0.91	0.75	0.93
	(0.04)**	(0.15)**	(0.18)**
ΔAIP_{-1}			−2.59
			(2.29)
ΔPRI_{-1}			−5.36
			(4.97)
ΔSTK_{-1}			0.91
			(1.51)
RUS_{-1}			−5.43
			(5.67)
RUK_{-1}			−4.09
			(6.88)
AR^2	.91	.93	.94
DW	1.62	1.75	1.98

Note. Each equation was estimated using ordinary least squares. Equations (3.2) and (3.3) included seasonal dummy variables; Eq. (3.1) did not. Standard errors are in parentheses.

  a ΔG and ΔC represent the 1-month gold flow and currency flow only, not the average over 3 months as in the models of Tables 1 and 2.

  * Significant at the 0.05 level (one-tail test).

  ** Significant at the 0.01 level (one-tail test).

The coefficient on ΔC in Eq. (3.2) is still significantly different from 0, but is also significantly different from 1.0 (at the 0.05 level).

Equation (3.3) includes the independent variables used to gauge the Fed's open-market policy response as additional explanatory variables. None of the coefficients on these variables is significantly different from zero. Nor does their inclusion improve the overall fit of the model, as measured by the adjusted R^2. Thus, as Toma's study implies, the Fed's response to its policy goals was not reflected in the behavior of FRC. Because they were offset by the other forms of FRC outstanding, open-market operations did not produce systematic changes in bank reserves or in the supply of money. Thus when the Fed bought government securities, perhaps in response to a recession, it failed to buy enough of them to increase total FRC. In fact it appears that the Fed's strategy was to purchase just enough securities to drive the other forms of FRC close to zero and then to suspend its operations. In other words, the Fed quit buying just at the point where further purchases would begin to increase total FRC. If this same strategy was used during the depression, it would help to explain why monetary policy did not lead to economic recovery.

POLICY CONSISTENCY

One debate which persists about monetary policy during the Great Depression is whether or not Fed behavior during the depression was consistent with that of the 1920s. Friedman and Schwartz (1963) contend that the death of Benjamin Strong in 1928 and subsequent institutional changes marked a distinct change in Fed performance. Trescott (1982) agrees, stressing the effects of changes in the Open Market Investment Committee in early 1930. However, Wicker (1966) and Brunner and Meltzer (1968) argue there was no change in the quality of policy making, and that monetary policy during the depression was consistent with that of the 1920s.[36]

As a simple test of policy consistency, I forecast the Fed's holdings of government securities from October 1929 to February 1933 from Eq. (1.2) and (1.4). Using Eq. (2.2) and (2.3), I made similar forecasts of the sum of Fed government security and bankers acceptance holdings (FOM) and of the stock of unborrowed reserves (UR). These forecasts and the actual levels of each series are plotted in Figs. 1–4. Regardless of which variable is used to measure the Fed's policy intent, beginning in mid-1930 the forecast levels are much larger than the actual levels. Does this mean that there was indeed a change in policy regime with the onset of the depression?

Undoubtedly there are multiple reasons for the apparent shift in Fed policy between 1924–1929 and the early 1930s. Friedman and Schwartz document that officials of the Federal Reserve Bank of New York generally favored more expansionary policies during the depression than did other Fed officials. And they argue persuasively that the Fed would have been more responsive to the downturn had the New York Bank not lost much of its power following Benjamin Strong's death.[37]

Wicker (1966) and Brunner and Meltzer (1968) argue that there was no inconsistency in Fed policy. They contend that the Fed employed a procyclical policy strategy. That strategy focused on the volume of discount loans and nominal interest rates as policy guides, and since these variables fell sharply in 1930–1931, Fed officials inferred that money was easy and that open-market purchases were unnecessary.[38] Wicker writes:

[36] See Bordo (1987) for a further review of this debate.

[37] Friedman and Schwartz (1963, pp. 367–391).

[38] Wicker argues also that it had not been Fed policy to respond to economic fluctuations from 1924 to 1929, so the Fed's lack of action in 1930–1931 was not inconsistent with earlier policy.

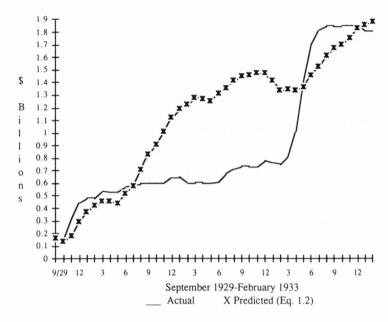

FIG. 1.   Federal Reserve holdings of U.S. Government securities and forecast holdings based on Eq. (1.2), September 1929–February 1933.

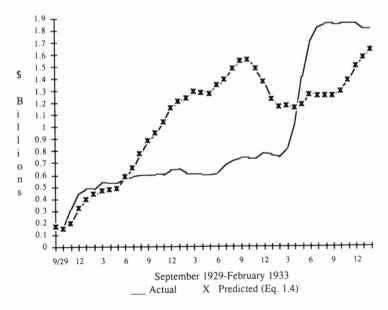

FIG. 2.   Federal Reserve holdings of U.S. Government securities and forecast holdings based on Eq. (1.4), September 1929–February 1933.

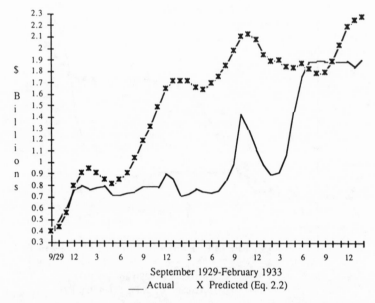

September 1929-February 1933
___ Actual   X Predicted (Eq. 2.2)

Fig. 3. Federal Reserve holdings of U.S. Government securities and bankers acceptances and forecast holdings based on Eq. (2.2), September 1929–February 1933.

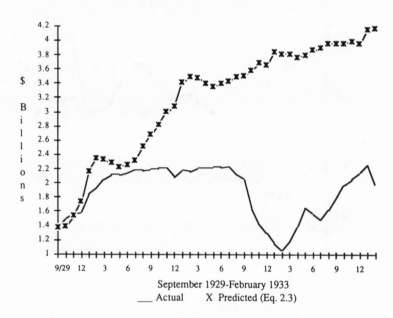

September 1929-February 1933
___ Actual   X Predicted (Eq. 2.3)

Fig. 4. Unborrowed reserves of Federal Reserve member banks and forecast unborrowed reserves based on Eq. (2.3), September 1929–February 1933.

It was Harrison's (Governor of the Federal Reserve Bank of New York) opinion that so long as the New York member banks remained practically out of debt, there was no justification for forcing further funds upon the market. To this position he adhered unswervingly throughout 1930 and 1931.[39]

And he argues:

It ought to be clear that the New York Bank did not at this time (1930) contemplate substantial purchases of government securities. Its objective was limited in scope and did not go beyond the goal set out by Burgess and Strong in the nineteen-twenties—that is, to eliminate the indebtedness of the New York and Chicago banks.[40]

Benjamin Strong's testimony in 1926 illustrates the importance he attached to discount loan volume as a policy guide, and supports Wicker's and Brunner and Meltzer's conclusion that there was not a change in Fed behavior. Referring to open-market purchases in 1924, Strong testified:

I think the guide . . . was whether the New York banks were completely out of debt or not. . . . We continued to buy after the New York banks had completely liquidated their borrowings from us.[41]

Table 4 compares the Fed's actions during the economic downturn of 1929–1931 with those taken during the recessions of 1924 and 1927. In addition to the Fed's government security holdings (GS) and its discount rate (DR), the table also gives the Index of Industrial Production (AIP), discount borrowing of all member banks (DL), borrowing by reporting member banks in New York City (DL(NYC)), and the bankers acceptance rate (RUS). Relative to the decline in output, the Fed bought few government securities in 1930–1931. But, if the Fed's strategy during an economic downturn was to buy securities only as necessary to reduce discount loans to some minimal level, then it would seem that there was not a change in system policy.

The Fed's purchases in 1924 and 1927 were soon followed by economic recoveries, leading Fed officials (and later studies) to conclude that the purchases had contributed to the upturns. Their apparent successes suggest further that the Fed would not have changed procedures in 1930 when faced with another recession. However, the apparently easy monetary conditions of 1930–1931 did not lead to recovery, and in April 1932 the Fed began a new program of substantial open-market purchases.[42]

[39] Wicker (1966, p. 153).

[40] Wicker (1966, p. 156).

[41] House of Representatives (1926, p. 336).

[42] Despite the worsening depression and a sharp increase in discount loans in the fourth quarter of 1931, the Fed did not buy government securities. Its justification was a lack of

TABLE 4
A Comparison of Fed Policy during Three Downturns

Date	AIP	GS	DR	DL	DL(NYC)	RUS
Jul 1929	124	147	5.0	1096	319	5.13
Oct 1929	118	154	6.0	885	74	5.13
Jan 1930	106	485	4.5	501	39	3.94
Apr 1930	104	530	3.5	231	17	2.94
Jul 1930	93	583	2.5	226	0	1.88
Oct 1930	88	602	2.5	196	6	1.88
Jan 1931	83	647	2.0	253	5	1.56
Apr 1931	88	600	2.0	155	0	1.50
Jul 1931	82	674	1.5	169	0	0.88
Oct 1931	73	733	3.5	614	74	2.25
Apr 1923	106	229	4.5	658	123	4.1?
Jul 1923	104	97	4.5	834	143	4.13
Oct 1923	99	91	4.5	873	121	4.13
Jan 1924	100	118	4.5	574	85	4.06
Apr 1924	95	274	4.5	489	45	4.00
Jul 1924	84	467	3.5	315	13	2.00
Oct 1924	95	585	3.0	240	28	2.19
Jan 1925	105	464	3.0	275	32	3.00
Oct 1926	111	306	4.0	663	84	3.88
Jan 1927	107	310	4.0	481	76	3.69
Apr 1927	108	341	4.0	447	78	3.63
Jul 1927	106	381	4.0	454	59	3.56
Oct 1927	102	506	3.5	424	75	3.19
Jan 1928	107	512	3.5	465	94	3.38

Note. GS, DL, and DL(NYC) are in $ millions. DR and RUS are in %. For variable definitions and sources, see Appendix.

Friedman and Schwartz argue that Fed was hesitant to buy securities, but was pressured by Congress to do so.[43] Epstein and Ferguson (1984) concur, but argue also that member banks wanted the Fed to support bond prices.[44] Although New York City member banks were out of debt and held excess reserves throughout much of 1932, borrowing by all member banks was high.[45] Nevertheless, because New York City banks were already out of debt, the Fed's purchases were not consistent with a strategy of simply eliminating the indebtedness of those banks. However, the change in strategy was really very slight. According to Wicker

gold reserves. However, Friedman and Schwartz (1963) doubt this reason (pp. 399–406). Nevertheless, the Glass–Steagall Act of 1932 removed the constraint.

[43] Friedman and Schwartz (1963, p. 332).
[44] Epstein and Ferguson (1984, pp. 966–967).
[45] Discount loans volume averaged $516 million in 1932. By contrast, in 1930 and 1931 the average volumes were $256 million and $324 million, respectively.

(1966) and to Chandler (1971), the Fed measured the effects of its purchases by the excess reserve position of New York banks, and by mid-1932 had begun to set explicit excess reserve targets.[46] In essence, the Fed's strategy had evolved from one of judging credit conditions by the behavior of discount loan volume to one of targeting "free reserves," i.e., excess reserves less borrowed reserves. And by using open-market operations to control free reserves, the Fed believed that it could influence market interest rates. Although the Fed made substantial open-market purchases in 1932, it continued to rely on bank reserve positions and market interest rates as policy guides. Thus, to the extent that the Fed's policy strategy had changed, it was simply a minor modification.[47]

CONCLUSION

In support of Friedman and Schwartz (1963), the evidence presented in this paper indicates from 1924 to 1929 the Federal Reserve attempted to limit economic fluctuations with open-market operations. But it also suggests the Fed sought to check stock market speculation and to assist Great Britain to return to the gold standard.

Friedman and Schwartz contend that the Fed's failure to make substantial open-market purchases during the depression indicates that there had been a significant change in policy regime. And forecasts of system open-market holdings for 1930–1933 based on policy models estimated from 1924 to 1929 are much larger than actual Fed security holdings. However, when these comparisons are considered in light of the Fed's policy strategy, it seems doubtful that a significant change in regime did occur.

The Fed's strategy involved the use of open-market operations to influence discount loan volume which, in the Fed view, led to changes in market interest rates. This strategy was not developed to the point where the Fed set specific operating targets for discount loans and interest rates, but the Fed watched these variables closely as indicators of monetary conditions. And since both discount loans and interest rates where historically low in 1930–1931, the Fed believed that money was easy and significant open-market purchases were unnecessary. Even when the Fed was forced to modify its strategy and to buy a substantial volume of securities in 1932, the modification was slight, with the focus on the excess reserves, rather than the borrowed reserves, of member banks in principal cities.

[46] Wicker (1966, pp. 172–184), and Chandler (1971, pp. 198–204).

[47] Meigs (1962) analyzes the flaws in the Fed's use of a free reserves strategy during the 1950s and 1960s and points out the similarities between that strategy and the Fed's use of borrowed reserves as a policy guide during the 1920s and early 1930s. Wheelock (1988a) considers further the flaws in the Fed's use of borrowed reserves as an indicator during the depression.

This paper also supports Toma's (1989) finding that during the 1920s open-market operations had no significant impact on total Federal Reserve Credit outstanding. This evidence suggests further that the Fed's failures during the depression were due to its policy strategy. In response to an economic downturn, the Fed would buy a volume of securities sufficient to reduce discount loans to near zero. Once this had occurred, no further purchases were made. However, Toma's research implies that only open-market purchases made after discount loans had fallen to zero would have been effective. Thus the Fed's strategy prescribed that open-market purchases be ended just at the point where they would begin to have an impact on Federal Reserve Credit outstanding, bank reserves, and the money supply. Therefore it appears that the failure of the Fed to make large open-market purchases during the depression, especially in 1930–1931, and hence for the failure of monetary policy to lead to economic recovery, was due to the development and continued use of a flawed policy strategy.

APPENDIX
Variable Definitions and Data Sources

AIP   Index of Industrial Production (seasonally adjusted) (Federal Reserve Board, *Annual Report*, pp. 173–179).

C   Currency in circulation (*Banking and Monetary Statistics*, pp. 370–371).

DL   Discount loans of all member banks (*Banking and Monetary Statistics*, pp. 370–371).

DL(NYC)   Discount loans of reporting banks in New York City (*Banking and Monetary Statistics*, pp. 168–174).

DR   Discount rate of the Federal Reserve Bank of New York (*Banking and Monetary Statistics*, pp. 440–441).

FOM   Sum of Federal Reserve government security and bankers acceptance holdings (*Banking and Monetary Statistics*, pp. 370–371).

FRC   Federal Reserve Credit (sum of DL and FOM only) (*Banking and Monetary Statistics*, pp. 370–371).

G   Monetary gold stock (*Banking and Monetary Statistics*, pp. 370–371).

GS   Federal Reserve holdings of government securities (*Banking and Monetary Statistics*, pp. 370–371).

PRI   All Commodities Price Index (*Federal Reserve Bulletin*, various issues).

RUK   Bankers acceptance interest rate in London (*Banking and Monetary Statistics*, p. 656).

RUS   Bankers acceptance interest rate in New York (*Banking and Monetary Statistics*, p. 450).

RR   RUS-RUK.

STK   Standard and Poor's stock price index (*Banking and Monetary Statistics*, pp. 480–481).

UR   Unborrowed reserves, the difference between total member bank reserves and member bank discount loans (*Banking and Monetary Statistics*, pp. 370–371).

All data except index numbers are monthly averages of daily figures.

REFERENCES

Board of Governors of the Federal Reserve System (1943), *Banking and Monetary Statistics*.

Bordo, M. D. (1987), "The Contribution of *A Monetary History of the United States 1867–1960* to Monetary History." Presented at "Money in Historical Perspective: A Conference in Honor of Anna J. Schwartz," New York (October).

Brunner,K., and Meltzer, A. H. (1968), "What Did We Learn from the Monetary Experience of the United States in the Great Depression?" *Canadian Journal of Economics* 1(2), 334–348.

Burgess, W. R. (1946), *The Reserve Banks and the Money Market*. New York: Harper & Brothers.

Chandler, L. V. (1958), *Benjamin Strong, Central Banker*. Washington, DC: Brookings Institution.

Chandler, L. V. (1971). *American Monetary Policy 1928–1941*. New York: Harper & Row.

Epstein, G., and Ferguson, T. (1984), "Monetary Policy, Loan Liquidation, and Industrial Conflict: The Federal Reserve and the Open-Market Operations of 1932." *Journal of Economic History* 44(4), 957–983.

Field, A. J. (1984a), "Asset Exchanges and the Transactions Demand for Money." *American Economic Review* 74(1), 43–59.

Field, A. J. (1984b), "A New Interpretation of the Onset of the Great Depression." *Journal of Economic History* 64(1), 489–498.

Friedman, M., and Schwartz, A. J. (1963), *A Monetary History of the United States, 1967–1960*. New York: National Bureau of Economic Research.

Goldfeld, S. M., and Chandler, L. V. (1986), *The Economics of Money and Banking*. New York: Harper & Row. 9th ed.

Hamilton, J. D. (1987), "Monetary Factors in the Great Depression." *Journal of Monetary Economics* 19, 145–169.

Meigs, A. J. (1962), *Free Reserves and the Money Supply*. Chicago: Univ. of Chicago Press.

Miron, J. A. (1986), "Financial Panics, the Seasonality of the Nominal Interest Rate, and the Founding of the Fed. *American Economic Review* 76(1), 124–140.

Riefler, W. (1930), *Money Rates and Money Markets in the United States*. New York: Harper & Brothers.

Toma, M. (1989), "The Policy Effectiveness of Open Market Operations in the 1920s." *Explorations in Economic History, 26, 99–116.

Trescott, P. B. (1982), "Federal Reserve Policy in the Great Depression: A Counterfactual Assessment." *Explorations in Economic History* 19, 211–220.

United States House of Representatives (1926), *Stabilization*. Hearings before the Committee on Banking and Currency, 69th Congress, 1st Session.

Wheelock, D. C. (1988a), "The Demand for Federal Reserve Credit: The Key to Fed Errors in the Great Depression?" Presented at the Western Economic Association Meetings, Los Angeles, California, July 1988.

Wheelock, D. C. (1988b), "Interest Rate Seasonality, Financial Panics, and Federal Reserve Policy during the Great Depression." Unpublished manuscript.

Wicker, E. (1966), *Federal Reserve Monetary Policy 1917–1933*. New York: Random House.

ACKNOWLEDGMENTS

Cuff, Robert D. "Harry Garfield, the Fuel Administration, and the Search for a Cooperative Order During World War I." *American Quarterly* 30 (1978): 39–53. Reprinted with permission of the author, and The American Studies Association, publisher. Copyright 1978. Courtesy of Yale University Sterling Memorial Library.

Cuff, Robert D. "United States Mobilization and Railroad Transportation: Lessons in Coordination and Control, 1917–1945." *Journal of Military History* 53 (1989): 33–50. Reprinted with the permission of the Virginia Military Institute. Courtesy of Yale University Sterling Memorial Library.

Drake, Douglas C. "Herbert Hoover, Ecologist: The Politics of Oil Pollution Control, 1921–1926." *Mid-America* 55 (1973): 207–28. Reprinted with the permission of Loyola University. Courtesy of *Mid-America*.

Fickle, James E. "Defense Mobilization in the Southern Pine Industry: The Experience of World War I." *Journal of Forest History* 22 (1978): 206–23. Reprinted with the permission of the Forest History Society. Courtesy of the Forest History Society.

Garvey, Daniel E. "Secretary Hoover and the Quest for Broadcast Regulation." *Journalism History* 3 (1976): 66–70, 85. Courtesy of Yale University Sterling Memorial Library.

Grin, Carolyn. "The Unemployment Conference of 1921: An Experiment in National Cooperative Planning." *Mid-America* 55 (1973): 83–107. Reprinted with the permission of Loyola University. Courtesy of *Mid-America*.

Hawley, Ellis W. "The Discovery and Study of a 'Corporate Liberalism.'" *Business History Review* 52 (1978): 309–20. Reprinted with the permission of the Harvard Business School. Courtesy of Yale University Sterling Memorial Library.

Hawley, Ellis W. "Herbert Hoover and American Corporatism, 1929–1933." In Martin L. Fausold and George T. Mazuzan, eds., *The Hoover Presidency: A Reappraisal* (Albany, NY: SUNY Press, 1974): 101–19. Reprinted with the permission of the State University of New York Press. Courtesy of Yale University Sterling Memorial Library.

Hawley, Ellis W. "Herbert Hoover, the Commerce Secretariat, and the Vision of an 'Associative State,' 1921–1928." *Journal of American History* 61 (1974): 116–40. Reprinted with the permission of the *Journal of American History*. Courtesy of Yale University Sterling Memorial Library.

Hawley, Ellis W. "Herbert Hoover and Economic Stabilization, 1921–22." In *Herbert Hoover as Secretary of Commerce: Studies in New Era Thought and Practice* (Iowa City, IA: University of Iowa Press, 1981): 43–79. Reprinted with the permission of the University of Iowa Press. Courtesy of Yale University Sterling Memorial Library.

Hawley, Ellis W. "Three Facets of Hooverian Associationalism: Lumber, Aviation, and Movies, 1921–1930." In Thomas K. McCraw, ed., *Regulation in Perspective* (Cambridge, MA: Harvard Business School, 1981): 95–123. Reprinted with the permission of Harvard Business School Press. Courtesy of Yale University of Law.

Kane, N. Stephen. "American Businessmen and Foreign Policy: The Recognition of Mexico, 1920–1923." *Political Science Quarterly* 90 (1975): 293–313. Reprinted with the permission of the author and The Academy of Political Science. Courtesy of Yale University Sterling Memorial Library.

Keller, Robert R. "Supply-Side Economic Policies During the Coolidge-Mellon Era." *Journal of Economic Issues* 16 (1982): 773–90. Reprinted with the permission of the Association of Evolutionary Economics. Courtesy of the Association of Evolutionary Economics.

Koistinen, Paul A.C. "The 'Industrial-Military Complex' in Historical Perspective: The InterWar Years." *Journal of American History* 56 (1970): 819–39. Reprinted with the permission of the *Journal of American History*. Courtesy of Yale University Sterling Memorial Library.

McQuaid, Kim. "Young, Swope and General Electric's 'New Capitalism': A Study in Corporate Liberalism, 1920–33." *American Journal of Economics and Sociology* 36 (1977): 323–34. Reprinted with the permission of the *American Journal of Economics and Sociology*. Courtesy of Yale University Sterling Memorial Library.

Parrini, Carl. "Anglo-American Corporatism and the Economic Diplomacy of Stabilization in the 1920s." *Reviews in American History* 6 (1978): 379–87. Reprinted with the permission of Johns Hopkins University Press. Courtesy of Yale University Sterling Memorial Library.

Reagan, Patrick D. "From Depression to Depression: Hooverian National Planning, 1921–1933." *Mid-America* 70 (1988): 35–60. Reprinted with the permission of Loyola University. Courtesy of *Mid-America*.

Robbins, William G. "Voluntary Cooperation vs. Regulatory Paternalism: The Lumber Trade in the 1920s." *Business History Review* 56 (1982): 358–79. Reprinted with the permission of the Harvard Business School. Courtesy of Yale University Sterling Memorial Library.

Wheelock, David C. "The Strategy, Effectiveness, and Consistency of Federal Reserve Monetary Policy 1924–1933." *Explorations in Economic History* 26 (1989): 453–76. Copyright by Academic Press, Inc. Courtesy of Yale University Sterling Memorial Library.